Discovery and the Market Process
Toward an Understanding of the Business & Economic Environment
Third Edition

Barry Brownstein
Deborah Brownstein

University of Baltimore

 McGraw Hill **Custom Publishing**

Boston   Burr Ridge, IL   Dubuque, IA   Madison, WI   New York   San Francisco   St. Louis
Bangkok   Bogotá   Caracas   Lisbon   London   Madrid
Mexico City   Milan   New Delhi   Seoul   Singapore   Sydney   Taipei   Toronto

DISCOVERY AND THE MARKET PROCESS
Toward an Understanding of the Business & Economic Environment

McGraw-Hill's College Custom Series consists of products that are produced from camera-ready copy. Peer review, class testing, and accuracy are primarily the responsibility of the author(s).

4 5 6 7 8 9 0 QSR QSR 0 9 8

ISBN-13: 978-0-07-354212-6
ISBN-10: 0-07-354212-1

Editor: Elaine Manke
Production Editor: Susan Culbertson
Cover Design: Maggie Lytle
Printer/Binder: Quebecor World

CONTENTS

INTRODUCTION TO THE THIRD EDITION

Barry and Deborah Brownstein

As we write this introduction, in March 2005, the NCAA college basketball tournament is about to begin. During this time the *Wall Street Journal* published an intriguing article focusing on Mike Krzyzewski's work at Duke. One point in the article "Leadership as Layup" especially caught our attention. Using basketball as a metaphor for business, the article observes: "Players must make decisions on the court rather than wait for orders from the sidelines. In both business and basketball, the question is how to manage in a way that employees make smart decisions, work together and ultimately succeed." The dean at Duke's business school added: "Management needs to be different from old-style General Motors."

Even though Peter Drucker and others began to write about the importance of knowledge workers as early as the 1950s, Dee Hock, founder and former CEO of Visa, has observed that: "The most abundant, least expensive, most underutilized, and constantly abused resource in the world is human ingenuity."

Why would organizations underutilize their human resources? To be sure it is not deliberate. Instead it is simply the inadvertent outcome of the wrong ideas they hold about how their organizations can operate most efficiently. Many organizations continue to be organized along hierarchical principles with very complex rules. Many organizations continue to treat their employees as "interchangeable components of a great machine." The idea that employees function best when management gives employees simple rules and then gets out of the way would seem at the very least to be naïve and at worst dangerously absurd.

Dee Hock has summed up brilliantly the idea that relinquishing control can create more, rather than less, organizational intelligence when he observed that: "Simple, clear purpose and principles give rise to complex, intelligent behavior. Complex rules and regulations give rise to simple, stupid behavior." Many of the readings in this third edition will help us understand the reasoning behind his observation.

Indeed, with competition coming at us from all parts of the globe, an organization that does not utilize fully its organizational intelligence is doomed to have a very rough time competing. They simply are ill-equipped to interpret the business environment that they face, and they have no tools to respond to it.

This third edition of the reader keeps the core readings from the first and second editions which help us understand the key economic principles that facilitate healthy economies, as well as healthy organizations. To those core readings we have added several new and important readings that provide examples of these principles.

A challenge for each of us is to get out of the "box" we are in. Our "box" consists of our beliefs, many of which we are unaware. We cannot get out of our "box" until we see the "box" that we are in. The act of "seeing" our beliefs allows us to reconsider erroneous ideas that we may have. In the chapter, "Our Models Define Our World" that we include from their new book *The Power of Impossible Thinking,* Jerry Wind and Colin Crooks help us see the boxes we are in by helping us understand where our "mental models" of the world come from.

We are pleased to include a chapter, "The Difference Difference Makes," from the best-selling book *The Wisdom of Crowds* by James Surowiecki. In this book Surowiecki describes many practical applications of a key insight of Nobel Laureate Friedrich Hayek. Hayek's insight that useful knowledge is dispersed is developed in his essay "The Use of Knowledge in Society," which is also in this reader. Given that knowledge is dispersed, Surowiecki writes: "If you can assemble a diverse group of people who possess varying degrees of knowledge and insight, you're better off entrusting it with major decisions rather than leaving it to the hands of one or two people."

Harvey Seifter is the executive director of the Orpheus Chamber Orchestra. Orpheus is a world famous conductorless orchestra organized on the principles of self-organization. In a chapter, "Put Power in the Hands of the People Doing the Work," from his book *Leadership Ensemble,* Seifter describes how JP Morgan Chase created a decentralized organization "that allowed decisions to be made where the customers were, no matter where in the world they might be."

In the chapter, "Self-Organization and the Corporation" that we included from *Surfing on the Edge of Chaos,* Richard Pascale, Mark Millemann and Linda Gioja give many examples of how the principles of self-organization can be applied. Especially interesting is their analysis of "information-age warfare." They contrast the leadership style of Generals George Patton and Bernard Montgomery and quote Patton: "Never tell people how to do things. Tell them what to do and they will surprise you with their ingenuity."

Michael McMaster's chapter "Design for Emergence" from *The Praxis Equation* has proven to be so valuable to students that in this edition of *Discovery and the Market Process* we decided to include a second chapter: "Organizing for Forever." In this new chapter McMaster offers guidelines for an organization's long-term survival in an ever changing business environment.

T. Irene Sanders challenges the classical mechanical view of the universe in "Butterflies and Hurricanes" a chapter from her book *Strategic Thinking and the New Science*. She helps us understand that "we do not live in a static, linear cause-effect world" and helps us explore the implications of that understanding.

Finally, we include in this third edition Brink Lindsey's chapter "The Rule of Lawlessness" from his book *Against the Dead Hand* which discusses why economic development is slow in much of the third world. Without a legal system that enforces property rights there simply can be no way that a market is fully able to develop.

The aim of all of these new essays, as well as the holdover essays from the second edition is to increase the reader's understanding of the economy and the business environment, as well as how to successfully manage and lead. Although all of these essays do not directly focus on the latter goal, the more leveraged a framework that the essay presents the more its ideas are applicable on all levels. This is why an essay that may seem abstract initially frequently can be more rewarding in its applicability than an essay that provides many examples. In this reader we strove to seek a balance in both types of essays: abstract and applied. We hope you enjoy your reading.

INTRODUCTION TO THE
SECOND EDITION

Barry and Deborah Brownstein

Since the publication of the first edition of *Discovery and the Market Process* two major events have influenced the development of the second edition. The first is an explosion of books and articles that use the theoretical framework in this book as a guide to business management. The second is the development of exclusively web-based courses.

In the latter decades of the 20th Century, change in the business environment began to accelerate. Markets became global and technology increased the speed of communication and access to information. Prior to this era of rapid change, as Mark Youngblood puts it, "The problems and conditions that (managers) faced lent themselves to simple, linear analysis and solutions, and a command and control management style. These were convergent problems, where application of analytical problem-solving techniques converged on a single 'right' solution." In the rougher waters of today, gone are the days of calm sailing through a business environment characterized by linearity and predictability.

Given this change in business climate, Dee Hock, the legendary founder and former CEO of Visa, has observed: "We can't run 21st century society with 17th century notions of organization." Instead, Tom Petzinger writes: "The new model for organizations is the biological world, where uncontrolled actions produce stunningly efficient and robust results, all through adaptation and self-organization." Business leaders, who Petzinger calls "the new pioneers," are embracing the emerging field of complexity science and growing new understandings as to how synergistic interdependent systems that are self-organizing can provide insights into business management. The collection of essays in this second edition of our reader is unique in that is provides a foundation for understanding the capacity of markets and firms to self-organize.

All complex adaptive or self-organizing systems need simple rules to govern them. Paradoxically we find that the simpler the rules, the more complex is the resultant order. A central question to ponder as you read this collection of essays is, what simple rules will facilitate a complex order in your own organization? In this new edition of the reader, Michael Lissack and Johan Roos provide their ideas on this important topic in "Use Simple Guiding Principles." This is a chapter from their recently published book *The Next Common Sense: Mastering Corporate Complexity Through Coherence*. Lissack and Roos's chapter complements Murray Rothbard's classic essay "Justice and Property Rights" which focuses on the simple rules that facilitate complex, robust, healthy market systems.

In this new edition of the reader we are very pleased to reprint in its entirety the monograph *Introduction to Market Based Management* by Wayne Gable and Jerry Ellig. In their monograph, which is certain to be a classic, Gable and Ellig show how the insights of Nobel Laureate Friedrick Hayek into market processes are applicable at the level of the firm. Carried over from the first edition of the reader are such classics as Hayek's essays "Cosmos and Taxis" and "The Use of Knowledge in Society." Gable and Ellig brilliantly extend to management practices the powerful insights in these essays by Hayek. This is not just theoretical. These ideas are being used in Koch Industries among other firms. Pick up a current issue of *Fast Company* and see how many firms are trying similar ideas.

In part, what Gable and Ellig are concerned with in management, and Hayek in markets, is how to utilize knowledge that is inherently dispersed and can never be centralized. As Gable and Ellig point out in this monograph, "It is no accident that today's most innovative and successful management techniques are those that mobilize the vast knowledge dispersed throughout organizations. Their success points to the need for an overall approach to management that continually uncovers and mobilizes this knowledge."

Michael McMaster is one of the foremost theorists and practitioners of the new thinking in management in the world. We are pleased to include in this edition of the reader a chapter from his book *The Praxis Equation: Design Principles for Intelligent Organization*. In "Design For Emergence" McMaster asks the fundamental question: "Do we use an engineering approach for our company—one that tends to produce predictability, exactness and control? Or, do we design for emergence—one that will bring forth adaptability, innovation and things that are yet beyond our imagination?"

Included in this edition of the reader are two chapters from *Dialogue: Creating and Sustaining Collaborative Partnerships at Work* by Linda Ellinor and Glenna Gerard. Physicist David Bohm did much to reveal the generative capacity of dialogue. Ellinor and Gerard show how Bohm's insights into dialogue are very useful for increasing coherence and complexity in an organization. As Mike McMaster also points out, "crucial to the effective operation of any enterprise is to make sense of things, interpret, create meaning, and act on an individual basis in ways that are coordinated with the whole." Sustained dialogue is a key to generating such alignment of purpose.

For over two years at the University Of Baltimore our MBA has been offered over the Internet. This reflects an accelerating nationwide trend. The challenge of teaching on the web is how to use the inherent collaborative capacity of the Internet in order to create a rich learning environment. Dialogue helps in this regard too. We particularly like Mike McMaster's definition of dialogue as, "A conversation in which the intention is to generate something in the conversation itself that did not exist in any one of the participants before the conversation began." By following the simple rules of dialogue and conversing with each other through course-based Forums we increase our understanding. Since one of the goals of any organization in today's global markets is to increases its innovative capability and coherence, by practicing dialogue we learn a skill that is increasingly valued in today's job market.

Carried over from the first edition of the reader are many classic essays. Our criteria for keeping an essay and for adding a new essay were simple: Would a reading of the essay increase the reader's understanding of markets and/or their organization? Would multiple readings increase this understanding even further? And has the essay stood the test of time (or is it likely to)? We hope you enjoy this collection of readings as much as we do.

INTRODUCTION

Barry and Deborah Brownstein

U ntil recently economics and business curricula tended to be narrowly focused, compartmentalized subjects. In order to give students a systemic understanding of the field they are studying, innovative courses have begun to spring up that are more interdisciplinary in nature. We have designed this reader to be a resource for those who seek a systemic understanding of the role that free markets play in the economy and the ethical underpinnings of these markets. Now more than ever, such an integrative perspective is needed.

> To the layman untrained in economics, the market economy presents a bewildering face. It consists of numerous individuals each intent on his own goals, giving no concern to the overall social implications of his pursuits. No central coordinating agency controls or even monitors the innumerable independent production and exchange decisions made by these countless individuals. It is no wonder that the market economy seems to be nothing but a jungle of clashing discordant individual activities. From this perspective, government regulation fills a simple and obvious need: to introduce a modicum of coordination into these otherwise chaotic conditions.[1]
>
> —*Israel Kirzner*

Perhaps Israel Kirzner is being kind. Misunderstandings about the market process are not limited to "layman untrained in economics" but are also prevalent in academia, business and government. It is the admittedly ambitious, but attainable goal of this reader that a study of these essays will provide the reader a systemic understanding of the market process. While the chief perspective of the readings is economics, this collection of essays also draws on philosophical, political, and psychological theories. These essays will help the reader understand the effects of public policies as they impact, in intended and unintended ways, the domestic and global marketplace. Perhaps more importantly the reader will gain insight into the ethical underpinnings of free markets and gain insights into their own beliefs about market. These readings will help uncover and make explicit assumptions that are often implicit in theories and in our own mental maps of the world. This challenges readers to know better their own minds and builds personal integrity. The approach taken here is consistent with emerging views in mainstream economics, particularly 1993 Nobel laureate Douglas North. "Economic choices are a function of how people perceive the world," said North. The *Wall Street Journal* further quotes North as saying, "people have subjective mental models" and that beliefs a society has in common aren't analyzed enough in traditional economics. We believe it is only by being aware and reflective about one's beliefs does one have the freedom to make mindful ethical choices and exercise personal responsibility.

Specifically the reader is designed to promote an understanding of:

- An ethical paradigm that stresses that the quality of an individual's decisions is affected by the quality of one's thinking and that belief and insight shape one's responses to life's challenges,

- The consequences of thought systems and beliefs as they effect issues of political-economy,

- The nature of rights, both human rights and property rights, and social justice,

- The role and impact of prices and profits in a market economy,

- The use of knowledge in society and the market conditions which promote the integration of knowledge,

- Entrepreneurial discovery which fuels dynamic change and adaptation in the market and the effects of government regulation on this discovery process,

- The effects of the growing volume of world trade, and

- Political-economy and ethical considerations in such issues as health care and environmental problems.

Without Friedrich Hayek's contributions to economics, this reader would not be possible. His seminal contributions resulted in his receiving the Nobel Prize in 1974. For the business or economics student Hayek's importance to understanding markets grows ever larger. Business guru Tom Peters writes of Hayek: " Why spend so much time on Hayek? Simple. To fail to appreciate—in the fullest sense of that term—the richness, passion and raggedness of the market mechanism is to be unprepared to lead a firm (or a regional or national economy)—especially in today's unhinged global marketplace."[2]

The first part of this reader is titled *The Individual, Property Rights and Society: The Basis for Free Markets* and begins with a psychological reading that explains the role of insight. With that reading and Emerson's classic essay "Self-Reliance," the reader understands that the individual is the decision maker and that the quality of one's decisions is affected by the quality of one's thinking. An understanding of insight has direct relevance to entrepreneurial discovery which is discussed later in the reader. Hayek's classic essay "Individualism: True and False" refutes "the silliest of the common misunderstandings (about individualism); the belief that individualism postulates (or bases its arguments on the assumptions of) the existence of isolated or self-contained individuals, instead of starting from men whose whole nature and character is determined by their existence in society." Emerson's essay has been subject to similar misunderstandings. "Cosmos and Taxis" introduces to the reader the contrast between spontaneous order and planned order. The careful reader will be forced to confront the core belief of many social scientists that the good order is one "which has been made by somebody putting the elements of a set in their places or directing their movements." From that point the reader introduces rights as a basis for any market using Rothbard's "Justice and Property Rights." Murray Rothbard writes: "For the free-market economy, as complex as the system appears to be on the surface, is yet nothing more than a vast network of voluntary and mutually agreed-upon two-person or two-party exchanges of property titles. . . ."[3] The importance of a clear and precise demarcation of property rights for the market economy . . . [is essential to] the allocation of resources and in preventing or compensating for unwanted imposition of 'external costs.' "[4] " 'Social' or Distributive Justice" which is from Hayek's *Law, Legislation and Liberty* discusses whether the role of government should be to rig outcomes or simply to insure fair rules to play the game. Hayek writes, "the enforcement of any image of 'social justice' inevitably destroys that freedom of personal decisions on which all morals must rest."[5] This rounds out a discussion of the ethical basis for free-markets. Armed with the understanding presented here, the reader begins to see that the government-business partnership accepted as axiomatic by many could be objected to on efficiency and equity grounds. The dichotomy Hayek presents between equity based on outcomes or conduct helps students see their own beliefs on "social justice" and traces through the systemic consequences of outcome based public policies. The next part of this reader focuses on efficiency considerations.

Perhaps Hayek's greatest and certainly most quoted contribution to economics is his seminal essay "The Use of Knowledge in Society." This essay is essential to understand that the core economic problem is "a problem of how to secure the best use of resources known to any of the members of society, for ends whose relative importance only those individuals know."[6] For those readers who have previous economic training this is obviously in stark contrast to neo-classical economics with its assumption of given knowledge and its reduction of the economic problem to allocative choices. In reading this essay the reader may find it useful to characterize centrally planned versus competitive systems in terms of (1) how the economic problem is defined, (2) the type of information that is used, and (3) how quickly it is used, in response to (4) how change in the economy is perceived by the relevant decision makers.

The readings in this section discuss the meaning of competition. We, along with many others, believe "the Austrian view of competition and entrepreneurship is critical to understanding the contemporary business environment. The conventional textbook model of perfect competition is incapable of producing real competitive behavior, because competition in the real world is a dynamic process of change and adaptation. . . . Anyone who claims that 'competitive firms' cut costs or introduce new products is implicitly employing a dynamic theory of competition."[7] The neo-classical model of perfect competition simply cannot produce this behavior.

A central theme in this reader is a discussion of the market process, the role of the entrepreneur and of discovery. In Kirzner's essays entrepreneurial discovery is compared and contrasted with neo-classical economics calculative economizing activity. He discusses the limits of rationality. He sets out the qualities of good entrepreneurship and describes how entrepreneurial alertness is fundamentally different from the resources ordinarily employed in decision making. Kirzner describes the impact that government regulation has on the entrepreneurial discovery process and economic growth.

Hayek describes in *The Road to Serfdom* the dangers to democracy of central planning. This reader includes two chapters from this 1944 work which Milton Friedman calls "a true classic" and Thomas Sowell calls "a landmark work." Useful to an understanding of the economic and business environment is Hayek's discussion of "the general interest." It is an impossibility to specify a complete system of human values upon which any definition of "the general interest" depends. An understanding of the business environment is enhanced by understanding that the rule of law necessitates formal rules which limit the *ad hoc* powers of government. These are qualitatively distinct from substantive rules of government proposed by social planners.

Part III presents applications of the theoretical framework presented in Parts I and II. While the applications discussed are related to the environment, health care and international trade, the framework presented in these readings can be infinitely generalized. Indeed, a measure of the comprehension of these readings is the ability to generalize to other applications.

A Note on Reading the Reader

We have also designed this reader to build critical thinking skills. These skills include the ability to uncover and articulate hidden assumptions behind judgments, decisions and actions; to recognize faulty reasoning and biases in perceptions; to trace through cause and effect beyond primary effects to secondary effects and thus to analyze systems; to reframe a problem from many points of view and to synthesize ideas. The nature of the ideas presented will prompt the reader to reflect on their own beliefs and professional and ethical values. Readers will gain a deeper understanding of the mental models in their own minds and what is truly meaningful to them.

Reading original works instead of a textbook engages students in the great debates of our time and demonstrates that knowledge and beliefs change. We believe this sparks enthusiasm for life-long learning.

> The development of general ability for independent thinking and judgment should always be placed foremost.
>
> *—Albert Einstein*

> Some people will never learn anything for this reason: because they understand everything too soon.
>
> *—Alexander Pope*

For many this will be your initial exposure to reading original pieces of critical thinking as opposed to second or third hand textbook presentations. A few words about what to expect are in order. Initially you may find the readings difficult. You might long for the familiar formulas and graphs of a traditional textbook. Adam Robinson in his outstanding book, *What Smart Students Know,* tells the the story involving the famous physicist Nells Bohr. Bohr tells a scientist in his audience that "if he wasn't confused and bewildered by the presentation, he hadn't been paying attention."[8] While we hope these essays don't provoke such an extreme reaction, as Robinson writes, "if your brain isn't a little shaken up by something new, you've missed the point."[9]

We encourage the reader to have respect for the process of learning. For most readers several readings of the more difficult essays are necessary to begin to understand them. Hayek's prose which may be difficult at first encounter soon becomes a welcome treasure of rich ideas to return to again and again. Hayekian scholar Chiaki Nishiyama writes: "once readers master Hayekian terminology and his innovative way of thinking, they find it surprisingly easy to appreciate his arguments, none of which is self-evident at first glance. The so-called great discoveries and widely accepted 'truths' are almost without exception rather easy to understand. So it is with the Hayekian order of ideas."[10]

In the final analysis though this reader is a beginning not an end. To understand and learn is a lifetime's journey and because a central insight of Hayek's work is that an individual can never have the whole of knowledge this journey of understanding is ever unfolding.

Notes

1. Israel Kirzner, "Competition, Regulation, and the Market Process," *Policy Analysis* no. 18 (Cato Institute, Washington, DC 1982), p. 1.

2. Tom Peters, *Liberation Management* (New York: Alfred Knopf, 1992), p. 501.

3. Murray Rothbard, "Justice and Property Rights" in *Property in a Humane Society* (La Salle, Illinois: Open Court, 1974), p. 114.

4. Ibid., p. 102.

5. Friedrich Hayek, *Law, Legislation and Liberty,* V2 (Chicago: University of Chicago Press, 1976), p. 99.

6. Friedrich Hayek, "The Use of Knowledge in Society" in *Individualism and Economic Order* (Chicago: Henry Regnery Co., 1972), p. 78.

7. Professor Jerry Ellig of George Mason University.

8. Adam Robinson, *What Smart Students Know* (New York: Crown, 1993), p. 133.

9. Ibid.

10. Chiaki Nishiyama and Kurt Leube ed. *The Essence of Hayek* (Stanford: Hoover Institution Press, 1984), p. xxxviii.

ACKNOWLEDGMENTS

Part I: Kinds of Order, The Individual, Property Rights and Rules

"Our Models Define Our World" by Yoram Wind and Colin Crook with Robert Gunther from *The Power of Impossible Thinking: Transform the Business of Your Life and the Life of Your Business*. Copyright © 2005 by Pearson Education, Inc. Publishing as Wharton School Publishing. Reprinted with permission.

"The Connection Between Conversation, Leadership, and Cultures of Collaboration and Partnership" by Linda Ellinor and Glenna Gerard from *Dialogue*. John Wiley and Sons, 1998. Copyright © by Linda Ellinor and Glenna Gerard.

"What is Dialogue?" by Linda Ellinor and Glenna Gerard from *Dialogue*. John Wiley and Sons, 1998. Copyright © by Linda Ellinor and Glenna Gerard.

"Wisdom, Insight, and Psychological Change" by Rick Suarez, Roger Mills and Darlene Stewart from *Sanity, Insanity and Common Sense*. Copyright © 1980, 1982 by E.M. Suarez, Roger C. Mills and Darlene Stewart. Reprinted by permission of Ballantine Books, a division of Random House, Inc.

"Cosmos and Taxis" by Friedrich A. Hayek from *Law, Legislation and Liberty*. Copyright © 1973 by F.A. Hayek. Reprinted by permission of The University of Chicago Press.

"Self-Organization and the Corporation" by Richard T. Pascale, Mark Millemann, and Linda Gioja from *Surfing the Edge of Chaos: The Laws of Nature and the New Laws of Business*. Published by Crown Business, Random House, Inc. Copyright © 2000 by Richard T. Pascale, Mark Millemann, and Linda Gioja. Reprinted with permission.

"Individualism: True or False" by Friedrich Hayek from *The Essence of Hayek*. Copyright © 1948 by The University of Chicago Press.

"Self-Reliance" by Ralph Waldo Emerson from *Self-Reliance*.

Part II: Knowledge, Emergence, and The Market Process

Part III: The Rule of Law and Regulation

Thanks

Our appreciation to Elaine Manke, Sue Culbertson, and Teresa Hicks of McGraw-Hill for their invaluable assistance on this revision and for that priceless feeling of knowing that you are in the best of hands.

Part I

KINDS OF ORDER, THE INDIVIDUAL, PROPERTY RIGHTS AND RULES

OUR MODELS DEFINE
OUR WORLD

Yoram Wind and Colin Crook with Robert Gunther

> In the old world, managers make products. In the new world,
> managers make sense of things.
> —John Seely Brown[1]

It's midnight, and you hear a loud radio in the apartment downstairs. Last week the quiet old man who lived there passed away, and you've been concerned about the arrival of the next tenant. You never know who might move in, and you've heard some real horror stories from your college friends. In an apartment house, the wrong neighbors can make your life miserable.

Now your worst fears have come true. The rock music plays on and on. You toss and turn, looking at the clock. At 12:30 a.m., you decide to wait just a little longer. Even if your new neighbor is a jerk, you are reluctant to turn your first meeting into a fight. At 1:00 a.m., the radio is blaring just as loud. What kind of party are they throwing down there? You've got to get up for work tomorrow. How can a person be so ignorant? So you walk down to lecture this idiot on common courtesy. You knock heavily on the door, and it swings open.

You are surprised to find the apartment completely bare. There is no sign of your new neighbor. There isn't even a sign of furniture. So you walk in. In the back room you find some drop cloths and paint cans. Plugged into one wall, you see a boom box cranked up full.

There is no neighbor, just a careless painter who left the radio on when he left for the day. The new tenant hasn't even arrived yet. The ignorant neighbor that you invented based on the noise vanishes into air, but the anger and other emotions you felt are still very real. You have trouble settling down and going back to sleep because you are still angry at this neighbor, a neighbor who exists only in your mind. You created this evil figure to explain the loud music, and he took on a life of his own. If you hadn't gone down and knocked on the door, you might have lived with this illusion for days.

Your mental models shape the way you see the world. They help you to quickly make sense of the noises that filter in from outside, but they can also limit your ability to see the true picture. They are with you always and, like your neighbors, can be a great help or can keep you up at night without reason.

What are mental models, and how do they shape your understanding and define the world you live in?

Can the wrong mental model kill you? Over the past quarter century, more than 150 children have died in the United States after their parents chose not to provide medical treatment because of their religious beliefs.[2] The parents belonged to one of some 20 religious groups whose teachings deny the use of traditional medical care, relying instead on faith healing. The results are often tragic.

In April 1986, two-year-old Robyn Twitchell died of a bowel obstruction in Boston, Massachusetts. His parents, Christian Scientists, took the boy to a church practitioner who prescribed only prayer. The child's condition worsened. He had difficulty eating and sleeping. He was shaking and vomiting. Five days after the onset of the illness, he became unresponsive. The parents and the practitioner continued to trust in prayer up to the time of his death. The parents were convicted in July 1990 of manslaughter.

Experts testified that the condition could have been treated with a simple operation to remove the twisting of the bowel, an operation that would have very likely saved the child's life. This procedure, based on a surgical model of treating disease, was not considered by the boy's parents because of the mental model they held about the causes and treatment of disease. In a certain sense, the boy's death was due to the way they made sense of the world.

This story is not presented to pass judgment on the parents for their tragic decision or criticize their religious beliefs. It does offer an example of a single decision that is viewed through divergent models—the parents' beliefs and the medical perspective that the courts used in ruling on the case. In the court's opinion, the outcome of following the parents' model was very likely much worse than the outcome that could have been achieved from following a medical model.

While their impact is rarely so sharply defined as in this case, our mental models can affect our lives, careers and relationships; the prosperity of our businesses; and the quality of life in our societies. Almost every aspect of our lives is shaped in some way by how we make sense of the world. Our thinking and our actions are affected by the mental models we hold. These models define our limits or open our opportunities. Despite their power and pervasiveness, these models are usually virtually invisible to us. We don't realize they are there at all.

We believe that what we see is reality rather than something we create inside our heads. The parents of Robyn Twitchell believed that prayer alone was going to cure him. For them, this was reality. The surgeons who could have treated the child saw the case through a completely different set of eyes, as did the criminal justice system. We might think of mental models as something abstract or academic—to be studied and explained like optical illusions—but in this case and many others these models clearly are anything but academic. They not only shape what we see and how we understand the world but also how we act in it. In a real sense, what we think is what we see, and what we see is what we think.

How do the models you use to understand your life keep you locked in certain patterns of thought or prevent you from seeing solutions that are right in front of you? What are the potentially negative effects of your current models? How could you change your models to improve the quality of your life?

Rethinking IBM's Research Model

Models also limit or open new opportunities in business. In the early 1990s, the head of research at IBM, Jim McGroddy, came to visit one of the authors (Colin Crook), who was then chief technology officer at Citicorp. McGroddy faced a serious challenge. IBM was losing billions of dollars every year. How could the research program help turn this situation around?

Crook discussed the information-technology value chain that was guiding IT development at Citibank. This value chain had three basic levels: at the bottom were atoms and basic math; in the middle was technology, such as storage, displays and chips; and at the top were customer solutions. What was really important, he said, was the work on these customer solutions, and that was where Citicorp was differentiating itself from rivals.

McGroddy realized that this focus on customer solutions had been largely ignored by IBM Research. Most of the company's attention was on basic research at the bottom level or on technology in the middle. The company had become insular and product-focused, losing touch with its customers. This realization led to a reorganization of IBM Research and the creation of a new strategic area focusing on services, applications and solutions. IBM's successful turnaround was driven by research in that category, which increased from nearly zero in 1990 to more than 25 percent in 2001. This dovetailed nicely with the launch of new chairman Lou Gerstner's global services initiative, which became the fastest growing area for IBM.[3]

IBM may not have recognized it, but its research had been driven by a technocentric mental model. When this model was recognized and challenged, new opportunities could be seen, the organization could be redesigned and the business could be transformed (a transformation that was, of course, much broader than R&D). What looked like an R&D problem could be rethought from the perspective of the market. What looked like a difficult technological problem could be reconsidered as a challenge of business design.

Compartmentalization of Business and Personal Life

We recently spoke with a successful manager who remarked that when she needs to hire a new employee, she inevitably turns to a headhunter. But in her personal life, she trusts to chance to find a life partner. It is a similar challenge of finding the right person with the right characteristics and chemistry, but she applies a completely different approach because she has a different mental model for her personal and business life. She would never think about going into a single's bar and hoping to stumble across the perfect vice president of marketing, but she will in her personal life. Because of this artificial wall, she was much less creative in thinking about her personal life (and less successful in filling the position for a life partner) than in her business life where she routinely found great people to fill key positions.

One of the limiting frames we have is the separation of business and personal life, even as these two worlds are merging together. Look at how many TV entertainment programs have a work setting for portraying stories of personal lives. As the lines between business and personal lives blur, there are opportunities for shifting our thinking within business and personal life and across the two. We can borrow mental models from one area and apply them to the other to change the way we see both aspects of our lives.

Domestic Emerging Markets

To take another example, consider how most companies view inner-city markets. These markets tend to be areas with low incomes, high crime rates and other risks or costs—in short, they are seen as a marketer's nightmare. Even as major companies are waking up to the potential of emerging markets around the world, inner-city markets are still largely neglected. Yet, as Michael Porter has pointed out, these markets have distinctive advantages and hidden opportunities if we look more closely.[4] While income may be lower, population density is much higher so "spending power per acre" is comparable to more affluent parts of the city. These markets are in strategic locations and often present demographics segments that are crucial to future market growth.

If we were to reframe the inner city as "domestic emerging markets," what new possibilities would this open? What strategies that are being used to address emerging markets in China and India might be applied in the cities of the United States and other developed nations with good effect? This simple shift in the way we view these markets could open new possibilities for strategies and new potential for growth.

How do your models for your industry and business prevent you from recognizing opportunities and realizing the full value of your organization?

The Parallel Universes in Our Minds

The brain, weighing on average just around three pounds, has a complexity of structure and function that we are only just beginning to understand. Estimates vary, but we have around 100 billion neurons, which communicate via perhaps several hundred trillion synapses. The whole brain is awash in a swirl of neurochemicals, and lightning storms of electrical activity flicker across it, as millions of sensory signals from the eyes, ears, nose, mouth and skin are thrown into the mix.

It is a wonder we can even think. And yet we do. A linear processing machine bombarded with this flood of stimulation would probably shut right down. The brain is quite different. It somehow makes sense out of the welter of flashing signals. The human mind engages in daily magic tricks that make David Copperfield look like a parlor act. Studies in neuroscience indicate that the sense we make of external things is based in small part on what we see outside and in large part on the patterns located in our minds.

Mkanig Snese from Nsosnese

As Lewis Carroll demonstrated in the "brillig" and "slithy toves" of his poem *Jabberwocky,* it takes only a little bit of context for our marvelous sense-making abilities to draw meaning from absolute gibberish. With a little effort, the following statement, circulating online, should make this point clear. While neither the study nor the university are formally identified, the words, however garbled, speak for themselves:

Aoccdrnig to rscheearch at an Elingsh uinervtisy, it deosn't mttaer in waht oredr the ltteers in a wrod are, olny taht the frist and lsat ltteres are at the rghit pcleas. The rset can be a toatl mses and you can sitll raed it wouthit a porbelm. Tihs is bcuseae we do not raed ervey lteter by ilstef, but the wrod as a wlohe.

Ask yourself: Does the rest of your life have this many holes that you are not seeing?

The mind appears to do this, in part, *by choosing to ignore some of the external world.* American neurophysiologist Walter Freeman discovered that the neural activity due to sensory stimuli disappears in the cortex. Our eyes and ears are constantly gathering information, but our mind is not really processing all of it (see sidebar, "Mkanig Snese from Nsosnese"). This stimulation flows into the brain, where what seems to be an internally related pattern appears, which the brain uses to represent the external situation.

The brain takes in the information about the world through the senses and then discards most of it, using it principally to evoke a parallel world of its own. Each brain creates its own world, which is internally consistent and complete. Perception is not a linear process of information reception, processing, storage and recall. Instead it is a very complex, interactive, subjective and evocative process.

It is as if a visitor came to the front door and rang the bell, and the person inside, by a quick glance through the fisheye peephole, formed a complete profile of the person outside, without opening the door. We know from experience that we have the ability to form snap judgments about people immediately—and that these judgments are sometimes wrong. Yet this process is extraordinarily efficient and effective, which is why there are peepholes in doors in the first place. Unlike a baby first learning about the world, we don't have to try to make sense of every new piece of information. Given a few lines, we can fill in the entire image. This ability to respond intuitively to what we see is crucial to quick thinking and action. (In Chapter 10 we discuss the power and limitations of intuition.)

Building Our Brains

The brain has developed and changed throughout human evolution, and its layered structure clearly shows this, starting deep within with the oldest "reptilian" part and moving out through the "limbic" system to the "neocortex," the seat of rational behavior.

Our own brains change and evolve over time, with neurons constantly dying and being recreated, synapses being destroyed and created anew. The brain selects and reinforces or weakens certain synapses to forge the complex neural structures that determine our thinking. Then we reshape these neural "models" through experience, education and training.

The newborn child has a fundamental but only rudimentary capacity to make sense of the signals, probably derived from genetic instructions. Subsequent experience works upon this genetic foundation. The child's first, urgent task is to quickly develop the capacity to make sense of these confusing signals. Within the first two years, most children appear to develop this capability. The process involved is to understand where the stimulus comes from and then categorize the signal as some specific case of a more general pattern. A mix of shadows and colors is recognized as a ball. The face hovering above the baby is recognized as the mother—but then all similar faces are also seen as mother until the model is refined. The child is able to form a holistic sense without getting bogged down in the details. This categorization is key. These experiences are also retained in the form of memory—complex patterns spread across the brain that are not representational but are evoked by other patterns and external stimuli.

As the internal worlds in the child's mind become richer, the external world recedes. Freeman's experiments show that the balance tips from the outside to the inside. The brain's own models replace the input signals from external sources. When the brain confronts a new experience, it calls up a complex neural activity or "mental model" that seems to be its nearest equivalent. We see the absence of these models in the child's wonder at the simplest of experiences. We feel their presence when we express regret about the familiar routines and ruts that sometimes determine our lives in adulthood. The development of mental models is, in a certain sense, a demarcation line between childhood and maturity. We increasingly live in a familiar world that can be considered as a benign illusion—benign, because it helps us move through the world efficiently, but an illusion nonetheless.

We eventually lose all awareness that these "models" are in fact internal illusions. We accept them as external reality and act on them as if they were. If they are good models, in most circumstances they more than adequately permit the mind to handle external reality. But here a danger creeps in. When the world changes in important ways, we can find ourselves with a model that is completely irrelevant to the current situation. We find ourselves wearing our street clothes when we are thrown off the deck of a ship. What we need at that point is a wet suit and lifejacket.

Where "Models" Come From

Constant training shapes and refines our "models." A jazz musician or modern artist probably has a very different view of many aspects of the world than, say, a scientist or engineer. Even training doesn't fully explain our models. Not every musician or engineer will look at the world in the same way. A breakthrough thinker like Albert Einstein might have much more in common with a modern artist than with some of his colleagues in science. Some individual scientists may creatively push the limits; others may work in a well-defined area of study. Some CFOs may be risk averse while others are daring to the point of danger. Their approaches are shaped by their personality (genetics), education, training, influence of others and other experiences.

We can gain insights into our "mental models" by looking at where they come from. There has been a long debate about the influence of nature versus nurture in shaping our thinking. At the moment, it appears increasingly likely that nature, in the form of genetics, plays a significant role in determining who we are. Many of the basic capabilities of the brain, such as language, appear to be predetermined at birth by virtue of the genetics we inherit.

Clearly we are born with some hardware and hard wiring that influences the way we see the world. Mood disorders offer an extreme example of how these chemical and genetic differences can color the way we see the world. While genetic research and pharmaceutical interventions are offering new ways to change the structure and chemicals of our thinking, their exact impact on mental models is unclear. As much as we might like to find one, there is no pill or genetic theory for changing our mental models, although at some point in the future development of science it may fall within the realm of possibility. There also seems to be considerable flexibility in the human mind in overcoming the limitations of nature.

Genetics appear to provide the fundamental basis of who we are and what we can do, and then experience plays a major role in shaping these capabilities, strengthening some and weakening others. Thus a number of forces of "nurture" shape and reshape our "mental models," including:

- *Education.* Our education shapes our mental models very broadly and forms a foundation that molds our world view. A scientist learns to approach the world in a different way than a jazz musician. This broad education is often the least visible force shaping our mindset. We surround ourselves with people of similar background. A liberal arts education aims in many ways to give people a common language and world view from which to operate, so it is very easy for this educational foundation to blend into the environment like a chameleon on a rock. While deepening knowledge in a subject area is one kind of learning, learning about mental models represents a second kind of learning (see sidebar, "A Second Kind of Learning").

- *Training.* Related to education is the specific training we receive to deal with transitions or handle new tasks. A computer programmer might learn a programming language, or an artist might learn to work in metal sculpture. This training is more specific and more visible than education, and more easily changed. Still, we often get into a rut in our training that is very difficult to break out of, even when the world around us has changed significantly.

- *Influence of others.* We are all influenced by mentors, experts, family and friends. These individuals, their philosophy of life and approach to problems affect us deeply in how we approach our own challenges. We are also influenced by the books we've read. For example, a child who grows up reading all of H. G. Wells' novels might be influenced by this experience to become a scientist. We are influenced by people in our immediate environment—first by parents, friends and teachers and later by supervisors and coworkers—who push us in new directions or encourage us to achieve more, challenging our own views of ourselves. We also are influenced by broader trends in society, as were many people who grew up in the 1960s. finally, we are influenced by mass culture in a world in which MTV can transfer fashion trends around the globe in a matter of hours.

- *Rewards and incentives.* Our mental models and actions are shaped by the rewards we receive for holding them. These rewards can be tangible, such as direct financial gain, or less tangible ones, such as social approval.

- *Personal experience.* Some artists and scientists are self-taught. They create their own style through personal experience, which makes it easier to think outside the mainstream. The tradition of apprenticeship is also based on a process of combining learning from both experience and a mentor or expert craftsman.

In addition to the specifics of what we learn in our education, we also develop capabilities for *learning how to learn* that help us to make sense of our experiences. Our own successes and failures can dramatically shape our view of the world. Personal encounters can have a major impact on how we view life overall or in specific areas. How we cope with mistakes and learn from our successes affects how we approach every new challenge. Severe ordeals, such as imprisonment in a concentration camp or traumatic childhood abuse, may affect our world view throughout our lives. Some people find their worlds crushed and limited by these misfortunes. Others respond by developing a determination and drive that carries them not only across their present hurdles but also to new levels of success.

Today's experience quickly becomes tomorrow's theology. This is why generals are often fighting the last war. They have shaped their policies based on their past equipment and military strategy, carefully learning lessons from debriefings on the last battlefield that may no longer be relevant on the current one (although post-mortems can be a valuable source of insights as long as we recognize that the world may change). Experience can be a double-edged sword.

Models for the Moment

Some of our models are very broad, held by members of an entire nation, political party or religious group, while others are very localized and specific. A broader model such as a belief in democracy or communism affects the mental models of followers, influencing their beliefs and behavior as well as the entire structure of society and economic life. Not all our models are on such a grand scale. Our background and philosophical beliefs often affect how we see the world, but we also apply situation-specific models. A fire drill or airplane evacuation routine is an example of a situation-specific model. Whatever our backgrounds, training and experience, we all look for the nearest exit, put on our oxygen mask if it is deployed from the ceiling or inflate our life vests.

In this case, the goal is to give everyone a common model that seems to be best practice in responding to a particular emergency. But when passengers on the flights of 9/11 were faced with a situation that was not on the cards in the seatbacks, they needed to improvise and create a model based on their experience, drawing upon past experiences such as sports, military training, stories or movies.

In many cases, our background and experience determine how we will respond in a particular situation. When Johnson & Johnson made its famous decision to pull its product off the shelves in response to the Tylenol scare in 1982 (when an unknown tamperer laced the capsules with cyanide, killing seven people in Chicago), the company's actions were based on a firmly embedded set of values embodied in the corporate "credo." It set a course of action that was consistent with its core mental model—that if it put its customers and other stakeholders first, returns to shareholders would naturally follow.

Sometimes our responses to specific challenges ultimately transform our broader models. Consider the long-held opposition to big government by the U.S. Republican party. In the face of terrorist attacks and scandals on Wall Street early in the new millenium, the Republican administration expanded government staffing, budgets and powers to meet these new threats to national economic stability. The proponents of reducing government had actually expanded it. The specific actions, designed to meet the challenges of the moment, ultimately undermined the broader model.

This view of the application of models for the moment is in contrast to approaches such as Meyers-Briggs, which attempts to define a specific individual style of approaching decisions. While the recognition of the different cognitive styles (such as perceptive/receptive, or systematic/intuitive) is an important one, we are not necessarily static in how we apply these approaches. An individual may work through a variety of styles in addressing specific challenges or responding to specific situations.

A Second Kind of Learning

There is a lot of discussion about the importance of creating what Peter Senge and others have called a "learning organization." We recognize the importance in personal development of continuing to engage in what Stephen Covey refers to as "sharpening the saw." But in the application of these ideas to our business and personal lives, we often fail to make a distinction about two kinds of learning.

The first kind of learning, which is far more common and more easily achieved, is to deepen our knowledge within an existing mental model or discipline.

The second kind of learning is focused on new mental models and on shifting from one to another. It does not deepen knowledge in a specific model but rather looks at the world outside the model and adopts or develops new models to make sense of this broader world. Sometimes we don't need to merely "sharpen" the saw; we need to throw it out to pick up a power tool. If we are focused only on sharpening, then we might not see the opportunity to apply new technology that can radically change the way we approach the task. The sharpest saw in the tool box may be no match for a powerful new approach based on a new way of looking at the world.

This book focuses primarily on this second kind of learning. It is not just doing a better job at the current task but asking whether it is the right approach and how we might be able to change it. It is not the kind of learning that results from an engineer's taking the 100th course in engineering, but rather the kind that comes from her taking a first course in jazz, which allows her to look at engineering problems from a completely new perspective. Learning about new mental models is much more challenging and complex, but crucial in an environment of rapid change and uncertainty.

Avoiding Obsolescence

During the painful layoffs and restructuring at Citicorp in the early 1990s, we witnessed the following uncomfortable scene: A talented computer programmer in his forties, facing the loss of his position, was shocked to find that he was no longer needed because his skills in COBOL programming were obsolete. This bolt came totally out of the blue, because he was a good programmer. He just hadn't kept up. Not only this, but as he worked through outplacement, he discovered to his horror that his skills were no longer valuable to *anyone*. He had been cruising along in his career, unaware of the changes around him, and now he found that the road he was traveling led right off a cliff.

Could this programmer have been better prepared if he hadn't been locked in an outdated mindset? Even if he couldn't have prevented his dismissal, could he at least have been better able to move forward afterward?

If the world remained static, we might be able to remain blissfully unaware of our models. Like our primitive hunter-gatherer ancestors, our basic instinct and experience would serve us well from childhood throughout our relatively short lives. But today the world changes ever more rabidly, and we need to be able to recognize our own models, to know whether and how to change them, to act quickly, and to influence the models of others.

Like the programmer in the example above, we often don't see the need to change until we experience the pink slip, the divorce, the lawsuit or the heart attack. Then, if it is not too late, we wake up to see that our old mental models no longer work. (Surprisingly, even these shocks sometimes are not enough.)

It doesn't have to be this way. You can consciously change your mental models before the world forces you to do so. Some of the people at Citicorp, including many who ultimately survived the job cuts, made a conscious effort to immerse themselves in the outside world. They explored different aspects of technology, such as new programming languages and techniques, and brought these new perspectives to their work. They actively challenged their own mental models and those around them. They continued to develop new and useful mindsets that were valuable to the organization. They became leaders of the transformations that were needed to turn the company around.

At any given point, we have a choice in how we view the world. But we are not always aware of these choices. The models we have developed through our education and experience are often invisible to us until it is too late.

In a changing environment, we can either transform ourselves or be transformed. Every day individuals in their work and personal lives prove that it is possible to change before life itself gives them a painful wakeup call. But to transform our lives, we have to first transform our minds. Our mental models determine what we are able to see and do.

The Consequences of Models

We live in a world of great risk and great possibilities. We have unprecedented opportunities to blend the best of the old and new, to open up new perspectives and connect to different fields of knowledge, like sampling from a buffet. Yet it is a risky business to abandon our old views of the world. We have seen the traditional views of religion, family, institutions and belief in capitalism eroded in recent years, with some positive consequences but also some degree of chaos rushing into the vacuum. When we depart from the dry land in business or personal life, we are subject to the crosswinds and crosscurrents of whatever crackpot ideas and fads come toward us. If we can navigate this passage to new mindsets, we will have opportunities to discover new worlds with rich potential.

Our true work, as John Seely Brown points out in the quote that opens this chapter, is making sense. It is not just for managers in business but for everyone in business, politics and personal life. As in a detective story, we are in a race against time, against clever rivals who deliberately or inadvertently create decoy trails to throw us off the scent. In a world of deep complexity and extensive information, this work of making sense has never been harder—or more important. Unlike most detective stories, this one does not have a simple (The butler did it!) answer at the end, unless we discover it or create it. It does not even have an ending. The world we see today could undergo a gestalt flip tomorrow. We can get better at this process of making sense—and the first step is recognizing that there is a process at all.

Some will argue that the world is already far too complicated for us to make sense of it. they act as if we need to just keep our heads down, focus on the track in front of our feet and keep moving. That may work for a limited time (until some freight train comes barreling down the track we're walking on). But our strength as human beings is our power to make sense, adapt to a fabulously complex world and quickly decide on a practical course of action. This is how we have survived and progressed since the age of the sabertooth tiger. It is how we can succeed in today's complex world.

In today's complicated and uncertain environment, the greatest dangers are not from beasts prowling around outside. More often than not they are in our own minds, our inability to see our own limits and to see things differently. It is these internal beasts that we seek to better understand—and learn to live with, if not to tame—in the pages of this book.

Impossible Thinking

- What are your mental models that shape your thinking? How are your models different from those of others?
- What are a few recent decisions, personal or professional, in which you can identify the role of mental models in how you framed the problem or developed your solution?
- How has your own education and experience affected your mental models?
- What are the potential blindspots of your models and experience?
- How can you seek out new perspectives and experience to help challenge or change your current models?

Notes

1. Address to Complexity Conference in Phoenix, Arizona, and February 1997.

2. "Death by Religious Exemption." *Massachusetts Citizens for Children*. January 1992. <http://www.masskids.org/peama/religion_1cases.html>.

3. Thanks to Robert Buderi for reviving this example in "The Once and Future Industrial Research." *26th Annual Colloquium on Science and Technology Policy*. Washington, DC. 3—4 May 2001.

4. Porter, Michael E. "The Competitive Advantage of the Inner City," *Harvard Business Review* (May-June 1995), pp. 55-71.

THE CONNECTION BETWEEN CONVERSATION, LEADERSHIP, AND CULTURES OF COLLABORATION AND PARTNERSHIP

Linda Ellinor and Glenna Gerard

> Eighty percent of the people who fail at work do so for one reason: they do not relate well to other people.
>
> —Robert Bolton
> *People Skills*

The High Cost and Frustration of Poor Communication[1]

Millions of dollars are lost every day by organizations simply because of the limited and ineffective ways we have learned to communicate.[2] Think back to meetings you have attended lately that were long, dry, boring, and unproductive. Think of the countless numbers of hours that you sit in such meetings where nothing new is put forward, or certain members monopolize the air time, or everyone goes away with different understandings of what took place, or where power plays prevented any real or authentic conversation to take place. All of these and more are the repetitive norm in most organizations today. If you figure that we pay people a lot of money to engage in such conversations, think of the bottom-line ramifications of conversing in these ways.

Limitations in How We Develop our Leaders

Vast sums of money are also spent every year by organizations on executive and leadership development. Many organizations assume that because they pay their managers large salaries they ought to be investing in their ongoing growth and development. But, think back to the last time you attended a program of this sort. How much of what was covered were you able to apply when you returned to work? If you attended an outdoor or outward-bound program, you probably learned certain things about teamwork and the value of taking personal risks. Or, if you attended an awareness program, you may have been given insight into your strengths and weaknesses as a leader. Other programs stress leadership skills and theories that can be valuable. How much did any of what you may have learned affect your day-to-day behaviors when you returned? Can you say that you manage and lead differently now? Were the changes you made lasting ones?

The Difficulty of Building Cultures of Collaboration and Partnership

We talk a lot today about the importance of building collaboration and partnership in our organizations. We sense that a movement towards these qualities will make a difference in our ability to achieve higher productivity and a better quality of work life; but, with all the increases in workload on employees from downsizings, layoffs, and restructuring, we don't seem to be making much headway towards cultures of collaboration and partnership. These qualities don't fit into our short-term needs for handling the spiraling amount of work that must get done.

In fact, in our rush to accomplish rising levels of work, we rely even more strongly on what in the West has been our cultural mainstay: Individual effort and heroism. With beating the competition, winning, and the Puritan work ethic pumping through our veins, we find ourselves unconsciously continuing to reward our workers based on *these* qualities rather than on the alternative norms of collaboration and partnership. Being pushed up against the wall for results creates ambivalence and confusion around any movement towards these later norms.

Even if we are clear about the need for change, it is often less clear *how* to bring it about. Weaving the qualities of collaboration and partnership into traditional competitive management practices can seem like mixing water and oil. We don't know how to do it.

We write what we want to see into vision and mission statements. We send individual managers to workshops that support the values we want to see in our firms. We make structural changes leading to more decentralized control. But after we do all these things, we realize that little has fundamentally changed. We still encounter the same old patterns in our meetings; the same competitive, uncooperative stuff, such as one-upmanship, the need to be right, the usual power plays that typify win/lose over others. "What is going on," we ask ourselves. "Why aren't the new norms around teamwork and collaboration taking hold?"

Linking Communication, Leadership and Cultures of Collaboration and Partnership

A larger question may be how developing communication skills, leadership, and cultures of collaboration are all interconnected and can't be done effectively without treating them as one comprehensive whole.

By not seeing how they link and overlap, we address them piecemeal and overlook powerful ways they reinforce and impact each other. For instance, consider that the way we communicate is rooted in the shared norms we hold regarding competition and the role of the individual in getting the results we want. If we assume that in most organizations, competition and individualism still reign supreme, then it is little wonder that most of our meetings and conversations with others are chock-full of innuendoes and manners of speech that emphasize who is right, who is wrong, power plays, and gamesmanship. How could it be any different? We are so used to these ways of interacting that we just assume they are the natural order of things. We are not conscious of the underlying mind-sets that drive these ways of interrelating.

Communication is at the root in what needs changing in leadership development. We can help leaders see the value of teamwork and of motivating subordinates to higher levels of performance, but until we help them change the ways in which they communicate with their subordinates, little that is fundamental will be different. Theory, self-awareness, and outdoor activities that promote experiential learning are effective as far as they go. But, these forms of leadership development leave off where long-lasting behavioral change needs to begin. The behaviors that will make a difference are ones such as how leaders listen and develop the trust of others, and how they challenge team members to think productively together and surface problems before they become crises.

Think about leaders or managers you have known whose technical skills were extraordinary but whose people skills were lacking. If, in communicating with others, they always have to have the final say, if they ignore or discount others, or are disrespectful and arrogant, they will not be effective in their work with others. Eventually, such managers reach a plateau. They alienate people to the point where no one wants to work with them anymore. At this point they have three options available to them: 1) they can move to another job where they will most likely experience the same pattern playing out, 2) they can modify their job in ways that rely more on their technical versus people skills, or 3) they can bite the bullet and develop their people skills.

Finally, consider how communication itself is fundamental in the movement to a culture of collaboration and partnership. After all, it is in how we speak with one another that we experience respect from others and whether we are being heard. But, we can only speak in these ways if we have the corresponding attitudes and values about other people that support this kind of respect and integrity. It is our values and attitudes that drive how we speak and listen. They drive the overall culture that we create together through the ways in which we converse.

If we are to change the ways in which we communicate with one another, we must find a way to surface the underlying values and mental models that keep us locked into limited ways of speaking and listening. In the United States and other western-based cultures, this usually means examining our shared assumptions around competition and individual effort versus collaboration and partnership to see when and where we might be out of balance. Then we need to begin to practice behaviors that support the changes we would like to see, those that might give us more of the balance we desire between these two value sets. Dialogue is a process that can help us do just that.

An Answer for Our Times: Dialogue

For now, think of dialogue as a communications practice that actually bridges communication, leadership, and culture. It is a powerful form of conversation that helps us meet the dilemmas we face by transforming the consciousness of those who engage in it. Let's consider some key elements of this change process.

Relationships: The Critical Factor

Generally, it is the quality of our relationships that makes the critical difference in getting the results we are looking for at work. Having said this, it is also true that we are culturally blind to this critical factor. Why? Because we "attend" to the results of our work and not to how we get the results through working with others. Our relationships with others are often the last thing we consciously focus on. In our rush to complete our work, we may not realize the damage we do to some of the most important relationships we have.

Through ongoing practice of dialogue, we can breathe new life into our relationships. Dialogue helps us pay continuous attention to the ways in which we work with others. It safeguards the glue that binds us together in getting our work done.

It does this by building deeper and deeper levels of trust and understanding about who each of us is and how best we can blend and synchronized our work together. It helps us transcend the limitations of formal job roles and status. By seeing who each of us is *personally* and all that we bring to the table, we are able to take full advantage of all the relationships that help us get our work done.

Trust is built by taking the time to deeply listen to one another and to get to know one another. This is the secret of high-performance teams, whether they be related to sports, music, or work.

Moving Beyond the Level of the Individual to Our Shared Mental Models

Dialogue moves us beyond the individual to a focus on the larger social and cultural context in which we live and work. It is a natural evolution that expands on what has too often been a singular focus on the individual to the social systems in which work is actually being performed.

The larger core dilemmas of our times—such as alienation in the workplace, integration of diversity, running from one crisis to another, or making sense of increasing levels of complexity—can no longer be addressed piecemeal and only at the individual level. These seemingly intractable organizational problems can only be chipped away if seen through the lens of a system as a whole entity. Dialogue is by its nature such a lens. It works to bring integration and wholeness of perspective into the day-to-day decisions we make. By illuminating our shared mental models, dialogue helps surface and make conscious the shared underlying assumptions and belief systems that tie us all together into larger systems. We become more conscious of and have more choices around how we approach and solve systemic dilemmas.

Dialogue as Practice Field

Part of the power of dialogue is that it creates a practice field. Just as an orchestra or any performing art or team sport needs practice and rehearsal for peak performance, so do we all when it comes to changing and enhancing the quality of relationships that helps us get our work done.

Practice is pivotal in developing competence around the new behaviors we desire. Practicing dialogue brings into relief our underlying behaviors and patterns of communication. We are able to see directly what works and what needs changing. From this place of greater awareness, we are then able to make the agreements we need with one another to move towards desired changes.

In the past, it has been common to send individuals off to workshops and programs that develop new skills and ways of working. Dialogue reverses this approach. In dialogue, we practice a set of skills and behaviors in the very groups and teams we work with. The more we practice dialogue in these intact groups and teams, the faster the behaviors, norms, and thinking patterns that support them begin to shift.

Bridging the Competitive Work Ethic with Collaboration and Partnership

Dialogue can help to dispel our ambivalence toward change. Coming out of a worldview that can hold the tension between competition individualism and collaborative partnership, it expands our notions of how organizations work. This expanded worldview arises from an understanding of how chaos theory, self-organizing systems, and quantum physics affect our concepts of social behavior. In nature, both competition and collaboration exist simultaneously, but collaboration is how most leaps in evolution occur. What are the implications for organizations? Competition is an appropriate strategy in certain contexts. But, if we want to see quantum leaps in productivity and results, we need to expand our repertoire to include collaboration.

Dialogue is a process that can help us embrace more of our human potential by learning how to bring in the qualities of cooperation and balance them with our natural urge to compete. In a sense, dialogue is a new way of "being" in a relationship that will help all of us "be" more in whatever situation we confront. It gives us another approach for working together, for handling conflict, for making decisions, and solving problems. It also helps us create alignment in our visions of our work together. Altogether, dialogue can build more flexibility and scope into our organizations today. We can think of it as fitting into a natural evolutionary progression that moves us beyond strict reliance on competition and individual effort to cooperation between people.

Unleashing Motivation through the Re-infusion of Meaning

Dialogue provides ongoing forums for re-infusing the workplace with meaning, which drives motivation. Too often our workplaces become dry and sterile environments because we make little time for that which is human. Our meetings and conversations lack life because our attention is solely on the work at hand and the drive for results. We lose a fuller focus on why we are engaged in doing the work in the first place. In leaving time for the ongoing inquiry into the "why," we can reenchant the workplace with the meaning that is needed for excitement and energy to come back where it may have been lost. Everyone who works as part of an organization or team today needs to feel how what they do is making a difference to the whole. In our rush for results, this is too often overlooked. Dialogue, when it is practiced routinely, can continuously keep our individual and collective juices flowing and the energy level high.

Building In Collective Thinking Capacity

Dialogue uncovers and makes clear the often unseen thinking patterns that block us from making lasting change in recurring problems. We usually see a problem occurring and rush into action before we have sorted things out more comprehensively. We get locked into problem/action/new problem cycles. We continue to get the same basic results, although we try numerous different approaches to solve it. Groups that practice dialogue over time actually develop a capability for collective thinking that can move them beyond this kind of vicious cycling.

Slowing Down to Go Faster

It is rare today that we provide the time and space for thoughtful and reflective conversations to take place. In our fast-paced rush to action, bringing in more thoughtful and reflective forms of speaking may seem somewhat odd or out-of-place. But, it is exactly because the pace of our lives is constantly accelerating, that dialogue is most needed. One of the greatest benefits of dialogue is that it slows the pace of our conversation down so that we can see what is behind all of the rushing around anyways. We stop fire fighting, stand back and consider what started the fires in the first place. Dialogue can help us see new and creative directions rather than just doing what we always have done before when there is no time to consider other possibilities for the future. Slowing down becomes a source of ongoing renewal and generativity.[3]

The New Sciences and Dialogue

The new sciences of chaos theory, self-organizing systems, and quantum physics tell us about the value of dialogue in the modern world. They point out how both the roots of, as well as the solution to, our current dilemmas spring from the very worldviews we hold. Images and ways of working based on seventeenth-century physics are now limiting us as we try to meet twenty-first-century challenges. The old, or Newtonian, views of how to organize and manage organizations are not only insufficient for facing our core dilemmas, but are, in certain cases, the cause of them. The new, or quantum, worldview tells us that the nature of our world is relational. Rather than being made up solely of parts, it is based on the interconnection between the parts. Reality is one seamless whole and cannot be reduced. Analytic/reductionistic ways of thinking about organizations that brought us fixed job descriptions and hierarchical chains of command can still serve us, but only in specific contexts and over a limited time frame. At a certain point, we need more expansive ways of operating that take paradox and shared meaning into account. The new sciences actually point to the absolute necessity of shared leadership if we are to take on the multifaceted, complex, and systemic problems of our day. Again, dialogue is a process that is tailor-made for this task.

The Overall Promise of Dialogue

None of us today can ignore the escalating problems we are confronting from expanding levels of complexity and the increasing speed of modern times. Nor can we continue to work in ways that alienate us from one another and from those we serve and manage. The new sciences tell us that the speed and complexity we are presently experiencing will only increase in the future. They tell us, too, that the only way we will be able to meet these challenges is to figure out how to unleash the full creative potential found within our human systems. The secret appears to be found in paying more attention to the quality of relationships and to the underlying culture and collective thinking patterns that help us get our work done. This is the promise of creating and sustaining cultures of collaboration and partnership through dialogue.

As dialogue is practiced over time, we discover 1) greater levels of authenticity showing up, 2) better decisions being made, and 3) improved morale and alignment forming around shared work. More personal initiative and leadership are exercised outside of the formal hierarchy. As people begin to see more of the whole of what is being accomplished together, they each see where he/she can add more value. People stop waiting for someone else to *tell* them what to do.

Notes

1. We use the term communication here as the broader category in which conversation is a form. Communication encompasses written, verbal, and nonverbal forms. We normally talk about dialogue being a conversational form of communication, but dialogue can also bring in the nonverbal as well.

2. The exact amount of dollars would be impossible to estimate. Perhaps it is billions of dollars.

3. Generativity is the capacity of a person(s) or process to originate, to participate in the unfolding of emergent forms and futures.

WHAT IS DIALOGUE?

Linda Ellinor and Glenna Gerard

> I give a meaning to the word 'dialogue' that is somewhat different from what is commonly used. The derivations of words often help to suggest a deeper meaning.
>
> —David Bohm
> *On Dialogue*

Like a river that has no beginning and no end, there is no single clear definition of dialogue. Where aspects of it have sprung up in the past it has usually led to cultures that honor and respect individuals and the relationships that unite everyone into families and communities. The Greek roots of dialogue are *dia* (through) and *logos* (meaning). Although this definition may sound obtuse, it is the meanings that we share that form the very basis for understanding one another at all. It is also the root of our culture—all those ways of doing things, artifacts, symbols, and words and language—that tie us into a common heritage.

Dialogue helps us bridge the increasing diversity found within modern organizations today. It is through the exploration of meaning that we learn who each person is and how we can work together appropriately. Reflect back on a time when you may have been with people from a foreign country and didn't understand what was going on around you. You probably felt like an outsider, a bit in the dark and left out of things. Not only might you have experienced a language barrier, but a whole range of cultural meanings separating you from the others. Even if you spent a very long time with these people, studying their language and customs, you might still have felt like an outsider. This is because you have not been a part of the "meaning pool" or cultural experience over any significant period of time. Although an extreme example, this is the basis of what it feels like to be a part of a minority in any organization today where you have not grown up a member of whatever forms the majority. Dialogue can help us move beyond cultural stereotypes and develop a sense of shared meaning because then we learn who one another is authentically.

It's helpful to compare the roots of dialogue with the roots of a more commonly found form of conversation in organizations today—discussion. This comparison helps us understand dialogue by understanding what it is not. We generally do not find either pure dialogue or discussion in normal conversation; you might think of them as two poles of a conversation continuum. Although we tend to move between both, we usually are unaware of when we do so. We can improve the quality of our communication just by becoming more conscious of when and where to employ each one.

A Contrast with Discussion

The roots of *discussion* are the same as the roots of *percussion* and *concussion*. All three connote a fragmenting or shattering. The other root of *discussion*, "discus," connotes a disc being thrown against a wall and breaking apart. So, in contrasting dialogue with discussion, we can say that dialogue is about gathering or unfolding meaning that comes from many parts, while discussion is about breaking the whole down into many parts.

Think about the focus of attention in some of the meetings you have attended lately. Were people trying to learn from one another so that they could see what was going on from a larger perspective, or were they trying to justify, explain, or defend their personal perspective? When the underlying dynamic in a meeting is to learn and expand what is known about something or to generate new perspectives from the views of many, the conversation tends toward the dialogic end of the continuum. And, conversely, when the dynamic is about finding one solution or the best alternative among many, it tends towards the discussion end.

Let's look at the characteristics of what we might label as pure dialogic communication or pure discussion and its close, more extreme cousin, debate:

The Conversation Continuum	
Dialogue	**Discussion/Debate**
Seeing the *whole* among the parts	Breaking issues/problems into *parts*
Seeing the *connections* between the parts	Seeing *distinctions* between the parts
Inquiring into assumptions	*Justifying/defending* assumptions
Learning through inquiry and disclosure	*Persuading, selling, telling*
Creating *shared* meaning among many	Gaining agreement on *one* meaning

The main question to ask yourself when you are wondering if the conversation is more dialogic or more discussion-based is whether the main intention of those taking part in it is to push towards closure and choose one perspective; or, if it is to primarily learn from each other and build shared meaning that includes all perspectives. When there is a strong push for a conclusion or to find one solution, people tend toward discussion. When there is no push for a conclusion or a solution, people find it safer to offer differing views without any need to justify "rightness," and it will have more of a dialogic flavor.

When and Why Would Dialogue versus Discussion Be Used?

Because most conversations include a mixture of both dialogic and discussion-based ways of communicating, it is a good idea to get clear on the different objectives or intentions behind both forms. In this way, you can engage each form, depending on the context in which you find yourself.

For instance, if you were calling a meeting together of your peers from different parts of your organization to talk about a joint problem that has arisen, you might ask yourself the following:

- Am I calling the meeting to figure out what immediate action to take?

- Or, am I calling the meeting to learn from everyone about the nature of the problem?

If it is the former, then people will naturally fall into discussion. If it is the latter, and people are clear that you are not trying to solve the problem at this point, you may notice more of a dialogic quality to the meeting.

What often happens in the above scenario is that since people are not consciously aware of the difference between dialogue and discussion, they will think that they have been called to the meeting for both purposes—to learn about the problem *and* to take immediate action. The limitation that this assumption imposes is that these two intentions don't mix very well. Like oil and water, they foster different dynamics and lead to very different end results. In most organizations today, if the purpose of a meeting is not made clear at the outset and there is something obvious to be decided, most groups engage in discussion rather than dialogue. Our need for action and immediate decisions make this so.

Divergent versus Convergent Conversation

Dialogue encourages an opening up about problems, issues, or topics. Because it *expands* what is being communicated by opening up many different perspectives, we call it *divergent* conversation. This is in contrast to discussion or debate that is about *narrowing* down the conversation to one end result. It is trying to come to closure so that everyone knows what to do. Because of this narrowing down, we call this *convergent* conversation. Discussion converges on one point versus dialogue opening to different points.

In most meetings held today in the West, we use convergent, or a discussion-based form of communication. And, when our objective is mainly to converge on the one right answer, we may be missing a large part of the whole picture as depicted below.

We depict the proportions in the following pie chart as we do because it is our strong intuition that if we spent more of our time in dialogic-based conversation first, we wouldn't need to spend as much time in discussion. We would have a larger vision or perspective about whatever it is we are trying to figure out.

Today, the pie is probably reversed with discussion taking up the major portion. Think how often in your experience there is a problem that has surfaced and everyone is gathered together to figure out what to do. Because the problem seems so menacing and urgent, little time is given to any kind of in-depth look at what is causing it, or how everyone is affected by it. Rather, in the rush to action, a decision is made that only later has to be aborted because it doesn't get at the root of things.

If a group or a team dialogues about such a problem or an issue first, by the time a solution must be selected, chances are the process will go more quickly. The choice may almost "choose itself."

Consider the amount of time that you and those you work with spend between the two. Are you constantly trying to rush to a decision and closure about whatever is "up" in your work situation, or do you take more time and explore what is the nature itself of what is "up"? If you reverse the proportions towards the latter, even though it may seem counter-intuitive to you just now, you may find things go a bit more easily in the long run.

Try This: Practice Expanding and Filling in the Circle

When a problem crops up, rather than trying to figure out what action to take immediately, build a bit more time into your decision-making process. Call a meeting of all those who are affected by the problem (or as many as practical). Tell them that you are not going to make a decision about what to do immediately. Ask them to reflect on what they consider to be the nature of the problem from their perspective and to be prepared to contribute this in the meeting.

When everyone has gathered, open by asking them to take turns speaking about the problem. Let them know that there will be no back-and-forth conversation until everyone has had a chance to speak at least once.

Depending on how much time there is available after everyone has spoken, open the meeting up for comments. Remind the group that the objective of the meeting is to learn about what the problem is about and not to make a decision. If you notice people trying to come to a conclusion, you may have to remind them of this objective. At the end, allow ten minutes to collect the key learnings. If you meet again with the same people for decision-making purposes, bring a copy of these key learnings with you to review before you begin.

Whether you meet to dialogue about a problem or about trying to come up with a new way of doing things to make improvements, you may notice a strong tendency to fall back into discussion or to converge on one solution. In western culture, this is common because of our "results and action-oriented" ethos. It is why it takes a while for groups to catch on. As people become accustomed to the difference in intention between discussion and dialogue, and they see the results they get after engaging in dialogue, it gets easier to maintain dialogue without unconsciously falling back into discussion. Participants learn to monitor themselves as to what conversational form needs to be used depending on the situation and need for a decision.

Advocacy and Inquiry in Dialogue

From what we have said so far about the distinction between dialogue and discussion, you might think that advocacy wouldn't occur in dialogue and that inquiry wouldn't occur in discussion. But, this isn't so.

What determines when and how these aspects of conversation show up, is the intention behind their use. In dialogue, advocacy is quite appropriate if it is to offer some perspective for the purpose of the group's learning. The intention is *not* to force the group to come around to your perspective as the right one, but rather to build shared meaning. It is just the reverse in discussion, where advocacy is intended to persuade and convince the others that your perspective is the right or best one, not just to add another perspective.

In dialogue, we use inquiry for the purpose of digging deeper into whatever we are talking about. We use it to ask about one another's assumptions and underlying thinking. We use it to clarify and expand what we know about something. Again, our overall intention in inquiring is to *learn* more.

Inquiry in discussion is used typically to learn enough about what the others are thinking so that we might better convince or advocate our own position. In this case, our use of inquiry is to gather enough ammunition to shoot down the other's opinion while elevating our own.

Other Defining Qualities of Dialogue

There are many other defining characteristics and qualities of dialogue. We speak more in depth about these in Part II. We list some below to give you a flavor for what is generally present when dialogue is practiced. None of these characteristics in and of themselves makes a conversation a dialogue. Rather, it is all of them combined that give it its unique feel and quality:

- Suspension of judgment

- Release of the need for specific outcomes

- An inquiry into and an examination of underlying assumptions

- Authenticity

- A slower pace with silence between speakers

- Listening deeply to self, others, and for collective meaning

The Many Faces of Dialogue

There are many forms and ways in which dialogue shows up in the world today. Some of them are based on the work of David Bohm, and others are not. While we (The Dialogue Group) largely take our inspiration from Bohm, we also recognize and draw from other disciplines and traditions such as Jungian and Gestalt psychology, western philosophy, eastern meditation practice, indigenous and Greek societies, Quaker religious and business practices, and others. And we, along with a host of colleagues and peers, are continuing to evolve new ways to work with dialogue. It is important to note that just as no two conversations are ever the same even between the same people, no two dialogues are ever the same in the same way. Each time dialogue is practiced, groups invent what works best for them.

What have we tried to do in this chapter is to give you a feel for what seems most universal about the many forms that dialogue takes.

Bohm's ideas have served as a platform for dialogue's current re-emergence in organizations. While it is not our intention to be inclusive of all those who are introducing dialogue into organizations, we do want to mention the work being done by The Dialogue Project out of MIT. Dr. William Isaacs, its director, has been conducting research, which is meant to advance what is known about how dialogue can be integrated into ongoing organizational practices, particularly in the field of organizational learning.[1]

There are other institutions and organizations that are also doing work with dialogue that go beyond the domain of the organization. Some of the contexts in which dialogue is being explored and practiced are interreligious groups, conflict resolution and mediation work, educational and public domain work, and therapeutic and small-group settings.

What all of these diverse forms of dialogue seem to share is the intention to promote learning, growth, understanding, healing, and renewal of those engaging in it.

Notes

1. Dr. Isaacs is completing a book titled *The Art of Thinking Together* which will be published by Doubleday (NY) in 1998. The book develops a theory of dialogue as well as a set of principles for its practice and will contain examples from large system change efforts within institutions and corporations conducted over several years.

WISDOM, INSIGHT, AND PSYCHOLOGICAL CHANGE

Rick Suarez, Roger Mills and Darlene Stewart

Throughout time, humanity has sought to understand the words of the enlightened people of this world who have tried to improve the human condition. People have searched for the magic ingredient that would help them change conditions of mental disturbance and interpersonal conflict to conditions of mental health and cooperation. Such knowledge would be known by its results, but a look at human social and psychological conditions suggests that the desired change has come grudgingly over thousands of years and is microscopic. When progress in the human condition is compared to technological advancement, we find that our understanding of human psychological behavior has grown at a snail's pace. The words of the wise, which we revere, profess, and often quote, have remained words and have never become reality for most people. Why? What is missing?

The factor that has been missing in humanity's understanding has been the psychological recognition that perceptions, feelings, and behaviors are shaped by thoughts. As we have noted in earlier chapters, people have tried to understand life from the perspective of whatever thought system they acquired during their life. For this reason, it has been next to impossible for people to profit from what those who have achieved a deeper understanding of life have tried to convey. The reason for this is simple. At higher levels of consciousness, people see life in a simpler, less complex, and, in essence, more truthful way. These individuals, in touch with common sense, have a clearer picture of life. Now, someone who is in a different reality, one that is at a lower level of understanding, relatively devoid of common sense, would see the actions of the other as being wiser. This is why at many points in history, people with an extraordinary degree of common sense, relative to their contemporaries, have been referred to as being "wise." These wise men or women have been thought to possess something called "wisdom." So what is wisdom?

Wisdom and Mental Health

Wisdom is a level of intelligence, innate in every human being, which is deeper and more comprehensive than what we associate with an IQ score. Wisdom exists outside of individualized frames of reference, which is why it has not been more readily realized by a humanity that is wedded to fixed patterns of thinking and perceptions of reality. When wisdom is realized by an individual, it frees him from his own fixed views of life and guides that person toward the attainment of selfesteem, peace of mind, happiness, creativity, and productivity. In other words, wisdom shows the individual how to live in the state of mental health.

What we have begun to realize in the course of our studies is that wisdom is synonymous with understanding thought, reality, emotions, and levels of consciousness. Thus, when we read accounts of truly wise people, it becomes apparent that they were mentally healthy in a way that was so far beyond the realm of what was normal in their time, that their contemporaries (at varying levels of consciousness) either viewed them as a blessing or as a threat. In either case, people have always found it very difficult to listen to what the wise have said about how life works.

What we are saying is simply this: These wise people that we have revered were people who broke the barrier of humanity's thought-created reality and realized that humanity's problems were indeed thought-created. Wisdom, in essence, is mental health, and mental health, as we have noted, is a state of mind in which the human being understands the psychological principles of human reality. This is why the "wise," irrespective of culture, warned people about the perils of judging what is "out there." They were warning us about judging our own perceptions or misperceptions. They told people to look within for wisdom, noting that it did not exist in the realm of what mankind perceives to be real. And all pointed toward the feeling of love and goodwill as the route to a better reality.

Wisdom and Insight

The realization of wisdom occur in a very natural and spontaneous manner which is sometimes dramatic, but more frequently subtle. Sometimes wisdom is realized through an insight that breaks into our thought like a light being turned on in a dark room; other times wisdom appears quietly, as though a new thought crept silently into our awareness without our suspecting its importance at first, and later we cannot recall how it came. It was simply there, complete, obvious, relevant. When wisdom is realized, it reveals the unknown. It may show us a missing piece or an appropriate answer that seems so simple and obvious that we wonder how we could not see it before. The conscious state that provides the perspective to see obvious, positive answers is what we are calling common sense.

Everyone has had flashes of wisdom but some people have manifested it more consistently than others. The experience and expression of wisdom has been a haphazard affair because until now no one has understood this intelligence as a psychological factor. Most people have placed wisdom beyond the reach of their lives. Yet there are undeniable clues that wisdom is already within each human being. For example who could deny that a person in a mentally healthy state of mind acts wiser than when that person is in a lower state of mind. Who could deny that a person behaves wiser in a good mood than in a bad mood?

The beginning of wisdom is the realization that the human being has the ability to think. Everyone would agree of course, that human beings think. However, very few people realize that ability as a creative, voluntary function. People experience their ability to think as a passive review of data that is being imposed upon them. To see that the human mind has the ability to create thoughts and project them into forms that we call experience, is to understand that we can consciously nurture our mental health. Wisdom reveals to the individual that through the ability to think, that individual is creating the separate reality that becomes his life. Such understanding allows the individual to see beyond his personal frame of reference and find the common sense answers to life's questions.

The Experience of Insight

Wisdom cannot be realized through mental struggle or the intellectual process of trying to figure out our problems. The reason that wisdom is not more frequently recognized is that human beings have traditionally idolized intellectual and analytical reasoning, and wisdom does not come from these thought patterns. We have missed wisdom because we have learned to think in terms of our problems, to be "realistic," and to sort through our stored information for the answers that we seek. We have literally been looking for our answers in the wrong place without knowing it. All that we can think about is what is programmed into our biological computer.

This is not to say that our thought system has no use. Of course it does. As we have repeatedly noted, it is the perfect tool for accessing useful memory so that we don't forget our language or how to get to work, our telephone number or where to put the dishes when we take them out of the dishwasher. In other words, our thought system is our biological computer and it should be used to help us out in the same way that we utilize a personal computer. We would not consult our personal computer to tell us what to do when our teenager is taking drugs or how to make up with our sweetheart. This would be an obvious misuse of the computer. In the same way, we learn not to use our thought system for things that are beyond its capabilities.

When we realize knowledge that is beyond the software of our biological computer, this is called the experience of insight. Once we experience insight, we realize our capability to drop habits of anxiety, fear, insecurity, and worry. Once we do this we start to live in a more positive feeling level. This feeling level allows us to see things with clarity and objectivity. We regain our self-esteem and our sense of humor and move naturally into states of mind where we feel increased joy and appreciation for the simple things in life. Enjoying what we have opens us to beauty and possibilities that were unseen before. Gratitude for what we have increases the positive feelings which lead us deeper into states of mind where wisdom and insight are found.

Wisdom comes through insight, which is the act of seeing within ourselves and recognizing how our psychological functioning works. Wisdom is not to be found in information. Neither can wisdom depend on an idea, concept, theory, opinion, or belief because all of these things vary from individual to individual, theorist to theorist, profession to profession, culture to culture. Wisdom is not derived from the content of a frame of reference. Rather, the first step toward true wisdom involves the realization that other realities exist. Wisdom is the knowledge that beliefs and ideas are merely thoughts that can lock people into certain perceptions, feelings, and behaviors. Wisdom is a higher vantage point that is unobstructed by personal beliefs, attitudes, opinions, and biases. Wisdom is the intelligence of consciousness that exists before the creation of thought content. For this reason, wisdom cannot be taught to one person by another. It must be realized through the experience of insight. It is difficult, if not impossible, for one person to communicate insight to another person, because wisdom is not a thinking process. Wisdom is the spontaneous appearance of knowledge.

To understand wisdom, we can look at the two distinct approaches that people take in putting a jigsaw puzzle together. The more insecurity we have about completing the puzzle, the more we focus on the separate pieces of the puzzle and the more difficulty we have in putting the pieces together. When we lose sight of the overall picture we get lost in the parts. It is a simple case of not being able to see the forest for the trees. However, the moment that we relax and begin to enjoy the puzzle, the easier it becomes to see what pieces are out of place. As we begin to work, not so much with the separate pieces, but with the whole picture, our view becomes broader, more objective. As we find more missing pieces, the picture becomes more complete, and we are able to see each piece in relation to the whole picture. In states of wisdom, we have an objective clarity that guides us to see a bigger picture rather than to spend our time trying to figure out each piece. In an analogous way, wisdom helps us keep the details of life in perspective.

We ask our computer to do an impossible task when we ask it to tell us the meaning of life. The moment we see the futility of trying to use our thought system in this way, we cease to struggle, we relax, and our wisdom and common sense emerge naturally. We begin to know the experience of insight. It is insight that helps us realize facts about the workings of our thought systems, so we are able to see beyond our existing frames of reference. Insights show us how the conditioning process works. They show us what a thought is and what a belief is so that we are no longer at the mercy of perceptions resulting from beliefs and conditional thinking. Insights show us how we move from one belief system to another or, more to the point, how we move from one reality to another. Insights, similar to the ones that we used to learn a language when we were babies, show us the simplicity of life. Insights are a function of a higher level of consciousness, a level where we are guided by positive feeling and effortless knowing that allows us to live the lives that we want to have and to be successful and happy, regardless of the beliefs, opinions, or biases of the people around us.

By definition, an insight must be fresh, useful, and positive. An insight will never produce negativity or fear. Negativity is a sign that a person is responding to negative conditioning. Conditioning and insight are mutually exclusive and it is important to a person's mental health to be able to distinguish one from the other. A true insight will always show a better, more positive understanding than was previously seen. A true insight is a highlight, a purely pleasurable experience that increases our feelings of well-being and self-esteem. If a negative thought intrudes upon our awareness, bringing with it a feeling of repulsion, dread or fear, the negative feelings immediately tell us that we have tapped into conditioning from the past and are going in the opposite direction of our mental health.

A perfect example of an insight occurred in 1928. For nearly a century, researchers had been desperately searching for something that would kill the various kinds of bacteria that cause deadly infections. The scientific search for such a compound involved, among other things, growing colonies of the types of bacteria that were known to be pathogenic. One fateful day, while inspecting the cultures of bacteria growing in petri dishes, the director of a lab noticed that one of his dishes had been contaminated. Earlier that week he had opened that dish to extract some of the bacteria. When he did, some stray mold must have contaminated the bacterial colony. This was not an uncommon occurrence; it happened in all laboratories and all that a researcher could do was to contain his anger and frustration, discard the contaminated colony, and begin all over again. This particular researcher had experienced this same situation many times in his career. On this occasion, however, before discarding the dish as he was accustomed to doing, he held it up to the light and took another look at the green mold that had ruined his experiment. To his astonishment, he noted that for a considerable distance around the mold, the bacterial colony was undergoing lysis—something was dissolving the bacteria! The researcher, of course, was Alexander Fleming and the mold was penicillin. What had "ruined" this man's research was the answer he was seeking. One can only be grateful that on this one occasion, a human being took one look beyond his disappointment. So what began as a disaster, from the point of view of Fleming's conditioned thinking, ended up being one of the greatest scientific discoveries of the century.

While the above example shows how an insight can result in a breakthrough in the physical health of humanity, an insight can also assist an individual in attaining more mental health in everyday life, by shedding new light on his or her problems.

A person's conditioning might lead her to react negatively in a certain situation. Take, for example, a client named Ann, a teacher who had come to therapy because of job-related stress. On her way to therapy one day, Ann was caught in a rush hour traffic jam. As usual, she began to think the negative thoughts that were so familiar to her. She became tense, angry, and hostile toward other drivers. In her frustration, she began to honk her horn and make insulting comments to other drivers. All of a sudden, one of the drivers, a young man in the car next to hers, looked at her and said, "Lady, take it easy." Ann's initial reaction was to become enraged, but then she remembered where she was going. She realized she was late for a session where she hoped to find some peace of mind. Ann very quickly recognized that what she had been told by her therapist was not only applicable to the classroom, but also to her reality in her car. With this realization, Ann sat back, put some good music on her cassette player, and dropped all her thoughts of needing to hurry. She realized that if she was going to arrive late, she might as well arrive with her wellbeing intact. This was a turning point for Ann, who for the first time in her life began to see the difference between habit and insight. (As it turned out, Ann arrived 20 minutes late, but had to wait another 20 minutes, as her therapist was also stuck in traffic!)

The individual who experiences such an insight enters into a more positive reality than the one she lived in prior to the insight. What makes the examples of Alexander Fleming and Ann noteworthy is that both exemplify insight. So whether one achieves indirect relief through an insight of how to stop an infection or gains direct relief by realizing that one is inflicting oneself with negative thinking, the end result is the same: A new reality is found.

Adding the dimension of wisdom and insight to psychology is analogous to adding a third dimension to a two-dimensional geometry. It is a shift to a larger, more encompassing, more objective frame of reference. This broader frame of reference includes what was there before, and more. It gives a new meaning and significance to what was previously experienced.

Psychological Frames of Reference and Change

Before wisdom is realized, people live in their beliefs. A belief system is a psychological frame of reference that limits and distorts our vision of life, and leads to habitual behaviors. It is possible to make a horizontal shift within a frame of reference, which simply means moving from one belief system to another. A person's reality can be changed, to a new conditioned reality. This, of course, will change the pattern of behavior. It must be emphasized that this change is not to a new level of understanding reality, but is a shift at the same level to a different pattern. The process by which an individual is conditioned to a new set of beliefs without being aware of it is called a "conversion process." Such conversion processes do not involve any real change in the level of understanding, but are simply ways in which individuals transfer their insecurities from one thought pattern or set of beliefs to another.

If we look at conversion or reconditioning processes, we find that these processes always involve certain "commitment mechanisms" that ensure that people adhere to and identify with a particular ideology or belief system. In order to be converted to certain beliefs, people are subjected to initiations that involve highlighting their fears and inducing embarrassment, emotional catharsis, and emotional or physical exhaustion. These techniques are used to make people feel that they cannot have wellbeing or selfesteem without belonging to the group. These procedures foster a we/they mentality that excludes the rest of the world from their group. This intensifies the pressure to conform to the group's behavioral, moral, and attitudinal norms, or to face the insecurity of being rejected from the group. Conversions can never involve a shift to a higher level of understanding because this would obviate people attaching their well-being or security to a belief system.

On the other hand, there is another order of change, one that does not merely involve substituting one belief for another. This is the kind of shift that is involved in realizing wisdom or common sense. The shift to a psychological frame of reference of wisdom involves no conversion processing or reconditioning. This is a vertical shift that involves having an insight or realization about the existence and nature of the frames of reference of conditioned beliefs. When people have this realization, they move to a higher level or perspective where they are able to live outside of their conditioning. There is no need for individuals at these higher levels to attach themselves to any particular group, ideology, or movement, as they have little need to base their self-esteem or well-being on anything outside of themselves.

Moving from the psychological frame of reference created by a thought system to the frame of reference of wisdom is not a parallel movement across the same level, but a vertical transfer to a new level. This vertical shift can be compared to a change in understanding that happens in elementary school. In first grade, the teacher wanted us to learn the principle of addition. Since a principle cannot be articulated, the teacher presented us with example after example to show the result of the principle. At first, not knowing the principle of addition, we had no choice but to practice, drill, and memorize examples that were presented to us by the teacher. But at some point, we had an insight that showed us the comprehensive picture behind all the examples that the teacher had presented. From that moment on, we were able to add an endless variety of numbers, not from practice, but from a realization of the logical relationships involved in the problem. With this realization, we moved from a conditioned frame of reference to the larger, unconditioned frame of reference.

Learning the principle of addition is a recapitulation of learning to live life successfully. We are all taught to try to be loving, grateful, courteous, patient, fair, just, forgiving, understanding, and respectful of others. But how many people are successful at arriving at these correct answers when faced with the problems that they encounter in the course of their life? Very few. The reason for this is that these qualities are not techniques or causes, they are effects. They are the effects of living at a level of consciousness where one sees that every human being is acting according to the limits of his or her understanding. It is obvious that at any given moment, it is impossible for someone to be nonjudgmental, patient, loving, or forgiving if their level of consciousness is such that the reality they are feeling and perceiving is threatening, hurtful, harmful, or hostile. What few people realize is that all the positive attributes that people try so hard to live up to, as well as all those negative attributes which we try to suppress, are attributes of our level of consciousness rather than our beliefs. So the answer lies in raising one's level of consciousness above the level where we are constantly trying to be good by fighting off our negative desires. Figure 5 graphically depicts how our level of consciousness typically manifests itself. The upper half of this diagram denotes levels of consciousness where people see realities that are positive and thus elicit from them what most of us consider virtues, while the lower half denotes levels of consciousness where the realities that are perceived are more negative in nature and thus elicit all of humanity's shortcomings.

Insights are one of the natural outcomes of living in an unconditioned frame of reference. These insights give us working knowledge of the principles of thought, separate realities, levels of consciousness, and the role of feelings. As people advance through levels of consciousness, they learn to move through realities. True responsibility becomes a fact as individuals realize that the world is not what is really affecting them, but that they are, in fact, shaping their own experience in life through their own thinking. This is the beginning of wisdom, common sense, and mental health.

FIGURE 5: The Characteristics of Conditioned and Unconditioned Frames of Reference

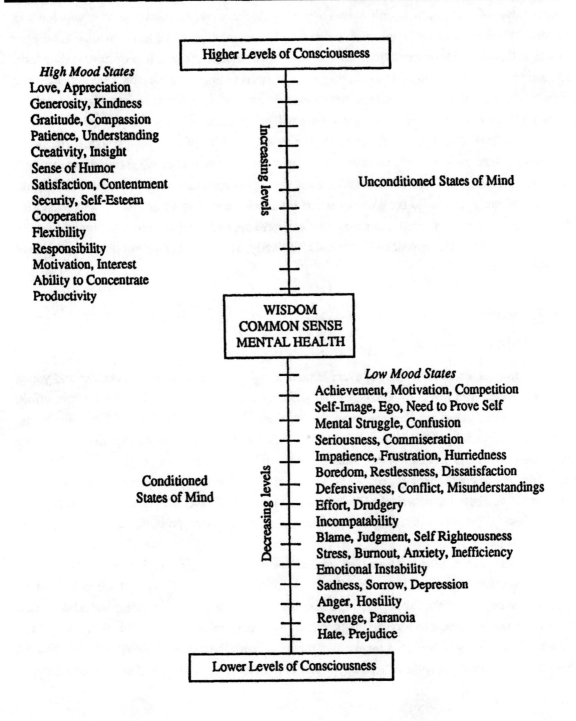

High Mood States
Love, Appreciation
Generosity, Kindness
Gratitude, Compassion
Patience, Understanding
Creativity, Insight
Sense of Humor
Satisfaction, Contentment
Security, Self-Esteem
Cooperation
Flexibility
Responsibility
Motivation, Interest
Ability to Concentrate
Productivity

Higher Levels of Consciousness

Increasing levels

Unconditioned States of Mind

WISDOM
COMMON SENSE
MENTAL HEALTH

Low Mood States
Achievement, Motivation, Competition
Self-Image, Ego, Need to Prove Self
Mental Struggle, Confusion
Seriousness, Commiseration
Impatience, Frustration, Hurriedness
Boredom, Restlessness, Dissatisfaction
Defensiveness, Conflict, Misunderstandings
Effort, Drudgery
Incompatability
Blame, Judgment, Self Righteousness
Stress, Burnout, Anxiety, Inefficiency
Emotional Instability
Sadness, Sorrow, Depression
Anger, Hostility
Revenge, Paranoia
Hate, Prejudice

Conditioned
States of Mind

Decreasing levels

Lower Levels of Consciousness

Wisdom, by the process of insight, reveals the futility of trying to solve a problem at the same level at which the problem was created by thought and perceived as reality. When this is recognized, an individual realizes that any method, technique, or ritual that comes out of thinking at a lower level of consciousness only serves to perpetuate the level of consciousness at which it was created. When we attempt to use information to solve our problems, we fail to realize the deeper principle that all problems result from thinking in an insecure state of mind. In problematic situations, the solutions involve using common sense to take whatever immediate measures are indicated and then to drop the thought of the problem so that we will be free to move into higher levels of consciousness where an obvious, simple answer will be apparent.

We have all had the experience of trying to solve a problem by mental struggle. No matter how hard or how long we think, the answer will not come. However, once we give up trying to think about it and relax, watch television, or take a walk, the answer appears spontaneously in our thoughts. Reports of major scientific breakthroughs are filled with accounts of scientists who exhausted themselves trying to figure out a complex problem, gave up, and put their minds on something else, only to have the solution appear suddenly and effortlessly. This is an example of how the process of insight works.

Learning and Insight

Insights are a natural part of every human being's experience in life. As babies and young children, we learned to walk and talk, tie our shoes, and climb stairs all without conscious effort. Learning was effortless and pleasurable because we were experiencing life from within, with nothing in the way of learning and enjoyment. We did not think about or judge these experiences; thus we were unaware of the fact that we were "learning" anything. We were simply enjoying life. However, as we developed our thought system, we became so identified with it that we forgot about the insight experience and began to experience life from the perspective of other people's beliefs and expectations. Then the process of learning became attached to our thinking process, and we began to run into difficulties.

This is why children can learn languages with ease but for most adults it is a struggle. The trouble is that adults try to learn from the perspective of the language they already know. Their inability to let go of one to experience another impedes their learning. We have seen six-year-olds, who had used their natural process of insight to become fluent in two languages, suddenly have a "learning disability" in school after being conditioned by insecure thought. These "learning-disabled" students became fluent in two languages without teachers, without programmed learning, without memorization or drill. Learning by insight, mastery of two languages was part of their play. But in the classroom, the function of insight is replaced by the memorization and utilization of information. When this happens, spontaneous learning is impede by compulsive thinking. We take the pleasure out of learning and make it difficult. From this point on, experiencing life from within—using insight—rather than from the thought system becomes the exception to the rule.

It takes some degree of courage to look at what we believe and to realize that much of what we believe to be true about how human beings function is based on misperceptions that have been handed down to us. But this realization must happen before we are willing to let go of the old to make way for something new. We have to be willing to do this before we can move into a larger realm of knowing that is not dependent on the stored information in our biological computer. Once we realize that there is more to life than what we think, our thought process softens, we become emotionally relaxed, and we discover new, positive feelings that indicate that we are in a state of mental health. These positive feelings bring us not only creativity, satisfaction, and happiness, but also a source of knowledge.

Wisdom has nothing to do with IQ scores or station in life. It has nothing to do with information or the ability to develop sophisticated or complex technology. In fact, many of our mental problems are a direct result of not being able to understand our own information and technologies. The deeper knowledge which we refer to as wisdom is not a thinking process. People who idolize their fixed forms of thinking will have difficulty accessing wisdom because thinking, and the insecurity that this thinking produces, is what actually obscures or denies the view within. When we return to the state of innocence of thought that we had as children, we will learn effortlessly, as we did then, all that is necessary for us to have happy, mentally healthy, and successful lives.

To date, very few individuals have even come close to understanding the words of the wise because the principle or essence of what the wise were trying to convey has been hidden by the separate reality of conditioned associations to the language they used—each using whatever words and terms were common to their culture. People have not been able to hear past language or culture. The link that has been missing is the psychological knowledge of thought, separate realities, levels of consciousness, and emotions. This knowledge is the necessary ingredient that begins to decipher the stories, parables, and statements of the wise. It allows the individual to listen beyond the cultural relativity of language to hear the universal wisdom behind the words. The beauty of wisdom, or true mental health, is that when any degree of wisdom is realized, one's level of sanity increases and one can never be as psychologically lost as before. Even more beautiful is the realization that no matter how wise one becomes, there is always more.

COSMOS AND TAXIS

Friedrich A. Hayek

> The man of system . . . seems to imagine that he can arrange the different members of a great society with as much ease as the hand arranges the different pieces upon a chessboard. He does not consider that the pieces upon the chessboard have no other principle of motion besides that which the hand impresses upon them; but that, in the great chessboard of human society, every single piece has a principle of motion of its own, altogether different from that which the legislature might choose to impress upon it. If those two principles coincide and act in the same direction, the game of human society will go on easily and harmoniously, and is very likely to be happy and successful. If they are opposite or different, the game will go on miserably and the society must be at all times in the highest degree of disorder.
>
> —*Adam Smith**

The Concept of Order

The central concept around which the discussion of this book will turn is that of order, and particularly the distinction between two kinds of order which we will provisionally call 'made' and 'grown' orders. Order is an indispensable concept for the discussion of all complex phenomena, in which it must largely play the role the concept of law plays in the analysis of simpler phenomena.[1] There is no adequate term other than 'order' by which we can describe it, although 'system', 'structure' or 'pattern' may occasionally serve instead. The term 'order' has, of course, a long history in the social sciences,[2] but in recent times it has generally been avoided, largely because of the ambiguity of its meaning and its frequent association with authoritarian views. We cannot do without it, however, and shall have to guard against misinterpretation by sharply defining the general sense in which we shall employ it and then clearly distinguishing between the two different ways in which such order can originate.

By 'order' we shall throughout describe *a state of affairs in which a multiplicity of elements of various kinds are so related to each other that we may learn from our acquaintance with some spatial or temporal part of the whole to form correct expectations concerning the rest, or at least expectations which have a good chance of proving correct.*[3] It is clear that every society must in this sense possess an order and that such an order will often exist without having been deliberately created. As has been said by a distinguished social anthropologist, 'that there is some order, consistency and constancy in social life, is obvious. If there were not, none of us would be able to go about our affairs or satisfy our most elementary needs.'[4]

Living as members of society and dependent for the satisfaction of most of our needs on various forms of cooperation with others, we depend for the effective pursuit of our aims clearly on the correspondence of the expectations concerning the actions of others on which our plans are based with what they will really do. This matching of the intentions and expectations that determine the actions of different individuals is the form in which order manifests itself in social life; and it will be the question of how such an order does come about that will be our immediate concern. The first answer to which our anthropomorphic habits of thought almost inevitably lead us is that it must be due to the design of some thinking mind.[5] And because order has been generally interpreted as such a deliberate *arrangement* by somebody, the concept has become unpopular among most friends of liberty and has been favored mainly by authoritarians. According to this interpretation order in society must rest on a relation of command and obedience, or a hierarchical structure of the whole of society in which the will of superiors, and ultimately of some single supreme authority, determines what each individual must do.

This authoritarian connotation of the concept of order derives, however, entirely from the belief that order can be created only by forces outside the system (or 'exogenously'). It does not apply to an equilibrium set up from within[6] (or 'endogenously') such as that which the general theory of the market endeavours to explain. A spontaneous order of this kind has in many respects properties different from those of a made order.

The Two Sources of Order

The study of spontaneous orders has long been the peculiar task of economic theory, although, of course, biology has from its beginning been concerned with that special kind of spontaneous order which we call an organism. Only recently has there arisen within the physical sciences under the name of cybernetics a special discipline which is also concerned with what are called self-organizing or self-generating systems.[7]

The distinction of this kind of order from one which has been made by somebody putting the elements of a set in their places or directing their movements is indispensable for any understanding of the processes of society as well as for all social policy. There are several terms available for describing each kind of order. The made order which we have already referred to as an exogenous order or an arrangement may again be described as a construction, an artificial order or, especially where we have to deal with a directed social order, as an *organization*. The grown order, on the other hand, which we have referred to as a self-generating or endogenous order, is in English most conveniently described as a *spontaneous order*. Classical Greek was more fortunate in possessing distinct single words for the two kinds of order, namely *taxis* for a made order, such as, for example, an order of battle,[8] and *kosmos* for a grown order, meaning originally 'a right order in a state or a community'.[9] We shall occasionally avail ourselves of these Greek words as technical terms to describe the two kinds of order.

It would be no exaggeration to say that social theory begins with—and has an object only because of—the discovery that there exist orderly structures which are the product of the action of many men but are not the result of human design. In some fields this is now universally accepted. Although there was a time when men believed that even language and morals had been "invented" by some genius of the past, everybody recognizes now that they are the outcome of a process of evolution whose results nobody foresaw or designed. But in other fields many people still treat with suspicion the claim that the patterns of interaction of many men can show an order that is of nobody's deliberate making; in the economic sphere, in particular, critics still pour uncomprehending ridicule on Adam Smith's expression of the 'invisible hand' by which, in the language of his time, he described how man is led 'to promote an end which was no part of his intentions'.[10] If indignant reformers still complain of the chaos of economic affairs, insinuating a complete absence of order, this is partly because they cannot conceive of an order which is not deliberately made, and partly because to them an order means something aiming at concrete purposes which is, as we shall see, what a spontaneous order cannot do.

We shall examine later (see volume 2, chapter 10) how that coincidence of expectations and plans is produced which characterizes the market order and the nature of the benefits we derive from it. For the moment we are concerned only with the fact that an order not made by man does exist and with the reasons why this is not more readily recognized. The main reason is that such orders as that of the market do not obtrude themselves on our senses but have to be traced by our intellect. We cannot see, or otherwise intuitively perceive, this order of meaningful actions, but are only able mentally to reconstruct it by tracing the relations that exist between the elements. We shall describe this feature by saying that it is an abstract and not a concrete order.

The Distinguishing Properties of Spontaneous Orders

One effect of our habitually identifying order with a made order or *taxis* is indeed that we tend to ascribe to all order certain properties which deliberate arrangements regularly, and with respect to some of these properties necessarily, possess. Such orders are relatively *simple* or at least necessarily confined to such moderate degrees of complexity as the maker can still survey; they are usually *concrete* in the sense just mentioned that their existence can be intuitively perceived by inspection; and, finally, having been made deliberately, they invariably do (or at one time did) *serve a purpose* of the maker. None of these characteristics necessarily belong to a spontaneous order or *kosmos*. Its degree of complexity is not limited to what a human mind can master. Its existence need not manifest itself to our senses but may be based on purely *abstract* relations which we can only mentally reconstruct. And not having been made it *cannot* legitimately be said to *have a particular purpose,* although our awareness of its existence may be extremely important for our successful pursuit of a great variety of different purposes.

Spontaneous orders are not necessarily complex, but unlike deliberate human arrangements, they may achieve any degree of complexity. One of our main contentions will be that very complex orders, comprising more particular facts than any brain could ascertain or manipulate, can be brought about only through forces inducing the formation of spontaneous orders.

Spontaneous orders need not be what we have called abstract, but they will often consist of a system of abstract relations between elements which are also defined only by abstract properties, and for this reason will not be intuitively perceivable and not recognizable except on the basis of a theory accounting for their character. The significance of the abstract character of such orders rests on the fact that they may persist while all the particular elements they comprise, and even the number of such elements, change. All that is necessary to preserve such an abstract order is that a certain structure of relationships be maintained, or that elements of a certain kind (but variable in number) continue to be related in a certain manner.

Most important, however, is the relation of a spontaneous order to the conception of purpose. Since such an order has not been created by an outside agency, the order as such also can have no purpose, although its existence may be very serviceable to the individuals which move within such order. But in a different sense it may well be said that the order rests on purposive action of its elements, when 'purpose' would, of course, mean nothing more than that their actions tend to secure the preservation or restoration of that order. The use of 'purposive' in this sense as a sort of 'teleological shorthand', as it has been called by biologists, is unobjectionable so long as we do not imply an awareness of purpose of the part of the elements, but mean merely that the elements have acquired regularities of conduct conducive to the maintenance of the order—presumably because those who did act in certain ways had within the resulting order a better chance of survival than those who did not. In general, however, it is preferable to avoid in this connection the term 'purpose' and to speak instead of 'function'.

Spontaneous Orders in Nature

It will be instructive to consider briefly the character of some spontaneous orders which we find in nature, since here some of their characteristic properties stand out most clearly. There are in the physical world many instances of complex orders which we could bring about only by availing ourselves of the known forces which tend to lead to their formation, and never by deliberately placing each element in the appropriate position. We can never produce a crystal or a complex organic compound by placing the individual atoms in such a position that they will form the lattice of a crystal or the system based on benzol rings which make up an organic compound. But we can create the conditions in which they will arrange themselves in such a manner.

What does in these instances determine not only the general character of the crystal or compound that will be formed but also the particular position of any one element in them? The important point is that the regularity of the conduct of the elements will determine the general character of the resulting order but not all the detail of its particular manifestation. The particular manner in which the resulting abstract order will manifest itself will depend, in addition to the rules which govern the actions of the elements, on their initial position and on all the particular circumstances of the immediate environment to which each of them will react in the course of the formation of that order. The order, in other words, will always be an adaptation to a large number of particular facts which will not be known in their totality to anyone.

We should note that a regular pattern will thus form itself not only if the elements all obey the same rules and their different actions are determined only by the different positions of the several individuals relatively to each other, but also, as is true in the case of the chemical compound, if there are different kinds of elements which act in part according to different rules. Whichever is the case, we shall be able to predict only the general character of the order that will form itself, and not the particular position which any particular element will occupy relatively to any other element.

Another example from physics is in some respects even more instructive. In the familiar school experiment in which iron filings on a sheet of paper are made to arrange themselves along some of the lines of force of a magnet placed below, we can predict the general shape of the chains that will be formed by the filings hooking themselves together; but we cannot predict along which ones of the family of an infinite number of such curves that define the magnetic field these chains will place themselves. This will depend on the position, direction, weight, roughness or smoothness of each of the iron filings and on all the irregularities of the surface of the paper. The forces emanating from the magnet and from each of the iron filings will thus interact with the environment to produce a unique instance of a general pattern, the general character of which will be determined by known laws, but the concrete appearance of which will depend on particular circumstances we cannot fully ascertain.

In Society, Reliance on Spontaneous Order Both Extends and Limits Our Powers of Control

Since a spontaneous order results from the individual elements adapting themselves to circumstances which directly affect only some of them, and which in their totality need not be known to anyone, it may extend to circumstances so complex that no mind can comprehend them all. Consequently, the concept becomes particularly important when we turn from mechanical to such 'more highly organized' or essentially complex phenomena as we encounter in the realms of life, mind and society. Here we have to deal with 'grown' structures with a degree of complexity which they have assumed and could assume only because they were produced by spontaneous ordering forces. They in consequence present us with peculiar difficulties in our effort to explain them as well as in any attempt to influence their character. Since we can know at most the rules observed by the elements of various kinds of which the structures are made up, but not all the individual elements and never all the particular circumstances in which each of them is placed, our knowledge will be restricted to the general character of the order which will form itself. And even where, as is true of a society of human beings, we may be in a position to alter at least some of the rules of conduct which the elements obey, we shall thereby be able to influence only the general character and not the detail of the resulting order.

This means that, though the use of spontaneous ordering forces enables us to induce the formation of an order of such a degree of complexity (namely comprising elements of such numbers, diversity and variety of conditions) as we could never master intellectually, or deliberately arrange, we will have less power over the details of such an order than we would of one which we produce by arrangement. In the case of spontaneous orders we may, by determining some of the factors which shape them, determine their abstract features, but we will have to leave the particulars to circumstances which we do not know. Thus, by relying on the spontaneously ordering forces, we can extend the scope or range of the order which we may induce to form, precisely because its particular manifestation will depend on many more circumstances than can be known to us—and in the case of a social order, because such an order will utilize the separate knowledge of all its several members, without this knowledge ever being concentrated in a single mind, or being subject to those processes of deliberate coordination and adaptation which a mind performs.

In consequence, the degree of power of control over the extended and more complex order will be much smaller than that which we could exercise over a made order or *taxis*. There will be many aspects of it over which we will possess no control at all, or which at least we shall not be able to alter without interfering with—and to that extent impeding—the forces producing the spontaneous order. Any desire we may have concerning the particular position of individual elements, or the relation between particular individuals or groups, could not be satisfied without upsetting the overall order. The kind of power which in this respect we would possess over a concrete arrangement or *taxis* we would not have over a spontaneous order where we would know, and be able to influence, only the abstract aspects.

It is important to note here that there are two different respects in which order may be a matter of degree. How well ordered a set of objects or events is depends on how many of the attributes of (or the relations between) the elements we can learn to predict. Different orders may in this respect differ from each other in either or both of two ways: the orderliness may concern only very few relations between the elements, or a great many; and, second, the regularity thus defined may be great in the sense that it will be confirmed by all or nearly all instances, or it may be found to prevail only in a majority of the instances and thus allow us to predict its occurrence only with a certain degree of probability. In the first instance we may predict only a few of the features of the resulting structure, but do so with great confidence; such an order would be limited but may still be perfect. In the second instance we shall be able to predict much more, but with only a fair degree of certainty. The knowledge of the existence of an order will however still be useful even if this order is restricted in either or both these respects; and the reliance on spontaneously ordering forces may be preferable or even indispensable, although the order towards which a system tends will in fact be only more or less imperfectly approached. The market order in particular will regularly secure only a certain probability that the expected relations will prevail, but it is, nevertheless, the only way in which so many activities depending on dispersed knowledge can be effectively integrated into a single order.

Spontaneous Orders Result from their Elements Obeying Certain Rules of Conduct

We have already indicated that the formation of spontaneous orders is the result of their elements following certain rules in their responses to their immediate environment. The nature of these rules still needs fuller examination, partly because the word 'rule' is apt to suggest some erroneous ideas, and partly because the rules which determine a spontaneous order differ in important respects from another kind of rules which are needed in regulating an organization or *taxis*.

On the first point, the instances of spontaneous orders which we have given from physics are instructive because they clearly show that the rules which govern the actions of the elements of such spontaneous orders need not be rules which are 'known' to these elements; it is sufficient that the elements actually behave in a manner which can be described by such rules. The concept of rules as we use it in this context therefore does not imply that such rules exist in articulated ('verbalized') forms, but only that it is possible to discover rules which the actions of the individuals in fact follow. To emphasize this we have occasionally spoken of 'regularity' rather than of rules, but regularity, of course, means simply that the elements behave according to rules.

That rules in this sense exist and operate without being explicitly known to those who obey them applies also to many of the rules which govern the actions of men and thereby determine a spontaneous social order. Man certainly does not know all the rules which guide his actions in the sense that he is able to state them in words. At least in primitive human society, scarcely less than in animal societies, the structure of social life is determined by rules of conduct which manifest themselves only by being in fact observed. Only when individual intellects begin to differ to a significant degree will it become necessary to express these rules in a form in which they can be communicated and explicitly taught, deviant behaviour corrected, and differences of opinion about appropriate behaviour decided. Although man never existed without laws that he obeyed, he did, of course, exist for hundreds of thousands of years without laws he 'knew' in the sense that he was able to articulate them.

What is of still greater importance in this connection, however, is that not every regularity in the behaviour of the elements does secure an overall order. Some rules governing individual behavior might clearly make altogether impossible the formation of an overall order. Our problem is what kind of rules of conduct will produce an order of society and what kind of order particular rules will produce.

The classical instance of rules of the behaviour of the elements which will not produce order comes from the physical sciences: it is the second law of thermodynamics or the law of enthropy, according to which the tendency of the molecules of a gas to move at constant speeds in straight lines produces a state for which the term 'perfect disorder' has been coined. Similarly, it is evident that in society some perfectly regular behaviour of the individuals could produce only disorder: if the rule were that any individual should try to kill any other he encountered, or flee as soon as he saw another, the result would clearly be the complete impossibility of an order in which the activities of the individuals were based on collaboration with others.

Society can thus exist only if by a process of selection rules have evolved which lead individuals to behave in a manner which makes social life possible. It should be remembered that for this purpose selection will operate as between societies of different types, that is, be guided by the properties of their respective orders, but that the properties supporting this order will be properties of the individuals, namely their propensity to obey certain rules of conduct on which the order of action of the group as a whole rests.

To put this differently: in a social order the particular circumstances to which each individual will react will be those known to him. But the individual responses to particular circumstances will result in an overall order only if the individuals obey such rules as will produce an order. Even a very limited similarity in their behaviour may be sufficient if the rules which they all obey are such as to produce an order. Such an order will always constitute an adaptation to the multitude of circumstances which are known to all the members of that society taken together but which are not known as a whole to any one person. This need not mean that the different persons will in similar circumstances do precisely the same thing; but merely that for the formation of such an overall order it is necessary that in some respects all individuals follow definite rules, or that their actions are limited to a certain range. In other words, the responses of the individuals to the events in their environment need be similar only in certain abstracts aspects to ensure that a determinate overall order will result.

The question which is of central importance as much for social theory as for social policy is thus what properties the rules must possess so that the separate actions of the individuals will produce an overall order. Some such rules all individuals of a society will obey because of the similar manner in which their environment represents itself to their minds. Other they will follow spontaneously because they will be part of their common cultural tradition. But there will be still others which they may have to be made to obey, since, although it would be in the interest of each to disregard them, the overall order on which the success of their actions depends will arise only if these rules are generally followed.

In a modern society based on exchange, one of the chief regularities in individual behaviour will result from the similarity of situations in which most individuals find themselves in working to earn an income; which means that they will normally prefer a larger return from their efforts to a smaller one, and often that they will increase their efforts in a particular direction if the prospects of return improve. This is a rule that will be followed at least with sufficient frequency to impress upon such a society an order of a certain kind. But the fact that most people will follow this rule will still leave the character of the resulting order very indeterminate, and by itself certainly would not be sufficient to give it a beneficial character. For the resulting order to be beneficial people must also observe some conventional rules, that is, rules which do not simply follow from their desires and their insight into relations of cause and effect, but which are normative and tell them what they ought to or ought not to do.

We shall later have to consider more fully the precise relation between the various kinds of rules which the people in fact obey and the resulting order of actions. Our main interest will then be those rules which, because we can deliberately alter them, become the chief instrument whereby we can affect the resulting order, namely the rules of law. At the moment our concern must be to make clear that while the rules on which a spontaneous order rests, may also be of spontaneous origin, this need not always be the case. Although undoubtedly an order originally formed itself spontaneously because the individuals followed rules which had not been deliberately made but had arisen spontaneously, people gradually learned to improve those rules; and it is at least conceivable that the formation of a spontaneous order relies entirely on rules that were deliberately made. The spontaneous character of the resulting order must therefore be distinguished from the spontaneous origin of the rules on which it rests, and it is possible that an order which would still have to be described as spontaneous rests on rules which are entirely the result of deliberate design. In the kind of society with which we are familiar, of course, only some of the rules which people in fact observe, namely some of the rules of law (but never all, even of these) will be the product of deliberate design, while most of the rules of morals and custom will be spontaneous growths.

That even an order which rests on made rules may be spontaneous in character is shown by the fact that its particular manifestation will always depend on many circumstances which the designer of these rules did not and could not know. The particular content of the order will depend on the concrete circumstances known only to the individuals who obey the rules and apply them to facts known only to them. It will be through the knowledge of these individuals both of the rules and of the particular facts that both will determine the resulting order.

The Spontaneous Order of Society is Made Up of Individuals and Organizations

In any group of men of more than the smallest size, collaboration will always rest both on spontaneous order as well as on deliberate organization. There is no doubt that for many limited tasks organization is the most powerful method of effective coordination because it enables us to adapt the resulting order much more fully to our wishes, while where, because of the complexity of the circumstances to be taken into account, we must rely on the forces making for a spontaneous order, our power over the particular contents of this order is necessarily restricted.

That the two kinds of order will regularly coexist in every society of any degree of complexity does not mean, however, that we can combine them in any manner we like. What in fact we find in all free societies is that, although groups of men will join in organizations for the achievement of some particular ends, the coordination of the activities of all these separate organizations, as well as of the separate individuals, is brought about by the forces making for a spontaneous order. The family, the farm, the plant, the firm, the corporation and the various associations, and all the public institutions including government, are organizations which in turn are integrated into a more comprehensive spontaneous order. It is advisable to reserve the term 'society' for this spontaneous overall order so that we may distinguish it from all the organized smaller groups which will exist within it, as well as from such smaller and more or less isolated groups as the horde, the tribe, or the clan, whose members will at least in some respects act under a central direction for common purposes. In some instances it will be the same group which at times, as when engaged in most of its daily routine, will operate as a spontaneous order maintained by the observation of conventional rules without the necessity of commands, while at other times, as when hunting, migrating, or fighting, it will be acting as an organization under the directing will of a chief.

The spontaneous order which we call a society also need not have such sharp boundaries as an organization will usually possess. There will often be a nucleus, or several nuclei, of more closely related individuals occupying a central position in a more loosely connected but more extensive order. Such particular societies within the Great Society may arise as the result of spatial proximity, or of some other special circumstances which produce closer relations among their members. And different partial societies of this sort will often overlap and every individual may, in addition to being a member of the Great Society, be a member of numerous other spontaneous suborders or partial societies of this sort as well as of various organizations existing within the comprehensive Great Society.

Of the organizations existing within the Great Society one which regularly occupies a very special position will be that which we call government. Although it is conceivable that the spontaneous order which we call society may exist without government, if the minimum of rules required for the formation of such an order is observed without an organized apparatus for their enforcement, in most circumstances the organization which we call government becomes indispensable in order to assure that those rules are obeyed.

This particular function of government is somewhat like that of a maintenance squad of a factory, its object being not to produce any particular services or products to be consumed by the citizens, but rather to see that the mechanism which regulates the production of those goods and services is kept in working order. The purposes for which this machinery is currently being used will be determined by those who operate its parts and in the last resort by those who buy its products.

The same organization that is charged with keeping in order an operating structure which the individuals will use for their own purposes, will, however, in addition to the task of enforcing the rules on which that order rests, usually be expected also to render other services which the spontaneous order cannot produce adequately. These two distinct functions of government are usually not clearly separated; yet, as we shall see, the distinction between the coercive functions in which government enforces rules of conduct, and its service functions in which it need merely administer resources placed at its disposal, is of fundamental importance. In the second it is one organization among many and like the others part of a spontaneous overall order, while in the first it provides an essential condition for the preservation of that overall order.

In English it is possible, and has long been usual, to discuss these two types of order in terms of the distinction between 'society' and 'government'. There is no need in the discussion of these problems, so long as only one country is concerned, to bring in the metaphysically charged term 'state'. It is largely under the influence of continental and particularly Hegelian thought that in the course of the last hundred years the practice of speaking of the 'state' (preferably with a capital 'S'), where 'government' is more appropriate and precise, has come to be widely adopted. That which acts, or pursues a policy, is however always the organization of government; and it does not make for clarity to drag in the term 'state' where 'government' is quite sufficient. It becomes particularly misleading when 'the state' rather than 'government' is contrasted with 'society' to indicate that the first is an organization and the second a spontaneous order.

The Rules of Spontaneous Orders and the Rules of Organization

One of our chief contentions will be that, though spontaneous order and organization will always coexist, it is still not possible to mix these two principles of order in any manner we like. If this is not more generally understood it is due to the fact that for the determination of both kinds of order we have to rely on rules, and that the important differences between the kinds of rules which the two different kinds of order require are generally not recognized.

To some extent every organization must rely also on rules and not only on specific commands. The reason here is the same as that which makes it necessary for a spontaneous order to rely solely on rules: namely that by guiding the actions of individuals by rules rather than specific commands it is possible to make use of knowledge which nobody possesses as a whole. Every organization in which the members are not mere tools of the organizer will determine by commands only the function to be performed by each member, the purposes to be achieved, and certain general aspects of the methods to be employed, and will leave the detail to be decided by the individuals on the basis of their respective knowledge and skills.

Organization encounters here the problem which any attempt to bring order into complex human activities meets: the organizer must wish the individuals who are to cooperate to make use of knowledge that he himself does not possess. In none but the most simple kind of organization is it conceivable that all the details of all activities are governed by a single mind. Certainly nobody has yet succeeded in deliberately arranging all the activities that go on in a complex society. If anyone did ever succeed in fully organizing such a society, it would no longer make use of many minds but would be altogether dependent on one mind; it would certainly not be very complex but extremely primitive—and so would soon be the mind whose knowledge and will determined everything. The facts which could enter into the design of such an order could be only those which were known and digested by this mind; and as only he could decide on action and thus gain experience, there would be none of that interplay of many minds in which alone mind can grow.

What distinguishes the rules which will govern action within an organization is that they must be rules for the performance of assigned tasks. They presuppose that the place of each individual in a fixed structure is determined by command and that the rules each individual must obey depend on the place which he has been assigned and on the particular ends which have been indicated for him by the commanding authority. The rules will thus regulate merely the detail of the action of appointed functionaries or agencies of government.

Rules of organization are thus necessarily subsidiary to commands, filling in the gaps left by the commands. Such rules will be different for the different members of the organization according to the different roles which have been assigned to them, and they will have to be interpreted in the light of the purposes determined by the commands. Without the assignment of a function and the determination of the ends to be pursued by particular commands, the bare abstract rule would not be sufficient to tell each individual what he must do.

By contrast, the rules governing a spontaneous order must be independent of purpose and be the same, if not necessarily for all members, at least for whole classes of members not individually designated by name. They must, as we shall see, be rules applicable to an unknown and indeterminable number of persons and instances. They will have to be applied by the individuals in the light of their respective knowledge and purposes; and their application will be independent of any common purpose, which the individual need not even know.

In the terms we have adopted this means that the general rules of law that a spontaneous order rests on aim at an abstract order, the particular or concrete content of which is not known or foreseen by anyone; while the commands as well as the rules which govern an organization serve particular results aimed at by those who are in command of the organization. The more complex the order aimed at, the greater will be that part of the separate actions which will have to be determined by circumstances not known to those who direct the whole, and the more dependent control will be on rules rather than on specific commands. In the most complex types of organizations, indeed, little more than the assignment of particular functions and the general aim will be determined by command of the supreme authority, while the performance of these functions will be regulated only by rules—yet by rules which at least to some degree are specific to the functions assigned to particular persons. Only when we pass from the biggest kind of organization, government, which as organization must still be dedicated to a circumscribed and determined set of specific purposes, to the overall order of the whole of society, do we find an order which relies solely on rules and is entirely spontaneous in character.

It is because it was not dependent on organization but grew up as a spontaneous order that the structure of modern society has attained that degree of complexity which it possesses and which far exceeds any that could have been achieved by deliberate organization. In fact, of course, the rules which made the growth of this complex order possible were initially not designed in expectation of that result; but those people who happened to adopt suitable rules developed a complex civilization which then often spread to others. To maintain that we must deliberately plan modern society because it has become so complex is therefore paradoxical, and the result of a complete misunderstanding of these circumstances. The fact is, rather, that we can preserve an order of such complexity not by the method of directing the members, but only indirectly by enforcing and improving the rules conducive to the formation of a spontaneous order.

We shall see that it is impossible, not only to replace the spontaneous order by organization and at the same time to utilize as much of the dispersed knowledge of all its members as possible, but also to improve or correct this order by interfering in it by direct commands. Such a combination of spontaneous order and organization it can never be rational to adopt. While it is sensible to supplement the commands determining an organization by subsidiary rules, and to use organizations as elements of a spontaneous order, it can never be advantageous to supplement the rules governing a spontaneous order by isolated and subsidiary commands concerning those activities where the actions are guided by the general rules of conduct. This is the gist of the argument against 'interference' or 'intervention' in the market order. The reason why such isolated commands requiring specific actions by members of the spontaneous order can never improve but must disrupt that order is that they will refer to a part of a system of interdependent actions determined by information and guided by purposes known only to the several acting persons but not to the directing authority. The spontaneous order arises from each element balancing all the various factors operating on it and by adjusting all its various actions to each other, a balance which will be destroyed if some of the actions are determined by another agency on the basis of different knowledge and in the service of different ends.

What the general argument against 'interference' thus amounts to is that, although we can endeavour to improve a spontaneous order by revising the general rules on which it rests, and can supplement its results by the efforts of various organizations, we cannot improve the results by specific commands that deprive its members of the possibility of using their knowledge for their purposes.

We will have to consider throughout this book how these two kinds of rules have provided the model for two altogether different conceptions of law and how this has brought it about that authors using the same word 'law' have in fact been speaking about different things. This comes out most clearly in the contrast we find throughout history between those to whom law and liberty were inseparable[11] and those to whom the two were irreconcilable. We find one great tradition extending from the ancient Greeks and Cicero[12] through the Middle Ages[13] to the classical liberals like John Locke, David Hume, Immanuel Kant[14] and the Scottish moral philosophers, down to various American statesmen[15] of the nineteenth and twentieth centuries, for whom law and liberty could not exist apart from each other; while to Thomas Hobbes, Jeremy Bentham[16] and many French thinkers[17] and the modern legal positivists law of necessity means an encroachment on freedom. This apparent conflict between long lines of great thinkers does not mean that they arrived at opposite conclusions, but merely that they were using the word 'law' in different senses.

The Terms 'Organism' and 'Organization'

A few comments should be added on the terms in which the distinction examined in this chapter has most commonly been discussed in the past. Since the beginning of the nineteenth century the terms 'organism' and 'organization' have been frequently used to contrast the two types of order. As we have found it advisable to avoid the former term and to adopt the latter in a specific sense, some comments on their history may be appropriate.

It was natural that the organismal analogy should have been used since ancient times to describe the spontaneous order of society, since organisms were the only kinds of spontaneous order with which everybody was familiar. Organisms are indeed a kind of spontaneous order and as such show many of the characteristics of other spontaneous orders. It was therefore tempting to borrow such terms as 'growth', 'adaptation', and 'function' from them. They are, however, spontaneous orders of a very special kind, possessing also properties which by no means necessarily belong to all spontaneous orders; the analogy in consequence soon becomes more misleading than helpful.[18]

The chief peculiarity of organisms which distinguishes them from the spontaneous orders of society is that in an organism most of the individual elements occupy fixed places which, at least once the organism is mature, they retain once and for all. They also, as a rule, are more or less constant systems consisting of a fixed number of elements which, although some may be replaced by equivalent new ones, retain an order in space readily perceivable with the senses. They are, in consequence, in the terms we have used, orders of a more concrete kind than the spontaneous orders of society, which may be preserved although the total number of elements changes and the individual elements change their places. This relatively concrete character of the order of organisms shows itself in the fact that their existence as distinct wholes can be perceived intuitively by the senses, while the abstract spontaneous order of social structures usually can only be reconstructed by the mind.

The interpretation of society as an organism has almost invariably been used in support of hierarchic and authoritarian views to which the more general conception of the spontaneous order gives no support. Indeed, since Menenius Agrippa, on the occasion of the first secession of the Roman plebs, used the organismal metaphor to justify the privileges of a particular group, it must have been used innumerable times for similar purposes. The suggestion of fixed places assigned to particular elements according to their distinct 'functions', and the much more concrete determination of the biological structures as compared with the abstract character of the spontaneous structures of society, have indeed made the organismal conception of very questionable value for social theory. It has been abused even more than the term 'order' itself when interpreted as a made order or *taxis*, and has frequently been used to defend a hierarchical order, the necessity of 'degree', the relation of command and obedience, or the preservation of established positions of particular individuals, and for this reason has rightly become suspect.

The term 'organization', on the other hand, which in the nineteenth century was frequently used in contrast to 'organism' to express the distinction we have discussed,[19] and which we shall retain to describe a made order or *taxis*, is of comparatively recent origin. It seems to have come into general use at the time of the French Revolution, with reference to which Kant once observed that 'in a recently undertaken reconstruction of a great people into a great state the word *organization* has been frequently and appropriately used for the institution of the magistracies and even the whole state.'[20] The word became characteristic of the spirit of the Napoleonic period[21] and became the central conception in the plans for the 'reconstruction of society' of the chief founders of modern socialism, the Saint Simonians, and of Auguste Comte.[22] Until the term 'socialism' came into general, use 'the organization of society as a whole' was in fact the accepted way of referring to what we now describe as socialism.[23] Its central role, particularly for French thinking during the early part of the nineteenth century, was clearly seen by the young Ernest Renan, who in 1849 could speak of the ideal of a 'scientific organization of mankind as the last word of modern science and its daring but legitimate ambition'.[24]

In English, the word appears to have come into general use around 1790 as a technical term for a 'systematic arrangement for a definite purpose'.[25] But it was the Germans who adopted it with particular enthusiasm and to whom it soon appeared to express a peculiar capacity in which they believed themselves to excel other people. This even led to a curious rivalry between French and German scholars, who during the First World War conducted a slightly comic literary dispute across the fighting lines as to which of the two nations had the stronger claim to possessing the secret of organization.[26]

In confining the term here to a made order or *taxis* we follow what seems to have become the general use in sociology and especially in what is known as 'organization theory'.[27] The idea of organization in this sense is a natural consequence of the discovery of the powers of the human intellect and especially of the general attitude of constructivist rationalism. It appeared for a long time as the only procedure by which an order serviceable to human purposes could be deliberately achieved, and it is indeed the intelligent and powerful method of achieving certain known and foreseeable results. But as its development is one of the great achievements of constructivism, so is the disregard of its limits one of its most serious defects. What it overlooks is that the growth of that mind which can direct an organization, and of the more comprehensive order within which organizations function, rests on adaptations to the unforeseeable, and that the only possibility of transcending the capacity of individual minds is to rely on those superpersonal 'self-organizing' forces which create spontaneous orders.

Notes

*Adam Smith, *The Theory of Moral Sentiments* (London, 1759), Part 6, ch. 2, penultimate paragraph. It deserves to be noted that this passage contains some of the basic concepts and terms we shall have to use throughout this book: the conception of a spontaneous order of the *Great Society* as contrasted with a deliberate *arrangement* of the elements; the distinction between *coincidence* and *opposition* between the rules (*principles of motion*) inherent in the elements and those imposed upon them by legislation; and the interpretation of the social process as a *game* which will go on smoothly if the two kinds of rules are in concord but will produce *disorder* if they are in conflict.

1. See my essay on 'The theory of complex phenomena', in F. A. Hayek, *Studies in Philosophy, Politics and Economics* (London and Chicago, 1967, henceforth referred to as *S.P.P.E.*). It was in fact at first entirely the result of methodological considerations that led me to resume the use of the unpopular concept of 'order': see also F. A. Hayek, *The Counter Revolution of Science* (Chicago, 1952), p. 39: 'If social phenomena showed no order except in so far as they were consciously designed, there would indeed be no room for a theoretical science of society and there would be, as is often maintained, only problems of psychology.' In recent discussion the term 'system' is often used in much the same sense in which I use here 'order', which still seems to me preferable.

2. It would seem that the currency of the concept of order in political theory goes back to St Augustine. See in particular his dialogue *Ordo* in J. P. Migne (ed) *Patrologiae cursus completus sec. lat.* 32/47 (Paris, 1861-2), and in a German version *Die Ordnung*, trans. C. J. Peel, fourth edition (Paderborn, 1966).

3. See L. S. Stebbing, *A Modern Introduction to Logic* (London, 1933), p. 228: 'When we know how a set of elements is ordered, we have a basis for inference.' See also Immanuel Kant, *Werke* (Akademie Ausgabe), *Nachlass*, vol 6, p. 669: 'Ordnung ist die Zusammenfügung nach Regeln.'

4. See E. E. Evans Pritchard, *Social Anthropology* (London, 1951), p. 49; see also ibid., p. 19:

    It is evident that there must be uniformities and regularities in social life, that society must have some sort of order, or its members could not live together. It is only because people know the kind of behaviour expected of them, and what kind of behaviour to expect from others, in the various situations of life, and coordinate their activities in submission to rules and under the guidance of values that each and all are able to go about their affairs. They can make predictions, anticipate events, and lead their lives in harmony with their fellows because every society has a form or pattern which allows us to speak of it as a system, or structure, within which, and in accordance with which, its members live their lives.

5. See L. S. Stebbing, op. cit., p. 229: 'Order is most *apparent* where man has been at work.'

6. See J. Ortega y Gasset, *Mirabeau o el politico* (1927), in *Obras Completas* (Madrid, 1947) vol. 3, p. 603: 'Orden no es una presión que desde fuera se ejerce sobra la sociedad, sin un equilibrio que se suscita en su interior.'

7. See H. von Foerster and G. W. Zopf, Jr (eds) *Principles of Self-Organization* (New York, 1962) and, on the anticipation of the main conceptions of cybernetics by Adam Smith, cf. G. Hardin, *Nature and*

Man's Fate (New York, 1961), p. 54; and Dorothy Emmet, *Function, Purpose and Powers* (London, 1958), p. 90.

8.   See H. Kuhn, 'Ordnung im Werden und Zerfall', in K. Ruhn and F. Wiedmann (eds), *Das Problem der Ordnung* (Sechster Deutscher Kongress für Philosophie, Munich, 1960, publ. Meisenheim am Glan, 1962), especially p. 17.

9.   See Werner Jaeger, *Paideia: The Ideals of Greek Culture*, trans. G. Highet, vol. I, second edition (New York, 1945), p. 110, about 'Anaximander of Miletus transferring the concept of *diké* from the social life of the city-state to the realm of nature.... This is the original of the philosophical idea of cosmos: for the word originally signified the *right order* in a state or in a community'; and ibid., p. 179: 'So the physicist's cosmos became by a curious retrogression in thought, the pattern of anemia in human society.' See also the same author's 'Praise of law' in P. Sayre (ed), *Interpretations of Modern Legal Philosophies: Essays in Honor of Roscoe Pound* (New York, 1947), especially p. 358:

A world thus 'justified' could be called rightly by another term taken over from the social order, a cosmos. That word occurs for the first time in the language of the Ionian philosophers; by taking this step and extending the rule of *diké* to reality as a whole they clearly revealed the nature of Greek legal thought and showed that it was based on the relationship of justice to being.

And ibid., p. 361: 'The law on which it [the *polis*] was founded was not a mere decree but the *nomos*, which originally meant the sum total of that which was respected by all living custom with regard to what is right and wrong'; and ibid., p. 365 on the fact that even during the period of the dissolution of the old Greek faith in law: 'the strict relationship of the *nomos* to the nature of the cosmos was not universally questioned.'

For Aristotle, who connects *nomos* with *taxis* rather than *kosmos* (see *Politics*, 1287a 18 and especially 1326a, 30: *ho te gar nomos taxis tis esti*), it is characteristically inconceivable that the order resulting from the *nomos* should exceed what the orderer can survey, 'for who will command its over-swollen multitude in war? or who will serve as its herald, unless he had the lungs of Stentor?' The creation of order in such a multitude is for him a task only the gods can achieve. Elsewhere (*Ethics*, IX, x, §3) he even argues that a state, i.e. an ordered society, of a hundred thousand people is impossible.

10.   Adam Smith, *Wealth of Nations*, edited by E. Cannan, vol. I, p. 421.

11.   See G. Sartori, *Democratic Theory* (Detroit, 1962), p. 306:

Western man for two and a half millennia has sought liberty in the law.... [Yet] the widespread skepticism about the value of the juridical protection of liberty is not unjustified. The reason for this is that our conception of law has changed; and that, as a consequence, law can no longer give us the protection that it did give us in the past.

12. See Philo of Alexandria, *Quod omnis probus liber sit,* 452, 45, Loeb edition, vol. IX, p. 36: '*hosoi de meta nomou zosin, eleuteroi*'. On freedom in ancient Greece see in particular Max Pohlenz, *The Idea of Freedom in Greek Life and Thought* (Dordrecht, 1962). On Cicero and the Roman concept of liberty generally see U. von Lübtow, *Blüte und Verfall der römischen Freikeit* (Berlin, 1953); Theo Mayer-Maly, 'Rechtsgeschichte der Freiheitsidee in Antike und Mittelalter', *Österreichische Zeitschrift für öffentliches Recht,* N.F. VI, 1956; and G. Crifo, 'Su alcuni aspetti della libertà in Roma', *Archivio Giuridico 'Filippo Serafini',* sesta serie, xxiii, 1958.

13. See R. W. Southern, *The Making of the Middle Ages* (New Haven, 1953), p. 107 *et seq.:*

The hatred of that which was governed, not by rule, but by will, went very deep in the Middle Ages.... The higher one rose towards liberty, the more the area of action was covered by law, the less it was subject by will.... Law was not the enemy of freedom; on the contrary, the outline of liberty was traced by the bewildering variety of law which was slowly evolved during our period.... High and low alike sought liberty by insisting on enlarging the number of rules under which they lived.... It was only when the quality of freedom was articulated by being attached to the status of knight, burgess or baron that it could be observed, analysed and measured.... Liberty is a creation of law, and law is reason in action; it is reason which makes men, as we should say, ends in themselves. Tyranny, whether of King John or of the Devil, is a manifestation of the absence of law.

14. Most emphatically, perhaps, Adam Ferguson, *Principles of Moral and Political Science* (Edinburgh, 1792), vol. 2, p. 258 *et seq.:*

Liberty or freedom is not, as the origin of the name may seem to imply, an exemption from all restraint, but rather the most effectual application of every just restraint to all the members of a free state, whether they be magistrates or subjects.

It is under just restraints only that every person is safe, and cannot be invaded, either in the freedom of his person, his property, or innocent action.... The establishment of a just and effectual government is of all circumstances in civil society the most essential to freedom: that everyone is justly said to be free in proportion as the government under which he resides is sufficiently powerful to protect him, at the same time that it is sufficiently restrained and limited to prevent the abuse of this power.

15. Daniel Webster is credited with the statement that 'Liberty is the creature of law, essentially different from the authorized licentiousness that trespasses on right'; and Charles Evans Hughes with that 'Liberty and Law are one and inseparable'. There are many similar statements by continental legal scholars of the last century, e.g. Charles Beudant, *Le Droit individuel et l'état* (Paris, 1891), p. 5: 'Le

Droit, au sens le plus général du mot, est la science de la liberté'; and Karl Binding who argued somewhere that 'Das Recht ist eine Ordnung menschlicher Freiheit.'

16. See J. Bentham, 'Principles of the civil code', in *Theory of Legislation,* edited by C. K. Ogden (London, 1931), p. 98: 'Laws cannot be made except at the expense of liberty.' Also in *Deontology* (London and Edinburgh, 1834), vol. 2, p. 59:

There are few words which, with its derivations, have been more mischievous than this word liberty. When it means anything beyond mere caprice and dogmatism, it means good government; and if good government had had the good fortune to occupy the same place in the public mind which has been occupied by liberty, the crimes and follies which have disgraced and retarded the progress of political improvement would hardly have been committed. The usual definition of liberty—that it is the right to do everything that the law does not forbid—shows with what carelessness words are used in ordinary discourse or composition; for if the laws are bad, what becomes of liberty? and if the laws are good, where is its value? Good laws have a definite intelligible meaning; they pursue an evidently useful end by obviously appropriate means.

17. See for example, Jean Salvaire, *Autorité et liberté* (Montpellier, 1932), p. 65 *et seq.*, who argues that 'the complete realization of liberty is, in fact, nothing else but the complete abolition of law.... Law and liberty are mutually exclusive'.

18. Edmund Burke, 'Letter to W. Elliot' (1795), in *Works* (London, 1808), vol. 7, p. 366:

These analogies between bodies natural and politick, though they may sometimes illustrate arguments, furnish no arguments for themselves. They are but too often used under the colour of a specious philosophy, to find apologies for the despair of laziness and pusillanimity, and to excuse the want of all manly efforts when the exigencies of our country call for them the more loudly.

19. For a characteristic use of the contrast between 'organism' and 'organization' see Adolf Wagner, *Grundlegung der politischen Ökonomie, I. Grundlagen der Volkswirtschaft* (Leipzig, 1876), § § 149 and 299.

20. See Immanuel Kant, *Kritik der Urteilshraft* (Berlin, 1790), Part 2 section I, § 6sn.: 'So hat man sich bei einer neuerlich unternommenen gänzlichen Umbildung eines grossen Volkes zu einem Staat des Wortes *Organisation* haüfig für Einrichtung der Magistraturen usw. und selbst des ganzen Staatskörpers sehr schicklich bedient.'

21. See H. Balzac, *Autre étude de femme*, in *La Comédie Humaine*, Pleiade edition, vol. 3, p. 226: 'Organiser, par example, est un mot de l'Empire et qui contient Napoléon tout entier.'

22. See, for example, the journal edited by H. de Saint Simon and Auguste Comte called *Organisateur*, reprinted in *Oeuvres de Saint Simon et d'Enfantin* (Paris, 1865-78), vol. 20, especially p. 220, where the aim of the work is described as 'D'imprimer au XIX siècle le caractère organisateur'.

23. See in particular Louis Blanc, *Organisation du travail* (Paris, 1839), and H. Ahrens, *Rechtsphilosophie*, fourth edition (Vienna, 1852) on 'organization' as the magic word of the communists and socialists; see also Francis Lieber, 'Anglican and Gallican liberty' (1848), in *Miscellaneous Writings* (Philadelphia, 1881), vol 2, p. 385:

    The fact that Gallican liberty expects everything from *organization*, while Anglican liberty inclines to development, explains why we see in France so little improvement and expansion of institutions; but when improvements are attempted, a total abolition of the preceding state of things—a beginning *ab ovo*—a rediscussion of the first elementary principles.

24. See Ernest Renan, *L'Avenir de la Science* (1890), in *Oeuvres complètes* (Paris, 1949), vol. 3, p. 757: 'ORGANISER SCIENTIFIQUEMENT L'HUMANITE, tel est donc le dernier mot de la science moderne, telle est son audacieuse mais légitime prétention.'

25. See *Shorter Oxford Dictionary*, s.v. 'organization', which shows, however, that the term was already used by John Locke.

26. Jean Labadie (ed), *L'Allemagne, a -t-elle secret de l'organisation?* (Paris, 1916).

27. See Dwight Waldo, 'Organization theory: an elephantine problem', *Public Administration Review*, xxx, 1961, and reprinted in *General Systems, Yearbook of the Society for General System Research*, VII 1962, the preceding volume of which contains a useful collection of, articles on the theory of organization.

SELF-ORGANIZATION AND THE CORPORATION

Richard T. Pascale, Mark Millemann, and Linda Gioja

V isa, the largest credit card network in the world, took form in the late 1970s under the guidance of one of complexity's earliest corporate proponents, Dee Hock. As CEO, Hock applied the principles of self-organization to this struggling enterprise and, as they say, the rest is history.[1] Starting from behind, Visa seized a huge competitive advantage over its rivals and continues to extend its lead to this day. With almost 100 million cardholders and three-quarters of a trillion dollars of point-of-sale volume annually, Visa claims half of the credit card market. Its nearest rival, MasterCard, has 31 percent.[2]

Visa represents self-organization in almost a pure form. Its decentralized structure relies almost exclusively on self-interest as the primary incentive. The transactional nature of members' relationship to the clearing center and to one another suffices to cause the right things to happen and the simplest structures to prevail.[3]

To apply the concepts of self-organization and emergence broadly, we must demonstrate their relevance to social systems. Most organizations require that a balance be struck between self-interest and community interest. Transaction costs increase. Decision making can not be entirely delegated to the organizations' members.

We discussed earlier how the self-organizing potential of a living system is enhanced by (1) devolving power to the nodes, (2) establishing rich connections to form networks, and (3) enriching the value of those networks with information that sparks further evolution. The examples that follow will illustrate how these parameters play out in more complicated corporate contexts.

Imagine a continuum of complexity. We began with Tupperware and Visa, organizations in which self-organization and emergence are fueled largely by self-interest and manifest in the purest and most straightforward form. Mid-continuum are organizations that are highly dependent on the self-organization of members, but also rely on connections between participants that are based on both social as well as economic ties. Alcoholics Anonymous provides an example. Further along the continuum are larger societal systems. Silicon Valley will be used as an illustration. Finally, we look at a more traditional organization, the U.S. Army, which has explicitly harnessed self-organization and emergence as essential components of its day-to-day strategic capability.

Self-Organization and Self-Help

Self-organization and emergence play a pivotal role in the nonprofit sphere. Such entities usually pay very low salaries and rely extensively on volunteers. An analysis of the pioneer self-help group, Alcoholics Anonymous, reveals much about the formation and functioning of such organizations.

"AA," as it is known, was formed in 1935 through a chance encounter between a physician and a stockbroker, both of whom were recovering alcoholics.[4] Emergence needs a ripe issue. In this case, the issue was the problem of addictive drinking within a society that minimized, joked about, or denied its existence. Beneath this veneer festered a great deal of suffering. Societal awakening was necessary to redefine alcoholism as a disease. The condition also required innovative strategies for healing. As discussed earlier, such factors provide the grist for emergence.

Self-organization and emergence flourish with simple rules and structure. AA's founders invented such rules through the "12-step" process, an extraordinary contribution in its own right. Step one requires the alcoholic to openly admit to a problem with alcohol. Subsequent steps require each member to work methodically through a therapeutic program of self-acceptance and spiritual surrender. Alcoholics Anonymous also devised an elegantly simple structure and operating principles. The philosophy holds, among other things, that participants are a brotherhood and must share the burden of maintaining their AA chapter. AA intentionally operates from hand-to-mouth with no fund raising, grants, or publicity that might allow members to rest on their laurels. Each chapter is only as viable as its active membership. There is no hierarchy, no paid staff, and no endowment.

AA's 12-step program and its organizing principles have been codified by many similar organizations. In effect, it has become the DNA of a whole new organizational species.

In the 1980s, social scientist Gregory Bateson conducted an extensive study of AA. One of his most interesting observations focused on emergence. He found that AA's therapeutic intervention had no precedent; it was a quantum leap against the backdrop of the psychotherapeutic techniques of the time.[5] AA addressed an unmet societal need and ignited a contagion of interest. Within a few years of its inception, AA chapters could be found throughout the United States and in many other nations. This broad social movement just seemed to materialize out of thin air.

AA's institutional significance in the self-help sphere is comparable to the innovation of the Federal Reserve Board as a quasi-independent guardian of the U.S. economy. Over the past six decades, the AA model has fostered hundreds of self-help and activist organizations around the world. MAAD (Mothers Against Drunk Driving) has almost single-handedly brought an end to lenient sentences for drunk drivers. MAAD has catalyzed public awareness, altered the drinking norms of our society, and made the term "designated Drive" a staple of our vocabulary.[6] Other self-organizing groups support victims of spouse and child abuse and patients facing the ravages of terminal disease. In the United States, two million people are involved with some aspect of Alcoholics Anonymous each day. Worldwide, at least thirty million individuals are directly involved with self-help organizations.[7]

The Emergence of Silicon Valley

Self-organization and emergence are not confined to any one company or industry. We find these factors at work in societies and economies. The thousands of highly specialized but tightly networked entrepreneurs who comprise the fashion industry of Northern Italy are an example.[8] A second is closer to home.

Self-organization in Silicon Valley occurs in two ways: (1) university scientists, entrepreneurs, and investors continuously self-organize to form start-ups; and (2) corporations, academic institutions, and venture capital firms self-organize to form strategic alliances, partnerships, and temporary project teams. *Emergence* likewise occurs in several characteristic ways. The Valley has been the spawning ground of emerging technology. Historically, it was the magnet that drew together the components and subsystems for personal computers. Today, it is a diverse coalescing site for the elements of biotechnology, microprocessors, and bioelectronics. The Valley has also fostered emergent business platforms such as e-commerce and, most recently, start-ups designed with an initial public offering (IPO) and imminent wealth creation in mind rather than near-term products, profit, or staying power. Finally, the Valley has been the source of emergent business practices—perpetual disequilibrium, fast pace, obsession with the big "after-next" idea—and a cauldron of talent and energy that seems continuously fueled by its own adrenaline.

Silicon Valley is home to one-third of the 100 largest technology companies created in the United States since 1965. The market value of these companies increased by $25 billion between 1986 and 1990 alone, dwarfing the $1 billion increase of their Boston-based Route-128 counterparts. Although the two regions employed workforces of roughly the same size in 1975, Silicon Valley businesses generated some 150,000 new technology jobs during the ensuing fifteen years—triple the number created along Route 128.[9] Venture-capital investments from January 1996 through the first quarter of 1997 were $2.8 billion in Silicon Valley as opposed to $700 million in Boston.[10] Over three decades, the Valley has grown to encompass 2,000 square miles. The region loosely includes Marin County, San Francisco, Oakland, Berkeley, Palo Alto, San Jose, and Santa Cruz.

Recently, McKinsey and Company conducted a survey to measure the growth of the high-technology sector in industrialized economies. In the United States, the revenues increased 14 percent between 1990 and 1998. The nearest rival was Germany, at 2 percent. Most of the U.S.'s astonishing growth was driven by Silicon Valley.[11]

"Historians will record 1971 and 1972 as the years the U.S. economy tilted west," writes Virginia Postrel, a columnist for *Forbes* magazine. "In those years, venture-capital firms began sprouting up in the region south of San Francisco to find young companies with information-technology products—often in the form of computers or their software—either on a desktop or on a silicon chip. Technology, silicon, talent, venture capital were the propellants of an engine that has generated more wealth in the past 20 years than the rest of the nation combined."[12]

As noted earlier, Silicon Valley combines the ingredients of emergence: sparks of innovation (including, but not limited to, the stream of discoveries pouring forth from Stanford University and the University of California at Berkeley); technology; capital; heterogeneity (intellectual and ethnic); and an upbeat and stimulating physical, intellectual, and spiritual climate. One interesting facet of self-organization in Silicon Valley is the remarkable and ever changing set of partnerships. This pattern of cooperation and coevolution distinguishes the area from less successful counterparts along Boston's Route 128 and elsewhere. "On the East Coast," says one observer, "there's still the perception [a dying perception] that we can do it alone. 'We'll just keep adding people and keep the core competence in-house.'"[13] Important potential partners like the Massachusetts Institute of Technology (MIT) stand somewhat aloof from the entrepreneurial fray. Early on, Stanford and the University of California decided to join forces with companies. One of Stanford's first deans of engineering launched a program in which the school and nearby companies exchanged talent and co-managed projects in return for royalties—a program that continues to this day.

In Silicon Valley, both academic and business leaders actively cultivate strategic alliances. Among other things, this allows these institutions to cope with risk by sharing it. Species gain resilience by banding together, sharing resources, and working in tandem. If one leg of a network buckles, others can keep it intact.

This web of self-organizing relationships has become a conscious operating model for the Valley. It gives the region a meta-intelligence insofar as expertise and intellectual properties aren't just held within a company but are spread around through cross-pollination by firms and self-employed individuals. For example, Sun Microsystems, Inc., draws on independent programmers to develop applications for Java. Netscape Communications Corporation turns its new releases over at no charge to the Internet community (in return, the early users become the Beta test). A recent *Fortune* article diagrammed the labyrinth of financial holdings, joint board appointments, and common venture capital holdings among some of the more prominent Silicon Valley venture capital firms. On average, each of the twenty firms in the report had ten shared connections, and some, such as Netscape, had sixteen.[14]

Genetic mixing within the Valley is fueled by constant employee turnover. "When employees join a company, they are passionately committed to it," states a partner of one of the Valley's largest venture capital firms, Paul Koontz. But employees can magically lose that loyalty on very short notice. Then they "go and rev up an equally passionate commitment to somebody else."[15] With serial employment the norm, firms compete intensely; at the same time, they cooperate, learn from, and partner with one another.

* * *

The stories of AA and Silicon Valley contain the common features of colorful anecdote. Such illustrations have one shortcoming: They can relegate the application of living systems principles to the colorful fringe of the organizational world rather than to the mainstream of management experience.

The relevance and application of the principles of living systems are much more than a practice of last resort. In adaptive circumstances, these principles should be the first recourse. The U.S. Army adopted precisely this outlook.

There is method in our madness in featuring the U.S. Army to illustrate how enduring organizational capabilities can be built on the dual properties of self-organization and emergence. The Army is above suspicion insofar as it is highly unlikely that these ideas could be applied casually or permissively. Beginning in the late 1980s, several generations of the Army's senior leaders studied and consciously embraced the ideas of self-organization and emergence and began to apply them as an alternative model to the Army's command-and-control legacy. They have since distilled them down to protocols that have served the Army well in sustaining its vitality over time.

For many, the juxtaposition of *U.S. Army* with *self-organization* and *transformation* amounts to a contradiction in terms. Our stereotypes warrant reexamination. General Gordon R. Sullivan, recently retired Chief of Staff of the Army, explains:

> The paradox of war in the Information Age is one of managing massive amounts of information and resisting the temptation to over-control it. The competitive advantage is nullified when you try to run decisions up and down the chain of command. All platoons and tank crews have real-time information on what is going on around them, the location of the enemy, and the nature and targeting of the enemy's weapons system. Once the commander's intent is understood, decisions must be devolved to the lowest possible level to allow these frontline soldiers to exploit the opportunities that develop.[16]

General Sullivan's words echo themes that we have discussed throughout this chapter.

Information-age warfare provoked the Army to harness self-organization and incorporate it as a central tenet of battlefield "doctrine" (the Army's term for *strategy*). The Army has pursued this by improving (1) the quality of the *nodes* (via higher-quality soldiers and superb training) and (2) the efficacy of *connections* that electronically tie together all the members of a fighting unit. Characteristically, the Army has codified these intentions so that these capabilities can be replicated.

The loosing of self-organizing impulses on the battlefield does not mean that tank crews fly helicopters or that soldiers spontaneously decide to support Kurdish rebels against Baghdad. To focus the lens of complexity, the Army invented an important managerial distinction called *Commander's Intent*. This is the foundation for action. Commander's Intent defines the scope of an engagement. The concept traces its origins to legendary General George S. Patton, a fatality of World War II.

"Never tell people *how* to do things," he once said, "Tell them *what* to do and they will surprise you with their ingenuity."[17] (This philosophical difference, by the way, was at the crux of his clashes with British General Bernard L. Montgomery.) Under this construct, combat units are encouraged to improvise and initiate, but always within the larger structure of the Commander's Intent. When that intent is clearly communicated, fighting units can exploit opportunities that arise, or regroup when things don't go exactly as planned.

The Army brought urgency to its reinvention efforts by simulating a form of "competition" peculiar to a military monopoly. True, the Army has little direct "competition," insofar as armed conflicts are rare. Indeed, the Army's leaders are well aware of the fact that the military services languish during periods of peace and then misapply the last recent war's doctrine to the technology and unique tactical challenges of the next.

What is remarkable about the U.S. Army in the decades since the Vietnam War is that it has sidestepped this pitfall by making technological obsolescence "the enemy" in its quest for continuous renewal. The accuracy and lethality of smart weapons pose a diabolical challenge; the massing of troops and material (which is, after all, what armies traditionally do) accomplishes little more than providing one's enemy with a large and vulnerable target. In addition, the advent of distributed information allows the foot soldier or tank commander in the field to know roughly as much about what's going on as the generals in the command center. If this information is properly managed, soldiers on the front lines are able to make decisions in real time. Given the right tools, they can exploit opportunities and improvise in highly advantageous ways. This competitive advantage is squandered if one conforms to the traditional Army doctrine of first running all decisions past headquarters. Herein lies the case for self-organization.

"New routes" are important to the Army because, at the strategic level, new routes are needed to fight wars in the information age. At the tactical level, soldiers can devise new routes to victory on the battlefield.

One of the Army's most significant contributions to management practice occurs at three highly unusual U.S. Army training centers: (1) Fort Irwin, California (mechanized warfare); (2) Fort Polk, Louisiana (guerrilla insurgence); and (3) Hoenfelds, Germany (peace-keeping and humanitarian relief). These facilities are sufficiently remarkable to have been studied by senior executives from Shell, Sears, Motorola, and General Electric, as well as by senior delegations from every country in Western Europe, Russia, and most nations of Asia, Latin America, and the Middle East. Perfected over the past fifteen years, they are widely recognized to have almost single-handedly transformed one of the largest employers in the United States, in a manner that has great relevance for business.[18]

Let us zoom in on the training that is under way at the National Training Center (NTC) in California's Mojave Desert. Over a grueling two-week period, an Army brigade of 3,000 to 4,000 people (equivalent to a fully integrated business unit within a corporation), from bottom to top, go head-to-head with a competitor of like size in a simulation so realistic that no participant comes away unscathed. It alters forever the way executives lead and the way a front line performs.

Critical to the impact of the experience is a cadre of 600 instructors, one of whom is assigned to every person with leadership or supervisory responsibilities. These "observer/controllers," as they are called, shadow their counterparts through day after twenty-hour day of intense activity, provide personal coaching, and facilitate a team debriefing called the After Action Review (AAR). An AAR helps participants to understand what went wrong and how to correct the shortcomings. The AARs are in fact where the tank treads touch the terrain—exploiting the teachable moments of an exercise that ranges across 650,000 acres and costs $1 million a day.

A number of factors have contributed to the Army's extraordinary and sustained transformation. But observers inside and outside of the military agree that the NTC and its satellite facilities have been the crucible in which the transformation has come together. Since the NTC was established, more than half a million Army personnel have rotated through its programs several times. In fact, most upper and middle officers and NCOs have had as many as five NTC experiences. As one officer stated, "Before the NTC, we used to kid ourselves. The training was highly subjective. But the NTC experience leaves no room for debate. Day after day, you are confronted with the hard evidence of discrepancies between intentions and faulty execution, between what you wanted the enemy to do and what he actually did."[19]

One of the most remarkable aspects of the Army's transformation is that it has been sustained over a long period of time—it has weathered the vicissitudes of numerous executive transitions. Since the mid 1970s, the U.S. Army has had to respond to the sifting policies of six different Republican and Democratic administrations, eight Secretaries of Defense, ten Secretaries of the Army, and a succession of six different Army Chiefs of Staff (the top ranking general and de facto chief executive of the Army).

How could any organization successfully undergo a prolonged transition with its leadership deck continuously shuffled? Even under the most ideal circumstances (which those enumerated above surely were not), how can an institution with so many organizational constraints (public-sector disincentives; a booming economy that siphons off the best talent while the Army remains hobbled by frozen pay and benefits structures; a 60 percent annual turnover among the troops; severe downsizing; and a deeply entrenched command-and-control tradition) achieve the best-in-class status it now enjoys and fundamentally alter its leadership style and culture?

The short answer to these questions is that the Army has done a superb job of utilizing the guidelines enumerated in this and previous chapters. Through its orchestration of the six factors described below, it has cultivated a great deal of continuity in its reinvention efforts, despite shifts in funding levels and in policies at the top.

Specifically, these factors are:

1. *Disequilibrium* is guaranteed by the grueling twenty-hour-a-day schedule at the NTC. Humiliating defeats at the hands of a superior "enemy," physical exhaustion, and the relentless discipline of the AAR work to unfreeze the organization and move it far out of its comfort zone.

2. *The edge of chaos* is an apt image for the participants' experience. Disequilibrium is *amplified* by fatigue and by mounting evidence that success is dependent on how well fighting units can integrate their proficiency at routine maneuvers with a new requirement: their ability to improvise. *Damping* feedback is provided by the training that has preceded the NTC experience. Soldiers have been drilled to perform tasks under specific conditions to achieve certain standards. The AARs use specific battlefield events, supported by compelling and unambiguous data, to orchestrate "teachable moments."

3. *Strange attractors* are ingeniously exploited by the Army to avoid the historical trap of a decline during peacetime:

   - The Army perpetually reminds itself of the terrible humiliation of Vietnam and is determined not to repeat it. ("Never again" is a mantra taken deeply to heart.)
   - By identifying "Information Age Warfare" and "The Digital Battlefield" as real and present dangers the Army stays focused on the threat of obsolescence.

   These big-picture attractors, as important as they are, have not kept the Army from attending to aspirations that appeal to individual soldiers. Other attractors are "Service to Nation" (an important consideration to many who volunteer) and "Be All That You Can Be." The latter is more than an ad slogan. It resonates with the desire of many soldiers to discover their latent potential. The Army authentically sees itself as a developmental institution—one that helps recruits build strengths so that they can return to the civilian world with maturity, skills, and a sense of possibility that were not present when they enlisted.

4. The Army's journey over its *fitness landscape* has been discussed. Its leaders recognized the need to abandon the "basin of attraction": conventional weapons, doctrine, conscripted soldiers, and command from the top. They sought a new fitness peak where the topography is shaped by smart weapons, electronically networked fighting units, nontraditional missions (e.g., Serbia, Haiti, Rwanda), and models that exploit the distributed intelligence and initiative of the front lines.

5. *Nodes and connections* are strengthened by higher-quality recruits (a continuous struggle in a prolonged boom economy), and superb training. Superior equipment and electronic linkages increased the flow of information that matters: real time and big picture. All this was fused together at the NTC. There, under the glaring light of the AARs, each of the nodes must stand and deliver; in the blazing sun and numbing cold, true teamwork is born. Lasting mutual respect and deep human connections are forged under these conditions.

6. *Freedom and discipline* are enacted through the NTC process. Freedom is defined within the boundaries of the Commander's Intent: When soldiers understand the overall objectives of each engagement, they are free to improvise. As noted, discipline is enforced through vigorous training before attending the NTC. A second level of discipline occurs through the rigorous self-examination of the AARs.

Emergence Without 20/20 Hindsight

The capacity to spot what is *emerging* (before it unfolds) is the acid test of how well one grasps the concept of emergence. Without hindsight, it is much harder, of course, but the exercise sharpens the mind. The key is to focus on arenas where there is a lot of "noise" or "heat," and where conversations and structural inconsistencies resemble interstellar debris that hasn't quite coalesced into a planet or star.

Consider the consulting industry. For close to two decades, it has grown at a rate of 20 to 25 percent each year, and it currently rings up annual fees of $30 billion.[20] Accompanying this growth is a curious irony: Clients buy more and pay more—and *complain* more. They decry the expense, fear their dependence, and protest that consultants "borrow your watch to tell you what time it is." The incongruity between words and actions alerts us to the possibility of an emergent issue.

What's going on?

Corporate downsizings during the past two decades may provide a partial explanation. Companies have kept just enough staff to handle ongoing business operations. When a special project arises or an unexpectedly high demand occurs, outside resources are needed. Some tasks require special expertise: reducing cycle time; providing change architecture; implementing software for enterprise resource planning; researching possible acquisitions. Those internally responsible benefit from advice provided by those familiar with the widest range of up-to-date applications across companies and industries. Because such expertise is hard to find and expensive to retain internally, consultants are hired.

What is emergent here is the need for *knowledge services*. Anachronistic stereotypes of consultants obscure this bona fide need. "Knowledge services" provide an efficient solution to an emergent need.

Another arena in which we see emergence-in-the-making is in societal contradictions toward adoption. Five million qualified parents in the most affluent nations of the world stand eager to adopt children. And fifteen million homeless children, mostly in economically deprived nations, stand in desperate need of support. In Africa alone, in the past ten years, 10.4 million children have become orphans after their parents' death from AIDS. These children, having lost their mothers (and, in most cases, their fathers), are essentially abandoned.[21] Most live in the streets.

For such youngsters' physical and mental suffering is acute. Many die in spirit, many die in flesh. Yet adopting these children remains extraordinarily difficult and fraught with legal, emotional, financial, and diplomatic perils. Note again the preconditions for emergence: heat and noise, unmet needs, and structural incongruities.

The problems begin as soon as a poor nation allows wealthier outsiders access to its abandoned children. The demand for youngsters is so intense that, in a remarkable short amount of time, criminal networks emerge to seal newborn infants—who *have* indigenous natural parents—from hospitals and sell them. Destitute women are paid to have babies. As these cruel and inhumane second-order effects become apparent, nations typically close their doors to adoption. They often impose restrictions on prospective parents that are so onerous as to relegate the remaining children to an untouchable category— "a problem too difficult to deal with." Such has been the case in Vietnam, Romania, the Philippines, the states of Russia, and most of sub-Saharan Africa.

Juxtapose this emergent-issue-waiting-to-happen with the outlawing of antipersonnel land mines. It is useful to reflect on the common patterns.

The hazard of antipersonnel mines was intractable until a host of agencies self-organized. The visibility and voice of Princess Diana, who raised the issue to public consciousness, aided the cause. As a result of many factors, significant strides were made in restricting the use of land mines, and, in 1998, a Nobel Peace Prize was awarded to several leaders who helped bridge from this emergent need to a remedy. In the new decade, the disconnect between those who desire to adopt children and youngsters who desperately need a home is likely to achieve the status of "an issue whose time has come." When that occurs, global policies and humane remedies are likely to follow.

Caveats

Successful application of the principles of living systems theory to human social systems does not mean that people left entirely to their own devices will miraculously self-organize and generate emergent outcomes. Neither logic nor experience supports this conclusion. The excesses and destructiveness of the Chinese Cultural Revolution are a case in point. Mao Tse-tung failed to articulate an adaptive challenge. He launched the Cultural Revolution in 1966 to restore a vibrant communist society, resist rightist leanings, and rout out the "Four Olds": old thinking, old culture, old habits, and old customs. But there were no boundaries to this Commander's Intent. Mao's "Little Red Book" provided ideological guidelines, but it lacked practical rules and behavioral limits for what became a prolonged uprising of the masses.[22] Many believe Mao intended that outcome. He prohibited education (middle school through university) for five years and ordered the military and the Party not to intervene in the rampages of the Red Guards. Insofar as unleashing the dark side of a society was the aim of Mao's design, the Cultural Revolution will stand as a perverse clinical experiment. It demonstrated the dark and explosive potential of self-organization without structure. Economic and social chaos followed, and it took a full five years after the Red Guard was dissolved to restore order.

Productive self-organization requires boundaries. Without them, self-organizing masses often regress into nihilism. China's Cultural Revolution destroyed all that stood out from, or above, the norm. The prolonged upheaval rent the fabric of Chinese society and spiraled toward the lowest common denominators. In this stark example, reckless and unchanneled self-organization tumbled from "the edge" into chaos itself, and set China back for decades.

It is also important to address the opposite extreme, where self-organization is sought and then throttled back through excessive control. The past thirty years' flirtation with "participative management" and "self-managed teams" is a case in point. These constructs rely, to some extent, on self-organization and emergence. But, like mushrooms, many of which look alike, reports of poisonings remind us that similarities can be dangerously deceptive.

Participative management and self-managed teams have had a disappointing thirty-year history. Too often, these techniques have been applied when management "knows the answer" but wants a little help or a superficial buy-in from the troops. In such circumstances, only limited space is allowed for contributions from the "intelligence in the nodes." The result: Three-quarters of the attempts at participative management fail. The problem rarely emanates from the workers. Usually, upper or middle management relegates these practices to the shop floor and makes sure they stay there. Participative management and self-managed teams have been hung out to dry on the hardwiring of social engineering. Self-organization and emergence will share precisely the same fate unless a living systems view is adopted as the context.[23]

Guidelines for Harnessing Self-Organization and Emergence

We have provided a half dozen organizational examples of self-organization and emergence in action. Let us summarize by distilling six general guidelines.

1. Decide whether self-organization and emergence are really needed. Do you face an Adaptive Challenge? Are new routes or new destinations sought? If nimbleness is required and discontinuous innovation is necessary, these dual properties can add value. Use the right tool for the right task.

2. Analyze the health of your network. Self-organization arises from networks that are fueled by nodes and connections. If you seek self-organization, enlarge the number of nodes and expect every organizational member to contribute (as the Army has done). Enrich the quality of the connections with simple routines and protocols that cement strong relationships (as was done at Tupperware and Alcoholics Anonymous and in the U.S. Army).

3. Remember the Goldilocks principle.[24] Neither too many rules or too few rules. The key to self-organization resides in a field of tension between discipline and freedom. Nature achieves this tension through selection pressures (which impose discipline) and by upending occurrences (such as chance mutations and environmental disruptions). In organizations, rules provide discipline. They can take the form of protocols; recall Tupperware's thick binder of party games and its tricks for identifying new recruits, or the Army's tasks, conditions, standards, and AARs. Freedom is reinforced by the power of a strange attractor (for example, Tupperware's commitment to enriching the lives of women, or the Army's challenge to recruits: "Be All That You Can Be").

4. Harness the power of requisite variety. Juxtapose people from different fields and backgrounds and let their varied work histories enrich the potential of self-organizing networks. This mixing cannot be done with abandon. But, as is evident in Silicon Valley, coevolution fosters unlikely forms of cooperation and can open the door to whole new worlds.

5. Look for the preconditions of emergence: the existence of "noise" or "heat" in the system; contradictions between words and actions; incongruencies between supply and demand; unexpressed needs. All hint at emergent possibilities and help to identify when an issue is bubbling toward the surface. "An idea whose time has come" is the conventional way we talk about emergence.

6. Self-organization and emergence should not be thought of exclusively as episodic occurrences. Self-organization can occur episodically (as it did at Sears), and emergence gives rise to periodic upwelling (for example, the global consensus to outlaw antipersonnel mines), but these properties of life have enduring power, as evidenced in Silicon Valley and the U.S. Army. When brought to the forefront of management consciousness, they can become sources of sustaining competitive advantage. They can exert a subtle influence—more akin to the way water wears away stone than the way dynamite blasts through granite.

* * *

Self-organization and emerging complexity are the twin engines in the evolution of all living things. But is an acquaintance with the laws of complexity required to harness them?

Our answer again is a qualified "Yes." Some challenges can be met with the management tools we have been depending on for ages. But this book is not about ordinary problems; rather, we are focusing on the adaptive challenges we encounter increasingly in the Information Age. For these challenges, familiar tools do not suffice.

In Chapter 9, we explore how managers can guide their organizations once they have tapped into their potential as living systems. The answer is not in detailed plans. One must learn to disturb an organization artfully. Avoid sledgehammers when feathers will do.

Notes

1. R. Pascale, Conversations with Dee Hock, Rescadero, California, 1997-1998; also see Dee Hock, "The One-Horned Cow," address to the American Bankers Association, July 18, 1993; also Steward Dougherty, "Visa International: The Management of Change," case study, Harvard Business School, 1981; also, Mitchell Waldrop, "The Trillion-Dollar Idea of Dee Hock," *Fast Company,* November 1996, pp. 76-86.

2. *Ibid.,* p. 70.

3. Waldrop, *ibid.,* p. 77.

4. R. Pascale, Conversation with Anthony Athos on the Gregory Bateson study of AA, San Francisco, California, April 29, 1997; also see F. Riessman and D. Carroll, *Redefining Self Help* (San Francisco: Jossey-Bass, 1995), pp. 13-15.

5. Pascale interview with Anthony Athos, Boston, Massachusetts, Winter 1993.

6. Pascale interview with Carol Moeller on history of MADD since its founding by Candy Lightner in 1981, Kona, Hawaii, March 1999.

7. F. Riessman and D. Carroll, *supra* note 4, p. ix.

8. Stephan H. Haeckel, *Adaptive Enterprises* (Boston, MA: Harvard Business School Press, 1999), p. 42.

9. Annalee Saxenian, "Lessons From Silicon Valley," *Technology Review,* Vol. 97, No. 5, 1994, p. 42. Also Virginia Postrel, "Resilience vs. Anticipation," *Forbes ASAP,* August 25, 1997, pp. 57-94.

10. *Ibid.,* p. 61.

11. R. Pascale, Conversation with Larry Kanarek, partner McKinsey & Co., Washington, DC, Winter 2000.

12. Virginia Postrel, "How the West Kicked Butt," *Forbes ASAP,* August 25, 1997, p. 55.

13. Postrel, "Resilience vs. Anticipation," *supra* note 9, p. 59. Also, Sanexian, *supra* note 9, pp. 42-51. Also, John Chisholm, "Silicon Valley vs. Route 128," *Unix Review,* Vol. 12, No. 11, October 1999, pp. 15-23.

14. Melanie Warner, "Inside the Silicon Valley Money Machine," *Fortune,* October 26, 1998, pp. 129-138.

15. Postrel, "Resilience vs. Anticipation," *supra* note 9, quoting Paul Koontz, p. 61.

16. R. Pascale, Conversations with General Gordon Sullivan and other Army officers. The Pentagon, Virginia: also at the National Training Center, Barstow, California, April 4-5, 1994, February 13-14 and May 6-7, 1995, and October 29, 1997.

17. George S. Patton, Jr., *War As I Knew It* (Boston: Houghton Mifflin, 1949), p. 357.

18. R. Rascale, Conversations with Sullivan, *supra* note 16.

19. R. Pascale, Conversations at the National Training Center, Barstow, California April 6-7, 1994, February 13-14, 1995, May 6-7, 1995.

20. Steffon Canback, "The Logic of Management Consulting," *Journal of Management Consulting,* 1998, p. 3; also, Jennifer Bresnahn, "The Latest in Suits," *C.I.O.,* p. 174, documents a 20% growth rate per year.

21. Illustrative of the type of media coverage that precedes an emergent issue, see Joan Oreck, "Wanted for Adoptions, Worldwide Standards," *Business Week,* June 14, 1999, p. 21. For documentation of numbers of AIDS orphans in Africa, see Jeffery Barthotel, "The Plague Years," *Newsweek,* January 17, 2000, pp. 34-35.

22.   Jasper Becker, "Zhou En Lai's Dark Secrets, *South China Morning Post,* May 26, 1996. Also, Mao's "Little Red Book," *Mao Tsetung, Quotations from Chairman Mao Tsetung* (Peking, China: Foreign Language Press, 1972). On the importance of structure to self organization, see Eric Beinhocker, "Strategy at the Edge of Chaos," *McKinsey Quarterly,* No. 1, 1997, pp. 30-34.

23.   See for example Bill Saporito, "The Revolt Against Working Smarter," *Fortune,* July 21, 1986, pp. 58-65. This article and other academic studies trace failure of these programs at General Motors Buick City, General Foods, P&G and Boeing.

24.   Reference to Goldilocks and the Three Bears. "The porridge needed to be neither too hot nor too cold." Courtesy of Murray Gell-Mann, quoting Seth Lloyd.

INDIVIDUALISM: TRUE AND FALSE

Friedrich A. Hayek

Du dix-huitième siècle et de la révolution, comme d'une source commune, étaient sortis deux fleuves: le premier conduisait les hommes aux institutions libres, tandis que le second les menait au pouvoir absolu.

—*Alexis de Tocqueville*

I

To advocate any clear-cut principles of social order is today an almost certain way to incur the stigma of being an unpractical doctrinaire. It has come to be regarded as the sign of the judicious mind that in social matters one does not adhere to fixed principles but decides each question "on its merits"; that one is generally guided by expediency and is ready to compromise between opposed views. Principles, however, have a way of asserting themselves even if they are not explicitly recognized but are only implied in particular decisions, or if they are present only as vague ideas of what is or is not being done. Thus it has come about that under the sign of "neither individualism nor socialism" we are in fact rapidly moving from a society of free individuals toward one of a completely collectivist character.

I propose not only to undertake to defend a general principle of social organization but shall also try to show that the aversion to general principles, and the preference for proceeding from particular instance to particular instance is the product of the movement which with the "inevitability of gradualness" leads us back from a social order resting on the general recognition of certain principles to a system in which order is created by direct commands.

After the experience of the last thirty years, there is perhaps not much need to emphasize that without principles we drift. The pragmatic attitude which has been dominant during that period, far from increasing our command over developments, has in fact led us to a state of affairs which nobody wanted; and the only result of our disregard of principles seems to be that we are governed by a logic of events which we are vainly attempting to ignore. The question now is not whether we need principles to guide us but rather whether there still exists a body of principles capable of general application which we could follow if we wished. Where can we still find a set of precepts which will give us definite guidance in the solution of the problems of our time? Is there anywhere a consistent philosophy to be found which supplies us not merely with the moral aims but with an adequate method for their achievement?

That religion itself does not give us definite guidance in these matters is shown by the efforts of the church to elaborate a complete social philosophy and by the entirely opposite results at which many arrive who start from the same Christian foundations. Though the declining influence of religion is undoubtedly one major cause or our present lack of intellectual and moral orientation, its revival would not much lessen the need for a generally accepted principle of social order. We still should require a political philosophy which goes beyond the fundamental but general precepts which religion or morals provide.

The title which I have chosen for this chapter shows that to me there still seems to exist such a philosophy—a set of principles which, indeed, is implicit in most of Western or Christian political tradition but which can no longer be unambiguously described by any readily understood term. It is therefore necessary to restate these principles fully before we can decide whether they can still serve us as practical guides.

The difficulty which we encounter is not merely the familiar fact that the current political terms are notoriously ambiguous or even that the same term often means nearly the opposite to different groups. There is the much more serious fact that the same word frequently appears to unite people who in fact believe in contradictory and irreconcilable ideals. Terms like "liberalism" or "democracy," "capitalism" or "socialism," today no longer stand for coherent systems of ideas. They have come to describe aggregations of quite heterogeneous principles and facts which historical accident has associated with these words but which have little in common beyond having been advocated at difficult times by the same people or even merely under the same name.

No political term has suffered worse in this respect than "individualism." It not only has been distorted by its opponents into an unrecognizable caricature—and we should always remember that the political concepts which are today out of fashion are known to most of our contemporaries only through the picture drawn of them by their enemies—but has been used to describe several attitudes towards society which have as little in common among themselves as they have with those traditionally regarded as their opposites. Indeed, when in the preparation of this paper I examined some of the standard descriptions of "individualism," I almost began to regret that I had ever connected the ideals in which I believe with a term which has been so abused and so misunderstood. Yet, whatever "individualism" may have come to mean in addition to these ideals, there are two good reasons for retaining the term for the view I mean to defend: this view has always been known by that term, whatever else it may also have meant at different times, and the term has the distinction that the word "socialism" was deliberately coined to express its opposition to individualism.[1] It is with the system which forms the alternative to socialism that I shall be concerned.

II

Before I explain what I mean by true individualism, it may be useful if I give some indication of the intellectual tradition to which it belongs. The true individualism which I shall try to defend began its modern development with John Locke, and particularly with Bernard Mandeville and David Hume and achieved full stature for the first time in the work of Josiah Tucker, Adam Ferguson, and Adam Smith and in that of their great contemporary, Edmund Burke— the man whom Smith described as the only person he ever knew who thought on economic subjects exactly as he did without any previous communication having passed between them.[2] In the nineteenth century I find it represented most perfectly in the work of two of its greatest historians and political philosophers: Alexis de Tocqueville and Lord Acton. These two men seem to me to have more successfully developed what was best in the political philosophy of the Scottish philosophers, Burke, and the English Whigs than any other writers I know; while the classical economists of the nineteenth century, or at least the Benthamites or philosophical radicals among them, came increasingly under the influence of another kind of individualism of different origin.

This second and altogether different strand of thought, also known as individualism, is represented mainly by French and other Continental writers—a fact due, I believe, to the dominant role which Cartesian rationalism plays in its composition. The outstanding representatives of this tradition are the Encyclopedists, Rousseau, and the physiocrats; and, for reasons we shall presently consider, this rationalistic individualism always tends to develop into the opposite of individualism, namely, socialism or collectivism. It is because only the first kind of individualism is consistent that

I claim for it the name of true individualism, while the second kind must probably be regarded as a source of modern socialism as important as the properly collectivist theories.[3]

I can give no better illustration of the prevailing confusion about the meaning of individualism than the fact that the man who to me seems to be one of the greatest representatives of true individualism, Edmund Burke, is commonly (and rightly) represented as the main opponent of the so-called "individualism" of Rousseau, whose theories he feared would rapidly dissolve the commonwealth "into the dust and powder of individuality,"[4] and that the term "individualism" itself was first introduced into the English language through the translation of one of the works of another of the great representatives of true individualism, de Tocqueville, who uses it in his *Democracy in America* to describe an attitude which he deplores and rejects.[5] Yet there can no doubt that both Burke and de Tocqueville stand in all essentials close to Adam Smith, to whom nobody will deny the title of individualist, and that the "individualism" to which they are opposed is something altogether different from that of Smith.

III

What, then, are the essential characteristics of true individualism? The first thing that should be said is that it is primarily a *theory* of society, an attempt to understand the forces which determine the social life of man, and only in the second instance a set of political maxims derived from this view of society. This fact should by itself be sufficient to refute the silliest of the common misunderstandings: the belief that individualism postulates (or bases its arguments on the assumption of) the existence of isolated or self-contained individuals, instead of starting from men whose whole nature and character is determined by their existence in society.[6] If that were true, it would indeed have nothing to contribute to our understanding of society. But its basic contention is quite a different one; it is that there is no other way toward an understanding of social phenomena but through our understanding of individual actions directed toward other people and guided by their expected behavior.[7] This argument is directed primarily against the properly collectivist theories of society which pretend to be able directly to comprehend social wholes like society, etc., as entities *sui generis* which exist independently of the individuals which compose them. The next step in the individualistic analysis of society, however, is directed against the rationalistic pseudo-individualism which also leads to practical collectivism. It is the contention that, by tracing the combined effects of individual actions, we discover that many of the institutions on which human achievements rest have arisen and are functioning without a designing and directing mind; that, as Adam Ferguson expressed it, "nations stumble poll establishments, which are indeed the result of human action but not the result of human design";[8] and that the spontaneous collaboration of free men often creates things which are greater than their individual minds can ever fully comprehend. This is the great theme of Josiah Tucker and Adam Smith, of Adam Ferguson and Edmund Burke, the great discovery of classical political economy which has become the basis of our understnding not only of economic life but of most truly social phenomena.

The difference between this view, which accounts for most of order which we find in human affairs as the unforeseen result of individual actions, and the view which traces all discoverable order to deliberate design is the first great contrast between the true individualism of the British thinkers of the eighteenth century and the so-called "individualism" of the Cartesian school.[9] But it is merely one aspect of an even wider difference between a view which in general rates rather low the place which reason plays in human affairs, which contends that man has achieved what he has in spite of the fact that he is only partly guided by reason, and that his individual reason is very limited and imperfect, and a view which assumes that Reason, with a capital R, is always fully and equally available to all humans and that everything which man achieves is the direct result of, and therefore subject to, the control of individual reason. One might even say that the former is a product of an acute consciousness of the limitations of the individual mind which induces an attitude of humility toward the impersonal and anonymous social processes by which individuals help to create things greater than they know, while the latter is the product of an exaggerated belief in the powers of individual reason and of a consequent contempt for anything which has not been consciously designed by it or is not fully intelligible to it.

The antirationalistic approach, which regards man not as a highly rational and intelligent but as a very irrational and fallible being, whose individual errors are corrected only in the course of a social process, and which aims at making the best of a very imperfect material, is probably the most characteristic feature of English individualism. Its predominance in English thought seems to me due largely to the profound influence exercised by Bernard Mandeville, by whom the central idea was for the first time clearly formulated.[10]

I cannot better illustrate the contrast in which Cartesian or rationalistic "individualism" stands to this view than by quoting a famous passage from Part II of the *Discourse on Method*. Descartes argues that "there is seldom so much perfection in works composed of many separate parts, upon which different hands had been employed, as in those completed by a single master." He then goes on to suggest (after, significantly, quoting the instance of the engineer drawing up his plans) that "those nations which, starting from a semi-barbarous state and advancing to civilization by slow degrees, have had their laws successively determined, and, as it were, forced upon them simply by experience of the hurtfulness of particular crimes and disputes, would by this process come to be possessed of less perfect institutions than those which, from the commencement of their association as communities, have followed the appointment of some wise legislator." To drive this point home, Descartes adds that in his opinion "the past pre-eminence of Sparta was due not to the pre-eminence of each of its laws in particular . . . but to the circumstance that, originated by a single individual, they all tended to a single end."[11]

It would be interesting to trace further the development of this social contract individualism or the "design" theories of social institutions, from Descartes through Rousseau and the French Revolution down to what is still the characteristic attitude of the engineers to social problems.[12] Such a sketch would show how Cartesian rationalism has persistently proved a grave obstacle to an understanding of historical phenomena and that it is largely responsible for the belief in inevitable laws of historical development and the modern fatalism derived from this belief.[13]

All we are here concerned with, however, is that this view, though also known as "individualism," stands in complete contrast to true individualism on two decisive points. While it is perfectly true of this pseudo-individualism that "belief in spontaneous social products was logically impossible to any philosophers who regarded individual man as the starting point and supposed him to form societies by the union of his particular will with another in a formal contract,"[14] true individualism is the only theory which can claim to make the formation of spontaneous social products intelligible. And, while the design theories necessarily lead to the conclusion that social processes can be made to serve human ends only if they are subjected to the control of individual human reason, and thus lead directly to socialism, true individualism believes on the contrary that, if left free, men will often achieve more than individual human reason could design or foresee.

This contrast between the true, antirationalistic and the false, rationalistsic individualism permeates all social thought. But because both theories have become known by the same name, and partly because the classical economists of the nineteenth century, and particularly John Stuart Mill and Herbert Spencer, were almost as much influenced by the French as by the English tradition, all sorts of conceptions and assumptions completely alien to true individualism have come to be regarded as essential parts of its doctrine.

Perhaps the best illustration of the current misconceptions of the individualism of Adam Smith and his group is the common belief that they have invented the bogey of the "economic man" and that their conclusions are vitiated by their assumption of a strictly rational behavior or generally by a false rationalistic psychology. They were, of course, very far from assuming anything of the kind. It would be nearer the truth to say that in their view man was by nature lazy and indolent, improvident and wasteful, and that it was only by the force of circumstances that he could be made to behave economically or carefully to adjust his means to his ends. But even this would be unjust to the very complex and realistic view which these men took of human nature. Since it has become fashionable to deride smith and his contemporaries for their supposedly erroneous psychology, I may perhaps venture the opinion that for all practical purposes we can still learn more about the behavior of men from the *Wealth of Nations* than from most of the more pretentious modern treatises on "social psychology."

However that may be, the main point about which there can be little doubt is that Smith's chief concern was not so much with what man might occasionally achieve when he was at his best but that he should have as little opportunity as possible to do harm when he was at his worst. It would scarcely be too much to claim that the main merit of the individualism which he and his contemporaries advocated is that it is a system under which bad men can do least harm. It is a social system which does not depend for its functioning on our finding good men for running it, or on all men becoming better than they now are, but which makes use of men in all their given variety and complexity, sometimes good and sometimes bad, sometimes intelligent and more often stupid. Their aim was a system under which it should be possible to grant freedom to all, instead of restricting it, as their French contemporaries wished, to "the good and the wise."[15]

The chief concern of the great individualist writers was indeed to find a set of institutions by which man could be induced, by his own choice and from the motives which determined his ordinary conduct, to contribute as much as possible to the need of all others; and their discovery was that the system of private property did provide such inducements to a much greater extent than had yet been understood. They did not contend, however, that this system was incapable of further improvement and, still less, as another of the current distortions of their arguments will have it, that there existed a "natural harmony of interests" irrespective of the positive institutions. They were more than merely aware of the conflicts of individual interests and stressed the necessity of "well-constructed institutions" where the "rules and principles of contending interests and compromised advantages"[16] would reconcile conflicting interests without giving any one group power to make their views and interests always prevail over those of all others.

IV

There is one point in these basic psychological assumptions which it is necessary to consider somewhat more fully. As the belief that individualism approves and encourages human selfishness is one of the main reasons why so many people dislike it, and as the confusion which exists in this respect is caused by a real intellectual difficulty, we must carefully examine the meaning of the assumptions it makes. There can be no doubt, of course, that in the language of the great writers of the eighteenth century it was man's "self-love," or even his "selfish interests," which they represented as the "universal mover," and that by these terms they were referring primarily to a moral attitude, which they thought to be widely prevalent. These terms, however, did not mean egotism in the narrow sense of concern with only the immediate needs of one's proper person. The "self," for which alone people were supposed to care, did as a matter of course include their family and friends; and it would have made no difference to the anything if it had included anything for which people in fact did care.

Far more important than this moral attitude, which might be regarded as changeable, is an indisputable intellectual fact which nobody can hope to alter and which by itself is a sufficient basis for the conclusions which the individualist philosophers drew. This is the constitutional limitation of man's knowledge and interests, the fact that he *cannot* know more than a tiny part of the whole of society and that therefore all that can enter into his motives are the immediate effects which his actions will have in the sphere he knows. All the possible differences in men's moral attitudes amount to little, so far as their significance for social organization is concerned, compared with the fact that all man's mind can effectively comprehend are the facts of the narrow circle of which he is the center; that, whether he is completely selfish or the most perfect altruist, the human needs for which he *can* effectively care are an almost negligible fraction of the needs of all members of society. The real question therefore, is not whether man is, or ought to be, guided by selfish motives but whether we can allow him to be guided in his actions by those immediate consequences which he can know and care for or whether he ought to be made to do what seems appropriate to somebody else who is supposed to possess a fuller comprehension of the significance of these actions to society as a whole.

To the accepted Christian tradition that man must be free to follow *his* conscience in moral matters if his actions are to be of any merit, the economists added the further argument that he should be free to make full use of *his* knowledge and skill, that he must be allowed to be guided by his concern for the particular things of which *he* knows and for which *he* cares, if he is to make as great a contribution to the common purposes of society as he is capable of making. Their main problem was how these limited concerns, which did in fact determine people's actions, could be made effective inducements to cause them voluntarily to contribute as much as possible to needs which lay outside the range of their vision. What the economists understood for the first time was that the market as it had grown up was an effective way of making man take part in a process more complex and extended than he could comprehend and that it was through the market that he was made to contribute "to ends which were no part of his purpose."

It was almost inevitable that the classical writers in explaining their contention should use language which was bound to be misunderstood and that they thus earned the reputation of having extolled selfishness. We rapidly discover the reason when we try to restate the correct argument in simple language. If we put it concisely by saying that people are and ought to be guided in their actions by *their* interests and desires, this will at once be misunderstood or distorted into the false contention that they are or ought to be exclusively guided by their personal needs or selfish interests, while what we mean is that they ought to be allowed to strive for whatever *they* think desirable.

Another misleading phrase, used to stress an important point, is the famous presumption that each man knows his interests best. In this form the contention is neither plausible nor necessary for the individualist's conclusions. The true basis of his argument is that nobody can know *who* knows best and that the only way by which we can find out is through a social process in which everybody is allowed to try and see what he can do. The fundamental assumption, here as elsewhere, is the unlimited variety of human gifts and skills and the consequent ignorance of any single individual of most of what is known to all the other members of society taken together. Or, to put this fundamental contention differently, human Reason, with a capital *R*, does not exist in the singular, as given or available to any particular person, as the rationalist approach seems to assume, but must be conceived as an interpersonal process in which anyone's contribution is tested and corrected by others. This argument does not assume that all men are equal in their natural endowments and capacities but only that no man is qualified to pass final judgment on the capacities which another possesses or is to be allowed to exercise.

Here I may perhaps mention that only because men are in fact unequal can we treat them equally. If all men were completely equal in their gifts and inclinations, we should have to treat them differently in order to achieve any sort of social organization. Fortunately, they are not equal; and it is only owing to this that the differentiation of functions need not be determined by the arbitrary decision of some organizing will but that, after creating formal equality of the rules applying in the same manner to all, we can leave each individual to find his own level.

There is all the difference in the world between treating people equally and attempting to make them equal. While the first is the condition of a free society, the second means, as de Tocqueville described it, "a new form of servitude."[17]

V

From the awareness of the limitations of individual knowledge and from the fact that no person or small group of persons can know all that is known to somebody, individualism also derives its main practical conclusion: its demand for a strict limitation of all coercive or exclusive power. Its opposition, however, is directed only against the use of *coercion* to bring about organization or association, and not against association as such. Far from being opposed to voluntary association, the case of the individualist rests, on the contrary, on the contention that much of what in the opinion of many can be brought about only by conscious direction, can be better achieved by the voluntary and spontaneous collaboration of individuals. The consistent individualist ought therefore to be an enthusiast for voluntary collaboration—wherever and whenever it does not degenerate into coercion of others or lead to the assumption of exclusive powers.

True individualism is, of course, not anarchism, which is but another product of the rationalistic pseudo-individualism to which it is opposed. It does not deny the necessity of coercive power but wishes to limit it—to limit it to those fields where it is indispensable to prevent coercion by others and in order to reduce the total of coercion to a minimum. While all the individualist philosophers are probably agreed on this general formula, it must be admitted that they are not always very informative on its application in specific cases. Neither the much abused and much misunderstood phrase of "laissez faire" nor the still older formula of "the protection of life, liberty, and property" are of much help. In fact, in so far as both tend to suggest that we can just leave things as they are, they may be worse than no answer; they certainly do not tell us what are and what are not desirable or necessary fields of government activity. Yet the decision whether individualist philosophy can serve us as a practical guide must ultimately depend on whether it will enable us to distinguish between the agenda and the nonagenda of government.

Some general rules of this kind which are of very wide applicability seem to me to follow directly from the basic tenets of individualism: If each man is to use *his* peculiar knowledge and skill with the aim of furthering the aims for which *he* cares, and if, in so doing, he is to make as large a contribution as possible to needs which are beyond his ken, it is clearly necessary, first, that he should have a clearly delimited area of responsibility and, second, that the relative importance to him of the different results he can achieve must correspond to the relative importance to others of the more remote and to him unknown effects of his action.

Let us first take the problem of the determination of a sphere of responsibility and leave the second problem for later. If man is to remain free to make full use of his knowledge or skill, the delimination of spheres of responsibility must not take the form of an assignation to him of particular ends which he must try to achieve. This would be imposing a specific duty rather than delimiting a sphere of responsibility. Nor must it take the form of allocating to him specific resources selected by some authority, which would take the choice almost as much out of his hands as the imposition of specific tasks. If man is to exercise his own gifts, it must be as a result of his activities and planning that his sphere of responsibility is determined. The solution to this problem which men have gradually developed and which antedates government in the modern sense of the word is the acceptance of formal principles, "a standing rule to live by, common to every one of that society"[18]—of rules which, above all, enable man to distinguish between mine and thine, and from which he and his fellows can ascertain what is his and what is somebody else's sphere of responsibility.

The fundamental contrast between government by rules, whose main purpose is to inform the individual what is his sphere of responsibility within which he must shape his own life, and government by orders which impose specific duties has become so blurred in recent years that it is necessary to consider it a little further. It involves nothing less than the distinction between freedom under the law and the use of the legislative machinery, whether democratic or not, to abolish freedom. The essential point is not that there should be some kind of guiding principle behind the actions of the government but that government should be confined to making the individuals observe principles which they know and can take into account in *their* decisions. It means, further, that what the individual may or may not do, or what he can expect his fellows to do or not to do, must depend not on some remote and indirect consequences which his actions may have but on the immediate and readily recognizable circumstances which he can be supposed to know. He must have rules referring to typical situations, defined in terms of what can be known to the acting persons and without regard to the distant effects in the particular instance—rules which, if they are regularly observed, will in the majority of cases operate beneficially— even if they do not do so in the proverbial "hard cases which make bad law."

The most general principle on which an individualist system is based is that it uses the universal acceptance of general principles as the means to create order in social affairs. It is the opposite of such government by principles when, for example, a recent blueprint for a controlled economy suggests as "the fundamental principle of organization . . . that in any particular instance the means that serves society best should be the one that prevails."[19] It is a serious confusion thus to speak of principle when all that is meant is that no principle but only expediency should rule; when everything depends on what authority decrees to be "the interests of society." Principles are a means to prevent clashes between conflicting aims and not a set of fixed ends. Our submission to general principles is necessary because we cannot be guided in our practical action by full knowledge and evaluation of all the consequences. So long as men are not omniscient, the only way in which freedom can be given to the individual is by such general rules to delimit the sphere in which the decision is his. There can be no freedom if the government is not limited to particular kinds of action but can use its powers in any ways which serve particular ends. As Lord Acton pointed out long ago: "Whenever a single definite object is made the supreme end of the State, be it the advantage of a class, the safety or the power of the country, the greatest happiness of the greatest number or the support of any speculative idea, the State becomes for the time inevitably absolute."[20]

VI

But, if our main conclusion is that an individualist order must rest on the enforcement of abstract principles rather the on the enforcement of specific orders, this still leaves open the question of the kind of general rules which we want. It confines the exercise of coercive powers in the main to one method, but it still allows almost unlimited scope to human ingenuity in the designing of the most effective set of rules; and, though the best solutions of the concrete problems will in most instances have to be discovered by experience, there is a good deal more that we can learn from the general principles of individualism with regard to the desirable nature and contents of these rules. There is, in the first instance, one important corollary of what has already been said, namely, that the rules, because they are to serve as signposts to the individuals in making their own plans, should be designed to remain valid for long periods. Liberal or individualist policy must be essentially long-run policy; the present fashion to concentrate on short-run effects, and to justify this by the argument that "in the long run we are all dead," leads inevitably to the reliance on orders adjusted to the particular circumstances of the moment in the place of rules couched in terms of typical situations.

We need, and get from the basic principles of individualism, however, much more definite aid than this for the construction of a suitable legal system. The endeavor to make man by the pursuit of his interests contribute as much as possible to the needs of other men leads not merely to the general principle of "private property"; it also assists us in determining what the contents of property rights ought to be with respect to different kinds of things. In order that the individual in his decisions should take account of all the physical effects caused by these decisions, it is necessary that the "sphere of responsibility" of which I have been speaking be made to comprise as fully as possible all the direct effects which his actions have on the satisfactions which other people derive from the things under his control. This is achieved on the whole by the simple conception of property as the exclusive right to use a particular thing where mobile effects, or what the lawyer calls "chattels," are concerned. But it raises much more difficult problems in connection with land, where the recognition of the principle of private property helps us very little until we know precisely what rights and obligations ownership includes. And when we turn to such problems of more recent origin as the control of the air or of electric power, or of inventions and of literary or artistic creations, nothing short of going back to *rationale* of property will help us to decide what should be in the particular instance the sphere of control or responsibility of the individual.

I cannot here go further into the fascinating subject of a suitable legal framework for an effective individualist system or enter into discussion of the many supplementary functions, such as assistance in the spreading of information and in the elimination of genuinely avoidable uncertainty,[21] by which the government might greatly increase the efficiency of individual action. I mention them merely in order to stress that there are further (and noncoercive!) functions of government beyond the mere enforcement of civil and criminal law which can be fully justified on individualist principles.

There is still, however, one point left, to which I have already referred, but which is so important that I must give it further attention. It is that any workable individualist order must be so framed not only that the relative remunerations the individual can expect from the different uses of his abilities and resources correspond to the relative utility of the result of his efforts to others but also that these remunerations correspond to the objective results of his efforts rather than to their subjective merits. An effectively competitive market satisfies both these conditions. But it is in connection with the second that our personal sense of justice so frequently revolts against the impersonal decisions of the market. Yet, if the individual is to be free to choose it is inevitable that he should bear the risk attaching to that choice and that in consequence he be rewarded, not according to the goodness or badness of his intentions, but solely on the basis of the value of the results to others. We must face the fact that the preservation of individual freedom is incompatible with a full satisfaction of our views of distributive justice.

VII

While the theory of individualism has thus a definite contribution to make to the technique of constructing a suitable legal framework and of improving the institutions which have grown up spontaneously, its emphasis, of course, is on the fact that the part of our social order which can or ought to be made a conscious product of human reason is only a small part of all the forces of society. In other words, that the state, the embodiment of deliberately organized and consciously directed power, ought to be only a small part of the much richer organism which we call "society," and that the former ought to provide merely a framework within which free (and therefore not "consciously directed") collaboration of men has the maximum of scope.

This entails certain corollaries on which true individualism once more stands in sharp opposition to the false individualism of the rationalistic type. The first is that the organized state on the one side, and the individual on the other, far from being regarded as the only realities, while all the intermediate formations and associations are to be deliberately suppressed, as was the aim of the French Revolution, the noncompulsory conventions of social intercourse are considered as essential factors in preserving the orderly working of human society. The second is that the individual, in participating in the social processes, must be ready and willing to adjust himself to changes and to submit to conventions which are not the result of intelligent design, whose justification in the particular instance may not be recognizable, and which to him will often appear unintelligible and irrational.

I need not say much on the first point. That true individualism affirms the value of the family and all the common efforts of the small community and group, that it believes in local autonomy and voluntary associations, and that indeed its case rests largely on the contention that much for which the coercive action of the state is usually invoked can be done better by voluntary collaboration need not be stressed further. There can be no greater contrast to this than the false individualism which wants to dissolve all these smaller groups into atoms which have no cohesion other than the coercive rules imposed by the state, and which tries to make all social ties prescriptive, instead of using the state mainly as a protection of the individual against the arrogation of coercive powers by the smaller groups.

Quite as important for the functioning of an individualist society as these smaller groupings of men are the traditions and conventions which evolve in a free society and which, without being enforceable, establish flexible but normally observed rules that make the behavior of other people predictable in a high degree. The willingness to submit to such rules, not merely so long as one understands the reason for them but so long as one has no definite reasons to the contrary, is an essential condition for the gradual evolution and improvement of rules of social intercourse; and the readiness ordinarily to submit to the products of a social process which nobody has designed and the reasons for which nobody may understand is also an indispensable condition if it is to be possible to dispence with compulsion.[22] That the existence of common conventions and traditions among a group of people will enable them to work together smoothly and efficiently with much less formal organization and compulsion than a group without such common background, is, of course, a commonplace. But the reverse of this, while less familiar, is probably not less true: that coercion can probably only be kept to a minimum in a society where conventions and tradition have made the behavior of man to a large extent predictable.[23]

This brings me to my second point: the necessity, in any complex society in which the effects of anyone's action reach far beyond his possible range of vision, of the individual submitting to the anonymous society and seemingly irrational forces of society—a submission which must include not only the acceptance of rules of behavior as valid without examining what depends in the particular instance on their being observed but also a readiness to adjust himself to changes which may profoundly affect his fortunes and opportunities and the causes of which may be altogether unintelligible to him. It is against these that modern man tends to revolt unless their necessity can be shown to rest upon "reason made clear and demonstrable to every individual." Yet it is just here that the understandable craving for intelligibility produces illusory demands which no system can satisfy. Man in a complex society can have no choice but between adjusting himself to what to him must seem the blind forces of the social process and obeying the orders of a superior. So long as he knows only the hard discipline of the market, he may well think the direction by some other intelligent human brain preferable; but, when he tries it, he soon discovers that the former still leaves him at least some choice, while the latter leaves him none, and that it is better to have a choice between several unpleasant alternatives than being coerced into one.

The unwillingness to tolerate or respect any social forces which are not recognizable as the product of intelligent design, which is so important a cause of the present desire for comprehensive economic planning, is indeed only one aspect of a more general movement. We meet the same tendency in the field of morals and conventions, in the desire to substitute an artificial for the existing languages, and in the whole modern attitude toward processes which govern the growth of knowledge. The belief that only a synthetic system of morals, an artificial language, or even an artificial society can be justified in an age of science, as well as the increasing unwillingness to bow before any moral rules whose utility is not rationally demonstrated, or to conform with conventions whose rationale is not known, are all manifestations of the same basic view which wants all social activity to be recognizably part of a single coherent plan. They are the results of that same rationalistic "individualism" which wants to see in everything the product of conscious individual reason. They are certainly not, however, a result of true individualism and may even make the working of a free and truly individualistic system difficult or impossible. Indeed, the great lesson which the individualistic philosophy teaches us on this score is that, while it may not be difficult to destroy the spontaneous formations which are the indispensable bases of a free civilization, it may be beyond our power deliberately to reconstruct such a civilization once these foundations are destroyed.

VIII

The point I am trying to make is well illustrated by the apparent paradox that the Germans, though commonly regarded as very docile, are also often described as being particularly individualistic. With some truth this so-called German individualism is frequently represented as one of the causes why the Germans have never succeeded in developing free political institutions. In the rationalistic sense of the term, in their insistence on the development of "original" personalities which in every respect are the product of the conscious choice of the individual, the German intellectual tradition indeed favors a kind of "individualism" little known elsewhere. I remember well how surprised and even shocked I was myself when as a young student, on my first contact with English and American contemporaries, I discovered how much they were disposed to conform in all externals to common usage rather than, as seemed natural to me, to be proud to be different and original in most respects. If you doubt the significance of such an individual experience, you will find it fully confirmed in most German discussions of, for example, the English public school system, such as you will find in Dibelius' well-known book on England.[24] Again and again you will find the same surprise about this tendency toward voluntary conformity and see it contrasted with the ambition of the young German to develop an "original personality," which in every respect expresses what he has come to regard as right and true. This cult of the distinct and different individuality has, of course, deep roots in the German intellectual tradition and, through the influence of some of its greatest exponents, especially Goethe and Wilhelm von Humboldt, has made itself felt far beyond Germany and is clearly seen in J. S. Mill's *Liberty*.

This sort of "individualism" not only has nothing to do with true individualism but may indeed prove a grave obstacle to the smooth working of an individualist system. It must remain an open question whether a free or individualistic society can be worked successfully if people are too "individualistic" in the false sense, if they are too unwilling voluntarily to conform to traditions and conventions, and if they refuse to recognize anything which is not consciously designed or which cannot be demonstrated as rational to every individual. It is at least understandable that the prevalence of this kind of "individualism" has often made people of good will despair of the possibility of achieving order in a free society and even made them ask for a dictatorial government with the power to impose on society the order which it will not produce itself.

In Germany, in particular, this preference for the deliberate organization and the corresponding contempt for the spontaneous and uncontrolled, was strongly supported by the tendency toward centralization which the struggle for national unity produced. In a country where what traditions it possessed were essentially local, the striving for unity implied a systematic opposition to almost everything which was a spontaneous growth and its consistent replacement by artificial creations. That, in what a recent historian has well described as a "desperate search for a tradition which they did not possess,"[25] the Germans should have ended by creating a totalitarian state which forced upon them what they felt they lacked should perhaps not have surprised us as much as it did.

IX

If it is true that the progressive tendency toward central control of all social processes is the inevitable result of an approach which insists that everything must be tidily planned and made to allow a recognizable order, it is also true that this tendency tends to create conditions in which nothing but an all-powerful central government can preserve order and stability. The concentration of all decisions in the hands of authority itself produces a state of affairs in which what structure society still possesses is imposed upon it by government and in which the individuals have become interchangeable units with no other definite or durable relations to one another than those determined by the all-comprehensive organization. In the jargon of the modern sociologists this type of society has come to be known as "mass society"—a somewhat misleading name, because the characteristic attributes of this kind of society are not so much the result of mere numbers as they are of the lack of any spontaneous structure other than that impressed upon it by deliberate organization, an incapacity to evolve its own differentiations, and a consequent dependence on a power which deliberately molds and shapes it. It is connected with numbers only in so far as in large nations the process of centralization will much sooner reach a point where deliberate organization from the top smothers those spontaneous formations which are founded on contacts closer and more intimate than those that can exist in the large unit.

It is not surprising that in the nineteenth century, when these tendencies first became clearly visible, the opposition to centralization became one of the main concerns of the individualist philosophers. This opposition is particularly marked in the writings of the two great historians whose names I have before singled out as the leading representatives of true individualism in the nineteenth century, de Tocqueville and Lord Acton; and it finds expression in their strong sympathies for the small countries and for the federal organization of large units. There is even more reason now to think that the small countries may before long become the last oases that will preserve a free society. It may already be too late to stop the fatal course of progressive centralization in the bigger countries which are well on the way to produce those mass societies in which despotism in the end comes to appear as the only salvation. Whether even the small countries will escape will depend on whether they keep free from the poison of nationalism, which is both an inducement to, and a result of, that same striving for a society which is consciously organized from the top.

The attitude of individualism to nationalism, which intellectually is but a twin brother of socialism, would deserve special discussion. Here I can only point out that the fundamental difference between what in the nineteenth century was regarded as liberalism in the English-speaking world and what was so called on the Continent is closely connected with their descent from true individualism and the false rationalistic individualism, respectively. It was only liberalism in the English sense that was generally opposed to centralization, to nationalism and to socialism, while the liberalism prevalent on the Continent favored all three. I should add, however, that, in this as in so many other respects, John Stuart Mill, and the later English liberalism derived from him, belong at least as much to the Continental as to the English tradition; and I know no discussion more illuminating of these basic differences than Lord Acton's criticism of the concessions Mill had made to the nationalistic tendencies of Continental liberalism.[26]

X

There are two more points of difference between the two kinds of individualism which are also best illustrated by the stand taken by Lord Acton and de Tocqueville by their views on democracy and equality toward trends which became prominent in their time. True individualism not only believes in democracy but can claim that democratic ideals spring from the basic principles of individualism. Yet, while individualism affirms that all government should be democratic, it has no superstitious belief in the omnicompetence of majority decisions, and in particular it refuses to admit that "absolute power may, by the hypothesis of popular origin, be as legitimate as constitutional freedom."[27] It believes that under a democracy, no less than under any other form of government, "the sphere of enforced command ought to be restricted within fixed limits";[28] and it is particularly opposed to the most fateful and dangerous of all current misconceptions of democracy—the belief that we must accept as true and binding for future developmental the views of the majority. While democracy is founded on the convention that the majority view decides on common action, it does not mean that what is today the majority view ought to become the generally accepted view—even if that were necessary to achieve the aims of the majority. On the contrary, the whole justification of democracy rests on the fact that in course of time what is today the view of a small minority may become the majority view. I believe, indeed, that one of the most important questions on which political theory will have to discover an answer in the near future is that of finding a line of demarcation between the fields in which the majority views must be binding for all and the fields in which on the contrary, the minority view ought to be allowed to prevail if it can produce results which better satisfy a demand of the public. I am, above all, convinced that, where the interests of a particular branch of trade are concerned, the majority view will always be the reactionary, stationary view and that the merit of competition is precisely that it gives the minority a chance to prevail. Where it can do so without any coercive powers, it ought always to have the right.

I cannot better sum up this attitude of true individualism toward democracy than by once more quoting Lord Acton: "The true democratic principle," he wrote, "that none shall have power over the people, is taken to mean that none shall be able to restrain or to elude its power. The true democratic principle, that the people shall not be made to do what it does not like, is taken to mean that it shall never be required to tolerate what it does not like. The true democratic principle, that every man's will shall be as unfettered as possible, is taken to mean that the free will of the collective people shall be fettered in nothing."[29]

When we turn to equality, however, it should be said at once that true individualism is not equalitarian in the modern sense of the word. It can see no reason for trying to make people equal as distinct from treating them equally. While individualism is profoundly opposed to all prescriptive privilege, to all protection, by law or force, of any rights not based on rules equally applicable to all persons, it also denies government the right to limit what the able or fortunate may achieve. It is equally opposed to any rigid limitation of the position individuals may achieve, whether this power is used to perpetuate inequality or to create equality. Its main principle is that no man or group of men should have power to decide what another man's status ought to be, and it regards this as a condition of freedom so essential that it must not be sacrificed to the gratification of our sense of justice or of our envy.

From the point of view of individualism there would not appear to exist even any justification for making all individuals start on the same level by preventing them from profiting by advantages which they have in no way earned, such as being born to parents who are more intelligent or more conscientious than the average. Here individualism is indeed less "individualistic" than socialism, because it recognizes the family as a legitimate unit as much as the individual; and the same is true with respect to other groups, such as linguistic or religious communities, which by their common efforts may succeed for long periods in preserving for their members material or moral standards different from those of the rest of the population. De Tocqueville and Lord Acton speak with one voice on this subject. "Democracy and socialism," de Tocqueville wrote, "have nothing in common but one word, equality. But notice the difference: while democracy seeks equality in liberty, socialism seeks equality in restraint and servitude."[30] And Acton joined him in believing that "the deepest cause which made the French revolution so disastrous to Liberty was its theory of equality"[31] and that "the finest opportunity ever given to the world was thrown away, because the passion for equality made vain the hope for freedom."[32]

XI

It would be possible to continue for a long time discussing further differences separating the two traditions of thought which, while bearing the same name, are divided by fundamentally opposed principles. But I must not allow myself to be diverted too far from my task of tracing to its source the confusion which has resulted from this and of showing that there is one consistent tradition which, whether you agree with me or not that it is "true" individualism, is at any rate the only kind of individualism which I am prepared to defend and, indeed, I believe, the only kind which can be defended consistently. So let me return, in conclusion, to what I said in the beginning: that the fundamental attitude of true individualism is one of humility toward the processes by which mankind has achieved things which have not been designed or understood by an individual and are indeed greater than individual minds. The great question at this moment is whether man's mind will be allowed to continue to grow as part of this process or whether human reason is to place itself in chains of its own making.

What individualism teaches us is that society is greater than the individual only in so far as it is free. In so far as it is controlled or directed, it is limited to the powers of the individual minds which control or direct it. If the presumption of the modern mind, which will not respect anything that is not consciously controlled by individual reason, does not learn in time where to stop, we may, as Edmund Burke warned us, "be well assured that everything about us will dwindle by degrees, until at length our concerns are shrunk to the dimensions of our minds."

Notes

1. Both the term "individualism" and the term "socialism" are originally the creation of the Saint-Simonians, the founders of modern socialism. They first coined the term "individualism" to describe the competitive society to which they were opposed and then invented the word "socialism" to describe the centrally planned society in which ail activity was directed on the same principle that applied within a single factory. See on the origin of these terms the present author's article on "The Counter-Revolution of Science," *Economica*, VII (new ser., 1941), 146.

2. R. Bisset, *Life of Edmund Burke* (2d ed., 1800), 11, 429. Cf. also W. C. Dunn, "Adam Smith and Edmund Burke: Complimentary Contemporaries," *Southern Economic Journal* (University of North Carolina), Vol. VII, No. 3 (January, 1941).

3. Carl Menger, who was among the first in modern times consciously to revive the methodical individualism of Adam Smith and his school, was probably also the first to point out the connection between the design theory of social institutions and socialism. See his *Untersuchungen über die Methode der Sozialwissenschaften* (1883), esp. Book IV, chap.2, toward the end of which (p. 208) he speaks of "a pragmatism which, against the intention of its representatives, leads inevitably to socialism."

   It is significant that the physiocrats already were led from the rationalistic individualism from which they started, not only close to socialism (fully developed in their contemporary Morelly's *Le Code de la nature* [1755]), but to advocate the worst despotism. "L'État fait des hommes tout ce qu'il veut," wrote Bodeau.

4. Edmund Burke, *Reflections on the Revolution in France* (1790), in *Works* (World's Classics ed.), IV, 105: " Thus the commonwealth itself would, in a few generations, be disconnected into the dust and powder of individuality, and at length dispersed to all winds of heaven." That Burke (as A. M. Osborne points out in her book on *Rousseau and Burke* [Oxford, 1940], p. 23), after he had first attacked Rousseau for his extreme "individualism," later attacked him for his extreme collectivism was far from inconsistent but merely the result of the fact that in the case of Rousseau, as in that of all others, the rationalistic individualism which they preached inevitably led to collectivism.

5. Alexis de Tocqueville, *Democracy in America*, trans. Henry Reeve (London, 1864), Vol. II, Book II, chap. 2, where de Tocqueville defines individualism as "a mature and calm feeling, which disposes

each member of the community to sever himself from the mass of his fellows, and to draw apart with his family and friends; so that, after he has thus formed a little circle of his own, he willingly leaves society at large to itself." The translator in a note to this passage apologizes for introducing the French term "individualism" into English and explains that he knows "no English word exactly equivalent to the expression." As Albert Schatz pointed out in the book mentioned below, de Tocqueville's use of the well-established French term in this peculiar sense is entirely arbitrary and leads to serious confusion with the established meaning.

6. In his excellent survey of the history of individualist theories the late Albert Schatz rightly concludes that "nous voyons tout d'abord avec évidence ce que l'individualisme n'est pas. C'est précisément ce qu'on croit communément qu'il est: un système d'isolèment dans l'estistence et une apologie de l'égoisme" (*L'Individualisme économique et social* [Paris 1907], p. 558). This book, to which I am much indebted, to be much more widely known as a contribution not only to the subject indicated by its title but to the history of economic theory in general.

7. In this respect, as Karl Pribram has made clear, individualism is a necessary result of philosophical nominalsim, while the collectivist theories have their roots in the "realist" or (as K. R. Popper now more appropriately calls it) "essentialist" tradition (Pribram, *Die Entstehung der individualistischen Sozialphilosophie* [Leipzig, 1912]) But this "nominalist" approach is characteristic only of true individualism while the false individualism of Rousseau and the physiocrats, in accordance with the Cartesian origin, is strongly "realist" or "essentialist."

8. Adam Ferguson, *An Essay on the History of Civil Society* (1st ed., 1767), p. 187. Cf. also ibid.: "The forms of society are derived from an obscure and distant origin; they arise, long before the date of philosophy, from the instincts, not from the speculations of man.... We ascribe to a previous design, what came to be known only by experience, what no human wisdom could foresee, and what, without the concurring humour and disposition of his age, no authority could enable an individual to execute" (pp. 187 and 188).

It may be of interest to compare these passages with the similar statements in which Ferguson's contemporaries expressed the same basic idea of the British economists:

Josiah Tucker, *Elements of Commerce* (1756), reprinted in *Josiah Tucker: A Selection from His Economic and Political Writings*, ed. R. L. Schuyler (New York 1931), pp. 31 and 92: "The main point is neither to extinguish nor to enfeeble self-love, but to give it such a direction that it may promote the public interest by promoting its own.... The proper design of this chapter is to show that the universal mover in human nature, self-love, may receive such a direction in this case (as in all others) as to promote the public interest by those efforts it shall make towards pursuing its own."

Adam Smith, *Wealth of Nations* (1776), ed. Cannan, I, 421: "By directing that industry in such a manner as its produce may be of the greatest value, he intends only his own gain, and he is in this, as in many other cases, led by an invisible hand to promote an end which was no part of his intention. Nor is it always the worse for the society that it was no part of it. By pursuing his own interest he frequently promotes that of the society more effectively than when he really intends to promote it." Cf. also *The Theory of Moral Sentiments* (1759), Part IV (9th ed., 1801), chap. i, p. 386.

Edmund Burke, *Thoughts and Details on Scarcity* (1795), in *Works* (World's classics ed.), VI, 9: "The benign and wise disposer of all things, who obliges men, whether they will or not, in pursuing their own selfish interests, to connect the general good with their own individual success."

After these statements have been held up for scorn and ridicule by the majority of writers for the last hundred years (C.E. Raven not long ago called the last-quoted statement by Burke a "sinister sentence"—see his *Christian Socialism* [1920], p. 34), it is interesting now to find one of the leading theorists of modern socialism adopting Adam Smith's conclusions. According to A. P. Lerner (*The Economics of Control* [New York, 1944], p. 67), the essential social utility of the price mechanism is that "if it is appropriately used it induces each member of society, while seeking his own benefit, to do that which is in the general social interest. Fundamentally this is the great discovery of Adam Smith and the Physiocrats."

9. Cf. Schatz, op. cit., pp 41- 42, 81, 378, 568-69, esp. the passage quoted by him (p. 41, n. 1) from an article by Albert Sorel ("Comment j'ai lu la 'Réforme sociale,' " in *Réforme sociale,* November 1, 1906, p. 614): "Quel que fut mon respect, assez commandé et indirect encore pour le *Discours de la methode,* je savais déja que de ce fameux discours il était sorti autant de déraison sociale et d'aberrations metaphysiques, d'abstractions et d'utopies, que de données positives, que s'il menait à Comte il avait aussie mené a Rousseau." On the influence of Descartes on Rousseau see further P. Janet, *Histoire de la science politique* (3d ed., 1887), p. 423; F. Bouillier, *Histoire de la philosophie cartésienne* (3d ed., 1868), p. 643 and H. Michel, *L'Idée de l'état* (3d ed., 1898), p. 68.

10. The decisive importance of Mandeville in the history of economics, long overlooked or appreciated only by a few authors (particularly Edwin Cannan and Albert Schatz), is now beginning to be recognized, thanks mainly to the magnificent edition of the *Fable of the Bees* which we owe to the late F. B. Kaye. Although the fundamental ideas of Mandeville's work are already implied in the original poem of 1705, the decisive elaboration and especially his full account of the origin of the division of labor, of money, and of language occur only in Part II of the *Fable* which was published in 1728 (see Bernard Mandeville, *The Fable of the Bees,* ed. F. B. Kaye [Oxford, 1924], II, 142, 287 - 88, 349 - 50). There is space here to quote only the crucial passage from his account of the development of the division of labor where he observes that "we often ascribe to the excellency of man's genius and the depth of his penetration, what is in reality owing to the length of time, and the experience of many generations, all of them very little differing from one another in natural parts and sagacity" (ibid., p. 142).

It has become usual to describe Giambattista Vico and his (usually wrongly quoted) formula, *homo non intelligendo fit omnia* (*Opere,* ed. G. Ferrari [2d ed.; Milan, 1854], V, 183), as the beginning of the antirationalistic theory of social phenomena, but it would appear that he has been both preceded and surpassed by Mandeville.

Perhaps it also deserves mention that not only Mandeville but also Adam Smith occupy honorable places in the development of the theory of language which in so many ways raises problems of a nature kindred to those of the other social sciences.

11. Réné Descartes, *A Discourse on Method* (Everyman's ed.), pp. 10 - 11.

12. On the characteristic approach of the engineer type of mind to economic phenomena compare the present author's study on "Scientism and the Study of Society," *Economica,* Vols. IX - XI (new ser., 1942 - 44), esp XI, 34 ff.

13. Since this lecture was first published I have become acquainted with an instructive article by Jerome Rosenthal on "Attitudes of Some Modern Rationalists to History (*Journal of the History of Ideas,* IV, No. 4, October 1943], 429-56), which shows in considerable detail the antihistorical attitude of Descartes and particularly his disciple Malebranche and gives interesting examples of the contempt expressed by Descartes in his *Recherche de la vérité par la lumière naturelle* for the study of history, languages, geography, and especially the classics.

14. James Bonar, *Philosophy and Political Economy* (1893), p. 85.

15. A. W. Benn, in his History of English Rationalism in the Nineteenth Century (1906), says rightly: "With Quesnay, following nature meant ascertaining by a study of the world about us and of its laws what conduct is most conducive to health and happiness; and the natural rights meant liberty to pursue the course so ascertained. Such liberty only belongs to the wise and good, and can only be granted to those whom the tutelary authority in the state is pleased to regard as such. With Adam Smith and his disciples, on the other hand, nature means the totality of impulses and instincts by which the individual members of society are animated; and their contentions is that the best arrangements result from giving free play to those forces in the confidence that partial failure will be more than compensated by successes elsewhere, and that the pursuit of his own interest by each will work out in the greatest happiness of all" (I, 289).

On this whole question see Elie Halevy, *The Growth of Philosophic Radicalism* (1928), esp. pp. 266 - 70.

The contrast of the Scottish philosophers of the eighteenth century with their French contemporaries is also brought out in Gladys Bryson's recent study on *Man and Society: The Scottish Enquiry of the Eighteenth Century* (Princeton, 1945), p. 145. She emphasizes that the Scottish philosophers "all wanted to break away from Cartesian rationalism, with its emphasis on abstract intellectualism and innate ideas," and repeatedly stresses the "anti-individualistic" tendencies of David Hume (pp. 106, 155)— using "individualistic" in what we call here the false, rationalistic sense. But she occasionally falls back into the common mistake of regarding them as "representative and typical of the thought of the century" (p. 176). There is still, largely as a result of an acceptance of the German conception of "the Enlightenment," too much inclination to regard the views of all the eighteenth-century philosophers as similar, whereas in many respects the differences between the English and the French philosophers of the period are much more important than the similarities. The common habit of lumping Adam Smith and Quesnay together, caused by the former belief that Smith was greatly indebted to the physiocrats, should certainly cease, now that this belief has been disproved by W. R. Scott's recent discoveries (see his *Adam Smith as Student and Professor* [Glasgow, 1937], p. 124). It is also significant that both Hume and Smith are reported to have been stimulated to their work by their opposition to Montesquieu.

Some suggestive discussion of the differences between the British and the French social philosophers of the eighteenth century, somewhat distorted, however, by the author's hostility toward the "economic liberalism" of the former, will be found in Rudolf Goldscheid, *Grundlinien zu einer Kritik der Willenskraft* (Vienna, 1905), pp. 32 - 37.

16. Edmund Burke, *Thoughts and Details on Scarcity* (1795), in *Works* (World's Classics ed.), VI, 15.

17. This phrase is used over and over again by de Tocqueville to describe the effects of socialism, but see particularly *Oeuvre complètes*, IX (1886), 541, where he says: "Si, en définitive, j'avais à trouver une formule générale pour exprimer ce que m'apparait le socialisme dans son ensemble, je dirais que c'est une nouvelle formule de la servitude." Perhaps I may be allowed to add that it was this phrase of de Tocqueville's which suggested to me the title of a recent book of mine.

18. John Locke, *Two Treatises of Government* (1690), Book II, chap. 4, §22: "Freedom of men under government is to have a standing rule to live by, common to every one of that society and made by the legislative power erected in it."

19. Lerner, op. cit., p. 5.

20. Lord Acton, "Nationality" (1862), reprinted in *The History of Freedom and Other Essays* (1907), p. 288.

21. The actions a government can expediently take to reduce really *avoidable* uncertainty for the individuals are a subject which has given rise to so many confusions that I am afraid to let the brief allusion to it in the text stand without some further explanation. The point is that, while it is easy to protect a particular person or group against the loss which might be caused by an unforeseen change, by preventing people from taking notice of the change after it has occurred, this merely shifts the loss onto other shoulders but does not prevent it. If, e.g., capital invested in very expensive plant is protected against obsolescence by new inventions by prohibiting the introduction of such new inventions, this increases the security of the owners of the existing plant but deprives the public of the benefit of the new inventions. Or, in other words, it does not really reduce uncertainty for society as a whole if we

make the behavior of the people more predictable by preventing them from adapting themselves to an unforeseen change in their knowledge of the world. The only genuine reduction of uncertainty consists in increasing its knowledge, but never in preventing people from making use of new knowledge.

22. The difference between the rationalistic and the true individualistic approach is well shown in the different views expressed by French observers on the apparent irrationality of English social institutions. While Henri de Saint-Simon, e.g., complains that "cent volumes *in folio*, de caractère plus fin, ne suffiraient pas pour rendre compte de toutes les inconséquences organiques qui existent en Angleterre" (*Oeuvres de Saint-Simon et d'Enfantin* [Paris, 1885 - 78], XXXVIII, 179), de Tocqueville retorts "que ces bizarreries des Anglais pussent avoir quelques rapports avec leurs libertés, c'est ce qui ne lui tombe point dans l'esprit" (*L'Ancien régime et la révolution* [7th ed.; Paris, 1866], p. 103).

23. Is it necessary to quote Edmund Burke once more to remind the reader how essential a condition for the possibility of a free society was to him the strength of moral rules? "Men are qualified for civil liberty," he wrote "in exact proportion to their disposition to put moral chains upon their own appetites; in proportion as their love of justice is above their rapacity; in proportion as their own soundness and sobriety of understanding is above their vanity and presumption; in proportion as they are more disposed to listen to the councils of the wise and good, in preference to the battery of knaves" (*A Letter to a Member of the National Assembly* [1791], in *Works* [World's Classics ed], IV, 319).

24. W. Dibelius, *England* (1923), pp. 464 - 68 of 1934 English translation.

25. E. Vermeil, *Germany's Three Reichs* (London, 1944), p. 224.

26. Lord Acton, "Nationality" (1862), reprinted in The History of Freedom, pp. 270 - 300.

27. Lord Acton, "Sir Erskine May's Democracy in Europe" (1878), reprinted in *The History of Freedom*, p. 78.

28. Lord Acton, *Lectures on Modern History* (1906), p. 10.

29. Lord Acton, "Sir Erskine May's Democracy in Europe," reprinted in *The History of Freedom*, pp. 93 - 94.

30. Alexis de Tocqueville, *Oeuvres complètes*, IX, 546.

31. Lord Acton, "Sir Erskine May's Democracy in Europe," reprinted in *The History of Freedom*, p. 88.

32. Lord Acton, "The History of Freedom in Christianity (1877), reprinted in *The History of Freedom*, p. 57.

SELF-RELIANCE

Ralph Waldo Emerson

"Ne te quaesiveris extra."

Man is his own star; and the soul that can
Render an honest and a perfect man,
Commands all light, all influence, all fate;
Nothing to him falls early or too late.
Our acts our angels are, or good or ill,
Our fatal shadows that walk by us still.
Epilogue to Beaumont and Fletcher's Honest Man's Fortune.

Cast the bantling on the rocks,
Suckle him with the shewolf's teat,
Wintered with the hawk and fox,
Power and speed be hands and feet.

I read the other day some verses written by an eminent painter which were original and not conventional. The soul always hears an admonition in such lines, let the subject be what it may. The sentiment they instil is of more value than any thought they may contain. To believe your own thought, to believe that what is true for you in your private heart is true for all men-that is genius. Speak your latent conviction, and it shall be the universal sense; for the inmost in due time becomes the outmost, and our first thought is rendered back to us by the trumpets of the Last Judgment. Familiar as the voice of the mind is to each, the highest merit we ascribe to Moses, Plato and Milton is that they set at naught books and traditions, and spoke not what men, but what *they* thought. A man should learn to detect and watch that gleam of light which flashes across his mind from within, more than the lustre of the firmament of bards and sages. Yet he dismisses without notice his thought, because it is his. In every work of genius we recognize our own rejected thoughts; come back to us with a certain alienated majesty. Great works of art have no more affecting lesson for us than this. They teach us to abide by our spontaneous impression with good-humored inflexibility then most when the whole cry of voices is on the other side. Else tomorrow a stranger will say with masterly good sense precisely what we have thought and felt all the time, and we shall be forced to take with shame our own opinion from another.

There is a time in every man's education when he arrives at the conviction that envy is ignorance; that imitation is suicide; that he must take himself for better or worse as his portion; that though the wide universe is full of good, no kernel of nourishing corn can come to him but through his toil bestowed on that plot of ground which is given to him to till. The power which resides in him is new in nature, and none but he knows what that is which he can do, nor does he know until he has tried. Not for nothing one face, one character, one fact, makes much impression on him, and another none. This sculpture in the memory is not without preestablished harmony. The eye was placed where one ray should fall, that it might testify of that particular ray. We but half express ourselves, and are ashamed of that divine idea which each of us represents. It may be safely trusted as proportionate and of good issues, so it be faithfully imparted, but God will not have his work made manifest be cowards. A man is relieved and gay when he has put his heart into his work and done his best; but what he has said or done otherwise shall give him no peace. It is a deliverance which does not deliver. In the attempt his genius deserts him; no muse befriends; no invention, no hope.

Trust thyself: every heart vibrates to that iron string. Accept the place the divide providence has found for you, the society of your contemporaries, the connection of events. Great men have always done so, and confided themselves childlike to the genius of their age, betraying their perception that the absolutely trustworthy was seated at their heart, working through their hands, predominating in all their being. And we are now men, and must accept in the highest mind the same transcendent destiny; and not minors and invalids in a protected corner, not cowards fleeing before a revolution, but guides, redeemers and benefactors, obeying the Almighty effort and advancing on Chaos and the Dark.

What pretty oracles nature yields to us on this text in the face and behavior of children, babes, and even brutes! That divided and rebel mind, that distrust of a sentiment because our arithmetic has computed the strength and means opposed to our purpose, these have not. Their mind being whole, their eye is as yet unconquered; and when we look in their faces we are disconcerted. Infancy conforms to nobody; all conform to it; so that one babe commonly makes four or five out of the adults who prattle and play to it. So God has armed youth and puberty and manhood no less with its own piquancy and charm, and made it enviable and gracious and its claims not to be put by, if it will stand by itself. Do not think the youth has no force, because he cannot speak to you and me. Hark! in the next room his voice is sufficiently clear and emphatic. It seems he knows how to speak to his contemporaries. Bashful or bold then, he will know how to make us seniors very unnecessary.

The nonchalance of boys who are sure of a dinner, and would disdain as much as a lord to do or say aught to conciliate one, is the healthy attitude of human nature. A boy is in the parlor what the pit is in the playhouse; independent, irresponsible, looking out from his corner on such people and facts as pass by, he tries and sentences them on their merits, in the swift, summary way of boys, as good, bad, interesting, silly, eloquent, troublesome. He cumbers himself never about consequences, about interests; he gives an independent, genuine verdict. You must court him; he does not court you. But the man is as it were clapped into jail by his consciousness. As soon as he has once acted or spoken with *éclat* he is a committed person, watched by the sympathy or the hatred of hundreds, whose affections must now enter into his account. There is no Lethe for this. Ah, that he could pass again into his neutrality! Who can thus avoid all pledges and, having observed, observe again from the same unaffected, unbiased, unbribable, unaffrighted innocence—must always be formidable. He would utter opinions on all passing affairs, which being seen to be not private but necessary, would sink like darts into the ear of men and put them in fear.

These are the voices which we hear in solitude, but they grow faint and inaudible as we enter into the world. Society everywhere is in conspiracy against the manhood of every one of its members. Society is a joint-stock company, in which the members agree, for the better securing of his bread to each shareholder, to surrender the liberty and culture of the eater. The virtue in most request is conformity. Self-reliance is its aversion. It loves not realities and creators, but names and customs.

Whoso would be a man, must be a nonconformist. He who would gather immortal palms must not be hindered by the name of goodness, but must explore if it be goodness. Nothing is at last sacred but the integrity of your own mind. Absolve you to yourself, and you shall have the suffrage of the world. I remember an answer which when quite young I was prompted to make to a valued adviser who was wont to importune me with the dear old doctrines of the church. On my saying, "What have I to do with the sacredness of traditions, if I live wholly from within?" my friend suggested—"But these impulses may be from below, not from above." I replied, "They do not seem to me to be such; but if I am the Devil's child, I will live then from the Devil." No law can be sacred to me but that of my nature. Good and bad are but names very readily transferable to that or this; the only right is what is after my constitution; the only wrong what is against it. A man is to carry himself in the presence of all opposition as if every thing were titular and ephemeral but he. I am ashamed to think how easily we capitulate to badges and names, to large societies and dead institutions. Every decent and well-spoken individual affects and sways me more than is right. I ought to go upright and vital, and speak the rude truth in all ways. If malice and vanity wear the coat of philanthropy, shall that pass? If an angry bigot assumes this bountiful cause of Abolition, and comes to me with his last news from Barbadoes, why should I not say to him, 'Go love thy infant; love thy wood-chopper; be good-natured and modest; have that grace; and never varnish your hard, uncharitable ambition with this incredible tenderness for black folk a thousand miles off. Thy love afar is spite at home.' Rough and graceless would be such greeting, but truth is handsomer than the affectation of love. Your goodness must have some edge to it else it is none. The doctrine of hatred must be preached, as the counteraction of the doctrine of love, when that pules and whines. I shun father and mother and wife and brother when my genius calls me. I would write on the lintels of the doorpost, *Whim*. I hope it is somewhat better than whim at last, but we cannot spend the day in explanation. Expect me not to show cause why I seek or why I exclude company. Then again, do not tell me, as a good man did today, of my obligation to put all poor men in good situations. Are they *my* poor? I tell thee, thou foolish philanthropist, that I grudge the dollar, the dime, the cent I give to such men as do not belong to me and to whom I do not belong. There is a class of persons to whom by all spiritual affinity I am bought and sold; for them I will go to prison if need be; but your miscellaneous popular charities; the education at college of fools; the building of meetinghouses to the vain end to which many now stand; alms to sots, and the thousand-fold Relief Societies; though I confess with shame I sometimes succumb and give the dollar, it is a wicked dollar, which by and by I shall have the manhood to withhold.

Virtues are, in the popular estimate, rather the exception than the rule. There is the man *and* his virtues. Men do what is called a good action, as some piece of courage or charity, much as they would pay a fine in expiation of daily non-appearance on parade. Their works are done as an apology or extenuation of their living in the world—as invalids and the insane pay a high board. Their virtues are penances. I do not wish to expiate, but to live. My life is for itself and not for a spectacle. I much prefer that it should be of a lower strain, so it be genuine and equal, than that it should be glittering and unsteady. I wish it to be sound and sweet, and not to need diet and bleeding. I ask primary evidence that you are a man, and refuse this appeal from the man to his actions. I know that for myself it makes no difference whether I do or forbear those actions which are reckoned excellent. I consent to pay for a privilege where I have intrinsic right. Few and mean as my gifts may be, I actually am, and do not need for my own assurance or the assurance of my fellows any secondary testimony.

What I must do is all that concerns me, not what the people think. This rule, equally arduous in actual and in intellectual life, may serve for the whole distinction between greatness and meanness.

It is the harder because you will always find those who think they know what is your duty better than you know it. It is easy in the world to live after the world's opinion; it is easy in solitude to live after our own; but the great man is he who in the midst of the crowd keeps with perfect sweetness the independence of solitude.

The objection to conforming to usages that have become dead to you is that it scatters your force. It loses your time and blurs the impression of your character. If you maintain a dead church, contribute to a dead Bible society, vote with a great party either for the government or against it, spread your table like base housekeepers—under all these screens I have difficulty to detect the precise man you are: and of course so much force is withdrawn from your proper life. But do your work, and I shall know you. Do your work, and you shall reinforce yourself. A man must consider what a blind-man's-bluff is this game of conformity. If I know your sect I anticipate your argument. I hear a preacher announce for his text and topic the expediency of one of the institutions of his church. Do I not know beforehand that not possibly can he say a new and spontaneous word? Do I not know that with all this ostentation of examining the grounds of the institution he will do no such thing? Do I not know that he is pledged to himself not to look but at one side, the permitted side, not as a man, but as a parish minister? He is a retained attorney, and these airs of the bench are the emptiest affectation. Well, most men have bound their eyes with one or another handkerchief, and attached themselves to some one of these communities of opinion. This conformity makes them not false in a few particulars, authors of a few lies, but false in all particulars. Their every truth is not quite true. Their two is not the real two, their four not the real four; so that every word they say chagrins us and we know not where to begin to set them right. Meantime nature is not slow to equip us in the prison uniform of the party to which we adhere. We come to wear one cut of face and figure, and acquire by degrees the gentlest asinine expression. There is a mortifying experience in particular, which does not fail to wreak itself also in the general history; I mean "the foolish face of praise," the forced smile which we put on in company where we do not feel at ease, in answer to conversation which does not interest us. The muscles, not spontaneously moved but moved by a low usurping willfulness, grow tight about the outline of the face, with the most disagreeable sensation.

For nonconformity the world whips you with its displeasure. And therefore a man must know how to estimate a sour face The bystanders look askance on him in the public street or in the friend's parlor. If this aversion had its origin in contempt and resistance like his own, he might well go home with a sad countenance; but the sour faces of the multitude, like their sweet faces have no deep cause, but are put on and off as the wind blows and a newspaper directs. Yet is the discontent of the multitude more formidable than that of the senate and the college. It is easy enough for a firm man who knows the world to brook the rage of the cultivated classes. Their rage is decorous and prudent, for they are timid, as being very vulnerable themselves. But when to their feminine rage the indignation of the people is added, when the ignorant and the poor are aroused, when the unintelligent brute force that lies at the bottom of society is made to growl and mow, it needs the habit of magnanimity and religion to treat it godlike as a trifle of no concernment.

The other terror that scares us from self trust is our consistency; a reverence for our past act or word because the eyes of others have no other data for computing our orbit than our past acts, and we are loth to disappoint them.

But why should you keep your head over your shoulder? Why drag about this corpse of your memory, lest you contradict somewhat you have stated in this or that public place? Suppose you should contradict yourself; what then? It seems to be a rule of wisdom never to rely on your memory alone, scarcely even in acts of pure memory, but to bring the past for judgment into the thousand-eyed present, and live ever in a new day. In your metaphysics you have denied personality to the Deity, yet when the devout motions of the soul come, yield to them heart and life, though they should clothe God with shape and color. Leave your theory, as Joseph his coat in the hand of the harlot, and flee.

A foolish consistency is the hobgoblin of little minds, adored by little statesmen and philosophers and divines. With consistency a great soul has simply nothing to do. He may as well concern himself with his shadow on the wall. Speak what you think now in hard words and tomorrow speak what tomorrow thinks in hard words again, though it contradict every thing you said today. 'Ah, so you shall be sure to be misunderstood. 'Is it so bad then to be misunderstood? Pythagoras was misunderstood, and Socrates, and Jesus, and Luther, and Copernicus, and Galileo, and Newton, and every pure and wise spirit that ever took flesh. To be great is to be misunderstood.

I suppose no man can violate his nature. All the sallies of his will are rounded in by the law of his being, as the inequalities of Andes and Himmaleh are insignificant in the curve of the sphere. Nor does it matter how you gauge and try him. A character is like an acrostic or Alexandrian stanza; read it forward, backward, or across, it still spells the same thing. In this pleasing contrite woodlife which God allows me, let me record day by day my honest thought without prospect or retrospect, and, I cannot doubt, it will be found symmetrical, though I mean it not and see it not. My book should smell of pines and resound with the hum of insects. The swallow over my window should interweave that thread or straw he carries in his bill into my web also. We pass for what we are. Character teaches above our wills. Men imagine that they communicate their virtue or vice only by overt actions, and do not see that virtue or vice emit a breath every moment.

There will be an agreement in whatever variety of actions, so they be each honest and natural in their hour. For of one will, the actions will be harmonious, however unlike they seem. These varieties are lost sight of at a little distance, at a little height of thought. One tendency unites them all. The voyage of the best ship is a zigzag line of a hundred tacks. See the line from a sufficient distance, and it straightens itself to the average tendency. Your genuine action will explain itself and will explain your other genuine actions. Your conformity explains nothing. Act singly, and what you have already done singly will justify you now. Greatness appeals to the future. If I can be firm enough today to do right and scorn eyes, I must have done so much right before as to defend me now. Be it how it will, do right now. Always scorn appearances and you always may. The force of character is cumulative. All the foregone days of virtue work their health into this. What makes the majesty of the heroes of the senate and the field, which so fills the imagination? The consciousness of a train of great days and victories behind. They shed a united light on the advancing actor. He is attended as by a visible escort of angels. This is it which throws thunder into Chatham's voice, and dignity. into Washington's port, and America into Adam's eye. Honor is venerable to us because it is no ephemera. It is always ancient virtue. We worship it today because it is not of today. We love it and pay it homage because it is not a trap for our love and homage, but is self-dependent, self derived, and therefore of an old immaculate pedigree, even if shown in a young person.

I hope in these days we have heard the last of conformity and consistency. Let the words be gazetted and ridiculous henceforward. Instead of the gong for dinner, let us hear a whistle from the Spartan fife. Let us never bow and apologize more. A great man is coming to eat at my house. I do not wish to please him; I wish that he should wish to please me. I will stand here for humanity, and though I would make it kind, I would make it true. Let us affront and reprimand the smooth mediocrity and squalid contentment of the times, and hurl in the face of custom and trade and office, the fact which is the upshot of all history, that there is a great responsible Thinker and Actor working wherever a man works; that a true man belongs to no other time or place, but is the centre of things. Where he is, there is nature. He measures you and all men and all events. Ordinarily every body in society reminds us of somewhat else, or of some other person. Character, reality, reminds you of nothing else; it takes place of the whole creation. The man must be so much that he must make all circumstances indifferent. Every true man is a cause, a country, and an age; requires infinite spaces and numbers and time fully to accomplish his design; and posterity seem to follow his steps as a train of clients. A man Caesar is born, and for ages after we have a Roman Empire. Christ is born, and millions of minds so grow and cleave to his genius that he is confounded with virtue and the possible of man. An institution is the lengthened shadow of one man; as, Monachism, of the Hermit Antony; the Reformation, of Luther; Quakerism, of Fox; Methodism, of Wesley; Abolition, of Clarkson. Scipio, Milton called "the height of Rome"; and all history resolves itself very easily into the biography of a few stout and earnest persons.

Let a man then know his worth, and keep things under his feet. Let him not peep or steal, or skulk up and down with the air of a charity boy, a bastard, or an interloper in the world which exists for him. But the man in the street, finding no worth in himself which corresponds to the force which built a tower or sculptured a marble god, feels poor when he looks on these. To him a palace, a statue, or a costly book have an alien and forbidding air, much like a gay equipage, and seem to say like that, "Who are you, Sir?" Yet they all are his, suitors for his notice, petitioners to his faculties that they will come out and take possession. The picture waits for my verdict; it is not to command me, but I am to settle its claims to praise. That popular fable of the sot who was picked up dead-drunk in the street, carried to the duke's house, washed and dressed and laid in the duke's bed, and, on his waking, treated with all obsequious ceremony like the duke, and assured that he had been insane, owes its popularity to the fact that it symbolizes so well the state of man, who is in the world a sort of sot, but now and then wakes up, exercises his reason and finds himself a true prince.

Our reading is mendicant and sycophantic. In history our imagination plays us false. Kingdom and lordship, power and estate, are a gaudier vocabulary than private John and Edward in a small house and common day's work; but the things of life are the same to both; the sum total of both is the same. Why all this deference to Alfred and Scanderbeg and Gustavus? Suppose they were virtuous; did they wear out virtue? As great a stake depends on your private act today as followed their public and renowned steps. When private men shall act with original views, the lustre will be transferred from the actions of kings to those of gentlemen.

The world has been instructed by its kings, who have so magnetized the eyes of nations. It has been taught by this colossal symbol the mutual reverence that is due from man to man. The joyful loyalty with which men have everywhere suffered the king, the noble, or the great proprietor to walk among them by a law of his own, make his own scale of men and things and reverse theirs, pay for benefits not with money but with honor, and represent the law in his person, was the hieroglyphic by which they obscurely signified their consciousness of their own right and comeliness, the right of every man.

The magnetism which all original action exerts is explained when we inquire the reason of self-trust. Who is the Trustee? What is the aboriginal Self, on which a universal reliance may be grounded? What is the nature and power of that science-baffling star, without parallax, without calculable elements, which shoots a ray of beauty even into trivial and impure actions, if the least mark of independence appear? The inquiry leads us to that source, at once the essence of genius, of virtue and of life, which we call Spontaneity or Instinct. We denote this primary wisdom as Intuition, whilst all later teachings are tuitions. In that deep force, the last fact behind which analysis cannot go, all things find their common origin. For the sense of being which in calm hours rises, we know not how, in the soul, is not diverse from things, from space, from light, from time, from man, but one with them and proceeds obviously from the same source whence their life and being also proceed. We first share the life by which things exist and afterwards see them as appearances in nature and forget that we have shared their cause. Here is the fountain of action and of thought. Here are the lungs of that inspiration which giveth man wisdom and which cannot be denied without impiety and atheism. We lie in the lap of immense intelligence, which makes us receivers of its truth and organs of its activity. When we discern justice, when we discern truth, we do nothing of ourselves, but allow a passage to its beams. If we ask whence this comes, if we seek to pry into the soul that causes, all philosophy is at fault. Its presence or its absence is all we can affirm. Every man discriminates between the voluntary acts of his mind and his involuntary perceptions, and knows that to his involuntary perceptions a perfect faith is due. He may err in the expression of them, but he knows that these things are so, like day and night, not to be disputed. My wilful actions and acquisitions are but roving; the idlest reverie, the faintest native emotion, command my curiosity and respect. Thoughtless people contradict as readily the statement of perceptions as of opinions, or rather much more readily; for they do not distinguish between perception and notion. They fancy that I choose to see this or that thing. But perception is not whimsical, but fatal. If I see a trait, my children will see it after me, and in course of time all mankind—although it may chance that no one has seen it before me. For my perception of it is as much a fact as the sun.

The relations of the soul to the divine spirit are so pure that it is profane to seek to interpose helps. It must be that when God speaketh he should communicate, not one thing, but all things; should fill the world with his voice; should scatter forth light, nature, time, souls, from the centre of the present thought; and new date and new create the whole. Whenever a mind is simple and receives a divine wisdom, old things pass away,-means, teachers, texts, temples fall; it lives now, and absorbs past and future into the present hour. All things are made sacred by relation to it,-one as much as another. All things are dissolved to their centre by their cause, and in the universal miracles petty and particular miracles disappear. If therefore a man claims to know and speak of God and carries you backward to the phraseology of some old mouldered nation in another country, in another world, believe him not. Is the acorn better than the oak to which is its fulness and completion? Is the parent better than the child into whom he has cast his ripened being? Whence then this worship of the past? The centuries are conspirators against the sanity and authority of the soul. Time and space are but physiological colors which the eye makes, but the soul is light: where it is, is day; where it was, is night; and history is an impertinence and an injury if it be any thing more than cheerful apologue or parable of my being and becoming.

Man is timid and apologetic; he is no longer upright; he dares not say 'I think,' 'I am,' but quotes some saint or sage. He is ashamed before the blade of grass or the blowing rose. These roses under my window make no reference to former roses or to better ones; they are for what they are; they exist with God today. There is no time to them. There is simply the rose; it is perfect in every moment of its existence. Before a leafbud has burst, its whole life acts; in the full-blown flower there is no more; in the leafless root there is no less. Its nature is satisfied and it satisfies nature in all moments alike. But man postpones or remembers; he does not live in the present, but with reverted eye laments the past, or, heedless of the riches that surround him, stands on tiptoe to foresee the future. He cannot be happy and strong until he too lives with nature in the present, above time.

This should be plain enough. Yet see what strong intellects dare not yet hear God himself, unless he speak the phraseology of I know not what David, or Jeremiah, or Paul. We shall not always set so great a price on a few texts, on a few lives. We are like children who repeat by rote the sentences of grandames and tutors, and, as they grow older, of the men of talents and character they chance to see—painfully recollecting the exact words they spoke; afterwards, when they come into the point of view which those had who uttered these sayings, they understand them and are willing to let the words go; for at any time they can use words as good when occasion comes. If we live truly, we shall see truly. It is as easy for the strong man to be strong, as it is for the weak to be weak. When we have new perception, we shall gladly disburden the memory of its hoarded treasures as old rubbish. When a man lives with God, his voice shall be as sweet as the murmur of the brook and the rustle of the corn.

And now at last the highest truth on this subject remains unsaid; probably cannot be said; for all that we say is the far-off remembering of the intuition. That thought by what I can now nearest approach to say it, is this. When good is near you, when you have life in yourself, it is not by any known or accustomed way; you shall not discern the footprints of any other; you shall not see the face of man; you shall not hear any name;--the way, the thought, the good, shall be wholly strange and new. It shall exclude example and experience. You take the way from man, not to man. All persons that ever existed are its forgotten ministers. Fear and hope are alike beneath it. There is somewhat low even in hope. In the hour of vision there is nothing that can be called gratitude, nor properly joy. The soul raised over passion beholds identity and eternal causation, perceives the self existence of Truth and Right, and calms itself with knowing that all things go well. Vast spaces of nature, the Atlantic Ocean, the South Sea; long intervals of time, years, centuries, are of no account. This which I think and feel underlay every former state of life and circumstances, as it does underlie my present, and what is called life and what is called death.

Life only avails, not the having lived. Power ceases in the instant of repose; it resides in the moment of transition from a past to a new state, in the shooting of the gulf, in the darting to an aim. This one fact the world hates; that the soul *becomes*; for that forever degrades the past, turns all riches to poverty, all reputation to a shame, confounds the saint with the rogue, shoves Jesus and Judas equally aside. Why, then, do we prate of self-reliance? Inasmuch as the soul is present there will be power not confident but agent. To talk of reliance is a poor external way of speaking. Speak rather of that which relies because it works and is. Who has more obedience than I masters me, though he should not raise his finger. Round him I must revolve by the gravitation of spirits. We fancy it rhetoric when we speak of eminent virtue. We do not yet see that virtue is Height, and that a man or a company of men, plastic and permeable to principles, by the law of nature must overpower and ride all cities, nations, kings, rich men, poets, who are not.

This is the ultimate fact which we so quickly reach on this as on every topic, the resolution of all into the ever-blessed ONE. Self-existence is the attribute of the Supreme Cause, and it constitutes the measure of good by the degree in which it enters into all lower forms. All things real are so by so much virtue as they contain. Commerce, husbandry, bunting, whaling, war eloquence, personal weight, are somewhat, and engage my respect as examples of its presence and impure action. I see the same law working in nature for conservation and growth. Power is, in nature, the essential measure of right. Nature suffers nothing to remain in her kingdoms which cannot help itself. The genesis and maturation of a planet, its poise and orbit, the bended tree recovering itself from the strong wind, the vital resources of every animal and vegetable, are demonstrations of the self-sufficing and therefore self-relying soul.

Thus all concentrates: let us not rove; let us sit at home with the cause. Let us stun and astonish the intruding rabble of men and books and institutions by a simple declaration of the divine fact. Bid the invaders take the shoes from off their feet, for God is here within. Let our simplicity judge them, and our docility to our own law demonstrate the poverty of nature and fortune beside our native riches.

But now we are a mob. Man does not stand in awe of man, nor is his genius admonished to stay at home, to put itself in communication with the internal ocean, but it goes abroad to beg a cup of water of the urns of other men. We must go alone. I like the silent church before the service begins, better than any preaching. How far off, how cool, how chaste the persons look, begirt each one with a precinct or sanctuary! So let us always sit. Why should we assume the faults of our friend, or wife, or father, or child, because they sit around our hearth, or are said to have the same blood? All men have my blood and I all men's. Not for that will I adopt their petulance or folly, even to the extent of being ashamed of it. But your isolation must not be mechanical, but spiritual, that is, must be elevation. At times the whole world seems to be in conspiracy to importune you with emphatic trifles. Friend, client, child, sickness, fear, want, charity, all knock; at once at thy closet door and say—'Come out unto us.' But keep thy state; come not into their confusion. The power men possess to annoy me I give them by a weak curiosity. No man can come near me but through my act "What we love that we have, but by desire we bereave ourselves of the love."

If we cannot at once rise to the sanctities of obedience and faith, let us at least resist our temptations; let us enter into the state of war and wake Thor and Woden, courage and constancy, in our Saxon breasts. This is to be done in our smooth times by speaking the truth. Check this lying hospitality and lying affection. Live no longer to the expectation of these deceived and deceiving people with whom we converse. Say to them, 'O father, O mother, O wife, O brother, O friend, I have lived with you after appearances hitherto. Henceforward I am the truth's. Be it known unto you that henceforward I obey no law less than the eternal law. I will have no covenants but proximities. I shall endeavor to nourish my parents, to support my family, to be the chaste husband of one wife—but these relations I must fill after a new and unprecedented way. I appeal from your customs. I must be myself. I cannot break myself any longer for you, or you. If you can love me for what I am, we shall be the happier. If you cannot, I will still seek to deserve that you should. I will not hide my tastes or aversions. I will so trust that what is deep is holy, that I will do strongly before the sun and moon whatever inly rejoices me and the heart appoints. If you are noble, I will love you; if you are not, I will not hurt you and myself by hypocritical attentions. If you are true, but not in the same truth with me, cleave to your companions; I will seek my own. I do this not selfishly but humbly and truly. It is alike your interest, and mine, and all men's, however long we have dwelt in lies, to live in truth. Does this sound harsh today? You will soon love what is dictated by your nature as well as mine, and if we follow the truth it will bring us out safe at last.'—But so may you give these friends pain. Yes, but I cannot sell my liberty and my power, to save their sensibility. Besides, all persons have their moments of reason, when they look out into the region of absolute truth; then will they justify me and do the same thing.

The populace think that your rejection of popular standards is a rejection of all standard, and mere antinomianism; and the bold sensualist will use the name of philosophy to gild his crimes. But the law of consciousness abides. There are two confessionals, in one or the other of which we must be shriven. You may fulfil your round of duties by clearing yourself in the *direct*, or in the *reflex* way. Consider whether you have satisfied your relations to father, mother, cousin, neighbor, town, cat and dog—whether any of these can upbraid you. But I may also neglect this reflex standard and absolve me to myself. I have my own stern claims and perfect circle. It denies the name of duty to many offices that are called duties. But if I can discharge its debts,it enables me to dispense with the popular code. If any one images that this law is lax, let him keep its commandment one day.

And truly it demands something godlike in him who has cast off the common motives of humanity and has ventured to trust himself for a taskmaster. High be his heart, faithful his will, clear his sight, that he may in good earnest be doctrine, society, law, to himself, that a simple purpose may be to him as strong as iron necessity is to others!

If any man consider the present aspects of what is called by distinction *society*, he will see the need of these ethics. The sinew and heart of man seem to be drawn out, and we are become timorous, desponding whimperers. We are afraid of truth, afraid of fortune, afraid of death, and afraid of each other. Our age yields no great and perfect persons. We want men and women who shall renovate life and our social state, but we see that most natures are insolvent, cannot satisfy their own wants, have an ambition out of all proportion to their practical force and do lean and beg day and night continually. Our housekeeping is mendicant, our arts, our occupations, our marriages, our religion we have not chosen, but society has chosen for us. We are parlor soldiers. We shun the rugged battle of fate, where strength is born.

If our young men miscarry in their first enterprises they lose all heart. If the young merchant fails, men say he is *ruined*. If the finest genius studies at one of our colleges and is not installed in an office within one year afterwards in the cities or suburbs of Boston or New York, it seems to his friends and to himself that he is right in being disheartened and in complaining the rest of his life. A sturdy lad from New Hampshire or Vermont, who in turn tries all the professions, who *teams it, farms it, peddles*, keeps a school, preaches, edits a newspaper, goes to Congress, buys a township, and so forth, in successive years, and always like a cat falls on his feet, is worth a hundred of these city dolls. He walks abreast with his days and feels no shame in not 'studying a profession,' for he does not postpone his life, but lives already. He has not one chance, but a hundred chances. Let a Stoic open the resources of man and tell men they are not leaning willows, but can and must detach themselves; that with the exercise of self-trust, new powers shall appear; that a man is the word made flesh, born to shed healing to the nations; that he should be ashamed of our compassion, and that the moment he acts from himself, tossing the laws, the books, idolatries and customs out of the window, we pity him no more but thank and revere him; and that teacher shall restore the life of man to splendor and make his name dear to all history.

It is easy to see that a greater self-reliance must work a revolution in all the offices and relations of men; in their religion; in their education; in their pursuits; their modes of living; their association; in their property; in their speculative views.

1. In what prayers do men allow themselves! That which they call a holy office is not so much as brave and manly. Prayer looks abroad and asks for some foreign addition to come through some foreign virtue, and loses itself in endless mazes of natural and supernatural, and mediatorial and miraculous. Prayer that craves a particular commodity, anything less than all good, is vicious. Prayer is the contemplation of the facts of life from the highest point of view. It is the soliloquy of a beholding and jubilant soul. It is the spirit of God pronouncing his works good. But prayer as a means to effect a private end is meanness and theft. It supposes dualism and not unity in nature and consciousness. As soon as the man is at one with God, he will not beg. He will then see prayer in all action. The prayer of the farmer kneeling in his field to weed it, the prayer of the rower kneeling with the stroke of his oar, are true prayers heard throughout nature, though for cheap ends. Caratach, in Fletcher's "Bonduca," when admonished to inquire the mind of the god Audate, replies—

His hidden meaning lies in our endeavors;
Our valors are our best gods.

Another sort of false prayers are our regrets. Discontent is the want of self-reliance: it is infirmity of will. Regret calamities if you can thereby help the sufferer; if not, attend your own work and already the evil begins to be repaired. Our sympathy is just as base. We come to them who weep foolishly and sit down and cry for company, instead of imparting to them truth and health in rough electric shocks, putting them once more in communication with their own reason. The secret of fortune is joy in our hands. Welcome evermore to gods and men is the self-helping man. For him all doors are flung wide; him all tongues greet, all honors crown, all eyes follow with desire. Our love goes out to him and embraces him because he did not need it. We solicitously and apologetically caress and celebrate him because he held on his way and scorned our disapprobation. The gods love him because men hated him. "To the persevering mortal," said Zoroaster, "the blessed Immortals are swift."

As men's prayers are a disease of the will, so are their creeds a disease of the intellect. They say with those foolish Israelites, "Let not God speak to us, lest we die. Speak thou, speak any man with us, and we will obey." Everywhere I am hindered of meeting God in my brother, because he has shut his own temple doors and recites fables merely of his brother's, or his brother's God. Every new mind is a new classification. If it prove a mind of uncommon activity and power, a Locke, a Lavoisier, a Hutton, a Bentham, a Fourier, it imposes its classification on other men, and lo! a new system. In proportion to the depth of the thought, and so to the number of the objects it touches and brings within reach of the pupil, is his complacency. But chiefly is this apparent in creeds and churches, which are also classifications of some powerful mind acting on the elemental thought of duty and man's relation to the Highest. Such is Calvinism, Quakerism, Swedenborgism. The pupil takes the same delight in subordinating every thing to the new terminology as a girl who has just learned botany in seeing a new earth and new seasons thereby. It will happen for a time that the pupil will find his intellectual power has grown by the study of his master's mind. But in all unbalanced minds the classification is idolized, passes for the end and not for a speedily exhaustible means, so that the walls of the system blend to their eye in the remote horizon with the walls of the universe; the luminaries of heaven seem to them hung on the arch their master built. They cannot imagine how you aliens have any right to see how you can see; 'It must be somehow that you stole the light from us.' They do not yet perceive that light, unsystematic, indomitable, will break into any cabin, even into theirs. Let them chirp awhile and call it their own. If they are honest and do well, presently their neat new pinfold will be too strait and low, will crack, will lean, will rot and vanish, and the immortal light, all young and joyful, million-orbed, million colored, will beam over the universe as on the first morning.

2. It is for want of self-culture that the superstition of Travelling, whose idols are Italy, England, Egypt, retains its fascination for all educated Americans. They who made England, Italy,

or Greece venerable in the imagination, did so by sticking fast where they were, like an axis of the earth. In manly hours we feel that duty is our place. The soul is no traveller; the wise man stays at home, and when his necessities, his duties, on any occasion call him from his house, or into foreign lands, he is at home still and shall make men sensible by the expression of his countenance that he goes, the missionary of wisdom and virtue, and visits cities and men like a sovereign and not like an interloper or a valet.

I have no churlish objection to the circumnavigation of the globe for the purposes of art, of study, and benevolence, so that the man is first domesticated, or does not go abroad with the hope of finding somewhat greater than he knows. He who travels to be amused, or to get somewhat which he does not carry, travels away from himself, and grows old even in youth among old things. In Thebes, in Palmyra, his will and mind have become old and dilapidated as they. He carries ruins to ruins.

Travelling is a fool's paradise. Our first journeys discover to us the indifference of places. At home I dream that at Naples, at Rome, I can be intoxicated with beauty, and lose my sadness. I pack my trunk, embrace my friends, embark on the sea and at last wake up in Naples, and there beside me is the stern fact, the sad self, unrelenting, identical, that I fled from. I seek the Vatican and the palaces. I affect to be intoxicated with sights and suggestions, but I am not intoxicated. My giant goes with me wherever I go.

3. But the rage of travelling is a symptom of a deeper unsoundness affecting the whole intellectual action. The intellect is a vagabond, and our system of education fosters restlessness. Our minds travel when our bodies are forced to stay at home. We imitate; and what is imitation but the travelling of the mind? Our houses are built with foreign taste; our shelves are garnished with foreign ornaments; our opinions, our tastes, our faculties, lean, and follow the Past and the Distant. The soul created the arts wherever they have flourished. It was in his own mind that the artist sought his model. It was an application of his own thought to the thing to be done and the conditions to be observed. And why need we copy the Doric or the Gothic model? Beauty, convenience, grandeur of thought and quaint expression are as near to us as to any, and if the American artist will study with hope and love the precise thing to be done by him, considering the climate, the soil, the length of the day, the wants of the people, the habit and form of the government, he will create a house in which all these will find themselves fitted, and taste and sentiment will be satisfied also.

Insist on yourself; never imitate. Your own gift you can present every moment with the cumulative force of a whole life's cultivation; but of the adopted talent of another you have only an extemporaneous half possession. That which each can do best, none but his Maker can teach him. No man yet knows what is, nor can, till that person has exhibited it. Where is the master who could have taught Shakespeare? Where is the master who could have instructed Franklin, or Washington, or Bacon, or Newton? Every great man is a unique. The Scipionism of Scipio is precisely that part he could not borrow. Shakespeare will never be made by the study of Shakespeare. Do that which is assigned to you, and you cannot hope too much or dare too much. There is at this moment for you an utterance brave and grand as that of the colossal chisel of Phidias, or trowel of the Egyptians, or the pen of Moses or Dante, but different from all these. Not possibly will the soul, all rich, all eloquent, with thousand-cloven tongue, deign to repeat itself; but if you can hear what these patriarchs say, surely you can reply to them in the same pitch of voice; for the ear and the tongue are two organs of one nature. Abide in the simple and noble regions of thy life, obey thy heart, and thou shalt reproduce the Foreworld again.

4. As our Religion, our Education, our Art look abroad, so does our spirit of society. All men plume themselves on the improvement of society, and no man improves.

Society never advances. It recedes as fast on one side as it gains on the other. It undergoes continual changes; it is barbarous, it is civilized, it is christianized, it is rich, it is scientific; but this change is not amelioration. For every thing that is given something is taken. Society acquires new arts and loses old instincts. What a contrast between the well-clad, reading, writing, thinking American, with a watch, a pencil and a bill of exchange in his pocket, and the naked New Zealander, whose property is a club, a spear, a mat and an undivided twentieth of a shed to sleep under! But compare the health of the two men and you shall see that the white man has lost his aboriginal strength. If the traveller tells us truly, strike the savage with a broad-axe and in a day or two the flesh shall unite and heal as if you struck the blow into soft pitch, and the same blow shall send the white to his grave.

The civilized man has built a coach, but has lost the use of his feet. He is supported on crutches, but lacks so much support of muscle. He has a fine Geneva watch, but he fails of the skill to tell the hour by the sun. A Greenwich nautical almanac he has, and so being sure of the information when he wants it, the man in the street does not know a star in the sky. The solstice he does not observe; the equinox he knows as little; and the whole bright calendar of the year is without a dial in his mind. His notebooks impair his memory; his libraries overload his wit; the insurance-office increases the number of accidents; and it may be a question whether machinery does not encumber; whether we have not lost by refinement some energy, by a Christianity, entrenched in establishments and forms, some vigor of wild virtue. For every Stoic was a Stoic; but in Christendom where is the Christian?

There is no more deviation in the moral standard than in the standard of height or bulk. No greater men are now than ever were. A singular equality may be observed between the great men of the first and of the last ages; nor can all the science, art, religion, and philosophy of the nineteenth century avail to educate greater men than Plutarch's heroes, three or four and twenty centuries ago.

Not in time is the race progressive. Phocion, Socrates, Anaxagoras, Diogenes, are great men, but they leave no class. He who is really of their class will not be called by their name, but will be his own man, and in his turn the founder of a sect. The arts and inventions of each period are only its costume and do not invigorate men. The harm of the improved machinery may compensate its good. Hudson and Behring accomplished so much in their fishing boats as to astonish Parry and Franklin, whose equipment exhausted the resources of science and art. Galileo, with an opera glass, discovered a more splendid series of celestial phenomena than any one since. Columbus found the New World in an undecked boat. It is curious to see the periodical disuse and perishing of means and machinery which were introduced with loud laudation a few years or centuries before. The great genius returns to essential man. We reckoned the improvements of the art of war among the triumphs of science, and yet Napoleon conquered Europe by the bivouac, which consisted of falling back on naked valor and disencumbering it of all aids. The Emperor held it impossible to make a perfect army, says Las Cases, "without abolishing our arms, magazines, commissaries and carriages, until, in imitation of the Roman custom, the soldier should receive his supply of corn, grind it in his hand-mill and bake his bread himself."

Society is a wave. The wave moves onward, but the water of which it is composed does not. The same particle does not rise from the valley to the ridge. Its unity is only phenomenal. The persons who make up a nation to-day, next year die, and their experience dies with them.

And so the reliance on Property, including the reliance on governments which protect it, is the want of self-reliance. Men have looked away from themselves and at things so long that they have come to esteem the religious, learned and civil institutions as guards of property, and they deprecate assaults on these, because they feel them to be assaults on property. They measure their esteem of each other by what each has, and not by what each is. But a cultivated man becomes ashamed of his property, out of new respect for his nature. Especially he a what he has if he see that is accidental—came to him by inheritance, or gift, or crime; then he feel that it is not having; it does not belong to him, has no root in him and merely lies there because no revolution or no robber takes it away. But which a man is, does always by necessity acquire; and the man acquires, is living property, which does not wait beck of rulers, or mobs, or revolutions, or fire, or storm, or bankruptcies, but perpetually renews itself wherever the man breathes. "Thy lot or portion of life," said the Caliph Ali, "is seeking after thee; therefore be at rest from seeking after it." Our dependence on these foreign goods leads us to our slavish respect for numbers. The political parties meet in numerous conventions; the greater the concourse and with each new uproar of announcement, The delegation from Essex! The Democrats from New Hampshire! The Whigs of Maine! the young patriot feels himself stronger than before by a new thousand of eyes and arms. In like manner the reformers summon conventions and vote and resolve in multitude. No so, O friends! will the God deign to enter and inhabit you, but by a method precisely the reverse. It is only as a man puts off all foreign support and stands alone that I see him to be strong and to prevail. He is weaker by every recruit to his banner. Is not a man better than a town? Ask nothing of men, and, in the endless mutation, thou only firm column must presently appear the upholder of all that surrounds thee. He who knows that power is inborn, that he is weak because he has looked for good out of him and elsewhere, and, so perceiving, throws himself unhesitatingly on his thought, instantly rights himself, stands in the erect position, commands his limbs, works miracles; just as a man who stands on his feet is stronger than a man who stands on his head.

So use all that is called Fortune. Most men gamble with her, and gain all, and lose all, as her wheel rolls. But do thou leave as unlawful these winnings, and deal with Cause and Effect, the chancellors of God. In the Will work and acquire, and thou hast chained the wheel of Chance, and shall sit hereafter out of fear from her rotations. A political victory, a rise of rents, the recovery of your sick or the return of your absent friend, or some other favorable event raises your spirits, and you think good days are preparing for you. Do not believe it. Nothing can bring you peace but yourself. Nothing can bring you peace but the triumph of principles.

JUSTICE AND PROPERTY RIGHTS

Murray N. Rothbard

I. The Failure of Utilitarianism

Until very recently, free-market economists paid little attention to the entities actually being exchanged on the very market they have advocated so strongly. Wrapped up in the workings and advantages of freedom of trade, enterprise, investment, and the price system, economists tended to lose sight of the things being exchanged on that market. Namely, they lost sight of the fact that when $10,000 is being exchanged for a machine, or $1 for a hula loop, what is actually being exchanged is the *title of ownership* to each of these goods. In short, when I buy a hula hoop for a dollar, what I am actually doing is exchanging my title of ownership to the dollar in exchange for the ownership title to the hula hoop; the retailer is doing the exact opposite.[1] But this means that economists' habitual attempts to be *Wertfrei*, or at the least to confine their advocacy to the processes of trade and exchange, cannot be maintained; for if I and the retailer are indeed to be free to trade the dollar for the hula hoop without coercive interference by third parties, then this can only be done if these economists will proclaim the justice and the propriety of my original ownership of the dollar and the retailer's ownership of the hula hoop.

In short, for an economists to say that X and Y should be free to trade Good A for Good B unmolested by third parties, he must *also* say that X legitimately and properly owns Good A and that Y legitimately owns Good B. But this means that the free-market economist must have some sort of theory of justice in property rights; he can scarcely say that X properly owns Good A without asserting some sort of theory of justice on behalf of such ownership.

Suppose, for example, that as I am about to purchase the hula hoop, the information arrives that the retailer had really stolen the hoop from Z. Surely not even the supposed *Wertfrei* economist can continue to endorse blithely the proposed exchange of ownership titles between myself and the retailer. For now we find that retailer Y's title of ownership is improper and unjust and that he must be forced to return the hoop to Z, the original owner. The economist can then only endorse the proposed exchange between myself and Z, rather than Y, for the hula hoop, since he has to acknowledge Z as the proper owner of title to the hoop.

In short, we have two mutually exclusive claimants to the ownership of the hoop. If the economist agrees to endorse only Z's sale of the hoop, then he is implicitly agreeing that Z has the just, and Y the unjust, claim to the hoop. And even if he continues to endorse the sale by Y, then he is implicitly maintaining *another* theory of property titles: namely, that theft is justified. Whichever way he decides, the economist cannot escape a judgment, a theory of justice in the ownership of property. Furthermore, the economist is not really finished when he proclaims the injustice of theft and endorses Z's proper title. For what is the justification for Z's title to the hoop? Is it only because he is a nonthief?

In recent years, free-market economists Ronald Coase and Harold Demsetz have begun to redress the balance and to focus on the importance of a clear and precise demarcation of property rights for the market economy. They have demonstrated the importance of such demarcation in the allocation of resources and in preventing or compensating for unwanted imposition of "external costs" from the actions of individuals. But Coase and Demsetz have failed to develop any theory of justice in these property rights; or rather, they have advanced two theories: one, that it "doesn't matter" *how* the property titles are allocated, so long as they are allocated precisely; and two, that the titles should be allocated to minimize "total social transaction costs," since a minimization of costs is supposed to be a *Wertfrei* way of benefitting all of society.

There is no space here for a detailed critique of the Coase-Demsetz criteria. Suffice it to say that even if, say, in a conflict over property titles between a rancher and a farmer for the same piece of land, even if the allocation of title "doesn't matter" for the allocation of resources (a point which itself could be challenged), it certainly matters from the point of view of the rancher and the farmer. And secondly, that it is impossible to weigh "total social costs" if we fully realize that all costs are subjective to the individuals and therefore cannot be compared interpersonally.[2] Here the important point is that Coase and Demsetz, along with all other utilitarian free-market economists, implicitly or explicitly leave it to the hands of government to define and allocate the titles to private property.

It is a curious fact that utilitarian economists, generally so skeptical of the virtues of government intervention, are so content to leave the fundamental underpinning of the market process—the definition of property rights and the allocation of property titles—wholly in the hands of government. Thus, if Smith, Jones, and Doe each own property and are about to exchange their titles, utilitarians simply assert that if these titles are *legal* (i.e., if the government puts the stamp of approval upon them), then they consider those titles to be justified; it is only if someone violates the government's definition of legality (e.g., in the case of Y, the thieving retailer) that utilitarians are willing to agree with the general and the governmental view of the injustice of such action. But this means, of course, that once again, the utilitarians have failed in their wish to escape having a theory of justice in property; actually they do have such a theory, and it is the surely simplistic one that *whatever government denies as legal is right.*

As in so many other areas of social philosophy, then, we see that utilitarians, in pursuing their vain goal of being *Wertfrei*, of "scientifically" abjuring any theory of justice, actually *have* such a theory, namely, putting their stamp of approval on whatever the process by which the government arrives at its allocation of property titles. Furthermore, we find that, as on many similar occasions, utilitarians in their vain quest for the *Wertfrei*, really conclude by endorsing as right and just whatever the government happens to decide, that is, by blindly apologizing for the *status quo*.[3]

Let us consider the utilitarian stamp of approval on government allocation of property titles. Can this approval possibly achieve en the limited utilitarian goal of certain and precise allocation of property titles? Suppose that the government endorses the existing titles to their property held by Smith, Jones, and Doe. Suppose then that a faction of government calls for the confiscation of these titles and redistribution of that property to Roe, Brown, and Robinson. The reasons for this program may stem from any number of social theories or even from the brute fact that Roe, Brown, and Robinson have greater political power than the original trio of owners. The reaction to this proposal by free-market economists and other utilitarians is predictable: they will oppose this proposal on the ground that definite and certain property rights, so socially beneficial, are being endangered. But suppose that the government, ignoring the protests of our utilitarians, proceeds anyway and redistributes these titles to property. Roe, Brown, and Robinson are *now* defined by the government as the proper and legal owners, while any claims to that property by the original trio of Smith, Jones, and Doe are considered improper and illegitimate, if not subversive. What now will be the reaction of our utilitarians?

It should be clear that since the utilitarians base their theory of justice in property only on *whatever the government defines* as legal, they can have no groundwork whatever for any call for restoring the property in question to its original owners. They can only, willy-nilly, and despite any emotional reluctance on their part, simply endorse the new allocation of property titles as defined and endorsed by government. Not only must utilitarians endorse the *status quo* of property titles, they must endorse whatever *status quo* exists and however rapidly the government decides to shift and redistribute such titles. Furthermore, considering the historical record, we may indeed say that relying upon government to be the guardian of property rights is like placing the proverbial fox on guard over the chicken coop.

We see, therefore, that the supposed defense of the free market and of property rights by utilitarians and free-market economists is a very weak reed indeed. Lacking a theory of justice that goes beyond the existing *imprimatur* of government, utilitarians can only go along with every change and shift of government allocation after the occur, no matter how arbitrary, rapid, or politically motivated such shifts might be. And since they provide no firm roadblock for governmental reallocations of property, the utilitarians, in the final analysis, can offer no real defense of property rights themselves. Since governmental redefinitions can and will be rapid and arbitrary, they cannot provide long-run certainty for property rights, and therefore they cannot even ensure the very social and economic efficiency which they themselves seek.[4] All this is implied in the pronouncements of utilitarians that any future free society must confine itself to whatever definitions of property titles the government may happen to be endorsing at that moment.

Let us consider a hypothetical example of the failure of utilitarian defense of private property. Suppose that somehow government becomes persuaded of the necessity to yield to a clamor for a free-market, *laissez-faire* society. Before dissolving itself, however, it redistributes property titles: granting the owernship of the entire territory of New York to the Rockefeller family, of Massachusetts to the Kennedy family, etc. It then dissolves, ending taxation and all other forms of government intervention in the economy. However, while taxation has been abolished, the Rockefeller, Kennedy, etc., families proceed to dictate to all the residents in what is now "their" territory, exacting what are now called "rents" over all the inhabitants.[5] It seems clear that our utilitarians could have no intellectual armor with which to challenge this new dispensation; indeed, they would have to endorse the Rockefeller, Kennedy, etc., holdings as "private property" equally deserving of support as the ordinary property titles which they had endorsed only a few months previously. All this because the utilitarians have no theory of justice in property beyond endorsement of whatever *status quo* happens to exist.

Consider, furthermore, the grotesque box in which the utilitarian proponent of freedom places himself in relation to the institution of human slavery. Contemplating that institution and the "free" market that once existed in buying, selling, and renting slaves, the utilitarian who must rely on the legal definition of property can only endorse slavery on the ground that the slave masters had purchased their slave titles legally and in good faith. Surely, any endorsement of a "free" market in slaves indicates the inadequacy of utilitarian concepts of property and the need for a theory of justice to provide a groundwork for property rights and a critique of existing official titles to property.

II. Toward a Theory of Justice in Property

We conclude that utilitarianism cannot be supported as a groundwork for property rights or, *a fortiori*, for the free-market economy. A theory of justice must be arrived at which goes beyond government allocations of property titles and which can therefore serve as a basis for criticizing such allocations. Obviously, in this space I can only outline what I consider to be the correct theory of justice in property rights. This theory has two fundamental premises: (a) the absolute property right of each individual in his own person, his own body: this may be called the *right of self-ownership;* and (b) the absolute right in material property of the person who first finds an unused material resource and then in some way occupies or transforms that resource by the use of his personal energy. This might be called the *homestead principle*—the case in which someone, in the phrase of John Locke, has "mixed his labour" with an unused resource. Let Locke summarize these principles:

> ...every man has a *property* in his own *person*. This nobody has any right to but himself. The *labour* of his body and the *work* of his hands, we may say, are properly his. Whatsoever, then, he removes out of the state that nature hath provided and left it in, he hath mixed his labour with it, and joined to it something that is his own, and thereby makes it his property. It being by him removed from the common state nature placed it in, it hath by this labour something annexed to it that excludes the common right of other men.[6]

Let us consider the first principle: the right to self-ownership. This principle asserts the absolute right of each man, by virtue of his (or her) being a human being, to "own" his own body; that is, to control that body free of coercive interference. Since the nature of man is such that each individual must use his mind to learn about himself and the world, to select values, and to choose ends and means in order to survive and flourish, the right to self-ownership gives each man the right to perform these vital activities without being hampered and restricted by coercive molestation.

Consider, then, the alternatives—the consequences of *denying* each man the right to own his own person. There are only two alternatives: either (1) a certain class of people, A, have the right to own another class, B; or (2) everyone has the right to own his equal quotal share of everyone else. The first alternative implies that while Class A deserves the rights of being human, Class B is in reality subhuman and therefore deserves no such rights. But since they *are* indeed human beings, the first alternative contradicts itself in denying natural human rights to one set of humans. Moreover, allowing Class A to own Class B means that the former is allowed to exploit, and therefore to live parasitically, at the expense of the latter; but, as economics can tell us, this parasitism itself violates the basic economic requirement for human survival: production and exchange.

The second alternative, which we might call "participatory communalism" or "communism," holds that every man should have the right to own his equal quotal share of everyone else. If there are three billion people in the world, then everyone has the right to own a three-billionth of every other person. In the first place, this ideal itself rests upon an absurdity: proclaiming that every man is entitled to own a part of everyone else and yet is not entitled to *own himself*. Secondly, we can picture the viability of such a world: a world in which *no* man is free to take any action whatever without prior approval or indeed command by *everyone else* in society. It should be clear that in that sort of "communist" world, no one would be able to do anything, and the human race would quickly perish. But if a world of zero self-ownership and 100 percent other-ownership spells death for the human race, then any steps in that direction also contravene the natural law of what is best for man and his life on earth.

Finally, however, the participatory communist world *cannot* be put into practice. For it is physically impossible for everyone to keep continual tabs on everyone else and thereby to exercise his equal quotal share of partial ownership over every other man. In practice, then, any attempt to institute universal and equal other-ownership is utopian and impossible, and supervision, and therefore control and ownership of others, would necessarily devolve upon a specialized group of people, who would thereby become a "ruling class." Hence, in practice, any attempt at communist society will automatically become class rule, and we would be back at our rejected first alternative.

We conclude, then, with the premise of absolute universal right of self-ownership as our first principle of justice in property. This principle, of course, automatically rejects slavery as totally incompatible with our primary right.[7]

Let us now turn to the more complex case of property in material objects. For even if every man has the right to self-ownership, people are not floating wraiths; they are not self-subsistent entities; they can only survive and flourish by grappling with the earth around them. They must, for example, *stand* on land areas; they must also, in order to survive, transform the resources given by nature into "consumer goods," into objects more suitable for their use and consumption. Food must be grown and eaten; minerals must be mined and then transformed into capital and finally into useful consumer goods, etc. Man, in other words, must own not only his own person, but also material objects for his control and use. How, then, should property titles in these objects be allocated?

Let us consider, as our first example, the case of a sculptor fashioning a work of art out of clay and other materials; and let us simply assume for the moment that he owns these materials while waiving the question of the justification for their ownership. Let us examine the question: *who* should own the work of art, as it emerges from the sculptor's fashioning? The sculpture is, in fact, the sculptor's "creation," not in the sense that he has created matter *de novo*, but in the sense that he has transformed nature-given matter—the clay—into another form dictated by his own ideas and fashioned by his own hands and energy. Surely, it is a rare person who, with the case put thus, would say that the sculptor does *not* have the property right in his own product. For if every man has the right to his own body, and if he must grapple with the material objects of the world in order to survive, then the sculptor has the right to own the product which he has made, by his energy and effort, a veritable *extension* of his own personality. He has placed the stamp of his person upon the raw material, by "mixing his labor" with the clay.

As in the case of the ownership of people's bodies, we again have three logical alternatives: (1) either the transformer, the "creator," has the property right in his creation; or (2) another man or set of men have the right to appropriate it by force without the sculptor's consent; or (3) the "communal" solution—every individual in the world has an equal, quotal share in the ownership of the sculpture. Again, put badly, there are very few who would not concede the monstrous injustice of confiscating the sculptor's property, either by one or more others, or by the world as whole. For by what right do they do so? By what right do they appropriate to themselves the product of the creator's mind and energy? (Again, as in the case of bodies, any confiscation in the supposed name of the world as a whole would in practice devolve into an oligarchy of confiscators.)

But the case of the sculptor is not qualitatively different from *all* cases of "production." The man or men who extracted the clay from the ground and sold it to the sculptor were *also* "producers;" they too mixed their ideas and their energy and their technological knowhow with the nature-given material to emerge with a useful product. As producers, the sellers of the clay and of the sculptor's tools also mixed their labor with natural materials to transform them into more useful goods and services. All the producers are therefore entitled to the ownership of their product.

The chain of material production logically reduces back, then, back from consumer goods and works of art to the first producers who gathered or mined the nature-given soil and resources to use and transform them by means of their personal energy. And use of the soil logically reduces back to the legitimate ownership by first users of previously unowned, unused, virginal, nature-given resources. Let us again quote Locke:

> He that is nourished by the acorns he picked up under an oak, or the apples he gathered from the trees in the wood, has certainly appropriated them to himself. Nobody can deny but the nourishment is his. I ask then, when did they begin to be his? When he digested? or when he ate? or when he boiled? or when he brought them home? or when he picked them

up? And 'tis plain, if the first gathering made them not his, nothing else could. That labour put the distinction between them and common. That added something to them more than Nature, the common mother of all, had done, and so they became his private right. And will any one say he had no right to those acorns or apples he thus appropriated because he had not the consent of all mankind to make them his? Was it a robbery thus to assume to himself what belonged to all in common? If such a consent as that was necessary, man had starved, notwithstanding the plenty God had given him.... Thus, the grass my horse has bit, the turfs my servant has cut, and the ore I have digged in my place, where I have a right to them in common with others, become my property without the assignation or consent of any body. The labour that was mine, removing them out of that common state they were in, hath fixed my property in them.[8]

If every man owns his own person and therefore his own labor, and if by extension he owns whatever material property he has "created" or gathered out of the previously unused, unowned "state of nature," then what of the logically final question: who has the right to own or control the earth *itself?* In short, if the gatherer has the right to own the acorns or berries he picks, or the farmer the right to own his crop of wheat or peaches, *who* has the right to own the land on which these things have grown? It is at this point that Henry George and his followers, who would have gone all the way so far with our analysis, leave the track and deny the individual's right to own the piece of land itself, the ground on which these activities have taken place. The Georgists argue that, while every man should own the goods which he produces or creates, since Nature or God created the land itself, no individual has the right to assume ownership of that land. Yet again we are faced with our three logical alternatives: either the land itself belongs to the pioneer, the first user, the man who first brings it into production; *or* it belongs to a group of others; *or* it belongs to the world as a whole, with every individual owning an equal quotal part of every acre of land. George's option for the last solution hardly solves his moral problem: for if the land itself should belong to God or Nature, then why is it more moral for every acre in the world to be owned by the world as a whole, than to concede individual ownership? In practice, again, it is obviously impossible for every person in the world to exercise his ownership of his three-billionth portion of every acre of the world's surface; in practice a small oligarchy would do the controlling and owning rather than the world as a whole.

But apart from those difficulties in the Georgist position, our proposed justification for the ownership of ground land is the same as the justification for the original ownership of all other property. For, as we have indicated, no producer *really* "creates" matter; he takes nature-given matter and transforms it by his personal energy in accordance with his ideas and his vision. But *this* is precisely what the pioneer—the "homesteader"—does when he brings previously unused land into his private ownership. Just as the man who makes steel out of iron and transforms that ore out of his know how and with his energy, and just as the man who takes the iron out of the ground does the same, so too does the homesteader who clears, fences, cultivates or builds upon the land. The homesteader, too, has transformed the character and usefulness of the nature-given soil by his labor and his personality. The homesteader is just as legitimately the owner of the property as the sculptor or the manufacturer; he is just as much a "producer" as the others.

Moreover, if the producer is *not* entitled to the fruits of his labor, who is? It is difficult to see why a newborn Pakistani baby should have a moral claim to a quotal share of ownership of a piece of Iowa land that someone has just transformed into a wheatfield—and vice versa of course for an Iowan baby and a Pakistani farm. Land in its original state is unused and unowned. Georgists and other land communalists may claim that the entire world population "really" owns it, but if no one has yet used it, it is in the real sense owned and controlled by no one. The pioneer, the homesteader, the first user and transformer of this land, is the man who first brings this simple valueless thing into production and use. It is difficult to see the justice of depriving him of ownership in favor of people who have never gotten within a thousand miles of the land and who may not even know of the existence of the property over which they are supposed to have a claim. It is even more difficult to see the justice of a group of outside oligarchs owning the property, and at the expense of expropriating the creator or the homesteader who had originally brought the product into existence.

Finally, no one can produce *anything* without the cooperation of ground land, if only to be used as standing room. No man can produce or create anything by his labor alone; he must have the cooperation of land and other natural raw material. Man comes into the world with just himself and the world around him—the land and natural resources given him by nature. He takes these resources and transforms them by his labor and mind and energy into goods more useful to man. Therefore, if an individual cannot own original land, neither can he in the full sense own any of the fruits of his labor. Now that this labor has been inextricably mixed with the land, he cannot be deprived of one without being deprived of the other.

The moral issue involved here is even clearer if we consider the case of animals. Animals are "economic land," since they are original nature-given resources. Yet will anyone deny full title to a horse to the man who finds and domesticates it? This is no different from the acorns and berries which are generally conceded to the gatherer. Yet in land, too, the homesteader takes the previously wild, undomesticated land, and tames it by putting it to productive use. Mixing his labor with land sites should give him just as clear a title as in the case of animals.

From our two basic axioms: the right of every man to self-ownership; and the right of every man to own previously unused natural resources that he first appropriates or transforms by his labor—the entire system of justification for property rights can be deduced. For if anyone justly owns the land himself and the property which he finds and creates, then he of course has the right to exchange that property for the similarly acquired just property of someone else. This establishes the right of free exchange of property, as well as the right to give one's property away to someone who agrees to receive it. Thus, X may own his person and labor and the farm he clears on which he grows wheat; Y owns the fish he catches; Z owns the cabbages he grows and the land under it. But then X has the right to exchange some of his wheat for some of Y's fish (if Y agrees) or Z's cabbages. And when X and Y make a voluntary agreement to exchange wheat for fish, then that fish becomes X's justly acquired property to do with what he wishes, and the wheat becomes Y's just property in precisely the same way. Further, a man may of course exchange not only the tangible objects he owns but also his own labor, which of course he owns as well. Thus, Z may sell his labor services of teaching farmer X's children in return for some of the farmer's produce.

We have thus established the property-right justification for the free-market process. For the free-market economy, as complex as the system appears to be on the surface, is yet nothing more than a vast network of voluntary and mutually agreed upon two-person or two-party exchanges of property titles, such as we have seen occurs between wheat and cabbage farmers, or between the farmer and the teacher. In the developed free-market economy, the farmer exchanges his wheat for money; the wheat is bought by the miller who processes and transforms the wheat into flour; the baker sells the bread to the wholesaler, who in turn sells it to the retailer, who finally sells it to the consumer. In the case of the sculptor, he buys the clay and the tools from the producers who dug the clay out of the ground or those who bought the clay from the original miners; and he bought his tools from the manufacturers who in turn purchased the raw material from the miners of iron ore.

How "money" enters the equation is a complex process; but it should be clear here that conceptually the use of money is equivalent to any useful commodity that is exchanged for wheat, flour, etc. Instead of money, the commodity exchanged could be cloth, iron or whatever. At each step of the way, mutually beneficial exchanges of property titles—to goods, services, or money—are agreed upon and transacted.

And what of the capital-labor relationship? Here, too, as in the case of the teacher selling his services to the farmer, the laborer sells his services to the manufacturer who has purchased the iron ore or to the shipper who has bought logs from the loggers. The capitalist performs the function of saving money to buy the raw material, and then pays the laborers in advance of sale of the product to the eventual customers.

Many people, including such utilitarian free-market advocates as John Stuart Mill, have been willing to concede the propriety and the justice (if they are not utilitarians) of the producer owning and earning the fruits of his labor. But they balk at one point: inheritance. If Roberto Clemente is ten times as good and "productive" a ballplayer as Joe Smith, they are willing to concede the justice of Clemente's earning ten times the amount; but what, they ask, is the justification for someone whose only merit is being born a Rockefeller inheriting far more wealth than someone born a Rothbard?

There are several answers that could be given to this question: for example, the natural fact that every individual must, of necessity, be born into a different condition, at a different time or place, and to different parents. Equality of birth or rearing, therefore, is an impossible chimera. But in the context of our theory of justice in property rights, the answer is to focus *not* on the recipient, not on the child Rockefeller or the child Rothbard, but to concentrate on the *giver*, the man who bestows the inheritance. For if Smith and Jones and Clemente have the right to their labor and their property and to exchange the titles to this property for the similarly obtained property of others, then they *also* have the right to give their property to whomever they wish. The point is not the right of "inheritance" but the right of *bequest*, a right which derives from the title to property itself. If Roberto Clemente owns his labor and the money he earns from it, then he has the right to give that money to the baby Clemente.

Armed with a theory of justice in property rights, let us now apply it to the often vexing question of how we should regard existing titles to property.

III. Toward a Critique of Existing Property Titles

Among those who call for the adoption of a free market and a free society, the utilitarians, as might be expected, wish to validate all existing property titles, as so defined by the government. But we have seen the inadequacy of this position, most clearly in the case of slavery, but similarly in the validation that it gives to *any* acts of governmental confiscation or redistribution, including our hypothetical Kennedy and Rockefeller "private" ownership of the territorial area of a state. But how much of a redistribution from existing titles would be implied by the adoption of our theory of justice in property, or of any attempt to put that theory into practice? Isn't it true, as some people charge, that all existing property titles, or at least all land titles, were the result of government grants and coercive redistribution? Would *all* property titles therefore be confiscated in the name of justice? And who would be granted these titles?

Let us first take the easiest case: where existing property has been stolen, as acknowledged by the government (and therefore by utilitarians) as well as by our theory of justice. In short, suppose that Smith has stolen a watch from Jones; in that case, there is no difficulty in calling upon Smith to relinquish the watch and to give it back to the true owner, Jones. But what of more difficult cases—in short, where existing property titles are ratified by state confiscation of a previous victim? This could apply either to money or especially to land titles, since land is a constant, identifiable, fixed quotal share of the earth's surface.

Suppose, first, for example, that the government has either taken land or money from Jones by coercion (either by taxation or its imposed redefinition of property) and has granted the land to Smith, or alternatively, has ratified Smith's direct act of confiscation. What would our policy of justice say then? We would say, along with the general view of crime, that the aggressor and unjust owner, Smith, must be made to disgorge the property title (either land or money) and give it over to its true owner, Jones. Thus, in the case of an identifiable unjust owner and the identifiable victim or just owner, the case is clear: a restoration to the victim of his rightful property. Smith, of course, must not be compensated for this restitution, since compensation would either be enforced unjustly on the victim himself or on the general body of taxpayers. Indeed, there is a far better case for the additional punishment of Smith, but there is no space here to develop the theory or punishment for crime or aggression.

Suppose, next, a second case, in which Smith has stolen a piece of land from Jones but that Jones has died; he leaves, however, an heir, Jones II. In that case, we proceed as before; there is still the identifiable aggressor, Smith, and the identifiable heir of the victim, Jones II, who now is the inherited just owner of the title. Again, Smith must be made to disgorge the land and turn it over to Jones II.

But suppose, a third, more difficult case; Smith is still the thief, but Jones and his entire family and heirs have been wiped out, either by Smith himself or in the natural course of events. Jones is intestate; what then should happen to the property? The first principle is that Smith, being the thief, cannot keep the fruits of his aggression; but in that case, the property becomes unowned and becomes up for grabs in the same way as any piece of unowned property. The "homestead principle" becomes applicable, in the sense that the first user or occupier of the newly declared unowned property becomes the just and proper owner. The only stipulation is that Smith himself, being the thief, is not eligible for this homesteading.[9]

Suppose now a fourth case, and one generally more relevant to problems of land title in the modern world. Smith is not a thief, nor has he directly received the land by government grant; but his *title* is derived from his ancestor who *did* so unjustly appropriate title to the property; the ancestor, Smith I, let us say, stole the property from Jones I, the rightful owner. What should be the disposition of the property now? The answer, in our view, completely depends on whether or not Jones' heirs, the surrogates of the identifiable victims, still exist. Suppose, for example, that Smith VI legally "owns" the land, but that Jones VI is still extant and identifiable. Then we would have to say that, while Smith VI himself is not a thief and not punishable as such, his *title* to the land, being solely derived from inheritance passed down from Smith I, does not give him true ownership, and that he too must disgorge the land—without compensation—and yield it into the hands of Jones VI.

But, it might protested, what of the improvements that Smiths II-VI may have added to the land? Doesn't Smith VI deserve compensation for these legitimately owned additions to the original land received from Jones I? The answer depends on the moveability or separability of these improvements. Suppose, for example, that Smith steals a car from Jones and sells it to Robinson. When the car is apprehended, then Robinson, though he purchased it in good faith from Jones, has no title better than Smith's which was nil, and therefore he must yield up the car to Jones without compensation. (He has been defrauded by Smith and must try to extract compensation out of Smith, *not* out of the victim Jones.) But suppose that Robinson, in the meantime, has improved the car? The answer depends on whether these improvements are separable from the car itself. If, for example, Robinson has installed a new radio which did not exist before, then he should certainly have the right to take it out before handing the car back to Jones. Similarly, in the case of land, to the extent that Smith VI has simply improved the land itself and mixed his resources inextricably with it, there is nothing he can do; but if, for example, Smith VI or his ancestors built new buildings upon the land, then he should have the right to demolish or cart away these buildings before handing the land over to Jones VI.

But what if Smith I did indeed steal the land from Jones I, but that all of Jones' descendants or heirs are lost in antiquity and cannot be found? What should be the status of the land then? In that case, since Smith VI is not himself a thief, he becomes the *legitimate* owner of the land on the basis of our homestead principle. For if the land is "unowned" and up for grabs, then Smith VI himself has been occupying and using it, and therefore he becomes the just and rightful owner on the homestead basis. Furthermore, all of his descendants have clear and proper title on the basis of being his heirs.

It is clear, then, that *even* if we can show that the origin of most existing land titles are in coercion and theft, the existing owners are still just and legitimate owners if (a) they themselves did not engage in aggression, and (b) if no identifiable heirs of the original victims can be found. In most cases of current land title this will probably be the case. *A fortiori*, of course, if we simply *don't know* whether the original land titles were acquired by coercion, then our homestead principle gives the current property owners the benefit of the doubt and establishes them as just and proper owners as well. Thus, the establishment of our theory of justice in property titles will not usually lead to a wholesale turnover of landed property.

In the United States, we have been fortunate enough to have largely escaped continuing aggression in land titles. It is true that originally the English Crown gave land titles unjustly to favored persons (e.g., the territory roughly of New York State to the ownership of the Duke of York), but fortunately these grantees were interested enough in quick returns to subdivide and sell their lands to the actual settlers. As soon as the settlers purchased their land, their titles were legitimate, and so were the titles of all those who inherited or purchased them. Later on, the U.S. government unfortunately laid claim to all virgin land as the "public domain," and then unjustly sold the land to speculators who had not earned a homestead title. But eventually these speculators sold the land to the actual settlers, and from then on the land title was proper and legitimate.[10]

In South America and much of the undeveloped world, however, matters are considerably different. For here, in many areas, an invading state conquered the lands of peasants and then parcelled out such lands to various warlords as their private fiefs, from then on to extract rent from the hapless peasantry. The descendants of the *conquistadores* still presume to own the land tilled by the descendants of the original peasants, people with a clearly just claim to ownership of the land. In this situation, justice requires the vacating of the land titles by these feudal or coercive landholders, (who are in a position equivalent to our hypothetical Rockefellers and Kennedys) and the turning over of the property titles without compensation to the individual peasants who are the true owners of their land.

Much of the drive for "land reform" by the peasantry of the undeveloped world is precisely motivated by an instinctive application of our theory of justice: by the apprehension of the peasants that the land they have tilled for generations is *their* land and that the landlord's claim is coercive and unjust. It is ironic, that, in these numerous cases, the only response of utilitarian free-market advocates is to defend existing land titles, regardless of their injustice, and to tell the peasants to keep quiet and "respect private property." Since the peasants are convinced that the property is *their* private title, it is no wonder that they fail to be impressed; but since they find the supposed champions of property rights and free-market capitalism to be their staunch enemies, they generally are forced to turn to the only organized groups that at least rhetorically champion their claims and are willing to carry out the required rectification of property titles—the socialists and communists. In short, from simply a utilitarian consideration of consequences, the utilitarian free-marketeers have done very badly in the undeveloped world, the result of their ignoring the fact that others than themselves, however inconveniently, *do* have a passion for justice. Of course, after socialists or communists take power, they do their best to collectivize peasant land, and one of the prime struggles of socialist society is that of the state *versus* the peasantry. But even those peasants who are aware of socialists duplicity on the land question may still feel that with the socialists and communists they *at least* have a fighting chance. And sometimes, of course, the peasants have been able to win and to force communist regimes to keep hands off their newly gained private property: notably in the cases of Poland and Yugoslavia.

The utilitarian defense of the *status quo* will then be *least* viable—and therefore the least utilitarian—in those situations where the *status quo* is the most glaringly unjust. As often happens, far more than utilitarians will admit, justice and genuine utility are here linked together.

To sum up: all existing property titles may be considered just under the homestead principle, *provided* (a) that there may never be any property in *people*; (b) that the existing property owner did not himself steal the property; and particularly (c) that any identifiable just owner (the original victim of theft or his heir) must be accorded his property.

It might be charged that our theory of justice in property titles is deficient because in the real world most landed (and even other) property has a past history so tangled that it becomes *impossible* to identify who or what has committed coercion and therefore who the current just owner may be. But the point of the "homestead principle" is that if we *don't know* what crimes have been committed in acquiring the property in the past, or if we don't know the victims or their heirs, then the current owner becomes the legitimate and just owner on homestead grounds. In short, if Jones owns a piece of land at the present time, and we don't know what crimes were committed to arrive at the current title, then Jones, as the current owner, becomes as fully legitimate a property owner of this land as he does over his own person. Overthrow of existing property title only becomes legitimate if the victims or their heirs can present an authenticated, demonstrable, and specific claim to the property. Failing such conditions, existing landowners possess a fully moral right to their property.

Notes

1. Economists failed to heed the emphasis on titles of ownership underlying exchange stressed by the social philosopher Spencer Heath. Thus: "Only those things which are *owned* can be exchanged or used as instruments of service or exchange. This exchange is not transportation; it is the transfer of ownership or title. This is a social and not a physical process." Spencer Heath, *Citadel, Market and Altar* (Baltimore: Science of Society Foundation, 1957), p. 48.

2. For a welcome recent emphasis on the subjectivity of cost, see James N. Buchanan, *Cost and Choice* (Chicago: Markham Pub. Co., 1969).

3. I do not mean to imply here that *no* social science of economic analysis can be *Wertfrei,* only that any attempt whatever to apply the analysis to the political arena, however remote, *must* involve and imply some sort of ethical position.

4. On the arbitrariness and uncertainty of all legislative law, see Bruno Leoni, *Freedom and the Law* (Los Angeles: Nash Pub. Co., 1972).

5.   The point here is not, of course, to criticize all rents *per se,* but rather to call into question the legitimacy of property titles (here landed property) derived from the coercive actions of government.

6.   John Locke, *An Essay Concerning the True, Original, Extent and End of Civil Government*, in E. Barker, ed., *Social Contract* (New York: Oxford University Press, 1948), pp. 17-18.

7.   Equally to be rejected is a grotesque proposal by Professor Kenneth E. Boulding, which however is a typical suggestion of a market-oriented utilitarian economist. This is a scheme for the government to allow only a certain maximum number of baby-permits per mother, but then to allow a "free" market in the purchase and sale of these baby rights. This plan, of course, denies the right of every mother over her own body. Boulding's plan may be found in Kenneth E. Boulding, *The Meaning of the 20th Century* (New York: Harper & Row, 1964). For a discussion of the plan, see Edwin G. Dolan, *TANSTAAFL: The Economic Strategy for Environmental Crisis* (New York: Holt, Rinehart & Winston, 1971), p. 64.

8.   Locke, *Civil Government*, p. 18.

9.   Neither is the government eligible. There is no space here to elaborate our view that government can never be the just owner of property. Suffice it to say here that the government gains its revenue from tax appropriation from production rather than from production itself, and hence that the concept of just property can never apply to government.

10.   This legitimacy, of course, does not apply to the vast amount of land in the West still owned by the federal government which it refuses to throw open to homesteading. Our response to this situation must be that the government should throw open all of its public domain to private homesteading without delay.

USE SIMPLE GUIDING PRINCIPLES

Michael Lissack and Johan Roos

The next common sense is about making simple rules interact to enable a coherent viewpoint to emerge, which will drive coherent actions.

"Only self-confident people can be simple," says Jack Welch. "Think about it. You get some engineer who is nervous and not too sure of himself. He can't explain his design to you in very simple terms, so he complicates it. If you're not simple you can't be fast, and if you're not fast you're dead in a global world. So everything we do [at GE] focuses on building self-confidence in people so they can be simple." Steve Case of AOL agrees when he says, "The essence of AOL is simplicity."

In the traditional "decision making is everything" business model, rules are used as a shortcut. In a complicated world, the trick was to cram more into less and to hide things that were uncomfortable. Rules provided a heuristic device so that thinking was less necessary and more time was available for deciding and acting. The intriguing thing about the old rules of business is that we succeeded in creating vast corporate empires in spite of them. Today's complexities did not happen overnight—weaving relations and dependencies takes time. Yet the old rules and their users carried on, oblivious.

Six Bad Rules

Let's look first at some of these traditional rules, or as we like to call them, six simple rules that lead to failure.

1. Treat business as if it were a war fought on a battlefield

This rule suggests that managers view business as a series of conflicts between companies in a market, between departments in a company, between groups in an organization, between individuals in a group and (by extension) between customers and vendors. What results? Managers build big empires and "armies" of employees to fight the war. Managers order the "troops" around, while the troops wait around for "marching orders." Customers become territory to be conquered rather than potential partners, and the competition is demonized into the "enemy."

2. View the corporation as a machine

This rule suggests that the corporation is a Rube Goldberg device in which employees are faceless cogs. Nobody is indispensable, and everybody is as replaceable as a spare part. Individual initiative, goals, and desires are completely subsumed by the demands of the corporate machine. What results? Managers create rigid organizations with rigid roles and rigid functions. Managers and workers alike become convinced that change is very difficult, similar to retooling a complicated machine. Managers are encouraged to think of themselves as "controllers" whose job it is to make sure that people follow the rules of the "system." Employees are treated in dehumanizing ways while the corporation centralizes control at the top.

3. Practice management as control

This rule suggests that the real job of the manager is to control employees' behaviors so that they do exactly what management wants them to do. Employees who disagree with a manager or refuse to do something are "insubordinate" and therefore dangerous. What results? Managers create organizations that can't adapt to new conditions because there are conflicting power structures, each of which is trying to "control" the corporation. Management gets involved in a supercharged political atmosphere where productive work becomes difficult. Individual initiative is killed in favor of a "let's wait and see what the boss says" mentality.

4. Treat your employees as children

This rule suggests that employees are too immature and foolish to be assigned real authority, and simply can't be trusted. If not restricted by complicated rules and regulations, they'll steal the company blind. What results? Employees develop a deep and abiding resentment toward management. They refuse to do anything until they're certain that they won't get blamed if something goes wrong. Employees spend more time "covering their butts" than doing productive work. Employees only work when they're being watched, if then.

5. To motivate, use fear

This rule suggests that employees only work because they're afraid of getting fired. Managers must therefore use the fear of getting fired, the fear of ridicule, or the fear of loss of privilege to motivate people. What results? Employees and managers alike become paralyzed, unable to make risky decisions or take courageous action. Work becomes a loathsome experience filled with truckling, ass-kissing, and compulsive corporate politicking.

6. Remember, change is nothing but pain

This rule suggests that managers and employees alike see change as complicated and difficult and something that companies only undergo if they're in desperate shape. What results? Reengineering, restructuring, and downsizing operations fail as people in the organization torpedo the change efforts to avoid the pain of change.

These rules don't allow for autonomy or for a context-dependent reaction to each situation. They do not allow room for interaction. And interaction is what the next common sense is all about.

Guiding Principles That Work

For a telling example of what the interaction of simple rules can achieve, consider Southwest Airlines. The airline began service in 1971 with flights to Houston, Dallas, and San Antonio. Southwest has grown to become the fourth largest US airline (in terms of domestic customers carried). It became a major airline in 1989 when it exceeded the billion-dollar revenue mark. What has made Southwest a success? Certainly, its strategy of being the shorthaul, low-fare, high-frequency, point-to-point carrier in its chosen markets has made a difference. But so too do the simple rules which Southwest transmits and expects of its employees: Trust, Interdependence, Genuineness, Empathy, Risk and Success.

Herb Kelleher, the chairman, says:

> We don't have many rules because I think that rules, in a lot of cases, are
> substitutes for management. Somebody wants a manual to hide behind instead of evaluating
> something on its merits. I've often advocated inconsistencies of corporate doctrine, and
> some people are astounded to hear that . . . Somebody's got to have the power to say, hey
> stop, whoa, this person is being ground up in the mills of the gods, and the mills weren't
> intended to grind this piece of grain. So we're not going to slavishly follow our remorseless
> rules.

The key to Southwest's policy is that if someone does make a judgment call, management gives
them full support, because they consider the person making the decision the expert in that situation.
Take the notion of hierarchy. Herb says:

> Avoid hierarchy to achieve productivity. A hierarchical organization breeds the
> idea that some people are superior to others because of their title and position alone. And I
> think most of us have known some pretty dumb rich people, and some pretty smart people
> who weren't rich—some pretty dishonest pillars of the church and some pretty honest
> gamblers. My only point is that title and position alone signify nothing about what you
> really are or what you're really worth.

If there is one word around which Southwest coheres it is family. Family does not tell the airline
where to fly next or what to charge, but it guides every employee's day-to-day understanding of
what it means to be part of the Southwest team. Treating people right is central to Southwest's
philosophy. For this reason, the company is renowned for taking special care to get to know those it
employs. Kelleher knows an astonishing percentage of his 12,000 employees' names, and can
recount details of past conversations—frequently asking about children, spouses or outside
interests.

Southwest values this caring attitude, as this classic quote from Herb illustrates:

> We want people who are "other" oriented. We don't want people who like to sit
> around and study their navel, no matter how pretty and lint free it may be.

Southwest coheres around family. Your firm may cohere around some other key value. The
important thing is to have some internalized notion among your team around which they cohere.

Why Simple Rules?

Where did all this emphasis on simple rules come from? After all, we live in a world that appears complex on the surface. The answer lies in a computer model—a model that one Craig Reynolds built in 1986. Craig wondered how birds and fish are able to travel in large groups and act as one unit. A flock of hundreds of birds can speed up in one direction, then suddenly, in unison, decrease their velocity and turn to follow a different route. No matter how complicated their acrobatic path, the birds always stay close together but never collide. Are they following a leader?

Many species of fish actually spend their entire lives in schools from the moment they are born. Schools are important. When fish travel as a school, it is more difficult for a predator to single out one fish to attack. Schools also allow the fish to find food more easily, and some species of fish travel in schools in order to protect an area that they have claimed for their own.

To quote Reynolds himself:

> In 1986 I made a computer model of coordinated animal motion such as bird flocks and fish schools. It was based on three dimensional computational geometry of the sort normally used in computer animation or computer aided design. I called the software boids. Each boid has direct access to the whole scene's geometric description, but reacts only to flockmates within a certain small radius of itself. The basic flocking model consists of three simple steering behaviors:
>
> 1 Separation: steer to avoid crowding local flockmates.
> 2 Alignment: steer towards the average heading of local flockmates.
> 3 Cohesion: steer to move toward the average position of local flockmates.
>
> In addition, the more elaborate behavioral model included predictive obstacle avoidance and goal seeking. Obstacle avoidance allowed the boids to fly through simulated environments while dodging static objects. For applications in computer animation, a low priority goal seeking behavior caused the flock to follow a scripted path.

Richard Dawkins in *The Selfish Gene* proposed that pack behavior follows the same rules as those of boids. A simple strategy for a predator is to chase the closest prey in its vicinity. This is in order to reduce the amount of energy that it must expend. The strategy for the prey is to keep as far away from its predators as possible. If predators only attack the closest prey, then all of the others should be safe. Each prey can be considered to have a "domain of danger" surrounding it. A lone individual would have a rather large domain of danger, while each individual in a pack would have a small domain of danger around it. The strategy of the prey then is to reduce its domain of danger as much as possible. This is accomplished by creating a pack, where each individual tries to reduce their own domain of danger. But, because those on the edges of the pack have a larger domain of danger than those in the center of the pack, those on the edges try to move inward, thus pushing those on the inside outward.

Simple rules could lead to complex behavior. This much seemed true. But most of the observers overlooked two critical details in Reynolds' description: the model is spatial with a predefined area and he used a "low priority goal seeking behavior" as an input. Leaving out these details leads to promising beginnings but problems in follow through.

The model as a whole—**simple rules interacting within a defined area starting with some goals**—has great promise. So instead of giving you more stories of how to program software creatures on your PC (unless you want a screensaver), we will discuss how to make sense of this model in your business. With luck, it will provide some vital insights.

Great Words—What Do They Mean?

Let's start with the word "rules." In designing boids, Reynolds did not mean to imply that we all must be like children at a military camp. Rules are not to be construed in the "this is allowed, but this other is forbidden" sense. Reynolds was not even talking about computer-type rules—the "if x, then y" of which programmers are so proud. The concept of rules in this instance is more a set of "guiding principles."

To us, the key aspect of rules in Reynolds' sense is that they are totally internalized and have become tacit. For example, "steer to avoid crowding" is a description of behavior as much as it is a prescription of "do this." The boid has internalized the rule and the rule has become part of the boid. They are now inseparable.

Notice that Reynolds used the word "cohesion" for his third rule. Cohesion, as in sticking together, is not only a rule for the flock as a whole, but also for each individual boid. Again, the rule is internalized. Every boid seeks to "cohere." As we prefer to put it: in human organizations, "coherence" is important to the individuals and the group; so too with boids.

Boids use rules that are "simple." As the opposite of complex, this word has a power well beyond its six letters. Notice that the rules are not in an "if, then" format. If they were in such a format, the rules would either have to be nearly infinite in number or infinite in length. How can we possibly describe enough if, thens to tell us (or boids) what to do in every possible situation?

The rule "steer to avoid crowding" does not say "when three other items are within two feet do x." Instead, the rule allows the boid a huge range of autonomy. The principle "avoid crowding" is made part of the boid. The "how" of "steering" is also part of the boid, but the interactions between the goal "avoid crowding," the how of "steering" and any other set of goals and hows which may also be part of the boid are left unspecified. This is the key to simple rules—**underspecify** to allow for autonomy and for a context-dependent reaction to every situation encountered. In the underspecification of a rule lies space for evolution, change, and that complexity word, emergence. Simple rules say something about principles for action but do not specify when to apply the principle, or to what extent, or which principles override any other.

Rules in Organizations

Someone once said that the lowest form of a civilized society is one based on the rule of law. Others have suggested that the more rules there are, the less trust there is in the organization. We agree with this, with a caveat. The only time an organization can exist without rules or laws is when complete virtue exists in each of the organization's members. Until that point comes, rules and laws must create a structure of trust and justice. Richard Epstein, in his *Simple Rules for a Complex World,* put it: "government works best when it establishes the rules of the road, not when it seeks to determine the composition of the traffic." In corporate settings, this translates into the idea that managers cannot micromanage all the time without really causing problems. The workers must internalize a few guiding principles and be allowed to get on with their job.

One consultant we know developed a list of rules that he thought would get good results in management if earnestly applied:

1   Attempt to give a lot of credit to the people around you.
2   Attempt to convince the people who work for you that you truly care about their future.
3   Attempt to give your organization clear goals and achievable objectives.

Are these rules simple? We don't think so. The concepts are not quite at the level of guiding principles, and the behavior does not quite get internalized. Notice that each of our friend's rules starts with the word "attempt." Reynolds didn't program the boids with "attempt." He gave them guiding principles and let them carry on.

So let's try a different friend's list:

1   Trust.
2   Respect.
3   Work towards a common goal.
4   Live in harmony.
5   Demand excellence.
6   Work hard.
7   Maintain perspective.
8   Come through.

These are simple. But the behavior they imply is complex. And they follow Reynolds' model. Underspecified to an extreme, they are probably useless if considered by themselves. Their power is in their interaction.

If a rule is to be an internalized guiding principle, it must be exhibited in behavior. Each of us has our own set of internal rules. Those who know us very well may be able to explicate for us what those rules are, but to relative strangers (including most of the people with whom we interact in the course of doing our work) such knowledge is hidden. If we want to build on the model of a flock of birds, a herd of sheep, or a school of fish, we must take into account the "others" with whom we interact. For all of us in the "flock" to be moving in the same direction, we need to be aware of the simple rules we all are following. So "making" the rules consists in articulating them for the awareness of the others with whom we will interact.

Simple rules work by interaction among numbers (be they of boids, sheep, or people). Complicated formulations of "if, thens" are great for a legal manual, but poor for trying to get a group to act. Action is the name of the game. Organizations are not the legal code expounded by the corporate office and memorialized in the 20-page memos that seem to come down from on high every week or so. **Instead, they are the day-to-day actions of the members of the network—employees, customers, suppliers, partners—doing something.** Simple rules are "made" by allowing those concerned to be aware of them. It does not have to be in words—international road signs work fine in their context—but it does have to be communicated.

Peter Scott-Morgan, in *The Unwritten Rules of the Game*, notes:

> You encourage people to act in a new way as a means to an end of achieving what is important to them. As they find that the new behavior is valuable in its own right, so the transition is consolidated. Yet the speed of change is far faster than if you only try to

encourage people to behave in the new way by attempting to convince them that the behavior is worthwhile in its own right. Try that and they may simply not agree with you.

Waving a sales sign in a parking lot, shouting about how nicely it is worded or the high quality of the reflective paint on its surface, will not encourage shoppers to leave spaces for the handicapped or for pregnant mothers. Giving them a reason to internalize the behavior pattern (perhaps by showing some poor soul struggling to make their way through an icy lot in a wheelchair while having to play dodgems with the oncoming cars) will not only get the job done but will help it to last for a long time.

Simple Rules Lead to Meaning Only Through Interaction

What is the "key value added" of Federal Express? As it tells us in commercials, "when it absolutely has to be there overnight." This is a simple rule, but its meaning comes from interaction with other rules.

For example, FedEx could not use the word "absolutely" without both engendering a relationship of trust and asking the same of the customer. Why is the FedEx tracking system so important? Because it allows the customer, if they doubt that trusting relationship, a means of checking up on what FedEx is doing. Respect also enters the picture by means of the Internet interface, which allows the customer **acting on their own** to enter FedEx's computer system and check on a package. The customer does not need to ask for assistance, their privacy is respected, and they are viewed as being able to handle the task. Sure, FedEx was able to save a lot of money because it no longer needed as many operators to handle tracking questions, but the gains it made in its customers' perspective of the company were just as important. The interaction of "get it there overnight," "trust," and "respect" has created a meaningful space in which FedEx and its customers interact.

The *Wall Street Journal's* Tom Petzinger wrote about this kind of interaction within a Lucent Technologies factory:

Lucent employs no formulas or fixed methods here; constant change is the only constant. But a few simple principles were evident during my visit.

1 Hire attitude over aptitude.
2 Create mission from above, methods from below.
3 Foster feedback.
4 Unite the inside and the outside.
5 Reward teamwork.

Though management establishes the mission, workers fulfill it. "If I give you an endgame," Ms. Mercer [the plant manager] says, "you can find your way there." Teams continually alter the manufacturing process and even the product design itself. A senior engineer named David Therrien, who compiled the original assembly procedures, no longer recognizes them. "My instructions were nothing but a starting place," he says . . . The plant follows a one-page list of working principles—not some vague mission statement in a wooden frame, but a contract signed by every employee committing them to speed, innovation, candor, deep respect for colleagues and other plainly stated goals. People cite the document as if it were the Bill of Rights.

And indeed, America's founding fathers treated the Bill of Rights in just this way—as a set of simple rules (guiding principles) that would interact to help shape a new society. It is not that the Bill of Rights is not a complex legal document—it is—but that people tend to internalize it as a quick set of guiding ideals: freedom of the press, freedom of speech, right of assembly etc. Most Americans are not aware of the section of the Bill of Rights which speaks of bills of attainder or habeas corpus or writs of mandamus—those parts are just not relevant to the day-to-day actions on which our attention gets focused.

At Petzinger's example of the Lucent plant, the results of simple rules being allowed to interact are striking:

> In the brutal global market for digital cellular base stations, high speed and low cost are everything. So how does this self-directed work force of 480 stack up? In two years it hasn't missed a single delivery deadline. And total labor costs represent an exceedingly low 3% of product cost . . . "We solve problems in hallways rather than conference rooms," says production manager Steve Sherman. The process is so fluid that none of the manufacturing equipment is bolted to the floor . . . "This business has been handed to us," says technician Tom Guggiari. "This business is ours."

Interaction Happens in Context

Recall that Reynolds' boids operate in the space of his personal computer. The Lucent folk are operating within the context not only of their factory but also within a broad network of customers, suppliers, partners and the local community. Context drives how the rules come together and interact. The reason for underspecifying rules is to allow the context to drive what happens.

We will come back to this point again and again. Its general name is "**situatedness**." Things happen, people interact, and the relevant part of the environment changes within some context which describes the situation. It is important to remember that while rules may be abstract, situations are not. People care about things that happen, events that occur, and actions that take place; not about steering a boid five degrees to the left in cyberspace.

Knowledge, models, and expertise are co-created by thinking people working in and with their environment. Since that environment is different for every organization, it doesn't work to take something that has been developed in one place and just transfer it wholesale to another place. Consultants and managers have tried that with program after program (BPR, TQM, zero-based budgeting, scenario planning, and the learning organization) and, as a result, have generated a well-earned cynicism among the nation's workforce as it watches these programs come and go without creating the desired change. Today's manager needs something different, something that will engage the whole system of the organization in figuring out what makes sense for that particular system. The answers, the expertise, need to be created by the context that is in need of that expertise. Don't take something that's "tried and true" and apply it in cookie-cutter fashion. If you are to make knowledge work for you, it must be knowledge that is appropriate to the situation and context and not what some book (even ours) recommends.

How do you motivate people? You don't. Instead, you trust that they come with their own desire to thrive. They will make adjustments and do what is necessary for them to flourish. In an organization, you don't have to "incentivize" anybody. You have to create the conditions under which they can thrive, i.e. context. Among the things that human beings naturally seek are the ability to contribute and to make a difference, and the ability to be involved in satisfying social relationships. If you design your organization around these criteria, it will have to be one in which people are not boxed into roles and rules (trapped into inappropriate contexts). The right context is one in which they feel that they can continue to grow, learn, and develop, and in which a variety of relationships are available to them.

Guidelines for Using Simple Guiding Principles

The next common sense is about making simple rules interact to enable a coherent viewpoint. Where the old common sense was about dealing with local situations and trying to "sort things out," the next common sense is about adopting a global viewpoint, allowing interactions to happen, which in turn will drive coherent actions.

- Always ground your guiding principles in values.

- Ensure that these guiding principles are aligned with the purpose, identity and values of individuals and those of the organization as a whole. Don't just cite guiding principles or hang them in a nice wooden frame. The guiding principles must encourage people to act in a certain way as a means to the end of achieving what is important to them. As people find that the new behavior is valuable in its own right and aligned with their values, these principles will be internalized in day-to-day actions.

- Use only guiding principles that are allowed to interact, like these two: "management sets the goal, workers fulfill it," and "reward teamwork." Underspecified guiding principles, like "work hard," are useless. Overspecification, like "if . . ., then . . ." makes guiding principles equally useless.

Management Principles

	Next common sense	Old common sense
The world	Complex	Complicated
Management	Guiding interactions	Leading entities
Simple principles	Adopting a global viewpoint, allowing interactions to happen	Dealing with local situations and trying to "sort things out"

'SOCIAL' OR DISTRIBUTIVE JUSTICE

Friedrich A. Hayek

> So great is the uncertainty of merit, both from its natural obscurity, and from the self-conceit of each individual, that no determinate rule of conduct could ever follow from it.
>
> *—David Hume**

> Welfare, however, has no principle, neither for him who receives it, nor for him who distributes it (one will place it here and another there); because it depends on the material content of the will, which is dependent upon particular facts and thereby incapable of a general rule.
>
> *—Immanuel Kant**

The Concept of 'Social Justice'

While in the preceding chapter I had to defend the conception of justice as the indispensable foundation and limitation of all law, I must now turn against an abuse of the word which threatens to destroy the conception of law which made it the safeguard of individual freedom. It is perhaps not surprising that men should have applied to the joint effects of the actions of many people, even where these were never foreseen or intended, the conception of justice which they had developed with respect to the conduct of individuals towards each other. 'Social' justice (or sometimes 'economic' justice) came to be regarded as an attribute which the 'actions' of society, or the 'treatment' of individuals and groups by society, ought to possess. As primitive thinking usually does when first noticing some regular processes, the results of the spontaneous ordering of the market were interpreted as if some thinking being deliberately directed them, or as if the particular benefits or harm different persons derived from them were determined by deliberate acts of will, and could therefore be guided by moral rules. This conception of 'social' justice is thus a direct consequence of that anthromorphism or personification on by which naive thinking tries to account for all self-ordering processes. It is a sign of the immaturity of our minds that we have not yet outgrown these primitive concepts and still demand from an impersonal process which brings about a greater satisfaction of human desires than any deliberate human organization could achieve, that it conform to the moral precepts men have evolved for the guidance of their individual actions.[1]

The use of the term 'social justice' in this sense is of comparatively recent date, apparently not much older than a hundred years. The expression was occasionally used earlier to describe the organized efforts to enforce the rules of just individual conduct,[2] and it is to the present day sometimes employed in learned discussion to evaluate the effects of the existing in situations of society.[3] But the sense in which it is now generally used and constantly appealed to in public discussion, and in which it will be examined in this chapter, is essentially the same as that in which the expression 'distributive justice' had long been employed. It seems to have become generally current in this sense at the time when (and perhaps partly because) John Stuart Mill explicitly treated the two terms as equivalent in such statements as that

> society should treat all equally well who have deserved equally well of it, that is, who have deserved equally well absolutely. This is the highest abstract standard of social and distributive justice; towards which all institutions, and the efforts of all virtuous citizens should be made in the utmost degree to converge.[4]

or that

> it is universally considered just that each person should obtain that (whether good or evil) which he deserves; and unjust that he should obtain a good, or be made to undergo an evil, which he does not deserve. This is perhaps the clearest and most emphatic form in which the idea of justice is conceived by the general mind. As it involves the idea of desert, the questions arises of what constitutes desert.[5]

It is significant that the first of these two passages occurs in the description of one of five meanings of justice which Mill distinguishes, of which four refer to rules of just individual conduct while this one defines a factual state of affairs which may but need not have been brought about by deliberate human action. Yet Mill appears to have been wholly unaware of the circumstance that in this meaning it refers to situations entirely different from those to which the other four meanings apply, or that this conception of 'social justice' leads straight to full- fledged socialism.

Such statements which explicitly connect 'social and distributive justice' with the 'treatment' by the society of the individuals according to their 'deserts' bring out most clearly its difference from plain justice, and at the same time the cause of the vacuity of the concept: the demand for 'social justice' is addressed not to the individual but to society—yet society, in the strict sense in which it must be distinguished from the apparatus of government, is incapable of acting for specific purpose, and the demand for 'social justice' therefore becomes a demand that the members of society should organize themselves in a manner which makes it possible to assign particular shares of the product of society to the different individuals or groups. The primary question then becomes whether there exists a moral duty to submit to a power which can co-ordinate the efforts of the members of society with the aim of achieving a particular pattern of distribution regarded as just.

If the existence of such power is taken for granted, the question of how the available means for the satisfaction of needs ought to be shared out becomes indeed a question of justice—though not a question to which prevailing morals provide an answer. Even the assumption from which most of the modern theorists of 'social justice' start, namely that it would require equal shares for all in so far as special considerations do not demand a departure from this principle, would then appear to be justified.[6] But the prior question is whether it is moral that men be subjected to the powers of direction that would have to be exercised in order that the benefits derived by the individuals could be meaningfully described as just or unjust.

It has of course to be admitted that the manner in which the benefits and burdens are apportioned by the market mechanism would in many instances have been regarded as very unjust *if* it were the result of a deliberate allocation to particular people. But this is not the case. Those shares are the outcome of a process the effect of which on particular people was neither intended nor foreseen by anyone when the institutions first appeared—institutions which were then permitted to continue because it was found that they improve for all or most the prospects of having their needs satisfied. To demand justice from such a process is clearly absurd, and to single out some people in such a society as entitled to a particular share evidently unjust.

The Conquest of Public Imagination By 'Social Justice'

The appeal to 'social justice' has nevertheless by now become the most widely used and most effective argument in political discussion. Almost every claim for government action on behalf of particular groups is advanced in its name, and if it can be made to appear that a certain measure is demanded by 'social justice', opposition to it will rapidly weaken. People may dispute whether or not the particular measure is required by 'social justice'. But that this is the standard which ought to guide political action, and that the expression has a definite meaning, is hardly ever questioned. In consequence, there are today probably no political movements of politicians who do not readily appeal to 'social justice' in support of the particular measures which they advocate.

It also can scarcely be denied that the demand for 'social justice' has already in a great measure transformed the social order and is continuing to transform it in a direction which those who called for it never forsaw. Though the phase has undoubtably helped occasionally to make the law more equal for all, whether the demand for justice in distribution has in any sense made society juster or reduced discontent must remain doubtful.

The expression of course described from the beginning the aspirations which were at the heart of socialism. Although classical socialism has usually been defined by its demand for the socialization of the means of production, this was for it chiefly a means thought to be essential in order to bring about a 'just' distribution of wealth; and since socialists have later discovered that this redistribution could in great measure, and against less resistance, be brought about by taxation (and government services financed by it), and have in practice often shelved their earlier demands, the realization of 'social justice' has become their chief promise. It might indeed be said that the main difference between the order of society at which classic liberalism aimed and the sort of society into which it is now being transformed is that the former was governed by principles of just individual conduct while the new society is to satisfy the demands for 'social justice'—or, in other words, that the former demanded just action by the individuals while the latter more and more places the duty of justice on authorities with power to command people what to do.

The phrase could exercise this effect because it has gradually been taken over from the socialist not only by all the other political movements but also by most teachers and preachers of morality. It seems in particular to have been embraced by a large section of the clergy of all Christian denominations, who, while increasingly losing their faith in a supernatural revelation, appear to have sought a refuge and consolation in a new 'social' religion which substitutes a temporal for a celestial promise of justice, and who hope that they can thus continue their striving to do good. The Roman Catholic church especially has made the aim of 'social justice' part of its official doctrine;[7] but the ministers of most Christian denominations appear to vie with each other with such offers of more mundane aims—which also seem to provide the chief foundation for renewed ecumenical efforts.

The various modern authoritarian or dictatorial governments have of course no less proclaimed 'social justice' as their chief aim. We have it on the authority of Mr. Andrei Sakharov that millions of men in Russia are the victims of a terror that 'attempts to conceal itself behind the slogan of social justice'.

The commitment to 'social justice' has in fact become the chief outlet for moral emotion, the distinguishing attribute of the good man, and the recognized sign of the possession of a moral conscience. Though people may occasionally be perplexed to say which of the conflicting claims advanced in its name are valid, scarcely anyone doubts that the expression has a definite meaning, describes a high ideal, and points to grave defects of the existing social order which urgently call for correction. Even though until recently one would have vainly sought in the extensive literature for an intelligible definition of the term,[8] there still seems to exist little doubt, either among ordinary people or among the learned, that the expression has a definite and well understood sense.

But the near-universal acceptance of a belief does not prove that it is valid or even meaningful any more than the general belief in witches or ghosts proved the validity of these concepts. What we have to deal with in the case of 'social justice' is simply a quasi-religious superstition of the kind which we should respectfully leave in peace so long as it merely makes those happy who hold it, but which we must fight when it becomes the pretext of coercing other men. And the prevailing belief in 'social justice' is at present probably the gravest threat to most other values of a free civilization.

Whether Edward Gibbon was wrong or not, there can be no doubt that moral and religious beliefs can destroy a civilization and that, where such doctrines prevail, not only the most cherished beliefs but also the most revered moral leaders, sometimes saintly figures whose unselfishness is beyond question, may become grave dangers to the values which the same people regard as unshakeable. Against this threat we can protect ourselves only by subjecting even our dearest dreams of a better world to ruthless rational dissection.

It seems to be widely believed that 'social justice' is just a new moral value which we must add to those that were recognized in the past, and that it can be fitted within the existing framework of moral rules. What is not sufficiently recognized is that in order to give this phrase meaning a complete change of the whole character of the social order will have to be effected, and that some of the values which used to govern it will have to be sacrificed. It is such a transformation of society into one of a fundamentally different type which is currently occurring piecemeal and without awareness of the outcome to which it must lead. It was in the belief that something like 'social justice' could thereby be achieved, that people have placed in the hands of government powers which it can now not refuse to employ in order to satisfy the claims of the ever increasing number of special interests who have learnt to employ the open sesame of 'social justice'.

I believe that 'social justice' will ultimately be recognized as a will-o'-the-wisp which has lured men to abandon many of the values which in the past have inspired the development of civilization—an attempt to satisfy a craving inherited from the traditions of the small group but which is meaningless in the Great Society of free men. Unfortunately, this vague desire which has become one of the strongest bonds spurring people of good will to action, not only is bound to be disappointed. This would be sad enough. But, like most attempts to pursue an unattainable goal, the striving for it will also produce highly undesirable consequences, and in particular lead to the destruction of the indispensible environment in which the traditional moral values alone can flourish, namely personal freedom.

The Inapplicability of the Concept of Justice to the Results of a Spontaneous Process

It is now necessary clearly to distinguish between two wholly different problems which the demand for social justice raises in a market order.

The first is whether within an economic order based on the market the concept of 'social justice' has any meaning or content whatever.

The second is whether it is possible to preserve a market order while imposing upon it (in the name of 'social justice' or any other pretext) some pattern of remuneration based on the assessment of the performance or the needs of different individuals or groups by an authority possessing the power to enforce it.

The answer to each of the questions is a clear no.

Yet it is the general belief in the validity of the concept of 'social justice' which drives all contemporary societies into greater and greater efforts of the second kind and which has a peculiar self-accelerating tendency: the more dependent the position of the individuals or groups is seen to become on the actions of government, the more they will insist that the governments aim at some recognizable scheme of distributive justice; and the more governments try to realize some preconceived pattern of desirable distribution, the more they must subject the position of the different individuals and groups to their control. So long as the belief in 'social justice' governs political action, this process must progressively approach nearer and nearer to a totalitarian system.

We shall at first concentrate on the problem of the meaning, or rather lack of meaning, of the term 'social justice', and only later consider the effects which the efforts to impose *any* preconceived pattern of distribution must have on the structure of the society subjected to them.

The contention that in a society of free men (as distinct from any compulsory organization) the concept of social justice is strictly empty and meaningless will probably appear as quite unbelievable to most people. Are we not all constantly disquited by watching how unjustly life treats different people and by seeing the deserving suffer and the unworthy prosper? And do we not all have a sense of fitness, and watch it with satisfaction, when we recognize a reward to be appropriate to effort or sacrifice?

The first insight which should shake this certainty is that we experience the same feelings also with respect to differences in human fates for which clearly no human agency is responsible and which it would therefore clearly be absurd to call injustice. Yet we do cry out against the injustice when a succession of calamities befalls one family while another steadily prospers, when a meritorious effort is frustrated by some unforseeable accident, and particularly if of many people whose endeavours seem equally great, some succeed brilliantly while others utterly fail. It is certainly tragic to see the failure of the most meritorious efforts of parents to bring up their children, of young men to build a career, or of an explorer or scientist pursuing a brilliant idea. And we will protest against such a fate although we do not know anyone who was to blame for it, or any way in which such disappointments can be prevented.

It is no different with regard to the general feeling of injustice about the distribution of material goods in a society of free men. Though we are in this case less ready to admit it, our complaints about the outcome of the market as unjust do not really assert that somebody has been unjust; and there is no answer to the question of *who* has been unjust. Society has simply become the new deity to which we complain and clamour for redress if it does not fulfil the expectations it has created. There is no individual and no cooperating group of people against which the sufferer would have a just complaint, and there are no conceivable rules of just individual conduct which would at the same time secure a functioning order and prevent such disappointments.

The only blame implicit in those complaints is that we tolerate a system in which each is allowed to choose his occupation and therefore nobody can have the power and the duty to see that the results correspond to our wishes. For in such a system in which each is allowed to use his knowledge for his own purposes[9] the concept of 'social justice' is necessarily empty and meaningless, because in it nobody's will can determine the relative incomes of the different people, or prevent that they can be partly dependent on accident. 'Social justice' can be giving a meaning only in a directed or 'command' economy (such as an army) in which the individuals are ordered what to do; and any particular conception of 'social justice' could be realized only is such a centrally directed system. It presupposes that people are guided by specific directions and not by rules of just individual contact. Indeed, no system of rules of just individual conduct, and therefore no free action of the individuals, could produce results satisfying any principle of distributive justice.

We are of course not wrong in perceiving that the effects of the processes of a free society on the fates of the different individuals are not distributed according to some recognizable principle of justice. Where we go wrong is in concluding from this that they are unjust and that somebody is to be blamed for this. In a free society in which the position of the different individuals and groups is not the result of anybody's design—or could, within such a society, be altered in accordance with a generally applicable principle—the differences in reward simply cannot meaningfully be described as just or unjust. There are, no doubt, many kinds of individual action which are aimed at affecting particular remunerations and which might be called just or unjust. But there are no principles of individual conduct which would produce a pattern of distribution which as such could be called just, and therefore also no possibility for the individual to know what he would have to do to secure a just remuneration of his fellows.

The Rationale of the Economic Game in Which Only the Conduct of the Players But Not the Result Can Be Just

We have seen earlier that justice is an attribute of human conduct which we have learnt to exact because a certain kind of conduct is required to secure the formation and maintenance of a beneficial order of actions. The attribute of justice may thus be predicated about the intended results of human action but not about circumstances which have not deliberately been brought about by men. Justice requires that in the 'treatment' of another person or persons, i.e. in the intentional actions affecting the well-being of other persons, certain uniform rules of conduct be observed. It clearly has no application to the manner in which the impersonal process of the market allocates command over goods and services to particular people: this can be neither just nor unjust, because the results are not intended or foreseen, and depend on a multitude of circumstances not known in their totality to anybody. The conduct of the individuals in that process may well be just or unjust; but since their wholly just actions will have consequences for others which were neither intended nor foreseen, these effects do not thereby become just or unjust.

The fact is simply that we consent to retain, and agree to enforce, uniform rules for a procedure which has greatly improved the chances of all to have their wants satisfied, but at the price of all individuals and groups incurring the risk of unmerited failure. With the acceptance of this procedure the recompense of different groups and individuals becomes exempt from deliberate control. It is the only procedure yet discovered in which information widely dispersed among millions of men can be effectively utilized for the benefit of all—and used by assuring to all an individual liberty desirable for itself on ethical grounds. It is a procedure which of course has never been 'designed' but which we have learnt gradually to improve after we had discovered how it increased the efficiency of men in the groups who had evolved it.

It is a procedure which, as Adam Smith (and apparently before him the ancient Stoics) understood,[10] in all important respects (except that normally it is not pursued solely as a diversion) is wholly analogous to a game, namely a game partly of skill and partly of chance. We shall later describe it as the game of catallaxy. It proceeds, like all games, according to rules guiding the actions of individual participants whose aims, skills, and knowledge are different, with the consequence that the outcome will be unpredictable and that there will regularly be winners and losers. And while, as in a game, we are right in insisting that it be fair and that nobody cheat, it would be nonsensical to demand that the results for the different players be just. They will of necessity be determined partly by skill and partly by luck. Some of the circumstances which make the services of a person more or less valuable to his fellows, or which may make it desirable that he change the direction of his efforts, are not of human design or foreseeable by men.

We shall in the next chapter have to return to the rationale of the discovery procedure which the game of competition in a market in effect constitutes. Here we must content ourselves with emphasizing that the results for the different individuals and groups of a procedure for utilizing more information than any one person or agency can possess, must themselves be unpredictable, and must often be different from the hopes and intentions which determined the direction and intensity of their striving; and that we can make effective use of that dispersed knowledge only if (as Adam Smith was also one of the first to see clearly)[11] we allow the principle of negative feedback to operate, which means that some must suffer unmerited disappointment.

We shall also see later that the importance for the functioning of the market order of particular prices or wages, and therefore of the incomes of the different groups and individuals, is not due chiefly to the effects of the prices on all of those who receive them, but to the effects of the prices on those for whom they act as signals to change the direction of their efforts. Their function is not so much to reward people for what they *have* done as to tell them what in their own as well as in general interest they *ought* to do. We shall then also see that, to hold out a sufficient incentive for those movements which are required to maintain a market order, it will often be necessary that the return of people's efforts do *not* correspond to recognizable merit, but should show that, in spite of the best efforts of which they were capable, and for reasons they could not have known, their efforts were either more or less successful than they had reason to expect. In a spontaneous order the question of whether or not someone has done the 'right' thing cannot always be a matter of merit, but must be determined independently of whether the persons concerned ought or could have known what was required.

The long and the short of it all is that men can be allowed to decide what work to do only if the remuneration they can expect to get for it corresponds to the value their services have to those of their fellows who receive them; and that *these values which their services will have to their fellows will often have no relations to their individual merits or needs.* Reward for merit earned and indication of what a person should do, both in his own and in his fellows' interest, are different things. It is not good intentions or needs but doing what in fact most benefits others, irrespective of motive, which will secure the best reward. Among those who try to climb Mount Everest or to reach the Moon, we also honour not those who made the greatest efforts, but those who got there first.

The general failure to see that in this connection we cannot meaningfully speak of the justice or injustice of the results is partly due to the misleading use of the term 'distribution' which inevitably suggests a personal distributing agent whose will or choice determines the relative position of the different persons or groups.[12] There is of course no such agent, and we use an impersonal process to determine the allocation of benefits precisely because through its operation we can bring about a structure of relative prices and remunerations that will determine a size and composition of the total output which assures that the real equivalent of each individual's share that accident or skill assigns to him will be as large as we know to make it.

It would serve little purpose to enquire here at greater length into the relative importance of skill and luck in actually determining relative incomes. This will clearly differ a great deal between different trades, localities and times, and in particular between highly competitive and less enterprising societies. I am on the whole inclined to believe that within any one trade or profession the correspondence between individual ability and industry is higher than is commonly admitted, but that the relative position of all the members of a particular trade or profession compared with others will more often be affected by circumstances beyond their control and knowledge. (This may also be one reason why what is called 'social' injustice is generally regarded as a graver fault of the existing order than the corresponding misfortunes of individuals.)[13] But the decisive point is not that the price mechanism does on the whole bring it about that rewards are proportioned to skill and effort, but that even where it is clear to us that luck plays a great part, and we have no idea why some are regularly luckier in guessing than others, it is still in the general interest to proceed on the presumption that the past success of some people in picking winners makes it probable that they will also do so in the future, and that it is therefore worthwhile to induce them to continue their attempts.

The Alleged Necessity of a Belief in the Justice of Rewards

It has been argued persuasively that people will tolerate major inequalities of the material positions only if they believe that the different individuals get on the whole what they deserve, that they did in fact support the market order only because (and so long as) they thought that the differences of remuneration corresponded roughly to differences of merit, and that in consequence the maintenance of a free society presupposes the belief that some sort of 'social justice' is being done.[14] The market order, however, does not in fact owe its origin to such beliefs, nor was originally justified in this manner. This order could develop, after its earlier beginnings had decayed during the middle ages and to some extent been destroyed by the restrictions imposed by authority, when a thousand years of vain efforts to discover substantively just prices or wages were abandoned and the late schoolmen recognized them to be empty formulae and taught instead that the prices determined by just conduct of the parties in the market, i.e. the competitive prices arrived at without fraud, monopoly and violence, was all that justice required.[15] It was from this tradition that John Locke and his contemporaries derived the classical liberal conception of justice for which, as has been rightly said, it was only 'the way in which competition was carried on, not its results',[16] that could be just or unjust.

It is unquestionably true that, particularly among those who were very successful in the market order, a belief in a much stronger moral justification of individual success developed, and that, long after the basic principles of such an order had been fully elaborated and approved by catholic moral philosophers, it had in the Anglo-Saxon world received strong support from Calvinist teaching. It certainly is important in the market order (or free enterprise society, misleadingly called 'capitalism') that the individuals believe that their well-being depends primarily on their own efforts and decisions. Indeed, few circumstances will do more to make a person energetic and efficient than the belief that it depends chiefly on him whether he will reach the goals he has set himself. For this reason this belief is often encouraged by education and governing opinion—it seems to me, generally much to the benefit of most of the members of the society in which it prevails, who will owe many important material and moral improvements to persons guided by it. But it leads no doubt also to an exaggerated confidence in the truth of this generalization which to those who regard themselves (and perhaps are) equally able but have failed must appear as a bitter irony and severe provocation.

It is probably a misfortune that, especially in the USA, popular writers like Samuel Smiles and Horatio Alger, and later the sociologist W.G. Sumner, have defended free enterprise on the ground that it regularly rewards the deserving, and it bodes ill for the future of the market order that this seems to have become the only defence of it which is understood by the general public. That it has largely become the basis of the self-esteem of the businessman often gives him an air of self-righteousness which does not make him more popular.

It is therefore a real dilemma to what extent we ought to encourage in the young the belief that when they really try they will succeed, or should rather emphasize that inevitably some unworthy will succeed and some worthy fail—whether we ought to allow the views of those groups to prevail with whom the over-confidence in the appropriate reward of the able and industrious is strong and who in consequence will do much that benefits the rest, and whether without such partly erroneous beliefs the large numbers will tolerate actual differences in rewards which will be based only partly on achievement and partly on mere chance.

There is No 'Value to Society'

The futile medieval search for the just price and just wage, finally abandoned when it was recognized that only that 'natural' price could be regarded as just which would be arrived at in a competitive market where it would be determined not by any human laws or decrees but would depend on so many circumstances that it could be known beforehand only by God,[17] was not the end of the search for that philosophers' stone. It was revived in modern times, not only by the general demand for 'social justice,' but also by the long and equally abortive efforts to discover criteria of justice in connection with the procedures for reconciliation or arbitration in wage disputes. Nearly a century of endeavours by public spirited men and women in many parts of the world to discover principles by which just wage rates could be determined have, as more and more of them acknowledge, produced not a single rule which would do this.[18] It is somewhat surprising in view of this when we find an experienced arbitrator like Lady Wootton, after admitting that arbitrators are 'engaged in the impossible task of attempting to do justice in an ethical vacuum,' because 'nobody knows in this context what justice is,' drawing from it the conclusion that the criteria should be determined by legislation, and explicitly demand a political determination of all wages and incomes.[19] One can hardly carry any further the illusion that Parliament can determine what is just, and I don't suppose the writer would really wish to defend the atrocious principle implied that all rewards should be determined by political power.

Another source of the conception that the categories of just and unjust can be meaningfully applied to the remunerations determined by the market is the idea that the different services have a determined and ascertainable 'value to society,' and that the actual remuneration frequently differs from the value. But though the conception of a 'value to society' is sometimes carelessly used even by economists, there is strictly no such thing and the expression implies the same sort of anthropomorphism or personification of society as the term 'social justice.' Services can have value only to particular people (or an organization), and any particular service will have very different values for different members of the same society. To regard them differently is to treat society not as a spontaneous order of free men but as an organization whose members are all made to serve a single hierarchy of ends. This would necessarily be a totalitarian system in which personal freedom would be absent.

Although it is tempting to speak of a 'value to society' instead of a man's value to his fellows, it is in fact highly misleading if we say, e.g., that a man who supplies matches to millions and thereby earns $200,000 a year is worth more 'to society' than a man who supplies great wisdom or exquisite pleasure to a few thousand and thereby earns $20,000 a year. Even the performance of a Beethoven sonata, a painting by Leonardo or a play by Shakespeare have no 'value to society' but a value only to those who know and appreciate them. And it has little meaning to assert that a boxer or a crooner is worth more to society than a violin virtuoso or a ballet dancer if the former renders services to millions and the latter to a much smaller group. The point is not that the true values are different, but that the values attached to the different services by different groups of people are incommensurable; all that these expressions mean is merely that one in fact receives a larger aggregate sum from a larger number of people than the other.[20]

Incomes earned in the market by different persons will normally not correspond to the relative values of their services to any one person. Although, in so far as any one of a given group of different commodities is consumed by any one person, he or she will buy so much of each that the relative values to them of the last units bought will correspond to their relative prices, many pairs of commodities will never by consumed by the same person: the relative price of articles consumed only by men and of articles consumed only by women will not correspond to the relative values of these articles to anybody.

The remunerations which the individuals and groups receive in the market are thus determined by what these services are worth to those who receive the (or, strictly speaking, to the last pressing demand for them which can still be satisfied by the available supply) and not by some fictitious 'value to society.'

Another source of the complaint about the alleged injustice of this principle of remuneration is that the remuneration thus determined will often be much higher than would be necessary to induce the recipient to render those services This is perfectly true but necessary if all who render the same service are to receive the same remuneration, if the kind of service in question is to be increased so long as the price still exceeds costs, and if anyone who wishes to buy or set it at the current price is to be able to do so. The consequence must be that all but the marginal sellers make a gain in excess of what was necessary to induce them to render the services in question—just as all but the marginal buyers will get what they buy for less than they were prepared to pay. The remuneration of the market will therefore hardly ever seem just in the sense in which somebody might endeavour justly to compensate others for the efforts and sacrifice incurred for his benefit.

The consideration of the different attitudes which different groups will take to the remuneration of different services incidentally also shows that the large numbers by no means grudge all the incomes higher than theirs, but generally only those earned by activities the functions of which they do not understand or which they even regard as harmful. I have never known ordinary people grudge the very high earnings of the boxer or torero, the football idol or the cinema star or the jazz king—they seem often even to revel vicariously in the display of extreme luxury and waste of such figures compared with which those of industrial magnates or financial tycoons pale. It is where most people do not comprehend the usefulness of an activity, and frequently because they erroneously regard it as harmful (the 'speculator'—often combined with the belief that only dishonest activities can bring so much money), and especially where the large earnings are used to accumulate a fortune (again out of the erroneous belief that it would be desirable that it should be spent rather than invested) that the outcry about the injustice of it arises. Yet the complex structure of the modern Great Society would clearly not work if the remunerations of all the different activities were determined by the opinion which the majority holds of their value—or indeed if they were dependent on any one person's understanding or knowledge of the importance of all the different activities required for the functioning of the system.

The main point is not that the masses have in most instances no idea of the values which a man's activities have to his fellows, and that it is necessarily their prejudices which would determine the use of the government's power. It is that nobody knows except in so far as the market tells him. It is true enough that our esteem of particular activities often differs from the value given to them by the market; and we express this feeling by an outcry about the injustice of it. But when we ask what ought to be the relative remunerations of a nurse and a butcher, of a coal miner and a judge at a high court, of the deep sea diver or the cleaner of sewers, of the organizer of a new industry and a jockey, of the inspector of taxes and the inventor of a life-saving drug, of the jet pilot or the professor of mathematics, the appeal to 'social justice' does not give us the slightest help in deciding—and if we use it it is no more than an insinuation that the others ought to agree with our view without giving any reason for it.

It might be objected that, although we cannot give the term 'social justice' a precise meaning, this need not be a fatal objection because the position may be similar to that which I have earlier contended exists with regard to justice proper: we might not know what is 'socially just' yet know quite well what is 'socially unjust'; and by persistently eliminating 'social injustice' whenever we encounter it, gradually approach 'social justice.' This, however, does not provide a way out of the basic difficulty. There can be no test by which we can discover what is 'socially unjust' because there is no subject by which such an injustice can be committed, and there are no rules of individual conduct the observance of which in the market order would secure to the individuals and groups the position which as such (as distinguished from the procedure by which it is determined) would appear just to us.[21] It does not belong to the categeory of error but to that of nonsense, like the term 'a moral stone'.

The Meaning of 'Social'

One might hope to get some help in the search for the meaning of 'social justice' by examining the meaning of the attribute 'social'; but the attempt to do so soon leads into a quagmire of confusion nearly as bad as that which surrounds 'social justice' itself.[22] Originally 'social' had of course a clear meaning (analogous to formations like 'national', 'tribal', or 'organizational'), namely that of pertaining to, or characteristic of the structure and operations of society. In this sense justice clearly is a social phenomenon and the addition of 'social' to the noun a pleonasm[23] such as if we spoke of 'social language'—though in occasional early uses it might have been intended to distinguish the generally prevailing views of justice from that held by particular persons or groups.

But 'social justice' as used today is not 'social' in the sense of 'social norms', i.e. something which has developed as a practice of individual action in the course of social evolution, not a product of society or of a social process, but a conception to be imposed upon society. It was the reference of 'social' to the whole of society, or to the interests of all its members, which led to its gradually acquiring a predominant meaning of moral approbation. When it came into general use during the third quarter of the last century it was meant to convey an appeal to the still ruling classes to concern themselves more with the welfare of the much more numerous poor whose interests had not received adequate consideration.[24] The 'social question' was posed as an appeal to the conscience of the upper classes to recognize their responsibility for the welfare of the neglected sections of society whose voices had till then carried little weight in the councils of government. 'Social policy' (or *Social-politik* in the language of the country then leading in the movement) became the order of the day, the chief concern of all progressive and good people, and 'social' came increasingly to displace such terms as 'ethical' or simply 'good'.

But from such an appeal to the conscience of the public to concern themselves with the unfortunate ones and recognize them as members of the same society, the conception gradually came to mean that 'society' ought to hold itself responsible for the particular material position of all its members, and for assuring that each received what was 'due' to him. It implied that the processes of society should be deliberately directed to particular results and, by personifying society, represented it as a subject endowed with a conscious mind, capable of being guided in its operation by moral principles.[25] 'Social' became more and more the description of the pre-eminent virtue, the attribute in which the good man excelled and the ideal by which communal action was to be guided.

But while this development indefinitely extended the field of application of the term 'social', it did not give it the required new meaning. It even so much deprived it of its original descriptive meaning that American sociologists have found it necessary to coin the new term 'societal' in its place. Indeed, it has produced a situation in which 'social' can be used to describe almost any action as publicly desirable and has at the same time the effect of depriving any terms with which it is combined of clear meaning. Not only 'social justice' but also 'social democracy', 'social market economy'[26] or the 'social state of law' (or rule of law—in German *sozialer Rechtsstaat*) are expressions which, through justice, democracy, the market economy or the *Rechtsstaat* have by themselves perfectly good meanings, the addition of the adjective 'social' makes them capable of meaning almost anything one likes. The word has indeed become one of the chief sources of confusion of political discourse and can probably no longer be reclaimed for a useful purpose.

There is apparently no end to the violence that will be done to language to further some ideal and the example of 'social justice' has recently given rise to the expression 'global justice'! Its negative, 'global injustice', was defined by an ecumenical gathering of American religious leaders as 'characterized by a dimension of sin in the economic, political, social, sexual, and class structures and systems of global society'![27] It would seem as if the conviction that one is arguing in a good cause produced more sloppy thinking and even intellectual dishonesty than perhaps any other cause.

'Social Justice' and Equality

The most common attempts to give meaning to the concept of 'social justice' resort to egalitarian considerations and argue that every departure from equality of material benefits enjoyed has to be justified by some recognizable common interest which these differences serve.[28] This is based on a specious analogy with the situation in which some human agency has to distribute rewards, in which case indeed justice would require that these rewards be determined in accordance with some recognizable rule of general applicability. But earnings in a market system, though people tend to regard them as rewards, do not serve such a function. Their rationale (if one may use this term for a role which was not designed but developed because it assisted human endeavour without people understanding how), is rather to indicate to people what they ought to do if the order is to be maintained on which they all rely. The prices which must be paid in a market economy for different kinds of labour and other factors of production if individual efforts are to match, although they will be affected by effort, diligence, skill, need, etc., cannot conform to any one of these magnitudes; and considerations of justice just do not make sense[29] with respect to the determination of a magnitude which does not depend on anyone's will or desire, but on circumstances which nobody knows in their totality.

The contention that all differences in earnings must be justified by some corresponding difference in deserts is one which would certainly not have been thought to be obvious in a community of farmers or merchants or artisans, that is, in a society in which success or failure were clearly seen to depend only in part on skill and industry, and in part on pure accident which might hit anyone—although even in such societies individuals were known to complain to God or fortune about the injustice of their fate. But, though people resent that their remuneration should in part depend on pure accident, that is in fact precisely what it must if the market order is to adjust itself promptly to the unavoidable and unforeseen changes in circumstances, and the individual is to be allowed to decide what to do. The now prevalent attitude could arise only in a society in which large numbers worked as members of organizations in which they were remunerated at stipulated rates for time worked. Such communities will not ascribe the different fortunes of its members to the operation of an impersonal mechanism which serves to guide the directions of efforts, but to some human power that ought to allocate shares according to merit.

The postulate of material equality would be a natural starting point only if it were a necessary circumstance that the shares of the different individuals or groups were in such a manner determined by deliberate human decision. In a society in which this were an unquestioned fact, justice would indeed demand that the allocation of the means for the satisfaction of human needs were effected according to some uniform principle such as merit or need (or some combination of these), and that, where the principle adopted did not justify a difference, the shares of the different individuals should be equal. The prevalent demand for material equality is probably often based on the belief that the existing inequalities are the effect of somebody's decision—a belief which would be wholly mistaken in a genuine market order and has still only very limited validity in the highly interventionist 'mixed' economy existing in most countries today. This now prevalent form of economic order has in fact attained its character largely as a result of governmental measures aiming at what was thought to be required by 'social justice'.

When the choice, however, is between a genuine market order, which does not and cannot achieve a distribution corresponding to any standard of material justice, and a system in which government uses its powers to put some such standard into effect, the question is not whether government ought to exercise, justly or unjustly, powers it must exercise in any case, but whether government should possess and exercise additional powers which can be used to determine the shares of the different members of society. The demand for 'social justice', in other words, does not merely require government to observe some principle of action according to uniform rules in those actions which it must perform in any case, but demands that it undertake additional activities, and thereby assume new responsibilities—tasks which are not necessary for maintaining law and order and providing for certain collective needs which the market could not satisfy.

The great problem is whether this new demand for equality does not conflict with the equality of the rules of conduct which government must enforce on all in a free society. There is, of course, a great difference between government treating all citizens according to the same rules in all the activities it undertakes for other purposes, and government doing what is required in order to place the different citizens in equal (or less unequal) material positions. Indeed, there may arise a sharp conflict between these two aims. Since people will differ in many attributes which government cannot alter, to secure for them the same material position would require that government treat them very differently. Indeed, to assure the same material position to people who differ greatly in strength, intelligence, skill, knowledge and perseverance as well as in their physical and social environment, government would clearly have to treat them very differently to compensate for those disadvantages and deficiencies it could not directly alter. Strict equality of those benefits which government could provide for all, on the other hand, would clearly lead to inequality of the material positions.

This, however, is not the only and not even the chief reason why a government aiming to secure for its citizens equal material positions (or any determined pattern of material welfare) would have to treat them very unequally. It would have to do so because under such a system it would have to undertake to tell people what to do. Once the rewards the individual can expect are no longer an appropriate indication of how to direct their efforts to where they are most needed, because these rewards correspond not to the value which their services have for their fellows, but to the moral merit or desert the persons are deemed to have earned, they lose the guiding function they have in the market order and would have to be replaced by the commands of the directing authority. A central planning office would, however, have to decide on the tasks to be allotted to the different groups or individuals wholly on grounds of expedience or efficiency and, in order to achieve its ends, would have to impose upon them very different duties and burdens. The individuals might be treated according to uniform rules so far as their rewards were concerned, but certainly not with respect to the different kinds of work they would have to be made to do. In assigning people to their different tasks, the central planning authority would have to be guided by considerations of efficiency and expediency and not by principles of justice or equality. No less than in the market order would the individuals in the common interest have to submit to great inequality—only these inequalities would be determined not by the interaction of individual skills in an impersonal process, but by the uncontradictable decision of authority.

As is becoming clear in ever increasing fields of welfare policy, an authority instructed to achieve particular results for the individuals must be given essentially arbitrary powers to make the individuals do what seems necessary to achieve the required result. Full equality for most cannot but mean the equal submission of the great masses under the command of some elite who manages their affairs. While an equality of rights under a limited government is possible and an essential condition of individual freedom, a claim for equality of material position can be met only by a government with totalitarian powers.[30]

We are of course not wrong when we perceive that the effects on the different individuals and groups of the economic processes of a free society are not distributed according to some recognizable principle of justice. Where we go wrong is in concluding from this that they are unjust and that somebody is responsible and to be blamed for this. In a free society in which the position of the different individuals and groups is not the result of anybody's design—or could within such a society not be altered in accordance with a principle of general applicability—the differences in rewards cannot meaningfully be described as just or unjust. There are, no doubt, many kinds of individual actions which are aimed at affecting particular remunerations and which might be regarded as unjust. But there are no principles of individual conduct which would produce a pattern of distribution which as such could be called just, and therefore also no possibility for the individual to know what he would have to do to secure a just remuneration of his fellows.

Our whole system of morals is a system of rules of individual conduct, and in a Great Society no conduct guided by such rules, or by decisions of the individuals guided by such rules, could produce for the individuals results which would appear to us as just in the sense in which we regard designed rewards as just or unjust: simply because in such a society nobody has the power or the knowledge which would enable him to ensure that those affected by his actions will get what he thinks right for them to get. Nor could anyone who is assured remuneration according to some principle which is accepted as constituting 'social justice' be allowed to decide what he is to do: remuneration indicating how urgent it was that a certain work should be done could not be just in this sense, because the need for work of a particular kind would often depend on unforeseeable accidents and certainly not on the good intentions or efforts of those able to perform it. And an authority that fixed remunerations with the intention of thereby reducing the kind and number of people thought necessary in each occupation could not make these remunerations 'just', i.e. proportionate to desert, or need, or the merits of any other claim of the persons concerned, but would have to offer what was necessary to attract or retain the number of people wanted in each kind of activity.

'Equality of Opportunity'

It is of course not to be denied that in the existing market order not only the results but also the initial chances of different individuals are often very different; they are affected by circumstances of their physical and social environment which are beyond their control but in many particular respects might be altered by some governmental action. The demand for equality of opportunity or equal starting conditions (*Startgerechtigkeit*) appeals to, and has been supported by, many who in general favour the free market order. So far as this refers to such facilities and opportunities as are of necessity affected by governmental decisions (such as appointments to public office and the like), the demand was indeed one of the central points of classical liberalism, usually expressed by the French phrase 'la carrière ouverte aux talents'. There is also much to be said in favour of the government providing on an equal basis the means for the schooling of minors who are not yet fully responsible citizens, even though there are grave doubts whether we ought to allow government to administer to them.

But all this would still be very far from creating real equality of opportunity, even for persons possessing the same abilities. To achieve this government would have to control the whole physical and human environment of all persons, and have to endeavour to provide at least equivalent chances for each; and the more government succeeded in these endeavours, the stronger would become the legitimate demand that, on the same principle, any still remaining handicaps must be removed—or compensated for by putting extra burden on the still relatively favoured. This would have to go on until government literally controlled every circumstance which could affect any person's well-being. Attractive as the phrase of equality of opportunity at first sounds, once the idea is extended beyond the facilities which for other reasons have to be provided by government, it becomes a wholly illusory ideal, and any attempt concretely to realize it apt to produce a nightmare.

'Social Justice' and Freedom under the Law

The idea that men ought to be rewarded in accordance with the assessed merits or deserts of their services 'to society' presupposes an authority which not only distributes these rewards but also assigns to the individuals the tasks for the performance of which they will be rewarded. In other words, if 'social justice' is to be brought about, the individuals must be required to obey not merely general rules but specific demands directed to them only. The type of social order in which the individuals are directed to serve a single system of ends is the organization and not the spontaneous order of the market, that is, not a system in which the individual is free because bound only be general rules of just conduct, but a system in which all are subject to specific directions by authority.

It appears sometimes to be imagined that a mere alteration of the rules of individual conduct could bring about the realization of 'social justice'. But there can be no set of such rules, no principles by which the individuals could so govern their conduct that in a Great Society the joint effect of their activities would be a distribution of benefits which could be described as materially just, or any other specific and intended allocation of advantages and disadvantages among particular people or groups. In order to achieve *any* particular pattern of distribution through the market process, each producer would have to know, not only whom his efforts will benefit (or harm), but also how well off all the other people (actually or potentially) affected by his activities will be as the result of the services they are receiving from other members of the society. As we have seen earlier, appropriate rules of conduct can determine only the formal character of the order of activities that will form itself, but not the specific advantages particular groups or individuals will derive from it.

This rather obvious fact still needs to be stressed since even eminent jurists have contended that the substitution of 'social' or distributive for individual or commutative justice need not destroy the freedom under the law of the individual. Thus the distinguished German legal philosopher Gustav Radbruch explicitly maintained that 'the socialist community would also be a *Rechtsstaat* [i.e., the Rule of Law would prevail there], although a *Rechtsstaat* governed not by commutative but by distributive justice.'[31] And of France it is reported that 'it has been suggested that some highly placed administrators should be given the permanent task of "pronouncing" on the distribution of national income, as judges pronounce on legal matters.'[32] Such beliefs, however, overlook the fact that no specific pattern of distribution can be achieved by making the individuals obey rules of conduct, but that the achievement of such particular pre-determined results require deliberate co-ordination of all the different activities in accordance with the concrete circumstances of time and place. It precludes, in other words, that the several individuals act on the basis of their own knowledge and in the service of their own ends, which is the essence of freedom, but requires that they be made to act in the manner which according to the knowledge of the directing authority is required for the realization of the ends chosen by that authority.

The distributive justice at which socialism aims is thus irreconcilable with the rule of law, and with that freedom under the law which the rule of law is intended to secure. The rules of distributive justice cannot be rules for the conduct towards equals, but must be rules for the conduct of superiors towards their subordinates. Yet though some socialists have long ago themselves drawn the inevitable conclusion that 'the fundamental principles of formal law by which every case must be judged according to general rational principles...obtains only for the competitive phase of capitalism,'[33] and the communists, so long as they took socialism seriously, had even proclaimed that 'communism means not the victory of socialist law, but the victory of socialism over any law, since with the abolition of classes with antagonistic interests, law will disappear altogether',[34] when, more than thirty years ago, the present author made this the central point of a discussion of the political effects of socialist economic policies,[35] it evoked great indignation and violent protests. But the crucial point is implied even in Radbruch's own emphasis on the fact that the transition from commutative to distributive justice means a progressive displacement of prive by public law,[36] since public law consists not of rules of conduct for private citizens but of rules of organization for public officials. It is, as Radbruch himself stresses, a law that subordinates the citizens to authority.[37] Only if one understands by law not the general rules of just conduct only but any command issued by authority (or any authorization of such commands by a legislature), can the measures aimed at distributive justice be represented as compatible with the rule of law. But this concept is thereby made to mean mere legality and ceases to offer the protection of individual freedom which it was originally intended to serve.

There is no reason why in a free society government should not assure to all protection against severe deprivation in the form of an assured minimum income, or a floor below which nobody need to descend. To enter into such an insurance against extreme misfortune may well be in the interest of all; or it may be felt to be a clear moral duty of all to assist, within the organized community, those who cannot help themselves. So long as such a uniform minimum income is provided outside the market to all those who, for any reason, are unable to earn in the market an adequate maintenance, this need not lead to a restriction of freedom, or conflict with the Rule of Law. The problems with which we are here concerned arise only when the remuneration for services rendered is determined by authority, and the impersonal mechanism of the market which guides the direction of individual efforts is thus suspended.

Perhaps the acutest sense of grievance about injustice inflicted on one, not by particular persons but by the 'system', is that about being deprived of opportunities for developing one's abilities which others enjoy. For this any difference of environment, social or physical, may be responsible, and at least some of them may be unavoidable. The most important of these is clearly inseparable from the institution of the family. This not only satisfies a strong psychological need but in general serves as an instrument for the transmission of important cultural values. There can be no doubt that those who are either wholly deprived of this benefit, or grew up in unfavourable conditions, are gravely handicapped; and few will question that it would be desirable that some public institution so far as possible should assist such unfortunate children when relatives and neighbours fail. Yet few will seriously believe (although Plato did) that we can fully make up for such a deficiency, and I trust even fewer that, because this benefit cannot be assured to all, it should, in the interest of equality, be taken from those who now enjoy it. Nor does it seem to me that even material equality could compensate for those differences in the capacity of enjoyment and of experiencing a lively interest in the cultural surroundings which a suitable upbringing confers.

There are of course many other irremediable inequalities which must seem as unreasonable as economic inequalities but which are less resented than the latter only because they do not appear to be man-made or the consequence of institutions which could be altered.

The Spatial Range of 'Social Justice'

There can be little doubt that the moral feelings which express themselves in the demand for 'social justice' derive from an attitude which in more primitive conditions the individual developed towards the fellow members of the small group to which he belonged. Towards the personally known member of one's own group it may well have been a recognized duty to assist him and to adjust one's actions to his needs. This is made possible by the knowledge of his person and his circumstances. The situation is wholly different in the Great or Open Society. Here the products and services of each benefit mostly persons he does not know. The greater productivity of such a society rests on a division of labour extending far beyond the range any one person can survey. This extension of the process of exchange beyond relatively small groups, and including large numbers of persons not known to each other, has been made possible by conceding to the stranger and even the foreigner the same protection of rules of just conduct which apply to the relations to the known members of one's own small group.

This application of the same rules of just conduct to the relations to all other men is rightly regarded as one of the great achievements of a liberal society. What is usually not understood is that this extension of the same rules to the relations to all other men (beyond the most intimate group such as the family and personal friends) requires an attenuation at least of some of the rules which are enforced in the relations to other members of the smaller group. If the legal duties towards strangers or foreigners are to be the same as those towards the neighbours or inhabitants of the same village or town, the latter duties will have to be reduced to such as can also be applied to the stranger. No doubt men will always wish to belong also to smaller groups and be willing voluntarily to assume greater obligations towards self-chosen friends or companions. But such moral obligations towards some can never become enforced duties in a system of freedom under the law, because in such a system the selection of those towards whom a man wishes to assume special moral obligations must be left to him and cannot be determined by law. A system of rules intended for an Open Society and, at least in principle, meant to be applicable to all others, must have a somewhat smaller content than one to be applied in a small group.

Especially a common agreement on what is the due status or material position of the different members is likely to develop only in the relatively small group in which the members will be familiar with the character and importance of each other's activities. In such small communities the opinion about appropriate status will also still be associated with a feeling about what one self owes to the other, and not be merely a demand that somebody provide the appropriate reward. Demands for the realization of 'social justice' are usually as a matter of course, though often only tacitly, addressed to national governments as the agencies which possess the necessary powers. But it is doubtful whether in any but the smallest countries standards can be applied nationally which are derived from the condition of the particular locality with which the individual is familiar, and fairly certain that few men would be willing to concede to foreigners the same right to a particular income that they tend to recognize in their fellow citizens.

It is true that in recent years concern about the suffering of large numbers in the poor countries has induced the electorates of the wealthier nations to approve substantial material aid to the former; but it can hardly be said that in this considerations of justice played a significant role. It is indeed doubtful whether any substantial help would have been rendered if competing power groups had not striven to draw as many as possible of the developing countries into their orbit. And it deserves notice that the modern technology which has made such assistance possible could develop only because some countries were able to build up great wealth while most of the world saw little change.

Yet the chief point is that, if we look beyond the limits of our national states, and certainly if we go beyond the limits of what we regard as our civilization, we no longer even deceive ourselves that we know what would be 'socially just', and that those very groups within the existing states which are loudest in their demands for 'social justice', such as the trade unions, are regularly the first to reject such claims raised on behalf of foreigners. Applied to the international sphere, the complete lack of a recognized standard of 'social justice', or of any known principles on which such a standard could be based, becomes at once obvious; while on a national scale most people still think that what on the level of the face-to-face society is to them a familiar idea must also have some validity for national politics or the use of the powers of government. In fact, it becomes on this level a humbug—the effectiveness of which with well-meaning people the agents of organized interests have learnt successfully to exploit.

There is in this respect a fundamental difference between what is possible in the small group and in the Great Society. In the small group the individual can know the effects of his actions on his several fellows, and the rules may effectively forbid him to harm them in any manner and even require him to assist them in specific ways. In the Great Society many of the effects of a person's actions on various fellows must be unknown to him. It can, therefore, not be the specific effects in the particular case, but only rules which define kinds of actions as prohibited or required, which must serve as guides to the individual. In particular, he will often not know who the individual people will be who will benefit by what he does, and therefore not know whether he is satisfying a great need or adding to abundance. He cannot aim at just results if he does not know who will be affected.

Indeed the transition from the small group to the Great or Open Society—and the treatment of every other person as a human being rather than as either a known friend or an enemy—requires a reduction of the range of duties we owe to all others.

If a person's legal duties are to be the same towards all, including the stranger and even the foreigner (and greater only where he has voluntarily entered into obligations, or is connected by physical ties as between parents and children), the legally enforceable duties to neighbour and friend must not be more than those towards the stranger. That is, all those duties which are based on personal acquaintance and familiarity with individual circumstances must cease to be enforceable. The extension of the obligation to obey certain rules of just conduct to wider circles and ultimately to all men must thus lead to an attenuation of the obligation towards fellow members of the same small group. Our inherited or perhaps in part even innate moral emotions are in part inapplicable to Open Society (which is an abstract society), and the kind of 'moral socialism' that is possible in the small group and often satisfies a deeply ingrained instinct may well be impossible in the Great Society. Some altruistic conduct aimed at the benefit of some known friend that in the small group might be highly desirable, need not be so in the Open Society, and may there even be harmful (as e.g. the requirement that members of the same trade refrain from competing with each other).[38]

It may at first seem paradoxical that the advance of morals should lead to a reduction of specific obligations towards others: yet whoever believes that the principle of equal treatment of all men, which is probably the only chance for peace, is more important than special help to visible suffering, must wish it. It admittedly means that we make our rational insight dominate over our inherited instincts. But the great moral adventure on which modern man has embarked when he launched into the Open Society is threatened when he is required to apply to all his fellowmen rules which are appropriate only to the fellow members of a tribal group.

Claims for Compensation for Distasteful Jobs

The reader will probably expect me now to examine in greater detail the particular claims usually justified by the appeal to 'social justice'. But this, as bitter experience has taught me, would be not only an endless but also a bootless task. After what has been said already, it should be obvious that there are no practicable standards of merit, deserts, or needs, on which in a market order the distribution of material benefits could be based, and still less any principle by which these different claims could be reconciled. I shall therefore confine myself to considering two arguments in which the appeal to 'social justice' is very commonly used. The first case is usually quoted in theoretical argument to illustrate the injustice of the distribution by the market process, though little is done about it in practice, while the second is probably the most frequent type of situation in which the appeal to social justice leads to government action.

The circumstance which is usually pointed out to demonstrate the injustice of the existing market order is that the most unpleasant jobs are commonly also the worst paid. In a just society, it is contended, those who have to dig coal underground or to clean chimneys or sewers, or who perform other unclean or menial tasks, should be remunerated more highly than those whose work is pleasurable.

It is of course true that it would be unjust if persons, although equally able as others to perform other tasks, were without special compensation assigned by a superior to such distasteful duties. If, e.g., in such an organization as an army, two men of equal capacity were made to perform different tasks, one of which was attractive and the other very unpleasant, justice would clearly require that the one who had regularly to perform the unpleasant duty should in some way be specially compensated for it.

The situation is entirely different, however, where people earn their living by selling their services to whoever pays best for them. Here the sacrifice brought by a particular person in rendering the service is wholly irrelevant and all that counts is the (marginal) value the services have to those to whom they are rendered. The reason for this is not only that the sacrifices different people bring in rendering the same kind of service will often be very different, or that it will not be possible to take account of the reason why some will be capable of rendering only less valuable services than others. But those whose aptitudes, and therefore also remunerations, will be small in the more attractive occupations will often find that they can earn more than they could otherwise by undertaking unpleasant tasks that are scorned by their more fortunate fellows. The very fact that the more unpleasant occupations will be avoided by those who can render services that are valued more highly by the buyers, will open to those whose skills are little valued opportunities to earn more than they otherwise could.

That those who have to offer to their fellows little that is valuable may have to incur more pain and effort to earn even a pittance than others who perhaps actually enjoy rendering services for which they are well paid, is a necessary concomitant of any system in which remuneration is based on the values the services have to the user and not an assessment of merit earned. It must therefore prevail in any social order in which the individual is free to choose whatever occupation he can find and is not assigned to one by authority.

The only assumption on which it could be represented as just that the miner working underground, or the scavenger, or slaughter-house workers, should be paid more highly than those engaged in more pleasant occupations, would thus be that this was necessary to induce a sufficient number of persons to perform these tasks, or that they are by some human agency deliberately assigned to these tasks. But while in a market order it may be a misfortune to have been born and bred in a village where formost the only chance of making a living is fishing (or for the women the cleaning of fish), it does not make sense to describe this as unjust. Who is supposed to have been unjust?—especially when it is considered that, if these local opportunities had not existed, the people in question would probably never have been born at all, as most of the population of such a village will probably owe its existence to the opportunities which enabled their ancestors to produce and rear children.

The Resentment of the Loss of Accustomed Positions

The appeal to 'social justice' which in practice has probably had the greatest influence is not one which has been much considered in literary discussion. The considerations of a supposed 'social injustice' which have led to the most far-reaching interference with the functioning of the market order are based on the idea that people are to be protected against an unmerited descent from the material position to which they have become accustomed. No other consideration of 'social justice' has probably exercised as widespread an influence as the 'strong and almost universal belief that it is unjuust to disappoint legitimate expectations of wealth. When differences of opinion arise, it is always on the question of what expectations are legitimate.' It is believed, as the same author says, 'that it is legitimate even for the largest classes to expect that no very great and sudden changes will be made to their detriment.'[39]

The opinion that long established positions create a just expectation that they will continue serves often as a substitute for more substantial criteria of 'social justice'. Where expectations are disappointed, and in consequence the rewards of effort often disproportionate to the sacrifice incurred, this will be regarded as an injustice without any attempt to show that those affected had a claim in justice to the particular income which they expected. At least when a large group of people find their income reduced as a result of circumstances which they could not have altered or foreseen, this is commonly regarded as unjust.

The frequent recurrence of such undeserved strokes of misfortune affecting some group is, however, an inseparable part of the steering mechanism of the market: it is the manner in which the cybernetic principle of negative feedback operates to maintain the order of the market. It is only through such changes which indicate that some activities ought to be reduced, that the efforts of all can be continuously adjusted to a greater variety of facts than can be known to any one person or agency, and that that utilization of dispersed knowledge is achieved on which the well-being of the Great Society rests. We cannot rely on a system in which the individuals are induced to respond to events of which they do not and cannot know without changes of the values of the services of different groups occurring which are wholly unrelated to the merits of their members. It is a necessary part of that process of constant adaptation to changing circumstances on which the mere maintenance of the existing level of wealth depends that some people should have to discover by bitter experience that they have misdirected their efforts and are forced to look elsewhere for a remunerative occupation. And the same applies to the resentment of the corresponding undeserved gains that will accrue to others for whom things have turned out better than they had reason to expect.

The sense of injury which people feel when an accustomed income is reduced or altogether lost is largely the result of a belief that they have morally deserved that income and that, therefore, so long as they work as industriously and honestly as they did before, they are in justice entitled to the continuance of that income. But the idea that we have morally deserved what we have honestly earned in the past is largely an illusion. What is true is only that it would have been unjust if anybody had taken from us what we have in fact acquired while observing the rules of the game.

It is precisely because in the cosmos of the market we all constantly receive benefits which we have not deserved in any moral sense that we are under an obligation also to accept equally undeserved diminutions of our incomes. Our only moral title to what the market gives us we have earned by submitting to those rules which makes the formation of the market order possible. These rules imply that nobody is under an obligation to supply us with a particular income unless he has specifically contracted to do so. If we were all to be consistently deprived, as the socialists propose to do, of all 'unearned benefits' which the market confers upon us, we would have to be deprived of most of the benefits of civilization.

It is clearly meaningless to reply, as is often done, that, since we owe these benefits to 'society', 'society' should also be entitled to allocate these benefits to those who in its opinion deserve them. Society, once more, is not an acting person but an orderly structure of actions resulting from the observation of certain abstract rules by its members. We all owe the benefits we receive from the operation of this structure not to anyone's attention to confer them on us, but to the members of society generally obeying certain rules in the pursuit of their interests, rules which include the rule that nobody is to coerce others in order to secure for himself (or for third persons) a particular income. This imposes upon us the obligation to abide by the results of the market also when it turns against us.

The chance which any individual in our society has of earning an income approximating that which he has now is the consequence of most individuals obeying the rules which secure the formation of that order. And though this order provides for most good prospects for the successful employment of their skills, this success must remain dependent also on what from the point of view of the individual must appear as mere luck. The magnitude of the chances open to him are not of his making but the result of others submitting to the same rules of the game. To ask for protection against being displaced from a position one has long enjoyed, by others who are now favoured by new circumstances, means to deny to them the chances to which one's own present position is due.

Any protection of an accustomed position is thus necessarily a privilege which cannot be granted to all and which, if it had always been recognized, would have prevented those who now claim it from ever reaching the position for which they now demand protection. There can, in particular, be no right to share equally in a general increase of incomes if this increase (or perhaps even their maintenance at the existing level) is dependent on the continuous adjustment of the whole structure of activities to new and unforeseen circumstances that will alter and often reduce the contributions some groups can make to the needs of their fellows. There can thus be in justice no such claims as, e.g., those of the American farmer for 'parity', or of any other group to the preservation of their relative or absolute position.

The satisfaction of such claims by particular groups would thus not be just but eminently unjust, because it would involve the denial to some of the chances to which those who make this claim owe their position. For this reason it has always been conceded only to some powerfully organized groups who were in the position to enforce their demands. Much of what is today done in the name of 'social justice' is thus not only unjust but also highly unsocial in the true sense of the word: it amounts simply to the protection of entrenched interests. Though it has come to be regarded as a 'social problem' when sufficiently large numbers clamour for protection of their accustomed position, it becomes a serious problem chiefly because, camouflaged as a demand for 'social justice', it can engage the sympathy of the public. We shall see in volume 3 why, under the existing type of democratic institutions, it is in practice inevitable that legislatures with unlimited powers yield to such demands when made by sufficiently large groups. This does not alter the fact that to represent such measures as satisfying 'social justice' is little more than a pretext for making the interest of the particular groups prevail over the general interest of all. Though it is now usual to regard every claim of an organized group as a 'social problem', it would be more correct to say that, though the long run interests of the several individuals mostly agree with the general interest, the interests of the organized groups almost invariably are in conflict with it. Yet it is the latter which are commonly represented as 'social'.

Conclusions

The basic contention of this chapter, namely that in a society of free men whose members are allowed to use their own knowledge for their own purposes the term 'social justice' is wholly devoid of meaning or content, is one which by its very nature cannot be *proved*. A negative assertion never can. One may demonstrate for any number of particular instances that the appeal to 'social justice' in no way assists the choices we have to make. But the contention that in a society of free men the term has no meaning whatever can only be issues as a challenge which will make it necessary for others to reflect on the meaning of the words they use, and as an appeal not to use phrases the meaning of which they do not know.

So long as one assumes that a phrase so widely used must have some recognizable meaning one may endeavour to prove that attempts to enforce it in a society of free individuals must make that society unworkable. But such efforts become redundant once it is recognized that such a society lacks the fundamental precondition for the application of the concept of justice to the manner in which material benefits are shared among its members, namely that this is determined by a human will—or that the determination of rewards by human will could produce a viable market order. One does not have to prove that something is impracticable which cannot exist.

What I hope to have made clear is that the phrase 'social justice' is not, as most people probably feel, an innocent expression of good will towards the less fortunate, but that it has become a dishonest insinuation that one ought to agree to a demand of some special interest which can give no real reason for it. If political discussion is to become honest it is necessary that people should recognize that the term is intellectually disreputable, the mark of demagogy or cheap journalism which responsible thinkers ought to be ashamed to use because, once its vacuity is recognized, its use is dishonest. I may, as a result of long endeavours to trace the destructive effect which the invocation of 'social justice' has had on our moral sensitivity, and of again and again finding even eminent thinkers thoughtlessly using the phrase,[40] have become unduly allergic to it, but I have come to feel strongly that the greatest service I can still render to my fellow men would be that I could make the speakers and writers among them thoroughly ashamed ever again to employ the term 'social justice'.

That in the present state of the discussion the continued use of the term is not only dishonest and the source of constant political confusion, but destructive of moral feeling, is shown by the fact that again and again thinkers, including distinguished philosophers,[41] after rightly recognizing that the term justice in its now predominant meaning of distributive (or retributive) justice is meaningless, draw from this the conclusion that the concept of justice itself is empty, and who in consequence jettison one of the basic moral conceptions on which the working of a society of free men rests. But it is justice in this sense which courts of justice administer and which is the original meaning of justice and must govern men's conduct if peaceful coexistence of free men is to be possible. While the appeal to 'social justice' is indeed merely an invitation to give moral approval to demands that have no moral justification, and which are in conflict with that basic rule of a free society that only such rules as can be applied equally to all should be enforced, justice in the sense of rules of just conduct is indispensable for the intercourse of free men.

We are touching here upon a problem which with all its ramifications is much too big to try to be examined here systematically, but which must at least be mentioned briefly. It is that we can't have any morals we like or dream of. Morals, to be viable, must satisfy certain requirements, requirements which we may not be able to specify but may only be able to find out by trial and error. What is required is not merely consistency, or compatibility of the rules as well as the acts demanded by them. A system of morals also must produce a functioning order, capable of maintaining the apparatus of civilization which it presupposes.

We are not familiar with the concept of non-viable systems of morals and certainly cannot observe them anywhere in practice since societies which try them rapidly disappear. But they are being preached, often by widely revered saintly figures, and the societies in decay which we can observe are often societies which have been listening to the teaching of such moral reformers and still revere the destroyers of their society as good men. More often, however, the gospel of 'social justice' aims at much more sordid sentiments: the dislike of people who are better off than oneself, or simply envy, that 'most anti-social and evil of all passions' as John Stuart Mill called it,[42] that animosity towards great wealth which represents it as a 'scandal' that some should enjoy riches while others have basic needs unsatisfied, and camouflages under the name of justice what has nothing to do with justice. At least all those who wish to despoil the rich, not because they expect that some more deserving might enjoy that wealth, but because they regard the very existence of the rich as an outrage, not only cannot claim any moral justification for their demands, but indulge in a wholly irrational passion and in fact harm those to whose rapacious instincts they appeal.

There can be no moral claim to something that would not exist but for the decision of others to risk their resources on its creation. What those who attack great private wealth do not understand is that it is neither by physical effort nor by the mere act of saving and investing, but by directing resources to the most productive uses that wealth is chiefly created. And there can be no doubt that most of those who have built up great fortunes in the form of new industrial plants and the like have thereby benefited more people through creating opportunities for more rewarding employment than if they had given their superfluity away to the poor. The suggestion that in these cases those to whom in fact the workers are most indebted do wrong rather than greatly benefit them is an absurdity. Though there are undoubtedly also other and less meritorious ways of acquiring large fortunes (which we can hope to control by improving the rules of the game), the most effective and important is by directing investment to points where they most enhance the productivity of labour—a task in which governments notoriously fail, for reasons inherent in non-competitive bureaucratic organizations.

But it is not only by encouraging malevolent and harmful prejudices that the cult of 'social justice' tends to destroy genuine moral feelings. It also comes, particularly in its more egalitarian forms, into constant conflict with some of the basic moral principles on which any community of free men must rest. This becomes evident when we reflect that the demand that we should equally esteem all our fellow men is irreconcilable with the fact that our whole moral code rests on the approval or disapproval of the conduct of others; and that similarly the traditional postulate that each capable adult is primarily responsible for his own and his dependents' welfare, meaning that he must not through his own fault become a charge to his friends or fellows, is incompatible with the idea that 'society' or government owes each person an appropriate income.

Though all these moral principles have also been seriously weakened by some pseudo-scientific fashions of our time which tend to destroy all morals—and with them the basis of individual freedom—the ubiquitous dependence on other people's power, which the enforcement of any image of 'social justice' creates, inevitably destroys that freedom of personal decisions on which all morals must rest.[43] In fact, that systematic pursuit of the *ignis fatuus* of 'social justice' which we call socialism is based throughout on the atrocious idea that political power ought to determine the material position of the different individuals and groups—an idea defended by the false assertion that this must always be so and socialism merely wishes to transfer this power from the privileged to the most numerous class. It was the great merit of the market order as it has spread during the last two centuries that it deprived everyone of such power which can be used only in arbitrary fashion. It had indeed brought about the greatest reduction of arbitrary power ever achieved. This greatest triumph of personal freedom the seduction of 'social justice' threatens again to take from us. And it will not be long before the holders of the power to enforce 'social justice' will entrench themselves in their position by awarding the benefits of 'social justice' as the remuneration for the conferment of that power and in order to secure to themselves the support of a praetorian guard which will make it certain that their view of what is 'social justice' will prevail.

Before leaving the subject I want to point out once more that the recognition that in such combinations as 'social', 'economic', 'distributive' or 'retributive' justice the term 'justice' is wholly empty should not lead us to throw the baby out with the bath water. Not only as the basis of the legal rules of just conduct is the justice which the courts of justice administer exceedingly important; there unquestionably also exists a genuine problem of justice in connection with the deliberate design of political institutions, the problem to which Professor John Rawls has recently devoted an important book. The fact which I regret and regard as confusing is merely that in this connection he employs the term 'social justice'. But I have no basic quarrel with an author who, before he proceeds to that problem, acknowledges that the task of selecting specific systems or distributions of desired things as just must be 'abandoned as mistaken in principle, and it is, in any case, not capable of a definite answer. Rather, the principles of justice define the crucial constraints which institutions and joint activities must satisfy if persons engaging in them are to have no complaints against them. If these constraints are satisfied, the resulting distribution, whatever it is, may be accepted as just (or at least not unjust).'[44] This is more or less what I have been trying to argue in this chapter.

Appendix to Chapter Nine: Justice And Individual Rights

The transition from the negative conception of justice as defined by rules of individual conduct to a 'positive' conception which makes it a duty of 'society' to see that individuals have particular things, is often effected by stressing the *rights* of the individual. It seems that among the younger generation the welfare institutions into which they have been born have engendered a feeling that they have a claim in justice on 'society' for the provision of particular things which it is the duty of that society to provide. However strong this feeling may be, its existence does not prove that the claim has anything to do with justice, or that such claims can be satisfied in a free society.

There is a sense of the noun 'right' in which every rule of just individual conduct creates a corresponding right of individuals. So far as rules of conduct delimit individual domains, the individual will have a right to his domain, and in the defence of it will have the sympathy and the support of his fellows. And where men have formed organizations such as government for enforcing rules of conduct, the individual will have a claim in justice on government that his right be protected and infringements made good.

Such claims, however, can be claims in justice, or rights, only in so far as they are directed towards a person or organization (such as government) which can act, and which is bound in its actions by rules of just conduct. They will include claims on people who have voluntarily incurred obligations, or between people who are connected by special circumstances (such as the relations between parents and children). In such circumstances the rules of just conduct will confer on some persons rights and on others corresponding obligations. But rules as such, without the presence of the particular circumstances to which they refer, cannot confer on anyone a right to a particular sort of thing. A child has a right to be fed, clad, and housed because a corresponding duty is placed on the parents or guardians, or perhaps a particular authority. But there can be no such right in the abstract determined by a rule of just conduct without the particular circumstances being stated which determine on whom the corresponding obligation rests. Nobody has a right to a particular state of affairs unless it is the duty of someone to secure it. We have no right that our houses do not burn down, nor a right that our products or services find a buyer, nor that any particular goods or services be provided for us. Justice does not impose on our fellows a general duty to provide for us; and a claim to such a provision can exist only to the extent that we are maintaining an organization for that purpose. It is meaningless to speak of a right to a condition which nobody has the duty, or perhaps even the power, to bring about. It is equally meaningless to speak of right in the sense of a claim on a spontaneous order, such as society, unless this is meant to imply that somebody has the duty of transforming that cosmos into an organization and thereby to assume the power of controlling its results.

Since we are all made to support the organization of government, we have by the principles determining that organization certain rights which are commonly called political rights. The existence of the compulsory organization of government and its rules of organization does create a claim in justice to shares in the services of government, and may even justify a claim for an equal share in determining what government shall do. But it does not provide a basis for a claim on what government does not, and perhaps could not, provide for all. We are not, in this sense, members of an organization called society, because the society which produces the means for the satisfaction of most of our needs is not an organization directed by a conscious will, and could not produce what it does if it were.

The time-honored political and civil rights which have been embodied in formal Bills of Right constitute essentially a demand that so far as the power of government extends it ought to be used justly. As we shall see, they all amount to particular applications of, and might be effectively replaced by, the more comprehensive formula that no coercion must be used except in the enforcement of a generic rule applicable to an unknown number of future instances. It may well be desirable that these rights should become truly universal as a result of all governments submitting to them. But so long as the powers of the several governments are at all limited, these rights cannot produce a duty of the governments to bring about a particular state of affairs. What we can require is that so far as government acts it ought to act justly; but we cannot derive from them any positive powers government ought to have. They leave wholly open the question whether the organization for coercion which we call government can and ought in justice be used to determine the particular material position of the several individuals or groups.

To the negative rights which are merely a complement of the rules protecting individual domains and which have been institutionalized in the charters of organization of governments, and to the positive rights of the citizens to participate in the direction of this organization, there have recently been added new positive 'social and economic' human rights for which an equal or even higher dignity is claimed.[45] These are claims to particular benefits to which every human being as such is presumed to be entitled without any indication as to who is to be under the obligation to provide those benefits or by what process they are to be provided.[46] Such positive rights, however, demand as their counterpart a decision that somebody (a person or organization) should have the duty of providing what the others are to have. It is, of course, meaningless to describe them as claims on 'society' because 'society' cannot think, act, value, or 'treat' anybody in a particular way. If such claims are to be met, the spontaneous order which we call society must be replaced by a deliberately directed organization: the cosmos of the market would have to be replaced by a taxis whose members would have to do what they are instructed to do. They could not be allowed to use their knowledge for their own purposes but would have to carry out the plan which their rulers have designed to meet the needs to be satisfied. From this it follows that the old civil rights and the new social and economic rights cannot be achieved at the same time but are in fact incompatible; the new rights could not be enforced by law without at the same time destroying that liberal order at which the old civil rights aim.

The new trend was given its chief impetus through the proclamation by President Franklin Roosevelt of his 'Four Freedoms' which included 'freedom *from* want' and 'freedom *from* fear' together with the old 'freedom *of* speech' and 'freedom *of* worship'. But it found its definite embodiment only in the *Universal Declaration of Human Rights* adopted by the General Assembly of the United Nations in 1948. This document is admittedly an attempt to fuse the rights of the Western liberal tradition with the altogether different conception deriving from the Marxist Russian Revolution.[47] It adds to the list of the classical civil rights enumerated in its first twenty-one articles seven further guarantees intended to express the new 'social and economic rights'. In these additional clauses 'every one, as a member of society' is assured the satisfaction of positive claims to particular benefits without at the same time placing on anyone the duty or burden of providing them. The document also completely fails to define these rights in such a manner that a court could possibly determine what their contents are in a particular instance. What, for instance, can be the legal meaning of the statement that every one 'is entitled to the realization . . . of the economic, social, and cultural rights indispensible for his dignity and free development of his personality' (Art. 22)? Against whom is 'every one' to have a claim to 'just and favourable conditions of work' (Art. 23 (I)) and to 'just and favourable employment' (Art. 23 (3))? What are the consequences of the requirement that every one should have the right 'freely to participate in the cultural life of the community and to share in the scientific advances and its benefits' (Art. 27 (I))? 'Every one' is even said to be 'entitled to a social and international order in which the rights and freedoms set forth in this Declaration are fully realized' (Art. 28)—on the assumption apparently that not only is this possible but that there exists now a known method by which these claims can be satisfied for all men.

It is evident that all these 'rights' are based on the interpretation of society as a deliberately made organization by which everybody is employed. They could not be made universal within a system of rules of just conduct based on the conception of individual responsibility, and so require that the whole of society be converted into a single organization, that is, made totalitarian in the fullest sense of the word. We have seen that rules of just conduct which apply to everybody alike but subject nobody to the commands of a superior can never determine what particular things any person is to have. They can never take the form of 'everybody must have so and so.' In a free society what the individual will get must always depend in some measure on particular circumstances which nobody can foresee and nobody has the power to determine. Rules of just conduct can therefore never confer on any person as such (as distinct from the members of a particular organization) a claim to particular things; they can bring about only opportunities for the acquiring of such claims.

It apparently never occurred to the authors of the Declaration that not everybody is an employed member of an organization whose right 'to just and favourable remuneration, including reasonable limitations of working hours and periodic holidays with pay' (Art. 24) can be guaranteed. The conception of a 'universal right' which assures to the peasant, to the Eskimo, and presumably to the Abominable Snowman, 'periodic holidays with pay' shows the absurdity of the whole thing. Even the slightest amount of ordinary common sense ought to have told the authors of the document that what they decreed as universal rights were for the present and for any foreseeable future utterly impossible of achievement, and that solemnly to proclaim them as rights was to play an irresponsible game with the concept of 'right' which could result only in destroying the respect for it.

The whole document is indeed couched in that jargon of organization thinking which one has learnt to expect in the pronouncement of trade union officials or the International Labour Organization and which reflects an attitude business employees share with civil servants and the organization men of the big corporations, but which is altogether inconsistent with the principles on which the order of a Great Society rests. If the document were merely the production of an international group of social philosophers (as in origin it is), it would constitute only somewhat disturbing evidence of the degree to which organization thinking has permeated the thinking of these social philosophers and how much they have become total strangers to the basic ideals of a free society. But its acceptance by a body of presumably responsible statesmen, seriously concerned with the creation of a peaceful international order, gives cause for much greater apprehension.

Organization thinking, largely as a result of the sway of the rationalist constructivism of Plato and his followers, has long been the besetting vice of social philosophers; perhaps it should therefore not surprise us that academic philosophers in their sheltered lives as members of organizations should have lost all understanding of the forces which hold the Great Society together and, imagining themselves to be Platonic philosopher-kings, should propose a reorganization of society on totalitarian lines. If it should be true, as we are told, that the social and economic rights of the Universal Declaration of Human Rights would today be 'accepted by the vast majority of American and British moralists,'[48] this would merely indicate a sorry lack of critical acumen on the part of these thinkers.

The spectacle, however, of the General Assembly of the United Nations solemnly proclaiming that *every* individual (!), 'keeping this Declaration constantly in mind' (!), should strive to insure the universal observation of those human rights, would be merely comic if the illusions which this creates were not so profoundly tragic. To see the most comprehensive authority which man has yet created undermining the respect it ought to command by giving countenance to the naive prejudice that we can create any state of affairs which we think to be desirable by simply decreeing that it ought to exist, and indulging in the self-deception that we can benefit from the spontaneous order of society and at the same time mould it to our own will, is more than merely tragic.[49]

The fundamental fact which these illusions disregard is that the availability of all those benefits which we wish as many people as possible to have depends on these same people using for their production their own best knowledge. To establish enforceable rights to the benefits is not likely to produce them. If we wish everybody to be well off, we shall get closest to our goal, not by commanding by law that this should be achieved, or giving everybody a legal claim to what we think he ought to have, but by providing inducements for all to do as much as they can that will benefit others. To speak of rights where what are in question are merely aspirations which only a voluntary system can fulfill, not only misdirects attention from what are the effective determinants of the wealth which we wish for all, but also debases the word 'right', the strict meaning of which it is very important to preserve if we are to maintain a free society.

Notes

*The first quotation is taken from David Hume, *An Enquiry Concerning the Principles of Morals*, sect. III, part II, *Works* IV, p. 187, and ought to be given here in its context: the

> most obvious thought would be, to assign the largest possessions to the most extensive virtue, and give every one the power of doing good proportioned to his inclination.... But were mankind to execute such a law; so great is the uncertainty of merit, both from its natural obscurity, and from the self-conceit of each individual, that no determinate rule of conduct would ever follow from it; and the total dissolution of society must be the immediate consequence.

*The second quotation is translated from Immanuel Kant (*Der Streit der Fakultäten* (1798), sect. 2, para. 6, note 2) and reads in the original: 'Wohlfahrt aber hat kein Prinzip, weder für den der sie empfängt, noch für den der sie austeilt (der eine setzt sie hierin, der andere darin); weil es dabei auf das *Materiale* des Willens ankommt, welches empirisch und so einer allgemeinen Regel unfähig ist.' An English translation of this essay in which the passage is rendered somewhat differently will be found in *Kant's Political Writings*, ed. H. Reiss, trs. H. B. Nisbett (Cambridge, 1970), p. 183, note.

1. Cf. P. H. Wicksteed, *The Common Sense of Political Economy* (London, 1910), p. 184: 'It is idle to assume that ethically desirable results will necessarily be produced by an ethically indifferent instrument.'

2. Cf. G. del Vecchio, *Justice* (Edinburgh, 1952), p. 37. In the eighteenth century the expression 'social justice' was occasionally used to describe the enforcement of rules of just conduct within a given society, so e.g. by Edward Gibbon, *Decline and Fall of the Roman Empire*, chapter 41 (World's Classics edn, vol. IV, p. 367).

3. E.g. by John Rawls, *A Theory of Justice* (Harvard, 1971).

4. John Stuart Mill, *Utilitarianism* (London, 1861), chapter 5, p.92; in H. Plamenatz, ed., *The English Utilitarians* (Oxford, 1949), p. 225.

5. *Ibid.*, pp. 66 and 208 respectively. Cf. also J. S. Mill's review of F. W. Newman, *Lectures on Political Economy*, originally published in 1851 in the *Westminster Review* and republished in *Collected Works*, vol. v (Toronto and London, 1967), p. 444: 'the distinction between rich and poor, so slightly connected as it is with merit and demerit, or even with exertion and want of exertion, is obviously unjust.' Also *Principles of Political Economy*, book II, ch. I, §, ed. W. J. Ashley (London, 1909), pp. 211ff.: 'The proportioning of remuneration to work done is really just only in so far as the more or less of the work is a matter of choice: when it depends on natural differences of strength and capacity, this principle of remuneration is itself an injustice, it gives to those who have.'

6. See e.g. A. M. Honoré, 'Social Justice' in *McGill Law Journal*, VIII, 1962 and revised version in R. S. Summers, ed., *Essays in Legal Philosophy* (Oxford, 1968), p. 62 of the reprint: 'The first [of the two propositions of which the principle of social justice consists] is the contention that *all men considered merely as men and apart from their conduct or choice have a claim to an equal share in all those things, here called advantages, which are generally desired and are in fact conducive to well-being.*' Also W. G. Runciman, *Relative Deprivation and Social Justice* (London, 1966), p. 261.

7. Cf. especially the encyclicals *Quadragesimo Anno* (1931) and *Divini Redemptoris* (1937) and Johannes Messner, 'Zum Begriff der sozialen Gerechtigkeit' in the volume *Die soziale Frage und der Katholizismus* (Paderborn, 1931) issued to commemorate the fortieth anniversary of the encyclical *Rerum Novarum*.

8.   The term 'social justice' (or rather its Italian equivalent) seems to have been first used in its modern sense by Luigi Taparelli d'Azeglio, *Saggio teoretico di diritto naturale* (Palermo, 1840) and to have been made more generally known by Antonio RosminiSerbati, *La costitutione secondo la giustizia sociale* (Milan, 1848). For more recent discussions cf. N. W. Willoughby, *Social Justice* (New York, 1909); Stephen Leacock, *The Unsolved Riddle of Social Justice* (London and New York, 1920); John A. Ryan, *Distributive Justice* (New York, 1916); L. T. Hobhouse, *The Elements of Social Justice* (London and New York, 1922); T. N. Carver, *Essays in Social Justice* (Harvard, 1922); W. Shields, *Social Justice, The History and Meaning of the Term* (Notre Dame Ind. 1941); Benevuto Donati 'che cosa è giustizia sociale?', *Archivio giuridico,* vol. 134, 1947; C. de Pasquier, 'La notion de justice sociale', *Zeitschrift für Schweizerisches Recht,* 1952; P. Antoine, 'Qu-est-ce la justice sociale?', *Archives de Philosophie,* 24, 1961; For a more complete list of this literature see G. del Vecchio, *op. cit.,* pp. 379.

In spite of the abundance of writings on the subject, when about ten years ago I wrote the first draft of this chapter, I found it still very difficult to find any serious discussion of what people meant when they were using this term. But almost immediately afterwards a number of serious studies of the subject appeared, particularly the two works quoted in note 6 above as well as R. W. Baldwin, *Social Justice* (Oxford and London, 1966), and R. Rescher, *Distributive Justice* (Indianapolis, 1966). Much the most acute treatment of the subject is to be found in a German work by the Swiss economist Emil Küng, *Wirtschaft und Gerechtigkeit* (Tübingen, 1967) and many sensible comments in H. B. Acton, *The Morals of the Market* (London, 1971), particularly p. 71: 'Poverty and misfortune are evils but not injustices'. Very important is also Bertrand de Jouvenel, *The Ethics of Redistribution* (Cambridge, 1951) as well as certain passages in his *Sovereignty* (London, 1957), two of which may here be quoted. P. 140: 'The justice now recommended is a quality not of a man and a man's actions, but of a certain configuration of things in social geometry, no matter by what means it is brought about. Justice is now something which exists independently of just men.' P. 164: 'No proposition is likelier to scandalise our contemporaries than this one: it is impossible to establish a just social order. Yet it flows logically from the very idea of justice, on which we have, not without difficulty, thrown light. To do justice is to apply, when making a share-out, the relevant serial order. But it is impossible for the human intelligence to establish a relevant serial order for all resources in all respects. Men have needs to satisfy, merits to reward, possibilities to actualize; even if we consider these three aspects only and assume that—what is not the case—there are precise *indicia* which we can apply to these aspects, we still could not weight correctly among themselves the three sets of *indicia* adopted.'

The at one time very famous and influential essay by Gustav Schmoller on 'Die Gerechtigkeit in der Volkswirtschaft' in that author's *Jahrbuch für Volkswirtschaft etc.,* vol. v, 1895 is intellectually most disappointing—a pretentious statement of the characteristic muddle of the do-gooder foreshadowing some unpleasant later developments. We know now what it means if the great decisions are to be left to the 'jeweilige Volksbewusstsein nach der Ordnung der Zwecke, die im Augenblick als die richtige erscheint' !

9.   Cf. note 7 to chapter VII above.

10.   Cf. Adam Smith, *The Theory of Moral Sentiments* (London, 1801), vol. II, part VII, sect. ii, ch. I, p. 198: 'Human life the Stoics appear to have considered as a game of great skill, in which, however, there was a mixture of chance or of what is vulgarly understood to be chance.' See also Adam Ferguson, *Principles of Moral and Political Science* (Edinburgh 1792) vol. I p. 7: 'The Stoics conceived of human life under the image of a Game, at which the entertainment and merit of the players consisted in playing attentively and well whether the stake was great or small.' In a note Ferguson refers to the *Discourses of Epictetus* preserved by Arrian, book II, ch. 5.

11.   Cf. G. Hardin, *Nature and Man's Fate* (New York, 1961), p. 55: 'In a free market, says Smith in effect, prices are regulated by negative feedback.' The much ridiculed 'miracle' that the pursuit of self-interest serves the general interest reduces to the self-evident proposition that an order in which the action of the elements is to be guided by effects of which they cannot know can be achieved only if they are induced to respond to signals reflecting the effects of those events. What was familiar to Adam Smith has belatedly been rediscovered by scientific fashion under the name of 'self-organizing systems'.

12.   See L. von Mises, *Human Action* (Yale, 1949), p. 255 note: 'There is in the operation of the market economy nothing which could properly be called distribution. Goods are not first produced and then distributed, as would be the case in a socialist state.' Cf. also M. R. Rothbard, 'Towards a Reconstruction of Utility and Welfare Economics' in M. Sennholz (ed.), *On Freedom and Free Enterprise* (New York, 1965), p. 231.

13.   Cf. W. G. Runciman, *op. cit.*, p. 274: 'Claims for social justice are claims on behalf of a group, and the person relatively deprived within an individual category will, if he is the victim of an unjust inequality, be a victim only of individual injustice.'

14.   See Irving Kristol, 'When Virtue Loses all Her Loveliness—Some Reflections on Capitalism and "The Free Society"', *The Public Interest*, no. 21 (1970), reprinted in the author's *On the Democratic Idea in America* (New York, 1972), as well as in Daniel Bell and Irving Kristol (eds), *Capitalism Today* (New York, 1970).

15.   Cf. J. Höffner, *Wirtschaftsethik und Monopole im 15. und 16. Fahrhundert* (Jena, 1941) und 'Der Wettbewerb in der Scholastik', *Ordo*, V, 1953; also Max Weber, *On Law in Economy and Society*, ed. Max Rheinstein (Harvard, 1954) pp. 295ff., but on the latter also H. M. Robertson, *Aspects on the Rise of Economic Individualism* (Cambridge, 1933) and B. Groethuysen, *Origines de l'esprit bourgeois en France* (Paris, 1927). For the most important expositions of the conception of a just price by the late sixteenth century Spanish Jesuits see particularly L. Molina, *De iustitia et de iure*, vol. 2, *De Contractibus* (Cologne, 1594), disp. 347, no. 3 and especially disp. 348, no. 3, where the just price is

defined as that which will form 'quando absque fraude, monopoliis, atque aliis versutiies, commu-niter res aliqua vendi consuevit pretio in aliqua regione, aut loco, it habendum est pro mensura et reg-ula judicandi pretium iustum rei illius in ea regione.' About man's inability to determine beforehand what a just price would be see also particularly Johannes de Salas, *Commentarii in Secundum Secun-dae D. Thomas de Contractibus* (Lyon, 1617), *Tr. de empt. et Vend.* IV, n. 6, p. 9: '. . . quas exacte comprehendere, et ponderare Dei est, not hominum'; and J. de Lugo, *Disputationes de Iustitia et Iure* (Lyon, 1643), vol. II d. 26 s. 4, n. 40; 'pretium iustum matematicum, licet sold Deo notum.' See also L. Molina, *op. cit.,* disp. 365, no. 9: 'omnesque rei publicae parses ius habent conscendendi ad gradum superiorem, si cuiusque sors id tulerit, neque cuiquam certus quidam gradus debitur, qui de-scendere et conscendere possit.' It would seem that H. M. Robertson (*op. cit.,* p. 164) hardly exagger-ates when he writes 'It would not be difficult to claim that the religion which favoured the spirit of capitalism was Jesuitry, not Calvinism.'

16. John W. Chapman, 'Justice and Fairness', *Nomos VI, Justice* (New York, 1963), p. 153. This Lockean conception has been preserved even by John Rawls, at least in his earlier work, 'Constitutional Lib-erty and the Concept of Justice', *Nomos VI, Justice* (New York, 1963), p. 117, note: 'If one assumes that law and government effectively act to keep markets competitive, resources fully employed, prop-erty and wealth widely distributed over time, and maintains a reasonable social minimum, then, if there is equality of opportunity, the resulting distribution will be just or at least not unjust. It will have resulted from the working of a just system . . . a social minimum is simply a form of rational in-surance and prudence.'

17. See passages quoted in note 15 above.

18. See M. Fogarty, *The Just Wage* (London, 1961).

19. Barbara Wootton, *The Social Foundation of Wage Policy* (London, 1962), pp. 120 and 162, and now also her *Incomes Policy, An Inquest and a Proposal* (London, 1974).

20. Surely Samuel Butler (Hudibras, II, I) was right when he wrote

    For what is worth in any thing
    But so much money as 'twill bring.

21. On the general problem of remuneration according to merit, apart from the passages by David Hume and Immanuel Kant placed at the head of this chapter, see chapter VI of my book *The Constitution of Lib-erty* (London and Chicago, 1960) and cf. also Maffeo Pantaleoni, 'L'atto economico' in *Erotemi di Economia* (2 vols, Padua, 1963), vol. I, p. 101:

    E tre sono le proposizioni che conviene comprendere bene:
    La prima è che il merito è una parole vuota di senso.

La seconda è che il concetto di giustizia è un polisenso che si presta a quanti paralogismi si vogliono ex amphibologia.

La terza è che la remunerazione non può essere commisurata da una produttività (marginale) capace di determinazione isolamente, cioè senza la simultanea determinazione della produttività degli altri fattori con i quali entra in una combinazione di complimentarità.

22.   On the history of the term 'social' see Karl Wasserrab, *Sozialwissenschaft und soziale Frage* (Leipzig, 1903); Leopold von Wiese, *Der Liberalismus in Vergangenheit und Zukunft* (Berlin, 1917), and *Sozial, Geistig, Kulturell* (Cologne, 1936); Waldemar Zimmermann, 'Das "Soziale" im geschichtlichen Sinn- und Begriffswandel' in *Studien zur Soziologie, Festgabe für L. von Wiese* (Mainz, 1948); L. H. A. Geck, *Über das Eindringen des Wortes 'sozial' in die deutsche Sprache* (Göttingen, 1963); and Ruth Crummemerl Zur Wortgeschichte von 'sozial' bis zur englischen Aufklärung', unpublished essay for the State examination in philology (Bonn, 1963). Cf. also my essay 'What is "Social"? What does it Mean?' in a corrected English version in my *Studies in Philosophy, Politics and Economics* (London and Chicago, 1967).

23.   Cf. G. del Vecchio, *op. cit.,* p. 37.

24.   Very instructive on this is Leopold von Wiese, D*er Liberalismus in Vergangenheit und Zukunft* (Berlin, 1917) pp. 115ff.

25.   Characteristic for many discussions of the issue by social philosophers is W. A. Frankena, 'The Concept of Social Justice', in *Social Justice,* ed. R. B. Brandt (New York, 1962), p. 4, whose argument rests on the assumption that 'society' *acts* which is a meaningless term if applied to a spontaneous order. Yet this anthropomorphic interpretation of society seems to be one to which utilitarians are particularly prone, although this is not often as naively admitted as by J. W. Chapman in the statement quoted before in note 21 to chapter VII.

26.   I regret this usage though by means of it some of my friends in Germany (and more recently also in England) have apparently succeeded in making palatable to wider circles the sort of social order for which I am pleading.

27.   Cf. the 'Statement of Conscience' received by the 'Aspen Consultation on Global Justice', an 'ecumenical gathering of American religious leaders' at Aspen, Colorado, 4-7 June 1974, which recognized that 'global injustice is characterised by a dimension of sin in the economic, political, social, racial, sexual and class structures and systems of global society.' *Aspen Institute Quarterly* (New York), no. 7, third quarter, 1974, p. 4.

28.   See particularly A. M. Honoré, *op. cit.* The absurdity of the contention that in a Great Society it needs moral justification if *A* has more than *B,* as if this were the result of some human artifice, becomes obvious when we consider not only the elaborate and complex apparatus of government which would

be required to prevent this, but also that this apparatus would have to possess power to direct the efforts of all citizens and to claim the products of those efforts.

29. One of the few modern philosophers to see this clearly and speak out plainly was R. G. Collingwood. See his essay on 'Economics as a philosophical science,' *Ethics* 36, 1926, esp. p. 74: 'A just price, a just wage, a just rate of interest, is a contradiction in terms. The question of what a person ought to get in return for his goods and labour is a question absolutely devoid of meaning.'

30. If there is any one fact which all serious students of the claims for equality have recognized it is that material equality and liberty are irreconcilable. Cf. A. de Tocqueville, *Democracy in America,* book II, ch. I (New York, edn 1946, vol. II, p. 87): democratic communities 'call for equality in freedom, and if they cannot obtain that, they still call for equality in slavery'; William S. Sorley, *The Moral Life and the Moral Worth* (Cambridge, 1911) p. 110: 'Equality is gained only by constant interference with liberty'; or more recently Gerhard Leibholz, 'Die Bedrohung der Freiheit durch die Macht der Gesetzgeber', in F*reiheit der Personlichkeit* (Stuttart, 1958), p. 80: 'Freiheit erzeugt notwendig Ungleichheit und Gleichheit notwendig Unfreiheit', are merely a few instances which I readily find in my notes. Yet people who claim to be enthusiastic supporters of liberty still clamour constantly for material equality.

31. Gustav Radbruch, *Rechtsphilosophie* (Stuttgart, 1956), p. 87: 'Auch das sozialistische Gemeinwesen wird also ein Rechtsstaat sein, ein Rechtsstaat freilich, der statt von der ausgleichenden von der austeilenden Gerechtigkeit beherrscht wird.'

32. See M. Duverger, *The Idea of Politics* (Indianapolis, 1966), p. 201.

33. Karl Mannheim, *Man and Society in an Age of Reconstruction* (London, 1940), p. 180.

34. P. J. Stuchka (President of the Soviet Supreme Court) in *Encyclopedia of State and Law* (in Russian, Moscow, 1927), quoted by V. Gsovski, *Soviet Civil Law* (Ann Arbor, Michigan, 1948), I, p. 70. The work of E. Paschukanis the Soviet author who has most consistently developed the idea of the disappearance of law under socialism, has been described by Karl Korsch in *Archiv sozialistischer Literatur*, III, (Frankfurt, 1966) as the only consistent development of the teaching of Karl Marx.

35. *The Road to Serfdom* (London and Chicago, 1944), chapter IV. For discussions of the central thesis of that book by lawyers see W. Friedmann, *The Planned State and the Rule of Law* (Melbourne, 1948), reprinted in the same author's *Law and Social Change in Contemporary Britain* (London, 1951). Hans Kelsen, 'The Foundations of Democracy', *Ethics* 66, 1955; Roscoe Pound, 'The Rule of Law and the Modern Welfare State', *Vanderbilt Law Review*, 7, 1953; Harry W. Jones, 'The Rule of Law and the Modern Welfare State', *Columbia Law Review*, 58, 1958; A. L. Good hart, 'The Rule of Law and Absolute Sovereignty', U*niversity of Pennsylvania Law Review*, 106, 1958.

36. G. Radbruch, *op. cit.,* p. 126.

37. Radbruch's conceptions of these matters are concisely summed up by Roscoe Pound (in his introduction to R. H. Graves, *Status in the Common Law*, London, 1953, p. XI): Radbruch

starts with a distinction between commutative justice, a correcting justice which gives back to one what has been taken away from him or gives him a substantial substitute, and distributive justice, a distribution of the goods of existence not equally but according to a scheme of values. Thus there is a contrast between coordinating law, which secures interests by reparation and the like, treating all individuals as equal, and subordinating law, which prefers some or the interests of some according to its measure of value. Public law, he says, is a law of subordination, subordinating individual to public interests but not the interests of other individuals with those public interests.

38. Cf. Bertrand de Jouvenel, *Sovereignty* (Chicago, 1957), p. 136:

The small society, as the milieu in which man is first found, retains for him an infinite attraction; he undoubtedly goes to it to renew his strength; but . . . any attempt to graft the same features on a large society is utopian and leads to tyranny. With that admitted, it is clear that as social relations become wider and more various, the common good conceived as reciprocal trustfulness cannot be sought in methods which the model of the small, closed society inspires; such a model is, in the contrary, entirely misleading.

39. Edwin Cannan, *The History of Local Rates in England*, 2nd edn (London, 1912), p. 162.

40. While one has become used to find the confused minds of social philosophers talking about 'social justice', it greatly pains me if I find a distinguished thinker like the historian Peter Geyl (*Encounters in History*, London, 1963, p. 358) thoughtlessly using the term. J. M. Keynes (*The Economic Consequences of Mr. Churchill*, London, 1925, *Collected Writings*, vol. IX, p. 223) also writes unhesitatingly that 'on grounds of social justice no case can be made for reducing the wages of the miners.'

41. Cf. e.g. Walter Kaufmann, *Without Guilt and Justice* (New York, 1973) who, after rightly rejecting the concepts of distributive and retributive justice, believes that this must lead him to reject the concept of justice altogether. But this is not surprising after even *The Times* (London) in a thoughtful leading article (I March 1957) apropos the appearance of an English translation of Josef Pieper's *Justice* (London, 1957) had observed that 'roughly, it may be said that in so far as the notion of justice continues to influence political thinking, it has been reduced to the meaning of the phrase "distributive justice" and that the idea of commutative justice has almost entirely ceased to influence our calculations except in so far it is embodied in laws and customs—in the maxims for instance of the Common Law— which are preserved from sheer conservatism.' Some contemporary social philosophers indeed beg the whole issue by so *defining* 'justice' that it includes only distributive justice. See e.g. Brian M. Barry, 'Justice and the Common Good', *Analysis*, 19, 1961, p. 80: 'although Hume uses the expression "rules of justice" to cover such things as property rules, *"justice" is now analytically tied to*

"desert" and "need", so that one could quite properly say that some of what Hume calls "rules of justice" were unjust' (italics added). Cf. *ibid.*, p. 89.

42.   J. S. Mill, *On Liberty*, ed. McCallum (Oxford, 1946), p. 70.

43.   On the destruction of moral values by scientific error see my discussion in my inaugural lecture as Visiting Professor at the University of Salzburg, *Die Irrtümer des Konstruktivismus und die Grundlagen legitimer Kritik gesellschaftlicher Gebilde* (Munich, 1970, now reprinted for the Walter Eucken Institute at Freiburg i.Brg. by J. C. B. Mohr, Tübingen, 1975).

44.   John Rawls, 'Constitutional Liberty and the Concept of Justice', *Nomos IV, Justice* (New York, 1963), p. 102 where the passage quoted is preceded by the statement that 'It is the system of institutions which has to be judged and judged from a general point of view.' I am not aware that Professor Rawls' later more widely read work *A Theory of Justice* (Harvard, 1971) contains a comparatively clear statement of the main point, which may explain why this work seems often, but as it appears to me wrongly, to have been interpreted as lending support to socialist demands, e.g. by Daniel Bell, 'On Meritocracy and Equality', *Public Interest*, Autumn 1972, p. 72, who describes Rawls' theory as 'the most comprehensive effort in modern philosophy to justify a socialistic ethic.'

Appendix To Chapter Nine

This appendix has been published as an article in the 75th anniversary issue of the Norwegian journal *Farmand* (Oslo, 1966).

45.   For discussions of the problem cf. the papers assembled in the *Philosophical Review*, April 1955 and in D. D. Raphael (ed.), *Political Theory and the Rights of Man* (London, 1967).

46.   See the *Universal Declaration of Human Rights* adopted by the General Assembly of the United Nations on 10 December 1948. It is reprinted, and the intellectual background of this document can be found, in the volume entitled *Human Rights, Comments and Interpretations*, a symposium edited by UNESCO (London and New York, 1945). It contains in the Appendix not only a 'Memorandum Circulated by UNESCO on the Theoretical Bases of the Rights of Men' (pp. 251-4), but also a 'Report of the UNESCO Committee on the Theoretical Bases of the Human Rights' (in other places described as the 'UNESCO Committee on the Principles of the Rights of Men'), in which it is explained that their efforts were directed towards reconciling the two different 'complementary' working concepts of human rights, of which one 'started, from the premises of inherent individual rights . . . while the other was based on Marxist principles', and at finding 'some common measure of the two tendencies'. 'This common formulation,' it is explained, 'must by some means reconcile the various divergent or opposing formulations now in existence'! (The British representatives on that committee were Professors H. J. Laski and E. H. Carr!).

47.   *Ibid.*, p. 22, Professor E. H. Carr, the chairman of the UNESCO Committee of experts, explains that 'If the new declaration of the rights of man is to include provisions for social services, for maintenance in childhood, in old age, in incapacity or in unemployment, it becomes clear that no society can guarantee the enjoyment of such rights unless it in turn has the right to call upon and direct the productive capacities of the individuals enjoying them'!

48.   G. Vlastos, 'Justice', *Revue Internationale de la Philosophie,* 1957, p. 331.

49.   On the whole document cf. Maurice Cranston, 'Human Rights, Real and Supposed' in the volume edited by D. D. Raphael quoted in note 45 above, where the author argues that 'a philosophically respectable concept of human rights has been muddied, obscured, and debilitated in recent years by an attempt to incorporate in it specific rights of a different logical category.' See also the same author's *Human Rights Today* (London, 1955).

Part II

KNOWLEDGE, EMERGENCE, AND THE MARKET PROCESS

THE USE OF KNOWLEDGE IN SOCIETY*

Friedrich A. Hayek

1

What is the problem we wish to solve when we try to construct a rational economic order? On certain familiar assumptions the answer is simple enough. *If* we possess all the relevant information, *if* we can start out from a given system of preferences, and *if* we command complete knowledge of available means, the problem which remains is purely one of logic. That is, the answer to the question of what is the best use of the available means is implicit in our assumptions. The conditions which the solution of this optimum problem must satisfy have been fully worked out and can be stated best in mathematical form:put at their briefest, they are that the marginal rates of substitution between any two commodities or factors must be the same in all their different uses.

This, however, is emphatically *not* the economic problem which society faces. And the economic calculus which we have developed to solve this logical problem, though an important step toward the solution of the economic problem of society, does not yet provide an answer to it. The reason for this is that the "data" from which the economic calculus starts are never for the whole society "given" to a single mind which could work out the implications and can never be so given.

The peculiar character of the problem of a rational economic order is determined precisely by the fact that the knowledge of the circumstances of which we must make use never exists in the concentrated or integrated form but solely as the dispersed bits of incomplete and frequently contradictory knowledge which all the separate individuals possess. The economic problem of society is thus not merely a problem of how to allocate "given" resources—if "given" is taken to mean given to a single mind which deliberately solves the problem set by these "data." It is rather a problem of how to secure the best use of resources known to any of the members of society, for ends whose relative importance only these individuals know. Or, to put it briefly, it is a problem of the utilization of knowledge which is not given to anyone in its totality.

This character of the fundamental problem has, I am afraid, been obscured rather than illuminated by many of the recent refinements of economic theory, particularly by many of the uses made of mathematics. Though the problem with which I want primarily to deal in this paper is the problem of a rational economic organization, I shall in its course be led again and again to point to its close connections with certain methodological questions. Many of the points I wish to make are indeed conclusions toward which diverse paths of reasoning have unexpectedly converged. But, as I now see these problems, this is no accident. It seems to me that many of the current disputes with regard to both economic theory and economic policy have their common origin in a misconception about the nature of the economic problem of society. This misconception in turn is due to an erroneous transfer to social phenomena of the habits of thought we have developed in dealing with the phenomena of nature.

2

In ordinary language we describe by the word "planning" the complex of interrelated decisions about the allocation of our available resources. All economic activity is in this sense planning; and in any society in which many people collaborate, this planning, whoever does it, will in some measure have to be based on knowledge which, in the first instance, is not given to the planner but to somebody else, which somehow will have to be conveyed to the planner. The various ways in which the knowledge on which people base their plans is communicated to them is the crucial problem for any theory explaining the economic process, and the problem of what is the best way of utilizing knowledge initially dispersed among all the people is at least one of the main problems of economic policy—or of designing an efficient economic system.

The answer to this question is closely connected with that other question which arises here, that of *who* is to do the planning. It is about this question that all the dispute about "economic planning" centers. This is not a dispute about whether planning is to be done or not. It is a dispute as to whether planning is to be done centrally, by one authority for the whole economic system, or is to be divided among many individuals. Planning in the specific sense in which the term is used in contemporary controversy necessarily means central planning—direction of the whole economic system according to one unified plan. Competition, on the other hand, means decentralized planning by many separate persons. The halfway house between the two, about which many people talk but which few like when they see it, is the delegation of planning to organized industries, or, in other words, monopolies.

Which of these systems is likely to be more efficient depends mainly on the question under which of them we can expect that fuller use will be made of the existing knowledge. This, in turn, depends on whether we are more likely to succeed in putting at the disposal of a single central authority all the knowledge which ought to be used but which is initially dispersed among many different individuals, or in conveying to the individuals such additional knowledge as they need in order to enable them to dovetail their plans with those of others.

3

It will at once be evident that on this point the position will be different with respect to different kinds of knowledge. The answer to our question will therefore largely turn on the relative importance of the different kinds of knowledge: those more likely to be at the disposal of particular individuals and those which we should with greater confidence expect to find in the possession of an authority made up of suitably chosen experts. If it is today so widely assumed that the latter will be in a better position, this is because one kind of knowledge, namely, scientific knowledge, occupies now so prominent a place in public imagination that we tend to forget that it is not the only kind that is relevant. It may be admitted that, as far as scientific knowledge is concerned, a body of suitably chosen experts may be in the best position to command all the best knowledge available—though this is of course merely shifting the difficulty to the problem of selecting the experts. What I wish to point out is that, even assuming that this problem can be readily solved, it is only a small part of the wider problem.

Today it is almost heresy to suggest that scientific knowledge is not the sum of all knowledge. But a little reflection will show that there is beyond question a body of very important but unorganized knowledge which cannot possibly be called scientific in the sense of knowledge of general rules: the knowledge of the particular circumstances of time and place. It is with respect to this that practically every individual has some advantage over all others because he possesses unique information of which beneficial use might be made, but of which use can be made only if the decisions depending on it are left to him or are made with his active co-operation. We need to remember only how much we have to learn in any occupation after we have completed our theoretical training, how big a part of our working life we spend learning particular jobs, and how valuable an asset in all walks of life is knowledge of people, of local conditions, and of special circumstances. To know of and put to use a machine not fully employed, or somebody's skill which could be better utilized, or to be aware of a surplus stock which can be drawn upon during an interruption of supplies, is socially quite as useful as the knowledge of better alternative techniques. The shipper who earns his living from using otherwise empty or half-filled journeys of tramp-steamers, or the estate agent whose whole knowledge is almost exclusively one of temporary opportunities, or the *arbitrageur* who gains from local differences of commodity prices—are all performing eminently useful functions based on special knowledge of circumstances of the fleeting moment not know to others.

It is a curious fact that this sort of knowledge should today be generally regarded with a kind of contempt and that anyone who by such knowledge gains an advantage over somebody better equipped with theoretical or technical knowledge is thought to have acted almost disreputably. To gain an advantage from better knowledge of facilities of communication or transport is sometimes regarded as almost dishonest, although it is quite as important that society make use of the best opportunities in this respect as in using the latest scientific discoveries. This prejudice has in a considerable measure affected the attitude toward commerce in general compared with that toward production. Even economists who regard themselves as definitely immune to the crude materialist fallacies of the past constantly commit the same mistake where activities directed toward the acquisition of such practical knowledge are concerned—apparently because in their scheme of things all such knowledge is supposed to "given." The common idea now seems to be that all such knowledge should as a matter of course be readily at the command of everybody, and the reproach of irrationality leveled against the existing economic order is frequently based on the fact that it is not so available. This view disregards the fact that the method by which such knowledge can be made as widely available as possible is precisely the problem to which we have to find an answer.

4

If it is fashionable to minimize the importance of the knowledge of the particular circumstances of time and place, this is closely connected with the smaller importance which is now attached to change as such. Indeed, there are few points on which the assumptions made (usually only implicitly) by the "planners" differ from those of their opponents as much as with regard to the significance and frequency of changes which will make substantial alterations of production plans necessary. Of course, if detailed economic plans could be laid down for fairly long periods in advance and then closely adhered to, so that no further economic decisions of importance would be required, the task of drawing up a comprehensive plan governing all economic activity would be much less formidable.

It is, perhaps, worth stressing that economic problems arise always and only in consequence of change. As long as things continue as before, or at least as they were expected to, there arise no new problems requiring a decision, no need to form a new plan. The belief that changes, or at least day-to-day adjustments, have become less important in modern times implies the contention that economic problems also have become less important. This belief in the decreasing importance of change is, for that reason, usually held by the same people who argue that the importance of economic considerations has been driven into the background by the growing importance of technological knowledge.

Is it true that, with the elaborate apparatus of modern production, economic decisions are required only at long intervals, as when a new factory is to be erected or a new process to be introduced? Is it true that, once a plant has been built, the rest is all more or less mechanical, determined by the character of the plant, and leaving little to be changed in adapting to the ever changing circumstances of the moment?

The fairly widespread belief in the affirmative is not, as far as I can ascertain, borne out by the practical experience of the businessman. In a competitive industry at any rate—and such an industry alone can serve as a test—the task of keeping cost from rising requires constant struggle, absorbing a great part of the energy of the manager. How easy it is for an inefficient manager to dissipate the differentials on which profitability rests and that it is possible, with the same technical facilities, to produce with a great variety of costs are among the commonplaces of business experience which do not seem to be equally familiar in the study of the economist. The very strength of the desire, constantly voiced by producers and engineers, to be allowed to proceed untrammeled by considerations of money costs, is eloquent testimony to the extent to which these factors enter into their daily work.

One reason why economists are increasingly apt to forget about the constant small changes which make up the whole economic picture is probably their growing preoccupation with statistical aggregates, which show a very much greater stability than the movements of the detail. The comparative stability of the aggregates cannot, however, be accounted for—as the statisticians occasionally seem to be inclined to do—by the "law of large numbers" or the mutual compensation of random changes. The number of elements with which we have to deal is not large enough for such accidental forces to produce stability. The continuous flow of goods and services is maintained by constant deliberate adjustments, by new dispositions made every day in the light of circumstances not known the day before, by B stepping in at once when A fails to deliver. Even the large and highly mechanized plant keeps going largely because of an environment upon which it can draw for all sorts of unexpected needs:tiles for its roof, stationery or its forms, and all the thousand and one kinds of equipment in which it cannot be self-contained and which the plans for the operation of the plant require to be readily available in the market.

This is, perhaps, also the point where I should briefly mention the fact that the sort of knowledge with which I have been concerned is knowledge of the kind which by its nature cannot enter into statistics and therefore cannot be conveyed to any central authority in statistical form. The statistics which such a central authority would have to use would have to be arrived at precisely by abstracting from minor differences between the things, by lumping together, as resources of one kind, items which differ as regards location, quality, and other particulars, in a way which may be very significant for the specific decision. It follows from this that central planning based on statistical information by its nature cannot take direct account of these circumstances of time and place and that the central planner will have to find some way or other in which the decisions depending on them can be left to the "man on the spot."

5

If we can agree that the economic problem of society is mainly one of rapid adaptation to changes in the particular circumstances of time and place, it would seem to follow that the ultimate decisions must be left to the people who are familiar with these circumstances, who know directly of the relevant changes and of the resources immediately available to meet them. We cannot expect that this problem will be solved by first communicating all this knowledge to a central board which, after integrating all knowledge, issues its orders. We must solve it by some form of decentralization. But this answers only part of our problem. We need decentralization because only thus can we insure that the knowledge of the particular circumstances of time and place will be promptly used. But the "man on the spot" cannot decide solely on the basis of his limited but intimate knowledge of the facts of his immediate surrounding. There still remains the problem of communicating to him such further information as he needs to fit his decisions into the whole pattern of changes of the larger economic system.

How much knowledge does he need to do so successfully? Which of the events which happened beyond the horizon of his immediate knowledge are of relevance to his immediate decision, and how much of them need he know?

There is hardly anything that happens anywhere in the world that *might* not have an effect on the decision he ought to make. But he need not know of these events as such, nor of *all* their effects. It does not matter for him *why* at the particular moment more screws of one size than of another are wanted, *why* paper bags are more readily available than canvas bags, or *why* skilled labor, or particular machine tools, have for the moment become more difficult to obtain. All that is significant for him is *how much more or less* difficult to procure they have become compared with other things with which he is also concerned, or how much more or less urgently wanted are the alternative things he produces or uses. It is always a question of the relative importance of the particular things with which he is concerned, and the causes which alter their relative importance are of no interest to him beyond the effect on those concrete things of his own environment.

It is in this connection that what I have called the "economic calculus" (or the Pure Logic of Choice) helps us, at least by analogy, to see how this problem can be solved, and in fact is being solved, by the price system. Even the single controlling mind, in possession of all the data for some small, self-contained economic system, would not—every time some small adjustment in the allocation of resources had to be made—go explicitly through all the relations between ends and means which might possibly be affected. It is indeed the great contribution of the Pure Logic Choice that it has demonstrated conclusively that even such a single mind could solve this kind of problem only be constructing and constantly using rates of equivalence (or "values," or "marginal rates of substitution"), that is, by attaching to each kind of scarce resource a numerical index which cannot be derived from any property possessed by that particular thing, but which reflects, or in which is condensed, its significance in view of the whole means-end structure. In any small change he will have to consider only these quantitative indices (or "values") in which all the relevant information is concentrated; and, by adjusting the quantities one by one, he can appropriately rearrange his dispositions without having to solve the whole puzzle *ab initio* or without needing at any stage to survey it at once in all its ramifications.

Fundamentally, in a system in which the knowledge of the relevant facts is dispersed among many people, prices can act to co-ordinate the separate actions of different people in the same way as subjective values help the individual to co-ordinate the parts of his plan. It is worth contemplating for a moment a very simple and commonplace instance of the action of the price system to see what precisely it accomplishes. Assume that somewhere in the world a new opportunity for the use of some raw material, say, tin, has arisen, or that one of the sources of supply of tin has been eliminated. It does not matter for our purpose—and it is significant that it does not matter—which of these two causes has made tin more scarce. All that the users of tin need to know is that some of the tin they used to consume is now more profitably employed elsewhere and that, in consequence, they must economize tin. There is no need for the great majority of them even to know where the more urgent need has arisen, or in favor of what other needs they ought to husband the supply. If only some of them know directly of the new demand, and switch resources over to it, and if the people who are aware of the new gap thus created in turn fill it from still other sources, the effect will rapidly spread throughout the whole economic system and influence not only all the uses of tin but also those of its substitutes and the substitutes of these substitutes, the supply of all the things made of tin, and their substitutes, and so on, and all this without the great majority of those instrumental in bringing about these substitutions knowing anything at all about the original cause of these changes. The whole acts as one market, not because any of its members survey the whole field, but because their limited individual fields of vision sufficiently overlap so that through many intermediaries the relevant information is communicated to all. The mere fact that there is one price for any commodity—or rather that local prices are connected in a manner determined by the cost of transport, etc.—brings about the solution which (it is just conceptually possible) might have been arrived at by one single mind possessing all the information which is in fact dispersed among all the people involved in the process.

6

We must look at the price system as such a mechanism for communicating information if we want to understand its real function—a function which, of course, it fulfils less perfectly as prices grow more rigid. (Even when quoted prices have become quite rigid, however, the forces which would operate through changes in price still operate to a considerable extent through changes in the other terms of the contract.) The most significant fact about this system is the economy of knowledge with which it operates, or how little the individual participants need to know in order to be able to take the right action. In abbreviated form, by a kind of symbol, only the most essential information is passed on and passed on only to those concerned. It is more than a metaphor to describe the price system as a kind of machinery for registering change, or a system of telecommunications which enables individual producers to watch merely the movement of a few pointers, as an engineer might watch the hands of a few dials, in order to adjust their activities to changes of which they may never know more than is reflected in the price movement.

Of course, these adjustments are probably never "perfect" in the sense in which the economist conceives of them in his equilibrium analysis. But I fear that our theoretical habits of approaching the problem with the assumption of more or less perfect knowledge on the part of almost everyone has made us somewhat blind to the true function of the price mechanism and led us to apply rather misleading standards in judging its efficiency. The marvel is that in a case like that of a scarcity of one raw material, without an order being issued, without more than perhaps a handful of people knowing the cause, tens of thousands of people whose identity could not be ascertained by months of investigation, are made to use the material or its products more sparingly; that is, they move in the right direction. This is enough of a marvel even if, in a constantly changing world, not all will hit off so perfectly that their profit rates will always be maintained at the same even or "normal" level.

I have deliberately used the word "marvel" to shock the reader out of the complacency with which we often take the working of this mechanism for granted. I am convinced that if it were the result of deliberate human design, and if the people guided by the price changes understood that their decisions have significance far beyond their immediate aid, this mechanism would have been acclaimed as one of the greatest triumphs of the human mind. Its misfortune is the double one that it is not the product of human design and that the people guided by it usually do not know why they are made to do what they do. But those who clamor for "conscious direction"—and who cannot believe that anything which has evolved without design (and even without our understanding it) should solve problems which we should not be able to solve consciously—should remember this: The problem is precisely how to extend the span of our utilization of resources beyond the span of the control of any one mind; and, therefore, how to dispense with the need of conscious control and how to provide inducements which will make the individuals do the desirable things without anyone having to tell them what to do.

The problem which we meet here is by no means peculiar to economics but arises in connection with nearly all truly social phenomena, with language and with most of our cultural inheritance, and constitutes really the central theoretical problem of all social science. As Alfred Whitehead has said in another connection, "It is a profoundly erroneous truism, repeated by all copy-books and by eminent people when they are making speeches, that we should cultivate the habit of thinking what we are doing. The precise opposite is the case. Civilization advances by extending the number of important operations which we can perform without thinking about them." This is of profound significance in the social field. We make constant use of formulas, symbols, and rules whose meaning we do not understand and through the use of which we avail ourselves of the assistance of knowledge which individually we do not possess. We have developed these practices and institutions by building upon habits and institutions which have proved successful in their own sphere and which have in turn become the foundation of the civilization we have built up.

The price system is just one of those formations which man has learned to use (though he is still very far from having learned to make the best use of it) after he had stumbled upon it without understanding it. Through it not only a division of labor but also a co-ordinated utilization of resources based on an equally divided knowledge has become possible. The people who like to deride any suggestion that this may be so usually distort the argument by insinuating that it asserts that by some miracle just that sort of system has spontaneously grown up which is best suited to modern civilization. It is the other way round: man has been able to develop that division of labor on which our civilization is based because he happened to stumble upon a method which made it possible. Had he not done so, he might still have developed some other, altogether different, type of civilization, something like the "state" of the termite ants, or some other altogether unimaginable type. All that we can say is that nobody has yet succeeded in designing an alternative system in which certain features of the existing one can be preserved which are dear even to those who most violently assail it—such as particularly the extent to which the individual can choose his pursuits and consequently freely use his own knowledge and skill.

7

It is in many ways fortunate that the dispute about the indispensability of the price system for any rational calculation in a complex society is now no longer conducted entirely between camps holding different political views. The thesis that without the price system we could not preserve a society based on such extensive division of labor as ours was greeted with a howl of derision when it was first advanced by von Mises twenty-five years ago. Today the difficulties which some still find in accepting it are no longer mainly political, and this makes for an atmosphere much more conducive to reasonable discussion. When we find Leon Trotsky arguing that "economic accounting is unthinkable without market relations"; when Professor Oscar Lange promises Professor von Mises a statue in the marble halls of the future Central Planning Board; and when Professor Abba P. Lerner rediscovers Adam Smith and emphasizes that the essential utility of the price system consists in inducing the individual, while seeking his own interest, to do what is in the general interest, the differences can indeed no longer be ascribed to political prejudice. The remaining dissent seems clearly to be due to purely intellectual, and more particularly methodological, differences.

A recent statement by Joseph Schumpeter in his *Capitalism, Socialism, and Democracy* provides a clear illustration of one of the methodological differences which I have in mind. Its author is pre-eminent among those economists who approach economic phenomena in the light of a certain branch of positivism. To him these phenomena accordingly appear as objectively given quantities of commodities impinging directly upon each other, almost, it would seem, without any intervention of human minds. Only against this background can I account for the following (to me startling) pronouncement. Professor Schumpeter argues that the possibility of a rational calculation in the absence of markets for the factors of production follows for the theorist "from the elementary proposition that consumers in evaluating ('demanding') consumers' goods *ipso facto* also evaluate the means of production which enter into the production of these goods."[1]

Taken literally, this statement is simply untrue. The consumers do nothing of the kind. What Professor Schumpeter's *"ipso facto"* presumably means is that the valuation of the factors of production is implied in, or follows necessarily from, the valuation of consumers' goods. But this, too, is not correct. Implication is a logical relationship which can be meaningfully asserted only of propositions simultaneously present to one and the same mind. It is evident, however, that the values of the factors of production do not depend solely on the valuation of the consumers' goods but also on the conditions of supply of the various factors of production. Only to a mind to which all these facts were simultaneously known would the answer necessarily follow from the facts given to it. The practical problem, however, arises precisely because these facts are never so given to a single mind, and because, in consequence, it is necessary that in the solution of the problem knowledge should be used that is dispersed among many people.

The problem is thus in no way solved if we can show that all the facts, *if* they were known to a single mind (as we hypothetically assume them to be given to the observing economist), would uniquely determine the solution; instead we must show how a solution is produced by the interactions of people each of whom possesses only partial knowledge. To assume all the knowledge to be given to a single mind in the same manner in which we assume it to be given to us as the explaining economists is to assume the problem away and to disregard everything that is important and significant in the real world.

That an economist of Professor Schumpeter's standing should thus have fallen into a trap which the ambiguity of the term "datum" sets to the unwary can hardly be explained as a simple error. It suggests rather that there is something fundamentally wrong with an approach which habitually disregards an essential part of the phenomena with which we have to deal: the unavoidable imperfection of man's knowledge and the consequent need for a process by which knowledge is constantly communicated and acquired. Any approach, such as that of much of mathematical economics with its simultaneous equations, which in effect starts from the assumption that people's *knowledge* corresponds with the objective *facts* of the situation, systematically leaves out what is our main task to explain. I am far from denying that in our system equilibrium analysis has a useful function to perform. But when it comes to the point where it misleads some of our leading thinkers into believing that the situation which it describes has direct relevance to the solution of practical problems, it is high time that we remember that it does not deal with the social process at all and that is no more than a useful preliminary to the study of the main problem.

Notes

*Reprinted from the *American Economic Review*, XXXV, No. 4 (September, 1945), 519-30.

1. *Capitalism, Socialism, and Democracy* (New York: Harper & Bros., 1942), p. 175. Professor Schumpeter is, I believe, also the original author of the myth that Pareto and Barone have "solved" the problem of socialist calculation. What they, and many others, did was merely to state the conditions which a rational allocation of resources would have to satisfy and to point out that these were essentially the same as the conditions of equilibrium of a competitive market. This is something altogether different from showing how the allocation of resources satisfying these conditions can be found in practice. Pareto himself (from whom Barone has taken practically everything he has to say), far from claiming to have solved the practical problem, in fact explicitly denies that it can be solved without the help of the market. See his *Manuel d'economie pure* (2d ed., 1927), pp. 233-34. The relevant passage is quoted in an English translation at the beginning of my article on "Socialist Calculation: The Competitive 'Solution,'" in *Economica,* VIII, No. 26 (new ser., 1940), 125; reprinted below as chapter viii.

THE DIFFERENCE DIFFERENCE MAKES: WAGGLE DANCES, THE BAY OF PIGS, AND THE VALUE OF DIVERSITY

James Surowiecki

I

In 1899, Ransom E. Olds opened the Olds Motor Works in Detroit, Michigan. Olds had been in the automobile business since the mid-1880s, when he built his first car, a steam-powered vehicle with three wheels. But success had remained elusive. After moving on to gasoline-powered cars, Olds started his own company in the early 1890s, but it floundered, leaving him nearly destitute. He was only able to start the Motor Works, in fact, by convincing a financier named Samuel Smith to put up nearly all the money. Olds got his company, but he also got a boss to whom he had to answer. This was a problem, because the two did not agree on what the Olds Motor Works should be making. Smith thought the company should cater to the high end of the market, building large, expensive cars with all the trimmings. Olds, though, was more intrigued by the possibility of building a car that could be marketed to the middle class. In 1900, the auto market was still minuscule—there were fewer than 15,000 cars on the road that year. But it seemed plausible that an invention as revolutionary as the car would be able to find a mass audience, if you could figure out a way to make one cheaply enough.

Olds couldn't commit himself to one idea though. Instead, he dabbled, building eleven different prototypes in the company's first year, including electric-powered cars in addition to steamers and internal-combustion-powered vehicles. It was a strategy that seemed destined for failure. But in March of 1901, bad luck lent a helping hand. Olds's factory burned down, and all the prototypes went up in flames. All, that is, but one—which happened to be right near the door, and to be light enough that the lone man present could push it to safety. The prototype that survived, fortuitously enough, was the inexpensive, low-cost model that Olds had imagined could be sold to a much larger market. In the wake of the fire, Olds rushed the prototype into production. The vehicle he produced was known as the "curved-dash Olds," since the floor curved up to form the dashboard. In design, it was an ungainly thing, a horseless carriage, started by a seat-side crank and steered by a tiller. It had two forward gears, one reverse, and a small, single-cylinder engine. It won no points for style. But at $600, it was within the reach of many Americans.

Though Olds was an engineer, he turned out to be something of a marketing whiz, too. He concocted elaborate publicity stunts—like sending a young driver eight hundred miles cross-country in an Olds to the Manhattan Auto Show—that won the attention of the press and of auto dealers while demonstrating to a still-skeptical public that the automobile was not just a gimmick. He drove a souped-up Olds in the first race at Daytona Beach. And in 1903, his company sold 4,000 vehicles , more than any other U.S. manufacturer, while two years later it sold 6,500 cars. Olds, it turned out, had designed the first mass-produced automobile in American history.

Olds's success came in the face of fierce competition. In that first decade of the twentieth century, there were literally hundreds of companies trying to make automobiles. And because there was no firm definition of what a car should look like, or what kind of engine it should have, those companies offered a bewildering variety of vehicles, including the aforementioned steamers and battery-powered cars. The victory of the gasoline-powered engine was not a foregone conclusion. Thomas Edison, for instance, had designed a battery-powered vehicle, and in 1899 one sage had offered the prediction that "the whole of the United States will be sprinkled with electric changing stations." At one point, a third of all the cars on U.S. roads were electric-powered. Similarly, steam-powered engines were seen by many as the most logical way to propel a vehicle, since steam obviously worked so well in propelling trains and boats. In the early part of the decade, there were more than a hundred makers of steam-powered cars, and the most successful of these, the Stanley Steamer, became legendary for its speed—in 1905, it went 127 miles per hour—and the comfort of its ride.

As the decade wore on, though, the contenders began to fade. Electric-powered cars couldn't go far enough without a recharge. Steam-powered cars took a long time to heat up. More important, though, the makers of gasoline-powered cars were the first to invest heavily in mass-production techniques and to figure out a way to reach the mass market. Olds had been the first automaker to buy different parts from different manufacturers, instead of making them all itself. Cadillac became the first manufacturer successfully to use standardized components, which cut down on the time and cost of manufacturing. And Ford, of course, revolutionized the industry with the moving assembly line and a relentless focus on producing one kind of car as cheaply as possible. By the time of World War

I, there were still more than a hundred automakers in America. But more than four hundred car companies had gone out of business or been acquired, including the Olds Motor Works, which had been bought by General Motors.

As for Olds himself, he never really got to enjoy the early success of his company since he left it after only a few years following a fight with Samuel Smith's sons. He eventually started a new car company called REO. But the moment had passed him by. What he had started, Henry Ford—who by World War I made almost half the cars in America—had finished. There was no more talk of steam- or electric-powered vehicles, and cars no longer came in a bewildering variety of shapes and sizes. Everyone knew what an automobile looked like. It looked like a Model T.

THE STORY OF THE early days of the U.S. auto industry is not an unusual one. In fact, if you look at the histories of most new industries in America, from the railroads to television to personal computers to, most recently, the Internet, you'll see a similar pattern. In all these cases, the early days of the business are characterized by a profusion of alternatives, many of them dramatically different from each other in design and technology. As time passes, the market winnows out the winners and losers, effectively choosing which technologies will flourish and which will disappear. Most of the companies fail, going bankrupt or getting acquired by other firms. At the end of the day, a few players are left standing and in control of most of the market.

This seems like a wasteful way of developing and selling new technologies. And, the experience of Google notwithstanding, there is no guarantee that at the end of the process, the best technology will necessarily win (since the crowd is not deciding all at once, but rather over time). So why do it this way?

For an answer, consider a hive of bees. Bees are remarkably efficient at finding food. According to Thomas Seeley, author of *The Wisdom of the Hive,* a typical bee colony can search six or more kilometers from the hive, and if there is a flower patch within two kilometers of the hive, the bees have a better-than-half chance of finding it. How do the bees do this? They don't sit around and have a collective discussion about where foragers should go. Instead, the hive sends out a host of scout bees to search the surrounding area. When a scout bee has found a nectar source that seems strong, he comes back and does a waggle dance, the intensity of which is shaped, in some way, by the excellence of the nectar supply at the site. The waggle dance attracts other forager bees, which follow the first forager, while foragers who have found less-good sites attract fewer followers and, in some cases, eventually abandon their sites entirely. The result is that bee foragers end up distributing themselves across different nectar sources in an almost perfect fashion, meaning that they get as much food as possible relative to the time and energy they put into searching. It is a collectively brilliant solution to the colony's food problem.

What's important, though, is the way the colony gets to that collectively intelligent solution. It does not get there by first rationally considering all the alternatives and then determining an ideal foraging pattern. It *can't* do this, because it doesn't have any idea what the possible alternatives—that is, where the different flower patches—are. So instead, it sends out scouts in many different directions and trusts that at least one of them will find the best patch, return, and do a good dance so that the hive will know where the food source is.

This is, it's important to see, different from the kind of problem solving that we looked at earlier. In the case of the ox-weighing experiment, or the location of the *Scorpion,* or the betting markets, or the IEM, the group's job was to decide among already defined choices or to solve a well-defined problem. In those cases, different members of the group could bring different pieces of information to bear on a problem, but the set of possible solutions was already, in a sense, determined. (Bush or Gore would become president; the Yankees or the Marlins would win the World Series.) In the case of problems like finding the most nectar-rich flower patches, though, the task is more complicated. It becomes a twofold process. First, uncover the possible alternatives. Then decide among them.

In the first stage of this process, the list of possible solutions is so long that the smart thing to do is to send out as many scout bees as possible. You can think of Ransom Olds and Henry Ford and the countless would-be automakers who tried and failed, then, as foragers. They discovered (in this case, by inventing) the sources of nectar—the gasoline-powered car, mass production, the moving assembly line—and then asked the crowd to render its verdict. You might even see Olds's publicity stunts as a kind of equivalent to the waggle dance.

One key to this approach is a system that encourages, and funds, speculative ideas even though they have only slim possibilities of success. Even more important, though, is diversity—not in a sociological sense, but rather in a conceptual and cognitive sense. You want diversity among the entrepreneurs who are coming up with the ideas, so you end up with meaningful differences among those ideas rather than minor variations on the same concept. But you also want diversity among the people who have the money, too. If one virtue of a decentralized economy is that it diffuses decision-making power (at least on a small scale) throughout the system, that virtue becomes meaningless if all the people with power are alike (or if, as we'll see in the next chapter, they become alike through imitation). The more similar they are, the more similar the ideas they appreciate will be, and so the set of new products and concepts the rest of us see will be smaller than possible. By contrast, if they are diverse, the chances that at least someone will take a gamble on a radical or unlikely idea obviously increases. Take the early days of radio, when three companies—American Marconi, NESCO, and De Forest Wireless Telegraphy—dominated the industry. American Marconi relied on investment banks to raise its capital from large private investors; NESCO was funded by two rich men from Pittsburgh; and De Forest Wireless Telegraphy was owned by small stockholders looking for a speculative gain. The variety of possible funding sources encouraged a variety of technological approaches.

Of course, even with diverse sources of funding, most endeavors will end up as failures. This was nicely expressed by Jeff Bezos, the CEO of Amazon, when he compared the Internet boom to the Cambrian explosion, which was the period in evolutionary history that saw the birth and the extinction of more species than any other period. The point is that you cannot, or so at least it seems, have one without the other. It's a familiar truism that governments can't, and therefore shouldn't try to, "pick winners." But the truth is that no system seems all that good at picking winners in advance. After all, tens of thousands of new products are introduced every year, and only a small fraction ever become successes. The steam-powered car, the picturephone, the Edsel, the Betamax, pen computing; companies place huge bets on losers all the time. What makes a system successful is its ability to recognize losers and kill them quickly. Or, rather, what makes a system successful is its ability to generate lots of losers and then to recognize them as such and kill them off. Sometimes the messiest approach is the wisest.

II

Generating a diverse set of possible solutions isn't enough. The crowd also has to be able to distinguish the good solutions from the bad. We've already seen that groups seem to do a good job of making such distinctions. But does diversity matter to the group? In other words, once you've come up with a diverse set of possible solutions, does having a diverse group of decision makers make a difference?

It does, in two ways. Diversity helps because it actually adds perspectives that would otherwise be absent and because it takes away, or at least weakens, some of the destructive characteristics of group decision making. Fostering diversity is actually more important in small groups and in formal organizations than in the kinds of larger collectives—like markets or electorates—that we've already talked about for a simple reason: the sheer size of most markets, coupled with the fact that anyone with money can enter them (you don't need to be admitted or hired), means that a certain level of diversity is almost guaranteed. Markets, for instance,, are usually prima facie diverse because they're made up of people with different attitudes toward risk, different time horizons, different investing styles, and different information. On teams or in organizations, by contrast, cognitive diversity needs to be actively selected, and it's important to do so because in small groups it's easy for a few biased individuals to exert undue influence and skew the group's collective decision.

Scott Page is a political scientist at the University of Michigan who has done a series of intriguing experiments using computer-simulated problem-solving agents to demonstrate the positive effects of diversity. For instance, Page set up a series of groups of ten or twenty agents, with each agent endowed with a different set of skills, and had them solve a relatively sophisticated problem. Individually, some of the agents were very good at solving the problem while others were less effective. But what Page found was that a group made up of some smart agents and some not-so-smart agents almost always did better than a group made up just of smart agents. You could do as well or better by selecting a group randomly and letting it solve the problem as by spending a lot of time trying to find the smart agents and then putting them alone on the problem.

The point of Page's experiment is that diversity is, on its own, valuable, so that the simple fact of making a group diverse makes it better at problem solving. That doesn't mean that intelligence is irrelevant—none of the agents in the experiment were ignorant, and all the successful groups had some high-performing agents in them. But it does mean that, on the group level, intelligence alone is not enough, because intelligence alone cannot guarantee you different perspectives on a problem. In fact, Page speculates, grouping only smart people together doesn't work that well because the smart people (whatever that means) tend to resemble each other in what they can do. If you think about intelligence as a kind of toolbox of skills, the list of skills that are the "best" is relatively small, so that people who have them tend to be alike. This is normally a good thing, but it means that as a whole the group knows less than it otherwise might. Adding in a few people who know less, but have different skills, actually improves the group's performance.

This seems like an eccentric conclusion, and it is. It just happens to be true. The legendary organizational theorist James G. March, in fact, put it like this: "The development of knowledge may depend on maintaining an influx of the naïve and the ignorant, and . . . competitive victory does not reliably go to the properly educated." The reason, March suggested, is that groups that are too much alike find it harder to keep learning, because each member is bringing less and less new information to the table. Homogeneous groups are great at doing what they do well, but they become progressively less able to investigate alternatives. Or, as March has famously argued, they spend too much time exploiting and not enough time exploring. Bringing new members into the organization, even if they're less experienced and less capable, actually makes the group smarter simply because what little the new members do know is not redundant with what everyone else knows. As March wrote, "[The] effect does not come from the superior knowledge of the average new recruit. Recruits are, on average, less knowledgeable than the individuals they replace. The gains come from their diversity."

III

The fact that cognitive diversity matters does not mean that if you assemble a group of diverse but thoroughly uninformed people, their collective wisdom will be smarter than an expert's. But if you can assemble a diverse group of people who posses varying degrees of knowledge and insight, you're better of entrusting it with major decisions rather than leaving them in the hands of one or two people, no matter how smart those people are. If this is difficult to believe—in the same way that March's assertions are hard to believe—it's because it runs counter to our basic intuitions about intelligence and business. Suggesting that the organization with the smartest people may not be the best organization is heretical, particularly in a business world caught up in a ceaseless "war for talent" and governed by the assumption that a few superstars can make the difference between an excellent and a mediocre company. Heretical or not, it's the truth: the value of expertise is, in many contexts, overrated.

Now, experts obviously exist. The play of a great chess player is qualitatively different from the play of a merely accomplished one. The great player sees the board differently, he processes information differently, and he recognizes meaningful patterns almost instantly. As Herbert A. Simon and W. G. Chase demonstrated in the 1970s, if you show a chess expert and an amateur a board with a chess game in progress on it, the expert will be able to re-create from memory the layout of the entire game. The amateur won't. Yet if you show that same expert a board with chess pieces irregularly and haphazardly placed on it, he will not be able to re-create the layout. This is impressive testimony to how thoroughly chess is imprinted on the minds of successful players. But it also demonstrates how limited the scope of their expertise is. A chess expert knows about chess, and that's it. We intuitively assume that intelligence is fungible, and that people who are excellent at one intellectual pursuit would be excellent at another. But this is not the case with experts. Instead, the fundamental truth about expertise is that it is, as Chase has said, "spectacularly narrow."

More important, there's no real evidence that one can become expert in something as broad as "decision making" or "policy" or "strategy." Auto repair, piloting, skiing, perhaps even management: these are skills that yield to application, hard work, and native talent. But forecasting an uncertain future and deciding the best course of action in the face of that future are much less likely to do so. And much of what we've seen so far suggests that a large group of diverse individuals will come up with better and more robust forecasts and make more intelligent decisions than even the most skilled "decision maker."

We're all familiar with the absurd predictions that business titans have made: Harry Warner of Warner Bros. pronouncing in 1927, "Who the hell wants to hear actors talk?," or Thomas Watson of IBM declaring in 1943, "I think there is a world market for maybe five computers." These can be written off as amusing anomalies, since over the course of a century, some smart people are bound to say some dumb things. What can't be written off, though, is the dismal performance record of most experts.

Between 1984 and 1999, for instance, almost 90 percent of mutual-fund managers underperformed the Wilshire 5000 Index, a relatively low bar. The numbers for bond-fund managers are similar: in the most recent five-year period, more than 95 percent of all managed bond funds underperformed the market. After a survey of expert forecasts and analyses in a wide variety of fields, Wharton professor J. Scott Armstrong wrote, "I could find no studies that showed an important advantage for expertise." Experts, in some cases, were a little better at forecasting than laypeople (although a number of studies have concluded that nonpsychologists, for instance, are actually better at predicting people's behavior than psychologists are), but above a low level, Armstrong concluded, "expertise and accuracy are unrelated." James Shanteau is one of the country's leading thinkers on the nature of expertise, and has spent a great deal of time coming up with a method for estimating just how expert someone is. Yet even he suggests that "experts' decisions are seriously flawed."

Shanteau recounts a series of studies that have found experts' judgments to be neither consistent with the judgments of other experts in the field nor internally consistent. For instance, the between-expert agreement in a host of fields, including stock picking, livestock judging, and clinical psychology, is below 50 percent, meaning that experts are as likely to disagree as to agree. More disconcertingly, one study found that the internal consistency of medical pathologists' judgments was just 0.5, meaning that a pathologist presented with the same evidence would, half the time, offer a different opinion.

Experts are also surprisingly bad at what social scientists call "calibrating" their judgments. If your judgments are well calibrated, then you have a sense of how likely it is that your judgment is correct. But experts are much like normal people: they routinely overestimate the likelihood that they're right. A survey on the question of overconfidence by economist Terrance Odean found that physicians, nurses, lawyers, engineers, entrepreneurs, and investment bankers all believed that they knew more than they did. Similarly, a recent study of foreign-exchange traders found that 70 percent of the time, the traders overestimated the accuracy of their exchange-rate predictions. In other words, it wasn't just that they were wrong; they also didn't have any idea how wrong they were. And that seems to be the rule among experts. The only forecasters whose judgments are routinely well calibrated are expert bridge players and weathermen. It rains on 30 percent of the days when weathermen have predicted a 30 percent chance of rain.

Armstrong, who studies expertise and forecasting, summarized the case this way: "One would expect experts to have reliable information for predicting change and to be able to utilize the information effectively. However, expertise beyond a minimal level is of little value in forecasting change." Nor was there evidence that even if most experts were not very good at forecasting, a few titans were excellent. Instead, Armstrong wrote, "claims of accuracy by a single expert would seem to be of no practical value." This was the origin of Armstrong's "seer-sucker theory": "No matter how much evidence exists that seers do not exist, suckers will pay for the existence of seers."

Again, this doesn't mean that well-informed, sophisticated analysts are of no use in making good decisions. (And it certainly doesn't mean that you want crowds of amateurs trying to collectively perform surgery or fly planes.) It does mean that however well-informed and sophisticated an expert is, his advice and predictions should be pooled with those of others to get the most out of him. (The larger the group, the more reliable its judgment will be.) And it means that attempting to "chase the expert," looking for the one man who will have the answers to an organization's problem, is a waste of time. We know that the group's decision will consistently be better than most of the people in the group, and that it will be better decision after decision, while the performance of human experts will vary dramatically depending on the problem they're asked to solve. So it is unlikely that one person, over time, will do better than the group.

Now, it's possible that a small number of genuine experts—that is, people who can consistently offer better judgments than those of a diverse, informed group—do exist. The investor Warren Buffett, who has consistently outperformed the S&P 500 Index since the 1960s, is certainly someone who comes to mind. The problem is that even if these superior beings do exist, there is no easy way to identify them. Past performance, as we are often told, is no guarantee of future results. And there are so many would-be experts out there that distinguishing between those who are lucky and those who are genuinely good is often a near-impossible task. At the very least, it's a job that requires considerable patience: if you wanted to be sure that a successful money manager was beating the market because of his superior skill, and not because of luck or measurement error, you'd need many years, if not decades, of data. And if a group is so unintelligent that it will flounder without the right expert, it's not clear why the group would be intelligent enough to recognize an expert when it found him.

We think that experts will, in some sense, identify themselves, announcing their presence and demonstrating their expertise by their level of confidence. But it doesn't work that way. Strangely, experts are no more confident in their abilities than average people are, which is to say that they are overconfident like everyone else, but no more so. Similarly, there is very little correlation between experts' self-assessment and their performance. Knowing and knowing that you know are apparently two very different skills.

If this is the case, then why do we cling so tightly to the idea that the right expert will save us? And why do we ignore the fact that simply averaging a group's estimates will produce a very good result? Richard Larrick and Jack B. Soll suggest that the answer is that we have had intuitions about averaging. We assume averaging means dumbing down or compromising. When people are faced with the choice of picking one expert or picking pieces of advice from a number of experts, they try to pick the best expert rather than simply average across the group. Another reason, surely, is our assumption that true intelligence resides only in individuals, so that finding the right person—the right consultant, the right CEO—will make all the difference. In a sense, the crowd is blind to its own wisdom. Finally, we seek out experts because we get, as the writer Nassim Taleb asserts, "fooled by randomness." If there are enough people out there making predictions, a few of them are going to compile an impressive record over time. That does not mean that the record was the product of skill, nor does it mean that the record will continue into the future. Again, trying to find smart people will not lead you astray. Trying to find *the* smartest person will.

IV

In part because individual judgment is not accurate enough or consistent enough, cognitive diversity is essential to good decision making. The positive case for diversity, as we've seen, is that it expands a group's set of possible solutions and allows the group to conceptualize problems in novel ways. The negative case for diversity is that diversity makes it easier for a group to make decisions based on facts, rather than on influence, authority, or group allegiance. Homogeneous groups, particularly small ones, are often victims of what the psychologist Irving Janis called "groupthink." After a detailed study of a series of American foreign-policy fiascoes, including the Bay of Pigs invasion and the failure to anticipate Pearl Harbor, Janis argued that when decision makers are too much alike—in worldview and mind-set—they easily fall prey to groupthink. Homogeneous groups become cohesive more easily than diverse groups, and as they become more cohesive they also become more dependent on the group, more insulated from outside opinions, and therefore more convinced that the group's judgment on important issues must be right. These kinds of groups, Janis suggested, share an illusion of invulnerability, a willingness to rationalize away possible counterarguments to the group's position, and a conviction that dissent is not useful.

In the case of the Bay of Pigs invasion, for instance, the Kennedy administration planned and carried out its strategy without ever really talking to anyone who was skeptical of the prospects of success. The people who planned the operation were the same ones who were asked to judge whether it would be successful or not. The few people who voiced caution were quickly silenced. And, most remarkably, neither the intelligence branch of the CIA nor the Cuban desk of the State Department was consulted about the plan. The result was a bizarre neglect of some of the most elemental facts about Cuba in 1961, including the popularity of Fidel Castro, the strength of the Cuban army, and even the size of the island itself. (The invasion was predicated on the idea that 1,200 men could take over all of Cuba.) The administration even convinced itself that the world would believe the United States had nothing to do with the invasion, though American involvement was an open secret in Guatemala (where the Cuban exiles were being trained).

The important thing about groupthink is that it works not so much by censoring dissent as by making dissent seem somehow improbable. As the historian Arthur Schlesinger Jr. put it, "Our meetings took place in a curious atmosphere of assumed consensus." Even if at first no consensus exists—only the appearance of one—the group's sense of cohesiveness works to turn the appearance into reality, and in doing so helps dissolve whatever doubts members of the group might have. This process obviously works all the more powerfully in situations where the group's members already share a common mind-set. Because information that might represent a challenge to the conventional wisdom is either excluded or rationalized as obviously mistaken, people come away from discussions with their beliefs reinforced, convinced more than ever that they're right. Deliberation in a groupthink setting has the disturbing effect not of opening people's minds but of closing them. In that sense, Janis's work suggests that the odds of a homogeneous group of people reaching a good decision are slim at best.

One obvious cost of homogeneity is also that it fosters the palpable pressures toward conformity that groups often bring to bear on their members. This seems similar to the problem of groupthink, but it's actually distinct. When the pressure to conform is at work, a person changes his opinion not because he actually believes something different but because it's easier to change his opinion than to challenge the group. The classic and still definitive illustration of the power of conformity is Solomon Asch's experiment in which he asked groups of people to judge which of three lines was the same size as a line on a white card. Asch assembled groups of seven to nine people, one of them the subject and the rest (unbeknownst to the subject) confederates of the experimenter. He then put the subject at the end of the row of people, and asked each person to give his choice out loud. There were twelve cards in the experiment, and with the first two cards, everyone in the group identified the same lines. Beginning with the third card, though, Asch had his confederates begin to pick lines that were clearly not the same size as the line on the white card. The subject, in other words, sat there as everyone else in the room announced that the truth was something that he could plainly see was not true. Not surprisingly, this occasioned some bewilderment. The unwitting subjects changed the position of their heads to look at the lines from a different angle. They stood up to scrutinize the lines more closely. And they joked nervously about whether they were seeing things.

Most important, a significant number of the subjects simply went along with the group, saying that lines that were clearly shorter or longer than the line on the card were actually the same size. Most subjects said what they really thought most of the time, but 70 percent of the subjects changed their real opinion at least once, and a third of the subjects went along with the group at least half the time. When Asch talked to the subjects afterward, most of them stressed their desire to go along with the crowd. It wasn't that they really believed the lines were the same size. They were only willing to say they were in order not to stand out.

Asch went on, though, to show something just as important: while people are willing to conform even against their own better judgment, it does not take much to get them to stop. In one variant on his experiment, for instance, Asch planted a confederate who, instead of going along with the group, picked the lines that matched the line on the card, effectively giving the unwitting subject an ally. And that was enough to make a huge difference. Having even one other person in the group who felt as they did made the subjects happy to announce their thoughts, and the rate of conformity plummeted.

Ultimately, diversity contributes not just by adding different perspectives to the group but also by making it easier for individuals to say what they really think. As we'll see in the next chapter, independence of opinion is both a crucial ingredient in collectively wise decisions and one of the hardest things to keep intact. Because diversity helps preserve that independence, it's hard to have a collectively wise group without it.

Notes

Pages 23-26: There has never been, as far as I can tell, a scholarly biography of Ransom Olds, but lively accounts of his career can be found in Duane Yarnell, *Auto Pioneering* (Lansing: privately printed, 1949); and Glenn Niemeyer, *Automotive Career of Ransom E. Olds* (East Lansing: Bureau of Business and Economic Research, 1963).

Pages 26-27: An excellent account of the waggle dance, and much else besides, can be found in Thomas Seeley, *The Wisdom of the Hive* (Harvard: Harvard University Press, 1996). A book worth reading.

Page 28: Rajiv Kumar Sah and Joseph E. Stiglitz, "Human Fallibility and Economic Organization," *American Economic Review* 75 (1985): 292-97.

Sah and Stiglitz, "The Architecture of Economic Systems: Hierarchies and Polyarchies," *American Economic Review* 76 (1986): 716-27.

Page 28-29: Jeff Bezos drew the analogy between the Cambrian explosion and the Internet in a number of places, including an interview in *Business Week* (September 16, 1999), http://www.businessweek.com/ebiz/9909/916bezos.htm.

Page 30: Scott Page describes this experiment in "Return to the Toolbox," unpublished paper (2002). Also see Scott Page and Lu Hong, "Problem Solving by Heterogeneous Agents," *Journal of Economic Theory* 97 (2001): 123-63.

Pages 30-31: The seminal paper is James G. March, "Exploration and Exploitation in Organizational Learning," *Organization Science* 2 (1991): 71-87. The quotes are from pages 86 and 79.

Pages 32-34: The study of chess players can be found in Herbert A. Simon and W. G. Chase, "Skill in Chess," *American Scientist* 61 (1973): 394-403. The Chase quote is from James Shanteau, "Expert Judgment and Financial Decision Making," paper prepared for *Risky Business: Risk Behavior and Risk Management,* edited by Bo Green (Stockholm: Stockholm University, 1995). This paper includes an excellent survey of expert studies. Also see Shanteau, "Domain Differences in Expertise," Kansas State University unpublished paper (2002), http://www.ksu.edu/psych/cws/downloads.htm.

Pages 33-34: The numbers on mutual-fund performance are from John Bogle, *John Bogle on Investing* (New York: McGraw Hill, 2001): 20.

J. Scott Armstrong, "The Seer-Sucker Theory: The Value of Experts in Forecasting," *Technology Review* 83 (June-July 1980): 16-24.

Shanteau, "Expert Judgment and Financial Decision Making": 2. See also Shanteau, "Why Do Experts Disagree," in *Risk Behaviour and Risk Management in Business Life,* edited by B. Green et al. (Dordrecht: Kluwer Academic Press, 2000): 186-96.

Terrance Odean, "Volume, Volatility, Price, and Profit When All Traders Are Above Average," *Journal of Finance* 53 (1998): 1887-934.

Pages 35-36: Richard Larrick and Jack B. Soll, "Intuitions About Combining Opinions: Misappreciation of the Averaging Principle," INSEAD working paper 2003/09/TM (2003), http://ged.insead.edu/fichiersti/inseadwp2003/2003-09.pdf.

Pages 36-38: The definitive account of groupthink can be found of course, in Irving Janis, *Groupthink: Psychological Studies of Policy Decisions and Fiascoes* (Boston: Houghton Mifflin, 1982). See also Irving Janis and Leon Mann, *Decision Making: A Psychological Analysis of Conflict, Choice, and Commitment* (New York: The Free Press, 1977).

Pages 38-39: Solomon Asch, *Social Psychology* (Englewood Cliffs, NJ: Prentice-Hall, Inc., 1952). See also Asch, "Effects of Group Pressure upon the Modification and Distortion of Judgments," *Groups Leadership and Men,* edited by Harold Guetzkow (New York: Russell & Russell, 1963 [1951]): 177-90.

DESIGN FOR EMERGENCE

Michael D. McMaster

A
s we explore the structures of our corporations with the intention of changing their organisational design, we have a fundamental choice to make. This choice will create our context, and therefore influence all our other choices. The choice we face is this: do we use an engineering approach for our company—one that intends to produce predictability, exactness and control? Or do we design for emergence—one that will bring forth adaptability, innovation and things that are as yet beyond our imagination? Something engineered tends to reduce complexity. Something designed to be emergent tends to increase it. The richness and diversity that come from increased connections and interactions are lost when we try to control form and content. Can two such different approaches co-exist within a corporation? Yes, there is a place for both. However, after the fundamental choice, one will provide the context for the other.

If an engineered approach reigns, we organise ourselves to produce predictable results, leaving little room for innovation, flexibility and creativity *in our day-to-day affairs*. All we need, to realise our intention using this approach, is for very little to change within or outside the corporation. As long as things stay the same as the original assumptions when the design was engineered, all will be well. When such an organisation is confronted with a major *unplanned for* change, breakdown is just ahead. An interesting version of this occurs when a company, or some part of it, has breakthroughs in productivity which are the source of major failures soon after. This can happen to an entire company or a small part of it. If it occurs at an individual level, the particularly productive individual is often ousted by the system.

If we decide to choose an emergent approach to guide our corporation, the corporation will organise itself to produce, and welcome, results that are unpredictable and yet robustly viable. This approach surrenders detailed prediction and control for general direction and adaptability. Innovation and creativity are *designed in*, and the expectation is for the unexpected. This sounds far more precarious than it is. During times of stable conditions, the cost and risk of such a design often seems higher than necessary. However, during times of rapid change, the ability to respond and adapt without loss of profit or identity becomes extremely valuable. Knowing this transforms the sense of risk and waste into a sense of robust viability and confidence.

Our Existing Models Determine How We See

Because carbon-based life is the life form that has succeeded on earth, we know a lot about it. As diverse as this magnificent planet seems, everything shares certain characteristics. When we think of life, we think of this particular kind of life. We understand this life form by understanding how the elements of it are organised. If another life form had also occurred and persisted along with carbon-based life, it would probably have had a very different nature, and its elements would have been organised in a very different way. With the existence of another form, our ability to imagine other possibilities of life would expand exponentially and our thinking would develop in remarkable ways.

Our corporations have used only one model in modern history. And because of this we think only in terms of hierarchy, positions of authority, command-and-control, and limited access to information. It's unimaginable to us that any significant progress can be made without very specific results produced from explicit processes of production and control. The only way we can imagine responsible action occurring is through a chain of command. (This includes the workforce as well as senior management—as evidenced by the demand for "clear direction from the top".)

Prior to the creation of joint stock corporations, which were created in England, no major trading venture was undertaken with another country without royal approval, participation and funding. But once joint stock corporations emerged, an explosion of commercial ventures was inevitable. The private arrangements that could be imagined and implemented were now limitless. This explosion had a rippling effect which influenced exploration and international trade dramatically. A new explosion of form is beginning.

It's easy to speculate about alternative forms of organisation, simply by referring to other situations—including nature. However, we find it difficult to take them seriously and the idea of putting them into practice is almost unconfrontable. When presented with an alternative, we can't imagine that it would work. Even if it's already working somewhere else, we still can't imagine it working in *our* situation. Changing to a new and unfamiliar basis for organising appears an insurmountable task.

There are now plenty of successful organisations available for observation. However, most people are not able to learn from them, and cannot grasp the distinct principles which put them on top. 3M has been a leading innovator for decades. Other companies are still not able to reproduce the level of new product development that they accomplish. Likewise, growth leader Visa, has left everyone in their dust for years. Dee Hock, its creator, has been sharing his design approach freely, but no one can capture his theory or Visa's success. The Topeka Kansas dog food plant has marched through decades as a productivity miracle. They have wowed management at conferences around the world. But not even its various owners have been able to see how the plant does it. Donnelley Mirrors dominated their industry, using a unique approach to organisation. Their attempt to share that approach had little, if any, impact on anyone. Disney's secret is taught thoroughly in their public courses, and still their comment on their own approach is that people won't understand the source of their success for another 20 years. Stora has 700 successful years under their belt, but few show an interest in their history, much less see how to extract the critical principles.

In the last 30 years, many executives have invested substantial resources of time and money studying Japan's miraculous achievements in quality and productivity. Unipart of the UK, along with a few other countries, took what they learned and went on to produce breakthroughs that surpassed the quality and productivity of the very companies they studied. However, the remainder of the companies which undertook such studies learned almost nothing.

The problem was that many of the executives viewed everything that they were studying through the lens of their own models, and failed to grasp what was right before their eyes. Many executives, excited about the possibility of a turn-around, gladly embraced and imported Japanese forms but failed to grasp the thinking and models out of which these forms emerged. I've seen this repeated in companies where a division or plant make changes which produce remarkable results, but the rest of the company is unable to learn from them. Just as General Motors failed to learn from its own NUMMI plant, many other companies fail to learn from turn-arounds, transformations and successes that occur within plants or divisions in their own systems.

Principle of a Guiding Metaphor

Why can so few learn from these corporate success stories and recreate what they have? What's the missing link? Answer: The successes have been created from a guiding metaphor that is very different to the guiding metaphor of our times, one that contains a particular way of viewing organisation. Most of the business world is using a guiding metaphor which fosters an engineered approach to organisation. When immersed in this way of thinking, one cannot understand or learn from an organisation that is being guided by a totally different type of design principle.

When operating from an engineering model, we reduce things into parts as though they were machines. We then proceed to construct or reconstruct something as desired. As we all know, this works beautifully for physical and material structures. The aid of this model is limitless when working with unchanging matter. In fact, it can be our most skilful tool at a certain level of operation. However, it is limiting and confining when applied to the processes of life. Because we have used an engineering metaphor for a long time, we have developed *stacked* metaphors, through which we pre-suppose our ways of organising and the way we expect people to function in organisations. The approach is ineffective because we are applying reductionist and linear approaches to non-reducible and non-linear entities. We blindly assume that hierarchy, authority, prediction and control are all necessary fundamental features of human organisation. Using these features, we go on to generate the meanings and applications which are also stacked metaphors that we have blindly taken for granted.

Engineering—Not a Guiding Metaphor for Intelligence

What we need as a guiding metaphor for our organisations is a model for organisational intelligence. This is indicated by such currently-popular terms as *the learning organisation* and *the knowledge-based company*. We must begin to see human organisation as human community, so that we can express fully the rich and limitless possibilities of our human endeavours together. To do this, we design principles that will bring forth the possibilities of living systems.

As complex, adaptive and intelligent beings, we combine, blend and mix in various ways to form entities that are themselves complex, adaptive and intelligent. We live and work in larger environments that are also complex and adaptive. Every one of these levels bears the qualities of living systems such as: identity, change, fluid boundaries, loose connections and unpredictability. The models we use must be able to manage the paradoxes that are part of every living system. Paradoxes such as developing a strong core *while* supporting and accessing the periphery;

John Seely Brown[1] of Xerox tells a story which illustrates the challenge of working with this type of paradox. Xerox has the challenge of developing the effectiveness of about 30,000 repair personnel. To do this, the company created centralised training programmes and countless manuals. When the company noticed that the difference between the best performance and the worst was enormous, it became obvious that their training approaches weren't working. So they set aside their mechanistic way of training and began a wild experiment—one based on living systems. They brought in an anthropologist to study the way the repair personnel *actually* worked, learned and shared knowledge. The study revealed that the programmes and manuals were a joke among the repair people. The study also revealed that for *complex* problems that required creativity and rigorous thinking, the learning and innovation occurred in the storytelling or *narratives* of the repair personnel.

maintaining *both* continuous change and reliable production; creating stable processes while *at the same time* challenging those processes, providing opportunities for individual expression *and* maintaining an identity independent of the individual.

Intelligence is a way of understanding the world by making patterns that create meaning. Our formal education and development systems are not set up to do this. Manuals are not put together in a way that supports the creation of meaning. Intelligence comes into being and creates *meaning* from dialogue, conversations, narratives, community and the *whole*. Use of storytelling and metaphor are the means of an effective apprenticeship, and are at the heart of how a master works. Humans remember stories and are guided in action by them.

The Nature of Knowledge

We tend to apply the engineering approach to information and learning—in fact, we use it for just about everything. We think that by giving information to people, whether in a classroom or a manual, we have given them knowledge. People don't learn through bits of information, they learn through meaning. But knowledge is *always and only* implicit and self-generated.[2] Knowledge is not something that gets transferred from one person to another. A model can be made explicit, but it will be missing the richness and depth necessary for application unless it is also captured in experience or narrative.

Xerox's response to their study was to provide radio communication between the repair personnel, so that they could be in constant contact with one another. A dramatic improvement in productivity and learning occurred. In fact, the project was so successful that it was applied throughout the company. But like any company rollout of a system—it worked far better in some places than others. This is where the real learning from their story begins.

What was missing in the rollout? It's important to see that if we ask this kind of question, we will arrive at an answer using the engineering methods of analysis and reduction that are the very source of the problem. The answers that we would come up with couldn't possibly make a difference. Let's consider that the source of many of the rollouts not working is in our guiding metaphor of organisation.

Let's return to the case of the Xerox repair force: A means of communicating was made available, and the way in which it was used *spontaneously emerged* from the everyday activities of the people at work. The system of communication evolved or *self-organised*—as living systems do. The whole process of *self-organisation* occurs through constant learning, development and innovation based on some key initial conditions. But, in the Xerox case as in many others, when it was clear that the system worked, the system got *engineered* so that the equipment *and the information* could be given to others. This isn't what happened in the original case. The initial case worked because it was developed in action, and emerged through experiences and stories. It emerged spontaneously. This emergence is missing in the usual rollout approach.

The source of success in the project was knowledge and intelligence. Not the intelligence of the individuals involved in each particular work community, but the intelligence of the community itself. The effective work communities were organised in ways that resembled living systems. They told stories and shared in ways that integrated the new with the current level of experience. They learned. They created knowledge. The source of success was the integration that took place through the free and natural processes of dialogue and social interaction. The ineffective work communities

---

When Xerox sent the anthropologist back out into the field to assess the situation, it became apparent that the work communities that showed dramatic improvement in their productivity and learning were the ones that experimented, and allowed the process to evolve naturally with those doing the work using some basic principles. The work communities which tried to use the equipment, instructions and materials exactly as they were issued, found that the package had little effect.

The difference in productivity and learning was not a result of the individuals. Nor was it a result of the package supplied. The difference occurred because of the dissimilar models of organisation within the divisions that received the package. The divisions that were more traditionally organised failed to adopt, adapt and learn. Those that were organised in more natural and free communities succeeded. In some cases, they even exceeded the results produced by the original group.

---

lacked the ability to integrate the new with the existing level of experience. Metaphors, stories and narratives were not part of how they worked together so they failed to create a community of understanding, one that could benefit from the package offered. Their approach was not organic but engineered.

Knowledge—Its Relationship to Identity and Freedom

This sketch of Xerox's experiment exposes the fact that the guiding metaphor that exists for most people, and most businesses, views learning, information and knowledge as material "bits of stuff." Information is treated like "chunks" that we can transfer because they exist independently of us. But information cannot be transferred. Most corporate attempts to share new knowledge fail because they think knowledge is a thing that gets passed from here to there. Much of the teaching in courses and workshops is a waste of time for the same reason. Learning is not a matter of shifting information or knowledge from one person to another—it is much more dynamic and emergent than that.

Most training programmes are ineffective because of the approach, or guiding metaphor, that is used for their delivery. The reason for this is that a mechanistic approach includes aspects that make it impossible for it to work. First, the content gets packaged as though it were *transferable*. No recognition is given to the fact that it has to be created within those for whom it is intended. Secondly, we treat the whole learning process as mechanistic and reductionist, which does not match the nature of human beings—complex, adaptive and independent. We fail to understand that learning emerges through the process of integration—it is this process which transforms information into knowledge. And finally, we fail to see the entire context within which the desired knowledge is to be applied. So even if the participants attain the intended results *in* the programme, they return to an environment that is inimical to the development and application of what they have learned. Also, because the programmes are not skillfully designed, they do not include sufficient preparation, or the support structures, for integrating the knowledge into the context.

Principle of Emergence

If we wish to position our corporations for a breakthrough in learning and innovation, we must understand that knowledge is an emergent phenomenon. Knowledge comes into being as a result of how we organise. For a breakthrough to occur, the periphery of the corporation must be given the tools and the freedom to act, and it must be supported in its choices. Balancing is essential

> When I look back over the past 30 years of my life, attending and then delivering countless company-sponsored courses for thousands of individuals, I can recall only a handful of people attending these courses whose managers requested that specific results be produced during or after the course. Equally few supported these people in producing these results. I can recall even fewer instances in which management requested or even supported the participant sharing what they had learned in these courses with their department or work team.
>
> In the last few years, our consulting group has designed and offered a management development programme which required a major commitment of time from every participant. We also required that participants enrol their own management in making a commitment to the results they intended to produce. Just about every participant thought our request was unusual, and a few even insisted that their management's approval was irrelevant. It's really not surprising that courses are not integrated into people's day-to-day work when management does not participate in the design of the process *or the results* of a course—even when they request their people to attend.

here, because at the same time as learning and innovation are occurring, the core of the corporation must retain its identity. This is possible when the core honours the periphery and supports its actions. What is also required is that the *core* consist of principles and values that are commonly understood rather than rules and prescriptions that are enforced.

The periphery is honoured when structures and practices are created that allow it to move to the centre and be heard. This supports being related *as an integral part of the whole rich community*, which in turn nurtures the periphery. In all living systems *knowing* is a function of experience, understanding and integration. By realising this, we see how critical relationships are. In social organisations, knowing is a socially constructed occurrence. For everything that is alive in our corporations (the individuals and the corporation itself), learning occurs interspersed throughout the whole as a result of social interaction and collaboration, not in isolation.

Learning Emerges from the Interplay of the Whole

We can see the relationship between knowledge and community by looking at the various relationships in a quadrant analysis. This matrix was developed by the Institute of Research on Learning at Xerox, and John Seely Brown. This provides a useful way of exploring the process of learning.

	INDIVIDUAL	COMMUNITY
EXPLICIT	✓✓	✓
IMPLICIT	✓	?

For most of us, our formal education had its foundations in the upper left-hand quadrant. It is the least effective method of learning and contains the smallest possibility for the development of knowledge. This is the domain of information transfer. It is an effective method when what needs to be learned is simple and very accessible. When the information is routine, well-developed, or already in practice in the community or corporation, this method will work. In most cases, a simple pamphlet or work aid will be an adequate teaching tool.

Of course, our earliest learning as children was nothing like this. We learned by implicit, intuitive means through exposure and "being in a community" where we were attempting to belong. There was little explicit teaching but enormous implicit learning.

When we introduce experiential or action-based approaches into our way of educating, we are learning in the way that is represented by the lower left-hand quadrant. Through action, we integrate what we are learning with the background of implicit knowledge already in existence. Integration with the implicit occurs because action emerges from a whole or pattern rather than from isolated, explicit information. The implicit can also be accessed by story, humour, metaphor, ritual, or the imagination.

The upper right-hand quadrant represents the formalising of group understanding by creating explicit processes, manuals, and similar tools that can be shared explicitly, checked against standards, and controlled externally. This is what has happened with much of the quality movement (TQM) and other similar approaches. Most of the current re-engineering methodologies pursue this means. The focus for "capturing the knowledge" is explicit and loses the implicit and social character from which it emerged. We often wonder why such promising initiatives lose their energy. This is why.

When we create participation within a group by engaging in conversation or by integrating something that is being learned into a community understanding, we are doing what is represented by the lower right-hand quadrant. Learning is stimulated by group action, which demands physical or mental co-ordination, or simple processes of dialogue. Dialogue is used here to distinguish conversational processes which create something in the thinking of each participant that is greater than what is explicit or individual, and remains emergent in the conversation itself.

The lower right-hand quadrant represents the place where knowledge of any great and lasting power is created. We are typically uncomfortable with the approaches in this domain because the guiding metaphor that most people and corporations embody demands explicit, rational and individualistic understanding and operation. This quadrant, however, represents implicit and social knowledge. It operates under different rules and processes. Even after we acknowledge the validity of this kind of knowledge—implicit/social—we still think we need to transfer the knowledge and the processes into a domain that is explicit/individual. The processes of the implicit/social quadrant are emergent and arise from the interplay of environment, process, metaphors, and historical knowledge of the participants in the particular community of learning.

Learning emerges from the interplay of the whole. Most of the educational habits that we are locked into are represented by one of the first three quadrants in the diagram, and we would benefit enormously by being able to access the types of learning process which best suit the complexity of learning and exploring of the implicit/social quadrant. When our focus is skewed towards a particular type of learning, then the emergent results will also be skewed and limited in particular ways.

Franchising, the century's most successful structure for marketing and delivery, offers valuable insights into implicit/social knowledge. If a franchise is to be successful, the approaches that they design must be unique and well conceived. However, once the system is up and running and individual franchises are sold, there is a wide variation in performance between the different franchisees once the initial growth burst has passed. This is largely due to the fact that franchisors do not understand the social and implicit nature of knowledge.

When a franchise is new, there is ample knowledge embedded in the model. Initially, the franchisor has figured out how to make sufficient new knowledge available to franchisees. However, in years to come, the only source of continued learning, development, and outstanding growth will be in the development of the social/implicit quadrant. This requires a shift in approach that is not understood by most franchisors. Although the change includes specific processes, it is much more about developing an understanding of the interplay that must take place for knowledge to emerge.

And for those of you who think franchising is just for low-priced services which minimise costs, consider the following: McDonald's had one of the fist corporate universities. About one-third of the GNP of the USA is sold by franchisees. British Airways is now franchising their airlines. And many companies not engaged in franchising are speaking of "the franchise" that their name and processes represent.

Dialogue Explores the Implicit & Unfolding Possibility

There is a common process that a team goes through as it forms. In its early stages, it develops social and linguistic practices. It develops a way of speaking that is accepted by the whole. This way of speaking forms the patterns of social interaction within the team. A fabric of social practices emerges, and it is composed of conversations and interpretations. The team begins to form identity and meaning which are consistent with the larger community at the same time as being a unique social creation of that team. What eventually comes into being is a *community of practice* in which the specific intentions and formal structures co-exist with emerging knowledge and the emergent structures of language and practice.

Only a small fraction of implicit knowledge can be converted to the explicit. Even though explicit information can be generated from implicit knowledge, a great deal is always omitted. *We cannot say everything*. Knowledge exists in an iterative, reflexive, self-referential world of complex relationships in which presuppositions diversely interconnected, and the levels of logic change endlessly, depending on where we are looking. The value of that which can be made explicit is dependent on the social and implicit for its context, meaning, and effectiveness in action.

Business Process Re-engineering takes direct aim at the explicit quadrants. Its widely varied results are a reflection of the implicit knowledge that is ignored in the process. If a BPR process is developed by a team or community which share an implicit understanding of a larger whole, it is likely to be effective. But if BPR is an analytic process conducted by those who do not share the implicit knowledge of the business, it is likely to be ineffective or worse. Where outside consultants go beyond supporting a team, and supply both the knowledge and the analysis, the process is almost bound to fail.

Principle of Distributed Knowledge

The rate at which we develop knowledge is crucial to our competitive success. In order to improve the rate at which organisational knowledge develops, the organisational design must enhance the amount of distributed, implicit knowledge contained within the company. This exceeds sharing existing chunks of knowledge. *The vast majority of distributed knowledge emerges from the interplay of different interpretations, different perspectives, and different content within a shared community of understanding.* Distributed knowledge emerges from interaction, rather than from any single point of storage, any collection of specific points (such as manuals), or any explicit memory of the whole.

An autocratically managed fashion company began a development programme with us intended to reorganise the firm in a way that would release the creative potential of all its employees. Until then, the company trend was for the older, traditionalist managers to make all the decisions and for the young, bright, creative people to do all the work.

The company's development programme included basic education in communication, dialogue and working in teams. A process of "re-engineering" was also initiated, which did not include any outside analytic help. Teams were formed, each having an older, experienced manager as an advisor, and displays of every major design project currently underway were created. The displays consisted of simple hand-drawn wall charts that were hung in designated public areas. Each employee was free to add to any chart from any project when they were moved to do so. When there were sufficient design contributions, the charts were deemed complete. The teams reconvened and refined the design of their respective project, which was again displayed on charts in a similar manner. By the end of the process—only a matter of months—new heights of quality were achieved, costs dropped, and everyone in the company now shared a new understanding of what was possible. This was accomplished by collaboration within a community—and the work increased the sense of community as well as increasing effectiveness.

The human medium for interactions which will create distributed knowledge is conversation and dialogue. Knowledge that does not require conversation becomes a mechanism which repeats automatically when conditions arise that call for it. This type of knowledge is contained in machinery, layout, process and routine. Emergent knowledge, which is generative and alive, resides as potential in the language of the members of the community. The implicit and social knowledge of a *community of practice or a community of competence* lives in its language, its practices (linguistic and physical), and its conversations. Dialogue is the process of exploring the implicit and unfolding possibilities that reside in the rich background of shared practice.

A Corporation as a Network of Conversations

Conversation is the generative force of a company. The challenge is to generate distinctions of conversation that are rich enough to produce vibrant and effective communities. These distinctions must be capable of producing a variety of actions appropriate to the circumstances and intentions. As we generate distinctions, we design them to have the ability to build understanding, learning and innovation into our everyday affairs.

The task of executives is two-fold: They must provide a *framework of interpretation* that is unique to the company, and they must maintain that framework as a dynamic structure. This framework is generated from the interplay of interpretations that they see as historically significant about the company, the industry, and the larger social communities of practice in which the company operates. The framework also includes an identity that is unique to that company, one which embodies the possibilities of those historically-based interpretations. The responsibilities of executives and leaders go on to include the creation of a language that is capable of opening doors to unique possibilities for the organisation and everyone in it.

When new employees enter a corporation that is designed for emergence, they bring with them ways of perceiving and speaking that don't match the community of practice that they are entering. Initiation programmes are required which alter an employee's old, and mostly automatic, structures of interpreting and ways of speaking into ones that are able to engage in the conversations currently alive in the corporation. Such programmes are a process of emergent evolution, in which the interplay both initiates the employee and provides opportunities for the integration of ideas into the mainstream of the corporation. In the reproduction process of any species, the constant intermingling of different gene pools provides biological variety. Organisational variety is created in much the same way, i.e., through the constant intermingling of different linguistic communities of practice.

Linguistic Patterns are the Building Blocks of Models

As we become clearer and more accepting of the idea that the model guiding our corporate actions is no longer sufficient for today's business world, we become concerned with the question, "How do we construct new models?" Those who have explored the area in any depth, won't be too surprised with the answer: "Construct conversations, engage in dialogue, change supporting structures, institute new practices and, above all, develop new ways of speaking." In order for a change to be successful, core principles will have to be in place. The problem for most companies is that they lack core principles that are sufficiently understood and adequately integrated.

If we look around at the actual results of most change processes in the corporate world, it's obvious that most of us are far from understanding the crafts involved. What we are witnessing in many of the moderately successful results that we see is a little artistry and a lot of luck or magic. Those that do succeed are either not able to transfer their work to others, or they are succeeding in one place and failing in another. Part of the problem is that we are using terminology that is bound to get us into trouble. For instance, the phrase *mental models* suggests that we are dealing with something that belongs to a person, is explicit, and is relatively complete. This perspective has little power or effectiveness when we are dealing with a social phenomenon such as corporate models.

Those who use the phrase, *mental models,* think that it refers to how things are viewed within individual minds, and that to change a model entails changing the content of those individual minds. But our representations of reality are much "messier" than that. We have many partial "models" that often conflict with one another. (This is not always a bad thing. In practice, it is a useful condition for adaptation.)

The "models" of a corporation have similar variety and often contradict one another. In a corporation, the "models" are revealed in its conversations. Language and conversations are the source of action within a corporation. To change the language and conversations that are the source of our actions, we do not need to access the models that are internal to the individual participants of that corporation. Our efforts at change can be successful by accessing things that are external to individuals and live in public conversation and language.

In order to facilitate the process of change, we should shift our attention from efforts to alter individual *mental models* to an inquiry about linguistic patterns, and how to start and maintain webs of conversation. Our conversations will begin to develop models, theories and guiding metaphors that will generate innovative joint activity within a community of practice. An ongoing pursuit of mastery in conversation and dialogue is our gateway to continual development and emergence, as well as a means of strengthening the company continually.

Approaching change through conversation also turns us away from the idea that there is one single explicit model, or even set of models, that is guiding an individual or a company. Rather, there are countless rather vague models that interact in different ways at different times and under different circumstances. All the models are incomplete and require connection with elements of other models to be understandable. So, there is no *mental model*, but instead intermingling linguistic elements that create approximate models for varying circumstances and intentions. Models appear to be different things at different times. Sometimes they're seen as the source of intention. At other times, they're seen as a guide to action; one that occurs as a result of an intention that has already been decided. Sometimes models conflict. All of this suggests that perhaps models are linguistic patterns of individuals, companies and communities that function as the building blocks of multiple models. These are both useful and expendable. *Models* act as interim hypotheses open to question and continual change.

Core Competencies

Our conversations with each other are social and emergent, and out of them arise core competencies. A core competency is a set of linguistic or conceptual building blocks that can be recombined with other building blocks to form new possibilities. To the extent that a core competency is associated with physical objects or knowledge such as processes, then that core competency has the tendency to become rigid due to lack of ongoing challenge. It does, however, provide a platform for future development as long as we bear in mind the difficulty of including anything in dialogue that has been reified into something concrete and established as *true* or *right*.

Core competencies are not explicit and individual. Neither are they neat packages of skills or capabilities. Rather, they are complex packages which can be chunked into various parts, recombined with other elements and made generally available for dynamic interaction. Most have failed to access this useful language of core competencies because they are still locked into a material perspective rather than an information and knowledge perspective.

When core competencies can be seen as the result of communities of practice and something emergent out of the social interaction of linguistic patterns, then we are free to invent and develop without the attachment and limitation implied in *mental models*. The source of innovation and creativity is the ability to engage in linguistic recombination on a social scale. When this is distributed throughout an organisation, an enterprise can flourish in any environment and maintain a robust identity.

Core competencies tend to come to be identified as the core of the company. Balance is difficult—the core has all the explicit formal authority, while the periphery has minimum power and no authority. Our challenge is to honour the periphery, so that it remains vibrant and robust. By doing so, the periphery is able to contribute to the continual emergence of the possibility of the company. This is the principle of enabling the periphery.

There are two major elements to consider in building core competencies. One is the relative *information value*, or unique idea, of your enterprise. The other is distributing this effectively throughout your organisation. If you are low on both, then you know it's time for serious and intense work or you will soon find yourselves on a very slippery downward slope. If you are high on information value but it is not widely distributed, then the economic value of your idea is minimised. If you are high on distributed knowledge but low on new ideas, then some concentrated effort on thinking abstractly or developing core principles will pay large dividends rapidly.

The success of franchising can be seen as an illustration of these elements. Successful new franchises have new ideas *and* they distribute them broadly throughout their system. Without both in full operation, a franchise will not succeed. Neither will your company.

Development of core competencies and the spread of new ideas fail due to the existence of structures which support the needs of those in authority. The formal and authorised possess power, and use that power to maintain itself. This will remain the case until the authorised see that the source of robust viability for the whole comes from the interplay of the periphery and the formal. Here is the basis for our design for organisational intelligence. The cost of enabling the periphery is not great. The periphery is enabled through conversation, dialogue and communication, rather than just improved facilities enhancement or equipment.

Enabling occurs by design and practice, not spending. For example, creating a forum for the *messages* heard at the periphery, and then creating a means to evaluate and pursue the most promising on an iterative basis is not expensive. Each successive stage of support for the periphery will require a greater level of support from the existing communities of practice. Our reward in this process is a robust periphery which engages passionately and gives willingly.

Principle of Levels

To enable the periphery, higher levels of the organisation must spend their energy, attention and conversation on higher level issues—key values, principles and ideas—and refrain from engaging in detail appropriately left to lower levels. In order to fully honour the interplay between the two major levels, the periphery, which is supported by the authorised, will also have to change their conversations. Normal conversations that support the periphery often conflict with conversations that support the authorised. The historical conflict has generated a social conversation *in the periphery* that disempowers the source of the whole. Structures of authority must maintain an awareness of this, so that the conflict can be dealt with in ways that increase the empowerment of the

---

Every successful leader struggles with resolving the "leader's paradox." When a company's leader has clear and unique ideas, a balance must occur between the expression of individual freedom and intelligence, and the clearer and more effective vision of the leader. The founders of very successful companies, such as Charles Koch of Koch Industries, are constantly struggling to share their own structures of interpretation, while at the same time encourgaging the freedom that is essential for realising the full potential of human intelligence. The particular distinction of relevance is that of levels. The leader's role is to provide high level or general principles and to resist the "interference" of engaging in lower level application. The distinctions being developed in this book are intended to provide a basis for resolving the paradox that faces many leaders.

---

emergent, and support a balance between the periphery and the authorised. Our challenge will be to ensure that what emerges is not converted into a means of serving the authority structures, thus cannibalising a process that would otherwise be creative.

Praxis Design Principles

1. Principle of a Guiding Metaphor

A company is made up of independently intelligent human beings who make sense and meaning in their own unique ways. We make sense by making patterns combining principles, information and detail. How we accomplish this is by relating information to larger models, schemata or metaphors. These larger views provide a context for interpreting the smaller elements. *A job of leadership is to provide a guiding metaphor which enables independent intelligent people to make sense of the important elements of a company's approach to business—in a co-ordinated way.* When well constructed, the guiding metaphor enables full creative interaction and yet aligns understanding in a sufficiently coherent manner.

2. Principle of Emergence

Knowledge is not a linear accumulation of information—or even experience. Knowledge emerges from the interaction of intelligence, from dialogue, where the elements create something new in the interaction. Such interactions produce knowledge by an act of integration with what is already known. *To generate knowledge which provides the base for innovation, there must be an increase in the connections between areas, levels or experience which produce things that cannot be integrated immediately. Only then can something new emerge.* What emerges will be only after a process of struggle at convergence, relating differences and connecting partial understandings to existing knowledge.

3. Principle of Distributed Knowledge

Intelligence, knowledge and teamwork are possible only when the elements from which they emerge are distributed, and able to act beyond the controlling limitations of a linear system. Only when intelligence is distributed among the members of a corporation (not equally but similarly), can the corporation realise its full intelligence. *Most knowledge emerges from the interplay of different interpretations, different perspectives, and different content within a shared community of understanding.* To increase intelligence, leadership, responsibility, relationship, or any other emergent phenomena, we must recognise that it is distributed throughout the corporation and we must nurture and access it, rather than inhibit it or attempt to designate the source as one specific place.

4. Principle of Levels

Fundamental to understanding emergence is the concept of levels. Each new characteristic, feature or state of being which emerges from earlier stages has its own requirements and ways of operating. Knowledge can be seen as non-linear hierarchies, or levels, which each require different levels of abstraction and complexity, and different cognitive operations. *When we fail to recognise the distinctions of levels, and demand information or engage in operations "belonging" to other levels, we create an interference in the working of that level.* Besides this frequent interfering, we often apply the thinking of lower levels to the new circumstances of higher levels and make great mistakes.

Notes

1. John Seely Brown shared this story in some detail at the '95 Conference, Complexity & Strategy. In his recently published book, *Seeing Differently,* he expands on his theories and his experience at Xerox.

2. This self-generation takes place in a community and cannot occur outside of social interaction. This seeming paradox does not invalidate the need to make meaning for oneself.

VIOLENT MARKET-INJECTION STRATEGIES

Tom Peters

> The thematic terms are . . . *autonomy, experiment,* and *diversity*. . . . The underlying source of the West's ability to attract the lightning of economic revolutions was a unique use of experiment in technology and organization.... The key elements of the system were the wide diffusion of the authority and resources necessary to experiment; an absence of more than rudimentary political and religious restrictions on experiment; and incentives which combined ample rewards for success . . . with the risk of severe penalties for failing to experiment.
>
> —*Nathan Rosenberg and L. E. Birdzell, Jr.*
> *How the West Grew Rich*

In the title of this section, you'll find markets *first*, innovation *second*. It's increasingly clear to me that in a topsy-turvy world, where all goods are more or less fashion goods, only egging on the market to fully buffet each and every part of the firm will increase (to a satisfactory level—maybe!) the possibility of corporate survival, and, occasionally, excellence.

Exalter of Untidiness

F. A. Hayek was that rare economist who was also a first-rate historian. And to the faithful economic historian, like the meritorious novelist, the mess is the story. Hayek describes fitful economic (and human) progress as a direct function of rich, volatile, unpredictable experimentation in the marketplace. (He calls the global economy "the most complex structure in the universe"—inherently incomprehensible.) It's not pretty, but it's increasingly clear that it works far better than any alternative.

Tumbling into Hayck—yes, I started reading him by accident, appropriately enough—was a profoundly exhilarating experience. He mustered hard empirical evidence to buttress his case (in those 22 volumes of collected works—I'm not through all of them yet). My introduction to Hayek made me vow that I'd never again accede to the forces of order—the dogmatic strategic planners, the hierarchists, the central controllers who try to convince us that order and success are handmaidens (oh, what a comforting illusion, as Hayek points out so eloquently); that if we can just get the plan right, goodness will surely follow. To revel in disorder and the joys of accidental discovery. That's the magic of Madison Avenue and of Hollywood. Of Silicon Valley and once, long ago, of Detroit.

Where's the Mess?

> After two years I have not been able to get rid of the smell of central planning.
> —*Vladimir Dloughy , Minister of the Economy, Czechoslovakia,*
> *on the offices he inherited from the Communist regime in 1988*

> There is no hope for the state enterprises.
> —*Anonymous Chinese economist, quoted in*
> *The New York Times December 18, 1991*

In 1991, I glanced at *Marketing Strategy: A Customer-driven Approach,* by Professor Steven P. Schnaars. Then I dug in. It's a useful brook, neatly summarizing the important positions taken by today's marketing and business strategy gurus: the successes and stumbles of the Boston Consulting Group's market share/"experience curve" approach in the 1970s; the pros and cons of Harvard professor Michael Porter's three "generic strategies"; the strengths and weaknesses of the PIMS (profit impact of market strategies) database. And so on.

I took notes. Then, as I prepared to write this section, I reviewed my scribblings on Hayek one last time—and ripped up my notes on *Marketing Strategy* with anguish, anger, even disgust.

Why? Nowhere in those tidy pages (presented as a primer for business students) was there even a hint of the richness, messiness, and uncertainty of markets. Of the disorder, fun, and enthusiasm—and agony and despair—of markets. (No, not untidiness "of" markets. Untidiness *is* markets.) To the contrary, the possibility of conquering markets with a sound plan and a little more market research could be found on any page. Not in *these* pages. You'll quickly find that messiness is the message here.

F. A. Hayek: The Mess is the Message

To understand innovation in a frantic world, like it or not, we need to go back to the economic basics. Not the dull basics of supply and demand curves that you and I first learned, but the real basics—the hurly-burly of economic life. Friedrich August von Hayek long ago dismissed traditional macroeconomic thinking, for he was the exceptional observer who examines the raw essence of markets. Consider the circumstances that led to the emergence of markets, upon which Hayek speculates in *The Fatal Conceit*:

> Only a few, relatively small localities would have provided small bands of hunters and gatherers all that even the most primitive tool-using groups need for a settled existence.... Without support from fellows elsewhere, most humans would find the places they wished to occupy either uninhabitable or able to be settled only very thinly. Those few relatively self-sustaining niches that did exist would likely be the first in any particular area to be permanently occupied and defended against intruders. Yet people living there would come to know of neighboring places that provided most but not all of their needs, and which would lack some substances that they would require only occasionally: flint, strings for their bows....
>
> Confident that such needs could be met by infrequent return visits to their present homes, they would stride out from their groups, and occupy some of these neighboring places, or other new territory even further away in other parts of the thinly populated continents on which they lived. The importance of these early movements of persons and of necessary goods cannot be gauged by volume alone. Without the availability of imports, even if they formed only an insignificant fraction of what was currently being consumed in any particular place, it would have been impossible for early settlers to maintain themselves, let alone to multiply. Return visits to replenish supplies would raise no difficulty so long as the migrants were still known to those who had remained at home.
>
> Within a few generations, however, descendants of these original groups would begin to seem strangers to one another; and those inhabiting the original more self-sustaining

localities would often begin to defend themselves and their supplies in various ways. To gain permission to enter the original territory for the purpose of obtaining whatever special substances could be obtained only there, visitors would, to herald their peaceful intentions and to tempt desires of its occupants, have had to bring presents. To be more effective, these gifts had best not satisfy everyday needs readily met locally, but would need to be enticingly new and unusual ornaments or delicacies. This is one reason why objects offered on one side of such transactions were, in fact, so often "luxuries"—which hardly means that the objects exchanged were not necessities to the other side. Initially, regular connections involving exchange of presents would probably have developed between families with mutual obligations of hospitality....

The transition from the practice of giving presents to such family members and relations to the appearance of more impersonal institutions of hosts or "brokers" who routinely sponsored such visitors and gained for them permission to stay long enough to obtain what they needed, and on to the practice of exchanging particular things at rates determined by their relative scarcity, was no doubt slow. But from the recognition of a minimum still regarded as appropriate, and of a maximum at which the transaction seemed no longer worthwhile, specific prices for particular objects will gradually have emerged.

In this description, the complexity of what Hayek calls the "extended [economic] order" appears. And along with it, and quickly at that, the "unknowability" in any exhaustive sense, of even the simplest extended order. The connections have already become far too rich and too dense to map.

Extended trade, Hayek observes, emerged before agriculture—in the Paleolithic Age some 30,000 years ago. To move trade beyond the narrow immediate locale, some small number of guiding traditions and rules proved essential. (It is important to note at the outset that those "rules" were not, as the term might imply the product of planning. Some societies accidentally fell into such practices, Hayek asserts. They prospered. The practices—"rules"— they had stumbled upon were copied and spread.) Above all, he avers, private property was the cornerstone for all that followed, the very basis for organized trade and thence the painful movement from small, isolated savage bands or tribes to widespread interdependent modern civilization.

The "extended order" began around the Mediterranean. Societies there were the first, according to Hayek, to accept a "person's rights to dispose [of property], thus allowing individuals to develop a dense network of commercial relations." Private property, Hayek insists, also enshrines, by definition, the primacy of decentralization. The right to dispose of one's assets provides the basis for dealing with—or not dealing with—others of one's choosing (the most fundamental definition of decentralization).

The intellectual problem that was Hayek's preoccupation (and amply illustrated by the long extract) is this: The dense, decentralized network that emerges quickly becomes unknowable. Moreover, the chief vehicle which moves economies and civilization forward is unplanned experimentation by and among millions of individuals (billions today) who do not know one another. Along the way, successful experiments are emulated. (Some very few experiments are immediately successful, for the "right" reasons—i.e., according to "plan." The rest that are successful emerge, over time, for the "wrong" —i.e., unplanned, unimagined, mostly unimaginable—reasons.) Unsuccessful experiments, the vast majority, simply drop by the wayside. Thus the process of economic expansion is humbling, irrational, and—in principle—not amenable to centralized planning and control. "Order generated without design," Hayek wrote, "can far outstrip plans men consciously contrive." He adds that the "extended [economic] order resulted not from human design or intention but spontaneously.... Evolution leads us ahead precisely in bringing about much that we could not intend or foresee."

(Hayek's use of "evolution" and terms derived from evolutionary theory such as "blind variation," "adaptation" and "selection" is no accident. Indeed, he takes pains to point out that Darwin was singularly influenced, 20 years prior to publication of *Origin of the Species,* by reading Adam Smith's *The Wealth of Nations*. The proper credit for evolutionary theory may lie almost as much with Smith's brilliant notion of the "invisible hand" as with Darwin's rich observations during the voyage of the *Beagle*.)

But those, yesterday or today, who are under the spell of the invisible hand are faced with a dilemma: First, they/we cannot fully "understand" how the market works, given its extensive nature. Second, the market serves no purpose "that one can specify fully in advance." And third, it produces results that are "not immediately observable" (i.e., results clouded by those tangles of causes and effects). But these three properties, Hayek points out, are *the* defining bases of testable, modern scientific hypotheses. That is, this extended, unknowable, unplannable, unspecifiable market order flies squarely in the face of the Enlightenment, of Cartesian logic and of scientific reasoning—all that has defined intellectual "progress" for the last several hundred years.

Part of the problem is egocentrism. "Intelligent people," Hayek wrote, ". . . tend to over-value intelligence and to suppose that we must owe all advantages and opportunities that civilization offers to deliberate design." To the contrary, Hayek insists, for instance, that Europe's "extraordinary expansion in the Middle Ages" was a product of "political anarchy." The anarchy per se produced the diversity which led directly to modern economic "order." The rowdy capitalist towns of the Renaissance in northern Italy, southern Germany, the Low Countries, and England were an inexplicable new species—which launched modern market economics.

Joyous Anarchy

So much of economic success—Silicon Valley, Taipei, Hong Kong, Guangdong, Hollywood—has to do with anarchy. The "magic" of Silicon Valley lies as much in the bars and the squash courts as in Stanford University's fertile labs. It is the anarchy itself that "produces" the high volume of chance connections, the oft-told motivational fables. It is the energy from the critical mass—a statistical artifact, product of the law of large numbers—that makes Silicon Valley what it is, and makes it almost uncopyable. You could physically construct a Silicon Brasilia, but you'd be hard-pressed to initiate the wild, untrammeled growth that created California's matchless economic hot spot.

On the one hand, Hayek argues persuasively that rules are imperative to progress (in very small number: private property, enforceability of contracts). On the other hand, freedom is maximized—as is wealth and the fruits of civilization in general—precisely because these rules are *impersonal*. They guide vast numbers of relationships among large numbers of people unknown to one another; their content and minimalist nature spawn decentralization rather than centralization. And maximizing decentralization, Hayek claims, by definition maximizes experiments—thereby maximizing the number of "blind variations" (the evolutionary model) from which unpredictable but useful outcomes (called "selective retention") can occasionally occur.

Hayek further claims that "all evolution rest[s] on competition.... [Useful knowledge] arises in a process of experimental interaction of widely dispersed, different and even conflicting beliefs of millions of individuals.... [Rules aimed at] repressing differentiation due to luck . . . would have scotched most discoveries." Hayek cites the preeminent philosopher of science, Karl Popper, who wrote in *Conjectures and Refutations* that there can be no final knowledge, only "suggestions" (hypotheses or conjectures) which are supported for a time, then subsequently overturned (refuted) by better but still necessarily inconclusive "suggestions"/conjectures. "Our aim," Popper added in a passage admiringly quoted by Hayek, "must be to make our successive mistakes as quickly as possible."

Which leads us back to Hayek's disdain for modern macroeconomic reasoning. He contends that it "conceals the character of competition as a discovery process." (Some maintain that the connection of markets and spontaneous discovery is Hayek's most profound contribution.) Hayek hammers away at the importance of disorderly decentralization as "the only way to make use of [widely] dispersed information in its great variety.... Decentralized control of resources, . . . through [privately owned] property, leads to the generation and use of more information than is possible under central direction. [As Popper said,] 'To the naive mind, that conceives of order only as product of deliberate arrangement, it may seem absurd that in complex condtions order and adaptation to the unknown can be achieved more effective by decentralizing decisions.' "

Yet another problem for rationalists, Hayek says, is that diversity wants/tastes/values—which directly creates relative scarcity, and indirectly creates the price mechanism—is "not an attribute or physical property possessed by things." It is completely subjective. (Fashion!) The creation of products, markets, and trade itself is "simply" a by-product of playing up to different tastes among different individuals. "To serve a constantly changing scale of values," Hayek acknowledges, "may indeed seem repulsive." Economists, he asserts, have wrongheadedly regarded the daily elbowing among merchants in the marketplace as "superfluous . . . a methodological mistake . . . Activities that appear to add to available wealth 'out of nothing,' without physical creation and by merely rearranging what already exists, stink of sorcery."

Why spend so much time on Hayek? Simple. To fail to appreciate—in the fullest sense of that term—the richness, passion, and raggedness of the market mechanism is to be unprepared to lead a firm (or a regional or national economy)—especially in today's unhinged global marketplace. There is doubt that economists and planners don't much like bawdy capitalists. There's no place in the Chase Econometrics Model (or the General Motors strategic plan) for destabilizers like today's Steve Jobs, Ted Turner, Al Neuharth, or yesterday's Thomas Edison, J. P. Morgan, Andrew Carnegie.

Propositions from Hayek

- Liberty/wealth ("civilization") is due to "extended order"—i.e., trade over distance where producers and distributors and buyers are *not known to one another*.

- The extended order is based on a few overarching "rules"—e.g., private property, enforceable contracts. (The rules did not emerge as the product of planning!)

- Following a few uniform, impersonal rules maximizes variety. Variety (the product of competition/decentralization) in turn is the key to discovery and hence the creation of wealth.

- *Intangibles*—money and banking, differing tastes—are *the* basis for the extended order. *All* value (trade) is a function of intangibles/human relationships, *not* physical properties (e.g., intrinsic "quality" of the objects per se).

- Value stems from rearrangement/rearrangers. Brokers, etc., are *more* important than "producers."

- Growth stems from trial and error, competition, the survival of (and imitation of) the successful. (The successful seldom know they will be successful. Success invariably stems from unintended consequences, from endless strings of unpredictable causes and effects.)

- Decentralization/decentralized processing of information (and the trial-and-error, often "lucky" discovery of preferences/tastes) is the key to the extended order. More information, *by far*, can be processed more quickly in a "disorganized" (decentralized) system—i.e., more chance, unpredictable-in-advance connections occur, which lead to more "blind variations," thence, eventually, more "selective retention." (Not for sure, of course. "Selective retention" is a probabilities game.)

- Success doesn't necessarily come to those who "deserve it" and is not a matter of "fairness"—because of the complexity of the system, which leads to long chains of unintended consequences, with *long-term* effects which can rarely if ever be anticipated at the moment by even the most brilliant prognosticator.

BUTTERFLIES AND HURRICANES

T. Irene Sanders

> A truly stable system expects the unexpected,
> is prepared to be disrupted, waits to be transformed.
> —Tom Robbins
> *Even Cowgirls Get the Blues*

Wayne Gretzky, recognized as the world's best hockey player, says that the key to his success is that he doesn't skate toward the puck, but instead tries to anticipate where its going and get there ahead of it. The same thing could be said about great leaders—they anticipate where change is going and make sure their organizations get there first.

Here, at the transition point between millennia, we are faced with the challenge of anticipating and responding to change in a world that is increasingly more interconnected. As our need to anticipate change has become more urgent, science has made a quantum leap in its own understanding about the dynamics of change.

The new *science of chaos theory and complexity* is providing us with information about the dynamics of the real world in which our decisions are being made. And in addition to helping us anticipate and respond to change, the new science has provided us with another option—the ability to *influence* change as it is emerging.

With the new science we have an innovative model for developing *insight* about the present and *foresight* about the future. As we cross the threshold into the twenty-first century, we finally have a way to develop the much-needed skill of *strategic thinking*—a skill that will allow us to see and influence the future, today.

In order to lead change, you have to understand it. Just like athletes must understand their games. But until now, all we've had are techniques designed to stabilize what feels like an endless roller-coaster ride of change. This is like having a playbook without understanding the subtleties of the game that create the dynamic or constantly changing *field of play*.

In the last decade, a lot of effort has been focused on identifying and managing internal change processes designed to make organizations more competitive. This is known as *planned* change. You decide to do something different, such as *re*inventing, *re*structuring or *re*engineering, and develop a plan to carry it out. These are ongoing large-scale efforts designed to make organizations more effective in responding to the changes, challenges, and opportunities in their larger *external* environment.

Leaders, focused on organizational transformation, internal-change agents, and change-management consultants and trainers have worked together over the last ten years to build a library of case studies on successful internal change efforts. They have demonstrated what works and what doesn't. These experts in the *human side of change* have compiled playbooks filled with ideas, principles, processes, and techniques designed to help managers and employees build commitment to change and maintain productivity, while moving forward with the least amount of resistance.

But it's easy to let the *internal* change process become the primary focus of attention, because results are tangible and the process manageable, when compared to the constant changes and uncertainties swirling around outside the window. It feels safer to hunker down in familiar territory and wait out the storm. But we've all experienced that sudden unplanned something that seems to come out of nowhere, like a gust of wind that blows the door open. It forces us to drop what we're doing in order to come up with a quick and effective response. And we know from experience that when change comes as a surprise, it takes more resources to identify and implement an effective response. It also has the potential to create huge power outages or disconnections throughout an organization.

As the executive team changes its priorities or makes decisions that require the organization to move quickly, middle managers are still working on the last set of priorities in addition to the *re*-YouNameIt change process, while front-line employees are just beginning to get the message about changes needed two weeks ago. Everyone points to someone or something else as the source of confusion.

But is there another way to understand change? One that would get us out of this vicious fire-fighting cycle? One that stops the divisiveness and gets everyone on the same team? One that helps everyone understand the relationship between your internal change efforts and the complexities in the world around them? One that connects each person and each function to the organization's evolving A-list priorities? One that supports long-term strategies and quick maneuvers? One that helps us anticipate change, see the options, and make wise choices—before a crisis arises? And finally, one that allows us to create or influence change to our advantage?

The answer is YES. At last, we can take a deep breath and exhale.

If we lift our eyes and our thinking, everything we see and experience can be thought of as happening within a larger system. And the key to understanding the dynamics of the "big picture" is to see the larger system in a coherent and realistic way. Edward Lorenz, a research meteorologist and mathematician working at the Massachusetts Institute of Technology in the early 1960s, knew this as he started the next run on his computer and left the room to get a cup of coffee. Trying to come up with a weather model that would help meteorologists provide accurate forecasts was beginning to seem like a fool's game. All he had to do was look out the window to understand the futility of his efforts. While his weather models forecast the same weather day after day, the weather outside changed constantly. He was thinking about all of this as he sat back down at his desk.[1]

Lost in his own thoughts, it took him a minute or two to notice that something was different. Instead of the usual rolling pattern coming from the tracing device he had hooked up to his (what we would now call primitive) computer, the tracings were fluctuating widely. The printout looked like the electrocardiogram (EKG) of a hospital patient whose heart is fibrillating out of control.

He tried to figure out what was going on. His intuition told him that something significant was happening, but as he replayed his actions just before leaving the room, nothing was different. He'd done everything just like he'd done it a hundred times before. Except, that he had abbreviated one of the numbers he was using to represent atmospheric conditions. Instead of .506127 he had rounded it to .506, typed it in, and left it to run while he walked down the hall to the coffeepot. What he discovered when he returned was one of the first clues to a new science that would revolutionize the way we think about change.

As we saw in the previous chapter, from the seventeenth century to the early part of this century science believed that the universe was static and operated like a huge machine with clockwork precision. Change, they believed, was caused by outside forces acting on solid lifeless particles of matter like the action of the cue ball on the eight ball in a game of pool. The universe, they believed, was characterized by order, which could be recognized, understood, and measured through the use of mathematics.

This classical mechanical-mathematical view of the world required that scientists develop narrowly focused research questions. Focusing their attention and then joining the results from one experiment to the results of the next was an approach based on the central tenet of the mechanistic view—only by understanding the parts could one make sense of the whole.

Mathematics is the basic language or tool that undergirds all scientific disciplines. It allows scientists to convert their questions from words to numbers and symbols. It's scientific shorthand, and it's language we nonscientists have adapted for our own everyday uses. Without mathematics we would have a hard time balancing our checkbooks, giving directions, following a recipe, making a telephone call, or keeping track of who's winning the basketball game.

Math helps us make sense of and organize the world in very specific ways. One of the ways it does this is by helping us recognize patterns. For example, my editor's office in New York is easier to find by looking first for the coordinates "6th Avenue between 48th and 49th Streets," then for the street address, "1230 Avenue of the Americas (which is also 6th Ave.)," and finally for his location in that building, "11th floor." Each of these numbers helps me identify a pattern of organization that leads me to his door. Just like the number on your boarding pass tells you how to locate your seat on the airplane. Numbers are also clues that lead us to a point where we can see a pattern of organization. For example, every spring when we fill out the dreaded income tax forms, we are creating a picture of our financial pattern over the last year. In simple ways, numbers help us see and understand patterns, reach conclusions, and make decisions. This is also what they do for scientists.

Mathematics is the tool that helps scientists uncover the hidden patterns in nature, which are clues to how the world is organized and by what patterns of organization or principles it operates.[2] Mathematics is the imposition of man-made logic on nature's creation. It is a highly refined tool, but it is not reality.

Mathematical equations can at best only serve as highly idealized representations of events in the real world. As Benoit Mandelbrot, a pioneering mathematician working at IBM in the late 1960s and '70s, put it: "Clouds are not spheres, mountains are not cones, coastlines are not circles, and bark is not smooth, nor does lightning travel in a straight line."[3]

The techniques of mathematical *approximation,* the type of rounding and shaving implied by Mandelbrot's statement, were designed to help scientists screen out nature's irregularities and stabilize the variables in question in order to study them. This is similar to a carpenter's shaving and planing. A carpenter ignores the small differences and irregularities in a piece of lumber in favor of its approximate linear qualities, which allow it to fit with the next board and the next, eventually forming the frame of a house. The underlying assumption is that small differences are insignificant, and in many cases that assumption proved to be *useful*. Translating the motions of planets, comets, or other natural phenomena into approximate linear equations provided scientists with new insights and led to many of science's great discoveries. But it also created the belief in a predictable, linear, cause-effect world in which overlooking small differences in favor of mathematical approximation was more than just useful, it defined reality.

In the early part of this century, the success of this approach led French scientist Marquis Pierre-Simon de Laplace and others to adopt a perspective known as a scientific determinism, which says that through mathematics it is possible to predict everything that will happen by just knowing the existing conditions at an earlier point in time and projecting those into the future.[4] In a static mechanically efficient universe this perspective seemed to make sense.

Lorenz's weather program was based on this classical deterministic model. Given a set of approximate linear equations representing the weather conditions last Tuesday, it projected those into the future and came up with, guess what? A forecast that predicted approximately the same weather next Tuesday as last Tuesday, and every Tuesday after that into infinity. Clearly, something was missing.

What Lorenz discovered is that a deterministic system—a simple system which follows fixed, precise laws—can display what looks like erratic or random behavior because of its *sensitive dependence on initial conditions*. In the classic deterministic model, the future is merely an extension of the past. There is no room for chance, changing conditions, or creativity. It's a straight line from the present to

---

the future. What Lorenz found is that in systems like the weather or the Indianapolis 500 a straight line is not the reality.

In *nonlinear dynamical* systems, the variables cannot be taken apart and added back together again like a child's building blocks; A+B does not equal C. In these types of systems, things never happen the same way twice. A small change in one variable will create changes in another and another, because the variables are interacting constantly and changing in response to each other. Lorenz discovered that nonlinear dynamical systems are teeming with creative potential and sensitivity to new influences. This sensitivity to new influences means that change can be introduced at almost any point. In other words, the possibilities for creativity, innovation, and change are infinite.

This *sensitive dependence on initial conditions,* he found starts an interactive process known metaphorically as the *Butterfly Effect.* The Butterfly Effect describes the image of a butterfly flapping its wings in Asia and causing a hurricane in the Atlantic, which is a metaphor for how small changes or events create complex results. The Butterfly Effect was a major breakthrough in understanding how small systems interact with large systems. A small change in the initial conditions of one system multiply upward, expanding into larger and larger systems, changing conditions all along the way, eventually causing unexpected consequences at a broader level sometime in the future. That's why the slight difference in his weather model caused by rounding just one variable from .506127 to .506 was enough to create a thunderstorm instead of sun in next week's forecast. It also explains why the physical and psychological conditioning of athletes is so important. In a game of basketball, for example, the initial conditions are changing constantly as each player experiences varying levels of physical exhaustion, focus, and pressure to perform. In a sense, each player is a small system whose starting conditions at any point in time influence the dynamics of the next play and the next, eventually determining the outcome of the larger system—the overall game and its final score.

It would have been easy for Lorenz to stop here and give up any hope of developing a forecasting model for the weather. Nonlinearity had long been the nemesis of mathematicians, as nonlinear equations were almost impossible to solve. But setting aside his expertise as a meteorologist and listening to his instincts as a mathematician, he sensed something more. A sort of geometric architecture to the randomness in the weather tracings he'd produced by tinkering with the system's initial equations—an order within the disorder. So, he decided to follow his intuition by studying a simpler type of nonlinear system: convection.

Remember that Lorenz's original interest was in predicting the weather. So, in studying convection, the type of nonlinear heating, cooling, and rolling process that takes place when you add cream to a hot cup of coffee or when cool air touches a hot radiator, he was searching for a nonlinear system that could be represented by just a few equations. Since it was the future he was interested in, he wanted to see what would happen when he tried to predict the future state of a simple nonlinear system. He came up with a set of three equations that represented the variables in a simplified convection system and used his tracing device to create a *picture* of that system.

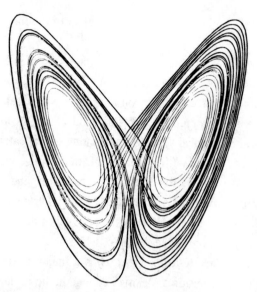

The Lorenz Attractor. The first picture of the order hidden within the behavior of a nonlinear system. Compliments of Edward N. Lorenz.

Lorenz used a technique that had been developed half a century before by French mathematician Jules-Henri Poincaré. Poincaré invented a mathematical concept known as phase space, where all the possible motions of a dynamical system could be represented by a geometric shape. By translating numbers into shapes he demonstrated that it is possible to create a picture of a system's behavior over time. Poincaré's geometrization of dynamics demonstrated the power of imagery in mathematics[5] and was an early predecessor to the recent field of scientific visualization—the ability to translate numbers into pictures through the use of high-speed computers and computer graphics.

This simple image, resembling the wings of a butterfly or an owl's mask, is known as the Lorenz Attractor. The most remarkable thing about this image is that it allowed scientists to *see*, for the first time, the order, shape, or structure hidden within the behavior of a nonlinear system. This is the picture that's worth a thousand words.

There are three important findings represented in this image. First, because the system is deterministic, it is possible to know its initial conditions. What's difficult, because the system is also nonlinear, is predicting its future state. Because it is nonlinear, it would be easy to assume that its long term behavior would be random and disorderly. But remember that Lorenz's intuition told him that there was something hidden beneath the apparent randomness. So, using the three nonlinear equations for convection, he created a picture of the *behavior of the system over time*. This image represents all the possible outcomes of the three equations. And what it shows is that *there is a type of self-organizing pattern, shape, or structure that becomes obvious when the behavior of the system is seen as a whole. There is order hidden beneath the disorder.*

After you see the pattern, the obvious next question is "What creates the pattern and holds the system together?" *The pattern arises because the variables in the system are attracted to and interact with each other in a unique way.* The attraction of the variables creates the edges or boundaries of the pattern, and the interactive relationship of the variables creates the internal design that never repeats itself.

And finally, this image represents a shift made possible by the power of computer graphics. In the past, scientists and mathematicians would try to *solve* nonlinear equations or *predict* the future of a nonlinear system in terms of a singular outcome or state. What this image shows us is that *while it may not be possible to solve or predict the future of a nonlinear system, it is possible to provide a qualitative description of its characteristics and behavior as a whole over time.* Ian Stewart describes this shift in perspective: "[T]his approach again changes the meaning of 'solve.' First that word meant 'find a formula.' Then its meaning changed to 'find approximate numbers.' Finally it has in effect become 'tell me what the solutions look like.' . . . [T]his move toward an explicitly qualitative theory is not a retreat but a major advance. For the first time, we are starting to understand nature's patterns in their own terms."[6] Analyzing a nonlinear system by describing its behavior and characteristics as a whole over time is known as qualitative analysis.

Although Lorenz is now recognized as one of the earliest pioneers in the development of *chaos theory,* a new type of mathematics explaining the complex behavior of nonlinear systems, the implications of his work were not immediately understood. In a sense they were isolated findings in a field still being fertilized for the harvest to come.

Until recently, the different scientific disciplines and specialties did not communicate between and among themselves. It's as if each were a smokestack operating independently from the others. Their research intermingled only when someone stood outside and looked for similarities across the columns of smoke drifting into the atmosphere. And what one would have seen, beginning in the early part of this century, were the sparks of a revolution in the making.

The strict deterministic view of the world promoted by Laplace began to shift in the early part of the twentieth century. Einstein's theory of general relativity, which he proposed in 1915, provided a new theory of gravity based on the idea that space-time is not flat, but curved. In his theory, both space and time are not static, but *dynamic,* affecting and affected by everything that happens in the universe.[7] This was a dramatic departure from the fixed deterministic view of the universe supported by Laplace, and it paved the way for Edwin Hubble's discovery in 1929 that the universe is not static, but expanding in all directions.

This discovery opened the door for rapid advances in astronomy and physics. Max Planck's quantum theory of energy and Werner Heisenberg's uncertainty principle led to a reformulation of mechanics known as quantum mechanics or quantum physics, which describes the behavior of particles at the subatomic level. Stated simply, quantum physics says that the smallest particles are not solid static lifeless bits of matter, but are instead pulsating bundles of energy known as quanta, whose behavior is impossible to measure or predict with absolute certainty, because they exist and interact in a quantum or energetic state that has a number of potential outcomes.[8]

In quantum physics, you can observe an outcome but only make guesses about the interactions of the particles involved and the path they took to that result. Quantum physics is based on a type of mathematics that helps scientists identify *probabilities*. The probabilities or potential outcomes arise out of the *dynamics* of the whole.

The recognition that the fundamental structure of the universe is dynamic behavior expressed as a whole, through its interconnections and relationships, was a dramatic departure from classical mechanics, where the parts determine the actions of the whole. With quantum physics, Laplace's fixed deterministic universe was replaced by an active universe filled with energy, interconnections, and creative potential. The linear, clockwork view of the world was transformed by science's recognition that at its most fundamental level the world is an energetic field of connections, relationships, and patterns of interaction. This discovery raised a whole set of new questions. If, at its most basic level, the world is made out of particles whose structure is actually expressed as a web of energetic relationships and patterns of interaction, what are the implications for how we view life at the macro level?

As much as science tries to be exact, it never can be. Science is an ongoing spiral of discovery, contradictions, gaps, partial answers, conclusions, and more discovery. Exploring nature is like trying to put together a jigsaw puzzle without the picture on the box top to guide you. The important thing to recognize is that gaps and inconsistencies generate new questions, which lead to new discoveries. For example, quantum physics and Einstein's theory of gravity, known as general relativity, are recognized as two of the three major scientific revolutions this century (chaos theory is the third), but they are inconsistent with each other. The search for a grand unified theory (GUT), which scientists believe will reconcile them, is one of science's greatest challenges.

Examples of other discoveries and theories that helped to lay the foundation for a whole new way of thinking about change include the discovery that our galaxy is only one among an infinite number of galaxies still being discovered today by the increasing power of land-based and satellite-based telescopes; the discovery of dense gravitational fields known as black holes; the discovery of dark matter, that unknown something that makes up an estimated 90 percent of the universe; the discovery of other planets with evidence of life-supporting elements; and the theory of an explosion, known as the Big Bang, which brought the universe into being.

While the disciplines of astronomy and physics moved forward, important advances were also being made in other scientific disciplines. For example, the biological theory of evolution, developed by Charles Darwin and first published in 1859, provided an explanation about how change occurs within and across species. Over the years, this theory has grown from its original concepts of random mutation and natural selection, also known as the survival of the fittest, to include the current ideas of niche adaptation and punctuated equilibrium.[9]

Modern evolutionary biologists believe that plants and animals adapt to their specific location, function, and set of circumstances within a complex living ecosystem, which itself survives and adapts as a whole through its intricate network of interdependent relationships. Today the exciting scientific debates are not over the validity of the theory, as they were in its earlier days, although the creationists occasionally stir that pot, but over the *dynamics* or "hows," of the process.

For well over a century, evolution has been the biological model for the development of life on earth and, with the acceptance of the Big Bank theory in the early 1970s, it became the model for the development of the universe as a whole. Evolutionary biology and evolutionary cosmology converged to create a new model within which to explore nature's creativity—one more step in the breakthrough that was to come.

The natural world is filled with a variety of rich textures, shapes, and patterns—the rough bark on a tree, the long graceful limbs of a fern, stepping-stones across a stream. Yet, the richness of the real world could only be appreciated in the abstract by classical science. Scientists could identify the elements in a molecule of water, H_2O, but not the dynamics at work in a waterfall. New approaches were needed for exploring mysteries that they saw all around them—variations in cloud patterns, fluctuations in weather and wildlife populations, and changes in the rate and flow of mountain streams.

The common wisdom among scientists, even into the late 1970s, was that these questions could not be answered. Questions such as these were nonlinear and involved looking at the irregularities that mathematical approximation tried to screen out, as well as at a number of interdependent connections and relationships that scientists traditionally tried to break into component parts. In other words, these types of questions were better left unasked, because they were too frustrating. Science did not have the tools or the type of mathematics that would make these questions solvable.

By the early 1970s, science had become highly specialized and compartmentalized. Each discipline had many subspecialties pursuing very narrow lines of research with little communication among them. The narrower the research, the greater the prestige. Answering broad everyday questions required dealing directly with nature's unruliness. So instead, scientists developed their infamous "ivory tower" image by isolating themselves from the day-to-day by pursuing highly specialized research questions, which conformed more easily to mathematical modeling. Fueling this approach was the stiff competition for research funds, the lifeblood of any scientist, which were also focused at this more esoteric level.

But even with intense pressure to conform, there were renegades, scientists who were growing bored and restless with safe and what they considered irrelevant science. What they longed for was a new form of scientific freedom. Observing the world through a microscope with higher and higher levels of magnification is one way to learn. But these restless ones recognized that this approach eliminated much of the world outside their windows. They began to ask themselves if another approach could work. Could you also learn by stepping back and observing the world through a wide-angle lens? What could be learned by tackling those nightmarish nonlinear questions about nature's irregularities?

Those who would later be recognized as *chaos* pioneers began to probe these questions, even though they were warned against this by their colleagues. Like explorers facing unknown territory, they each followed their inner urgings and moved forward. Physics, biology, mathematics, astronomy, meteorology—all provided paths, first into *chaos* and then into *complexity*.

In everyday language the word "chaos" is used to describe conditions that appear to be highly disorganized, turbulent, or volatile. It's an active word that implies changeability and movement. It's a word used more and more to describe the state of world affairs. Now science has given it a new and deeper meaning.

Chaos theory is the popular name for dynamical systems theory, or nonlinear studies. Nonlinear dynamical systems are systems that, like the weather, move, grow, or change. It's difficult to predict the outcome or future state of a nonlinear system, because the variables are interacting and changing constantly in response to each other. The behavior of a nonlinear system is not a straight line. As it turns out, *most of the world is made up of nonlinear systems* and dynamical systems theory, or chaos theory is a new mathematical approach that allows scientists to study the *behavior* of nonlinear systems.

The weather along the eastern slope of the Rocky Mountains is a good example of a nonlinearity. Meteorologists there struggle to provide the public with at least a hint of what to expect during the day. Cold air, flowing down into the United States from Canada, collides near Denver with the warm jet stream air, creating volatile moisture and temperature conditions so extreme that in the foothills it's not unusual to see a cloudless blue sky turn gray with a sudden snow shower and then blue again, all within half an hour.

Over the last three decades, many individuals contributed to the development of chaos theory. Through their research, and the use of high-speed computers and computer graphics, scientists began to see and understand the dynamics of work behind the apparent randomness of nonlinear systems, and the pieces of the puzzle began to fit together. New concepts, techniques, and descriptions of nonlinear systems started to appear in research papers worldwide, eventually forming the framework for this new approach to answering those frustrating questions about nonlinearity. And this is what they found.

Most of the world is made up of nonlinear dynamical systems. The world is more nonlinear than it is linear, and nonlinear dynamical systems have several unique properties that make them recognizable. *First, beneath the seemingly chaotic behavior of a nonlinear system, there is order.* The term "order" does not refer to characteristics such as quiet, calm, or good, but refers instead to a type of self-organizing pattern, shape, or structure. The shape is created by the attraction or active relationship of the variables making up the system.

The concepts of attractor and attraction are important to understand. In its purest definition, an *attractor* is the end state or final behavior toward which a dynamical system moves. And that end state is either predictable or unpredictable. A *predictable attractor* is the end state into which a system *settles*. For example, if you throw a handful of marbles into a bowl, they will eventually all come to rest at the bottom. The bottom of the bowl is the attractor, a specific point. In other cases, the attractor is a cycle, as in the back-and-forth movement of a pendulum in a grandfather clock. You cannot predict the path of each marble nor the immediate behavior of a pendulum brought to a standstill by a mischievous child who grabs the swinging arm and then gives it a hard push. But you can predict the final outcome or behavior of each system: a pool of marbles at the bottom of the bowl and the pendulum's eventual return to cyclic motion.

Then there are *chaotic systems that never settle into a predictable or steady state* and those are said to have *strange attractors*. A graphic representation of such a system will reveal a complicated pattern or shape, where the internal design never repeats itself. Chaos theory describes the behavior of chaotic nonlinear systems and their strange attractors.

The Lorenz Attractor is a strange attractor, as would be the attractor for a hurricane. A tornado is another example of an energy system held together by a strange attractor. No external container or funnel gives a tornado its unique form. This dynamic, coherent, and focused system with a recognizable shape is created by the interaction of the variables making up the tornado. The attraction and force of the variables hold the system together and move it along its path of destruction at speeds of up to 200 miles per hour or more until it eventually loses its energy and disperses.

You may sense some flexibility in how the term strange attractor is used. The term "strange attractor" describes the behavior of the force of forces that hold the system variables in place. The strange attractor coalesces the energy and creates the system boundaries, while at the same time allowing dynamic activity within those boundaries. The shape of a hurricane or tornado provides evidence that a strange attractor is present, as do computer-generated pictures such as the Lorenz Attractor, which demonstrates the behavior of a chaotic system over time. The pictures provide evidence that a strange attractor exists. And because each strange attractor creates a unique shape, it is common to also hear the picture referred to as a "strange attractor."

Imagine walking down Main Street in the town where you live. You see a seemingly mismatched couple strolling arm in arm. What is the attraction that keeps them together? People usually are attracted to each other for many reasons. Those reasons or elements create an attraction that holds their relationship together. And like the dynamics in a game of basketball, all of those elements are interacting constantly to create the dynamics of the overall system or relationship. If we could create a graphic image of their relationship over time, it would have its own unique shape, or strange attractor.

If we translated these concepts into the business world, we would ask ourselves "What elements create the dynamics of a business or an industry and give it its unique shape and characteristics? What connections and relationships hold the system together and create the structure beneath the visible activity?" Understanding that beneath disorder there is order allowed scientists to look at the world with new eyes and ask new questions. How does the order or structure arise?

Lorenz discovered that nonlinear systems display *a sensitive dependence on initial conditions. Nonlinear systems, he found, are teeming with creative potential and sensitivity to new influences.* Because of this sensitivity to new influences, change can be introduced at almost any point, and the possibilities for creativity and innovation are infinite. He also found that through the Butterfly Effect, small changes multiply upward, expanding into larger and larger systems, changing conditions all along the way, eventually causing unexpected consequences at a broader level sometime in the future. *A nonlinear system responds to changes in itself through a type of feedback loop, set in motion by the Butterfly Effect. Through this process, small changes can produce complex results.*

An example of the Butterfly Effect occurs in the movie *Outbreak,* when an African monkey is brought to the United States and sold illegally to an exotic animal trader. Unknown to everyone, the monkey is carrying the deadly Ebola virus. The drama begins when the monkey infects its owner through a scratch on the arm, setting in motion a viral outbreak that threatens to kill the entire U.S. population within days. The scratch on the arm was a small event that multiplied up and out with enormous consequences.

As scientists began to understand the dynamics of nonlinear systems, they began to ask more questions about the interactions in and among systems. How do changes, such as evolution, fluctuations, and extinction, occur? What other dynamics are involved? *How do order and structure arise in the midst of constant change?* These questions brought them to the next level of understanding and to the concept of *complex adaptive systems.*

Complex adaptive systems (CAS) are open nonlinear evolutionary systems, such as a rain forest, that are constantly processing and incorporating new information. Their existence and structure depend on the constant flow of energy and new information, making it *impossible to know all of the initial conditions at any point in time.* These are systems that exist at the boundary between chaos and order. Instead of settling into a predictable or steady state like the back and forth motion of a pendulum, or ultimately dissipating like a hurricane or tornado, these types of systems adapt to change, thus their name *complex* adaptive *systems.*

In a complex adaptive system, change is constant because of the flow of new information, but dramatic change occurs when something tips the balance. *If* the system is sensitive to the new information, it goes through a period of *adaptation* out of which a new pattern or shape *emerges*. And, sometimes the changes are dramatic enough to be recognized as transformative—the system before the change is vastly different from the system after the change.

Imagine looking at a National Geographic video about a South American rainforest. It is humid, lush with vegetation and filled with the sounds of birds and other animals. It remains in this state of dynamic or active equilibrium until new information enters the system. Something happens to disturb it, such as commercial plant harvesting. Now, in your mind fast-forward the tape. You see that because the rain forest was sensitive to the new information, it has been pushed into a chaotic period or a period of instability.

Fast-forward the scene again to a place ten years in the future. Here you see that *adaptation* has occurred and a new state of equilibrium has been reached. Some plants and animals are gone, but others are thriving and new species or hybrids have emerged. The rain forest has adapted to the *edge of chaos,* poised and ready for new information.

Evolutionary biology is providing new insights about how systems such as this evolve and adapt. Stuart Kauffman reminds us that "the edge-of-chaos image arises in coevolution as well, for as we evolve, so do our competitors; to remain fit, we must adapt to their adaptations."[10]

Chaos theory describes how a sensitive dependence on initial conditions contains the potential for change through the Butterfly Effect. Complexity theory describes how order and structure arise through the process of adaptation set in motion by new information, which tips the balance and pushes the system into a chaotic episode. In complex adaptive systems, complexity theory incorporates and depends on the details of chaos theory. In other words, chaos is not something that just happens in an otherwise orderly world. It is the mechanism through which change is initiated and organized. It is the way the world creates the rich diversity that we see all around us.

In summary:

- We do not live in a static, linear cause-effect world. We live in a world made up of nonlinear dynamical systems. Our world is full of motion, change, and emerging events.
- The world may appear to be disorderly. But beneath the apparent disorder there is order. The term "order" does not refer to characteristics such as quiet, calm, or good, but refers instead to a self-organizing pattern, shape, or structure.
- The patterns or shapes are created by the attraction or active relationship of the elements or components of the system.
- We may experience disorder, but we need to ask ourselves, What is beneath the surface? What connections, relationships, and patterns of interaction are creating the structure beneath the visible activity?
- Because nonlinear systems display a *sensitive dependence on initial conditions,* a small event in one system can cause tremendous turbulence in another through the Butterfly Effect.
- In *complex adaptive systems,* which have the ability to process and incorporate new information, change occurs through a process of *adaptation.* Through this process a new self-organizing pattern or shape emerges.

Notes

1.   Gleick (1987), p. 11-31. The references to Edward Lorenz are adapted from Gleick's description of these same events. His book is the best introduction to the people, their work, and the discoveries that brought chaos theory into focus. I highly recommend it.
2.   Steward (1995).
3.   Mandelbrot (1983), p. 1.
4.   Hawking (1987), p. 53.
5.   Stewart (1995), p. 113-15; Capra (1996), p. 126-28.
6.   Stewart (1995), p. 58-59.
7.   Hawking (1987), p. 29-33.
8.   Hawking (1987).
9.   Kauffman (1995); Capra (1996).
10.   Kauffman (1996), p. 27.

UNCERTAINTY, DISCOVERY, AND HUMAN ACTION

A STUDY OF THE ENTREPRENEURIAL PROFILE IN THE MISESIAN SYSTEM

Israel M. Kirzner

A central element in the economics of Ludwig von Mises is the role played by the entrepreneur and the function fulfilled by entrepreneurship in the market process. The character of that process for Mises is decisively shaped by the leadership, the initiative, and the driving activity displayed and exercised by the entrepreneur. Moreover, in an intellectual edifice built systematically on the notion of individual *human action*—on the manner in which reasoning human beings interact while seeking to achieve their individual purposes—it is highly significant that Mises found it of relevance to emphasize that each human actor is always, in significant respects, an entrepreneur.[1] The present paper seeks to explore the character of Misesian entrepreneurship, with special reference to the influence exercised by the inescapable uncertainty that pervades economic life. Both at the level of isolated individual human action and at the level of entrepreneurial activity in market context, I shall be concerned to determine the extent to which the Misesian entrepreneur owes his very existence and his function to the unpredictability of his environment and to the ceaseless tides of change that undergird that unpredictability.

On the face of it, this question may not seem worthy of new research. Mises, it may be pointed out, expressed himself quite clearly on numerous occasions to the effect that the entrepreneurial function is inseparable from speculation with respect to an uncertain future. For example he wrote that "the entrepreneur is always a speculator."[2] Or again, he wrote that "entrepreneur means acting man in regard to the changes occurring in the data of the market."[3] Moreover, when Mises points out that every individual acting man is an entrepreneur, this is because "every action is embedded in the flux of time and thus involves a speculation."[4] In other words, the entrepreneurial element cannot be abstracted from the notion of individual human action, because the "uncertainty of the future is already implied in the very notion of action. That man acts and that the future is uncertain are by no means two independent matters, they are only two different modes of establishing one thing."[5]

Thus it might seem that the essentiality of uncertainty for the Misesian entrepreneur hardly needs to be established anew. Certainly any thought of questioning that essentiality must, it might appear, be quickly dismissed.

What I shall argue in this chapter is not that the role of uncertainty in the function of the Misesian entrepreneur may be any less definitive than these clear-cut statements imply, but that this role is a more subtle one than may on the surface appear to be the case. It is this subtlety in the role played by uncertainty in the Misesian system, I believe, that sets that system apart in significant respects from the views of other economists (such as Knight or Shackle) who have emphasized the phenomenon of uncertainty in the context of the market.

The Background of the Present Exploration

In earlier forays into the field of the Misesian entrepreneur, I developed an interpretation of the entrepreneurial function in which the role of uncertainty, while recognized and certainly not denied, was not emphasized. This failure to emphasize uncertainty was quite deliberate and was indeed explicitly acknowledged.[6] Instead of emphasizing the uncertainty in which entrepreneurial activity is embedded, these earlier treatments stressed the element of *alertness to hitherto unperceived opportunities* that is, I argued, crucial for the Misesian concept of entrepreneurship.[7] Since my position explicitly recognized the element of change and uncertainty while it claimed to be able to explicate the elusive quality of entrepreneurship without need to emphasize the uncertainty element, it is perhaps not surprising that my treatment has drawn fire from two different perspectives. A number of critics have felt rather strongly that failure to emphasize the role of uncertainty renders my understanding of entrepreneurship fundamentally defective. At least one critic, on the other hand, has been persuaded by my exposition of entrepreneurship to the point that even my frugal references to uncertainty as an inescapable characteristic of the entrepreneurial scene appear altogether unnecessary and are seen as producing confusion. Since all these critics are basically in agreement with me, I believe, on the broad accuracy of the general entrepreneurial character of the market process that I ascribe to Mises, it has for some time been my hope to delve into these questions more thoroughly. Some further brief recapitulation of these earlier discussions seems in order as an introduction to our present exploration.

My emphasis on alertness to hitherto unperceived opportunities as the decisive element in the entrepreneurial function stemmed from my pursuit of a didactic purpose. This purpose was to distinguish the analysis of the market *process* (a process in which the entrepreneur plays the crucial role) as sharply as possible from the analysis of equilibrium states (in which all scope for entrepreneurial activity has been assumed away). In equilibrium, it turns out, all market decisions have somehow come already into complete mutual coordination. Market participants have been assumed to be making their respective decisions with perfectly correct information concerning the decisions that all other participants are making at the same time.[8] So long as the underlying present consumer attitudes and production possibilities prevail, it is clear that we can rely on the very same set of decisions being made in each of an indefinite number of future periods. On the other hand, in the absence of such complete equilibrium coordination of decisions, a market process is set in motion in which market participants are motivated to learn to anticipate more accurately the decisions of others; in this process the entrepreneurial, profit-motivated discovery of the gaps in mutual coordination of decisions is a crucial element. Entrepreneurial activity drives this market process of mutual discovery by a continually displayed alertness to profit opportunities (into which the market automatically translates the existing gaps in coordination). Whereas entrepreneurial activity is indeed speculative, the pursuit of profit opportunities is a purposeful and deliberate one, the "emphasis on the element of alertness in action [was] intended to point out that, far from being numbed by the inescapable uncertainty of our world, men *act upon their judgments of* what opportunities have been left unexploited by others."[9]

In developing this aspect of entrepreneurship I was led to emphasize the capture of pure entrepreneurial profit as reducible essentially to the exploitation of arbitrage opportunities. Imperfect mutual awareness on the part of other market participants had generated the emergence of more than one price for the same bundle of economic goods; the entrepreneur's alertness to the profit opportunity presented by this price discrepancy permits him to win these profits (and, in so doing, tends to nudge the prices into closer adjustment with each other). In so emphasizing the arbitrage character of pure profit, emphasis was deliberately withdrawn from the speculative character of entrepreneurial activity that wins pure profit by correctly anticipating *future* price movements.[10]

A number of (otherwise friendly) critics expressed serious reservations concerning my deliberate lack of stress on the speculative character of entrepreneurial activity. Henry Hazlitt pointed out that my repeated references to the entrepreneur's perceiving of opportunities fail to make clear that at best the entrepreneur *thinks* that he perceives opportunities: that what an entrepreneur "acts on may not be a perception but a *guess*."[11] Murray Rothbard has endorsed a discussion by Robert Hébert in which my definition of the entrepreneur is sharply distinguished from that of Mises: "Mises conceives of the entrepreneur as the uncertainty bearer.... To Kirzner, on the other hand, entrepreneurship becomes reduced to the quality of *alertness*; and uncertainty seems to have little to do with the matter."[12] Although conceding that my treatment of the entrepreneur has "a certain amount of textual justification in Mises," Rothbard sees this not as providing genuine support for my reading of the Misesian entrepreneur but as being the result of a "certain uncharacteristic lack of clarity in Mises' discussion of entrepreneurship."[13]

In a most thoughtful paper several years ago, Lawrence H. White too deplored my deliberate failure to emphasize uncertainty in the analysis of entrepreneurship. This treatment, White argues, fosters neglect of important features of entrepreneurial activity that arise precisely from the passage of time and from the uncertainty generated by the prospect of unanticipated changes bound to occur during the journey to the future. To compress entrepreneurial activity into an arbitrage box is, in particular, to fail to recognize the highly important part played by entrepreneurial *imagination*.[14]

On the other hand, my treatment of entrepreneurship has been criticized by J. High from a diametrically opposite point of view. High accepts the definition of entrepreneurship in terms of alertness to opportunities for pure profit. He proceeds to point out that "nothing in this definition requires uncertainty. The definition requires ignorance, because the opportunity has not been discovered earlier: it requires error, because the opportunity could have been discovered earlier, but the definition does not require uncertainty."[15] High is therefore critical of passages in which uncertainty is linked specifically with entrepreneurship.[16]

Clearly the role of uncertainty in the entrepreneurial environment, and in particular its relationship to the entrepreneur's alertness to error, demands further explication. What follows may not satisfy my critics (from both wings). I trust, however, that my discussion of some of the perhaps less obvious links between uncertainty and alertness will, if it does not quite absolve me of the charge of intransigence, at least bear witness to my grateful acknowledgment of the very deep importance of the problems raised by my critics.

Our inquiry will be facilitated by a careful examination of the sense in which each individual engaging in human action is, as already cited from Mises, exercising entrepreneurship.[17] Or to put the issue somewhat differently, it will be helpful to explore more precisely what it is that distinguishes human action from purely calculative, allocative, economizing activity.

I have argued in earlier work that the concept of human action emphasized by Mises includes an ineradicable entrepreneurial element that is absent from the notion of economizing, of the allocation of scarce resources among competing ends, that was articulated by Lord Robbins.[18] On the face of it there appear to be two distinct aspects of Misesian human action that might be considered to set it apart from Robbinsian economizing activity. We shall have to ask whether these are indeed two distinct aspects of human action and how they relate to the entrepreneurial element that human action contains (but which Robbinsian allocative activity does not). These two aspects of human action (not present in economizing activity) may be identified as (1) the element in action that is beyond the scope of "rationality" as an explanatory tool, and (2) the element in action that constitutes discovery of error. Let us consider these in turn.

The Limits of Rationality

Perhaps the central feature of purely economizing activity is that it enables us to explain behavior by reference to the postulate of rationality. With a given framework of ranked goals sought, and of scarce resources available to be deployed, rationality (in the narrow sense of consistency of behavior with the relevant given ranking of ends) ensures a unique pattern of resource allocation; decision making can be fully understood in the light of the given ends-means framework. There is no part of the decision that cannot be accounted for; given the framework, the decision taken is fully determined (and therefore completely explained); any other decision would have been simply unthinkable.

On the other hand, the notion of Msesian human action embraces the very adoption of the ends means framework to be considered relevant. The adoption of any particular ends-means framework is a step which is logically (although not necessarily chronologically) prior to that of allocating means consistently with the given ranking of ends. If the human decision is to be perceived as including the selection of the ends-means framework, then we have an element in that decision that cannot, of course, be explained by reference to rationality. Consistency in action is not sufficient to account for that ranking of ends in terms of which consistency itself is to be defined. Thus the totality of human action cannot, even in principle, be explained on the basis of rationality. A science of human action cannot fail to acknowledge—even after full recognition of the formidable explanatory power of the postulate of rationality—that human history, depending as it does on unexplained adoption of goals and awareness of means, contains a strong element of the unexplained and even the spontaneous. These are themes that have, of course, been extensively developed by G. L. S. Shackle: "Choice and reason are things different in nature and function, reason *serves* the chosen purposes, not performs the selection of them."[19] "A man can be supposed to act always in rational response to his 'circumstances' but those 'circumstances' can, *and must*, be in part the creation of his own mind.... In this loose-textured history, men's choices of action being choices action being choices among thoughts which spring indeterminately in their minds, we can deem them to *initiate* trains of events in some real sense."[20]

In an earlier era, much criticism of the role of the rationality postulate in economic theory focused on the place of apparently nonrational behavior, behavior arising out of impetuous impulse or out of unthinking habit.[21] It is simply unrealistic, these criticisms ran, to assume that economic activity represents the exclusive result of deliberation. Man acts all too often without careful deliberation; he does not weigh the costs and benefits of his actions. This is not the place to evaluate these criticisms or deal with the debates that they engendered three-quarters of a century ago and more. But it is perhaps important to point out that limits of rationality discussed in this section have little to do with the arguments based on impulsiveness and on habit bondage. It is not at all being argued here that human action involves the *thoughtless* selection of goals. Human decision making may of course involve the most agonizingly careful appraisal of alternative courses of action to choose what seems likely to offer the most estimable of outcomes. In emphasizing that the rationality postulate is unable to explain the selection of the relevant ends-means framework, I am not suggesting that that selection occurs without deliberation, but merely that the results of that deliberation cannot be predicted on the basis of the postulate of consistency; that deliberation is essentially creative. One may predict the answer that a competent mathematician will arrive at when he tackles a given problem in computation (in the same way that one may know in advance the answer to that problem that will be yielded by an electronic computer); but one cannot, in the same way, predict which computational problem the mathematician will deliberately choose to tackle (as one may not be able to predict which problems will be selected to be fed into the electronic computer).

The matter may be presented in an alternative version. One may always distinguish, within each human decision, an element into which thought enters in self-aware fashion from an element into which thought enters without self awareness. A man desires a specific goal with great eagerness; but deliberation persuades him, let us imagine, that it is in his interest not to reveal that eagerness to others (say, because others might then spitefully wish to deny that goal to him). The studied nonchalance with which he masks his pursuit of the goal exhibits scope for both element: (1) his apparent nonchalance is indeed deliberate and studied, he knows precisely the reason why it is important that he pretend lack of interest; but (2) he may not be at all self-aware as to how he arrived at this judgment to act on the assumption that others may spitefully seek to frustrate his achievement. He simply decides to act. His decision is to refrain from naively pursuing with evident eagerness what he eagerly desires; but his decision is yet naive in the sense that he has not, for example, sought (as reasons having to do with long-term strategy might well suggest) to ostentatiously pretend unawareness of the spitefulness of the others. No matter how calculative a man's behavior may be, it seems impossible to avoid having accepted, without calculation, some framework within which to self-consciously engage in cost-benefit comparisons. A man decides to display behavior a. We may call the mental activity of making that decision activity b. Now the man *may* have decided (in the course of decision-making activity c) to engage in decision making activity b (or he may have simply and impulsively engaged in decision-making activity b). But even if engaging in decision-making activity b (as a result of which behavior a was chosen) was itself the outcome of "higher" decisions, at some level our decision maker's highest decision was made quite unselfconsciously.

This extra-Robbinsian aspect of human action, the aspect which involves the creative, unpredictable selection of the ends-means framework, can also be usefully stated in terms of *knowledge*. Given his knowledge of the relevant ends-means framework, man's decision can be predicted without doubt; it is simply a matter of computation. To the extent, however, that man must "decide" what it is, so to speak, that he knows, and that this determination is not in general based ineluctably on other knowledge unambiguously possessed, man's behavior is not at all predictable. What a man believes himself to know is not itself the result of a calculative decision.[22] This expression of the notion of the existence of limits to rationality will facilitate our insight into the important linkage that exists between these limits and the phenomenon of uncertainty.

In the absence of uncertainty it would be difficult to avoid the assumption that each individual does in fact already know the circumstances surrounding his decision. Without uncertainty, therefore, decision making would no longer call for any imaginative, creative determination of what the circumstances really are. Decision making would call merely for competent calculation. Its results could, in general, be predicted without doubt. Human judgment would have no scope. "With uncertainty absent, man's energies are devoted altogether to doing things; . . . in a world so built . . . it seems likely that . . . all organisms [would be] automata."[23] "If man knew the future, he would not have to choose and would not act. He would be like an automaton, reacting to stimuli without any will of its own."[24] Thus the extra-Robbinsian aspect of human action, the aspect responsible for rendering human action unpredictable and incompletely explainable in terms of rationality, arises from the inherent uncertainty of human predicament. If, then, one chooses to identify entrepreneurship with the function of making decisions in the face of an uncertain present or future environment, it certainly appears that Misesian human action does (while Robbinsian economizing does not) include an entrepreneurial element.

But before making up our minds on this point, we must consider that second element, mentioned at the end of the preceding section, that distinguishes Misesian human action from Robbinsian allocative decision making.

The Discovery of Error

To draw attention to this element in human action I shall draw on an earlier paper in which I attempted to identify what might represent "entrepreneurial profit" in successful individual action in a Crusoe context.[25] Entrepreneurial profit in the Crusoe context, it turned out, can be identified only where Crusoe discovers that he has up until now attached an erroneously low valuation to resources over which he has command. Until today Crusoe has been spending his time catching fish with his bare hands. Today he has realized that he can use his time far more valuably by building a boat or making a net. "He has discovered that he had placed an incorrectly low value on his time. His reallocation of his labor time from fishing to boat-building is an entrepreneurial decision and, assuming his decision to be a correct one, yields pure profit in the form of additional value discovered to be forthcoming from the labor time applied."[26] This (Crusonian) pure profit arises from the circumstance that at the instant of entrepreneurial discovery Menger's law is violated. Menger's law teaches that men value goods according to the value of the satisfactions that depend on possession of those goods. This law arises from man's propensity to attach the value of ends to the means needed for their achievement. At the moment of entrepreneurial discovery Crusoe realizes that the ends achievable with his labor time have higher value than the ends he had previously sought to achieve:

> The value Crusoe has until now attached to his time is *less* than the value of the ends he now seeks. This discrepancy is, at the level of the individual, pure profit.... Once the old ends-means framework has been completely and unquestionably replaced by the new one, of course, it is the value of the new ends that Crusoe comes to attach to his means.... But, during the instant of an entrepreneurial leap of faith . . . there is scope for the discovery that, indeed, the ends achieved are more valuable than had hitherto been suspected. *This*, is the discovery of pure (Crusonian) entrepreneurial profit.[27]

Scope for entrepreneurship thus appears to be grounded in the possibility of discovering error. In the market context, the state of general equilibrium, providing as it does absolutely no scope for the discovery of profitable discrepancies between prices and costs, affords no opportunity for entrepreneurial discovery and turns out to be populated entirely by Robbinsian maximizers. In the same way, it now appears, the situation in which Crusoe is errorlessly allocating his resources—with the value of ends being fully and faultlessly attached to the relevant means in strict accordance with Menger's law— affords no scope for the entrepreneurial element in human action. Human action, without scope for the discovery of error, collapses into Robbinsian allocative activity.

Clearly this way of identifying the entrepreneurial element that is present in Misesian human action but absent in Robbinsian economizing activity fits in well with the approach that defines entrepreneurship as alertness to hitherto unperceived opportunities.[28] In the market context entrepreneurship is evoked by the presence of as yet unexploited opportunities for pure profit. These opportunities are evidence of the failure of market participants, up until now, to correctly assess the realities of the market situation. At the level of the individual too, it is then attractive to argue, an entrepreneurial element in action is evoked by the existence of as yet unexploited private opportunities. To act entrepreneurially is to identify situations overlooked until now because of error.

Uncertainty and/or Discovery

Our discussion has led us to identify two apparently distinct elements in human action, each of which possesses plausible claims as constituting that entrepreneurial element in action that sets it apart from purely calculative economizing activity: (1) On the one hand we saw that it appears plausible to associate entrepreneurship with the department within human action in which the very framework for calculative economizing activity is, in an open-ended, uncertain world, selected as being relevant. It is here that we would find scope for the unpredictable, the creative, the imaginative expressions of the human mind—expressions that cannot themselves be explained in terms of the postulate of consistency. Thus entrepreneurship, at the Crusoe level, arises uniquely and peculiarly from the circumstance that, as a result of the inescapable uncertainty of the human predicament, acting man cannot be assumed to be sure of the framework relevant for calculative activity. He must, using whatever entrepreneurial gifts he can display, *choose* a framework. (2) On the other hand, as we have seen, it appears perhaps equally plausible to associate entrepreneurship with that aspect of human action in which the alert individual realizes the existence of opportunities that he has up until now somehow failed to notice. Scope for entrepreneurship, at the Crusoe level, arises then not from the present uncertainty that must now be grappled with in decision making but from earlier error from which entrepreneurial discovery must now provide protection.

I must emphasize that these alternative identifications of the entrepreneurial element in action do appear, at least on a first scrutiny, to be genuinely different from one another. It is of course true that past error (from which, on the one view, we look to entrepreneurial discovery to provide a rescue) may be attributed to the pervasive uncertainty that characterizes our world (and to the inevitably kaleidic changes responsible for that uncertainty). But to discover hitherto unnoticed opportunities (unnoticed because of past failure to pierce correctly the fog of uncertainty) does not at all seem to be the same task as that of selecting between alternative present scenarios for the future within which calculative activity is to be undertaken. Moreover, whatever the possible reasons for past error, error itself implies merely ignorance, not necessarily uncertainty.[29] To escape ignorance is one thing; to deal with uncertainty is another.

This tension that we have discovered at the level of human action in the Crusoe context, between present uncertainty and earlier error as sources of entrepreneurship, is clearly to be linked immediately with our more general exploration in this chapter. This chapter is concerned with determining the extent to which the Misesian entrepreneur is to be perceived as the creature of uncertainty. The tension we have now discovered between present uncertainty and earlier error corresponds exactly to the disagreement we encountered between those who see the Misesian entrepreneur as essentially the bearer of market uncertainty and those who see him as the discoverer of earlier market errors. It is my contention that our awareness of this apparent tension can in fact shed light on certain subtleties in the concept of entrepreneurship likely otherwise to be overlooked. My procedure to develop this claim will be as follows: I will seek to show that, on a deeper understanding of the meaning of uncertainty and of the discovery of error at the level of individual action, the tension between them dissolves in a way that will reveal the full significance of entrepreneurial alertness at the level of the individual. Thereafter I will pursue the analogy between the scope of entrepreneurship at the individual level and that of entrepreneurship at the level of the market, drawing on this analogy to identify precisely the relative roles, in market entrepreneurship, of uncertainty and of alertness.

Action and Alertness

Man acts, in the light of the future as he envisages it, to enhance his position in that future. The realized consequences of man's actions, however, flow from the impact of those actions on the actual (as contrasted with the envisaged) course of future events. The extent to which man's plans for the enhancement of his prospects are fulfilled depends on the extent to which the future as he has envisaged it corresponds to the future as it in fact occurs. There is no natural set of forces or constraints assuring correspondence between the envisaged future and the realized future. The two may, it seems at first glance, diverge from one another with complete freedom. The future course of events is in general certainly not constrained by past forecasts; nor, unfortunately, are forecasts constrained by the actual future events these forecasts seek to foretell. On the face of it, then, with nothing to guarantee correspondence between the actual future and the future as it is envisaged, it might seem as if successful action were entirely a matter of good fortune. Indeed, if man is aware of this apparent lack of ability to envisage the future correctly except as a matter of sheer good fortune, it is not clear why (apart from the joys of gambling itself) man bothers to act at all. But of course the overwhelming fact of human history is that man does act, and his choices are made in terms of an envisaged future that, although by no means a photographic image of the future as it will actually unfold, is yet not entirely without moorings in regard to that realized future. "To be genuine, choice must be neither random nor predetermined. There must be some grounds for choosing, but they must be inadequate; there must be some possibility of predicting the consequences of choice, but none of perfect prediction."[30] "The essence of the situation is action according to *opinion*, . . . neither entire ignorance nor complete and perfect information, but partial knowledge."[31] The genuine choices that do, I am convinced, make up human history express man's conviction that the future as he envisages it does hold correspondence, in some degree, to the future as it will in fact unfold. The uncertainty of the future reflects man's awareness that this correspondence is far from complete; the fact that he acts and chooses at all reflects his conviction that this correspondence is far from negligible. Whence does this correspondence, incomplete though it may be, arise? If there are no constraints assuring correspondence, how is successful action anything but the sheerest good fortune?

The answer to this dilemma surely lies in the circumstance that man is *motivated* to formulate the future as he envisages it, as accurately as possible. It is not a matter of two unfolding tapestries, one the realized future, the second a fantasized series of pictures of what the first might look like. Rather, acting man really does try to construct his picture of the future to correspond to the truth as it will be realized. He really does try to glimpse the future, to peer through the fog. He is thus motivated to *bring about* correspondence between the envisaged and the realized futures. Not only are man's purposeful efforts to better his condition responsible for his choices as constructed against a given envisaged future, that purposefulness is, perhaps even more importantly, responsible for the remarkable circumstance that that envisaged future does overlap significantly with the future as it actually unfolds. (Of course, these forecasts need not be made, explicitly, prior to action; they are embedded, possibly without self-awareness, in action itself.) I call this motivated propensity of man to formulate an image of the future man's alertness. Were man totally lacking in alertness, he could not act at all: his blindness to the future would rob him of any framework for action. (In fact, were man totally lacking in potential for *alertness*, it would be difficult to identify a notion of error altogether: were unalert man to act, it would not be on the basis of an erroneously forecast future. It would be on the basis of no relevant forecast at all. Not recognizing that he might— had he been more alert—have avoided the incorrect picture of the future, he could not in any meaningful sense blame himself for having erred.)

It will surely be acknowledged that this alertness— which provides the only pressure to constrain man's envisaged future toward some correspondence with the future to be realized—is what we are searching for under the phrase "the entrepreneurial element in human action."

Robbinsian allocation activity contains no such element, because within the assigned scope of such defined activity no possible divergence between a future as envisaged and a future to be realized is considered. What is incomplete in the notion of purely allocative activity is surely to be found precisely in this abstraction from the desperately important element of entrepreneurship in human action.

It should be observed that the entrepreneurial alertness we have identified does not consist merely in "seeing" the unfolding of the tapestry of the future in the sense of seeing a preordained flow of events. Alertness must, importantly, embrace the awareness of the ways the human agent can, by imaginative, bold leaps of faith, and determination, in fact *create* the future for which his present acts are designed. As I shall argue in a subsequent section, this latter expression of entrepreneurial alertness does not affect its essential formal character—which remains that of ensuring a tendency for the future context envisaged as following present action to bear some realistic resemblance to the future as it will be realized.

In understanding this entrepreneurial element in human action, we must notice, two aspects of it: (1) We note what provides the scope for entrepreneurship. This scope is provided by the complete freedom with which the future as envisaged might, without entrepreneurial alertness, diverge from the future as it will in fact be. Entrepreneurial alertness has a function to perform. (2) We note what provides the incentive that switches on entrepreneurial alertness. This incentive is provided by the lure of pure entrepreneurial profit to be grasped in stepping from a less accurately envisaged future to a more accurately envisaged one. Each step taken in moving toward a vision of the future that overlaps more significantly with the truth is not merely a step toward truth (that is, a positive entrepreneurial success); it is also a profitable step (that is, a step that enhances the value of the sources with which action is available to be taken).

Viewed from this perspective, the tension between the uncertainty environment in which action occurs, on the one hand, and the discovery-of-error aspect of action, on the other, can be seen to dissolve at a glance. These two aspects of action can be seen immediately as merely two sides of the same entrepreneurial coin. If uncertainty were merely an unpleasant condition of life to which man must passively adjust, then it would be reasonable to distinguish between the quite separate activities of bearing uncertainty on the one hand and of discovering error on the other. Escaping from current errors is one thing; grappling with the uncertainty of the future is another. But, as we have noticed, to choose means to *endeavor*, under the incentive to grasp pure profit, to identify a more truthful picture of the future. Dealing with uncertainty is motivated by the profit to be won by avoiding error. In this way of viewing the matter the distinction be seen escaping current enor and avoiding potential future error is unimportant. The discovery of error is an interesting feature of action because it offers incentive. It is this incentive that inspires the effort to pierce the fog of uncertainty that shrouds the future. To deal with uncertainty means to seek to overcome it by more accurate prescience; to discover error is merely that aspect of this endeavor that endows it with incentive attraction. The imagination and creativity with which man limits his envisaged future are inspired by the pure gains to be won in ensuring that that envisaged future is in fact no less bright than that which can be made the truth.

We shall find in the next section that these insights surrounding entrepreneurship at the level of individual action have their exact counterparts in entrepreneurship in the market context. It will be useful to summarize briefly the key points we have learned about individual entrepreneurship:

1. Entrepreneurship in individual action consists of the endeavor to secure greater correspondence between the individual's future as he envisages it and his future as it will in fact unfold. This endeavor consists in the individual's alertness to whatever can provide clues to the future. This alertness, broadly conceived, embraces those aspects of imagination and creativity through which the individual may himself *ensure* that his envisaged future will be realized.

2. Scope for entrepreneurship is provided by the uncertainty of the future. For our purposes uncertainty means that, in the absence of entrepreneurial alertness, an individual's view of the future may diverge with total freedom from the realized future. In the absence of entrepreneurial alertness it is only sheer chance that can be responsible for successful action.

3. Incentive for the "switching on" of entrepreneurial alertness is provided by the pure gain (or avoidance of loss) to be derived from replacing actions based on less accurate prescience by action based on the more realistically envisaged future. The avoidance of entrepreneurial error is not merely a matter of being more truthful, it happens also to be profitable.

Entrepreneurship in the Market

Our examination of the entrepreneurial element in individual action permits us to see the role of entrepreneurship in the market in a fresh light. We shall discover, in the market context, elements that correspond precisely to their analogues in the individual context. Let us consider what happens in markets.

In a market, exchanges occur between market participants.[32] In the absence of perfect mutual knowledge, many of the exchanges are inconsistent with one another. Some sales are made at low prices when some buyers are buying at high prices. Some market participants are not buying at all because they are unaware of the possibility of buying at prices low enough to be attractive; some are refraining from selling because they are unaware of the possibility of selling at prices high enough to be attractive. Clearly the actions of these buyers and sellers are, from the perspective of omniscience, uncoordinated and inconsistent. We notice that, although the assumption of perfect knowledge that is necessary for market equilibrium would constrain different transactions in the market to complete mutual consistency, the actuality of imperfect knowledge permits these different transactions in different parts of the market to diverge with apparently complete freedom. What alone tends to introduce a modicum of consistency and coordination into this picture, preventing a situation in which even the slightest degree of coordination could exist only as a matter of sheerest chance, is market entrepreneurship, inspired by the lure or pure market profit. We are now in a position to identify, in the market context, elements that correspond to key features already identified in the context of individual entrepreneurship.

Corresponding to uncertainty as it impinges on individual action, we have market discoordination. The freedom with which an individual's envisaged future may diverge from the future to be realized corresponds precisely to the freedom with which transactions made in one part of the market may diverge from transactions made elsewhere. In the absence of entrepreneurship it is only out of the purest chance that market transactions by different pairs of buyers and sellers are made on anything but the most wildly inconsistent terms. There is nothing that constrains the mutually satisfactory price bargain reached between one pair of traders to bear any specific relation to corresponding bargains reached between other pairs of traders.

Corresponding to error at the level of the individual, we have price divergence at the level of the market. Perfect knowledge (such as in Robbinsian individual allocative activity) precludes error. Market equilibrium (implied by universal perfect knowledge) precludes price divergences.

The individual entrepreneurial element permits the individual to escape from the distressing freedom with which divergences between envisaged futures and realized futures may occur; the entrepreneur fulfills the same function for the market. The function of the entrepreneur is to bring different parts of the market into coordination with each other. The market entrepreneur bridges the gaps in mutual knowledge, gaps that would otherwise permit prices to diverge with complete freedom.

Corresponding to the incentive for individual entrepreneurship provided by more realistic views of the future, we have at the market level the incentive provided by opportunities for pure entrepreneurial profit. Market profit consists in the gap between prices generated by error and market inconsistency—just as the source for private gain is to be discovered in a present divergence between the imagined and the actual future.

The following are propositions, in the context of the market, that concern entrepreneurship; they correspond precisely to those stated at the conclusion of the preceding section.[33]

1°. Entrepreneurship in the market consists in the function of securing greater consistency between different parts of the market. It expresses itself in entrepreneurial alertness to what transactions are in fact available in different parts of the market. It is only such alertness that is responsible for any tendency toward keeping these transactions in some kind of mutual consistency.

2°. Scope for market entrepreneurship is provided by the imperfect knowledge that permits market transactions to diverge from what would be a mutually consistent pattern.

3°. Incentive for market entrepreneurial activity is provided by the pure gain to be won by noticing existing divergences between the prices at which market transactions are available in different parts of the market. It is the lure of market profits that inspires entrepreneurial alertness.

Time, Uncertainty, and Entrepreneurship

My analogy between entrepreneurship at the level of the individual and entrepreneurship in the market emphasized only the most salient respects of the analogy. Certain additional features of the entrepreneurial function in the market need to be dealt with more extensively. In the individual context the divergence (which it is the function of entrepreneurship to limit) was a divergence between anticipated and realized future. Its source in uncertainty was immediately apparent. In the market context the divergence (which it is the function of entrepreneurship to limit) was a divergence between the transactions in different parts of the market. Its source was stated in terms of imperfect mutual knowledge among market participants. Its relationship to uncertainty was not asserted. This requires both amplification and modification.

My statements concerning market entrepreneurship were couched in terms of the market for a single commodity within a single period. It should be clear that nothing essential is lost when our picture of the market is expanded to include many commodities and, in particular, the passage of time. This should of course not be understood to mean that the introduction of the passage of time does not open up scope for additional insights. I merely argue that the insights we have gained in the single-period context for entrepreneurship are not to be lost sight of in the far more complex multiperiod case.

When we introduce the passage of time, the dimensions along which mutual ignorance may develop are multiplied. Market participants in one part of today's market not only may be imperfectly aware of the transactions available in another part of that market, they also may be imperfectly aware of the transactions that will be available in next year's market. Absence of consistency between different parts of today's market is seen as a special case of a more general notion of inconsistency that also includes inconsistency between today's transactions and those to be transacted next year. A low price today may be in this sense inconsistent with the high prices that will prevail next year. Scope for market entrepreneurship, in the context of the passage of time, arises then from the need to coordinate markets also across time. Incentive for market entrepreneurship along the intertemporal dimension is provided not by arbitrage profits generated by imperfectly coordinated present markets but, more generally, by the speculative profits generated by the as yet imperfectly coordinated market situations in the sequence of time. And, of course, the introduction of entrepreneurial activity to coordinate markets through time introduces, for individual entrepreneurs engaged in market entrepreneurship, precisely the considerations concerning the uncertain future that we have, until now, considered only in the context of the isolated individual.

It is because of this last circumstance that we must acknowledge that the introduction of the passage of time, although leaving the overall formal function of market entrepreneurship unchanged, will of course introduce substantial modification into the way we must imagine entrepreneurship to be exercised concretely. It is still the case, as noted, that the entrepreneurial function is that of bringing about a tendency for transactions in different parts of the market (conceived broadly now as including transactions entered into at different times) to be made in greater mutual consistency. But whereas in the case of entrepreneurship in the single-period market (that is, the case of the entrepreneur as arbitrageur) entrepreneurial alertness meant alertness to present facts, in the case of multi period entrepreneurship alertness must mean alertness to the future. It follows that market entrepreneurship in the multiperiod case introduces uncertainty as facing the entrepreneur not only as in the analogy offered in the preceding section—where the market analogue for uncertainty turned out to be the freedom with which transactions in different parts of today's market may unconstrainedly diverge from being mutually consistent—but also in the simple sense of the entrepreneur's awareness of the freedom with which his own envisaged future (concerning future market transactions) may diverge from the realized future. In particular the futurity that entrepreneurship must confront introduces the possibility that the entrepreneur may, by his own creative actions, in fact *construct* the future as *he* wishes it to be. In the singleperiod case alertness can at best discover hitherto overlooked current facts. In the multiperiod case entrepreneurial alertness must include the entrepreneur's perception of the way creative and imaginative action may vitally shape the kind of transactions that will be entered into in future market periods.

Thus the exercise of entrepreneurial alertness in the multiperiod market context will indeed call for personal and psychological qualifications that were unneeded in the single-period case. To be a successful entrepreneur one must now possess those qualities of vision, boldness, determination, and creativity that we associated earlier with the entrepreneurial element in isolated individual action with respect to an uncertain future. There can be no doubt that in the concrete fulfillment of the entrepreneurial function these psychological and personal qualities are of paramount importance. It is in this sense that so many writers are undoubtedly correct in linking entrepreneurship with the courage and vision necessary to *create* the future in an uncertain world (rather than with merely seeing what stares one in the face).

However, the function of market entrepreneurship in the multiperiod context is nonetheless still that spelled out in the preceding section. What market entrepreneurship accomplishes is a tendency for transactions in different parts of the market (including the market at different dates) to become coordinated. The incentive that inspires this entrepreneurial coordination is the lure of pure profit—the difference in market values resulting from hitherto less complete coordination. These insights remain true for the multiperiod case no less than for the arbitrage case. For some purposes it is no doubt important to draw attention to the concrete psychological requirements on which successful entrepreneurial decision making depends. But for other purposes such emphasis is not required; in fact such emphasis may divert attention from what is, from the perspective of the overall functioning of the market system, surely the essential feature of entrepreneurship: its market-coordinative properties.

Let us recall that at the level of the individual, entrepreneurship involved not merely bearing uncertainty but also overcoming uncertainty. Uncertainty is responsible for what would, in the absence of entrepreneurship, be a failure to perceive the future in a manner sufficiently realistic to permit action. Entrepreneurship, so to speak, pushes aside to some extent the swirling fogs of uncertainty, permitting meaningful action. It is this function of entrepreneurship that must be kept in view when we study the market process. The uncertainty that characterizes the environment within which market entrepreneurship plays its coordinative role must be fully recognized; without it there would be no need and no scope for entrepreneurship. But an understanding of what entrepreneurship accomplishes requires us to recognize not so much the extent to which uncertainty is the ineradicable feature of human existence as the extent to which both individual action and social coordination through the market can occur significantly despite the uncertainty of the future (and in spite also of the uncertainty analogue that would, in the absence of the arbitrageur, fog up even the single-period market).

Further Reflections on Uncertainty and Alertness

Thus we can see how those writers who have denied that the pure entrepreneurial role involves the bearing of uncertainty were both correct and yet at least partly irrelevant. Both J. A. Schumpeter[34] and J. B. Clark insisted that only the capitalist bears the hazards of business; the pure entrepreneur has, by definition, nothing to lose.[35] No doubt all this is true, as far as it goes, but what is important about linking the entrepreneur with the phenomenon of uncertainty is not that it is the entrepreneur who accepts the disutilities associated with the assumption of the hazards of business in an uncertain world. What is important is that the entrepreneur, motivated by the lure of pure profits, attempts to pierce these uncertainties and endeavors to see the truth that will permit profitable action on his part.

A number of economists may be altogether unwilling to accept the notion of alertness with respect to uncertain future. In fact many may wish to reject the very formulation I have employed to schematize the uncertainty of the future. For me uncertainty means the essential freedom with which the envisaged future may diverge from the realized future. Entrepreneurial alertness means the ability to impose constraints on that freedom, so that the entrepreneur's vision of the future may indeed overlap, to some significant extent, with that future he is attempting to see. But many will be unwilling to treat the future as something to be seen at all. "The present is uniquely determined. It can be seen by the eyewitness.... What is the future but the void? To call it the future is to concede the presumption that it is already 'existent' and merely waiting to appear. If that is so, if the world is determinist, then it seems idle to speak of choice."[36] Similarly, many are unwilling to see the entrepreneur as "alert to opportunities" if this terminology implies that future opportunities already "exist" and are merely waiting to be grasped. "Entrepreneurial projects are not waiting to be sought out so much as to be thought up."[37]

What perhaps needs to be emphasized once again is that in using phrases such as "grasping future opportunities," "seeing the future correctly or incorrectly," or the "divergence between the envisaged future and the realized future" I do not wish to imply any determinacy regarding the future. No doubt, to say that one sees the future (with greater or lesser accuracy) is to employ a metaphor. No doubt that future that one "sees" is a future that may in fact be constructed significantly by one's action, which is supposed to be informed by that very vision. But surely these metaphors are useful and instructive. To dream realistically in a way that inspires successful, creative action is to "see correctly" as compared with the fantasies that inspire absurd ventures or the cold water poured by the unduly timid pessimist that stunts all efforts at improvement. "The future, " we have learned, "is unknowable, though not unimaginable."[38] To acknowledge the unknowability of the future is to acknowledge the essential indeterminacy and uncertainty surrounding human existence. But surely in doing so we need not consign human existence to wholly uncoordinated chaos. To speak of entrepreneurial vision is to draw attention, by use of metaphor, to the formidable and benign coordinative powers of the human imagination. Austrian economists have, in principled fashion, refused to see the world as wholly knowable, as suited to interpretation by models of equilibrium from which uncertainty has been exhausted. It would be most unfortunate if, in pursuing this refusal, economists were to fall into a no less serious kind of error. This error would be the failure to understand how entrepreneurial individual actions, and the systematic market forces set in motion by freedom for entrepreneurial discovery and innovation, harness the human imagination to achieve no less a result than the liberation of mankind from the chaos of complete mutual ignorance. Mises's concept of human action and his analysis of the role of entrepreneurial market processes surely remain, in this regard, unique and as yet insufficiently appreciated contributions to the profound understanding of human society.

Notes

1. L. von Mises, *Human Action* (New Haven: Yale University Press, 1949), p. 253.

2. Ibid., p. 288.

3. Ibid., p. 255.

4. Ibid., p. 254.

5. Ibid., p. 105.

6. Israel M. Kirzner, *Competition and Entrepreneurship,* (Chicago: University of Chicago Press, 1973), pp. 86-87.

7. Ibid., chap.2. See also Israel M. Kirzner, *Perception, Opportunity, and Profit* (Chicago: University of Chicago Press, 1979), chap. 10.

8. F. A. Hayek, *Individualism and Economic Order* (London: Routledge and Kegan Paul, 1949), p. 42.

9. Kirzner, *Competition and Entrepreneurship,* pp. 86-87 (italics in original).

10. Such activity was subsumed under arbitrage by pointing out the formal similarity between (1) buying and selling in different markets today and (2) buying and selling in different markets at different dates (see Kirzner, *Competition and Entrepreneurship,* pp. 85-86).

11. Henry Hazlitt, review of *Competition and Entrepreneurship*, in *Freeman* 24 (December 1974: 759. Similar concerns seem to be expressed in a review of *Competition and Entrepreneurship* by Percy L. Greaves, Jr., in *Wertfrei* no. 2 (Spring 1974), esp. pp. 18-19.

12. See unpublished paper by Murray N. Rothbard, "Professor Hébert on Entrepreneurship," pp. 1-2. Quoted with permission.

13. Ibid., p. 7.

14. L. H. White, "Entrepreneurship, Imagination, and the Question of Equilibrium," unpublished paper (1976). See also L. H. White, "Entrepreneurial Price Adjustment" (paper presented at Southern Economic Association meetings, Washington, D.C., November 1978), p. 36, n. 3.

15. J. High, review article on *Perception, Opportunity, and Profit* in *Austrian Economics Newsletter 2*, 3 (Spring 1980): 14.

16. High's criticisms of my references to uncertainty as a characteristic of the entrepreneurial environment focus most specifically on what he believes to be my use of uncertainty to "serve as the distinguishing characteristic between entrepreneurship and luck" (ibid.). Here there seems to be a definite misunderstanding of my position. Far from the presence of the uncertainty surrounding entrepreneurship being what separates entrepreneurial profit from the lucky windfall, almost the exact reverse is the case. What marks entrepreneurial profit as different from the lucky windfall is that the former was, despite the (inevitable) uncertainty that might have discouraged the entrepreneur, in fact deliberately pursued. Where luck confers gain it may well reflect the circumstance that the uncertainty of this gain deterred the actor from even dreaming of winning it. High's reading apparently resulted from his understanding a passage that he cites (from Kirzner, *Perception, Opportunity, and Profit*, pp. 159-60) to represent the case of a purely lucky gain. In fact the passage cited does not refer to luck at all. If one knows that one's labor can convert low-valued leisure into high-valued apples, the apples one so gains through one's hard work do not constitute a lucky windfall. The point of the cited passages is that Menger's law shows there is no value gain at all derived from that labor, since one would already have attached the higher value of the ends to the available means. My discussion in this chapter, however, proceeds on the assumption that High's unhappiness at my treatment of uncertainty in entrepreneurship does not rest solely on the validity of the way I distinguish entrepreneurial profits from windfall gains.

17. Mises, *Human Action*, p. 253.

18. See Kirzner, *Competition and Entrepreneurship*, pp. 32-35. See also Kirzner, *Perception, Opportunity, and Profit*, pp. 166-68.

19. G.L.S. Shackle, *Epistemics and Economics* (Cambridge: Cambridge University Press, 1972), p. 136 (italics in original).

20. Ibid., p. 351.

21. See also Israel M. Kirzner, *The Economic Point of View* (Princeton: Van Nostrand, 1960), p. 167.

22. See also Kirzner, *Perception, Opportunity, and Profit*, chap. 9.

23. F.H. Knight, *Risk, Uncertainty and Profit* (New York: Houghton Mifflin, 1921), p. 268.

24. Mises, *Human Action*, p. 105.

25. See Kirzner, *Perception, Opportunity, and Profit*, chap. 10, esp. pp. 158-64.

26. Ibid, p. 162.

27. Ibid., p. 163.

28. See, for example, Kirzner, *Competition and Entrepreneurship*, p. 39.

29. See note 15 of this chapter.

30. B.J. Loasby, *Choice, Complexity and Ignorance* (Cambridge: Cambridge University Press, 1976), p. 5.

31. Knight, *Risk, Uncertainty and Profit*, p. 199.

32. Our discussion proceeds in terms of the market for a single commodity. It could be couched, without altering the essentials in any respect, in more general terms. See also the subsequent section of this chapter.

33. The three pairs of statements may be viewed as additions to the two lists of twelve statements developing the analogy between the individual and the market provided in Kirzner, *Perception, Opportunity, and Profit*, chap. 10, pp. 170-72, 173-75.

34. J.A. Schumpeter, *The Theory of Economic Development* (Cambridge: Harvard University, 1934), p. 137; J.A. Schumpeter, *History of Economic Analysis* (Oxford: Oxford University, 1954), p. 556. See also S.M. Kanbur, "A Note on Risk Taking, Entrepreneurship and Schumpeter," *History of Political Economy* 12 (Winter 1980): 489-98.

35. J.B. Clark, "Insurance and Business Profit," *Quarterly Journal of Economics* 7 (October 1892): 46 (cited in Knight, *Risk, Uncertainty, and Profit*, p. 38).

36. Shackle, *Epistemics and Economics*, p. 122.

37. White, "Entrepreneurship, Imagination," p. 7.

38. L.M. Lachmann, "From Mises to Shackle: An Essay," *Journal of Economic Literature* 14 (March 1976): 59.

PROFIT AND LOSS*

Ludwig Von Mises

A. The Economic Nature of Profit and Loss

1. The Emergence of Profit and Loss

In the capitalist system of society's economic organization the entrepreneurs determine the course of production. In the performance of this function they are unconditionally and totally subject to the sovereignty of the buying public, the consumers. If they fail to produce in the cheapest and best possible way those commodities which the consumers are asking for most urgently, they suffer losses and are finally eliminated from their entrepreneurial position. Other men who know better how to serve the consumers replace them.

If all people were to anticipate correctly the future state of the market, the entrepreneurs would neither earn any profits nor suffer any losses. They would have to buy the complementary factors of production at prices which would, already at the instant of the purchase, fully reflect the future prices of the products. No room would be left either for profit or for loss. What makes profit emerge is the fact that the entrepreneur who judges the future prices of the products more correctly than other people do buys some or all of the factors of production at prices which, seen from the point of view of the future state of the market, are too low. Thus the total costs of production—including interest on the capital invested—lag behind the prices which the entrepreneur receives for the product. This difference s entrepreneurial profit.

On the other hand, the entrepreneur who misjudges the future prices of the products allows for the factors of production prices which, seen from the point of view of the future state of the market, are too high. His total costs of production exceed the prices at which he can sell the product. This difference is entrepreneurial loss.

Thus profit and loss are generated by success or failure in adjusting the course of production activities to the most urgent demand of the consumers. Once this adjustment is achieved, they disappear. The prices of the complementary factors of production reach a height at which total costs of production coincide with the price of the product. Profit and loss are ever present features only on account of the fact that ceaseless change in the economic data makes again and again new discrepancies, and consequently the need for new adjustments originate.

2. The Distinction Between Profits and Other Proceeds

Many errors concerning the nature of profit and loss were caused by the practice of applying the term profit to the totality of the residual proceeds of an entrepreneur.

Interest on the capital employed is not a component part of profit. The dividends of a corporation are not profit. They are interest on the capital invested plus profit or minus loss.

The market equivalent of work performed by the entrepreneur in the conduct of the enterprise's affairs is entrepreneurial quasi-wages but not profit.

If the enterprise owns a factor on which it can earn monopoly prices, it makes a monopoly gain. If this enterprise is a corporation, such gains increase the dividend. Yet they are not profit proper.

Still more serious are the errors due to the confusion of entrepreneurial activity and technological innovation and improvement.

The maladjustment the removal of which is the essential function of entrepreneurship may often consist in the fact that new technological methods have not yet been utilized to the full extent to which they should be in order to bring about the best possible satisfaction of consumers' demand. But this is not necessarily always the case. Changes in the data, especially in consumers' demand, may require adjustments which have no reference at all to technological innovations and improvements. The entrepreneur who simply increases the production of an article by adding to the existing production facilities a new outfit without any change in the technological method of production is no less an entrepreneur than the man who inaugurates a new way of producing. The business of the entrepreneur is not merely to experiment with new technological methods, but to select from the multitude of technologically feasible methods those which are best fit to supply the public in the cheapest way with the things they are asking for most urgently. Whether a new technological procedure is or is not fit for this purpose is to be provisionally decided by the entrepreneur and will be finally decided by the conduct of the buying public. The question is not whether a new method is to be considered as a more "elegant" solution of a technological problem. It is whether, under the given state of economic data, it is the best possible method of supplying the consumers in the cheapest way.

The activities of the entrepreneur consist in making decisions. He determines for what purpose the factors of production should be employed. Any other acts which an entrepreneur may perform are merely accidental to his entrepreneurial function. It is this that laymen often fail to realize. They confuse the entrepreneurial activities with the conduct of the technological and administrative affairs of a plant. In their eyes not the stockholders, the promotors and speculators, but hired employees are the real entrepreneurs. The former are merely idle parasites who pocket the dividends.

Now nobody ever contended that one could produce without working. But neither is it possible to produce without capital goods, the previously produced factors of further production. These capital goods are scarce, i.e., they do not suffice for the production of all things which one would like to have produced. Hence the economic problem arises: to employ them in such a way that only those goods should be produced which are fit to satisfy the most urgent demands of the consumers. No good should remain unproduced on account of the fact that the factors required for its production were used—wasted—for the production of another good for which the demand of the public is less intense. To achieve this is under capitalism the function of entrepreneurship that determines the allocation of capital to the various branches of production. Under socialism it would be a function of the state, the social apparatus of coercion and oppression. The problem whether a socialist directorate, lacking any method of economic calculation, could fulfill this function is not to be dealt with in this essay.

There is a simple rule of thumb to tell entrepreneurs from non-entrepreneurs. The entrepreneurs are those on whom the incidence of losses on the capital employed falls. Amateur-economists may confuse profits with other kinds of intakes. But it is impossible to fail to recognize losses on the capital employed.

3. Non-Profit Conduct of Affairs

What has been called the democracy of the market manifests itself in the fact that profit-seeking business is unconditionally subject to the supremacy of the buying public.

Non-profit organizations are sovereign unto themselves. They are, within the limits drawn by the amount of capital at their disposal, in a position to defy the wishes of the public.

A special case is that of the conduct of government affairs, the administration of the social apparatus of coercion and oppression, viz. the police power. The objectives of government, the protection of the inviolability of the individuals' lives and health and of their efforts to improve the material conditions of their existence, are indispensable. They benefit all and are the necessary prerequisite of social cooperation and civilization. But they cannot be sold and bought in the way merchandise is sold and bought; they have therefore no price on the market. With regard to them there cannot be any economic calculation. The costs expended for their conduct cannot be confronted with a price received for the product. This state of affairs would make the officers entrusted with the administration of governmental activities irresponsible despots if they were not curbed by the budget system. Under this system the administrators are forced to comply with detailed instructions enjoined upon them by the sovereign, be it a self-appointed autocrat or the whole people acting through elected representatives. To the officers limited funds are assigned which they are bound to spend only for those purposes which the sovereign has ordered. Thus the management of public administration becomes bureaucratic, i. e., dependent on definite detailed rules and regulations.

Bureaucratic management is the only alternative available where there is no profit and loss management.[1]

4. The Ballot of the Market

The consumers by their buying and abstention from buying elect the entrepreneurs in a daily repeated plebiscite as it were. They determine who should own and who not, and how much each owner should own.

As is the case with all acts of choosing a person—choosing holders of public office, employees, friends or a consort—the decision of the consumers is made on the ground of experience and thus necessarily always refers to the past. There is no experience of the future. The ballot of the market elevates those who in the immediate past have best served the consumers. However, the choice is not unalterable and can daily be corrected. The elected who disappoints the electorate is speedily reduced to the ranks.

Each ballot of the consumers adds only a little to the elected man's sphere of action. To reach the upper levels of entrepreneurship he needs a great number of votes, repeated again and again over a long period of time, a protracted series of successful strokes. He must stand every day a new trial, must submit anew to reelection as it were.

It is the same with his heirs. They can retain their eminent position only by receiving again and again confirmation on the part of the public. Their office is revocable. If they retain it, it is not on account of the deserts of their predecessor, but on account of their own ability to employ the capital for the best possible satisfaction of the consumers.

The entrepreneurs are neither perfect nor good in any metaphysical sense. They owe their position exclusively to the fact that they are better fit for the performance of the functions incumbent upon them than other people are. They earn profit not because they are clever in performing their tasks, but because they are more clever or less clumsy than other people are. They are not infallible and often blunder. But they are less liable to error and blunder less than other people do. Nobody has the right to take offense at the errors made by the entrepreneurs in the conduct of affairs and to stress the point that people would have been better supplied if the entrepreneurs had been more skillful and prescient. If the grumbler knew better, why did he not himself fill the gap and seize the opportunity to earn profits? It is easy indeed to display foresight after the event. In retrospect all fools become wise.

A popular chain of reasoning runs this way: The entrepreneur earns profit not only on account of the fact that other people were less successful than he in anticipating correctly the future state of the market. He himself contributed to the emergence of profit by not producing more of the article concerned; but for intentional restriction of output on his part, the supply of this article would have been so ample that the price would have dropped to a point at which no surplus of proceeds over costs of production expended would have emerged. This reasoning is at the bottom of the spurious doctrines of imperfect and monopolistic competition. It was resorted to a short time ago by the American Administration when it blamed the enterprises of the steel industry for the fact that the steel production capacity of the United States was not greater than it really was.

Certainly those engaged in the production of steel are not responsible for the fact that other people did not likewise enter this field of production. The reproach on the part of the authorities would have been sensible if they had conferred on the existing steel corporations the monopoly of steel production. But in the absence of such a privilege, the reprimand given to the operating mills is not more justified than it would be to censure the nation's poets and musicians for the fact that there are not more and better poets and musicians. If somebody is to blame for the fact that the number of people who joined the voluntary civilian defense organization is not larger, then it is not those who have already joined but only those who have not.

That the production of a commodity p is not larger than it really is, is due to the fact that the complementary factors of production required for an expansion were employed for the production of other commodities. To speak of an insufficiency of the supply of p is empty rhetoric if it does not indicate the various products m which were produced in too large quantities with the effect that their production appears now, i.e., after the event, as a waste of scarce factors of production. We may assume that the entrepreneurs who instead of producing additional quantities of p turned to the production of excessive amounts of m and consequently suffered losses, did not intentionally make their mistake.

Neither did the producers of p intentionally restrict the production of p. Every entrepreneur's capital is limited; he employs it for those projects which, he expects, will, by filling the most urgent demand of the public, yield the highest profit.

An entrepreneur at whose disposal are 100 units of capital employs, for instance, 50 units for the production of p and 50 units for the production of q. If both lines are profitable, it is odd to blame him for not having employed more, e. g., 75 units, for the production of p. He could increase the production of p only by curtailing correspondingly the production of q. But with regard to q the same fault could be found by the grumblers. If one blames the entrepreneur for not having produced more p, one must blame him also for not having produced more q. This means: one blames the entrepreneur for the facts that there is a scarcity of the factors of production and that the earth is not a land of Cockaigne.

Perhaps the grumbler will object on the ground that he considers p a vital commodity, much more important than q, and that therefore the production of p should be expanded and that of q restricted. If this is really the meaning of his criticism, he is at variance with the valuations of the consumers. He throws off his mask and shows his dictatorial aspirations. Production should not be directed by the wishes of the public but by his own despotic discretion.

But if our entrepreneur's production of q involves a loss, it is obvious that his fault was poor foresight and not intentional.

Entrance into the ranks of the entrepreneurs in a market society, not sabotaged by the interference of government or other agencies resorting to violence, is open to everybody. Those who know how to take advantage of any business opportunity cropping up will always find the capital required. For the market is always full of capitalists anxious to find the most promising employment for their funds and in search of the ingenious newcomers, in partnership with whom they could execute the most remunerative projects.

People often failed to realize this inherent feature of capitalism because they did not grasp the meaning and the effects of capital scarcity. The task of the entrepreneur is to select from the multitude of technologically feasible projects those which will satisfy the most urgent of the not yet satisfied needs of the public. Those projects for the execution of which the capital supply does not suffice must not be carried out. The market is always crammed with visionaries who want to float such impracticable and unworkable schemes. It is these dreamers who always complain about the blindness of the capitalists who are too stupid to look after their own interests. Of course, the investors often err in the choice of their investments. But these faults consist precisely in the fact that they preferred an unsuitable project to another that would have satisfied more urgent needs of the buying public.

People often err very lamentably in estimating the work of the creative genius. Only a minority of men are appreciative enough to attach the right value to the achievement of poets, artists and thinkers. It may happen that the indifference of his contemporaries makes it impossible for a genius to accomplish what he would have accomplished if his fellow-men had displayed better judgment. The way in which the poet laureate and the philosopher *á la mode* are selected is certainly questionable.

But it is impermissible to question the free market's choice of the entrepreneurs. The consumers' preference for definite articles may be open to condemnation from the point of view of a philosopher's judgment. But judgments of value are necessarily always personal and subjective. The consumer chooses what, as he thinks, satisfies him best. Nobody is called upon to determine what could make another man happier or less unhappy. The popularity of motor cars, television sets and nylon stockings may be criticized from a "higher" point of view. But these are the things that people are asking for. They cast their ballots for those entrepreneurs who offer them this merchandise of the best quality at the cheapest price.

In choosing between various political parties and programs for the commonwealth's social and economic organization most people are uninformed and groping in the dark. The average voter lacks the insight to distinguish between policies suitable to attain the ends he is aiming at and those unsuitable. He is at a loss to examine the long chains of aprioristic reasoning which constitute the philosophy of a comprehensive social program. He may at best form some opinion about the short-run effects of the policies concerned. He is helpless in dealing with the long run effects. The socialists and communists in principle often assert the infallibility of majority decisions. However, they belie their own words in criticizing parliamentary majorities rejecting their creed, and in denying to the people, under the one party system, the opportunity to choose between different parties.

But in buying a commodity or abstaining from its purchase there is nothing else involved than the consumer's longing for the best possible satisfaction of his instantaneous wishes. The consumer does not—like the voter in political voting—choose between different means whose effects appear only later. He chooses between things which immediately provide satisfaction. His decision is final.

An entrepreneur earns profit by serving the consumers, the people, as they are and not as they should be according to the fancies of some grumbler or potential dictator.

5. *The Social Function of Profit and Loss*

Profits are never normal. They appear only where there is a maladjustment, a divergence between actual production and production as it should be in order to utilize the available material and mental resources for the best possible satisfaction of the wishes of the public. They are the prize of those who remove this maladjustment; they disappear as soon as the maladjustment is entirely removed. In the imaginary construction of an evenly rotating economy there are no profits. There the sum of the prices of the complementary factors of production, due allowance being made for time preference, coincides with the price of the product.

The greater the preceding maladjustments, the greater the profit earned by their removal. Maladjustments may sometimes be called excessive. But it is inappropriate to apply the epithet "excessive" to profits.

People arrive at the idea of excessive profits by confronting the profit earned with the capital employed in the enterprise an measuring the profit as a percentage of the capital. This method is suggested by the customary procedure applied in partnerships and corporations for the assignment of quotas of the total profit to the individual partners and shareholders. These men have contributed to a different extent to the realization of the project and share in the profits and losses according to the extent of their contribution.

But it is not the capital employed that creates profits and losses. Capital does not "beget profit" as Marx thought. The capital goods as such are dead things that in themselves do not accomplish anything. If they are utilized according to a good idea, profit results. If they are utilized according to a mistaken idea, no profit or losses result. It is the entrepreneurial decision that creates either profit or loss. It is mental acts, the mind of the entrepreneur, from which profits ultimately originate. Profit is a product of the mind, of success in anticipating the future state of the market. It is a spiritual and intellectual phenomenon.

The absurdity of condemning any profits as excessive can easily be shown. An enterprise with a capital of the amount c produced a definite quantity of p which it sold at prices that brought a surplus of proceeds over costs of s and consequently a profit of n per cent. If the entrepreneur had been less capable, he would have needed a capital of $2c$ for the production of the same quantity of p. For the sake of argument we may even neglect the fact that this would have necessarily increased costs of production as it would have doubled the interest on the capital employed, and we may assume that s would have remained unchanged. But at any rate s would have been confronted with $2c$ instead of c and thus the profit would have been only $n/2$ per cent of the capital employed. The "excessive" profit would have been reduced to a "fair" level. Why? Because the entrepreneur was less efficient and because his lack of efficiency deprived his fellow-men of all the advantages they could have got if an amount c of capital goods had been left available for the production of other merchandise.

In branding profits as excessive and penalizing the efficient entrepreneurs by discriminatory taxation, people are injuring themselves. Taxing profits is tantamount to taxing success in best serving the public. The only goal of all production activities is to employ the factors of production in such a way that they render the highest possible output. The smaller the input required for the production of an article becomes, the more of the scarce factors of production is left for the production of other articles. But the better an entrepreneur succeeds in this regard, the more is he vilified and the more is he soaked by taxation. Increasing costs per unit of output, that is, waste, is praised as a virtue.

The most amazing manifestation of this complete failure to grasp the task of production and the nature and functions of profit and loss is shown in the popular superstition that profit is an addendum to the costs of production, the height of which depends uniquely on the discretion of the seller. It is this belief that guides governments in controlling prices. It is the same belief that has prompted many governments to make arrangements with their contractors according to which the price to be paid for an article delivered is to equal costs of production expended by the seller increased by a definite percentage. The effect was that the purveyor got a surplus the higher, the less he succeeded in avoiding superfluous costs.

Contracts of this type enhanced considerably the sums the United States had to expend in the two World Wars. But the bureaucrats, first of all the professors of economics who served in the various war agencies, boasted of their clever handling of the matter.

All people, entrepreneurs as well as nonentrepreneurs, look askance upon any profits earned by other people. Envy is a common weakness of men. People are loath to acknowledge the fact that they themselves could have earned profits if they had displayed the same foresight and judgment the successful businessman did. Their resentment is the more violent, the more they are subconsciously aware of this fact.

There would not be any profits but for the eagerness of the public to acquire the merchandise offered for sale by the successful entrepreneur. But the same people who scramble for these articles vilify the businessman and call his profit illgot.

The semantic expression of this enviousness is the distinction between earned and unearned income. It permeates the textbooks, the language of the laws and administrative procedure. Thus, for instance, the official Form 201 for the New York State Income Tax Return calls "Earnings" only the compensation received by employees and, by implication, all other income, also that resulting from the exercise of a profession, unearned income. Such is the terminology of a state whose governor is a Republican and whose state assembly has a Republican majority.

Public opinion condones profits only as far as they do not exceed the salary paid to an employee. All surplus is rejected as unfair. The objective of taxation is, under the ability-to-pay principle, to confiscate this surplus.

Now one of the main functions of profits is to shift the control of capital to those who know how to employ it in the best possible way for the satisfaction of the public. The more profits a man earns, the greater his wealth consequently becomes, the more influential does he become in the conduct of business affairs. Profit and loss are the instruments by means of which the consumers pass the direction of production activities into the hands of those who are best fit to serve them. Whatever is undertaken to curtail or to confiscate profits, impairs this function. The result of such measures is to loosen the grip the consumers hold over the course of production. The economic machine becomes, from the point of view of the people, less efficient and less responsive.

The jealousy of the common man looks upon the profits of the entrepreneurs as if they were totally used for consumption. A part of them is, of course, consumed. But only those entrepreneurs attain wealth and influence in the realm of business who consume merely a fraction of their proceeds and plough back the much greater part into their enterprises. What makes small business develop into big business is not spending, but saving and capital accumulation.

6. Profit and Loss in the Progressing and in the Retrogressing Economy

We call a stationary economy an economy in which the per head quota of the income and wealth of the individuals remains unchanged. In such an economy what the consumers spend more for the purchase of some articles must be equal to what they spend less for other articles. The total amount of the profits earned by one part of the entrepreneurs equals the total amount of losses suffered by other entrepreneurs.

A surplus of the sum of all profits earned in the whole economy above the sum of all losses suffered emerges only in a progressing economy, that is in an economy in which the per head quota of capital increases. This increment is an effect of saving that adds new capital goods to the quantity already previously available. The increase of capital available creates maladjustments insofar as it brings about a discrepancy between the actual state of production and that state which the additional capital makes possible. Thanks to the emergence of additional capital, certain projects which hitherto could not be executed become feasible. In directing the new capital into those channels in which it satisfies the most urgent among the previously not satisfied wants of the consumers, the entrepreneurs earn profits which are not counterbalanced by the losses of other entrepreneurs.

The enrichment which the additional capital generates goes only in part to those who have created it by saving. The rest goes, by raising the marginal productivity of labor and thereby wage rates, to the earners of wages and salaries and, by raising the prices of definite raw materials and food stuffs, to the owners of land, and, finally, to the entrepreneurs who integrate this new capital into the most economical production processes. But while the gain of the wage earners and of the landowners is permanent, the profits of the entrepreneurs disappear once this integration is accomplished. Profits of the entrepreneurs are, as has been mentioned already, a permanent phenomenon only on account of the fact that maladjustments appear daily anew by the elimination of which profits are earned.

Let us for the sake of argument resort to the concept of national income as employed in popular economics. Then it is obvious that in a stationary economy no part of the national income goes into profits. Only in a progressing economy is there a surplus of total profits over total losses. The popular belief that profits are a deduction from the income of workers and consumers is entirely fallacious. If we want to apply the term deduction to the issue, we have to say that this surplus of profits over losses as well as the increments of the wage earners and the landowners is deducted from the gains of those whose saving brought about the additional capital. It is their saving that is the vehicle of economic improvement, that makes the employment of technological innovations possible and raises productivity and the standard of living. It is the entrepreneurs whose activity takes care of the most economical employment of the additional capital. As far as they themselves do not save, neither the workers nor the landowners contribute anything to the emergence of the circumstances which generate what is called economic progress and improvement. They are benefited by other peoples' saving that creates additional capital on the one hand and by the entrepreneurial action that directs this additional capital toward the satisfaction of the most urgent wants on the other hand.

A retrogressing economy is an economy in which the per head quota of capital invested is decreasing. In such an economy the total amount of losses incurred by entrepreneurs exceeds the total amount of profits earned by other entrepreneurs.

7. The Computation of Profit and Loss

The originary praxeological categories of profit and loss are psychic qualities and not reducible to any interpersonal description in quantitative terms. They are intensive magnitudes. The difference between the value of the end attained and that of the means applied for its attainment is profit if it is positive and loss if it is negative.

Where there are social division of efforts and cooperation as well as private ownership of the means of production, economic calculation in terms of monetary units becomes feasible and necessary. Profit and loss are computable as social phenomena. The psychic phenomena of profit and loss, from which they are ultimately derived, remain, of course, incalculable intensive magnitudes.

The fact that in the frame of the market economy entrepreneurial profit and loss are determined by arithmetical operations has misled many people. They fail to see that essential items that enter into this calculation are estimates emanating from the entrepreneur's specific understanding of the future state of the market. They think that these computations are open to examination and verification or alteration on the part of a disinterested expert. They ignore the fact that such computations are as a rule an inherent part of the entrepreneur's speculative anticipation of uncertain future conditions.

For the task of this essay it suffices to refer to one of the problems of cost accounting. One of the items of a bill of costs is the establishment of the difference between the price paid for the acquisition of what is commonly called durable production equipment and its present value. This present value is the money equivalent of the contribution this equipment will make to future earnings. There is no certainty about the future state of the market and about the height of these earnings. They can only be determined by a speculative anticipation on the part of the entrepreneur. It is preposterous to call in an expert and to substitute his arbitrary judgment for that of the entrepreneur. The expert is objective insofar as he is not affected by an error made. But the entrepreneur exposes his own material well-being.

Of course, the law determines magnitudes which it calls profit and loss. But these magnitudes are not identical with the economic concepts of profit and loss and must not be confused with them. If a tax law calls a magnitude profit, it in effect determines the height of taxes due. It calls this magnitude profit because it wants to justify its tax policy in the eyes of the public. It would be more correct for the legislator to omit the term profit and simply to speak of the basis for the computation of the tax due.

The tendency of the tax laws is to compute what they call profit as high as possible in order to increase immediate public revenue. But there are other laws which are committed to the tendency to restrict the magnitude they call profit. The commercial codes of many nations were and are guided by the endeavor to protect the rights of creditors. They aimed at restricting what they called profit in order to prevent the entrepreneur from withdrawing to the prejudice of creditors too much from the firm or corporation for his own benefit. It was these tendencies which were operative in the evolution of the commercial usages concerning the customary height of depreciation quotas.

There is no need today to dwell upon the problem of the falsification of economic calculation under inflationary conditions. All people begin to comprehend the phenomenon of illusory profits, the offshoot of the great inflations of our age.

Failure to grasp the effects of inflation upon the customary methods of computing profits originated the modern concept of *profiteering*. An entrepreneur is dubbed a profiteer if his profit and loss statement, calculated in terms of a currency subject to a rapidly progressing inflation, shows profits which other people deem "excessive." It has happened very often in many countries that the profit and loss statement of such a profiteer, when calculated in terms of a noninflated or less inflated currency, showed not only no profit at all but considerable losses.

Even if we neglect for the sake of argument any reference to the phenomenon of merely inflation induced illusory profits, it is obvious that the epithet profiteer is the expression of an arbitrary judgment of value. There is no other standard available for the distinction between profiteering and earning fair profits than that provided by the censor's personal envy and resentment.

It is strange indeed that an eminent logician, the late L. Susan Stebbing, entirely failed to perceive the issue involved. Professor Stebbing equated the concept of profiteering to concepts which refer to a clear distinction of such a nature that no sharp line can be drawn between extremes. The distinction between excess profits or profiteering, and "legitimate profits," she declared, is clear, although it is not a sharp distinction.[2] Now this distinction is clear only in reference to an act of legislation that defines the term excess profits as used in its context. But this is not what Stebbing had in mind. Se explicitly emphasized that such legal definitions are made "in an arbitrary manner for the practical purposes of administration." She used the term *legitimate* without any reference to legal statutes and their definitions. But is it permissible to employ the term legitimate without reference to any standard from the point of view of which the thing in question is to be considered as legitimate? And is there any other standard available for the distinction between profiteering and legitimate profits than one provided by personal judgments of value?

Professor Stebbing referred to the famous *acervus* and *calvus* arguments of the old logicians. Many words are vague insofar as they apply to characteristics which may be possessed in varying degrees. It is impossible to draw a sharp line between those who are bald and those who are not. It is impossible to define precisely the concept of baldness. But what Professor Stebbing failed to notice is that the characteristic according to which people distinguish between those who are bald and those who are not is open to a precise definition. It is the presence or the absence of hair on the head of a person. This is a clear and unambiguous mark of which the presence or absence is to be established by observation and to be expressed by propositions about existence. What is vague is merely the determination of the point at which nonbaldness turns into baldness. People may disagree with regard to the determination of this point. But their disagreement refers to the interpretation of the convention that attaches a certain meaning to the word baldness. No judgments of value are implied. It may, of course, happen that the difference of opinion is in a concrete case caused by bias. But this is another thing.

The vagueness of words like bald is the same that is inherent in the indefinite numerals and pronouns. Language needs such terms as for many purposes of daily communication between men an exact arithmetical establishment of quantities is superfluous and too bothersome. Logicians are badly mistaken in attempting to attach to such words whose vagueness is intentional and serves definite purposes the precision of the definite numerals. For an individual who plans to visit Seattle the information that there are many hotels in this city is sufficient. A committee that plans to hold a convention in Seattle needs precise information about the number of hotel beds available.

Professor Stebbing's error consisted in the confusion of existential propositions with judgments of value. Her unfamiliarity with the problems of economics, which all her otherwise valuable writings display, led her astray. She would not have made such a blunder in a field that was better known to her. She would not have declared that there is a clear distinction between an author's "legitimate royalties" and "illegitimate royalties." She would have comprehended that the height of the royalties depends on the public's appreciation of a book and that an observer who criticizes the height of royalties merely expresses his personal judgment of value.

B. The Condemnation of Profit

1. Economics and the Abolition of Profit

Those who spurn entrepreneurial profit as "unearned" mean that it is lucre unfairly withheld either from the workers or from the consumers or from both. Such is the idea underlying the alleged "right to the whole produce of labor" and the Marxian doctrine of exploitation. It can be said that most governments—if not all—and the immense majority of our contemporaries by and large endorse this opinion although some of them are generous enough to acquiesce in the suggestion that a fraction of profits should be left to the "exploiters."

There is no use in arguing about the adequacy of ethical precepts. They are derived from intuition; they are arbitrary and subjective. There is no objective standard available with regard to which they could be judged. Ultimate ends are chosen by the individual's judgments of value. They cannot be determined by scientific inquiry and logical reasoning. If a man says, "This is what I am aiming at whatever the consequences of my conduct and the price I shall have to pay for it may be," nobody is in a position to oppose any arguments against him. But the question is whether it is really true that this man is ready to pay any price for the attainment of the end concerned. If this latter question is answered in the negative, it becomes possible to enter into an examination of the issue involved.

If there were really people who are prepared to put up with all the consequences of the abolition of profit, however detrimental they may be, it would not be possible for economics to deal with the problem. But this is not the case. Those who want to abolish profit are guided by the idea that this confiscation would improve the material well-being of all non-entrepreneurs. In their eyes the abolition of profit is not an ultimate end but a means for the attainment of a definite end, viz., the enrichment of the non-entrepreneurs. Whether this end can really be attained by the employment of this means and whether the employment of this means does not perhaps bring about some other effects which may to some or to all people appear more undesirable than conditions before the employment of this means, these are questions which economics is called upon to examine.

2. The Consequences of the Abolition of Profit

The idea to abolish profit for the advantage of the consumers involves that the entrepreneur should be forced to sell the products at prices not exceeding the costs of production expended. As such prices are, for all articles the sale of which would have brought profit, below the potential market price, the available supply is not sufficient to make it possible for all those who want to buy at these prices to acquire the articles. The market is paralyzed by the maximum price decree. It can no longer allocate the products to the consumers. A system of rationing must be adopted.

The suggestion to abolish the entrepreneur's profit for the benefit of the employees aims not at the abolition of profit. It aims at wresting it from the hands of the entrepreneur and handing it over to his employees.

Under such a scheme the incidence of losses incurred falls upon the entrepreneur, while profits go to the employees. It is probable that the effect of this arrangement would consist in making losses increase and profits dwindle. At any rate, a greater part of the profits would be consumed and less would be saved and ploughed back into the enterprise. No capital would be available for the establishment of new branches of production and for the transfer of capital from branches which—in compliance with the demand of the customers—should shrink into branches which should expand. For it would harm the interests of those employed in a definite enterprise or branch to restrict the capital employed in it and to transfer it into another enterprise or branch. If such a scheme had been adopted half a century ago, all the innovations accomplished in this period would have been rendered impossible. If, for the sake of argument, we were prepared to neglect any reference to the problem of capital accumulation, we would still have to realize that giving profit to the employees must result in rigidity of the once attained state of production and preclude any adjustment, improvement and progress.

In fact, the scheme would transfer ownership of the capital invested into the hands of the employees. It would be tantamount to the establishment of syndicalism and would generate all the effects of syndicalism, a system which no author or reformer ever had the courage to advocate openly.

A third solution of the problem would be to confiscate all the profits earned by the entrepreneurs for the benefit of the state. A one hundred per cent tax on profits would accomplish this task. It would transform the entrepreneurs into irresponsible administrators of all plants and workshops. They would no longer be subject to the supremacy of the buying public. They would just be people who have the power to deal with production as it pleases them.

The policies of all contemporary governments which have not adopted outright socialism apply all these three schemes jointly. They confiscate by various measures of price control a part of the potential profits for the alleged benefit of the consumers. They support the labor unions in their endeavors to wrest, under the ability-to-pay principle of wage determination, a part of the profits from the entrepreneurs. And, last but not least, they are intent upon confiscating, by progressive income taxes, special taxes on corporation income and "excess profits" taxes, an ever increasing part of profits for public revenue. It can easily be seen that these policies if continued will very soon succeed in abolishing entrepreneurial profit altogether.

The joint effect of the application of these policies is already today rising chaos. The final effect will be the full realization of socialism by smoking out the entrepreneurs. Capitalism cannot survive the abolition of profit. It is profit and loss that force the capitalists to employ their capital for the best possible service to the consumers. It is profit and loss that make those people supreme in the conduct of business who are best fit to satisfy the public. If profit is abolished, chaos results.

3. The Anti-Profit Arguments

All the reasons advanced in favor of an anti-profit policy are the outcome of an erroneous interpretation of the operation of the market economy.

The tycoons are too powerful, too rich and too big. They abuse their power for their own enrichment. They are irresponsible tyrants. Bigness of an enterprise is in itself an evil. There is no reason why some men should own millions while others are poor. The wealth of the few is the cause of the poverty of the masses.

Each word of these passionate denunciations is false. The businessmen are not irresponsible tyrants. It is precisely the necessity of making profits and avoiding losses that gives to the consumers a firm hold over the entrepreneurs and forces them to comply with the wishes of the people. What makes a firm big is its success in best filling the demands of the buyers. If the bigger enterprise did not better serve the people than a smaller one, it would long since have been reduced to smallness. There is no harm in a businessman's endeavors to enrich himself by increasing his profits. The businessman has in his capacity as a businessman only one task: to strive after the highest possible profit. Huge profits are the proof of good service rendered in supplying the consumers. Losses are the proof of blunders committed, of failure to perform satisfactorily the tasks incumbent upon an entrepreneur. The riches of successful entrepreneurs is not the cause of anybody's poverty; it is the consequence of the fact that the consumers are better supplied than they would have been in the absence of the entrepreneur's effort. The penury of millions in the backward countries is not caused by anybody's opulence; it is the correlative of the fact that their country lacks entrepreneurs who have acquired riches. The standard of living of the common man is highest in those countries which have the greatest number of wealthy entrepreneurs. It is to the foremost material interest of everybody that control of the factors of production should be concentrated in the hands of those who know how to utilize them in the most efficient way.

It is the avowed objective of the policies of all present-day governments and political parties to prevent the emergence of new millionaires. If this policy had been adopted in the United States fifty years ago, the growth of the industries producing new articles would have been stunted. Motorcars, refrigerators, radio sets and a hundred other less spectacular but even more useful innovations would not have become standard equipment of most of the American family households.

The average wage earner thinks that nothing else is needed to keep the social apparatus of production running and to improve and to increase output than the comparatively simple routine work assigned to him. He does not realize that the mere toil and trouble of the routinist is not sufficient. Sedulousness and skill are spent in vain if they are not directed toward the most important goal by the entrepreneur's foresight and are not aided by the capital accumulated by capitalists. The American worker is badly mistaken when he believes that his high standard of living is due to his own excellence. He is neither more industrious nor more skillful than the workers of Western Europe. He owes his superior income to the fact that his country clung to "rugged individualism" much longer than Europe. It was his luck that the United States turned to an anti-capitalistic policy as much as forty or fifty years later than Germany. His wages are higher than those of the workers of the rest of the world because the capital equipment per head of the employee is highest in America and because the American entrepreneur was not so much restricted by crippling regimentation as his colleagues in other areas. The comparatively greater prosperity of the United States is an outcome of the fact that the New Deal did not come in 1900 or 1910, but only in 1933.

If one wants to study the reasons for Europe's backwardness, it would be necessary to examine the manifold laws and regulations that prevented in Europe the establishment of an equivalent of the American drug store and crippled the evolution of chain stores, department stores, super markets and kindred outfits. It would be important to investigate the German Reich's effort to protect the inefficient methods of traditional *Handwerk* (handicraft) against the competition of capitalist business. Still more revealing would be an examination of the Austrian *Gewerbepolitik,* a policy that from the early eighties on aimed at preserving the economic structure of the ages preceding the Industrial Revolution.

The worst menace to prosperity and civilization and to the material well-being of the wage earners is the inability of union bosses, of "union economists" and of the less intelligent strata of the workers themselves to appreciate the role entrepreneurs play in production. This lack of insight has found a classical expression in the writings of Lenin. As Lenin saw it all that production requires besides the manual work of the laborer and the designing of the engineers is "control of production and distribution," a task that can easily be accomplished "by the armed workers." For this accounting and control "have been *simplified* by capitalism to the utmost, till they have become the extraordinarily simple operations of watching, recording and issuing receipts, within the reach of everybody who can read and write and knows the first four rules of arithmetic."[3] No further comment is needed.

4. The Equality Argument

In the eyes of the parties who style themselves progressive and leftist the main vice of capitalism is the inequality of incomes and wealth. The ultimate end of their policies is to establish equality. The moderates want to attain this goal step by step; the radicals plan to attain it at one stroke, by a revolutionary overthrow of the capitalist mode of production.

However, in talking about equality and asking vehemently for its realization, nobody advocates a curtailment of his own present income. The term equality as employed in contemporary political language always means upward levelling of one's income, never downward levelling. It means getting more, not sharing one's own affluence with people who have less.

If the American automobile worker, railroadman or compositor says equality, he means expropriating the holders of shares and bonds for his own benefit. He does not consider sharing with the unskilled workers who earn less. At best, he thinks of equality of all American citizens. It never occurs to him that the peoples of Latin America, Asia and Africa may interpret the postulate of equality as world equality and not as national equality.

The political labor movement as well as the labor union movement flamboyantly advertise their internationalism. But this internationalism is a mere rhetorical gesture without any substantial meaning. In every country in which average wage rates are higher than in any other area, the unions advocate insurmountable immigration barriers in order to prevent foreign "comrades" and "brothers"' from competing with their own members. Compared with the anti-immigration laws of the European nations, the immigration legislation of the American republics is mild indeed because it permits the immigration of a limited number of people. No such normal quotas are provided in most of the European laws.

All the arguments advanced in favor of income equalization within a country can with the same justification or lack of justification also be advanced in favor of world equalization. An American worker has no better title to claim the savings of the American capitalist than has any foreigner. That a man has earned profits by serving the consumers and has not entirely consumed his funds but ploughed back the greater part of them into industrial equipment does not give anybody a valid title to expropriate this capital for his own benefit. But if one maintains the opinion to the contrary, there is certainly no reason to ascribe to anybody a better right to expropriate than to anybody else. There is no reason to assert that only Americans have the right to expropriate other Americans. The big shots of American business are the scions of people who immigrated to the United States from England, Scotland, Ireland, France, Germany and other European countries. The people of their country of origin contend that they have the same title to seize the property acquired by these men as the American people have. The American radicals are badly mistaken in believing that their social program is identical or at least compatible with the objectives of the radicals of other countries. It is not. The foreign radicals will not acquiesce in leaving to the Americans, a minority of less than 7% of the world's total population, what they think is a privileged position. A world government of the kind the American radicals are asking for would try to confiscate by a world income tax all the surplus an average American earns above the average income of a Chinese or Indian worker. Those who question the correctness of this statement, would drop their doubts after a conversation with any of the intellectual leaders of Asia.

There is hardly any Iranian who would qualify the objections raised by the British Labor Government against the confiscation of the oil wells as anything else but a manifestation of the most reactionary spirit of capitalist exploitation. Today governments abstain from virtually expropriating—by foreign exchange control, discriminatory taxation and similar devices—foreign investments only if they expect to get in the next years more foreign capital and thus to be able in the future to expropriate a greater amount.

The disintegration of the international capital market is one of the most important effects of the antiprofit mentality of our age. But no less disastrous is the fact that the greater part of the world's population looks upon the United States—not only upon the American capitalists but also upon the American workers—with the same feelings of envy, hatred, and hostility with which, stimulated by the socialist and communist doctrines, the masses everywhere look upon the capitalists of their own nation.

5. Communism and Poverty

A customary method of dealing with political programs and movements is to explain and to justify their popularity by referring to the conditions which people found unsatisfactory and to the goals they wanted to attain by the realization of these programs.

However, the only thing that matters is whether or not the program concerned is fit to attain the ends sought. A bad program and a bad policy can never be explained, still less justified by pointing to the unsatisfactory conditions of its originators and supporters. The sole question that counts is whether or not these policies can remove or alleviate the evils which they are designed to remedy.

Yet almost all our contemporaries declare again and again: If you want to succeed in fighting communism, socialism and interventionism, you must first of all improve peoples' material conditions. The policy of *laissez faire* aims precisely at making people more prosperous. But it cannot succeed as long as want is worsened more and more by socialist and interventionist measures.

In the very short run the conditions of a part of the people can be improved by expropriating entrepreneurs and capitalists and by distributing the booty. But such predatory inroads, which even the *Communist Manifesto* described as "despotic" and as "economically insufficient and untenable," sabotage the operation of the market economy, impair very soon the conditions of all the people and frustrate the endeavors of entrepreneurs and capitalists to make the masses more prosperous. What is good for a quickly vanishing instant, (i.e., in the long run) result in most detrimental consequences.

Historians are mistaken in explaining the rise of Nazism by referring to real or imaginary adversities and hardships of the German people. What made the Germans support almost unanimously the twenty-five points of the "unalterable" Hitler program was not some conditions which they deemed unsatisfactory, but their expectation that the execution of this program would remove their complaints and render them happier. They turned to Nazism because they lacked common sense and intelligence. They were not judicious enough to recognize in time the disasters that Nazism was bound to bring upon them.

The immense majority of the world's population is extremely poor when compared with the average standard of living of the capitalist nations. But this poverty does not explain their propensity to adopt the communist program. They are anti-capitalitic because they are blinded by envy, ignorant and too dull to appreciate correctly the causes of their distress. There is but one means to improve their material conditions, namely, to convince them that only capitalism can render them more prosperous.

The worst method to fight communism is that of the Marshall Plan. It gives to the recipients the impression that the United States alone is interested in the preservation of the profit system while their own concerns require a communist regime. The United States, they think, is aiding them because its people have a bad conscience. They themselves pocket this bribe but their sympathies go to the socialist system. The American subsidies make it possible for their governments to conceal partially the disastrous effects of the various socialist measures they have adopted.

Not poverty is the source of socialism, but spurious ideological prepossessions. Most of our contemporaries reject beforehand, without having ever studied them, all the teachings of economics as aprioristic nonsense. Only experience, they maintain, is to be relied upon. But is there any experience that would speak in favor of socialism?

Retorts the socialist: But capitalism creates poverty; look at India and China. The objection is vain. Neither India nor China has ever established capitalism. Their poverty is the result of the absence of capitalism.

What happened in these and other underdeveloped countries was that they were benefited from abroad by some of the fruits of capitalism without having adopted the capitalist mode of production. European, and in more recent years also American, capitalists invested capital in their areas and thereby increased the marginal productivity of labor and wage rates. At the same time these peoples received from abroad the means to fight contagious diseases, medications developed in the capitalist countries. Consequently mortality rates, especially infant mortality, dropped considerably. In the capitalist countries this prolongation of the average length of life was partially compensated by a drop in the birth rate. As capital accumulation increased more quickly than population, the per head quota of capital invested grew continuously. The result was progressing prosperity. It was different in the countries which enjoyed some of the effects of capitalism without turning to capitalism. There the birth rate did not decline at all or not to the extent required to make the per head quota of capital invested rise. These nations prevent by their policies both the importation of foreign capital and the accumulation of domestic capital. The joint effect of the high birth rate and the absence of an increase in capital is, of course, increasing poverty.

There is but one means to improve the material well-being of men, viz., to accelerate the increase in capital accumulated as against population. No psychological lucubrations, however sophisticated, can alter this fact. There is no excuse whatever for the pursuit of policies which not only fail to attain the ends sought, but even seriously impair conditions.

6. The Moral Condemnation of the Profit Motive

As soon as the problem of profits is raised, people shift it from the praxeological sphere into the sphere of ethical judgments of value. Then everybody glories in the aureole of a saint and an ascetic. He himself does not care for money and material well-being. He serves his fellowmen to the best of his abilities unselfishly. He strives after higher and nobler things than wealth. Thank God, he is not one of those egoistic profiteers.

The businessmen are blamed because the only thing they have in mind is to succeed. Yet everybody—without any exception—in acting aims at the attainment of a definite end. The only alternative to success is failure; nobody ever wants to fail. It is the very essence of human nature that man consciously aims at substituting a more satisfactory state of affairs for a less satisfactory. What distinguishes the decent man from the crook is the different goals they are aiming at and the different means they are resorting to in order to attain the ends chosen. But they both want to succeed in their sense. It is logically impermissible to distinguish between people who aim at success and those who do not.

Practically everybody aims at improving the material conditions of his existence. Public opinion takes no offense at the endeavors of farmers, workers, clerks, teachers, doctors, ministers, and people from many other callings to earn as much as they can. But it censures the capitalists and entrepreneurs for their greed. While enjoying without any scruples all the goods business delivers, the consumer sharply condemns the selfishness of the purveyors of this merchandise. He does not realize that he himself creates their profits by scrambling for the things they have to sell.

Neither does the average man comprehend that profits are indispensable in order to direct the activities of business into those channels in which they serve him best. He looks upon profits as if their only function were to enable the recipients to consume more than he himself does. He fails to realize that their main function is to convey control of the factors of production into the hands of those who best utilize them for his own purposes. He did not, as he thinks, renounce becoming an entrepreneur out of moral scruples. He chose a position with a more modest yield because he lacked the abilities required for entrepreneurship or, in rare cases indeed, because his inclinations prompted him to enter upon another career.

Mankind ought to be grateful to those exceptional men who out of scientific zeal, humanitarian enthusiasm or religious faith sacrificed their lives, health and wealth, in the service of their fellow-men. But the philistines practice self deception in comparing themselves with the pioneers of medical X-ray application or with nuns who attend people afflicted with the plague. It is not self-denial that makes the average physician choose a medical career, but the expectation of attaining a respected social position and a suitable income.

Everybody is eager to charge for his services and accomplishments as much as the traffic can bear. In this regard there is no difference between the workers, whether unionized or not, the ministers and teachers on the one hand and the entrepreneurs on the other hand. Neither of them has the right to talk as if he were Francis d'Assisi.

There is no other standard of what is morally good and morally bad than the effects produced by conduct upon social cooperation. A—hypothetical—isolated and self-sufficient individual would not in acting have to take into account anything else than his own well-being. Social man must in all his actions avoid indulging in any conduct that would jeopardize the smooth working of the system of social cooperation. In complying with the moral law man does not sacrifice his own concerns to those of a mythical higher entity, whether it is called class, state, nation, race or humanity. He curbs some of his own instinctive urges, appetites and greed, that is his shortrun concerns, in order to serve best his own—rightly understood or long-run—interests. He foregoes a small gain that he could reap instantly lest he miss a greater but later satisfaction. For the attainment of all human ends, whatever they may be, is conditioned by the preservation and further development of social bonds and interhuman cooperation. What is an indispensable means to intensify social cooperation and to make it possible for more people to survive and to enjoy a higher standard of living is morally good and socially desirable. Those who reject this principle as un-Christian ought to ponder over the text: "That thy days may be long upon the land which the Lord thy God giveth thee." They can certainly not deny that capitalism has made man's days longer than they were in the precapitalistic ages.

There is no reason why capitalists and entrepreneurs should be ashamed of earning profits. It is silly that some people try to defend American capitalism by declaring: "The record of American business is good; profits are not too high." The function of entrepreneurs is to make profits; high profits are the proof that they have well performed their task of removing maladjustments of production.

Of course, as a rule capitalists and entrepreneurs are not saints excelling in the virtue of self-denial. But neither are their critics saintly. And with all the regard due to the sublime self-effacement of saints, we cannot help stating the fact that the world would be in a rather desolate condition if it were peopled exclusively by men not interested in the pursuit of material well-being.

7. The Static Mentality

The average man lacks the imagination to realize that the conditions of life and action are in a continual flux. As he sees it, there is no change in the external objects that constitute his well-being. His world view is static and stationary. It mirrors a stagnating environment. He knows neither that the past differed from the present nor that there prevails uncertainty about future things.

He is at a complete loss to conceive the function of entrepreneurship because he is unaware of this uncertainty. Like children who take all the things the parents give them without asking any questions, he takes all the goods business offers him. He is unaware of the efforts that supply him with all he needs. He ignores the role of capital accumulation and of entrepreneurial decisions. He simply takes it for granted that a magic table appears at a moment's notice laden with all he wants to enjoy.

This mentality is reflected in the popular idea of socialization. Once the parasitic capitalists and entrepreneurs are thrown out, he himself will get all that they used to consume. It is but the minor error of this expectation that it grotesquely overrates the increment in income, if any, each individual could receive from such a distribution. Much more serious is the fact that it assumes that the only thing required is to continue in the various plants production of those goods they are producing at the moment of the socialization in the ways they were hitherto produced. No account is taken of the necessity to adjust production daily anew to perpetually changing conditions. The dilettante-socialist does not comprehend that a socialization effected fifty years ago would not have socialized the structure of business as it exists today but a very different structure. He does not give a thought to the enormous effort that is needed in order to transform business again and again to render the best possible service.

This dilettantish inability to comprehend the essential issues of the conduct of production affairs is not only manifested in the writings of Marx and Engels. It permeates no less the contributions of contemporary psuedo-economics.

The imaginary construction of an evenly rotating economy is an indispensable mental tool of economic thinking. In order to conceive the function of profit and loss, the economist constructs the image of a hypothetical, although unrealizable, state of affairs in which nothing changes, in which tomorrow does not differ at all from today and in which consequently no maladjustments can arise and no need for any alteration in the conduct of business emerges. In the frame of this imaginary construction there are no entrepreneurs and no entrepreneurial profits and losses. The wheels turn spontaneously as it were. But the real world in which men live and have to work can never duplicate the hypothetical world of this mental makeshift.

Now one of the main shortcomings of the mathematical economists is that they deal with this evenly rotating economy—they call it the static state—as if it were something really existing. Prepossessed by the fallacy that economics is to be treated with mathematical methods, they concentrate their efforts upon the analysis of static states which, of course, allow a description in sets of simultaneous differential equations. But this mathematical treatment virtually avoids any reference to the real problems of economics. It indulges in quite useless mathematical play without adding anything to the comprehension of the problems of human acting and producing. It creates the misunderstanding as if the analysis of static states were the main concern of economics. It confuses a merely ancillary tool of thinking with reality.

The mathematical economist is so blinded by his epistemological prejudice that he simply fails to see what the tasks of economics are. He is anxious to show us that socialism is realizable under static conditions. As static conditions, as he himself admits, are unrealizable, this amounts merely to the assertion that in an unrealizable state of the world socialism could be realizable. A very valuable result, indeed, a hundred years of the joint work of hundreds of authors, taught at all universities, publicized in innumerable textbooks and monographs and in scores of allegedly scientific magazines!

There is no such thing as a static economy. All the conclusions derived from preoccupation with the image of static states and static equilibrium are of no avail for the description of the world as it is and will always be.

C. The Alternative

A social order based on private control of the means of production cannot work without entrepreneurial action and entrepreneurial profit and, of course, entrepreneurial loss. The elimination of profit, whatever methods may be resorted to for its execution, must transform society into a senseless jumble. It would create poverty for all.

In a socialist system there are neither entrepreneurs nor entrepreneurial profit and loss. The supreme director of the socialist commonwealth would, however, have to strive in the same way after a surplus of proceeds over costs as the entrepreneurs do under capitalism. It is not the task of this essay to deal with socialism. Therefore it is not necessary to stress the point that, not being able to apply any kind of economic calculation, the socialist chief would never know what the costs and what the proceeds of his operations are.

What matters in this context is merely the fact that there is no third system feasible. There cannot be any such thing as a nonsocialist system without entrepreneurial profit and loss. The endeavors to eliminate profits from the capitalist system are merely destructive. They disintegrate capitalism without putting anything in its place. It is this that we have in mind in maintaining that they result in chaos.

Men must choose between capitalism and socialism. They cannot avoid this dilemma by resorting to a capitalist system without entrepreneurial profit. Every step toward the elimination of profit is progress on the way toward social disintegration.

In choosing between capitalism and socialism people are implicitly also choosing between all the social institutions which are the necessary accompaniment of each of these systems, its "superstrucure" as Marx said. If control of production is shifted from the hands of entrepreneurs, daily anew elected by a plebiscite of the consumers, into the hands of the supreme commander of the "industrial armies" (Marx and Engels) or of the "armed workers" (Lenin), neither representative government nor any civil liberties can survive. Wall Street, against which the self-styled idealists are battling, is merely a symbol. But the walls of the Soviet prisons within which all dissenters disappear forever are a hard fact.

Notes

*A paper prepared for the meeting of the Mont Pèlerin Society held in Beauvallon, France, September 9 to 16, 1951. Available same year in English as separate booklet from Libertarian Press—out of print.

1. Cf. Mises, *Human Action*, Yale University Press, 1949, pages 305-307; *Bureaucracy*, Yale University Press, 1944, Pages 40-73.

2. Cf. L. Susan Stebbing, *Thinking to Some Purpose*. (Pelican Books A44), pages 185-187.

3. Lenin, *State and Revolution*, 1917 (Edition by International Publishers, New York, pages 83-84). The italics are Lenin's (or the communist translator's).

ORGANISING FOR FOREVER

Michael D. McMaster

Our corporate visions are too shallow. As visions they fail to inspire us. They do not begin to touch the depths of what concerns the human beings that participate in each and every company. People care about the future. We aspire to contribute to the future of our families and communities. We long to have a meaningful relationship with the world.

In the process of creating our visions statements, or other expressions of corporate possibility, what is really important to people becomes obscured. What genuinely concerns most of us? Are they issues about the direction of our career or the level of security our future holds? Are we deeply concerned about whether or not we will have an opportunity to bring the values and principles that are important to us to our working lives? It's not a question of one thing or another—we want all these things and more.

It seems that what individuals in large corporations most long for is to be able to be intelligent participants in the activities and intentions of the enterprise. We want things to make sense. We hunger for a meaning for our actions. A vision statement can't do all this. However, such a possibility may lie within the richness and complexity that will emerge out of a set of simple principles. Collectively, these operating principles may offer the inspiration and guidance we all wish to bring to the choices and actions of our working lives.

Corporations are Forever

The institutions people create outlive individual human beings. In fact, they can live as long as social systems favour this kind of institution. We have had conditions suitable for corporations, in their various forms, for hundreds of years. Although the forms and types of incorporating entities may be changing, there is no indication that they are about to disappear.

It is not social or legal conditions which challenge the possibility of an extended lifetime for corporations. The elements of design and practice are what threaten their existence. Most of today's corporations lack the adaptability necessary to be successful in their current environment. They also lack what it will take to survive in future environments. Given how brief the average life span has been for companies during the last century, it's obvious that survival has not been an easy matter. And yet, some companies have provided amply for their immediate survival, as they grow into the future for decades or even centuries.

A corporation can come into being and dissolve, with satisfactory returns as its sole interest. But our corporations have the possibility of being alive and pulsating with potential. They are living systems. They are social. And they are intimately interconnected with everything in the world. We can settle for an accumulation of financial wealth, or we can reach for more—self-expression, greater knowledge, and being able to contribute to our families and society. Our corporations have the potential to become entities with a multitude of concerns. They also have the potential for extending themselves well into the future—maybe even forever. A life span which is longer than the working lives of the participants in the corporation should be a natural occurrence for any well-designed and intelligently-operated corporation.

Corporations—Complex and Adaptive

A corporation is a living system, both complex and adaptive. It is complex because it is composed of—and emergent from—complex human beings contributing to the greater complexity of markets and society. It is adaptive because a part of being an intelligent system is the ability to develop, expand, and exchange information within an ever-changing environment. A complex adaptive system moves in the direction of maintaining its own life. It does this by the simple act of recombining. Out of recombination emerges the new, and a renewal of the old. From that, the extension of a system's life emerges. A corporation is considered successful if it lives longer than its founders and offers employment for generations to come. If a corporation intends to live a long, healthy life—one that will be able to meet the ever-changing faces of the world—learning, adapting and innovating will have to become a natural part of its life.

Why use employment as a measure of success? There's much more to it than the obvious factor of financial benefit. A corporation provides productive opportunity, not only for its founders, but for more and more people as it grows. The corporation is our institutional form of extending productive capacity far beyond what is possible if individuals were working alone. Something comes out of the whole that is greater than the individual parts could produce. Our corporations provide more than the obvious goods and services. They offer a lever for individual contribution to our communities and the world at large.

Today, the average life span of a company is not as long as that of its founders or members. But this is not a problem, because we have created structures to carry forward co-operative production. This is effective complexity at the level of markets. An effective complex adaptive system is something that has the inherent capacity to continue indefinitely in varying expressions, no matter what happens to the individual elements.

Although the life span of most corporations is brief, some have stood the test of time. (One such corporation has been in existence for over 700 years.) The small elite group of long-lived survivors exhibits such a substantial difference in the quality of their performance that they deserve investigation. Shell Corporation conducted such a study. In their look at long-lived companies, they found only 40 corporations of significant size whose identity had remained intact for over 100 years. Their study also revealed that the average life span of other corporations was only about 40 years. When Shell conducted its study, Arie de Geus was Coordinator of Group Planning for the company. From this study, he has developed an analysis of the design principles responsible for the success of the long-lived companies[i]. What follows is a similar look at corporations, but it will be from my perspective of intelligent systems and complexity.

If we ask, "What generates consistent patterns of survival for a corporation?", we can begin to formulate a set of simple design principles that act as *attractors* for survival and success. These principles will organise the intelligence of human beings working together in productive endeavours. When I suggested this idea to Murray Gell-Mann of the Santa Fe Institute, he referred to these *attractors* as "selection influences".

The Inherited Model

In order to benefit fully from seeing corporations as systems that are alive and intelligent, we'll need to shed all our old views about corporations. Our assortment of views is comprised of just about everything we've learned in business school, popular opinion, and almost every experience we've had as executives, managers, and people at work. These views influence how we see corporations and how we work in the midst of them. Because of these views, we relate to corporations as economic and legal entities with no intelligence of their own.

So it's not surprising that executives make dispassionate decisions based solely on calculations of profits. Or that they see the corporation as a combination of labour, capital, and land—all of which must be optimised. *Labour* no longer means *people* (individual human beings) to most executives. Decisions to cut labour and add machinery are based purely on costs. As evidence of how all-pervasive these views are, most people reading this are probably thinking, "Of course! How else could it be?"

The objective here is not to suggest that there is anything wrong with thinking this way, or that different actions should be taken. The point at the moment, is to show that we *do* think this way.

See if these notions don't also ring true:

- Shareholders provide the capital and they deserve the greatest possible return on their money.
- Hiring-firing decisions should be based on straight economic considerations.
- Management should attempt to minimise costs and maximise revenues continually.
- Approaching business in the aforesaid way is rational, goal-oriented and economic.

Viewing our corporations in this way has no depth—it lacks the reality of complexity. This is not to say that the limited view held by most people in business is not a part of what a corporation is, or that this perspective doesn't enter into the picture when conducting business—we're simply settling for a particular and narrow perspective. Plus, we're oversimplifying. And in doing so, we leave ourselves with little basis for good decision-making in areas of greater complexity such as timing, balance, knowledge development and strategy.

There is nothing wrong with our old way of thinking. Nor is there anything wrong with a narrow or *objective* perspective, except that it offers so little when working with a shifting, dynamic, complex corporation; an entity made up of human beings—each of which is also changing and complex. But in this narrower, almost mechanical, view of corporations, there is the implication that we are being rational in our choices, to the extent that we only consider the material, measurable aspects of the situation. It is here that people get lost and the humanity of a corporation disappears.

Human beings are curious, creative, and giving individuals. Put two together and marvellous things can emerge. Collectively, our endeavours can be profound and almost unimaginable. When institutions, our vehicles for collective endeavours, constrain, manipulate, or deceive, they conflict with our natural human capacities and our need to express them. Great difficulties are sure to occur. Depending on the extent of the institution's inhumanity, something will destroy it; be it the force of a market or a government. The more our corporations conflict with the human character and contemporary social condition, the shorter the life of the corporation.

Purpose Beyond Survival

What constitutes corporate success? This is a question that has been asked for a very long time. The most common response has been, "return on investment". The fact that the question is still being asked suggests other possibilities. Perhaps the most common responses fail to distinguish between necessary conditions and measures of success. The *purpose* of life is not to breathe or eat. We don't measure our success in life by those functions, even though it's necessary to breathe and eat.

As people, it is essential to create more energy than we expend in order to renew ourselves. If it costs more to eat than we earn, we won't survive. The same holds true for corporations. If they spend more on the production of goods than those goods can be sold for, the corporation won't survive. This is the *condition* of life—not the purpose of life. Purpose suggests value. Purpose implies that life can include much more than attention to one's own survival. By adding purpose we bring much more than attention to one's own survival. By adding purpose we bring meaning, value and contribution to our lives. Purpose, from this perspective, is possible only when there are more resources available than are required for survival.

Survival is a useful measure of success in that a corporation will have had to contribute something to the community in order for it to have earned a long life. As individuals, we want to participate in, and contribute to, our community. As members of a community, we want to provide institutions that facilitate participation and contribution, which in turn improves the overall quality of life in the community. Although many fail to see this, corporations are the main institutions for doing this.

Profit is necessary for survival. It is also a way to measure the level of economic benefit that is being provided by the people in the corporation. Corporations make their place in the world by providing value, and the economic measures of this provide feedback about that value. This does not mean that every time there is profit a contribution was made to the community or society. We know all too well that profits often result from social harm. Few appreciate profit as a function of the larger social culture and its mechanisms.

Using Nature's Principles to Design

Countless observations are made when science looks at the world. For instance, in the world of complex adaptive systems, the interaction of independent agents around attractors will result in the emergence of reliable and effective entities. Let's consider what design principles will act as a set of robust attractors to create satisfactory patterns of corporate life. Corporations created and managed from principles that are in agreement with human nature can look forward to a better chance of survival and success. Corporations created and managed from principles that have their roots purely in economics, or engineering, will come and go.

Let's develop a few qualities that would be appropriate design principles for operating any corporation. Our approach in doing this is not to reiterate what has already been discovered and then expand on it. Instead, our approach is to invent principles. We'll use synthesis rather than analysis. Pretend that there is no way to access the elite group of long-lived corporations, but that we do have access to the social conditions of our times. From the information that we gather about the current environment, we invent principles that provide an understanding of what we see around us and inform us in how to act in the midst of it.

Design principles will not be specific to a particular kind of business, nor will they include the basic operations (equivalent to breathing and eating). That is, in creating principles, we are assuming that the company has been sustained thus far by its ability to produce a product or service at a profit. We are intending the principles for the design and operation of a viable entity of some size and history, not the initial formulation of a corporation. The principles will be applicable to a start-up, but a start-up will have other concerns which are more important, i.e., producing, selling, and the other operations of basic survival. The principles will also apply to a corporation which requires turnaround, such as one facing bankruptcy. Again, however, such a corporation will be more concerned with the basic operations of survival. These design principles are being invented for corporations engaged in currently viable operations.

As we invent a set of design principles to inform and guide the operations of the company in a manner consistent with complexity, there will be no particular order to the principles. They will not be hierarchical. We are intending emergent evolution, not linear production. The interplay between the principles creates the whole. The balance between them will provide the robustness, even though at different times, particular ones will be more in the spotlight. Thinking that one is more important or must come first is the kind of thinking we are attempting to replace.

In attempting to understand how design principles organise our operations, a useful analogy to look at is a grouping of magnets. If iron filings are thrown at a few magnets placed in a specific relationship to one another, the filings will create a predictable pattern, even though the exact location of each filing is unpredictable. The regularity of the patterns that occur each time the filings are thrown, comes from the interaction of the magnet fields, and the specific, but chance, distribution of filings. By varying the strength of the magnets, we can vary the pattern. Irrespective of how strong or weak any particular magnet becomes, no single magnet is solely responsible for determining the patterns that form. The patterns are a result of the *interplay* of the set of magnets. Likewise, the emergent patterns of the corporation are the result of the interplay of the design principles acting as a set of *attractors*.

What allows a corporation to be viable at any point in time? We know that there are products or services that it can sell at a profit. There are others that can be sold making no profit, and some it cannot sell at all. We also know that their profitable items are only such if they are produced in a particular way. In short, at any point in time a corporation has a limited set of products to sell, and ways of producing them, in order to make a profit.

Principle of Entrepreneurship

Every thriving business has a unique body of knowledge which can be combined with the resources of the surrounding community, such that something is created to contribute to the general welfare of that community. The body of knowledge unique to that company includes accumulated experience, skilled individuals, physical production equipment, purchasing know-how, systems and processes. The collective knowledge of the company also encompasses the knowledge held by the larger industry, and by the community of potential customers (they know the product or service, where to get it, and the reputation of the supplier). The corporation has established a network of knowledge and relationships, and together they integrate what is available with what is wanted. This, above all else, adds value to the community and creates a viable corporation.

One of the principles in our set will be: *Develop and maintain knowledge that will integrate what already exists with things that will contribute to the quality of life within the community*. The business of a corporation exists in a network of tools and production processes, individuals and their skills, and people or institutions that are intent on improving their quality of life. What particular business a corporation is in, is not of primary importance to its long-term identity and survival. What is important is that the corporation should be in a business that integrates with what already exists and what will exist, so that it can provide a higher quality of life to a larger community. Anyone committed to doing a particular business will find that circumstances change, and soon they are no longer in business. Corporations with an extended lifetime are in business, any business, to participate and contributor. An appropriate name for this element is the *principle of entrepreneurship*.

Most executives fail to see the interactive nature of design principles. They create sets of principles, but then hold the set in a hierarchical way. The set is then communicated and worked with in that particular way. Other executives create lists of principles which reveal a certain disjointedness or lack of wholeness. Neither approach encourages the use of interpretation or intelligence. Nor do these approaches reveal that it is the interplay of the elements, in their rich possibility, that is the source of identity and a robust existence.

In his forthcoming book on *emergence*, John Holland of the Santa Fe Institute draws a comparison between design principles and board games. He points out that games similar to *Go* and *chess* have been around for thousands of years. These games still elicit people's fascination and study, even though they are composed of only a few very simple rules. He also notes that successful children's games and toys that have only a few parts—such as *Meccano* sets—can offer an infinite variety of forms, while others which have many intricate parts—such as *transformers*—are fascinating for a short time, then quickly become boring and are never played with again.

Corporations that have been in business for a very long period of time have all totally changed the type of business they are in at least once. Christian Salvesen, UK company, went from shipping to trucking to cold storage as an evolution of the technologies that they used in their first business. Stora started as a tin mining operation. The company has gone through a number of complete transformations, and is now a major pulp and paper company. The Hudson Bay Company of Canada began as a fur trading company; they are now a retail department store chain.

These patterns of sustainability indicate that operations based on a set of fundamental principles allow for and even demand change, while at the same time maintaining an identity.

Social Connection

Imagine that your life span equals that of your corporation. Also imagine that your corporation is Stora. So at the ripe old age of 700, what changes have you witnessed in the world around you? The world has become increasingly complex and now shows little resemblance to the days of your youth. You have watched the transformation of social systems, beliefs, customs, education, commerce, technology, and almost every field of human endeavour. Having witnessed the magnitude of change that you have, your perspective is extraordinary and unique. As one of the respected elders, what does your wisdom allow you to see?

From this perspective, you now understand that although change is constant, it is not regular or predictable. Over the duration of your life, the environment has been in constant flux and has transformed completely, numerous times. You can now see periods which appeared very stable, but were actually not. In those pockets of time that seemed steady, changes were simply smaller, remote from daily concerns, or isolated in specific areas. Not until later did you see that the changes occurring on the distant edges of your environment were going to have a significant impact on your company. The *structure of the future* was all around you, just difficult to see. At times transparent, the *structure of the future* remained hidden from awareness behind the pressing details of immediate concerns.

Principle of Social Connection

The ability to maintain a perspective of wisdom gives rise to another design principle: *Be sensitive to the whole social environment and maintain panoramic awareness of it*. Change indicators and clues of the potential direction are all woven into the social fabric created by a community and the people in it. Any business exists within a network, and that network interpenetrates a wider ecology of products, tools and people. This element for designing might be called the *principle of social connection*.

This elaborate, all-inclusive network is alive in language. Through conversation, the members of the business community interconnect with one another. This web stretches out into the context of the world at large. These conversations contain the seeds of change. Initiation of the new begins as a conversation. It mingles and then establishes itself within the already-familiar conversations. New stories, new sentences, new language, and new physical realities manifest, and they are transfused throughout the network via language.

Computers have yet to make their way into every sector of the world,. A skewed interpretation of what computers mean has prevented their entry into otherwise advanced communities. Project planners use computers extensively, but often cannot see the value of providing the workforce with direct access to planning (via computers). Argument, resistance and misunderstanding in the boardrooms of many large corporations demonstrate that they do not understand the meaning of information and

The single most important business process, in a world of information and knowledge, is conversation. When we think of processes, we usually think of the production process, how products are transported from one place to another, or how our policies document the way things are to be done. We seldom consider conversation as an important process.

Serving a customer can be seen as a network of conversations. This is very different to regarding the process as an exchange of information, let alone goods or services. Conversations are dynamic creations which unfold continuously and have lives of their own, rather than being fixed bits of information that can be passed around. At every moment, conversations are self-generative. If we are to understand the processes of human interaction, we must develop the capacity to engage in dialogue and be able to distinguish the various types and characteristics of conversations.

An example of this can be found in various alliancing initiatives. In the oil industry, where these alliances involve risks into billions of dollars, the parties have great trouble behaving in ways appropriate to alliances. They keep failing to distinguish between *negotiation conversations* (about specific financial matters, huge possible risks and government requirements, to name just a few areas) and *operating conversations*, where working as an alliance is expected to produce significant cost reductions. Part of the source of this failure is their inability to see that benefits will come from releasing information flows (communication) that are normally blocked and enabling co-operative learning and innovation that cannot happen across artificial boundaries. Those that are beginning to appreciate and act on these distinctions are making millions of extra dollars—and sharing those around. It is not a zero sum game any longer.

communication technology. For many board members, the idea of linking all levels and areas of a business is still considered novel, a waste of time, or even dangerous.

The main sources of awareness and sensitivity in our corporations are its very own people. They are the eyes and ears of a corporation—the ones who make frequent contact with the environment. Corporate structures, processes and practices then spread the information, absorbed through awareness and sensitivity, throughout the network of the corporation. This implies that if we want to be aware and sensitive to our environment, we must also be aware and sensitive to our people. In simple terms, we need to listen. It is essential that we create conditions which encourage people to be aware, and also to share the insights that follow from that awareness. Dialogue must be given a place of respect. Values and trust are the foundations for dialogue, and must be cultivated if we are to reap the benefits. From the executive suites to the shop floor, everyone must develop their ability to engage in dialogues that encourage understanding of the social environment—both inside and outside the company.

Principle of Resource Integrity

If a corporation is to live for a long time, inevitably its circumstances will change dramatically. Those changes will occur in technology, products, education, and every aspect of knowledge, including how that knowledge is applied. The company will go through difficult times as well as expansive and profitable ones. Purchase opportunities will appear on the horizon in the form of research, people, equipment or other companies. Many of the best opportunities will occur when the company is facing relatively hard times. Often, whenever there is major change, there is major opportunity, too. During such times, few corporations have the necessary resources ready to take advantage of the situation.

It is important, for sustaining adaptability to *maintain the ability to survive adversity and turn it into an advantage.* This strength will find its footing in policies of low debt, financial conservatism, and building financial strength for investing in the future. Great efforts must be made to maintain a reputation of unfaltering integrity in financial dealings. This means building a corporate character of prudence, honouring promises made by the corporation, and fulfiling all financial obligations as promised. This includes abandoning the practice of getting by with the minimum in order to provide small immediate advantages to the corporation. This is the principle of resource integrity.

A corporation, like any other complex adaptive phenomenon, survives by maintaining a core identity which allows flexibility. Balancing identity and flexibility is one of the constant challenges of survival. Resource integrity maintains an identity (of integrity in financial matters) while also offering the flexibility of financial strength. Such a corporation is not as subject to adverse surprises or general economic downturns as other companies, and has the advantage of being available for growth opportunities when others are not.

Principle of Enabling the Periphery

In a constantly shifting and unpredictable world, how can we access what we need to know in order to make a timely adjustment? It's difficult, because the clues and signals we need are subtle. Different people read them in different ways. Even more challenging, how can we maintain a stable

---

A profitable and highly successful retail grocery chain has undertaken the practice of paying *in advance of all payment terms.* This practice has been instrumental in the company's success. For obvious reasons, suppliers like to deal with them, and in return the grocers are always offered first bid on great deals. Their public identity as a company of financial integrity spans the marketplace. The grocery chain's practice is a violation of the advice of almost every financial wizard, but the results they are producing by their approach and thinking are recognised by the measures of those same wizards.

Resource integrity encompasses efficient use of resources in relation to the whole economy. Prices are the information generated in the marketplace to indicate success in this arena. Resource integrity also includes awareness of the ecological and social impact of resources used, waste, and products becoming obsolete. It demands impeccable management of non-material items such as information, knowledge, and relationships with individuals and communities. Our limited view of resources as something strictly physical has been a contributing factor in our misuse of both physical and social resources.

enterprise when we are constantly exploring new areas and challenging the current way of doing things? Certainly not everyone can stay in touch with all of the changes all of the time.

When the signals that we are looking for are weak and distributed, we need a suitable searching mechanism. The need to change is not hidden one moment and obvious the next. Many say that IBM should have seen the market changes coming. Others say that they *did,* but couldn't initiate the change. Perhaps it is more accurate to say that a small percentage of IBM's people saw the changes coming and understood their significance for IBM. They just couldn't get the ear of the company. *IBM* didn't see it coming—some of its people did.

It's important to note that corporate understanding is distributed. Those who see the changes coming see different signals in different ways, and have different interpretations of them. Many people may be right about the signals, but slightly off in their interpretation of them—so not listened to. Or the signals are weak because they are only a small part of the gestalt of the change. And finally, the pathways for communication are not well-designed and clear, so what is finally heard by the corporation is considered noise, and a distraction from the focus on things that are already successful in obvious ways.

Another factor that hinders flexibility and adaptability in a corporation is the idea of a structure of authority. This structure is seen as something which cannot be tampered with for fear of causing weakness. Over time, this structure has accumulated power and privilege, and has a very strong tendency to maintain itself for both structural and individual reasons. Any company of long standing has well-developed authority structures, and practices that maintain them. In order to perturb/disturb this system, signals have to be very loud and very clear. What appears to be deafness in these structures of authority is actually the design of the internal structures of interpretation.

We are led to the principle of *enabling the periphery and listening to its messages.* Namely, a corporation's ability to hear, and act on input, is at the periphery (at the edge). The ability to act on input is also at the periphery. Just like with human beings. Although much of a corporation's processing is done far from the periphery, sensing and action occur at the point of contact with the external world. This places the need for maximum flexibility and adaptability at the periphery. This principle might be called *valuing the periphery.*

Even more important, immediate feedback is only available at the periphery. It is there that actions come into direct and unmediated contact with people. As long as the periphery is connected to the core, in a substantial way, the action at the periphery can be trusted. This means of survival is already operating in large companies. Because it's unauthorised, it remains unacknowledged and ignored by default because it can't be controlled or managed. In either case, it's the source of continued survival—and we suppress it at our peril.

Complexity where emergence occurs, is often referred to as *the edge of chaos,* or *far from equilibrium,* or *at phase transition.* Each of these descriptions is attempting to describe the setting or the conditions which facilitate learning, adaptation and change. Emergence does not occur at a physical location. It is a domain in which detailed control does not exist, and yet something exists which maintains reliable patterns and sufficient connection to the whole.

A Core Enables Convergence

The centre or *core* of a corporation is not the top. A better way to describe its location is the place in the network of conversations where there is the greatest convergence of external and internal connections. The point of convergence is not a fixed or physical location, it is a space. If a corporation is healthy, the convergence will balance the external and the internal to form the most useful patterns of interpretation. The core will act as a provider of structures of interpretation, and a source of meaning. If a corporation is not healthy, the core's interpretation and meaning will not be based on convergence, but instead will translate in a way that maintains or protects either the internal state or the past. The corporation will *lose its mind*—lose its identity—by losing contact with the ever-changing environment.

When a corporation loses contact, it can manifest in very different ways. One is to build a protective shell around either the corporation, an executive, or the "top" of the corporation. The shell is impermeable, rigid, and eventually becomes brittle. When such a shell exists and a substantial breakdown occurs, it will do so on a sudden and surprising way. Surprising at least to those within the

---

Our consulting group recently received a phone call from one of our clients, an oil company, requesting that we help them develop a team that would create a sense of alliance between companies that were going to work together on a major oil project. The client requested that we create a structure to support ways of working in co-operation, and then teach this structure through an educational programme offered to all the partner companies participating in the project. Our client felt that such a programme was necessary because they thought that many of those in leadership roles in the partner companies were up to their old tricks and doing what they could to stay in control.

The client also requested that we enroll the person in charge of the oil project into the idea of creating alliance through an educational programme. We were warned that he would probably not want to co-operate, nor would he be interested in spending time or money on developing the alliance. But when I spoke with the person in charge, he said, "Of course, that's exactly what we need to do". To ensure that the alliance and educational programme were created, he urged me to make an international flight in order to speak directly with his boss. He was absolutely certain that his boss would be a tough sell on such an approach.

I spared myself the agony of a long flight and phoned his boss instead. Well, as you have probably guessed, the boss was enthusiastic about the approach. He wanted only one thing. He wanted me to coach him on how best to present the new approach for alliance to the oil company that had initially requested it!

Throughout this entire sequence, one that eventually ended in a full circle, not a single person had a clue about their relative inability to engage in an effective dialogue within their own structures, nor could they see the cost of such a handicap. The "normal" structures of authority and the practices that accompany them obscured what was possible through communication.

---

shell. Losing contact with the environment can manifest in another direction. This will occur in a situation where there were initially no strong fundamental values, theories or principles upon which the corporation was founded. This is common when the company started as a copy, or was a very popular type of business at a given time. This may also happen when the original founder had strong but inconsistent ideas that have been lost or perverted over time. When a substantial breakdown occurs in a corporation with this type of history, there will be increasing confusion and chaos. This will all be noticeable, and the end my even be in sight, but no effective action will present itself.

Our challenge is to design and organise so that we are making continual structural changes which bring the corporation into harmony with the environment. This harmony influences the nature of the business, methods of production, how we organise the flow of information, and the interactions of people. These must all interconnect in ways that are consistent with one another. Keeping the corporation in harmony with its environment is a task that is too big and too complex to be done at the top. Yet there is too much diversity and seeming chaos at the periphery, where work is being done. So now what?

Core values and principles are the magnets that attract and select information generated by the "chaos" of the periphery. The job of the core is not to control or even make sense, but to maintain the selection influences from which sense is made at the periphery.

Many experiments will be occurring at the periphery. These are to be encouraged, shown tolerance as they begin, protected and enabled as they continue to grow—and given hurdles to test their robustness. This process allows for a natural flow that embraces the life and death of new ideas, new processes, and whole new businesses.

The Hidden Facet

As in a gem, every facet is critical to the beauty of the whole. The interplay of the various design principles that we have explored begins to reveal itself. Each can be seen as a unique facet of the others. We have now created design principles that can emerge into a corporation which is financially sound, has unique and useful knowledge, is attuned to its social environment, and which is able to adapt by experiments at the periphery. Is there anything missing?

There is one more principle to discover. The difficulty is that it has been assumed, or pre-supposed, by the earlier ones. It's a condition which remains in the background, and one we tend to take for granted. In many ways, it's implied by our very existence and therefore difficult to see.

Put yourself again in the position of being responsible for a 700-year time span of your corporation. Imagine yourself responsible for the corporation—being the source of a satisfying and productive enterprise for individuals who participate in it, and responsible for those individuals being able to function effectively. Now go on to imagine that all the previously mentioned design principles are operating, and that the enterprise is healthy. As you consider the future and the amount of change that will occur in the environment and in the people that are part of your corporation, what will be your greatest challenge?

Let's inquire further. If the world doesn't appear to be changing rapidly and you are secure in your business, then a certain challenge won't arise. All that appears to be required is to keep what's already in existence functioning in a healthy way. (This may be harder than it seems because people want to develop and what exists now may not be sufficient over time.) However, the world *is* changing and changing significantly. The business you are in now will not be a viable business at some point in the future. The skills and values that you have in the company may not be viable in that future. Is the challenge getting clearer?

The challenge has to do with change itself. So why is change a challenge? What is the source of resistance to change? It's not that we don't know how to change. And it's not that we don't want to change, especially when we understand it, and know that it's the appropriate thing to do. The source of the resistance and difficulty has to be with *identity*.

Robust Identity

Principle of Identity

Identity is critical for survival, and this is the function of the core. The core influences the way in which the whole organises (the processes and structures of interpretation), so that an identity can be maintained. Our challenge during change is that we must maintain an identity, and at the same time adapt that identity. A corporation is not a random group with constantly changing membership or diverse purposes. It is a cohesive whole that is adapting, and at the same time it is a specific entity connected to a particular past.

Our last principle is: *Maintain a robust identity which is sufficiently resilient to adapt, and sufficiently structured to hold together.* An identity is a particular organisation of elements, with a particular history, that interacts with its environment in particular ways. An identity is the source of meaning and patterns. This is the principle of identity.

An identity is what allows for a being to be *something*. In order for the world to interact, it must interact *with* something. The world cannot interact with what it cannot identify. Nor can it interact for an extended period of time with something it does not have a historical fit with, therefore having no predictability in its future interaction.

An identity provides meaning or a structure of interpretation for an individual, a corporation or any social institution. It is a pattern that is distinguishable in an otherwise chaotic, rich swirl of stimulation. An employee of a corporation makes meaning of their actions and their surroundings in a particular way because of how they relate to the identity of their company. A marketplace or community does the same. We relate to each other by acknowledging the identity of the other (as

McDonald's is one of the big players in the fast-food league. Without a doubt, they are the reigning champ when it comes to hamburgers. They created the fast-food industry as we know it, and have always maintained a leadership role. Although this type of business may be very competitive at times, it's certainly not complicated. Currently in the industry there are countless other large, successful businesses, but none of them ever take the lead. So what does McDonald's have that the others don't? A different way to ask the question is: What does McDonald's have that the others can't copy, and turn around and use to beat McDonald's?

It's not just better quality, better service or better marketing. It's that they are unique. McDonald's has an identity. Granted, I'm not a food critic, and yet I trust my palette and my experience to tell me that Burger King cooks a hamburger just as well as McDonald's. But Burger king is missing the identity. They are a copy of the identity of McDonald's. It doesn't sound like a big difference, but it's all that is needed.

It doesn't hurt that McDonald's knows what business they are in—and it isn't hamburgers or even "fast food".

Corporations that have been successful for a significant period of time all have unique stories that create and keep alive a strong identity. VISA has more stories that contribute to a unique identity than Mastercard, Koch Industries has an approach to values, organisation and the marketplace that is unique in business. Disney may be the single most well-known corporate *identity* in the world. Levi-Strauss doesn't just have a well known brand, they have an identity.

Many of the stories are linked to a founder or particular leader from their early history. In others like Merck, they have emerged from the ranks. Although Southwest Airlines has a single leadership force, their identity seems to have *just happened* through an organic development of simple ideas. In all cases, their particular identity cannot be copied.

unique and separate), and continually making sense of how that identity is manifesting. Successful adaptation is the process of balancing an identity so that it fits with the culture.

When an identity is going through a process of adaptation, the attempt to balance predictability and change is a great challenge. If change is too dramatic and occurs too rapidly, identity is lost. If the change that occurs is too slight and at a pace that's too slow, circumstances pass you by, your value diminishes, and eventually you cease to exist. To create and maintain a long-living corporation we must concern ourselves seriously with the identity of the whole—the corporation. The individual people will come and go. (Remember, the length of a corporation's life can extend well beyond any human life.) But at any point in time, the people that comprise a company need to have a sense of who they are as a company, in much the same way as they require a sense of who they are as individual people.

The analogy of a standing wave is useful here. The particular drops of water that constitute a wave change constantly as it swells and ebbs. There is no *thing* that we can find which is a constant part of a wave. We can disturb the wave to such an extent that it goes out of existence. When we remove the disturbance, the wave returns. The wave is constantly being created by an interplay of forces within the water, and the structures through which those forces move. If we alter the structures, we alter the shape or even the existence of a wave.

The *identity challenge,* balancing stability and change, begins to resolve itself by allowing the periphery the freedom to experiment without central control of the details. If people at the periphery are connected to the identity of the corporation, then they can be trusted to take actions which will be consistent with the interests of the whole.

As we begin to work with balancing the identity of a corporation, we are able to manage the resistance, fear and reluctance that arise in the face of change. Interestingly enough, these resistant elements tend to dissolve in the midst of creating a robust, adaptive identity. Instead of pulling back from change, people move towards it. This is because they are being called by a sense of community and belonging that provides stability for the constant challenges of growth and development.

The robustness and viability at the periphery is created by the connection to the historical form of the whole, both in detail and principle. This connection is what makes one a member of a community. The connection to detail is in the language and stories of the culture and community. A corporation is a socially-constructed reality, which provides a basis of interpretation for its members. The basis of identity for a corporation is a set of design principles, a set of values, and an organisational structure that makes sense. As employees, we often seek rigid structures and ask for specific interpretations which, even when given to us, fail when the basics are not in place. I have seen this in senior executives as much as in anyone else in a company. When this occurs, it indicates that the executive is not the core, but perched precariously at the top.

When a corporation has a clear identity, individuals are free to choose to be members of the community, based on its identity, or to find another which is more suitable for them. The identities of individuals and corporations are able to meet when each takes the risk of choosing: taking the choice to be *somebody* specific, knowing that there are both costs and benefits to every choice. The choice of identity is profound. It cannot be based on weighing up the costs and benefits, even though we know that there will be both. We must choose *before* either can be known to any great degree.

The core of a healthy, viable, robust corporation is made up of those who can hold the most divergent information. They must also be able to provide an opportunity for convergence—one that integrates the historical character of the enterprise with the current and future environments. This need for convergence is occurring in the corporation at every moment. The main role of the core is to embody this convergence, and provide structures of meaning and interpretation for everyone in the corporation.

An integration of new design principles can be accomplished when every person in a company realises that they are both the periphery and the core, depending on the circumstances. Executives have a particular role to play at the core, but as individuals, they are also at the periphery of the core, and at the periphery through their many unique contacts with the outside world. When each person sees themselves as both periphery and core, and when they can distinguish what to bring to their role, an organisation of intelligence will occur—one that will provide the full intelligence possibility of a single institution which has emerged from the interaction of intelligent beings and their larger institutions.

Praxis Design Principles

1. Principle of Entrepreneurship

This principle organises the way in which we *develop and maintain knowledge, thereby integrating what already exists with things that will contribute to the overall quality of life for the community*. Entrepreneurial success arises out of recombining what is already known and successful, in order to create something new. Entrepreneurship takes advantage of increasing complexity by creating new integrations. It shows a level of mastery in its organisation of information and knowledge. To be entrepreneurial is to be connected and competent in dealing with the *structure of the future*. It also requires maintaining a *social connection*. Putting this principle into practice requires cultivating maximum awareness and sensitivity to the whole social environment.

2. Principle of Resource Integrity

This quality allows us to maintain the ability to survive adversity, and take advantage of it. Integrity refers to our relatedness to the whole; how we *fit*. This includes current economic structures as well as our relationships from the past. The nature of increasing complexity and the emergence of living systems is not linear, nor can it be accurately predicted. This implies an irregularity in the times of excess resources and times of want. *Maintaining internal and external integrity supports the continued survival of a corporation.* This includes integrity with financial resources, financial choices, and use of resources. How we use our resources for the duration of our life of production or service will be a critical factor in determining the longevity of a corporation.

3. Principle of Periphery Value

It's essential to enable the periphery and listen to its messages. We typically consider the periphery to be of less value when comparing it to the core. However, the very life of the whole is a balance between the environment and the core. The periphery connects the two. It is both a separating boundary and a connection to the larger systems of which we are a part. Our skin functions in the same way, as does the membrane of a cell. Whether it's a corporation or a body, *the information possibilities of the periphery are key to success and survival.* Because of our imbalanced focus on the centre or top in the past, we must focus on the periphery in order to establish balance.

4. Principle of Identity

Maintain a robust identity which is sufficiently resilient to adapt, and sufficiently structured to hold together. Such an identity is one of effective complexity, patterns, and structures of interpretation or meaning. *A carefully designed set of values and a nucleus of people (a community) create an identity.* Structure is a component of identity. But more importantly, structure will either facilitate or inhibit a balance between identity and change. A structure that is flexible enough to allow for continued emergence, evolution and increasing complexity is the challenge of the day. The structures of intelligent organisation are key to using the full intelligence of the people of any corporation.

Notes

i   Arie de Geus, The Living Company, *Harvard Business Review,* 1997.

THE ENIGMA OF ENTERPRISE

George Gilder

America's entrepreneurs live in a world with 4 billion poor people. Vulnerable men and women, these leaders of business command little political power or means of defense. Democratic masses or military juntas could take their wealth at will. Why, on a planet riven with famine, poverty, and disease, should this tiny minority be allowed to control riches thousands of times greater than their needs for subsistence and comfort? Why should a few thousand families command wealth far exceeding the endowments of most nations?

More specifically, why should William Kluge, the broadcasting tycoon, have $7 billion, and Suzie Saintly, the social worker, make $15,000 a year? Or why should Harry Helmsley command a fortune worth over a billion dollars and Harry Homeless live on a rug on a grate? Why should Bill Gates, the chairman of Microsoft, be worth over $7 billion while Dan Bricklin, the inventor of the pioneering Visicalc spreadsheet, is still working out of his home with one employee. And why should Michael Milken have ruled tides of billions while the president of the United States earns $200,000 a year?

Does any of this make sense?

In statistical terms, the issue arises just as starkly. Why should the top 1 percent of families own 20 percent of the nation's wealth, while the bottom 20 percent, awash in debts, have no measurable net worth at all?

On a global level, the disparity assumes a deadly edge. Why should even this bottom fifth of Americans be able to throw away enough food to feed a continent, while a million Ethiopians die

---

of famine?Why should the dogs and cats of American eat far better than the average citizen on this unfair planet?

We all know that life is not fair, but to many people, this is ridiculous. These huge disparities seem to defy every measure of proportion and property. They apparently correspond neither to need nor to virtue nor to IQ, nor to credentials, nor to education, nor to social contribution.

Most observers now acknowledge that capitalism generates prosperity. But the rich seem a caricature of capitalism. Look at the "Forbes Four Hundred" list of America's wealthiest people, for example, and hold your nose. Many of them are short and crabby, beaked and mottled, fat and foolish. At least 10 never finished high school and only 240 out of the 304 who went to college managed to graduate. A society may tolerate an aristocracy certified by merit. But capitalism exalts a strange riffraff with no apparent rhyme or reason.

Couldn't we create a system of capitalism without fat cats? Wouldn't it be possible to contrive an economy that is just as prosperous, but with a far more just and appropriate distribution of wealth?

Wouldn't it be a better world if rich entrepreneurs saw their winnings capped at, say $15 million? Surely Sam Walton's heirs, or Harry and Leona Helmsley, could make do on a million dollars or so a year of annual income, four or five times the salary of the president.

Most defenders of capitalism say no. They contend that the bizarre inequalities we see are an indispensable reflection of the processes that create wealth. They imply capitalism doesn't make sense, morally or rationally, but it does make wealth. So, they say, don't knock it.

The usual case for capitalism maintains that greed may drive Leona Helmsley or Ivan Boesky to behavior that attracts the scrutiny of official investigators. But, runs the argument, greed also makes the system go. Because greed is less trammeled in the United States than in Ethiopia, Harry on the grate eats better than the middle class of Addis Ababa.

This was essentially the argument of Adam Smith, the first and still most quoted apologist of capitalism. He declared that it is only from the entrepreneur's "luxury and caprice," his desire for "all the different baubles and trinkets in the economy of greatness," that the poor "derive that share of the necessities of life, which they would in vain have expected from his humanity or his justice."

In perhaps his most famous lines, Smith wrote of entrepreneurs:

> In spite of their natural selfishness and rapacity, though they mean only their own conveniency, though the sole end which they proposed from the labours of all the thousands they employ, be the gratification of their own vain and insatiable desires...they are led by an invisible hand...and without intending it, without knowing it, advance the interest of society.

Thus did capitalism's greatest defender write of the rich of his day. But more recent writers, from John Kenneth Galbraith to Robert Kuttner, speak of the rich wallowing in their riches and implicitly bilking the poor of the necessities of life.

What slanderous garbage it all is! This case for capitalism as a Faustian pact, by which we trade greed for wealth, is simple hogwash. America's entrepreneurs are not more greedy than Harry Homeless or Suzie Saintly. Even without making comparison to their opportunities for indolence, one can see that they work fanatically hard. In proportion to their holdings or their output, and their contributions to the human race, they consume less than any other group of people in the history of the world.

Far from being greedy, America's leading entrepreneurs—with some unrepresentative exceptions—display discipline and self-control, hard work and austerity that excel that in any college of social work, Washington think tank, or congregation of bishops. They are a strange riffraff, to be sure, because they are chosen not according to blood, credentials, education, or services rendered to the establishment. They are chosen for performance alone, for service to the people as consumers.

Greed is an appetite for unneeded and unearned wealth and power. The truly greedy seek comfort and security first. They seek goods and clout they have not earned. Because the best and safest way to gain unearned pay is to get the state to take it from others, greed leads, as by an invisible hand, toward ever more government action—to socialism, not capitalism. Socialism is in practice a conspiracy of the greedy to exploit the productive. To confuse the issue, the beneficiaries of government transfers of wealth smear their betters with the claim of avarice that they themselves deserve.

The rich in general have earned their money by contributions to the common weal that far exceed their income, or have inherited fortunes from forebears who did likewise. What is more, most entrepreneurs continue their work to enrich the world. Let us hail them and their wealth.

Greed is actually less a characteristic of Bill Gates than of Harry Homeless. Harry may seem pitiable. But he and his advocates insist that he occupy—and devalue—some of the planet's most valuable real estate. From the beaches of Santa Monica to the center of Manhattan, he wants to live better than most of the population of the world throughout human history but he does not want to give back anything whatsoever to the society that sustains him. He wants utterly unearned wealth. That is the essence of avarice. If you want to see a carnival of greed, watch Jesse Jackson regale an audience of welfare mothers on the "economic violence" of capitalism, or watch a conference of leftist college professors denouncing the economic system that provides their freedom, tenure, long vacations, and other expensive privileges while they pursue their Marxist ego-trip at the expense of capitalism.

America's entrepreneurs in no way resemble the plutocrats of socialist and feudal realms who get government to steal their winnings for them and then revel in their palaces with eunuchs and harems. The American rich, in general, cannot revel in their wealth because most of it is not liquid. It has been given to others in the form of investments. It is embodied in a vast web of enterprise that retains its worth only through constant work and sacrifice.

Bill Gates and most of the others live modestly. They give prodigally of themselves and their work. They reinvest their profits in productive enterprise that employs and enriches the world.

Nonetheless, the reason for the disparities between the Four Hundred and the Four Billion is not that the entrepreneurs work harder or better or forgo more consumption. Dismissing the charge that the Four Hundred engage in a carnival of greed, we do not explain the real reasons for their huge wealth.

Since Adam Smith, a host of theories have been offered in answer to the great enigma of capitalist inequality. There is the argument of rights: the creators of great wealth have a right to it. But the assertion of rights to vast fortunes created by thousands of people and protected by the state only repeats the enigma in more abstract terms.

Then there is the argument of carrots and sticks: Sam Walton's billions offered him a necessary incentive in the expansion of his stores through the South; Harry on the grate offers a cautionary message to passer-by to work hard and obediently. But the critics can plausibly answer, "Sure, we all need incentives...but $7 billion?" Finally, some apologists will say that Sam's billions were a reward for his brilliant entrepreneurship, while penury is the just outcome of alcoholism and improvidence. But Suzy Saintly, Dan Bricklin, and George Bush are neither improvident, nor necessarily less brilliant than Sam was.

All these arguments, too, are beside the point. The distributions of capitalism make sense, but not because of the virtue or greed of entrepreneurs or the invisible hand of the market. The reason is not carrots and sticks, or just deserts. The reason capitalism works is that the creators of wealth are granted the right and burden of reinvesting it—of choosing the others who are given it in the investment process.

The very process of creating wealth is the best possible education for creating more wealth. Every enterprise is an experimental test of an entrepreneurial idea. If it succeeds it yields a twofold profit: a financial increase and an enlargement of knowledge and learning. An economy can continue to grow only if its profits are joined with entrepreneurial knowledge. In general, wealth can grow only if the people who create it control it. Divorce the financial profits from the learning process and the economy stagnates. Like a tree or a garden, an economy grows by photosynthesis. Without the light of new knowledge and the roots of ownership, it withers.

The riches of the Four Hundred all ultimately stem from this entrepreneurial process. Well over half of them received no significant inherited wealth and most of the rest gained their fortunes from entrepreneurial parents.

Entrepreneurial knowledge has very little to do with certified expertise of advanced degrees or the learning of establishment schools. It has little to do with the gregarious charm or the valedictory scope of the students judged most likely to succeed in every high school class. The fashionably educated and cultivated spurn the kind of fanatically focused learning commanded by the Four Hundred. Wealth usually comes from doing what other people consider insufferably boring.

The treacherous intricacies of building codes or garbage routes or software languages or groceries, the mechanics of butchering sheep and pigs or frying and freezing potatoes, the mazes of high-yield bonds and low-collateral companies, the murky lore of petroleum leases or housing deeds or Far Eastern electronics supplies, the ways and means of pushing pizzas or insurance policies or hawking hosiery or pet supplies, the grind of grubbing for pennies in fast-food unit sales, the chemistry of soap or candy or the silicon/silicon dioxide interface, the endless round of motivating workers and blandishing union bosses and federal inspectors and the IRS and EPA: all are considered tedious and trivial by the established powers.

Most people think they are above learning the gritty and relentless details of life that allow the creation of great wealth. They leave it to the experts. But in general you join the Four Hundred not by leaving it to the experts but by creating new expertise, not by knowing what the experts know but by learning what they think is beneath them.

Because entrepreneurship overthrows establishments rather than undergirds them, the entrepreneurial tycoons mostly begin as rebels and outsiders. Often they live in out-of-the-way places—like Bentonville, Arkansas; Omaha, Nebraska; or Mission Hills, Kansas—mentioned in New York, at all, as the punch lines of comedy routines. When these entrepreneurs move into high society, they are usually inheritors on the way down.

In a sense, entrepreneurship is the launching of surprises. What bothers many critics of capitalism is that a group like the Forbes Four Hundred is too full of surprises. Sam Walton opens a haberdashery and it goes broke. He opens another and it works. He launches a shopping center empire in the rural South and becomes America's richest man. Who would have thunk it? Forrest Mars goes bankrupt, fails twice in other ventures, then builds a fortune in candy bars. Bill Gates drops out of Harvard and founds a software company that brings IBM into personal computers. J.R. Simplot makes his fortune in potatoes and then takes a flyer in his eighties on microchip technology, chipping in another $100 million to his portfolio.

This process of wealth creation is offensive to levelers and because it yields mountains of new wealth in ways that could not possibly be planned. But unpredictability is fundamental to free human enterprise. It defies every econometric model and socialist scheme. It makes no sense to most professors, who their positions by the systematic acquisition of credentials pleasing to the establishment above them. By definition, innovations cannot be planned. Leading entrepreneurs—from Jack Simplot to Michel Milken—did not ascend a hierarchy; they created a new one. They did not climb to the top of anything. They were pushed to the top by their own success. They did not capture the pinnacle, they became it.

This process creates wealth. But to maintain and increase it is nearly as difficult. A pot of honey attracts flies as well as bears. Bureaucrats, politicians, bishops, raiders, robbers, revolutionaries, short-sellers, managers, business writers, and missionaries all think they could invest money better than its owners. Owners are besieged on all sides by aspiring spenders—debauchers of wealth and purveyors of poverty in the name of charity, idealism, envy, or social change. In fact, of all the people on the face of the globe it is only the legal owners of businesses who have a clear interest in building wealth for others rather than spending it on themselves.

Leading entrepreneurs in general consume only a tiny portion of their holdings. Usually they are owners and investors. As owners, they are the ones damaged most by mismanagement or the exploitation or waste of their assets.

As long as Bill Gates is in charge of Microsoft, it will probably grow in value. But if you put Harry Homeless in charge of Microsoft—or if as Harry's proxy you put a government bureaucrat in charge—within minutes the company would be worth half its former value. As other software firms, such as Oracle and Lotus, discovered in the early 1990s, a software stock can lose most of its worth in minutes if fashions shift or investors distrust the management.

As a Harvard Business School study recently showed, even if you put "professional management" at the helm of great wealth, value is likely to grow less rapidly than if you give owners the real control. A manager of Microsoft might benefit from stealing from it or turning it into his own special preserve, making self-indulgent "investments" in company planes and playgrounds or favored foundations that were in fact his own disguised consumption. It is only Gates who would see his own wealth drop catastrophically if he began to focus less on his customers than on his own consumption. The key to his wealth is his resolution neither to spend nor to abandon it. In a sense, Gates is as much the slave as the master of Microsoft.

The government could not capture America's wealth even if it wished to. As Marxist despots and tribal socialists from Cuba to Angola have discovered to their huge disappointment, governments can expropriate wealth, but cannot appropriate it or redistribute it. In the United States as well, a left ward administration could destroy the value of the Four Hundred's property but could not seize it or pass it on. In general, the confiscated banks and savings and loans of recent years accelerated their losses under government management and regulation.

Under capitalism, wealth is less a stock of goods than a flow of ideas. Joseph Schumpeter propounded the basic rule when he declared capitalism a "form of change" that "never can be stationary." The landscape of capitalism may seem solid and settled and thus seizable; but capitalism is really a mindscape.

Volatile and shifting ideas, not heavy and entrenched establishments, constitute the source of wealth. There is no bureaucratic net or tax web that can catch the fleeting thoughts of Gordon Moore of Intel or Michael Milken, lately of Pleasanton.

Nonetheless, in this mindscape of capitalism, all riches finally fall into the gap between thoughts and things. Governed by mind but caught in matter, to retain its value an asset must afford an income stream that is expected to continue. The expectation can shift as swiftly as thought, but the things, alas, are all too solid and slow to change.

Sam Walton's shopping centers, Bill Gate's software copyrights, John Kluge's TV stations, Lester Crown's skyscrapers, David Packard's chip factories, Fred Trammel Crow's building projects, the Hunt brothers' oil and real estate, Warren Buffett's media stocks, Craig McCaw's cellular franchises, David Rockefeller's real estate and banking interests all could become shattered monuments of Ozymandias tomorrow. "Look on my works, ye Mighty and despair!" Shelley wrote in the voice of the king whose empires became mere mounds in the desert sands. Like the deep gas of Oklahoma, the commercial real estate of Houston, the steel mills of Pittsburgh, the railroad grid of New England, the great printing presses of a decade ago, the supercomputers of a year ago, the giant nuclear plants of yesteryear, or the sartorial rage of last week, the physical base of the Four Hundred can be a trap of wealth, not a treasure chest.

In recent years, for example, Arthur Rock's venture holdings, Austin Furst's videocassette rights, Ken Pontikes's computer leases, Roy Speer and Lowell Paxon's Home Shopping Network all tumbled out of the mindscape of value. Earlier years saw the demise of scores of oil and real estate fortunes in Texas and Oklahoma. The underlying oil and buildings did not change. In all these cases, the *things* stayed pretty much the same. But *thoughts* about them changed. Much of what was supremely valuable in 1980 plunged to near worthlessness by 1990.

Overseas interests could buy the buildings and the rapidly obsolescing equipment and patents of high-technology firms. But they would probably fail to reproduce the leadership, savvy, and loyalty lost in the sale. If the Japanese or Arabs bought all of Silicon Valley, for example, they might well do best by returning it to the production of apricots, oranges, and bedrooms for San Francisco. Capturing the worth of a company is incomparably more complex and arduous a task than purchasing it.

In the Schumpeterian mindscape of capitalism, the entrepreneurial owners are less captors than captives of their wealth. If they try to take it or exploit it, it will tend to evaporate. As Bill Gates puts it, he is "tied to the mast" of Microsoft. David Rockefeller devoted a lifetime of sixty hour weeks to his own enterprises. Younger members of the family wanted to get at the wealth, and now after the sale of Rockefeller Center to Mitsubishi they command much of it. But they will discover that they can keep it only to the extent that they serve it, and thereby serve others, rather than themselves.

Wealth is valuable only to the extent others think it will be valuable in the future. Its value depends on running a fortune for the needs of the customers rather than for the interests of the owners. Its worth will collapse overnight if the market believes that the firm is chiefly serving its owner rather than he serving it, or that it is chiefly being run for the managers rather than for the people who buy its wares. The minds of the customers are ultimately sovereign even over the mindscape of America's entrepreneurs.

In feudal and socialist realms, in the third world or behind the increasingly porous boundaries of communism, a register of the holdings of material things could capture a fixed distribution of wealth. There, riches reside chiefly in land, natural resources, police powers, and party offices, often held in perpetuity. Under socialism, a Forbes Four Hundred might represent a dominant establishment, combining both political and economic clout.

Socialist regimes try to guarantee the value of things rather than the ownership of them. Thus they tend to destroy the value, which depends on dedicated ownership. In the United States, however, the government guarantees only the right to property, not the worth of it.

The belief that wealth consists not in ideas, attitudes, moral codes, and mental disciplines, but in definable and static things that can be seized and redistributed, is the materialist superstition. It stultified the works of Marx and other prophets of violence and envy. It betrays every person who seeks to redistribute wealth by coercion. It balks every socialist revolutionary who imagines that by seizing the socalled means of production he can capture the crucial capital of an economy. It baffles nearly every conglomerator who believes he can safely enter new industries by buying rather than by learning them. The means of production of entrepreneurs are not land, labor, or capital, but minds and hearts.

The reason for the huge wealth gap between John Kluge and Suzie Saintly, between Harry Helmsley and Harry Homeless, between all the Four Hundred and George Bush, or between Bill Gates and inventor Dan Bricklin or any number of other worthy men and women, is entrepreneurial knowledge and commitment. Most of the richest individuals are bound to the masts of their fortunes. They are allowed to keep their wealth only as long as they give it to others in the form of investments. They know how to maintain and expand their holdings and the market knows of their knowledge. Thus they increase the wealth of America and the opportunities of even the poorest.

The wealth of America is not an inventory of goods; it is an organic, living entity, a fragile pulsing fabric of ideas, expectations, loyalties, moral commitments, visions. To vivisect it for redistribution would eventually kill it. As President Mitterand's French Technocrats discovered in the 1980s, the proud new socialist owners of complex systems of wealth soon learn that they are administering an industrial corpse rather than a growing corporation.

The single most important question for the future of America is how we treat our entrepreneurs. If we smear, harass, overtax, and over regulate them, our liberal politicians will be shocked and horrified to discover how swiftly the physical tokens of the means of production collapse into so much corroded wire, eroding concrete, scrap metal, and jungle rot. They will be amazed how quickly the wealth of America flees to other countries.

Most American entrepreneurs would stay in America. But the new global ganglion of telecommunications would allow them to invest their liquid funds elsewhere at the speed of light down a fiber-optic line. Young entrepreneurs, once determined to start in America the fortunes of future decades, instead would begin them overseas, or not begin them at all, clutching instead to the corpse of a stagnant establishment. Their own worth and the wealth of the United States would decline sharply in the process. But within a few years, other countries would begin to thrive where America once flourished. During recent decades, the secrets of the wealthy have been spreading across the increasingly global mindscape of capitalism.

Even the prospects of the poor in the United States and around the world above all depend on the treatment of the rich. If the rich are immobilized by socialism, the poor will suffer everywhere. High tax rates and oppressive regulations do not keep anyone from being rich. They prevent poor people from getting rich. But if the rich are respected and allowed to risk their wealth—and new rebels are allowed to rise up and challenge them—America will continue to be the land where the last regularly become first by serving others.

This is the spirit of enterprise—but it is best embodied not in the theory of a writer but in the life of an entrepreneur, a story that leads from the old frontier to the new.

INTRODUCTION TO MARKET-BASED MANAGEMENT

Wayne Gable and Jerry Ellig

With a foreword by
Charles G. Koch, Chairman and CEO, Koch Industries

About Charles G. Koch

Charles G. Koch has served since 1967 as chairman and CEO of Koch Industries, Inc., a $20 billion petroleum, chemical, agricultural, and financial services company based in Wichita, Kansas. For the past 25 years, he has worked to improve Koch industries' management systems by incorporating insights from economics, philosophy, history, psychology, and other disciplines. In 1991, Koch first began describing his management philosophy as "market-based management," and Koch Industries is currently working to develop and apply further the basic market-based management framework to its various businesses.

About the Authors

From 1991 to 1993, Dr. Wayne Gable was managing director for federal affairs and management research at Koch Industries, where his duties included helping to apply market process concepts to the development of management systems. In 1993, he became president of the Center for Market Processes (renamed the Mercatus Center at George Mason University in 1998), which has launched a major program to help organizations understand market-based management and develop their own market-based management systems. Gable is now the President of the Charles Koch Foundation.

Dr. Jerry Ellig, a professor at George Mason University's Program on Social and Organizational Learning, spent part of 1992 and 1993 at the Koch Management Center in Wichita, Kansas, where he researched market-based management ideas and helped develop programs for teaching market process analysis to upper and middle managers. Ellig is a Senior Research Fellow at the Mercatus Center at George Mason University and he teaches graduate courses at George Mason University on Market-Based Management and Economic Regulation.

Foreword

Twenty-five years ago, Koch Industries was a small company compared to what we are today. We had fewer than 700 employees, about 1,000 miles of pipeline, and operations focused on Kansas and Oklahoma. Since then, we've established a consistent record of profitable growth significantly above the industry average. We now have approximately 13,000 employees, our pipeline network exceeds 35,000 miles, and our revenues have grown a hundred-fold. We handle several million barrels of hydrocarbons daily, and we have operations in several countries around the world.

Because we've had consistently strong performance over the years, many people have looked at Koch Industries and asked, "How did they do it?" They found that a lot of the usual explanations fail to account for our success. We did not perform better because we had better assets than the competition. In fact, 25 years ago Koch's assets were quite modest compared to many of our competitors. Nor was it because we were smarter than our competitors; if anything, the bigger oil companies' well-known names gave them an edge in attracting people with the greatest potential. We are convinced that Koch Industries' success stems primarily from our management philosophy, which we call "market-based management."

I have personally practiced this philosophy for the past 25 years at Koch Industries. For much of this time the philosophy was more implicit—guiding my business decisions and those in which I was directly involved. The business and management decisions in which I was not directly involved were often market-based as well, but more through our shared values, culture and business analysis techniques than through a well-articulated management philosophy.

Then, several years ago, we recognized that in order for Koch Industries to continue to succeed we needed to take full advantage of this powerful approach to management. Our entire management team, and eventually our entire organization, needed to understand the framework of market-based management and strive to operate within it. We therefore undertook an initiative with three complementary objectives:

(1) to articulate the conceptual framework and principles of market-based management in a manner that could be understood by the entire organization,

(2) to educate Koch management and eventually the entire organization about these concepts and philosophies, and

(3) to examine all facets of Koch Industries—our values, organizational structure, incentive systems, and other practices—to ensure that each was consistent with the principles of market-based management.

We have made good progress toward the first objective, and this booklet covers most of the principles we believe are important. We have not progressed as far toward the second and third objectives, but where we have applied the framework the results have been powerful enough to convince us we are on the right path.

Our experience has shown that market-based management is a framework within which we can analyze, and even improve upon, other management concepts such as Total Quality Management and Re-Engineering. By testing these ideas and programs against the principles of market-based management, we are better able to discern which parts truly add value and then apply them in a manner that is consistent and complementary with our other ongoing efforts. This helps us avoid the "false start" and "flavor of the month" problems that have plagued so many other companies and management approaches.

For Koch Industries—and, I believe, for most businesses—constant rethinking and improvement are now more important than ever. The entire business world faces a revolution that will redefine the role of managers, companies, and entire industries. Developments of new technology and changes in consumer desires have always meant change for corporations, but the change occurring today is more fundamental, more rapid, and potentially more devastating than at any time since the industrial revolution. American industry must now deal with massive increases in regulation and other government-imposed burdens. In addition, computer and telecommunications technology have created an explosion of information available to consumers and a wide variety of new means for satisfying consumer desires. This information explosion has redefined the products and services customers want and the forms in which they want them.

Nor is this unprecedented scope and rate of change limited to the information technology industry. America's most traditional industries—from automobiles, to steel production, to retailing—are experiencing it, and there is no end in sight. Business firms must respond more rapidly than ever to changing customer values and to the rapid innovations of competitors.

This kind of rapid response requires new ways of anticipating, discovering and communicating customer desires to everyone in the organization, from the sales force to the accounting staff. Firms also need improved ways of mobilizing everyone's talents, abilities, and knowledge to serve the customer better. These needs require us to constantly redefine the way work is done. It is no longer enough for employees to come to work every day and work hard at assigned tasks; each day, each person needs to ascertain what he or she can do that creates the most value for customers. In the new environment, only the best managed companies will be able to survive and thrive.

At Koch Industries, we believe market-based management provides a framework that better enables us to meet these requirements. We strive to improve our approach by further educating ourselves about market concepts and by developing market-based solutions to problems common to all organizations. The co-authors of this booklet have both played a role in helping us develop our market-based management ideas. They and other researchers at the Mercatus Center at George Mason University are well suited to develop further and communicate market-based management to a wider audience in business, nonprofit institutions, and academia.

The power of using the market system as a model for management systems has been only partially tapped, even by companies like ours that have been working on it for many years. I believe there are tremendous opportunities to develop and apply market-based management, and I hope this booklet will generate a greater understanding of the concepts involved. The challenge to improve has never been greater than in today's competitive environment. And while the exact solution is different for each organization, our experience indicates that market-based management is an excellent framework for anyone working to meet that challenge.

—Charles G. Koch
Chairman and CEO, Koch Industries
Wichita, Kansas

Why "Market-Based" Management?[1]

The past decade has witnessed a dramatic change in both the business world and our broader society. From the Soviet Union to IBM, massive institutions that seemed permanent stumble—or even crumble—in the face of constantly changing political forces, business conditions and information technology.[2]

Now more than ever, business managers must struggle to coordinate the knowledge and decisions of tens of thousands of employees from all walks of life. Traditionally, many people have thought that business coordination problems could be solved by hiring better brains at the top of the organization. These "experts" would carefully analyze the company's situation and prepare detailed plans for everyone to implement. This type of solution rests on a boundless optimism that superior minds can foresee every major contingency and find a course of action that is best for all.

In company after company, this approach has failed miserably. It has failed not because business managers were inept or corrupt, but because they overlooked a fundamental reality: the knowledge needed for sensible business decisions is inherently dispersed among many people, and much of it cannot be communicated to a central location for use by "experts." As a result, attempts to centrally plan a complex organization fail when confronted by competing firms that develop better ways to mobilize the knowledge of their people.

But how can an organization tap the knowledge and coordinate the decisions of thousands of employees, if not through command-and-control management?

Contemporary political and economic events suggest an answer. Most economists recognize that the Soviet and Eastern European economies failed because a command-and-control system cannot coordinate the millions of economic decisions needed to produce adequate amounts of consumer goods, even simple ones like bread and shoes.[3] In other words, centralized planning of national economies failed for the same reasons that authoritarian business strategies failed: both approaches overlook the severe limitations to any individual's knowledge.[4] While executives are beginning to realize this fact, most corporations still look much more like centrally planned economies than market systems.

Centrally planned economies suffer from what Nobel prize-winning economist Friedrich Hayek called the "Fatal Conceit."[5] This conceit is the belief that leaders or technical experts know what is best for everyone, and that they can effectively manage society while ignoring what most individuals in society actually know and think. Whenever this philosophy has been tried in practice, it has led to disaster, because no person or committee can have all of the knowledge needed to plan a complex society. The conceit is indeed fatal, because centralized economic planning condemns

FREEDOM WORKS

For years, people fled from East to West Germany, and from the People's Republic of China to Hong Kong, in search of both freedom and prosperity. In both cases, people sought to escape the results of a command-based society in order to enjoy the fruits of a more market-based system. The data below show dramatic differences in physical well-being in countries that shared virtually identical cultures, educational levels, and ethnic heritages before adopting different economic systems. Over time, greater reliance on free markets in Hong Kong and West Germany produced huge differences in human well-being. Not only were living standards dramatically higher in the two market-oriented cases, but less measurable aspects of human well-being, such as individual freedom and human rights, were clearly far more desirable as well. Markets and individual freedom made a profound difference in economic and social well-being.

	Hong Kong	People's Republic of China	West Germany	East Germany
GDP per capita (1988)	$9,613	$301	$19,743	$5,256
Number of people per*:				
-Telephone	2.2	149.8	1.6	4.3
-Television	4.2	100.7	2.4	5.8
-Car	29.8	1,093.3	2.2	4.8
Life Expectancy				
-Women	79	71	78	76
-Men	73	68	72	70

Source: *The Economist Book of Vital World Statistics* (Times Books, 1990).

* These statistics do not adjust for product quality, which is much higher in West Germany and Hong Kong than in East Germany or China.

most individuals in society to poverty, greater risk of disease, shorter life spans, and less fulfilling lives.

Free societies, on the other hand, have produced the greatest increases in living standards in the history of humanity, because free markets allow individuals to act on their own dispersed knowledge. For striking examples, contrast Hong Kong and the People's Republic of China, or West and East Germany, as shown in the accompanying table. In both cases, the people share a common history and similar ethnic backgrounds; the principal difference is the economic system. For years, people risked their lives escaping from East to West Germany, and from China to Hong Kong, in search of a better life. These examples demonstrate the superiority of market-oriented systems.

Historical experience shows that market economies, which rely on the dispersed knowledge and independent judgment of numerous consumers and producers, consistently provide a dramatically higher quality of life than centrally planned economies. Given that reality, it makes sense to examine how market economies coordinate human activity, in order to glean lessons for improving business management. Unfortunately, many analysts in business and academia resist this approach, out of a belief that market concepts apply only "out there," beyond the boundaries of the firm. In this view, the principles of a free society apply in the external market, but the firm's internal affairs are the province of brilliant planners making command decisions.

We believe that this point of view misses several elements essential to understanding organizations. The belief that market principles apply only outside the firm resembles the belief that market principles work in international trade, but not for a national economy. The Soviet experience readily calls this belief into question. The problem with formerly socialist economies was not that they refrained from external trade, but that they failed to implement market principles *internally*. Similarly, we believe firms that fail to learn and adapt market principles internally will one day find themselves distant competitors to firms that do.

The experience of Koch Industries, a firm with which we are quite familiar, shows the power of a more market-based approach. A small crude oil gathering company 25 years ago, Koch's current annual revenues—around $20 billion—rank behind only Cargill's among privately held American companies. During the past few years, while the major oil companies laid off thousands of workers, Koch Industries was one of the few large companies in this industry to expand.

Koch has also pioneered attempts to turn market principles into a management philosophy. Throughout this booklet, we will employ Koch Industries as a case study in market-based management. Koch's executives would be the first to agree that their ideas are not the last word on the subject, but this company provides the best example we know of a large company that has tried to implement market-based management as a consistent framework.[6] We hope these examples will pique the interest of executives in other companies who are looking for innovative ways to mobilize each employee's unique knowledge and abilities.

Why is Market-Based Management Different?

On the surface, market-based management shares some similarities with total quality management, just-in-time inventory control, and other currently popular management practices. Like market-based management, these programs help organizations tap the dispersed and tacit knowledge of many employees. Tapping the creativity and knowledge spread throughout an organization is essential, yet extremely difficult in practice, as indicated by the growing number of companies that have abandoned total quality management in frustration.

Market-based management gives us more than a list of additional management tools. It provides an overall framework—a "paradigm" for understanding organizational problems. The market-based management framework helps us examine and evaluate the tools of just-in-time inventory, total quality management and other ideas for improving organizational performance.

The paradigm underlying market-based management is a method of understanding human action and interaction called "market process analysis." Market process analysis helps us understand how free societies organize themselves to allow people to live and work in harmony, while increasing the well-being of the entire society. The market process allows vast amounts of human activity to be undertaken independently, yet coordinated with the activities of others. This coordination, referred to by Adam Smith in the *Wealth of Nations* as the "invisible hand" and by Nobel laureate F.A. Hayek as "spontaneous order," is responsible for the vast increase in living standards that has occurred in many societies since the industrial revolution. This increase in human well-being resulted from the unleashing of individual initiative rather than from the actions of governments. The market system enabled people to create and distribute wealth on a scale never imagined by previous generations.[7]

A business firm is not just a piece of society, but a mini-society in its own right. Like societies that adopt market-based rules and cultures, organizations can vastly increase their effectiveness by using the market system as a guide for redesigning their own systems. In fact, during the past several decades, many of the most forward-looking management thinkers have de-emphasized hierarchy, authority, and other "command-oriented" management techniques that became common during the first half of this century. Early management thinkers tended to follow the command-oriented "scientific management" school of thought championed by Frederick Taylor.[8] The similarities between the Taylorist approach to management and Soviet-style "economic planning" are uncanny, and they are not coincidental. Both approaches arise from the same framework: a framework that can understand order and coordination only as the deliberate product of some planner's design. As a result, both Taylorism and centralized economic planning depend on the ability of a central authority, whether economy-wide or organization-wide, to accumulate, process, and act on vast amounts of knowledge.[9] And experience has proven both wrong.

Even the long-time defenders of Soviet-type systems have now declared them a massive failure. It is widely recognized that, no matter how intelligent and well-meaning the "authorities" are, and no matter how sophisticated their planning tools, there is simply no way for a government to "run" an economy. Many recent developments in management theory suggest that the same is true for organizations. Rather than emphasizing authority, hierarchy, management information, and "planning," more and more management thinkers are emphasizing decentralization, empowerment, organizational learning, cross-functional teams, consumer sovereignty, and other concepts that don't fit the "scientific management" mold.

In focusing on these concepts, executives knowingly or unknowingly incorporate key elements of a free society into their corporate cultures, informal rules, organizational structures and incentive systems. We believe there is a discernible evolution away from "scientific" management toward a more effective approach—market-based management. Market-based management is based on a fundamental understanding of how the market system enables a group of people to achieve cooperatively results that far exceed what they could have achieved separately.

To avoid misunderstanding, we should note some misconceptions that often come with the name "market-based management." First, market-based management does not mean a mindless copying of external market practices inside the firm. A key difference between the business firm and our broader society is that the business firm exists to accomplish some specific mission, whereas a free society exists only as a means of allowing individuals to accomplish their own goals. Market-based management focuses on discovering organizational structures, responsibilities, values, and incentives that motivate people to advance a common mission. It does not mean merely turning everyone in the firm loose to do whatever they think will make money.

Second, market-based management does not mean simply being "responsive to the market." In our discussions with business leaders, we frequently hear, "Of course we're market-based; we respond to our customers." Any effective management system should help a firm respond to its customers, but market-based management is much more than responding to customers.

Market-based management is also different from various proposals for "industrial democracy" and "participative management." It shares with these approaches a skepticism of centralized management, but offers different solutions to the managerial coordination problem. The goal of many democratic and participative systems is to give every employee a voice in major decisions, either directly or through elected representatives. This approach relies on everyone being well enough informed to contribute to most decisions—a situation just as unlikely as one person having sufficient knowledge to make most decisions. Market-based management, in contrast, seeks to divide up decision making, so that the person or team with the requisite knowledge and the right incentives makes each decision and bears ongoing responsibility for the outcome.

Finally, it would be a mistake to identify market-based management merely with the creation of competitive bidding or spot markets inside the firm. This misconception stems from a

---

view of markets as nothing more than a sea of rivalrous, atomistic competition. [10] In reality, markets are a complex blend of competition and cooperation. Likewise, a market-based firm should promote cooperation while channeling competition into activities that actually promote the common mission.

Six Key Systems in Markets and Organizations

The market-based approach to management draws heavily on lessons learned from market process analysis. Markets facilitate economic growth and social progress through a highly complex process. To provide a workable framework for understanding the implications for organizations, we have focused on six key elements of the market system: division of labor, property rights, rules of just conduct, the price system, free flow of ideas, and market incentives.

Within the firm, each of these concepts has a parallel element in management practice, as illustrated by the table on the following page. The *Mission System* helps identify and keep everyone focused on the things that this particular organization does particularly well. A well-defined system of *Roles and Responsibilities* functions like property rights in the market. They link independent judgment with proper accountability, both for business units and for individuals. An organization's *Values and Culture* establish a framework that helps guide people in making decisions, just as laws and cultural norms guide behavior in the broader society. In the marketplace, the price system summarizes a tremendous amount of knowledge about the relative scarcity and demand for resources; similarly inside the firm, *Internal Markets* give people access to crucial information that they have no other way of obtaining. People also acquire critical information through discourse, and *Open Communication* is as critical inside the firm as in a free society. Finally, in a free market, profit and loss indicate value added and provide incentives for improvement; the firm's *Compensation and Motivation* system should provide similar incentives.

Six Key Systems in Market Economies and Organizations

Market Economy	Organization
Division of Labor	Mission System
Property Rights	Roles and Responsibilities
Rules of Just Conduct	Values and Culture
Price System	Internal Markets
Free Flow of Ideas	Open Communication
Market Incentives	Compensation and Motivation

When all six of these systems function well in a society, the results are truly dramatic. Societies that have these six systems have achieved tremendous increases in human well-being by successfully utilizing the knowledge that is spread out among all of their people. We can refer to these results broadly as "social learning." Similarly, when the analogous systems function well inside the firm, "organizational learning" occurs; the firm finds more effective ways to mobilize the knowledge of its people in pursuit of its mission.

More and more organizations are realizing that, regardless of what businesses they are in, they must also be in the "knowledge business." They must focus on generating and mobilizing the knowledge of their employees.[12] To survive and thrive in today's business environment, an organization must be able to learn, adapt, and improve itself continuously. If it does not, its competitors will soon leave it far behind. While each of the six systems is critical for the market-based organization to develop and improve, managers should remember that the systems are highly interrelated. Attempts to improve organizational performance by focusing on only one system probably won't work.

Division of Labor and the Mission System

Free societies generate wealth by facilitating an ever more complex division of labor and knowledge. Such specialization enhances productivity, because it allows each person to focus on the activities that create the most value at the least cost. A firm's mission system helps identify the activities in which it should specialize for maximum long-term profitability. In addition, when a firm understands its own "core competencies," it then has a much better idea of how its various divisions or profit centers should interact in order to accomplish its overall mission. To see in greater detail how an organization can identify its core competencies, we need to see how the division of labor works in a market economy.

Division of Labor and Comparative Advantage

Division of labor increases productivity by allowing each person or firm to exploit a "comparative advantage." To understand the role of comparative advantage in creating wealth for society, think about two farmers: an Idaho potato grower and a Louisiana rice grower. They can produce more potatoes and rice if each specializes in one crop than if each tries to be self-sufficient in both crops. To see why, imagine what would happen if the Idaho farmer tried to grow rice. Because the Idaho climate is better for potatoes, the farmer would give up a lot of potatoes to grow just a little rice. Idaho-grown rice would be very expensive, because customers would have to offer the farmer a high price for rice to make up for the lost income from potatoes. Similarly, the Louisiana farmer would give up a lot of rice in order to grow just a few potatoes in a swampy rice paddy. Potatoes grown in Louisiana rice paddles would be expensive, because it would take a very high potato price to replace the income that the farmer could have earned from growing rice.

In economist's jargon, the Idaho farmer has a "comparative advantage" in growing potatoes, and the Louisiana farmer has a comparative advantage in growing rice. Both farmers are better off if they grow the crop for which they have a comparative advantage, then trade for the other things they need. The rice farmer gets cheaper potatoes, and the potato farmer gets cheaper rice.

David Ricardo, a 19th-century economist, first developed the concept of comparative advantage to explain international trade. In reality, the principle is much broader than that, because it explains why different people specialize in producing some things and then buy whatever else they need from other people. An auto worker who buys vegetables at the grocery store, visits the doctor for a prescription, and rents videos for entertainment is practicing the principle of comparative advantage.

People and organizations can have comparative advantages for many reasons besides climate and soil. Individuals are born with different types of abilities, and so there would be gains from specialization even if we all lived in the same climate. Experience and education can generate comparative advantage, as people invest in developing skills that let them do new things with less time and effort.

While the specialization of different people in different activities is good for the people themselves, it is also good for society in general. If lots of Idaho farmers "wasted" resources growing rice and Louisiana farmers wasted resources growing potatoes, all of society would suffer the consequences. As a society, we should want farmers to grow the things they are best suited to grow, so we can use our limited resources to produce other things we need. Societies with market systems outperform societies run by command, in part because the market system applies the principle of division of labor across the entire economy.

The Comparative Advantage of a Firm

Organizations too can possess comparative advantages, because groups of people can jointly develop capabilities to do certain things particularly well. Wal-Mart, for example, has excelled by developing superior communication and transportation links between individual stores, warehouses, and suppliers; the company has a comparative advantage in getting customers the merchandise they want quickly and efficiently.[13] But having a comparative advantage in something also implies comparative disadvantages in other activities. If Wal-Mart stopped running retail stores and went into the oil drilling industry, it would probably lose money, because its communication and transportation skills might not be very useful in oil drilling. Thus, Wal-Mart and other companies have a strong incentive to concentrate their efforts in those areas in which they can contribute most to society.

A firm, like an individual, makes the most profits over the long term when it specializes in activities that create the most value for customers at the least cost. The firm's mission system helps promote long-term profitability by identifying the organization's comparative advantages, enabling each employee to focus on enhancing them, and giving employees a better means of measuring whether their efforts have been successful.

As the Wal-Mart example suggests, the process of developing and enhancing comparative advantage is complex. Physical assets and technical skills are important, but equally important are systems that enable everyone in the organization to combine their skills and abilities to deliver value in ways that competitors cannot match. Organization, values, and communication all play a crucial role in the creation of comparative advantage. The firm's mission, therefore, should provide a basis for evaluating and improving all of these aspects of the organization.

What happens when a company chooses to specialize in activities in which it doesn't have a comparative advantage? The market system gives it clear feedback in the form of sustained losses. Competitors who *do* have a comparative advantage in the business will emerge, and the errant company will eventually be forced to improve or exit the business. Although this process may sound cruel, it is actually quite humane. A corporation that decides to specialize in a business in which it lacks a comparative advantage is actually wasting resources. The resources available for investment in productive activity are limited, and when a firm uses up more resources than necessary to create a given level of value for consumers, the extra resources it used are gone forever. The additional value they could have provided for consumers will never be seen by anyone.

Koch Industries' Mission System

The concept of comparative advantage has played a large role in guiding business leaders at Koch Industries. One senior executive often comments, "We used to think we were in the oil business; it turned out that we're in the purchasing, transportation, processing, sales, and trading businesses." When Koch's managers began to view the company's expertise as transportation and processing, they started doing a number of things differently. Koch exited the retail gasoline business years ago, because it believed that retailing requires expertise quite different from that required in other businesses. Similarly, the company does a very limited amount of oil exploration and production—and only when these activities clearly complement the core businesses.

Koch Industries has developed a methodology for discovering its comparative advantages, organizing activities, and measuring success. The Koch "mission system" is an ongoing process in which employees systematically improve their understanding of the firm's capabilities and markets, define goals, plan ways to achieve the goals, and monitor progress. Many firms have mission statements that are intended to inspire employees to work toward common goals. At Koch, the mission statement is used more for strategic planning than for motivational inspiration. A mission statement is just one aspect of the mission system, and it continually changes as employees' understanding of the firm's competitive position changes.

Koch Industries divides its mission system into four key elements. The first element, **Understanding the Business**, involves deciding what is realistically possible given the nature of the markets, the competition, the firm's resources, and its capabilities. This understanding comes from knowing the business, its history, relevant economic theory, management tools, and the firm's competitive advantage.[14] Relevant questions that help refine this understanding include:

- Who are the key customers in this industry?

- Which of our activities create value for which customers are willing to pay, and which do not?

- What criteria guide customer purchasing decisions?

- How do we rate on these criteria, compared to the competition?

- What additional services could we provide that the customer would be willing to buy?

- What influences prices in this industry?

- What are the "best practices" employed by anyone in this industry?

- What are the key activities necessary for success in this business?

- How will emerging industry trends and changing technology alter the ways our customers create value, and the ways we can create value for them?

- Which activities are most profitable, and which are unprofitable?

- Why are we making profits or losses?

- How can we improve profits or eliminate losses?

The second element, deciding **What to Do**, is fairly self-explanatory. Many company missions are too general, emphasizing factors like growth or improvement without an understanding of whether they are desirable or feasible, and without specifying the most profitable ways to target the firm's efforts. To create a mission, a business must really understand where it can create the most value at the least cost. The mission must also be realistic and specific enough that the business can measure its performance against the resulting price, quality, and service goals.

Planning **How to Do It** involves enunciating the concrete steps to accomplish the goals. Without this aspect of the mission system, the mission is just empty words that do nothing to help coordinate activities. The planning process should include strategies to advance the mission for each part of the business, including each division, product, facility, operation, and function.

The fourth element, **Monitoring Progress**, is extremely easy to do poorly but extremely important to do well. For each goal, businesses and individuals need to develop measures of progress in advancing the mission. That imperative places a premium on measuring results, not activities, and on defining quality before measuring quantity. In addition, all measures need to be related to the broad goal of providing the most value at the least cost. Business history is full of examples of firms that achieved poor results—or even failed—because they measured the wrong things. It is all too easy to measure the things that are easily measurable, rather than measuring the things that actually provide guidance in advancing the mission.

Paradoxically, the quest for meaningful measures may be most important in businesses where it is the most difficult. This is true because a thorough search for measures will often lead to a greater understanding of the business even if it fails to yield perfect measures. The more difficult a business is to define and measure, the more important a keen understanding of that business becomes.

The monitoring process must provide feedback that is accurate, timely, and in a form that can guide actions. In particular, businesses and individuals should be evaluated on measures that they can actually affect. A welder in an auto plant, for example, should be evaluated primarily on her activities that have the strongest impact on profitability. All too often, people like the welder are implicitly measured and rewarded according to criteria they cannot directly affect, such as the gross profit margin on cars or the total volume of cars sold, with little emphasis on individual performance. Measurement systems should evaluate contributions to both local and organization-wide performance, and rewards should be based on clearly understood criteria.

Earlier we described Adam Smith's concept of the "invisible hand," a metaphor for the way that people mutually adjust their decisions and activities to fit with those of others. It is useful to think of an organization's mission system as a "visible hand," which gives employees important information they need to work as a team in accomplishing common goals. Through a well-developed and well-defined mission system, an organization can achieve a harmony of interests among its employees very similar to the harmony of interests that exists in a market economy. This requires educating all employees on the organization's mission, helping them understand how it is relevant to them, and encouraging them to develop personal missions that support the common mission. Ultimately, each person's mission should answer the question, "What can I do to promote long-term profitability, consistent with the firm's overall mission?"

Summary: Division of Labor and the Mission System

	SOCIETY	ORGANIZATION
COMMAND	"Social engineers" determine where society should go and how it should get there.	Top management determines corporate mission and strategy in isolation from rest of organization.
	Social well-being depends on the ability of official planners to direct and coordinate productive activities of the entire society.	Corporate "plan" translated into structure, job descriptions, regulations, and policies handed down by top management.
	Individuals must act in strict accordance with official regulations or face punishment.	Despite rhetoric, corporate plan not open to question or revision by rank and file, or open only at high risk.
	Creativity and entrepreneurial activity reserved for those designated by social planners.	Creativity and entrepreneurship discouraged, except as directed from above.
	Individuals succeed or fail based on whether they meet with official approval or disapproval.	Individual success dependent on "pleasing" supervisors politically.
MARKET-BASED	Individuals are free to pursue their personal mission, as long as they respect others' rights.	Individuals and organizations develop mission to create value by focusing on comparative advantage.
	Entrepreneurs earn profits by producing products or services that benefit consumers.	Individuals rewarded for helping organization satisfy its customers.
	Through specialization and the division of labor, individuals migrate toward activities that utilize their particular knowledge and talents, benefiting themselves and society in general.	Firms developing comparative advantage and pleasing customers earn long-term profits.

Property Rights, Roles, and Responsibilities

In a market economy, the institution of private property plays a key role in promoting productive activity. Private property has three fundamental characteristics: individuals can decide how to use their property, they can earn income from it, and they can freely sell their property to someone else. Each of these aspects has a significant social role. Independent judgment harnesses the specific knowledge of time, place, and circumstances that no planner (or CEO!) can possibly possess. Income from private property gives the owner continuous feedback on how well he is satisfying customers. And the sale of property capitalizes the value of future earnings, so that people take into account the long-term consequences of their decisions.[15]

Independent Judgment Harnesses Knowledge

Every social system provides some means of organizing resources to satisfy human wants and needs. No mind or committee can possibly know the intensity of everyone's desires for various goods and services or all of the possible ways of providing them. But each person in society has important knowledge, especially about his own desires and abilities. Private property harnesses this knowledge by allowing people to make independent decisions about the uses to which resources will be put.

Voluntary trade involves not just an exchange of money and property, but an exchange of knowledge. For example, someone with 50 cents buys an apple because he values the apple more than the 50 cents. By paying the 50 cents, that person is declaring to the store owner, "This apple is more valuable to me than to you, and the 50 cents is more valuable to you than to me." Conversely, the store owner makes the trade if he values the 50 cents more than the apple; he is telling the customer, "I agree; the apple is more valuable to you, and the 50 cents is more valuable to me." If customers could just walk into stores and take apples without paying for them, we would never know who placed more value on the apple. Voluntary exchange ensures that resources do not change hands unless the person acquiring them values them more than the person giving them up.[16] Taken as a whole, the system of voluntary exchange enables millions of transactions of this type to generate knowledge about the most valuable use of resources in society.

Profit and Loss Provides Feedback

Voluntary exchange and private property provide strong incentives for businesses to serve consumers and strong feedback on the quality of service. In a free exchange, each person gains control over more valuable resources by giving the other something he wants more. This illustrates a fundamental principle of economics: to profit in a truly free market, firms have to find ways of delivering more value to customers while using fewer resources than their competitors. Once again, Adam Smith's "invisible hand" leads the profit seeker to act in ways that benefit society. "Total quality" gurus like Deming and Juran, who speak of defining quality in terms of customer desires, have rediscovered the "invisible hand." In a free market system, profits are the rewards for success in serving customers.

Profits earned in the marketplace signify that an enterprise has made a valuable contribution to society. Profits also give entrepreneurs with good judgment control over more resources so they can try creating value on an even larger scale. On the other hand, losses indicate that the firm has taken important resources and diminished their value. Losses also help separate people with poor judgment from the control of resources. One of the market's greatest strengths is its ability to match greater control over society's resources with those who have the best ability to make decisions. For centuries, social thinkers have misunderstood the role of profit in the market, yet no one has been able to design a social planning system which even comes close to performing as well.

Purchase and Sale Capitalize Future Effects

To see how the right to sell property makes people accountable for the long-term effects of their actions, think about contemporary situations where property is not private, and so people cannot profit from preserving the value of resources. The air is regarded as public property, and the government feels compelled to regulate air pollution precisely because there is no owner who bears responsibility for keeping the air clean. Similarly, many American rivers became choked with pollution because *no one owned them*; no one had a strong enough incentive to preserve their future value by preventing pollution. Ecologists call this type of situation "the tragedy of the commons," because when a resource is considered public or "common" property, no one has a strong incentive to conserve and protect it.

Private ownership, on the other hand, creates strong incentives to preserve the value of resources. In Scotland, for example, the water in privately owned streams is crystal clear. Why? Because the stream owners have a legal right to limit water pollution, and they do so in order to protect the revenues they earn from selling fishing licenses.

If the environmental examples sound too far-fetched, think of the different habits we often associate with homeowners and renters. Homeowners plant trees, install roofs that will last for 20 years, and buy long-lived, heavy appliances in part because these investments all increase the value of the home when it is sold. Renters, on the other hand, often have to place a deposit up front to cover any damage they might do to the property. Without the deposit, renters would have less incentive to care about the condition of the property after they leave; the deposit is a way of inducing them to act more like owners.

It is important to understand that, in describing the important roles played by the institution of private property and the system of profit and loss, we are *not* claiming that all profits are socially "deserved." Profits promote a harmony of interests between the individual and society in free markets that have not been politicized. But companies can also make huge profits when legal or regulatory barriers prevent effective competition, as in the case of a government-granted cartel or monopoly. This allows the corporation to replace market competition—producing greater value using fewer resources—with what might be called "political" competition. Individuals or companies can also profit through government subsidies. Here the value judgments (and resources) of consumers are replaced by the value judgment of the government and the resources of the taxpayer. In these cases, the profit-and-loss system is not allowed to function effectively.

Profits earned by creating value for consumers stem from the creation of wealth for society. Profits acquired through government stem from *redistribution* of wealth that someone else has created. Historian Franz Oppenheimer referred to the second strategy as the "political means" of profit.[17] Oppenheimer distinguished the political means from what he called the "economic means"—creating greater value for customers while using fewer resources than competitors. The possibility of profiting from the political means, and the extensive resources devoted to this strategy, make it difficult for us simply to look at the most profitable companies and conclude that they are necessarily superior to all others at creating value for society.

Implications for Business Units

To devise a market-based organizational structure, executives need to understand the beneficial characteristics of private property. The goal is not simply to *copy* the external market; we do not necessarily advocate making all workers buy their own tools or letting middle managers sublease their offices to outside customers. Rather, the goal is to understand the crucial functions played by private property in a market economy, and then allocate rights and responsibilities in ways that harness independent judgment, provide continuous feedback, and capitalize the future impact of current decisions.

At the business unit level, a firm can facilitate profit-and-loss calculation through the creation of profit centers. A profit center is a definable unit within a business, created from any set of activities for which financial statements can be prepared. Unlike independent firms, however, profit centers operate within the context of a larger organization. It would be a mistake simply to turn profit centers loose to do whatever makes profits, for then there is little reason for having them in the same firm. But how, then, does a company decide when to create a distinct profit center within the larger organization and when to spin it off as a totally separate entity?

Koch Industries tries to answer this question by evaluating profit centers not just on their own profitability, but also on the external benefits or costs they create for other profit centers. A business engaged in activities in which the company has a comparative advantage naturally falls within the company's "core." Other, noncore businesses are evaluated based on their positive or negative impact on the core businesses. For example, Koch retains some profit centers not because of their inherent profitability for the company, but because of their positive net impact on what Koch views as its core businesses. Similarly, parts of the company that are not profit centers at all, such as accounting and other "support" groups, are evaluated primarily on the value they create for the profit centers. This type of structure makes evaluation more difficult for Koch businesses than for independent firms in the marketplace. But complex and decentralized evaluation procedures are crucial for reaping the benefits of teamwork across multiple profit centers.

Implications for Individuals

Profit centers make separate pieces of the organization accountable for their actions, but to reap the full benefits of a market-based system, accountability must extend to the level of the individual. For individuals, well-defined roles and responsibilities inside the firm play a role similar to that of private property, and for many of the same reasons. Like private property, roles and responsibilities define the area within which a person or team is free to utilize local knowledge, make judgments, and bear the consequences.

All too often, things fail to get done in business organizations because everyone thought it was someone else's responsibility. The similarity between this situation and the "tragedy of the commons" is obvious. In effect, the activity in question was turned into public property. Since no one "owned" it, no one followed up to make sure it was done. Well-defined roles and responsibilities can prevent this type of problem by assigning a kind of "ownership" for every activity, action, and result.

In the free market, profit and loss continually reallocate control over resources to those skillful enough, or lucky enough, to please the customer more effectively than competitors. Like a society, an organization needs some way of assigning and reallocating roles and responsibilities. Koch Industries tries to reallocate roles and responsibilities based on an employee's demonstrated ability to make good decisions and satisfy customer needs.

Each person enters the company with control over a significant asset: his or her own abilities. Employees are expected to think in terms of the company's long-term profit and loss when deciding how to use their time. As people demonstrate sound judgment and good stewardship of corporate resources, they receive expanded authority to commit corporate resources to projects. This authority system applies both to internal resource allocation and external purchase decisions, and it has allowed Koch to abolish centrally approved budgets. In place of command-and-control budgeting, Koch tries to approximate the market's allocation through profits and losses. If a manager makes consistently poor business decisions over time, his authority to make future decisions eventually shrinks.

Well-defined roles should not be confused with detailed job descriptions. Historically, job descriptions in business have consisted of task lists. At their worst, these job descriptions have undermined teamwork and productivity—as when a store cashier refuses to sweep the floor because, "It's not in my job description." Roles and responsibilities, on the other hand, continually change as the external market, business mission, and employee's knowledge and capabilities change.

What should a market-based system of roles and responsibilities look like? While it would be impossible to define an exact system for all organizations, we can identify several appropriate characteristics:

1. An individual's roles and responsibilities should be based on the individual's mission, developed within the context of the relevant business unit and overall organizational mission.

2. Roles and responsibilities should be developed with an understanding of the individual's knowledge base and incentive structure. The individual should be allowed to make decisions or take actions which he or she is better qualified to make than anyone in the organization, and his or her compensation should be based on effectiveness in that role.

3. Specific roles and responsibilities should be determined (and changed when necessary) for articulated and well-understood reasons.

4. New situations are likely to arise over time, so there should be a clearly understood process for addressing and resolving questions of overlapping roles or gaps between roles. Incentive compensation should be based on an employee's contribution to working out conflicts in a positive way as well as on working within the current system.

5. Expectations of performance, including the measures to be used, should be communicated and clearly understood.

Summary: Property Rights, Roles, and Responsibilities

	SOCIETY	ORGANIZATION
COMMAND	Social planners make decisions that determine structure and pre-coordinate all activity.	Planners at top of firm determine structure based on expert knowledge.
	Orders are communicated downward through the hierarchy.	Orders are communicated downward through the hierarchy.
	Everyone follows the plan or suffers punishment.	Workers do as they are told according to the structure and plan of top management.
MARKET-BASED	Private property rights permit individual choice in use of resources (within legal guidelines).	Roles and responsibilities define sphere for individual responsibility and autonomy.
	Income from property (the system of profit and loss) provides continuous feedback.	Employee responsibilities grow or shrink with individual's record of success.
	Transferability of property leads to effective stewardship of resources.	Roles and responsibilities change as corporate mission or individual knowledge and skills change.

Rules, Values, and Culture

In every society, various written and unwritten rules of just conduct provide guidelines for acceptable behavior. Some societies have rules that reward hard work, innovation, and service to others; other societies have rules that reward indolence, conflict, and power-seeking. It's not hard to predict which of these societies have been more successful in increasing the well-being of their members. Sensible rules also make people's behavior more predictable to others, and this predictability helps all people accomplish their different goals.

A society's rules of just conduct can be divided into the formal and the informal. Formal rules are written laws, such as those against murder and theft. For these rules to be effective, most people must accept and follow them voluntarily. The gang wars during Prohibition and riots in Los Angeles illustrate what happens when a sizable number of people choose not to accept formal rules of just conduct.

If law-breaking becomes widespread, it is much harder for people to accomplish their goals, because the behavior of other people is too unpredictable. An urban store owner faced with the threat of looters, for example, will try to protect himself from this uncertainty by carrying a smaller stock of merchandise and charging higher prices to pay for a security system. As a result, the threat of looting harms not just the store owner, but all of the customers in the surrounding community.

Beyond the formal rules are informal rules of just conduct. These are the customs, codes of decency, and culture that exist in society. For example, most people try to give accurate directions to strangers who ask for directions. But if a substantial number of people enjoy giving out wrong directions—or just guess at the directions because they don't want to admit that they don't know—travelers find it harder to get to their destinations in a reasonable time. Few places have formal laws about giving directions, but there is an unspoken norm that says we should be honest when someone asks. Similarly, some companies' informal rules of just conduct include honoring their agreements, but others will break agreements if they can get away with it. Adherence to commonly acknowledged business ethics makes us all wealthier by reducing the amount of resources we have to devote to contract negotiation and enforcement.

Over time, a large number of rules and norms have evolved in our society.[18] Concepts like honesty, respect for private property, and keeping one's word play a significant role in advancing our standard of living, because they promote the types of long-term investment and risk-taking that enhance human welfare. A corn farmer, for example, fully plants his acreage because he knows where the boundaries are, and he knows others will respect them. If the boundaries are in dispute on one quarter of the property, he probably will not invest as much time and money in planting that area as he would in the areas where his property rights are certain. If a gang periodically burns his crop or if the government periodically confiscates it, he will invest less time and money in developing that farm. Many people in the modern world, from residents of America's inner cities to inhabitants of war-torn countries, are in a position little better than the farmer beset by bandits—and for similar reasons. Prosperity slips away when the rules of just conduct break down, because people lack the predictability needed to make long-term plans and investments.

Just as scientific progress changes our understanding of the physical world, learning and experience gradually change people's ideas about the appropriate rules of just conduct. Formal rules are subject to change by government, of course, but informal rules constantly evolve as well. Customs regarding smoking are a good example. It used to be considered impolite to ask someone to put out a cigarette; now, it's considered impolite to light up without asking if the smoke will bother anyone.

Corporate Values and Culture

Rules defining acceptable behavior make the actions of others in society more predictable and beneficial. Similarly, a company's values and culture can guide employees' actions in ways that advance the common mission. In emphasizing values and culture, we explicitly reject the popular idea that there exists a conflict between what is profitable and what is moral. In society and in organizations, moral principles serve the crucial function of guiding our decisions in ways that promote our long-term welfare. The relevant tradeoff is not what is right versus what is profitable; it is between long-term and short-term profitability. If an organization's moral principles are sound, doing the right thing also enhances profitability over the long term.

For an illustration of rules of just conduct, we turn again to Koch Industries. Some key concepts in Koch's written statement of corporate principles are humility, intellectual honesty, openness, receptiveness to new ideas, treating others with dignity and respect, recognizing and using everyone's unique knowledge and abilities, and instilling a commitment to the common mission.

Of course, any organization can pay lip service to these types of principles, and putting principles on paper but not in practice can seriously damage a corporation's underlying culture. But when actually followed in practice, principles like these can promote the trust and openness that allow organizations to tap tremendous employee knowledge and creativity. Employees who exhibit humility recognize that they do not have all the answers, and probably never will. Without humility, individual and organizational learning is difficult if not impossible. Intellectual honesty means people admitting what they don't know, acknowledging mistakes, and searching for evidence that contradicts their positions with as much vigor as they search for evidence that confirms their positions.

When principles like these are not followed, a corporate culture develops in which "information is power," and those who collect and hoard key information are rewarded with positions of greater authority. It is easy to see the damage that such a culture can do to an organization that needs to tap and integrate the dispersed knowledge of all its employees. Finding solutions to complex problems is all but impossible if an organization depends on one person collecting the relevant information. A culture of genuine humility and honesty must be established in order to achieve organizational learning and profitability.

The Koch principles may sound like common sense, but they contrast sharply with the informal culture in many organizations. Managers often face strong pressure to appear competent and put a positive spin on every development, even if it was a genuine mistake. When mistakes occur, people often ask, "How can we avoid blame?" instead of asking, "What can we learn?" Edgar Schein, an organizational learning specialist at MIT, has noted that even in organizations that encourage people to learn from mistakes, there is often an unspoken prohibition on making the same mistake more than once.[19] In such an environment, managers may analyze past mistakes, but the main thing they learn is to avoid activities that carry some risk of repeating a mistake. As a result, people shy away from taking healthy risks, and they lose the opportunity to recognize patterns of events that repeatedly generate the same types of mistakes.

A company's actual values and culture also exercise a heavy influence on managers' attitude toward change. If followed consistently, principles like humility, intellectual honesty, and receptiveness to new ideas encourage people to embrace change as an opportunity for improvement, instead of avoiding it as a threat. Yet in many organizations, people spend a great deal of time and effort resisting change, under the guise of weeding out "unwise" change. Values that promote openness to change are now more important than ever, because in the modern business environment to resist change is virtually to guarantee failure.

Summary: Rules, Values, and Culture

	SOCIETY	ORGANIZATION
COMMAND	Respect for official leadership.	Respect for top management.
	Refraining from criticism of official policies and regulations, and acceptance of plan for society.	Acceptance of corporate plan as "given." Attitude of compliance, often without commitment.
	Accumulation of power by hoarding key information.	Accumulation of power by hoarding key information.
	Obedience to official authority.	Obedience to corporate authority.
MARKET-BASED	Respect for private property and individual rights.	Respect for others' knowledge and expertise.
	Honesty in dealing with others.	Intellectual honesty and humility.
	Tolerance of alternative views and lifestyles.	Openness to new ideas or ways of accomplishing corporate mission.
	Respect for individual initiative and entrepreneurship.	Freedom to question current practices or suggest improvements.

The Price System and Internal Markets

In a society of independent decision makers, people need some means of coordinating their decisions with those of others. A free society lets millions of individuals simultaneously try to accomplish their various goals. Yet at the same time, people cooperate harmoniously to accomplish their goals better than they could by acting alone. Market prices play a large role in providing both the information and the incentives that make this mutually beneficial activity possible. Guided by prices, both business and consumers weigh alternatives and make choices in ways that take other people's plans and desires into account.[20]

The Power of Prices

The absence of gasoline lines during the Persian Gulf War powerfully demonstrates the price system's ability to promote coordination. When Saddam Hussein invaded Kuwait, a portion of the world's oil supply was temporarily cut off, and many people expected the Gulf war to reduce supply further. With less oil available, it was only sensible for people to conserve. The oil price increase following the invasion accomplished this conservation with a minimum of disruption. Millions of people simply looked at the higher price of gasoline, and they decided that some of their driving was not worth the increased cost. Each person decided whether and how much to conserve, and each person who conserved decided which activities to curtail. We did not need ration coupons, a national oil allocation scheme, or presidential speeches urging us to save energy; people just responded sensibly to the signal conveyed by prices.

Contrast this to America's experience during the Arab oil embargo of the 1970s, when government-imposed price controls prevented pump prices from rising to reflect the reduced supply of oil. Without a reliable price signal, American families had no way of knowing how much they should conserve, and they had much less incentive to conserve. Instead of conserving, many people wasted time and millions of gallons of gasoline waiting in line at filling stations for fuel that was sold at an artificially low price. Price controls prevented Americans from adjusting to the reality of a temporarily reduced oil supply.

The price system facilitates amazing coordination in a market economy. Every day, millions of people make all manner of decisions by comparing the prices they see with the benefits they expect from products or services. Not even the most powerful computer could make all of these decisions for society, but ordinary people can make decisions for themselves when aided by the information summarized in prices.

Bringing Prices Inside the Firm

The size and complexity of resource allocation decisions within firms sometimes rival the size and complexity of decisions in the external marketplace. Yet the typical business firm employs the price system only sparingly. Many companies do establish transfer prices for products that move between internal divisions, but the vast pool of resources known as "corporate overhead" usually carries no internal price. Indeed, a recent survey by Price Waterhouse revealed that most companies are only just beginning to tackle the problem of internal pricing for corporate services.[21] In many companies, resource allocation for services is managed by corporate bureaucracies that more closely resemble Soviet planning boards than entrepreneurial businesses.

During the past ten years, though, some firms have made major strides in developing internal market systems to guide internal resource allocation decisions.[22] The creation of internal markets stemmed from the realization that many "corporate overhead" functions have traditionally been treated like government-run utilities. Instead of receiving resources from customers who voluntarily decided to buy, these groups frequently received budgets from top management. To cover these costs, profit centers then paid arbitrary "overhead" allocations that bore little relationship to their actual use of corporate services, much less the value created by such services for the corporation. As a result, profit centers had every incentive to use as many corporate services as they could—even if a given project consumed more resources than the value it created.

This overuse of corporate services often created the impression that services were undersupplied—an impression that could be used to argue for spending *even more* on overhead services in the future. The predictable result was often a corporate overhead cost spiral, which many companies addressed through "across-the-board" budget cuts. Across-the-board cuts, arbitrary by their very nature, fail to take the relative value of particular corporate services into account. Yet without some kind of market-type evaluation system, most alternatives are relatively arbitrary.

Frequently, business leaders and economists dismiss internal market ideas with a brusque statement that firms exist to minimize transaction costs. Administrative fiat supposedly reduces transaction costs, and so there is seemingly no place for the price system inside the firm. But these objections ignore the "costs" of making decisions without the knowledge provided by prices. No one disputes the notion that, at some level, internal pricing creates more transaction costs than are profitable.[23] But some innovative companies have achieved tremendous increases in productivity by organizing internal service providers as business units charging explicit prices for specific services.

Koch Industries' internal market system provides an interesting example. Services provided under Koch's internal market system include accounting, training, government affairs, information services, legal, environmental compliance, and a variety of other functions. When confronted with explicit prices linked to discrete choices, business leaders face strong incentives to "buy" only those specific "overhead" services that are really worth the cost. During the past two years, a number of Koch corporate service groups have made major revisions in the types of services they offer, because internal markets have forced them to provide services that internal customers perceive as valuable.

Examples of these services include development of certain reports and studies requested by senior management. In the absence of prices for research and reports, top executives asked for a lot of information on sundry topics; various departments dutifully supplied them, assuming that management knew the costs and had decided the activity was worth the cost. In reality, executives had little idea what the company paid to generate these reports. When prices for these services were presented to management, it quickly scaled back its requests, and some types of reports were eliminated entirely. On the other hand, several new reports were developed jointly by the report "suppliers" and their "customers" in management. These documents now provide managers with much more useful information, such as information on business unit profitability rather than raw data. Yet they would probably not have been developed without the incentives created by the internal market system.

Like Koch's profit centers, its internal service providers are not merely freed to do whatever they think will produce revenue for themselves. They are currently nonprofit entities whose survival depends on their ability to offer services that internal customers are willing to buy. Initially, most of Koch's internal service providers did not have to compete with outside vendors. But as the internal market system has evolved, more and more outside contracting has taken place. Currently, if an internal customer wants to purchase from an outside supplier, the internal service group acts as advisor and purchasing agent. The internal agent is always the "supplier" in this system, although it may not necessarily be the specific "generator" of the service. Even the corporate chairman's office is operated as a profit center, purchasing some services deemed essential to the well-being of Koch Industries as a whole.

Obviously, Koch Industries' implementation of internal markets differs from that of many other companies. Many proposals for internal markets sound like trust-busting gone wild; when the whirl of decentralization finished, there seems little justification for keeping a bunch of independent business units inside the same firm. Koch's corporate services currently are nonprofit entities, not because the company's executives are certain that this is the best way of organizing internal markets, but because they are searching for a solution that captures the benefits of internal markets without sabotaging teamwork.

The transition to internal markets demonstrates some of the challenges Koch has encountered in implementing its management philosophy. Market-based management does not mean merely mimicking markets inside the firm. Rather, it requires managers to understand the major features of a market economy, then adapt these features as needed to improve management practice. Koch's combination of profit centers and nonprofit service groups, along with the evaluation criteria for managers, are an attempt to capture the benefits of a market economy while preserving the benefits of having these entities in one business firm.

Summary: Price System and Internal Markets

	SOCIETY	ORGANIZATION
COMMAND	Money prices either don't exist, or are determined politically and convey little information.	When internal prices exist, they tend to be used for manipulation rather than determining value.
	People "pay" by waiting in line, currying favor, etc.	Projects wait in line until internal service providers can get to them.
	Planners must substitute their knowledge for the knowledge contained in prices.	Top management determines the level of internal service investment, with very little knowledge of true value added.
	Bureaucracy often grows excessively.	Corporate overhead often grows excessively.
MARKET-BASED	Prices summarize information about scarcities and consumer values.	Internal markets convey similar information to market prices.
	Price changes indicate need for reallocation of resources.	Investment in corporate services is determined by value added, not politics.
	When consumers react, prices allow adjustments to occur "automatically."	Corporate staff grows or shrinks according to ability to serve internal customers, not set by arbitrary limits.

Generation and Communication of Knowledge

An effective organization must tap the vast and diffused knowledge held by its employees. Decisions must be made by certain people and should be based on the best available information. For many organizations, getting the right information into the hands of the right people can mean the difference between profitability and failure. Many companies now realize that, whatever other businesses they are in, they are also in a kind of "knowledge business." In the business of generating and communicating knowledge, market-based systems have major advantages over command-based alternatives.

The price system serves as a communication network that links and coordinates individual decisions in a market economy. Internal markets can help capture some of the benefits of the price system inside the organization. But in addition to prices, many other aspects of a free society also promote the generation and use of knowledge. Three important characteristics of knowledge help show the power of market-based management in generating and utilizing ideas: much knowledge is dispersed (or "local"), much knowledge is difficult to articulate (or "tacit"), and potential knowledge needs to be tested.

Much Knowledge is "Local"

Regardless of how decisions and information are communicated, a free society allows—and even requires—that key decisions be made by a vastly greater number of people than a command system. And since knowledge is, by its very nature, widely dispersed among individuals in society and organizations, a system that allows people with appropriate knowledge to make decisions also must permit fairly decentralized decisionmaking. This does not mean that *all* systems that promote decentralized decisions are good, only that any system which cannot accommodate decentralized decisionmaking fails to take full advantage of the knowledge contained in the system.

The power of the market system lies largely in placing decisionmaking power in the hands of those with the appropriate knowledge. In a market economy, we see dramatic decentralization of decisionmaking, but we also see some cases where one or a few people make decisions that affect vast collections of resources. In many cases, the appropriate level of decisionmaking is much closer to the customer than to corporate headquarters. But it would be a mistake to view market-based management as always requiring more decentralized decisionmaking. When decisionmaking authority is placed at too local a level, the decisionmaker lacks the appropriate knowledge because he "can't see the forest for the trees." This kind of misplaced authority can be just as disastrous for an organization as having top management make all decisions.

The important point is that, where the critical knowledge is local, the market system permits decisions to be made at the local level. A market-based organization needs to approximate this distribution of authority to achieve its potential. But appropriate distribution of authority is not enough. Even a person with the appropriate knowledge won't make the best decisions unless he or she has the proper incentives to do so. For this reason, the organization's incentive system must be developed to maintain the harmony of interests between the individual decisionmaker and the organization.

Much Knowledge is "Tacit"

Much of the most important knowledge contained in societies and organizations is inarticulable—or what philosopher of science Michael Polanyi calls "tacit." One example is knowledge of how to ride a bicycle. While many people know how to ride one, no one could articulate this knowledge in any complete way. Polanyi captures this state of affairs by saying, "We know a great deal that we cannot tell."[24] Another often-cited example of tacit knowledge is language. When we learn to talk as children, we also learn a complex set of grammatical rules that very few of us can articulate, but almost all of us use on a daily basis. Other direct examples from organization management might be the knowledge of how to achieve maximum output from an assembly line or get maximum quality from a given production procedure.

Management literature features plenty of examples of companies that have found ways to capture local and tacit knowledge. How? By permitting individual initiative, creativity, and experimentation. While a command system relies on an explicit, articulated set of regulations establishing which decisions will be made by which people (often even specifying the information on which the decision will be based), a more market-based system permits flexibility and creativity in accomplishing the overall goal. The recognition that much of the crucial knowledge needed for maximum performance lies beyond the reach of the manager implies an entirely different approach to getting a particular job done.

An example from Koch Industries demonstrates what happens when an organization mobilizes the knowledge of its employees. At one processing unit, managers achieved a large increase in production simply by telling the unit operator to produce as much as he thought the unit could produce, within safety and legal tolerances. Formerly, he had explicit instructions to produce the maximum amount that engineers said the unit was designed to produce within the same tolerances. Koch management acted on the possibility that the unit operator might have superior knowledge in his area of expertise. and they were right. In this case, a seemingly small change had major results.

Much Knowledge Is Untested

How an organization or a society deals with new and untested ideas can have a major impact on its performance. In fact, we believe that the way in which the former Soviet Union stifled creativity and innovation is directly linked to its eventual downfall. In a command economy, people fear speaking up, because they are often punished if they disagree with the official doctrine. This is an unavoidable feature of centralized economic planning, because ordinary individuals are not supposed to be able to improve on the government's economic plans. Such a system clearly limits the creation and communication of knowledge. For decades the Soviet Union discouraged (and often persecuted) individuals engaged in scientific inquiry that was not condoned by the government. The system was clearly based on the idea that the government "knew" what needed to be discovered, and any other intellectual pursuits ran counter to "progress."

As misguided as the Soviet system sounds, it is likely that the real problem was not irrational or stupid government officials, but rather the inevitable result of a command-based system. How different, in principle, was this system from a corporate system in which new ideas must be passed through multiple and hostile "channels" in order to be heard by top management? How likely are creative suggestions to occur in a company within which success comes from protecting divisional budgets, product "turf," or some other variable unrelated to tapping the knowledge of employees? And how many companies don't have at least some elements hostile to new and untested ideas? We believe no company is completely immune to Soviet-style suppression of new ideas, and it is therefore critical for each company to examine its own systems for finding and testing these ideas.

Does the common tendency for people to suppress new and threatening ideas imply that an new ideas should at least be tried? No. But the systems a company uses to generate new ideas and select those that will be tried should be designed to avoid as many command-based shortcomings as possible. For example, rather than designating a fixed "channel" through which an idea must pass (such as a specific person), a system of several possible avenues might be arranged. This would more closely approximate a market-type system, since the "idea entrepreneur" would be able to choose the reviewer least likely to be threatened by the new idea. The ideal idea reviewers would be people with credibility in the organization, but would be unlikely to behave as authoritarians.[25] The reviewers would also be responsible for advancing the organization's mission by helping generate new ideas, and they would be rewarded based on their success in this area.

Freedom of expression, multiple idea filters, and mutually agreed upon standards of evaluation are positive features of a non-authoritarian scientific community described by Michael Polanyi as a "society of explorers."[26] Polanyi contrasts this kind of society with what he calls a "dogmatic society," which corresponds to our concept of a command society. The society of explorers is not without standards for determining the quality of ideas, but it *is* without centrally directed standards and channels. The standards are mutually held and reinforced (and sometimes even changed) by the members of the society themselves. It is this kind of system that seems to produce the most innovative ideas and thinkers, and a market-based system of creating and communicating knowledge should take this ideal as a model.

Summary: Knowledge Generation and Communication

	SOCIETY	ORGANIZATION
COMMAND	New ideas and knowledge are unwelcome unless consistent with official "party line."	Decisions made by higher ranks and communicated "down" the hierarchy.
	Communication media are tightly controlled by authorities.	Communication takes place mainly through proper channels.
	Independent thinking is considered disruptive and dangerous to society.	New ideas are resisted; questioning managerial decisions is improper.
MARKET-BASED	Individuals are free to communicate and act on new ideas.	Decisions are made by those with best knowledge and right incentives.
	Entrepreneurs can mobilize resources to fulfill their visions if they can "sell" venture capitalists on their ideas.	New ideas are welcomed and "filtered" by people who have responsibility and incentives to help generate knowledge.
	Dissent from official dogma is safe; pathbreaking dissension can be highly rewarded.	All recognize that new knowledge may invalidate existing shared assumptions about business.
	Authority in any field of knowledge conferred by mutual agreement among peers.	"Authority" is conferred (or lost) by one's track record, not by political power or rank.

Incentives, Compensation, and Motivation

The Social Role of Profit

The market system is critical if people are to receive rewards for helping others accomplish their goals. The prospect of profit motivates entrepreneurs to seek ways of delivering the most value to consumers for the least cost. Through their purchases, customers reward those who do a better job of satisfying their needs using fewer resources.

Some critics of the market object that the business leader's obsession with profitability prompts companies to pursue only short-term goals. This objection ignores the way markets capitalize future profits into the price of assets. In a market system, transferable property rights create powerful incentives to conserve and care for valuable resources. For example, when a corn farmer sells his farm, the price he gets depends on its condition. He has an incentive to ensure future productivity, so he leaves it in a condition that minimizes future costs and maximizes future revenues. In other words, by doing things that make the farm fetch a higher price today, he ends up taking the needs of future generations into account. In the case of a corporation, it makes much more sense to maximize the long-term net present value of the corporate income stream than to maximize short-term earnings. The market system thus contains strong incentives to provide for the future.

In contrast, a farmer in a socialist system like the former Soviet Union received rewards for meeting his quotas, not for thinking about the future. He could use the land, but he could not sell it, and so he had little incentive to preserve or enhance the land's value for the future. Ultimately, he would leave the property in worse condition than when he received it. This principle explains why environmental problems in the formerly socialist countries dwarf those that we face in the West. In Eastern Europe, sulfur emissions from coal-burning factories have completely denuded some forests. Water in rivers is so loaded with toxic chemicals that it is not even fit for industrial use. These results stem directly from the incentive system: pushed to meet production quotas, people did the things they were rewarded to do and no more.

Personal Profit and Loss

Psychologists, economists, and others have produced mountains of theories and research about motivating people inside organizations.[27] Market-based management adds not another theory of motivation, but a framework for integrating the existing research and deciding which ideas are most useful.

Inside the firm, an effective motivation system conveys market signals to each employee. To fully understand the implications of this statement, we need to remember that the profit-and-loss mechanism accomplishes several things in our broader society. It offers the prospect of rewards, conveys information, and redistributes control over resources. Each of these elements has a parallel in an organization's motivation system.

Within organizations, no aspect of motivation generates as much controversy as the issue of rewards. Some people think of incentives in a very mechanical and superficial way, assuming that people are naturally lazy and that financial and material rewards are the main things that motivate them. The motivation issue then simply becomes a question of discovering the "right" amount of pay and perks to elicit the "right" amount of effort. Many authors and business leaders have reacted against this view, arguing that intrinsic motivation—the individual's desire to accomplish something—is the main force that drives achievement. Unfortunately, some take this sensible notion to the opposite extreme, asserting that material rewards do not matter much, as long as people have fulfilling work in a good environment. This notion sometimes surfaces in the political realm as well. It is used to justify an ideological agenda that seeks more egalitarian pay scales and more progressive income taxation.

Market-based management offers a third way, different from either of these two extreme views. In general, people do want to make a positive contribution and do the best job they can. In many cases, though, organizations give people incentives to do just the opposite, and it is an exceptional person who can resist these incentives for a long period of time. Nearly every organization has stories of heroic people who succeeded in doing their jobs in spite of the system. The goal of a market-based company should be to create a motivation and incentive system that will reinforce people's natural desire to do the right thing.

How does one decide what "doing the right thing" means? While we can't give blanket criteria, we can suggest the following:

- Properly defined roles and responsibilities, as indicated by the individual's and organization's mission, are critical.

- Measures should reinforce the "harmony of interests" created by the compatible missions of the individual and organization. When an employee's action benefits the organization, it should benefit the individual as well.

- Behavior important to the organization—such as adherence to codes of conduct, principles, and other personal characteristics—will be taken seriously only if included in employee evaluations.

- Use of multiple measures, rather than only one or two, will help minimize the natural tendency to slip into behavior that improves calculated performance rather than true performance.

Carefully developed measures are especially important in large organizations, where people may be quite insulated from direct contact with the external marketplace. It is here that the organization's incentive system, understood in the broadest possible sense, is most crucial as a means of conveying information. People in a big company may sincerely want to do their best to serve the customer, but they need meaningful feedback to guide them. Furthermore, verbal evaluation and discussion by themselves may not provide sufficient information to guide action, because "talk is cheap." When administered sensibly, tangible rewards—in the form of pay, bonuses, greater responsibility, or other benefits—help underscore the most important things an employee can do to serve customers.

There is a third, distinct reason that advancement and compensation should depend on results: the imperative of matching people with the most appropriate responsibilities. In the marketplace, a small business owner who successfully serves customers will often earn higher profits and have the opportunity to make even more resource allocation decisions in the future. This continual redistribution of resources serves the important social function of moving each decision into the hands of the person with the best knowledge and judgment. A career development and compensation system should attempt to replicate these aspects of the market economy. Employees who make greater contributions to profit should enjoy greater opportunities to determine their own work and make decisions about the use of company resources. Many psychologists have argued that this type of motivation system makes people work harder because they feel better about their work. Just as important, it helps the organization allocate decisionmaking authority to the right people.

Summary: Incentives, Compensation, and Motivation

	SOCIETY	ORGANIZATION
COMMAND	Compensation of individuals is according to the "plan" of society.	Compensation is based on seniority, title, number of employees managed, etc., rather than value added.
	Even if compensation is based on "contribution," evaluation is done by officials with very little knowledge of individual's true product.	Where compensation is based on measured performance, specific measures and targets are often developed by top corporate brass.
	Most conspicuous rewards are for compliance with official dogma, and for achieving a position of official authority.	Rewards for climbing corporate ladder are based on compliance with corporate plan and adherence to corporate dogma.
	Criticism of government or dissent from official dogma is punished severely.	Dissent from official assumptions is especially dangerous.
MARKET-BASED	Profit opportunities encourage entrepreneurs to serve consumers.	Changes in compensation are linked to mission, including helping overall organization and commitment to corporate values and culture.
	Successful entrepreneurs get control of more resources; unsuccessful ones are separated from control of resources.	Changes in responsibilities depend on employee's record in using resources to advance the mission.
	People have financial incentives to work in jobs where they can add the most value to society.	Employees are rewarded for moving to new jobs where they can better contribute to the mission.

The Result: Social and Organizational Learning

Ultimately, a free economy generates vast wealth because it effectively uses individuals' knowledge in decisions. This "social learning" is a crucial element in economic progress, because of the dispersed and tacit nature of economically useful knowledge. The more effectively a society uses knowledge, the higher its standard of living, because better know-how lets us satisfy more consumer desires using fewer resources.

Social Learning

The incentive problems in a command system are generally well recognized, but the knowledge problems of a command system are not. The market system has the highest rate of social learning of any economic system because its rules of just conduct and property rights systems help generate a rich flow of information from two important sources: verbal exchanges and market transactions.

Markets promote learning because consumer choices determine rewards for entrepreneurship. Society benefits from the individual knowledge each consumer reveals in market exchanges. When competition forces firms to improve their ability to satisfy consumer needs, learning occurs. Without consumer choice, there would be much less learning or coordination in society. Command systems find it much more difficult to tap dispersed knowledge and "learn," which is a key reason why command systems fail. This failure of centralized planning also helps explain why large firms that use command systems are so inefficient. They fail to use everyone's knowledge, precisely because they are centrally controlled.

If planners impede market decisionmaking, coordination must occur in some other way. The central authority typically tries to specify the quantity and quality of the things to be made. But typically, government planners find that their plans are unworkable because they lack the necessary knowledge. For instance, when Soviet planners expressed a nail factory's quota in tons of nails per month, the factory produced a glut of large nails but a shortage of small nails, because that was the easiest way to meet the quota. When the quota was set in numbers of nails per month, the factory produced millions of tiny nails but no large ones. Both of these results occurred because planners rewarded factory managers for meeting their quota, and so the managers found the least difficult way to achieve it. Even with quotas expressed in particular sizes of nails, there were shortages of some and surpluses of others—because the planners could not really know the total number of every type of nail that was needed.[28]

Even if the planners could have gotten everything exactly right once, neither consumer desires nor production technologies stand still. To plan an economy or an organization effectively, those in charge need to anticipate continual change and respond effectively. A market system, in contrast, does not require such an impossible collection of knowledge and power. Firms that are skilled at anticipating future trends reap profits, and the prospect of profit spurs business leaders to adjust to change.

Organizational Learning

Organizational learning is the business firm's counterpart to social learning. Great differences in the rates of learning among firms stem from organization and management, because organization and management determine how well the firm uses the knowledge of its people in decisions.[29]

The Japanese and American auto industries provide a well-known case in point. Compared to U.S. auto firms in the 1980s, the Japanese were twice as productive, had one-third fewer defects, maintained less than eight percent of the inventory, and required half as many people in product development.[30] Japanese firms achieved these results because they found better ways to marshal the knowledge of individual workers and work teams.

The Japanese emphasis on mobilizing the knowledge of workers, their rejection of the "scientific management" theories of Frederick Taylor, and their strong sense of the superiority of their techniques, all come through quite clearly in the following quotation from Konosuke Matsushita:

> We will win and you will lose. . . . Your companies are based on Taylor's principles. Worse, your heads are Taylorized too. You firmly believe that sound management means executives on the one side and workers on the other, on the one side men who think and on the other side men who can only work. For you, management is the art of smoothly transferring the executives' idea to the workers' hands.

> We have passed the Taylor stage. We are aware that business has become terribly complex. Survival is very uncertain in an environment filled with risk, the unexpected, and competition. Therefore, a company must have the constant commitment of the minds of all of its employees to survive. For us, management is the entire work force's intellectual commitment at the service of the company. . . . We know that the intelligence of a few technocrats—even very bright ones—has become totally inadequate to face these challenges. . . . Yes, we will win and you will lose. For you are not able to rid your minds of the obsolete Taylorisms that we never had.[31]

Mobilization of knowledge is critical in the Japanese systems. Strategies like just-in-time inventory management, pioneered by Toyota, can work only if companies organize work in ways that tap the dispersed knowledge of individual workers. Many Japanese auto firms accomplish this by making each worker or work team responsible for inspecting the parts they receive from the previous stage of production. When defects are discovered, the parts are returned to the previous stage for repairs—a significant form of immediate feedback. Since workers know that they will be held responsible for correcting problems appearing at their stage, they have strong incentives to minimize defects. Given this division of responsibilities, it is sensible for the individual worker to learn statistical process control and other techniques that enhance quality. But note that the result—low defect rates—stems from the definition of responsibilities, just as the productive results in a market economy stem from the underlying structure of property rights.

It is tempting for management to adopt command practices when employees fail to do exactly what is expected of them. The easy response is to try to specify exactly what the people will do. However, giving orders and ignoring the knowledge of the people in the organization will generate the wrong decisions, will hamper employee motivation, and will likely produce results about as spectacular as those in the now-defunct Soviet Union.

Conclusion

Because the key systems of organizations discussed in this booklet are so heavily interdependent, we suspect that the principal elements of market-based management probably need to be implemented as a coherent system in order to achieve their full potential. This conjecture is certainly consistent with the experience of Koch Industries. An incentive system, for example, makes little sense unless people first understand the organization's mission.[32] Similarly, an attempt to create internal markets without profit centers and carefully defined roles and responsibilities will create chaos.

Changing management approaches is one of the most difficult processes a corporation can initiate, and a transition from command-based to market-based management is as fundamental a change as an organization can make. Effective change requires a strong understanding of how the market process really works—not just how it works in textbooks—combined with a sense of how people will react to different structures and incentive systems. One of the biggest challenges in this process is combining business expertise with a strong knowledge of economic concepts. This combination, though rare, seems essential for continued development of the market-based approach.

This realization has shaped our approach to developing market-based management at the Mercatus Center at George Mason University. Market-based management is not an off-the-shelf program that business managers can buy and install. Rather, it is a perspective that permeates our approach to analyzing and improving major organizational systems. We invite interested executives to join with us in developing and applying market-based management, to help modern organizations fully tap the unique knowledge and expertise of all of their employees.

The nature of today's business environment shows that organizational change and improvement are not just smart choices—they are necessary for survival. Command-based societies have found themselves unable to survive when faced with market-based alternatives, and command-based companies will suffer the same fate when confronted with market-based competitors. It is no accident that today's most innovative and successful management techniques are those that mobilize the vast knowledge dispersed throughout organizations. Their success points to the need for an overall approach to management that continually uncovers and mobilizes this knowledge.

We believe the coming decades will see the paradigm of command and hierarchy replaced—in practice as well as in theory. The new paradigm will allow employees to apply their knowledge and skills with minimal "management" in the traditional sense. It may or may not be referred to as market-based management, but to work effectively it must be based on many of the principles described in this booklet. And while there is still much work to be done, market-based management clearly has the potential to serve as a guide for designing and building the organization of the future.

Notes

1. The authors have spent several years discussing market-based management with, and learning from, Charles Koch, Richard Fink, and Paul Brooks at Koch Industries. We wish to acknowledge the major role played by them in developing the concepts and tools of market-based management, including much of the material covered in this booklet.

2. For a sweeping analysis of these changes, see Richard McKenzie and Dwight Lee, *Quicksilver Capital* (New York: The Free Press, 1991).

3. Don Lavoie, *National Economic Planning: What is Left?* (Cambridge, MA: Ballinger Publishing, 1985); Peter Boettke, *Why Perestroika Failed* (London: Routledge, 1992).

4. Jerry Ellig and Don Lavoie, "Governments, Firms, and the Impossibility of Central Planning," in Paul Foss (ed.), *Introduction to Organization Theory* (Oslo: Norwegian University Press, forthcoming).

5.   Friedrich Hayek, *The Fatal Conceit* (Chicago: University of Chicago Press, 1990).

6.   See also Tyler Cowen and Jerry Ellig, "Market-Based Management at Koch Industries," Center for the Study of Market Processes Working Paper (June 24, 1993).

7.   Adam Smith, *An Inquiry Into the Nature and Causes of the Wealth of Nations* (Chicago: University of Chicago Press, 1976 [1904]); Friedrich Hayek, *Law, Legislation, and Liberty* (Chicago: University of Chicago Press, 1979).

8.   Frederick W. Taylor, *Principles of Scientific Management* (New York: Norton, 1911).

9.   In fact, two of the Soviet Union's "founding fathers," Lenin and Trotsky, admired the Taylorist system and saw centralized economic planning as a means of making all of society run as smoothly as a factory. See Peter Boettke, *The Political Economy of Soviet Socialism* (Boston: Kluwer Academic Publishers, 1990), pp. 105-6.

10. The overemphasis on "competitive" relative to "cooperative" forces in the market process, and the analytical errors that result, are examined by Richard Fink, *Price Theory and Pricing Practice* (Routledge, forthcoming).

11. We disagree with the notion that the essence of the firm is the substitution of command for market relationships. Readers concerned about this issue should see G.B. Richardson, "The Organisation of Industry," in Richardson, *Information and Investment* (Oxford: Clarendon Press, 1990).

12. Peter Senge, *The Fifth Discipline* (New York: Doubleday, 1990).

13. George Stalk, Philip Evans, and Lawrence Shulman "Competing on Capabilities: The New Rules of Corporate Strategy," *Harvard Business Review* (March-April 1992).

14. In this type of analysis, Koch executives have been influenced by Michael Porter, *Competitive Advantage* (New York: The Free Press, 1985), and Ludwig von Mises, *Human Action,* 3d Revised ed. (Chicago: Contemporary Books, 1966).

15. Randy E. Barnett, "The Function of Several Property and Freedom of Contract," *Social Philosophy & Policy,* 1992), pp. 62-94.

16. This value judgment is, of course, made in practice *before* the buyer consumes the product. The buyer may later regret his decision, but at the time of purchase the apple was worth more to him than the price.

17. Franz Oppenheimer, *The State* (New York: Vanguard Press, 1914), pp. 24-27.

18. Friedrich Hayek, *The Fatal Conceit* (Chicago: University of Chicago Press, 1992).

19. Edgar Schein, "How Can Organizations Learn Faster? The Challenge of Entering the Green Room," *Sloan Management Review* (Winter 1993), pp. 85-92.

20. Friedrich Hayek, "The Use of Knowledge in Society," in Hayek, *Individualism and Economic Order* (Chicago: University of Chicago Press, 1945).

21. Daniel P. Keegan and Patrick D. Howard, "Making Transfer Pricing Work for Services," *Journal of Accountancy* (March 1988), pp. 96-103.

22. William Halal, Ali Geranmayeh, and John Proudehnad, *Internal Markets: Bringing the Power of Free Enterprise Inside the Organization* (New York: Wiley, 1993).

23. For a detailed analysis of transaction cost and pricing issues, see Jerry Ellig, "Internal Pricing for Corporate Services," Center for the Study of Market Processes Working Paper (Sept. 17, 1993).

24. Michael Polanyi, *The Tacit Dimension* (New York: Doubleday, 1983), p. 61.

25. Don Lavoie and Bill Tulloh, "The Use of Knowledge in Organizations," Center for the Study of Market Processes Working Paper (1993).

26. Michael Polanyi, *The Tacit Dimension* (New York: Doubleday, 1983), p. 83.

27. For example, see Frederick Herzberg, "One More Time: How Do You Motivate Employees?," *Harvard Business Review* (Sept.-Oct. 1987), pp. 109-120, and George P. Baker, Michael C. Jensen, and Kevin J. Murphy, "Compensation and Incentives: Practice vs. Theory," *Journal of Finance* (July 1988), pp. 593-616.

28. Thomas Sowell, *Knowledge and Decisions* (New York: Basic Books, 1980).

29. Ray Stata, "Organizational Learning: The Key to Management Innovation," *Sloan Management Review* (Spring 1989), pp. 63-74.

30. James P. Womack, Daniel T. Jones, and Daniel Roos, *The Machine That Changed the World* (New York: Rawson Associates, 1990).

31. Konosuke Matsushita, "The Secret is Shared," *Manufacturing Economics* (February, 1988), p. 15.

32. Acceptance of an incentive system can also depend on the organization's values and culture. For an example, see Kenneth W. Chilton, "The Double-Edged Sword of Administrative Heritage: The Case of Lincoln Electric" (St. Louis: Center for the Study of American Business, July 1993).

About the Mercatus Center at George Mason University

The Mercatus Center at George Mason University is an education, research, and outreach organization that works with scholars, policy experts, and government officials to bridge academic theory and real-world practice.

Mercatus ("mer-KAY-tus") is the Latin term used to describe the bustling activity associated with markets, trade, and commerce. A Latin name is fitting because in classical society, the world of action and the world of learning were unified. In addition, Roman thought emphasized the fallibility of man and the need for competitive dialogue. Mercatus seeks to foster this dialogue and to highlight the dynamic experimentation and innovation that are essential features of the market process.

Mercatus is at the core of a vibrant community of students, scholars, and decisionmakers. Our staff works with this community to build and apply an understanding of how individuals cooperate through the market and political processes. Our affiliations with other innovative organizations at George Mason enhance these efforts.

The Mercatus Center bridges academic theory and real world practice through efforts in the following areas:

- **Research**: Mercatus scholars conduct research to enhance our knowledge of how people live and work together. Based on that research, they work with decision-makers to develop practical solutions to real-world problems.

- **Outreach**: through innovative programs and publications, Mercatus helps public decisionmakers develop analytical tools with which to address society's problems.

- **Education**: to foster scholarly inquiry into the nature of the market process, Mercatus supports academic research and nurtures graduate students who will become tomorrow's idea leaders.

The Mercatus Center is located in George Mason University's new building on the Arlington Campus, along with the George Mason University School of Law, the Law and Economics Center, and the Institute for Humane Studies.

The past decade has witnessed a dramatic change in both the business world and our broader society. From the Soviet Union to IBM, massive institutions that seemed permanent stumble—or even crumble—in the face of constantly changing political forces, business conditions, and information technology. The Soviet economic system collapsed largely because a command economy fails to use effectively the knowledge dispersed among millions of individual citizens. This booklet shows how forward-looking businesses can avoid the Soviet Union's fate by harnessing market principles to mobilize the knowledge of their employees.

Mercatus Center at George Mason University
3401 North Fairfax Drive
Suite 450
Arlington, Virginia 22201-4433

PUT POWER IN THE HANDS OF THE PEOPLE DOING THE WORK

Harvey Seifter and Peter Economy

> Powerlessness corrupts.
> Absolute powerlessness corrupts absolutely.
> —ROSABETH MOSS KANTER,
> PROFESSOR, HARVARD BUSINESS SCHOOL

In recent years, most managers have become very familiar with the mantra of empowerment. According to this mantra, employers who give every worker the responsibility for performing meaningful tasks and the authority to get jobs done are rewarded with an empowered workforce composed of contented and loyal employees, who in turn make their customers happy as well. However, while many companies have taken on the symbolic trappings of empowerment by trimming multiple levels of management and giving nonmanagerial workers new titles and job descriptions, how many have granted employees real, meaningful power?

The truth is that few employees—even among so-called empowered corporations—have any say in setting the goals and direction of the companies they work for. In most organizations, authority to decide what products and services to provide to customers, and how best to provide them, still remains closely held by management at levels far removed from either product creation or service delivery. A Gallup survey of twelve hundred U.S. workers demonstrates that the reality of worker empowerment is quite different than the story touted by today's "enlightened" businesses. While an impressive 66 percent of survey respondents reported that their managers asked them to *get involved* in decision making, only 14 percent felt that they had actually been given real authority.[1] Apparently, it's one thing to talk about empowerment, but it's another to give it.

The symphony orchestra is a particularly stark example of the virtually complete powerlessness still facing so many knowledge workers. A conductor communicates with the more than one hundred musicians "reporting" to him by standing on an elevated platform and waving a stick of wood at them. This communication is essentially one-way since individual musicians rarely—if ever—express an idea or opinion to the conductor. Orchestral musicians are constantly required to conform, and they are usually denied an individual sense of accomplishment. For example, in a traditional orchestra, an important element of the job of violinist number 26 is to make absolutely sure that his bow flies off the strings of his instrument at precisely the same nanosecond as violinists number 25 and number 27. If he does his job well, violinist 26's immediate feedback (and reward) is to be ignored by the conductor altogether. Creativity, engagement in the process, and employee satisfaction don't really enter into the equation.

Unfortunately, to many workers in a wide variety of industries, this scenario will sound all too familiar. At the very least, top-down tyranny in the workplace leads to poor morale, low retention rates, and significant opportunity costs for the entire organization. In extreme cases, the results can include poor products and inadequate services, leading to less than satisfactory customer experiences. Clearly, organizations that put power in the hands of the people doing the work enjoy a substantial competitive advantage over those who do not.

The Principle

Empowerment means many things to many companies. At Target department stores, it means giving cashiers the authority to ask customers if they know the price of an unmarked item and then, if it sounds reasonable, entering that price in the cash register without further approval from management. Customers save time while paying for their purchases, employees are happier because they know that management trusts their judgment, and managers are freed up to concentrate on more productive tasks. At aerospace giant Boeing, a "no messenger" rule puts an enormous amount of power in the hands of workers: members of employee teams are *required* to make their own decisions concerning matters within their purview. To reinforce this, team members are not permitted to take unresolved issues to supervisors for a decision.

When we talk about putting power in the hands of the people doing the work, we are specifically suggesting giving workers the ability to exercise some measure of authority over such areas as setting work schedules and environment, developing and executing budgets, hiring and firing employees, determining what products and services will be developed and sold, and participating in the development of mission, strategy, and goals. Companies that do so will garner:

- Increased employee engagement in their jobs
- Improved worker morale in response to increased management trust
- New ideas, fresh energy, and increased employee commitment to achieving the corporation's goals
- Decreased employee absenteeism and rates of turnover

As we in Orpheus and banking giant J. P. Morgan Chase have seen, the benefits of putting power in the hands of the people doing the work go far beyond simply building a happy workforce.

Orpheus: A Democracy at Work

Unlike most orchestras, Orpheus has a strong and deeply rooted democratic tradition. By careful design, our twenty-seven permanent musicians wield real power over the creative and artistic process, and they have a significant voice in the organization's overall direction. Our musicians decide for themselves who will lead them onstage, and who will represent them on the board and within the administrative management. In a *New York Times* interview, oboist Matthew Dine described Orpheus's working environment as a place where "anyone can say anything they want and generally they do. During the discussions the interpretation forms itself. That doesn't mean that we have control over everything. Spontaneous things happen onstage, and sometimes after a performance we're saying, 'How did we do that?' But we go out knowing we're ready."[2]

Empowering musicians was—and still is—a radical innovation in the orchestra world. After nearly thirty years of experience, we can summarize the extraordinary results as follows: empowerment gives us the ability to maximize the talents of highly skilled individuals throughout our organization, and it improves our performance across the full spectrum of our activities.

The Chamber Music Paradigm

The founders of Orpheus required a model that was fundamentally different from the ridged and hierarchical structures of traditional orchestras, which were populated with authoritarian conductors, star soloists, and anonymous instrumentalists. To find it, they had to look to classical music's other group performance scenario—chamber music—for clues.

Solo performers are, along with conductors, the stars of the field. They have virtually unrestricted power over their own performances, and they exert a substantial amount of control over other musician's work as well. Not surprisingly, soloists frequently grow accustomed to dominating the final product, and come to believe that the role of every other musician onstage is to support their work. Orchestral musicians, on the other hand, are expected to follow direction as quickly, efficiently, and unobtrusively as possible. Technical proficiency and reliability are the most important factors in job performance.

The vast majority of musicians begin their careers as aspiring soloists, but only a small number possess the requisite mix of talent, charisma, endurance, and bravado needed to succeed. Although some musicians choose to play in orchestras because that experience most closely corresponds to their interests and temperaments, most orchestral musicians end up on this professional track either because teachers directed them to it, or because they were forced there by intense competition.

In many respects, the role of a soloist closely resembles that of a star salesperson, engineer, or software developer in the corporate world. Some amount of impetuousness, individuality, and originality is not only expected but encouraged in these business "soloists"—especially if the result is increased sales or product breakthroughs for the company. In business, they orchestral musician's role falls to the bulk of so-called rank-and-file workers. Regardless of how challenging their jobs may be, or how much creativity and originality may go into their performance, most workers are expected to simply do their jobs in compliance with company policies and procedures. While workers in some companies have a voice in setting goals and defining their jobs, most do not and often managers can overrule or "improve" employee-set goals.

Orpheus's founders discovered their inspiration in chamber music, a world grounded in democracy, where power along with responsibility, leadership, and motivation lie entirely in the hands of the people doing the work. Chamber musicians take personal responsibility for their performances while relying, to an astounding degree, on trust in the other musicians to determine the quality and character of the group's finished product.

In chamber ensembles, musicians bring their own ideas, energies, passions, and creativity to their music-making, working in close and fundamentally equal collaboration with other musicians and exercising self-evaluation to improve performance. Each participant individually negotiates the balance between independent thinking and teamwork. Many orchestral musicians and even instrumental soloists also belong to one or more chamber groups, not for financial benefit or professional advantage (indeed, they may not even perform chamber music for the public) but rather for their own pleasure.

Chamber musicians experience feelings of collegiality, shared purpose, and decision-making authority. These are powerful motivational forces that have broad applicability to the challenge of managing today's knowledge workers; clearly, chamber ensembles serve as a perfect analogue for business's self-managing teams.

Our unique approach brings this chamber music ideal to the experience of playing in an orchestra. In Orpheus, the orchestra stars, and every member gets the opportunity to solo. For a performance to reach its full potential, everyone has to be fully engaged.

The Fundamentals

During Orpheus's early years, our founding members identified a set of fundamental rules to guide them as they created a new orchestral structure. According to Norma Hurlburt, former executive vice president and general manager of Orpheus, these guidelines served either to give power to the musicians or help exercise power effectively:

- Management does not impose its vision on the musicians.
- Disputes are settled by vote of all members.
- Membership in the orchestra is decided by orchestra members.
- Interaction in rehearsal is essential, with civility and trust valued as operating norms.[3]

With these guidelines, Orpheus built a culture for employee authority, a necessary groundwork for finding a new way of making music and doing business. Thirty years later, they still apply.

Diffusing the Conductor's Authority

The absence of a conductor at the front of the orchestra does not mean that we have jettisoned authority. In fact, the reality is quite the opposite. Says violinist Ronnie Bauch, "No orchestra exists without direction, and the absence of a conductor as central authority figure doesn't mean that power doesn't exist. Power *needs* to exist. The unique thing about Orpheus is that power is divided up. At the basis of what we do, diversity is our strength. Empowering individual musicians allows Orpheus to draw on the leadership potential of everyone in the organization."

In Orpheus, we continuously disperse the conductor's traditional power and authority among everyone in the orchestra, and all members own an equal share. Members play active roles in key decision-making processes, including selecting music, determining the orchestra's interpretation, and finding the best way to contribute their specialized skills to the group as a whole. Working together on a self-managed basis, the musicians decide who will be invited to join our group (and, perhaps, who will be invited to leave), designate leaders for each piece, plan and implement rehearsal processes, and make the hundreds of interpretive decisions that shape the final performance. "Of course," says Bauch, "the trick is to coordinate all this diverse opinion and input."

Granting members the conductor's authority enhances our musical product by allowing us to draw on the expertise and leadership ability of many highly skilled musicians. It also creates an environment where employees know their contributions are welcome and valued. According to Orpheus bassoonist Frank Morelli, "What's special about Orpheus is the fact that, like a chamber ensemble, we work out our own interpretation, and we've been able to have an impact on artistic decisions such as personnel and repertoire. In Orpheus, one doesn't feel like a cog in a wheel. We are enfranchised, what we do is highly valued and it has the potential of having an impact upon the result. That puts us in a different frame of mind as far as how we can—and are expected to—contribute to the situation."

The average tenure in our orchestra is eighteen years and growing. While our members do occasionally choose to leave the group, most consider their participation in Orpheus to be the most exciting and fulfilling aspect of their professional lives, and will do whatever it takes to protect their tenure. High on the list of reasons for this dedication is empowerment.

For double-bass player Don Palma, a founding member, a brief foray into the world of conducted orchestras proved to be an experience that he didn't soon wish to repeat. Says Palma, "I took one year off from Orpheus at the very beginning and went to the Los Angeles Philharmonic. I just hated it. I didn't like to be told what to do all the time, being treated like my only value was just to sit there and be a good soldier. I felt powerless to affect things, particularly when they were not going well. I felt frustrated, and there was nothing I could seem to do to help make things better." As a member of Orpheus, however, life is quite different. In Palma's words, "Orpheus keeps me involved. I have some measure of participation in the direction the music is going to take. I think that's why a lot of us have stayed involved for so long."

The Power of Decentralization

In the past, businesses could maintain competitive advantage by concentrating power and decision making at the very top of the organization. Those days are now behind us. According to business researchers Eli Cohen and Noel Tichy, "In slower, more predictable times, command-and-control hierarchies weren't such a bad idea. They provided a simple system for consistent decision making: All questions were passed up the ladder to the same small group of people, and their decisions were handed back down. But in the current wired-together global marketplace, pleasing customers and making a profit are functions of quick thinking and agile action. In the time it takes for a question to be passed up the ladder and a decision handed back down, a customer may have gone elsewhere, or the opportunity may be lost."[4]

Gonzalo de Las Heras, executive vice president of international banking giant Banco Santander Centro Hispano (BSCH) and chairman of the Orpheus board of trustees, believes that the power of decentralized decision making is a key advantage of our organization, one that can help *any* business stay ahead of the competition. According to Las Heras, "What I've found in business is that some employees—particularly young people—don't want to decide on their own, because they're afraid. Of course, if you just sit passively, receive orders, and carry them out, you won't produce change or innovation, regardless of how much talent you bring to your endeavors. We have to encourage employees to create, to speak up and to find new and better ways of doing things, by making them partners. People fight much harder for the decision that they've made themselves. They feel that they own it. They work harder on making it a success because it's their own decision." As the speed of business continues to accelerate, the ability to foster innovation in a changing environment is a key ingredient in successful organizations.

The Product of Empowerment

Like the members of a string quartet, the twenty-seven members of Orpheus are directly responsible for many of our organization's most fundamental and important product decisions. It's the musicians who figure out how to adapt Friday night's successful performance in a four-hundred-seat hall in Easton, Pennsylvania, to the special needs of Carnegie Hall with its twenty-eight hundred seats, and implement the changes in an hour or two on Saturday morning.

To do so, we have developed formal structures to ensure that musicians have real power throughout the organization and participate in all important decisions.

Orpheus is a nonprofit corporation and, by law, the board of trustees is the ultimate repository of authority within our organization. Our board acts in much the same capacity as the board of directors in a for-profit corporation (with the important difference that our board is responsible to the "public trust" rather than to shareholders), working to ensure that Orpheus will remain financially, organizationally, and artistically viable over the long run.

The board officially defines and safeguards our mission, exercises fiduciary responsibility, oversees administrative management, and acts as a critical link between Orpheus and the community. In 1998, we added musicians to the board in order to deepen the connection between the orchestra's organizational and creative decisions. With elected representatives on the board, every member of the orchestra knows that no aspect of the organization is "off limits." The musicians have full access to information concerning our plans and operations, and they are directly involved in the most sensitive decisions regarding budgets, finances, product development, and strategic planning.

We have also discovered that adding musicians to the board helps us to recruit new trustees who, as generous volunteers, are in constant demand by Orpheus—and our competitors. The opportunity to sit next to great musicians, as well as top business leaders, has proven to be a powerful tool for building Orpheus's board, and our entire organization benefits.

Management, our twelve-member administrative team, is responsible for running the business and we have broad authority to perform our duties independent of the day-to-day supervision or approval of the board. That covers a lot of ground, since each year we develop and implement a complex operating plan covering more than one hundred events. For example, during the 1999-2000 season, Orpheus produced a five-concert subscription series at Carnegie Hall; performed more than sixty concerts in cities throughout North America, Europe, and Asia; participated in national television and radio broadcasts experienced by more than 8 million people; recorded or released five new CDs; and taught more than twenty-five hundred public school students in New York City.

Each year, the musicians elect three members to participate in the management team. As "artistic directors," their primary role is to propose and develop future projects, ideas, and initiatives, working closely with me to shape the orchestra's products and services through a process of collaboration and consent. This structure also assures informal musician involvement in many areas of Orpheus, and we encourage everyone on the administrative team to seek input from members of the orchestra on all of their projects. Though a new marketing person might be surprised to learn that she is expected to consult a clarinet player about how to plan an Orpheus subscription brochure, she soon learns that musicians—who perform in front of thousands of people at Orpheus concerts, night after night—often have valuable insight into how people respond to the orchestra, and why.

J.P. Morgan Chase & Company: Making Decisions Where the Customers Are

Firms that specialize in global financial transactions live in a complex environment that is heavily regulated, both by internal management controls and by external laws and statutes. But, while the natural tendency within such firms might be to enforce strong limits to employee authority, some have found that empowering individual workers, as we do in Orpheus, can enhance their capacity to successfully and efficiently manage complexity while creating a sense of employee "ownership."

As one of the oldest and most prestigious banks in the world, J. P. Morgan & Company set the trends that others in the financial services industry followed for more than a century. Founded in 1861 by J. Pierpont Morgan, the firm financed and helped build some of America's most important companies, including U.S. Steel, General Electric, American Telephone & Telegraph (AT&T), and many others. Although government legislation after the stock market crash of 1929 required J. P. Morgan to spin off the investment banking side of the business (forming Morgan Stanley in the process) J. P. Morgan & Company continued to thrive and grow.

J. P. Morgan's good fortunes took a sharp downward turn in the mid-1990s, however, as a flurry of mergers and acquisitions in the financial sector created increasingly larger institutions offering broader ranges of products and services. As Morgan turned down potential mergers with Citibank (which went on to become a part of Citigroup, Inc.), Merrill Lynch & Company, and Dean Witter (which later merged with Morgan Stanley to create Morgan Stanley Dean Witter), its share price began to fall behind other securities firms. In 1999, Wall Street punished the firm as shares fell 12 percent from May through the end of the year. During this same period, Goldman Sachs Group's shares rose 35 percent, and Morgan Stanley's shares increased 37 percent.[5]

Potential deals with a variety of financial institutions, including Goldman Sachs, HSBC Holdings PLC, Travelers Corporation, First Union Corporation, Deutsche Bank, and others, were explored; as each fell through for one reason or another, J. P. Morgan's management felt increasing pressure to find a partner and make a deal on its own terms, before the company was forced to accept an unfavorable takeover.

In 2000, Chase Manhattan agreed to acquire J. P. Morgan in a stock swap valued at the time at $30 billion. At the time of the merger with Chase Manhattan, J. P. Morgan & Company offered a full range of commercial banking and investment services internationally, including banking, financial advisory, securities underwriting, trading, and investment fund management services. In fiscal year 1999 the company saw revenues of $18.1 billion and employed more than fifteen thousand people. With more than ninety thousand people located in sixty different countries around the world, the newly formed J. P. Morgan Chase & Company ranked as the second-largest bank in the United States.

Though there were a variety of reasons why Chase Manhattan was interested in acquiring J. P. Morgan—including its venerable name, rich history, and sterling roster of clients—one key factor was the Morgan "culture" of developing long-term relationships with clients, built on a tradition of impeccable and responsive service.

A Flat Organization

Banks and financial institutions have traditionally reveled in hierarchies and ironclad central control. One of premerger J. P. Morgan's hallmarks was its decentralized organization that allowed decisions to be made where the customers were, no matter where in the world they might be. Morgan's approach stood in stark contrast to the multiple layers of supervisors, branch managers, district managers, assistant vice presidents, vice presidents, and senior vice presidents typically involved in the decision-making process at Morgan's competitors.

J. P. Morgan has taken a radically different approach to their organizational chart, one that mirrors Orpheus's in some important ways instead of endless layers of management separating clients from the very employees who can make decisions on their behalf, J. P. Morgan's flat organizational structure allows only four levels of employees worldwide: managing directors, vice presidents, associates, and analysts. But, while Morgan's formal, title-based hierarchy is already fairly flat, the organization's *real* hierarchy is often much flatter. According to Claus Loewe, managing director of J. P. Morgan Chase's operation in Frankfurt, Germany, "In many cases, the actual hierarchy of reporting lines is down to two or three, nor four. In this office, there is a management committee, and there are certain team leaders, and then the rest of the organization—that's as flat as it comes."

With fewer lines of reporting, employees have a greater voice in how they get their jobs done. Says Oliver Bender, an associate in the London office, "I have a certain framework, and within that framework I have a lot of freedom in what I can do and what I would like to do. And even if it's not within my framework, people will still listen to me and consider my opinions because they value my contribution."

J. P. Morgan Chase maintains a flat hierarchy that cuts across the entire company, and individual business units are vested with great autonomy. Says Loewe, "The management committee represents all of the businesses that we have in Germany, plus what we call a chief operating officer whose job is to look after our mid- and back-office operations. Each of the members of the management committee runs his own business in a very autonomous way."

Serving Clients with Authority

In Germany, J. P. Morgan Chase GmbH handles four separate and distinct lines of business: corporate finance (providing funds for business growth through loans and other debt instruments), risk management (helping clients understand, measure, and manage financial risk in their various business endeavors), underwriting (advising clients on fixed-income and equity transactions), and private banking (discretionary asset management and advising clients on specific investment strategies). In each of these lines of business, except private banking where the company deals with individuals directly, J. P. Morgan Chase's clients are institutional, meaning governments and government agencies, financial institutions (such as insurance companies and asset managers), and industrial corporations. J. P. Morgan Case developed three policies for putting power in the hands of their employees, in each of these business lines:

1. The company grants its employees extensive autonomy vis-à-via their own client strategies, while expecting their employees to take responsibility for achieving the organization's goals. According to Claus Loewe, "The guy who runs, for example, a markets business here, and who therefore deals with all of the investor clients in the German market, has complete freedom in terms of how he invests his resources—where he spends his time and how he focuses his team." As a part of granting employees power, J. P. Morgan Chase expects them to meet certain clearly identified and commonly shared targets including "share of wallet" (the percentage of client's assets under J. P. Morgan Chase control), economic value added, and new client acquisitions. Once an employee agrees to the targets for a specific year, they are made a part of the employee's plan, and he or she has complete freedom to decide how to reach those objectives. According to Jörn Caumanns, an analyst in the Frankfurt office of J. P. Morgan, "I have a senior banker who tells me which clients we want to target. How I achieve these targets is more or less up to me." This flexibility allows employees to make decisions as they interact with clients, resulting in increased responsiveness. Continues Caumanns, "The client gets answers quicker because they don't have to run through the entire organization."

2. J. P. Morgan Chase grants its employees wide-ranging autonomy to pick and choose from among the company's many different products, which are increasingly international, super-regional, or global, and to determine how they are presented and sold to clients. Although employees can't randomly create new products—this would quickly lead to chaos—they are encouraged to find the right product mix for each of their clients. To do this well, employees must develop extensive knowledge of J. P. Morgan Chase's products, both in and beyond their office. The right mix, for example, might include an equity product in Germany and an entirely different product out of London. Employees operate within the guidelines of the products—size, risk and returns, thresholds and caps—but they solely determine how to apply them to each client's needs.

3. J. P. Morgan Chase provides its employees with the power of information through its Intranet and other technology tools. By gathering all of the company's analytical tools, transaction history, and product information, and making this information available globally and immediately, Morgan gives its employees greater ability to respond to client needs quickly, locally, and autonomously. Information systems and processes remove the limitations of geography and time, while creating a discipline in the organization's processes for clearing transactions, transferring monies, supporting client transactions, and other business. The power of information has also created a new kind of hierarchy within J. P. Morgan Chase, based on knowledge and experience. You won't find this hierarchy on any organization chart, but it's one that has become increasingly important to the company. At Morgan, information helps break down the formal walls that often separate offices from one another, and encourages employees to create their own teams and affiliations to respond to client needs. Says Claus Loewe, "If we have a client who requires a specific solution, for example, to raise money in Latin America, then we try to identify the person who best understands that region and another person who best understands the client. We will put them together in the team and they will run the entire transaction, creating a certain transaction-related hierarchy for a limited period of time. But, as employees go through this process on a regular basis, people quickly realize where the knowledge is. The result is an informal knowledge hierarchy that can be tapped to improve their performance and their response to clients." In this system based on knowledge and experience there is no senior, and there is no junior—there are only "knows" and "need to knows." Says Jörn Caumanns, "You're working in project teams consisting of managing directors, associates, and analysts, and everybody has a specific role. Working in teams with all levels of employees brings down the hierarchies you may have felt beforehand."

Tearing Down Walls

Of course, every organization has its formal and informal boundaries, and J. P. Morgan Chase is no different. Managing directors, for example, tend to spend a lot of their time communicating within their own community of managing directors; some may find it hard to pick up the phone or to go over and talk to an analyst, who may, in turn, find it difficult to simply walk into a managing director's office and speak his or her mind.

But J. P. Morgan Chase has taken a variety of steps to break down these natural interpersonal barriers and to open up a free exchange of information across the corporation, regardless of position and rank, to support the company's culture of collegiality, teamwork, and camaraderie. For example, managing directors invite small groups of analysts, vice presidents, and other employees to join them for breakfast to discuss important business issues in a relaxed environment, breaking down hierarchical boundaries and encouraging people to get to know each other and work together. Informal get-togethers and receptions create an "equality of ideas" and foster the kind of environment where people aren't afraid to cross organizational lines to accomplish their goals.

Senior members of the J. P. Morgan team make a point of involving junior employees in meetings, building their presentation skills and self-confidence in the process. Says Oliver Bender, "We have a regular Monday lunch meeting where people explain what's going on and the project leaders and the managing directors give a quick summary of what happened last week and what's going to happen this week. They often delegate this task to the associates in their teams to give them a platform to speak." Junior employees are also routinely brought along to client presentation meetings, even for the firm's most senior and most important clients. These employees have a unique opportunity to learn and to observe, and they are often able to add value to meetings when details are discussed that they were involved in preparing. The relationships that they inevitably form with clients serve them—and the firm—well.

Premerger J. P. Morgan twice landed on *Fortune* magazine's list of the "50 Best Companies for Minorities," and Morgan employees consistently report that they feel both challenged and rewarded in their jobs. According to Jörn Caumanns, the autonomy allowed him by J. P. Morgan is one of the key reasons for his long tenure with the firm. Says Caumanns, "I always thought this was the right job. A year ago, the responsibility and the independence that you were given at a New Economy company was unparalleled, but I feel more valuable here." Adds Oliver Bender, "Money is an important aspect of business life, but money doesn't compensate for a miserable life where you never see a client and never see the impact of your work. At J. P. Morgan, you have freedom of mind and freedom of speech and you can actually see what's happening with the work you're producing. It motivates me because I know that ultimately I'm more than a little wheel in a big machine."

Putting this Principle into Practice

Creating an environment where employees are truly empowered means loosening the reins on authority and giving employees access to resources that are usually controlled by managers. You may meet resistance from supervisors who believe they have earned a "turnkey" position—but the trust you give to and gain from employees at every level will garner better products and happier customers.

Five Steps for Loosening the Reins of Power

Step 1: Encourage decision making by *all* employees, not just a select few. There are leaders and followers in every organization; the key is to ensure that these roles don't get frozen in place. To accomplish this, delegate decision-making authority down to the lowest level possible, allow front-line workers to respond directly to customers and clients without constantly seeking management approval, and give employees at every level leadership opportunities that are built—even temporarily—into their job descriptions and backed up by decision-making authority. To allow employees to develop decision-making skills without being overwhelmed, consider assigning projects and tasks that allow workers to gradually build their leadership muscles. Examples might include studying a business opportunity or problem and presenting a proposal to top management, organizing a company event, launching a new customer-service initiative, or chairing an interdepartmental committee. One excellent example is W. L. Gore and Associates, where the so-called waterline principle encourages associates to make most routine decisions on their own, but protects Gore's overall position by requiring associates to consult with others when a decision could adversely affect the company's reputation or financial stability.

Step 2: Delegate tasks and authority widely. Sometimes it takes a life-changing event to help one realize the importance of delegating tasks and authority to employees. Linda Ellerbee, journalist and CEO of Lucky Duck Productions, tells this story: "My biggest mistake as a manager was holding control too tightly. When I started Lucky Duck Productions in 1987, I had no management experience. As a consequence, I did what many people who are new at running their own companies do? I wanted to be involved in every detail of the business at all times. I literally wanted to go into the editing room and cut every piece myself. We ran our company that way for nearly five years. Then in 1992, I was diagnosed with cancer. The timing couldn't have been worse. We had just gotten our first really big project—to produce a news series for kids on Nickelodeon cable. So the day after I was diagnosed, I had called in the entire staff, told them that I had cancer, and basically asked if they could try to hold things together until I was ready to take over again. And for months I wasn't well. But I learned a valuable lesson. I had hired really good people who were good at their jobs, and what they needed was for me to get out of their way. The company continued to thrive in my absence. I never tried to micromanage again."[6]

Step 3: Involve employees in determining the company's and their own goals. Employees who are involved in creating an organization's goals will feel invested in them, and will be much more likely to meet them. Since the beginning, Austin, Texas-based Whole Foods, pioneer of the natural foods supermarket concept, has made a point of involving employees, known by the company as "team members," in the development and periodic review of the organization's mission and core values. The Whole Foods mission statement, dubbed the Declaration of Interdependence, was originally created by sixty Whole Foods employees in 1985 and has been updated three times since then. Key to the Whole Foods mission is the belief that the company should exist not only to make a profit but also to serve its stakeholders: its customers, employees, investors, the environment, and the community. The result is a company that is the nation's number one natural foods chain in sales with annual revenue in excess of $1.5 billion.[7]

Step 4: Open up your books to all employees. At medical supplies distributor Physician's Sales and Service, Inc. (PSS), of Jacksonville, Florida, CEO Pat Kelly has long been a believer in the benefit of opening the books to all employees. The company's financials are not simply shared with employees, they are literally plastered all over the walls of PSS's branch offices, which serve more than ninety thousand physician's practices nationwide. Key financial data, including sales and gross margin per person and branch performance against financial targets, are shared with employees on a daily, weekly, and monthly basis, and employees take ownership for the numbers, the results they represent, and the refining of their work as needed. Founded in 1983, PSS has quickly grown into the nation's largest medical supplier to physicians, with annual sales in excess of $1.7 billion.[8]

Step 5: Create self-managing work teams (and stay out of the way). Teams that put real power and authority in the hands of employees can be a very powerful force within an organization. At General Electric's jet-engine assembly facility in Durham, North Carolina, self-managing work teams are the norm, not the exception. The members of these teams have unprecedented levels of authority and responsibility for determining how, when, and where they will do their jobs. Says technician Duane Williams, "We had to come up with our own schedule. We had the chance to order tools, tool carts, and so on. We had to figure out how the assembly line to make the engine should flow. We were put on councils for every part of the business. I was never valued that much as an employee in my life. I had never been at the point where I couldn't wait to get to work. But here, I couldn't wait to get to work every day. That's no BS."[9] These self-managing teams have an extraordinary track record of finding ways to build better products more efficiently than ever before.

Potential Traps and Landmines

- **Delegating authority without putting appropriate feedback mechanisms into place.** Delegating authority is more than just the best way to put power in the hands of the people doing the work; it is also a particularly effective way for managers to leverage their own efforts and increase their productivity. However, delegated authority without feedback mechanisms can quickly lead to disaster, especially if workers find themselves too far down the wrong path and fail to seek help when serious problems arise. Proper delegation involves more than just giving employees authority; it also requires setting up appropriate mechanisms for obtaining and integrating feedback, such as milestones, regular progress reports, status meetings, and other methods of communication. The best tools provide exactly the quantity of genuinely valuable information managers and other employees need, at a frequency that doesn't lead to employees spending more time preparing reports or attending meetings than doing their jobs.

- **Managers who delegate responsibility for certain jobs, projects, and tasks, but not the authority necessary to get them done.** Delegating tasks and responsibility requires managers to let go of a certain amount of personal and organizational power, and many managers simply lack the confidence and experience to delegate effectively. Proper delegation requires a grant of authority as well as responsibility; anything less will lead to worker frustration when others in the organization impede their efforts or simply refuse to cooperate. Assign authority (to make decisions, direct financial and other resources, and so forth) when delegating responsibility, and invite your employees to ask for more if they need it. Remember that in new workplace situations, managers are just as likely to need training and support as employees are. In spite of the advantages of delegating authority, many managers will find it difficult to delegate.

- **Forgetting that old habits die hard, and that it is far more difficult to undo years of hierarchy than you think.** It's easy to say that every manager and every organization should put power in the hands of the people doing the work, but for many companies evolutionary rather than revolutionary change offers the best course. Consider gradually increasing the scope of authority given to workers, while simultaneously fostering the confidence of managers in the abilities of their employees. Developing a culture of trust requires everyone in the company to buy into the process, from the very top level of management to front-line workers. To underscore the company's commitment to empowerment, make delegating authority part of every supervisor's performance rating, and be sure to provide training in effective delegation. The transition will take time.

- **Workers who do not take responsibility for the impact of their decisions.** With worker empowerment, decisions get made closer to customers and clients by the employees who know them best, and workers become progressively more competent and capable as they make decisions on their own. Remember, though, that worker empowerment only succeeds if employees assume personal responsibility for following through on assigned duties and for the decisions they make. Companies have to hold their workers to a high standard of accountability; workers must hold themselves to an equally high standard. This doesn't mean punishing workers whenever they drop the ball, but it does mean helping them learn from their mistakes and giving them the training and support they need to do the job right the next time.

Putting power in the hands of the people doing the work is at the very heart of the Orpheus Process, and this principle forms the foundation for all others. Many of Orpheus's and J. P. Morgan Chase's successes can be traced to empowering employees, trusting and allowing them to make creative decisions, and giving them authority to use their knowledge and skills.

Notes

1. "To Boost Performance, Turn Employees Loose," *On Achieving Excellence,* November 1991, 10.
2. Allan Kozinn, "Democracy and Anarchy in Concert," *New York Times,* 27 October 1999.
3. John Lubans, "Orpheus Chamber Orchestra," *Duke University Libraries Information Bulletin,* no. 413, 21 November 1997, 6-7.
4. Eli Cohen and Noel Tichy, "How Leaders Develop Leaders," *Training and Development,* 1 May 1997, 58.
5. Charles Gasparino and Jonathan Sapsford, "Hostage to History: As Morgan Persisted in Clinging to Its Past, Time Finally Ran Out," *Wall Street Journal,* 19 October, 2000, A1.
6. Staff, "My Biggest Mistake: Linda Ellerbee," *Inc.,* 1 January 1999.
7. Ed Carberry, "Hypergrowth Strategy: Create an Ownership Culture," *Inc.,* 1 December 1999.
8. John Case, "Corporate Culture," *Inc.,* 1 November 1996.
9. Charles Fishman, "Engines of Democracy," *Fast Company,* October 1999, 174.

Part III

THE RULE OF LAW AND REGULATION

PLANNING AND DEMOCRACY

Friedrich A. Hayek

> The statesman who should attempt to direct private people in what manner they ought to employ their capitals, would not only load himself with a most unnecessary attention, but assume an authority which could safely be trusted to no council and senate whatever, and which would nowhere be so dangerous as in the hands of a man who had folly and presumption enough to fancy himself fit to exercise it.
>
> —*Adam Smith*

The common features of all collectivist systems may be described, in a phrase ever dear to socialists of all schools, as the deliberate organization of the labors of society for a definite social goal. That our present society lacks such "conscious" direction toward a single aim, that its activities are guided by the whims and fancies of irresponsible individuals, has always been one of the main complaints of its socialist critics.

In many ways this puts the basic issue very clearly. And it directs us at once to the point where the conflict arises between individual freedom and collectivism. The various kinds of collectivism, communism, fascism, etc., differ among themselves in the nature of the goal toward which they want to direct the efforts of society. But they all differ from liberalism and individualism in wanting to organize the whole of society and all its resources for this unitary end and in refusing to recognize autonomous spheres in which the ends of the individuals are supreme. In short, they are totalitarian in the true sense of this new word which we have adopted to describe the unexpected but nevertheless inseparable manifestations of what in theory we call collectivism.

The "social goal," or "common purpose," for which society is to be organized is usually vaguely described as the "common good," the "general welfare," or the "general interest." It does not need much reflection to see that these terms have no sufficiently definite meaning to determine a particular course of action. The welfare and the happiness of millions cannot be measured on a single scale of less and more. The welfare of a people, like the happiness of a man, depends on a great many things that can be provided in an infinite variety of combinations. It cannot be adequately expressed as a single end, but only as a hierarchy of ends, a comprehensive scale of values in which every need of every person is given its place. To direct all our activities according to a single plan presupposes that every one of our needs is given its rank in an order of values which must be complete enough to make it possible to decide among all the different courses which the planner has to choose. It presupposes, in short, the existence of a complete ethical code in which different human values are allotted their due place.

The conception of a complete ethical code is unfamiliar, and it requires some effort of imagination to see what it involves. We are not in the habit of thinking of moral codes as more or less complete. The fact that we are constantly choosing between different values without a social code prescribing how we ought to choose does not surprise us and does not suggest to us that our moral code is incomplete. In our society there is neither occasion nor reason why people should develop common views about what should be done in such situations. But where all the means to be used are the property of society and are to be used in the name of society according to a unitary plan, a "social" view about what ought to be done must guide all decisions. In such a world we should soon find that our moral code is full of gaps.

We are not concerned here with the question whether it would be desirable to have such a complete ethical code. It may merely be pointed out that up to the present the growth of civilization has been accompanied by a steady diminution of the sphere in which individual actions are bound by fixed rules. The rules of which our common moral code consists have progressively become fewer and more general in character. From the primitive man, who was bound by an elaborate ritual in almost every one of his daily activities, who was limited by innumerable taboos, and who could scarcely conceive of doing things in a way different from his fellows, morals have more and more tended to become merely limits circumscribing the sphere within which the individual could behave as he liked. The adoption of a common ethical code comprehensive enough to determine a unitary economic plan would mean a complete reversal of this tendency.

The essential point for us is that no such complete ethical code exists. The attempt to direct all economic activity according to a single plan would raise innumerable questions to which the answer could be provided only by a moral rule, but to which existing morals have no answer and where there exists no agreed view on what ought to be done. People will have either no definite views or conflicting views on such questions, because in the free society in which we have lived there has been no occasion to think about them and still less to form common opinions about them.

Not only do we not possess such an all-inclusive scale of values: it would be impossible for any mind to comprehend the infinite variety of different needs of different people which compete for the available resources and to attach a definite weight to each. For our problem it is of minor importance whether the ends for which any person cares comprehend only his own individual needs, or whether they include the needs of his closer or even those of his more distant fellows—that is, whether he is egoistic or altruistic in the ordinary senses of these words. The point which is so important is the basic fact that it is impossible for any man to survey more than a limited field, to be aware of the urgency of more than a limited number of needs. Whether his interests center round his own physical needs, or whether he takes a warm interest in the welfare of every human being he knows, the ends about which he can be concerned will always be only an infinitesimal fraction of the needs of all men.

This is the fundamental fact on which the whole philosophy of individualism is based. It does not assume, as is often asserted, that man is egoistic or selfish or ought to be. It merely starts from the indisputable fact that the limits of our powers of imagination make it impossible to include in our scale of values more than a sector of the needs of the whole society, and that, since, strictly speaking, scales of value can exist only in individual minds, nothing but partial scales of values exist—scales which are inevitably different and often inconsistent with each other. From this the individualist concludes that the individuals should be allowed, within defined limits, to follow their own values and preferences rather than somebody else's; that within these spheres the individual's system of ends should be supreme and not subject to any dictation by others. It is this recognition of the individual as the ultimate judge of his ends, the belief that as far as possible his own views ought to govern his actions, that forms the essence of the individualist position.

This view does not, of course, exclude the recognition of social ends, or rather of a coincidence of individual ends which makes it advisable for men to combine for their pursuit. But it limits such common action to the instances where individual views coincide; what are called "social ends" are for it merely identical ends of many individuals—or ends to the achievement of which individuals are willing to contribute in return for the assistance they receive in the satisfaction of their own desires. Common action is thus limited to the fields where people agree on common ends. Very frequently these common ends will not be ultimate ends to the individuals but means which different persons can use for different purposes. In fact, people are most likely to agree on common action where the common end is not an ultimate end to them but a means capable of serving a great variety of purposes.

When individuals combine in a joint effort to realize ends they have in common, the organizations, like the state, that they form for this purpose are given their own system of ends and their own means. But any organization thus formed remains one "person" among others, in the case of the state much more powerful than any of the others, it is true, yet still with its separate and limited sphere in which alone its ends are supreme. The limits of this sphere are determined by the extent to which the individuals agree on particular ends; and the probability that they will agree on a particular course of action necessarily decreases as the scope of such action extends. There are certain functions of the state on the exercise of which there will be practical unanimity among its citizens; there will be others on which there will be agreement of a substantial majority; and so on, until we come to fields where, although each individual might wish the state to act in some way, there will be almost as many views about what the government should do as there are different people.

We can rely on voluntary agreement to guide the action of the state only so long as it is confined to spheres where agreement exists. But not only when the state undertakes direct control in fields where there is no such agreement is it bound to suppress individual freedom. We can unfortunately not indefinitely extend the sphere of common action and still leave the individual free in his own sphere. Once the communal sector, in which the state controls all the means, exceeds a certain proportion of the whole, the effects of its actions dominate the whole system. Although the state controls directly the use of only a large part of the available resources, the effects of its decisions on the remaining part of the economic system become so great that indirectly it controls almost everything. Where, as was, for example, true in Germany as early as 1928, the central and local authorities directly control the use of more than half the national income (according to an official German estimate then, 53 per cent), they control indirectly almost the whole economic life of the nation. There is, then, scarcely an individual end which is not dependent for its achievement on the action of the state, and the "social scale of values" which guides the state's action must embrace practically all individual ends.

It is not difficult to see what must be the consequences when democracy embarks upon a course of planning which in is execution requires more agreement than in fact exists. The people may have agreed on adopting a system of directed economy because they have been convinced that it will produce great prosperity. In the discussions leading to the decision, the goal of planning will have been described by some such term as "common welfare," which only conceals the absence of real agreement on the ends of planning. Agreement will in fact exist only on the mechanism to be used. But it is a mechanism which can be used only for a common end; and the question of the precise goal toward which all activity is to be directed will arise as soon as the executive power has to translate the demand for a single plan into a particular plan. Then it will appear that the agreement on the desirability of planning is not supported by agreement on the ends the plan is to serve. The effect of the people's agreeing that there must be central planning, without agreeing on the ends, will be rather as if a group of people were to commit themselves to take a journey together without agreeing where they want to go: with the result that they may all have to make a journey which most of them do not want at all. That planning creates a situation in which it is necessary for us to agree on a much larger number of topics than we have been used to, and that in a planned system we cannot confine collective action to the tasks on which we can agree but are forced to produce agreement on everything in order that any action can be taken at all, is one of the features which contributes more than most to determining the character of a planned system.

It may be the unanimously expressed will of the people that its parliament should prepare a comprehensive economic plan, yet neither the people nor its representatives need therefore be able to agree on any particular plan. The inability of democratic assemblies to carry out what seems to be a clear mandate of the people will inevitably cause dissatisfaction with democratic institutions. Parliaments come to be regarded as ineffective "talking shops," unable or incompetent to carry out the tasks for which they have been chosen. The conviction grows that if efficient planning is to be done, the direction must be "taken out of politics" and placed in the hands of experts—permanent officials or independent autonomous bodies.

The difficulty is well known to socialists. It will soon be half a century since the Webbs began to complain of "the increased incapacity of the House of Commons to cope with its work."[1] More recently, Professor Laski has elaborated the argument:

"It is common ground that the present parliamentary machine is quite unsuited to pass rapidly a great body of complicated legislation. The National Government, indeed, has in substance admitted this by implementing its economy and tariff measures not by detailed debate in the House of Commons but by a wholesale system of delegated legislation. A Labour Government would, I presume, build upon the amplitude of this precedent. It would confine the House of Commons to the two functions it can properly perform: the ventilation of grievances and the discussion of general principles of its measures. Its Bills would take the form of general formulae conferring wide powers on the appropriate government departments; and those powers would be exercised by Order in Council which could, if desired, be attacked in the House by means of a vote of no confidence. The necessity and value of delegated legislation has recently been strongly reaffirmed by the Donoughmore Committee; and its extension is inevitable if the process of socialization is not to be wrecked by the normal methods of obstruction which existing parliamentary procedure sanctions."

And to make it quite clear that a socialist government must not allow itself to be too much fettered by democratic procedure, Professor Laski at the end of the same article raised the question "whether in a period of transition to Socialism, a Labour Government can risk the overthrow of its measures as a result of the next general election"—and left it significantly unanswered.[2]

It is important clearly to see the causes of this admitted ineffectiveness of parliaments when it comes to a detailed administration of the economic affairs of a nation. The fault is neither with the individual representatives nor with parliamentary institutions as such but with the contradictions inherent in the task with which they are charged. They are not asked to act where they can agree, but to produce agreement on everything—the whole direction of the resources of the nation. For such a task the system of majority decision is, however, not suited. Majorities will be found where it is a choice between limited alternatives; but it is a superstition to believe that there must be a majority view on everything. There is no reason why there should be a majority in favor of any one of the different possible courses of positive action if their number is legion. Every member of the legislative assembly might prefer some particular plan for the direction of economic activity to no plan, yet no one plan may appear preferable to a majority to no plan at all.

Nor can a coherent plan be achieved by breaking it up into parts and voting on particular issues. A democratic assembly voting and amending a comprehensive economic plan clause by clause, as it deliberates on an ordinary bill, makes nonsense. An economic plan, to deserve the name, must have a unitary conception. Even if a parliament could, proceeding step by step, agree on some scheme, it would certainly in the end satisfy nobody. A complex whole in which all the parts must be most carefully adjusted to each other cannot be achieved through a compromise between conflicting views. To draw up an economic plan in this fashion is even less possible than, for example, successfully to plan a military campaign by democratic procedure. As in strategy it would become inevitable to delegate the task to the experts.

Yet the difference is that, while the general who is put in charge of a campaign is given a single end to which, for the duration of the campaign, all the means under his control have to be exclusively devoted, there can be no such single goal given to the economic planner, and no similar limitation of the means imposed upon him. The general has not got to balance different independent aims against each other; there is for him only one supreme goal. But the ends of an economic plan, or of any part of it, cannot be defined apart from the particular plan. It is the essence of the economic problem that the making of an economic plan involves the choice between conflicting or competing ends—different needs of different people. But which ends do so conflict, which will have to be sacrificed if we want to achieve certain others, in short, which are the alternatives between which we must choose, can only be known to those who know all the facts; and only they, the experts, are in a position to decide which of the different ends are to be given preference. It is inevitable that they should impose their scale of preferences on the community for which they plan.

This is not always clearly recognized, and delegation is usually justified by the technical character of the task. But this does not mean that only the technical detail is delegated, or even that the inability of parliaments to understand the technical detail is the root of the difficulty.[3] Alterations in the structure of civil law are no less technical and no more difficult to appreciate in all their implications; yet nobody has yet seriously suggested that legislation there should be delegated to a body of experts. The fact is that in these fields legislation does not go beyond general rules on which true majority agreement can be achieved, while in the direction of economic activity the interests to be reconciled are so divergent that no true agreement is likely to be reached in a democratic assembly.

It should be recognized, however, that it is not the delegation of law-making power as such which is so objectionable. To oppose delegation as such is to oppose a symptom instead of the cause and, as it may be a necessary result of other causes, to weaken the case. So long as the power that is delegated is merely the power to make general rules, there may be very good reasons why such rules should be laid down by local rather than by the central authority. The objectionable feature is that delegation is so often resorted to because the matter in hand cannot be regulated by general rules but only by the exercise of discretion in the decision of particular cases. In these instances delegation means that some authority is given power to make with the force of law what to all intents and purposes are arbitrary decisions (usually described as "judging the case on its merits").

The delegation of particular technical tasks to separate bodies, while a regular feature, is yet only the first step in the process whereby a democracy which embarks on planning progressively relinquishes its powers. The expedient of delegation cannot really remove the causes which make all the advocates of comprehensive planning so impatient with the impotence of democracy. The delegation of particular powers to separate agencies creates a new obstacle to the achievement of a single coordinated plan. Even if, by this expedient, a democracy should succeed in planning every sector of economic activity, it would still have to face the problem of integrating these separate plans into a unitary whole. Many separate plans do not make a planned whole—in fact, as the planners ought to be the first to admit, they may be worse than no plan. But the democratic legislature will long hesitate to relinquish the decisions on really vital issues, and so long as it does so it makes it impossible for anyone else to provide the comprehensive plan. Yet agreement that planning is necessary, together with the inability of democratic assemblies to produce a plan, will evoke stronger and stronger demands that the government or some single individual should be given powers to act on their own responsibility. The belief is becoming more and more widespread that, if things are to get done, the responsible authorities must be freed from the fetters of democratic procedure.

The cry for an economic dictator is a characteristic stage in the movement toward planning. It is now several years since one of the most acute of foreign students of England, the late Élie Halévy, suggested that, "if you take a composite photograph of Lord Eustace Percy, Sir Oswald Mosley, and

Sir Stafford Cripps, I think you would find this common feature—you would find them all agreeing to say: 'We are living in economic chaos and we cannot get out of it except under some kind of dictatorial leadership.' "[4] The number of influential public men whose inclusion would not materially alter the features of the "composite photograph" has since grown considerably.

In Germany, even before Hitler came into power, the movement had already progressed much further. It is important to remember that, for some time before 1933, Germany had reached a stage in which it had, in effect, had to be governed dictatorially. Nobody could then doubt that for the time being democracy had broken down and that sincere democrats like Bruning were no more able to govern democratically than Schleicher or von Papen. Hitler did not have to destroy democracy; he merely took advantage of the decay of democracy and at the critical moment obtained the support of many to whom, though they detested Hitler, he yet seemed the only man strong enough to get things done.

The argument by which the planners usually try to reconcile us with this development is that, so long as democracy retains ultimate control, the essentials of democracy are not affected. Thus Karl Mannheim writes:

> The only [sic] way in which a planned society differs from that of the nineteenth century is that more and more spheres of social life, and ultimately each and all of them, are subjected to state control. But if a few controls can be held in check by parliamentary sovereignty, so can many . . . . In a democratic state sovereignty can be boundlessly strengthened by plenary powers without renouncing democratic control.[5]

This belief overlooks a vital distinction. Parliament can, of course, control the execution of tasks where it can give definite directions, where it has first agreed on the aim and merely delegates the working-out of the detail. The situation is entirely different when the reason for the delegation is that there is no real agreement on the ends, when the body charged with the planning has to choose between ends of whose conflict parliament is not even aware, and when the most that can be done is to present to it a plan which has to be accepted or rejected as a whole. There may and probably will be criticism; but as no majority can agree on an alternative plan, and the parts objected to can almost always be represented as essential parts of the whole, it will remain quite ineffective. Parliamentary discussion may be retained as a useful safety valve and even more as a convenient medium through which the official answers to complaints are disseminated. It may even prevent some flagrant abuses and successfully insist on particular shortcomings being remedied. But it cannot direct. It will at best be reduced to choosing the persons who are to have practically absolute power. The whole system will tend toward that plebiscitarian dictatorship in which the head of the government is from time to time confirmed in his position by popular vote, but where he has all the powers at his command to make certain that the vote will go in the direction he desires.

It is the price of democracy that the possibilities of conscious control are restricted to the fields where true agreement exists and that in some fields things must be left to chance. But in a society which for its functioning depends on central planning this control cannot be made dependent on a majority's being able to agree; it will often be necessary that the will of a small minority be imposed upon the people, because this minority will be the largest group able to agree among themselves on the question at issue. Democratic government has worked successfully where, and so long as, the functions of government were, by a widely accepted creed, restricted to fields where agreement among a majority could be achieved by free discussion; and it is the great merit of the liberal creed that it reduced the range of subjects on which agreement was necessary to one on which it was likely to exist in a society of free men. It is now often said that democracy will not tolerate "capitalism." If "capitalism" means here a competitive system based on free disposal over private property, it is far more important to realize that only within this system is democracy possible. When it becomes dominated by a collectivist creed, democracy will inevitably destroy itself.

We have no intention, however, of making a fetish of democracy. It may well be true that our generation talks and thinks too much of democracy and too little of the values which it serves. It cannot be said of democracy, as Lord Acton truly said of liberty, that it "is not a means to a higher political end. It is itself the highest political end. It is not for the sake of a good public administration that it is required, but for the security in the pursuit of the highest objects of civil society, and of private life." Democracy is essentially a means, a utilitarian device for safeguarding internal peace and individual freedom. As such it is by no means infallible or certain. Nor must we forget that there has often been much more cultural and spiritual freedom under an autocratic rule than under some democracies— and it is at least conceivable that under the government of a very homogeneous and doctrinaire majority democratic government might be as oppressive as the worst dictatorship. Our point, however, is not that dictatorship must inevitably extirpate freedom but rather that planning leads to dictatorship because dictatorship is the most effective instrument of coercion and the enforcement of ideals and, as such, essential if central planning on a large scale is to be possible. The clash between planning and democracy arises simply from the fact that the latter is an obstacle to the suppression of freedom which the direction of economic activity requires. But in so far as democracy ceases to be a guaranty of individual freedom, it may well persist in some form under a totalitarian regime. A true "dictatorship of the proletariat," even if democratic in form, if it undertook centrally to direct the economic system, would probably destroy personal freedom as completely as any autocracy has ever done.

The fashionable concentration on democracy as the main value threatened is not without danger. It is largely responsible for the misleading and unfounded belief that, so long as the ultimate source of power is the will of the majority, the power cannot be arbitrary. The false assurance which many people derive from this belief is an important cause of the general unawareness of the dangers which we face. There is no justification for the belief that, so long as power is conferred by democratic procedure, it cannot be arbitrary; the contrast suggested by this statement is altogether false: it is not the source but the limitation of power which prevents it from being arbitrary. Democratic control *may* prevent power from becoming arbitrary, but it does not do so by its mere existence. If democracy resolves on a task which necessarily involves the use of power which cannot be guided by fixed rules, it must become arbitrary power.

Notes

1. Sidney and Beatrice Webb, *Industrial Democracy* (1897), p. 800 n.

2. H.J. Laski, "Labour and the Constitution," *New Statesman and Nation*, No. 81 (new ser.), September 10, 1932, p. 277. In a book (*Democracy in Crisis* [1933], particularly p. 87) in which Professor Laski later elaborated these ideas, his determination that parliamentary democracy must not be allowed to form an obstacle to the realization of socialism is even more plainly expressed: not only would a socialist government "take vast powers and legislate under them by ordinance and decree" and "suspend the classic formulae of normal opposition" but the "continuance of parliamentary government would depend on its [i.e., the Labour government's] possession of guarantees from the Conservative Party that its work of transformation would not be disrupted by repeal in the event of its defeat at the polls"!

    As Professor Laski invokes the authority of the Donoughmore Committee, it may be worth recalling that Professor Laski was a member of that committee and presumably one of the authors of its report.

3. It is instructive in this connection briefly to refer to the government document in which in recent years these problems have been discussed. As long as thirteen years ago, that is before England finally abandoned economic liberalism, the process of delegating legislative powers had already been carried to a point where it was felt necessary to appoint a committee to investigate "what safeguards are desirable or necessary to secure the sovereignty of Law." In its report the Donoughmore Committee (*Report of the [Lord Chancellor's] Committee in Ministers' Powers*, Cmd. 4060 [1932]) showed that even at that date Parliament had resorted "to the practice of wholesale and indiscriminate delegation" but regarded this (it was before we had really glanced into the totalitarian abyss!) as an inevitably and relatively innocuous development. And it is probably true that delegation as such need not be a dan-

ger to freedom. The interesting point is why delegation had become necessary on such a scale. First place among the causes enumerated in the report is given to the fact that "Parliament nowadays passes so many laws every year" and that "much of the detail is so technical as to be unsuitable for Parliamentary discussion." But if this were all there would be no reason why the detail should not be worked out *before* rather than after Parliament passes a law. What is probably in many cases a much more important reason why, "if Parliament were not willing to delegate law-making power, Parliament would be unable to pass the kind and quantity of legislation which public opinion requires" is innocently revealed in the little sentence that "many of the laws affect people's lives so closely that elasticity is essential"! What does this mean if not conferment of arbitrary power—power limited by no fixed principles and which in the opinion of Parliament cannot be limited by definite and unambiguous rules?

4.   "Socialism and the Problems of Democratic Parliamentarism," *International Affairs*, XIII, 501.

5.   *Man and Society in an Age of Reconstruction* (1940), p. 340.

PLANNING AND THE RULE OF LAW

Friedrich A. Hayek

> Recent studies in the sociology of law once more confirm that the fundamental principle of formal law by which every case must be judged according to general rational precepts, which have a few exceptions as possible and are based on logical subsumptions, obtains only for the liberal competitive phase of capitalism.
>
> —*Karl Mannheim.*

Nothing distinguishes more clearly conditions in a free country from those in a country under arbitrary government than the observance in the former of the great principles known as the Rule of Law. Stripped of all technicalities, this means that government in all its actions is bound by rules fixed and announced beforehand—rules which make it possible to foresee with fair certainty how the authority will use its coercive powers in given circumstances and to plan one's individual affairs on the basis of this knowledge.[1] Though this ideal can never be perfectly achieved, since legislators as well as those to whom the administration of the law is intrusted are fallible men, the essential point, that the discretion left to the executive organs wielding coercive power should be reduced as much as possible, is clear enough. While every law restricts individual freedom to some extent by altering the means which people may use in the pursuit of their aims, under the Rule of Law the government is prevented from stultifying individual efforts by *ad hoc* action. Within the known rules of the game the individual is free to pursue his personal ends and desires, certain that the powers of government will not be used deliberately to frustrate his efforts.

The distinction we have drawn before between the creation of a permanent framework of laws within which the productive activity is guided by individual decisions and the direction of economic activity by a central authority is thus really a particular case of the more general distinction between the Rule of Law and arbitrary government. Under the first the government confines itself to fixing rules determining the conditions under which the available resources may be used, leaving to the individuals the decision for what ends they are to be used. Under the second the government directs the use of the means of production to particular ends. The first type of rules can be made in advance, in the shape of *formal rules* which do not aim at the wants and needs of particular people. They are intended to be merely instrumental in the pursuit of people's various individual ends. And they are, or ought to be, intended for such long periods that it is impossible to know whether they will assist particular people more than others. They could almost be described as a kind of instrument of production, helping people to predict the behavior of those with whom they must collaborate, rather than as efforts toward the satisfaction of particular needs.

Economic planning of the collectivist kind necessarily involves the very opposite of this. The planning authority cannot confine itself to providing opportunities for unknown people to make whatever use of them they like. It cannot tie itself down in advance to general and formal rules which prevent arbitrariness. It must provide for the actual needs of people as they arise and then choose deliberately between them. It must constantly decide questions which cannot be answered by formal principles only, and, in making these decisions, it must set up distinctions of merit between the needs of different people. When the government has to decide how many pigs are to be raised or how many busses are to be run, which coal mines are to operate, or at what prices shoes are to be sold, these decisions cannot be deduced from formal principles or settled for long periods in advance. They depend inevitably on the circumstances of the moment, and, in making such decisions, it will always be necessary to balance one against the other the interests of various persons and groups. In the end somebody's views will have to decide whose interests are more important; and these views must become part of the law of the land, a new distinction of rank which the coercive apparatus of government imposes upon the people.

The distinction we have just used between formal law or justice and substantive rules is very important and at the same time most difficult to draw precisely in practice. Yet the general principle involved is simple enough. The difference between the two kinds of rules is the same as that between laying down a Rule of the Road, as in the Highway Code, and ordering people where to go; or, better still, between providing signposts and commanding people which road to take. The formal rules tell people in advance what action the state will take in certain types of situation, defined in general terms, without reference to time and place or particular people. They refer to typical situations into which anyone may get and in which the existence of such rules will be useful for a great variety of individual purposes. The knowledge that in such situations the state will act in a definite way, or require people to behave in a certain manner, is provided as a means for people to use in making their own plans. Formal rules are the merely instrumental in the sense that they are expected to be useful to yet unknown people, for purposes for which these people will decide to use for them, and in circumstances which cannot be foreseen in detail. In fact, that we do *not* know their concrete effect, that we do *not* know what particular ends these rules will further, or which particular people they will assist, that they are merely given the form most likely on the whole to benefit all the people affected by them, is the most important criterion of formal rules in the sense in which we here use this term. They do not involve a choice between particular ends or particular people, because we just cannot know beforehand by whom and in what way they will be used.

In our age, with its passion for conscious control of everything, it may appear paradoxical to claim as a virtue that under one system we shall know less about the particular effect of the measures the state takes than would be true under most other systems and that a method of social control should be deemed superior because of our ignorance of its precise results. Yet this consideration is in fact the rationale of the great liberal principle of the Rule of Law. And the apparent paradox dissolves rapidly when we follow the argument a little further.

This argument is twofold; the first is economic and can here only briefly be stated. The state should confine itself to establishing rules applying to general types of situations and should allow the individuals freedom in everything which depends on the circumstances of time and place, because only the individuals concerned in each instance can fully know these circumstances and adapt their actions to them. If the individuals are to be able to use their knowledge effectively in making plans, they must be able to predict actions of the state which may affect these plans. But if the actions of the state are to be predictable, they must be determined by rules fixed independently of the concrete circumstances which can be neither foreseen nor taken into account beforehand: and the particular effects of such actions will be unpredictable. If, on the other hand, the state were to direct the individual's actions so as to achieve particular ends, its action would have to be decided on the basis of the full circumstances of the moment and would therefore be unpredictable. Hence the familiar fact that the more the state "plans," the more difficult planning becomes for the individual.

The second, moral or political, argument is even more directly relevant to the point under discussion. If the state is precisely to foresee the incidence of its actions, it means that it can leave those affected no choice. Wherever the state can exactly foresee the effects on particular people of alternative courses of action, it is also the state which chooses between the different ends. If we want to create new opportunities open to all, to offer chances of which people can make what use they like, the precise results cannot be foreseen. General rules, genuine laws as distinguished from specific orders, must therefore be intended to operate in circumstances which cannot be foreseen in detail, and, therefore, their effect on particular ends or particular people cannot be known beforehand. It is in this sense alone that it is at all possible for the legislator to be impartial. To be impartial means to have no answer to certain questions—to the kind of questions which, if we have to decide them, we decide by tossing a coin. In a world where everything was precisely foreseen, the state could hardly do anything and remain impartial.

Where the precise effects of government policy on particular people are known, where the government aims directly at such particular effects, it cannot help knowing these effects, and therefore it cannot be impartial. It must, of necessity, take sides, impose its valuations upon people and, instead of assisting them in the advancement of their own ends, choose the ends for them. As soon as the particular effects are foreseen at the time a law is made, it ceases to be a mere instrument to be used by the people and becomes instead an instrument used by the lawgiver upon the people and for his ends. The state ceases to be a piece of utilitarian machinery intended to help individuals in the fullest development of their individual personality and becomes a "moral" institution—where "moral" is not used in contrast to immoral but describes an institution which imposes on its members its views on all moral questions, whether these views be moral or highly immoral. In this sense the Nazi or any other collectivist state is "moral," while the liberal state is not.

Perhaps it will be said that all this raises no serious problem because in the kind of questions which the economic planner would have to decide he need not and should not be guided by his individual prejudices but could rely on the general conviction of what is fair and reasonable. This contention usually receives support from those who have experience of planning in a particular industry and who find that there is no insuperable difficulty about arriving at a decision which all those immediately interested will accept as fair. The reason why this experience proves nothing is, of course, the selection of the "interests" concerned when planning is confined to a particular industry. Those most immediately interested in a particular issue are not necessarily the best judges of the interests of society as a whole. To take only the most characteristic case: when capital and labor in an industry agree on some policy of restriction and thus exploit the consumers, there is usually no difficulty about the division of the spoils in proportion to former earnings or on some similar principle. The loss which is divided between thousands or millions is usually either simply disregarded or quite inadequately considered. It we want to test the usefulness of the principle of "fairness" in deciding the kind of issues which arise in economic planning, we must apply it to some question where the gains and the losses are seen equally clearly. In such instances it is readily recognized that no general principle such as fairness can provide an answer. When we have to choose between higher wages for nurses or doctors and more extensive services for the sick, more milk for children and better wages for agricultural workers, or between employment for the unemployed or better wages for those already employed, nothing short of a complete system of values in which every want of every person or group has a definite place is necessary to provide an answer.

In fact, as planning becomes more and more extensive, it becomes regularly necessary to qualify legal provisions increasingly by reference to what is "fair" or "reasonable"; this means that it becomes necessary to leave the decision of the concrete case more and more to the discretion of the judge or authority in question. One could write a history of the decline of the Rule of Law, the disappearance of the *Rechtsstaat*, in terms of the progressive introduction of these vague formulas into legislation and jurisdiction, and of the increasing arbitrariness and uncertainty of, and the consequent disrespect for, the law and the judicature, which in these circumstances could not but become an instrument of policy. It is important to point out once more in this connection that this process of the decline of the Rule of Law had been going on steadily in Germany for some time before Hitler came into power and that a policy well advanced toward totalitarian planning had already done a great deal of the work which Hitler completed.

There can be no doubt that planning necessarily involves deliberate discrimination between particular needs of different people, and allowing one man to do what another must be prevented from doing. It must lay down by a legal rule how well off particular people shall be and what different people are to be allowed to have and do. It means in effect a return to the rule of status, a reversal of the "movement of progressive societies" which, in the famous phrase of Sir Henry Maine, "has hitherto been a movement from status to contract." Indeed, the Rule of Law, more than the rule of contract, should probably be regarded as the true opposite of the rule of status. It is the Rule of Law, in the sense of the rule of formal law, the absence of legal privileges of particular people designated by authority, which safeguards that equality before the law which is the opposite of arbitrary government.

A necessary, and only apparently paradoxical, result of this is that formal equality before the law is in conflict, and in fact incompatible, with any activity of the government deliberately aiming at material or substantive equality of different people, and that any policy aiming directly at a substantive ideal of distributive justice must lead to the destruction of the Rule of Law. To produce the same result for different people, it is necessary to treat them differently. To give different people the same objective opportunities is not to give them the same subjective chance. It cannot be denied that the Rule of Law produces economic inequality—all that can be claimed for it is that this inequality is not designed to affect particular people in a particular way. It is very significant and characteristic that socialists (and Nazis) have always protested against "merely" formal justice, that they have always objected to a law which had no views on how well off particular people ought to be,[2] and that they have always demanded a "socialization of the law," attacked the independence of judges, and at the same time given their support to all such movements as the *Freirechtsschule* which undermined the Rule of Law.

It may even be said that for the Rule of Law to be effective it is more important that there should be a rule applied always without exceptions than what this rule is. Often the content of the rule is indeed of minor importance, provided the same rule is universally enforced. To revert to a former example: it does not matter whether we all drive on the left- or on the right-hand side of the road so long as we all do the same. The important thing is that the rule enables us to predict other people's behavior correctly, and this requires that it should apply to all cases—even if in a particular instance we feel it to be unjust.

The conflict between formal justice and formal equality before the law, on the one hand, and the attempts to realize various ideals of substantive justice and equality, on the other, also accounts for the widespread confusion about the concept of "privilege" and its consequent abuse. To mention only the most important instance of this abuse—the application of the term "privilege" to property as such. It would indeed be privilege if, for example, as has sometimes been the case in the past, landed property were reserved to members of the nobility. And it is privilege if, as is true in our time, the right to produce or sell particular things is reserved to particular people designated by authority. But to call private property as such, which all can acquire under the same rules, a privilege, because only some succeed in acquiring it, is depriving the word "privilege" of its meaning.

The unpredictability of the particular effects, which is the distinguishing characteristic of the formal laws of a liberal system, is also important because it helps us to clear up another confusion about the nature of this system: the belief that its characteristic attitude is inaction of the state. The question whether the state should or should not "act" or "interfere" poses an altogether false alternative, and the term "laissez faire" is a highly ambiguous and misleading description of the principles on which a liberal policy is based. Of course, every state must act and every action of the state interferes with something or other. But that is not the point. The important question is whether the individual can foresee the action of the state and make use of this knowledge as a datum in forming his own plans, with the result that the state cannot control the use made of its machinery and that the individual knows precisely how far he will be protected against interference from others, or whether the state is in a position to frustrate individual efforts. The state controlling weights and measures (or preventing fraud and deception in any other way) is certainly acting, while the state permitting the use of violence, for example, by strike pickets, is inactive. Yet it is in the first case that the state observes liberal principles and in the second that it does not. Similarly with respect to most of the general and permanent rules which the state may establish with regard to production, such as building regulations or factory laws: these may be wise or unwise in the particular instance, but they do not conflict with liberal principles so long as they are intended to be permanent and are not used to favor or harm particular people. It is true that in these instances there will, apart from the long-run effects which cannot be predicted, also be short-run effects on particular people which may be clearly known. But with this kind of laws the short-run effects are in general not (or at least ought not to be) the guiding consideration. As these immediate and predictable effects become more important compared with the long-run effects, we approach the border line where the distinction, however clear in principle, becomes blurred in practice.

The Rule of Law was consciously evolved only during the liberal age and is one of its greatest achievements, not only as a safeguard but as the legal embodiment of freedom. As Immanuel Kant put it (and Voltaire expressed it before him in very much the same terms), "Man is free if he needs to obey no person but solely the laws." As a vague ideal it has, however, existed at least since Roman times, and during the last few centuries it has never been so seriously threatened as it is today. The idea that there is no limit to the powers of the legislator is in part a result of popular sovereignty and democratic government. It has been strengthened by the belief that, so long as all actions of the state are duly authorized by legislation, the Rule of Law will be preserved. But this is completely to misconceive the meaning of the Rule of Law. This rule has little to do with the question whether all actions of government are legal in the juridical sense. They may well be and yet not conform to the Rule of Law. The fact that someone has full legal authority to act in the way he does gives no answer to the question whether the law gives him power to act arbitrarily or whether the law prescribes unequivocally how he has to act. It may well be that Hitler has obtained his unlimited powers in a strictly constitutional manner and that whatever he does is therefore legal in the juridical sense. But who would suggest for that reason that the Rule of Law still prevails in Germany?

To say that in a planned society the Rule of Law cannot hold is, therefore, not to say that the actions of the government will not be legal or that such a society will necessarily be lawless. It means only that the use of the government's coercive powers will no longer be limited and determined by preestablished rules. The law can, and to make a central direction of economic activity possible must, legalize what to all intents and purposes remains arbitrary action. If the law says that such a board or authority may do what it pleases, anything that board or authority does is legal—but its actions are certainly not subject to the Rule of Law. By giving the government unlimited powers, the most arbitrary rule can be made legal; and in this way a democracy may set up the most complete despotism imaginable.[3]

If, however, the law is to enable authorities to direct economic life, it must give them powers to make and enforce decisions in circumstances which cannot be foreseen and on principles which cannot be stated in generic form. The consequence is that, as planning extends, the delegation of legislative powers to divers boards and authorities becomes increasingly common. When before the last war, in a case to which the late Lord Hewart has recently drawn attention, Mr. Justice Darling said that "Parliament had enacted only last year that the Board of Agriculture in acting as they did should be no more impeachable than Parliament itself," this was still a rare thing. It has since become an almost daily occurrence. Constantly the broadest powers are conferred on new authorities which, without being bound by fixed rules, have almost unlimited discretion in regulating this or that activity of the people.

The Rule of Law thus implies limits to the scope of legislation: it restricts it to the kind of general rules known as formal law and excludes legislation either directly aimed at particular people or at enabling anybody to use the coercive power of the state for the purpose of such discrimination. It means, not that everything is regulated by law, but, on the contrary, that the coercive power of the state can be used only in cases defined in advance by the law and in such away that it can be foreseen how it will be used. A particular enactment can thus infringe the Rule of Law. Anyone ready to deny this would have to contend that whether the Rule of Law prevails today in Germany, Italy, or Russia depends on whether the dictators have obtained their absolute power by constitutional means.[4]

Whether, as in some countries, the main applications of the Rule of Law are laid down in a bill of rights or in a constitutional code, or whether the principle is merely a firmly established tradition, matters comparatively little. But it will readily be seen that, whatever form it takes, any such recognized limitations of the powers of legislation imply the recognition of the inalienable right of the individual, inviolable rights of man.

It is pathetic but characteristic of the muddle into which many of our intellectuals have been led by the conflicting ideals in which they believe that a leading advocate of the most comprehensive central planning like H. G. Wells should at the same time write an ardent defense of the rights of man. The individual rights which Mr. Wellshopes to preserve would inevitably obstruct the planning which he desires. To some extent he seems to realize the dilemma, and we find therefore the provisions of his proposed "Declaration of the Rights of Man" so hedged about with qualifications that they lose all significance. While, for instance, his declaration proclaims that every man "shall have the right to buy and sell without any discriminatory restrictions anything which may be lawfully bought and sold," which is admirable, he immediately proceeds to make the whole provision nugatory by adding that it applies only to buying and selling "in such quantities and with such reservations as are compatible with the common welfare." But since, of course, all restrictions ever imposed upon buying or selling anything are supposed to be necessary in the interest of the "common welfare," there is really no restriction which this clause effectively prevents and no right of the individual that is safeguarded by it.

Or, to take another basic clause, the declaration states that every man "may engage in any lawful occupation" and that "he is entitled to paid employment and to a free choice whenever there is any variety of employment open to him." It is not stated, however, who is to decide whether a particular employment is "open" to a particular person, and the added provision that "he may suggest employment for himself and have his claim publicly considered, accepted or dismissed," shows that Mr. Wells is thinking in terms of an authority which decides whether a man is "entitled" to a particular position— which certainly means the opposite of free choice of occupation. And how in a planned world "freedom of travel and migration" is to be secured when not only the means of communication and currencies are controlled but also the location of industries planned, or how the freedom of the press is to be safeguarded when the supply of paper and all the channels of distribution are controlled by the planning authority, are questions to which Mr. Wells provides as little answer as any other planner.

In this respect much more consistency is shown by the more numerous reformers who, ever since the beginning of the socialist movement, have attacked the "metaphysical" idea of individual right sand insisted that in a rationally ordered world there will be no individual rights but only individual duties. This, indeed, has become the much more common attitude of our socalled "progressives,"and few things are more certain to expose one to the reproach of being a reactionary than if one protests against a measure on the grounds that it is a violation of the rights of the individual. Even a liberal paper like the *Economist* was a few years ago holding up to us the example of the French, of all people, who had learned the lesson that "democratic government no less than dictatorship must always [*sic*] have plenary powers in *posse*, without sacrificing their democratic and representative character. There is no restrictive penumbra of individual rights that can never be touched by government in administrative matters whatever the circumstances. There is no limit to the power of ruling which can and should be taken by a government freely chosen by the people and can be fully and openly criticized by an opposition."

This may be inevitable in wartime, when, of course, even free and open criticism is necessarily restricted. But the "always" in the statement quoted does not suggest that the *Economist* regards it as a regrettable wartime necessity. Yet as a permanent institution this view is certainly incompatible with the preservation of the Rule of Law, and it leads straight to the totalitarian state. It is, however, the view which all those who want the government to direct economic life must hold.

How even a formal recognition of individual rights, or of the equal rights of minorities, loses all significance in a state which embarks on a complete control of economic life, has been amply demonstrated by the experience of the various Central European countries. It has been shown there that it is possible to pursue a policy of ruthless discrimination against national minorities by the use of recognized instruments of economic policy without ever infringing the letter of the statutory protection of minority rights. This oppression by means of economic policy was greatly facilitated by the fact that particular industries or activities were largely in the hands of a national minority, so that many a measure aimed ostensibly against an industry or class was in fact aimed at a national minority. But the almost boundless possibilities for a policy of discrimination and oppression provided by such apparently innocuous principles as "government control of the development of industries" have been amply demonstrated to all those desirous of seeing how the political consequences of planning appear in practice.

Notes

1. According to the classical exposition by A. V. Dicey in *The Law of the Constitution* (8th ed.), p.198, the Rule of Law "means, in the first place, the absolute supremacy or predominance of regular law as opposed to the influence of arbitrary power, and excludes the existence of arbitrariness, of prerogative, or even of wide discretionary authority on the part of government." Largely as a result of Dicey's work the term has, however, in England acquired a narrower technical meaning which does not concern us here. The wider and older meaning of the concept of the rule or reign of law, which in England had become an established tradition which was more taken for granted than discussed, has been most fully elaborated, just because it raised what were new problems there, in the early nineteenth century discussion in Germany about the nature of the *Rechtsstaat*.

2. It is therefore not altogether false when the legal theorist of National Socialism, Carl Schmitt, opposes to the liberal *Rechsttaaat* (i.e. the Rule of Law) the National Socialist ideal of the *gerechte Staat* ("the just state")—only that the sort of justice which is opposed to formal justice necessarily implies discrimination between persons.

3. The conflict is thus *not*, as it has often been misconceived in nineteenth-century discussions, one between liberty and law. As John Locke had already made clear, there can be no liberty without law. The conflict is between different kinds of law—law so different that it should hardly be called by the same name: one is the law of the Rule of Law, general principles laid down beforehand, the "rules of the game" which enable individuals to foresee how the coercive apparatus of the state will be used, or what he and his fellow-citizens will be allowed to do, or made to do, in stated circumstances. The other kind of law gives in effect the authority power to do what it thinks fit to do. Thus the Rule of Law could clearly not be preserved in a democracy that undertook to decide every conflict of interests not according to rules previously laid down but "on its merits."

4. Another illustration of an infringement of the Rule of Law by legislation is the case of the bill of attainder, familiar in the history of England. The form which the Rule of Law takes in criminal law is usually expressed by the Latin tag *nulla poena sine lege*—no punishment without a law expressly

prescribing it. The essence of this rule is that the law must have existed as a general rule before the individual case arose to which it is to be applied. Nobody would argue that, when in a famous case in Henry VIII's reign Parliament resolved with respect to the Bishop of Rochester's cook that "the said Richard Rose shall be boiled to death without having the advantage of his clergy," this act was performed under the Rule of Law. But while the Rule of Law had become an essential part of criminal procedure in all liberal countries, it cannot be preserved in totalitarian regimes. There, as E. B. Ashton has well expressed it, the liberal maxim is replaced by the principles *nullum crimen sine poena*—no "crime" must remain without punishment, whether the law explicitly provides for it or not. "The rights of the state do not end with punishing law breakers. The community is entitled to whatever may seem necessary to the protection of its interests—of which observance of the law, as it stands, is only one of the more elementary requirements" (E.B. Ashton, *The Fascist, His State and Mind* [1937], p. 119). What is an infringement of "the interests of the community" is, of course, decided by the authorities.

THE RULE OF LAWLESSNESS

Brink Lindsey

Henry Ford's innovations in automobile production captured the centralizing imagination of the world. The assembly line, introduced at Ford's Highland Park facility in 1913, offered a dazzling display of top-down planning's productive power. Here was a rationally designed system in which every step of the production process and the role of every worker on the line had been specified and sequenced to achieve maximum possible efficiency. To the partisans of the Industrial Counterrevolution, it appeared that Ford had constructed a scale model of the centrally planned economy.

In particular, Ford's methods were celebrated throughout the Soviet Union—despite the American capitalist's strong personal antipathy toward communism. His 1922 autobiography *My Life and Work* ran through four printings there by 1925. Soviet managers studied Ford's philosophy of mass production alongside the teachings of Lenin. By 1927, Ford had supplied some 85 percent of all the trucks and tractors in the Soviet Union; the Fordson tractor inspired Fordson days and Fordson festivals in Soviet villages.[1]

In light of this history, it is a supreme irony that in rural northern India today, decades of mimicking Soviet-style policies have caused—of all things—the abandonment of the mass production of automobiles. Economic life there is so grotesquely deformed that pre-1913 production methods have once again become economically viable.

To find this strange anachronism, I set out with a colleague and a driver one morning in February 2001 to brave India's infamous rural roads. Leaving Delhi still murky with wood and dung smoke from the previous night's way through a chaos of cars, trucks, buses, motorcycles, three-wheeled "Vikrams," tractors, ox-carts, and camel carts. I even saw a man walking alongside the road with a bear on a leash—a traveling entertainer who worked his way from village to village. My colleague told me that this highway was actually a showpiece by Indian standards—at least it had a median strip. As we ventured onto smaller roads I quickly understood what he meant: With traffic on the two-lane roads undulating back and forth across both lanes to pass slow-moving tractors and camels or avoid potholes the size of bomb craters, dodging the oncoming traffic was like a video game come to life.

All along the way vehicles were overflowing with passengers—people sitting on top of a jeep-like "Mahindra," or standing on the floorboard of a van with the back door swinging open, or crammed into the back of a truck or camel cart. With a billion people, India has only around 40 million vehicles—two-, three-, and four-wheeled combined. It is a desperately poor country, to be sure, but in this particular respect the poverty is a matter of explicit policy. Vehicle prices are grossly inflated by punishingly high taxes: Total duties on used cars, for instance, are 180 percent. Although American, Japanese, and Korean auto companies now assemble vehicles in India, their products are well out of financial reach for most Indians.

With admirable ingenuity and initiative, rural Indians have decided to take matters into their own hands: They are now building their own automobiles. Known alternately as "jugaad," a "maruta," or a "boogi," the vehicle offers basic, barebones transportation for Indian farmers. It has no roof, the 10 to 14 horsepower engine must be hand-cranked and maxes out around 15 miles per hour, and the driver sits on a wooden bench. But the rear compartment—a plywood bed with wood-panel sides—has plenty of room for passengers or cargo. And with a price tag of only around $1,000, it is an unbeatable bargain.

We found boogi manufacturers in the remote village of Toda Bhim in eastern Rajasthan. There were no assembly lines, no factories at all—just three small mechanic's garages spaced out along the semi-paved road that runs through the village. The mechanics buy minivan spare parts—wheels, axles, transmissions, gear boxes, and steering—from markets in Delhi; they get their engines, made to power water pumps, from Agra; and they pick up steel for the chassis and wood for the framing from Jaipur. They cut and fit the framing and weld the chassis themselves and then assemble the rest; according to the mechanic we spoke with, one shop can turn out four or five boogis a month.

Technically, these vehicles are illegal under India's Motor Vehicles Act. They are not officially registered, they have no license plates, and they are supposedly subject to seizure by the highway patrol whenever they are found. But the law is roundly ignored. In addition to the mechanics in Toda Bhim who actually make the cars, we spoke with a dealer in the nearby town of Mahwa and several satisfied customers, and none reported any problems with the police. We even saw boogis puttering along the main Delhi-Agra highway, not 60 miles from the capital city.

The production of boogis is part of India's enormous "informal sector"—unsanctioned economic activity that is nonetheless tolerated by the authorities. You don't have to venture to out-of-the-way Toda Bhim to see informal enterprise in India. Just drive around the streets of Delhi and it will confront you at every turn and traffic light. At red lights your car will be accosted by merchants hawking various wares: Boxes of tissue paper are an especially popular item, along with balloons, maps, and even toy-sized snake charmer's baskets. You'll whizz past streetside fruit and vegetable stands and—with inexplicable frequency—pyramid stacks of motorcycle helmets for sale on the curbside. You'll pass pedaling peddlers, driving bicycle carts with loads of folded cardboard boxes, or lumber, or scrap metal. On weekends, impromptu markets spring up and take over a street; one I saw specialized in second-had clothes. And in the depressingly common garbage heaps alongside the road, you'll see scavengers rooting through the trash for things that can be recycled.

The informal sector dominates India's economic life. Only around 30 million people, or 9 percent of the labor force, work in the official, "organized" economy; everybody else, the other 91 percent, works informally. It is a breathtaking statistic: 91 percent of Indian workers operate off the books and outside the law.[2] Those 91 percent don't have the proper permits and licenses, most don't pay taxes, and few show up at all in the official economic statistics. At the same time, many are subject to incessant extortion by corrupt officials, few have any access to the courts for legal redress, and virtually none are eligible for bank loans or any other type of formal financing.

The Indian economy is thus characterized by an extreme dualism. In the organized economy, even after a decade of reforms, large-scale enterprises still groan under a crushing burden of rules, regulations, licenses, prohibitions, and taxes. Meanwhile, in the vast and sprawling shadow economy, subsistence farmers and small-scale entrepreneurs eke out their existence in the lawless void of anarchy. The Indian government is simultaneously doing far *too much* and *far too little:* On the formal sector it inflicts a gruesome excess of controls, while to the informal sector it fails to provide even the basic public good of legal protection.

These sins of commission and omission are closely interrelated. Many enterprises in the informal sector are there because they fled the onerous controls and inflated costs of the organized economy. Heavy taxes beget smuggling and avoidance; cumbersome and restrictive licensing procedures beget illicit, unlicensed enterprises; burdensome labor laws beget stunted companies that keep below the employment thresholds that trigger the laws' application.

The story of EDP Aids, an informal computer company in Delhi with ten employees, illustrates the interplay between the level of government controls and the extent of informal lawlessness. Adarsh Alreja, the founder and head of the company, told me he entered the business of manufacturing personal computers back in 1990—notwithstanding the fact that it was illegal to do so without a license. And because duties on computer parts exceeded 100 percent, he used mostly smuggled components. Despite a ridiculously low production volume by Western standards (EDP Aids never made more than about 700 PCs a year), he was able to sell his computers at half the price charged for imports or by his domestic, formal competitors. Even more amazing, his profit margin was a fat 20 to 30 percent. Before 1998, Alreja estimates, some 70 to 80 percent of PCs sold in India were informally manufactured. Here again, as with the boogis in Rajasthan, the perversity of top-down controls had led to the overthrow of mass production.

But then import duties on computers and parts started to fall—down to their present level of around 25 percent. Falling duties led to declining competitiveness and profits in the informal sector: By 2001, EDP Aids' price advantage had shrunk to 8 to 10 percent, and the profit margin had dwindled to 5 percent. Consequently, the company has all but abandoned manufacturing, assembling only around 50 PCs a year. It now concentrates on service and maintenance instead. Adarsh Alreja figures that, nationwide, the informal share of the PC market has dropped to 60 percent.

The lifting of import controls has thus succeeded in causing a partial shift away from informality. In spite of this, EDP Aids, and much of the Indian computer industry, remains outside the organized economy. Why? Complying with the excess tax regime to which formal companies are subject would be impossible; the company would have to request and undergo a formal inspection before shipping each piece of merchandise. Furthermore, by staying informal, EDP Aids can avoid making social welfare deductions from workers' paychecks—and thus entice better workers with higher take-home pay. Also, as the head of an informal enterprise, Adarsh Alreja can hire and fire workers as he sees fit without any interference from India's onerous labor laws.

Informality, though, carries heavy costs. Most obviously, productivity suffers grievously because of the inability to exploit scale economies. The production of a few automobiles a month, or a few computers a day, is an absurdity in light of currently available technology. If boogis and informal computers were mass-produced, they could be made for a fraction of the current cost—and sold for a fraction of the current price. But in the informal sector, such obvious and enormous productivity gains are unattainable. Any enterprise large enough to realize them would be too big for the authorities to ignore; it would be swept into the formal sector's tangle of rules and requirements, and so would lose the cost advantages that allowed it to expand in the first place. Furthermore, growth requires capital, and the enterprises in the shadow economy had no access to formal financing. All expansion must be financed out of cash flow, or from woefully inefficient informal sources at grossly inflated interest rates. Consequently, informal enterprises are stunted by lack of resources as well as the need to avoid the heavy burdens of formality. Profligate wastefulness—and the agonizing persistence of mass poverty—is the inevitable and tragic result.

* * *

India's informal sector is only an especially egregious example of a global phenomenon. In Latin America, for example, the sprawling *favelas* of Brazil are perhaps the most familiar face of a pervasive shadow economy. In Brazil, as well as Costa Rica, Honduras, Panama, and Venezuela, 40 percent or more of total employment is informal; in Bolivia and Paraguay the figure tops 50 percent, while roughly 65 percent of Guatemalans work outside the organized economy.[3] Meanwhile, in Southeast Asia, over 70 percent of workers in heavily rural Thailand and Indonesia operate in the informal sector. Even in urban areas, roughly half of Thai workers are informal.

Estimating the size of informal economic output is a task fraught with difficulty. How, after all, does one measure that which is officially ignored and, indeed, often strives to remain hidden? In one recent study, economists Friedrich Schneider and Dominik Enste tried, among other things, to compare official GDP statistics to estimates of GDP based on electricity consumption. There is a strong and well-established empirical relationship between electricity use and overall economic activity; accordingly, by comparing the official numbers to those predicted by power consumption, it is possible to get at least a rough idea of the size of the unofficial, or informal, economy.

Using this methodology, Schneider and Enste found that the informal sector contributes substantially to total output throughout the developing and transition economies. Here are some of their estimated ratios of shadow economy output to official GDP for select developing countries: Malaysia, 39 percent; Peru, 44 percent; Mexico, 49 percent; Philippines, 50 percent; Egypt, 68 percent; and Nigeria, 76 percent. Schneider and Enste used two different data sources to calculate average ratios of 20.9 percent and 31.6 percent for the transition economies of Central and Eastern Europe; in the former Soviet Union, the average ratio of informal output to official GDP ranged from 35.3 percent to 43.6 percent.[4]

Peruvian author and political advisor Hernando de Soto has done more than just about anybody to bring the informal sector and its workings to public attention. In his pioneering 1989 book *The Other Path,* he showed that private property and market exchange, far from being tools of oppression imposed upon the poor of Latin America, are in fact being generated spontaneously by those very poor to free themselves from unworkable collectivist policies. Large and vibrant informal economies—created by the humblest elements of society in the fact of official indifference and even hostility—are proof of market competition's indispensable usefulness. But what this people's capitalism lacks, argues de Soto, and what it desperately needs in order to fulfill its wealth-creating potential, is formal recognition and legal protection.

In his latest book, *The Mystery of Capital,* de Soto attempts to measure the amount of wealth locked up in informal sectors around the developing and postcommunist worlds. To simplify the task, he and his colleagues at the Institute for Liberty and Democracy in Lima looked only at informal real estate. In de Soto's native Peru, they estimate that 53 percent of people in urban areas and 81 percent of people in rural areas live in dwellings to which nobody has clear title. In the Philippines, the corresponding figures are 57 percent and 67 percent, respectively; in Haiti, 68 percent and 97 percent; and in Egypt, 92 percent and 83 percent.[5]

Although these informal properties are certainly modest, collectively they represent enormous treasure troves of untapped wealth. In the Philippines, for example, the estimated value of informal housing is $133 billion—or four times the total capitalization of the stock market, seven times all the deposits in commercial banks, nine times the capital of all the state-owned enterprises, and 14 times the value of all foreign direct investment. De Soto estimates that the total value of informal real estate in the world is an astonishing $9.3 trillion—20 times the total foreign direct investment in all developing and transition economies since 1989, 46 times all the World Bank loans for the past three decades, and 93 times the total official development assistance from all rich countries over the same time span.[6] Unfortunately, all of this vast potential capital remains trapped in legal limbo.

Those of us who live in rich countries are used to thinking of the "underground" economy as marginal—and indeed for us it largely is.[7] But in the poorer nations, where most of the world's population lives and works, it is a different story altogether. There, the informal sector has become a major, even dominant, presence in economic life. The disastrously dysfunctional policies of the old Third World, once trumpeted as salvation for the struggling masses, have in fact exiled great multitudes of the poor and uneducated to a kind of legal wilderness. Into that same wilderness have wandered large numbers of refugees from the collapse of communism's economic structures—and the failure to build in their stead functioning market institutions. In this wilderness there is survival, and escape from oppression, but self-sustaining economic development remains out of reach.

* * *

It is widely but mistakenly assumed that support for free markets equals hostility toward government. Economic liberals who advocate dismantling or reforming failed collectivist policies are routinely characterized by their opponents as spoiling for anarchy.

Even someone as generally sympathetic to markets as Thomas Friedman succumbs to this confusion. Although an enthusiastic champion of globalization, Friedman retains his allegiance to certain aspects of the collectivist legacy—notably top-down social welfare programs in the domestic sphere and International Monetary Fund bailouts internationally. In *The Lexus and the Olive Tree*, he heaps contempt upon anyone who would question his particular sacred cows. "I heard mean-spirited voices," he writes, "voices uninterested in any compromise, voices for whom the American government was some kind of evil enemy." In particular, he lampoons the freshman congressional Republicans who swept their party to legislative power in the elections of 1994:

> I said to myself, "Well, my freshman Republican friends, come to Africa—it's a freshman Republican's paradise." Yes sir, nobody in Liberia pays taxes. There's no gun control in Angola. There's no welfare as we know it in Burundi and no big government to interfere in the market in Rwanda. But a lot of their people sure wish there were.[8]

Friedman is thrashing a straw man. Economic liberals—"free market ideologues" or "market fundamentalists" as they are called by those who disagree with them on any particular point—are hostile only to the collectivist hypertrophy of government, not government itself. As I addressed in Chapter 3, economic liberals recognize that strong and effective government is essential to the vitality and proper functioning of markets. Specifically, the ongoing development of a healthy market order entails the articulation of an increasingly complex division of labor—one that unites large numbers of people, the vast majority of whom don't know each other and, indeed, are only dimly aware of each other, in cooperative projects that may take many years to bear fruit. That level of social cooperation is possible only within a framework of clear and reliable rules for acquiring, holding, and transferring property. The great public good of market competition depends in turn upon the public good of a well-constructed legal infrastructure—whose construction and maintenance require the agencies of government.

But due in no small part to the Industrial Counterrevolution, most people in the world live under governments that fail to provide the necessary legal infrastructure. The persistent influence of the dead hand can thus be seen in the fact that contemporary governments are doing too little as well as too much. The present-day program of economic liberalism, especially in developing and transition economies, calls for greater government activism in addition to greater restraint.

The existence of large informal sectors is only one symptom of a broader institutional failure. It is not just that legal systems exclude large areas of economic life; they also fail to serve well those areas they do cover. The formal sectors of poorer countries are plagued by inadequate and unreliable legal infrastructure. Unclear or conflicting definitions of rights, unreasonable costs and delays in obtaining legal relief, inadequate enforcement of legal rulings, and endemic corruption all hamper and distort economic development.

A widely cited study by economist Paulo Mauro attempts to quantify the consequences of poor legal institutions. Using indices (prepared by a private business intelligence firm) that measure bureaucracy, red tape, corruption, and judicial efficiency and integrity, the analysis points to a significant effect of inadequate legal systems on the amount of private investment, and thereby on the rate of economic growth. Specifically, an increase of one standard deviation in those indices (for example, a jump from Bangladesh's level of institutional quality to that of Uruguay's) would cause a jump in the investment rate of almost 5 percentage points, and a consequent jump in annual GDP growth by more than half a percentage point.[9]

To examine the problem of institutional failure in detail, take the case of Argentina. During the first age of globalization, it developed an immensely productive agricultural sector and rode the wave of export-led growth to become one of the wealthiest nations on earth. But as the international economy on which its fortunes rested disintegrated during the 1930s and '40s, this once liberal country succumbed to military dictatorship and Perónism—and steadily sank back into the economic backwardness from which it had earlier escaped. In the 1980s, the Industrial Counterrevolution in Argentina finally expired, not with a whimper, but with two bangs: first, the defeat in the Falklands War, which toppled the dictators and brought back democracy; and second, the debt crisis and hyperinflation that prompted, as a desperate last resort, the rediscovery of market-oriented policies.

Over the past decade or so, Argentina's pro-market reforms have been undeniably impressive— yet woefully inadequate. In the *Economic Freedom of the World* ratings, Argentina now scores well on many crucial elements of economic policy: 8.9 out of a possible score of 10 for monetary policy and price stability (up from a score of zero in 1985); 7.7 for the average rate of its import tariffs (up from 4.6 in 1985); and a perfect score of 10 for its privatization of government-owned enterprises (up from 4.0). Indeed, Argentina's overall score in the 2000 *Economic Freedom of the World* report ranked 12th out of 123 countries surveyed.[10]

But flourishing markets require more than good policies; they require good institutions as well. And on that score, unfortunately, Argentina's reforms have thus far accomplished virtually nothing: the country's legal and administrative infrastructure is a shambles of corruption and inefficiency. Transparency International releases an annual index of corruption levels around the world based on surveys of business people, academics, and risk analysts. In 2001, Argentina ranked a dismal 57th out of 91 countries—worse than Botswana, Namibia, Peru, Brazil, Bulgaria, and Colombia, and on the same level as notoriously corrupt China.[11] In a similar vein, the 2000 *Global Competitiveness Report,* coproduced by Harvard University and the World Economic Forum, surveyed business leaders from 4,022 firms in 59 countries for their perceptions of business conditions in those countries. Argentina ranked consistently near the bottom in the perceived quality of its legal and administrative institutions: 40th in the frequency of irregular payments to government officials; 54th in the independence of the judiciary; 55th in litigation costs; 45th in corruption in the legal system; and 54th in the reliability of police protection.[12]

The dilapidation of Argentina's institutional infrastructure is a continuing legacy of the Industrial Counterrevolution. Look, for example, at the crucial question of judicial independence. Prior to the descent into statism, justices of Argentina's Supreme Court enjoyed long tenures undisturbed by political interference. Thus, at the beginning of Juan Perón 's first administration Supreme Court justices averaged 12 years on the bench. Since 1960, the average tenure has dropped below four years. Since Perón, five of 17 presidents named every member of the Court during their term; prior to Perón, only President Mitre, the country's first constitutional president, enjoyed the same distinction. Before Perón, it was typical for a majority of the Court to have been appointed by presidents from the current political opposition; afterwards, that was no longer the case.[13] The Supreme Court, the supposed bulwark of the rule of law, was reduced to a mere creature of politics.

The present era of reform has brought little improvement. President Carlos Menem, who did so much to better Argentina's policies, persisted in traducing the integrity of its institutions. Faced with a politically hostile Supreme Court, Menem responded with a court-packing scheme: He expanded the Court from five to nine members and filled the new slots with political supporters. And his transgressions did not stop there: Allegations of corruption swirled throughout his two terms in office. Those charges finally caught up with him on June 7, 2001, when the former president was arrested for his role in an illegal arms shipments deal. Such is the sad state of Argentina's legal system that it is unclear whether the prosecution of Menem represents the first step in a long overdue cleanup—or whether it is merely an act of revenge by his political opponents now that they are in power.

On the day of Menem's arrest I happened to be in Rosario, Argentina's second largest city. A small but noisy group of pro-Menem demonstrators temporarily tangled traffic that afternoon—compounding the transportation woes I was experiencing as I scrambled to get back to Buenos Aires on the eve of a one-day, nationwide general strike. (The strike, by the way, had been scheduled well beforehand as a protest of Argentina's long-running recession, but was totally upstaged by the stunning news of the former president's legal troubles.) Putting aside the petty personal inconveniences, I could not have picked a more fortuitous time to be in Argentina. I was there, after all, to investigate up close the effect of the country's ramshackle institutions on its economic prospects.

Especially illuminating was my visit to the northwestern province of Tucumán. During the "dirty war" of the 1970s, Tucumán served as a refuge for pro-Castro guerillas and was roiled by bloody fighting. Today it is better known as home to the world's largest producer of lemons, as well as a now-declining sugar industry, and its problems are more prosaic: bloated and corrupt bureaucracy, and a backward and unreliable legal system.

The public sector in Tucumán serves primarily to enrich politicians and fund patronage jobs; the provision of public services is but an afterthought. Out of a formal work force of some 400,000, there are nearly 80,000 provincial and municipal government employees and another 10,000 federal government workers. Elected officials are able to siphon off small fortunes for themselves: The annual salary for provincial legislators is roughly $300,000.[14] Tucumán is by no means noteworthy for such abuses. A true standout is the impoverished province of Formosa on the country's northern border. There about half of all formally employed workers are on the government payroll, and many of them show up on the job only once a month—to collect their paychecks.[15]

Such profligacy lies at the root of Argentina's latest financial crisis. Government spending as a percentage of gross domestic product climbed from 9.4 percent in 1989 to 21 percent in 2000—despite the fact that sweeping privatizations were at the same time relieving the government of significant fiscal burdens.[16] Free-spending provincial officials bear much of the blame: Operating expenses at the provincial level rose 25 percent from 1995 to 2000 even though inflation was nonexistent.[17] The spending binge has driven the country's external debt above 50 percent of GDP and led many investors to conclude that default, and resulting severe economic hardship, are virtually inevitable.

Meanwhile, as the public sector balloons uncontrollably, vital government responsibilities go unfulfilled—among them, the provision of a legal system that promptly and reliably vindicates the rights of the citizenry. As a result, the acute financial traumas that now beset Argentina are compounded by deeper, chronic ills—namely, a business environment that is profoundly hostile to investment, dynamism, and growth. In San Miguel de Tucumán, the capital of Tucumán province, I spoke with Ignacio Colombres Garmendia, the head of a major law firm in town. "The legal system is absolutely vital for our region's economic development," he complained, "but the politicians are blind to it. It's hard to see what doesn't happen because of a bad legal climate, and so nobody knows about it. But every day I see deals collapse—I see potential investors who decide not to come to Tucumán—because of the legal risks. They call and ask me about this or that legal issue, and I have to tell them, and they say 'thank you very much' and that's the end of it. 'The world is a big place,' a client told me once, 'and we don't need Tucumán'"[18]

Colombres related numerous examples of legal dysfunction. Foreign investors in particular have suffered hardships when their rights were not protected. Phibro, a major U.S. commodities trading firm, decided to invest in the province, providing $20 million in financing to a local sugar mill secured by sugar inventory. When the mill ran into problems, workers seized the factory and refused to leave until they were paid. Phibro, a secured creditor, was prevented by the seizure from obtaining its collateral, and courts failed to order the workers to stand aside. Months went by before an accommodation was finally reached, and Phibro never came back to Tucumán. In another case, a French company won the bid to provide water service when the provincial utility was privatized. Bidders had been required to offer a very high level of service, so the French company needed to impose a significant rate hike. In the face of public complaints about the higher rates, government officials began to look for ways out of the contract, and ultimately encouraged customers to stop paying for their water service. Collection rates plummeted to 25 percent, whereupon the French company terminated service and sued the province. After two years, international arbitrators have referred the matter back to local courts.

Foreign investors do not suffer alone in Tucumán: Creditors generally face serious obstacles when attempting to collect on their debts. In particular, it takes an average of five years to foreclose on a commercial mortgage in Tucumán. Given the punishingly high interest rates that prevail now in Argentina, such delays can render even excellent collateral insufficient to cover the amount ultimately due. The net effect of a system that leaves investors and creditors so badly exposed is simple: less investment, less financing, and therefore less growth and opportunity.

The failures of the Argentine legal system cannot be chalked up to insufficient funding. Total federal, provincial, and municipal spending on the judiciary came to 0.54 percent of gross domestic product in 1939—up from 0.39 percent of GDP in 1980 with no apparent improvement in service. By contrast, total spending on federal, state, and local courts in the United States amounted to only 0.33 percent of GDP in 1993, or roughly half the level of spending in Argentina.[19] The problem lies, not in a lack of resources, but rather a lack of accountability. There is nobody in the government at any level who is responsible for ensuring the prompt and reliable administration of justice; there are no consequences for anyone in the system when the system breaks down. Under such conditions, a total disconnect between the public sector and the public good is all but inevitable.

* * *

What is the link between a country's legal system and its rate of economic growth? Good legal institutions facilitate market development by reducing transaction costs.[20] Finding partners with whom to conduct mutually beneficial exchanges, settling the terms of those exchanges, monitoring compliance with agreed-upon terms, and enforcing compliance with those terms—all of these transaction costs are obstacles that must be overcome before market activity can occur. Specifically, if such costs outweigh the benefits of particular market exchanges, those exchanges will generally not be pursued. Accordingly, the lower the transaction costs, the broader the range of potentially profitable exchange opportunities for market participants to discover and exploit.

Consider, by the way of analogy, the rise of the Internet. The explosion of new businesses unleashed by the advent and expansion of the World Wide Web is the emphatic response of entrepreneurs to a dramatic fall in transaction costs. Because of Internet technology, it has suddenly become much cheaper to bring together buyers and sellers of a wide range of products. As a result, entirely new types of businesses—such as Amazon.com, eBay, and Priceline on the business-to-consumer side, and EnronOnline on the business-to-business side—have sprung into existence to explore the vast but untested possibilities of e-commerce. Of course, how best to take advantage of the Internet's reduction of transaction costs is shrouded in uncertainty, and so it should be no surprise that the discovery process of the past few years has included many wrong turns and stumbles. For all the recent shakeouts, though, Internet technology has indisputably broadened economic horizons—and has done so by conquering previously insurmountable transaction costs.

The rules of property and contract, and the institutions that define and enforce them, may be thought of as a kind of original Internet. They roll back the tides of transaction costs to reveal vast new terrains of market opportunity—terrains that entrepreneurs can explore and then cultivate for the mutual enrichment of all. Specifically, enforceable property and contract rules dramatically expand not only the circle of people with whom dealings are possible but also the time horizons over which dealings can extend. When property rights are insecure and agreements are not legally binding, market participants will do business only with people they know and trust, or in situations where exchanges can be consummated face to face. All other possibilities are precluded by the high costs of monitoring an ensuring compliance. Good legal institutions slash those costs and thus allow a much more complex, and prosperous, division of labor than otherwise would be possible.

As the economist Mancur Olson was wise to point out, poor countries today are not struggling because of a general lack of markets:

> Those who live in low-income economies know that there are shops and market days in the villages, bazaars in the towns, and peddlers hawking their wares on the street. The number of shops and peddlers in a large, poor city such as Calcutta is almost uncountable. The largest number of markets that I have ever seen in one place was in far-from-prosperous Moscow in early 1992, where there were people buying and selling at almost every metro stop and street corner.[21]

Olson argued persuasively that underdevelopment reflects, not the absence of markets generally, but rather the absence of particular types of markets—namely, "socially contrived" or "property-rights-intensive" markets that arise and flower only with the help of appropriate, government-provided legal institutions. For example, capital-intensive industry—an essential component of Western prosperity—entails high fixed costs that must be amortized over many years. Industries of this type can never arise and develop spontaneously except where property rights are reasonably secure. Likewise, sophisticated financial markets (whose vital importance to wealth creation was reviewed in the previous chapter) are utterly dependent upon reliable contract enforcement.

In what are now the rich countries, property rights were sufficiently well defined and protected to allow industrialization and the phenomenal elevation of living standards that it provides. There have been important exceptions—notably, inadequate enforcement of creditor and investor rights has stunted the growth of capital markets everywhere outside the Anglo-Saxon countries—but overall the legal infrastructure upon which markets are based is firmly in place and has been for many decades, or, in some cases, centuries. For these fortunate countries, the great threat to markets has been an overlying burden of statist controls, not an inadequate foundation of legal institutions. It is understandable, therefore, why market critics in the advanced nations tend to think of economic liberalism as always antigovernment. Those essential government activities that undergird a liberal market order are, by and large, so routine and uncontroversial that they do not figure in the ongoing debate over the role of government. In that context, economic liberals are always seen demanding less government intervention, and so develops the misconception that "the less government, the better" is the sum and substance of their position.

But the situation is altogether different for roughly five billion of the earth's six billion people. In the underdeveloped world, it is the underdevelopment of legal institutions that is especially debilitating. In a continuum from bad to worse—from corrupt officials and inadequate courts, to laws so dysfunctional that many or most people are chased into the informal sector, to the arbitrary confiscations of kleptocratic misrule, to the chaos of Hobbesian anarchy—the poorer countries are all plagued by the insufficient protection of property and contract rights. Under these conditions, most economic activity is confined to what Olson called "spontaneous" or "self-enforcing" markets— markets based on personal relationships or face-to-face contact. But those markets, however resilient and durable, cannot produce the division of labor upon which affluence depends. They are a dead end, or at best a holding pattern.

In the early 1990s—as Latin America was overcoming its debt crisis with bold liberal reforms, and the former Soviet bloc was throwing off the shackles of communism—it appeared to many friends of markets that a golden age of economic growth was at hand. International investors swooned over the prospects of "emerging markets," and pundits proclaimed the arrival of a "borderless world." Disappointing results in recent years, though, have erased that naïve optimism, and, in many quarters, have made such terms as "neoliberalism" and "privatization" into epithets. What went wrong?

In the past two chapters, and in the chapter that follows this one, I make the case that the elimination of government controls over economic life has not progressed as far as most people believe. Despite real gains over the past two decades, state-owned enterprises, price and entry controls, and other barriers to competition remain depressingly pervasive. But that is not the whole story. Removing top-down controls is a necessary condition for robust and self-sustaining economic development, but it is not a sufficient one. In addition, governments must take the affirmative steps of creating and nurturing the legal institutions that underlie market competition. The widespread failure to do so has saddled poorer countries with a growth-stunting rule of lawlessness—yet another bitter legacy of the Industrial Counterrevolution.

Nowhere is that legacy more evident today than in Africa. Although he completely misreads the implications of the fact, Thomas Friedman is correct in identifying the tragic continent as the place where the absence of government is at its most wretched. Property rights, and even basic personal safety, are miserably insecure; as a consequence, the promise of globalization is more remote there than almost any place on earth.

At its worst Africa presents a picture of unmitigated chaos. In Rwanda, a genocidal rampage by Hutu tribe members against rival Tutsis in 1994 left up to a million people dead, forced two million out of the country, and displaced yet another million internally. A civil war in Sudan has dragged on since 1983; combat, famine, and disease have claimed an estimated two million lives. In Sierra Leone, a ghastly ten-year conflict between the government and the insurgent Revolutionary United Front has featured rape, mass amputations, and ritual cannibalism; the soldiers on both sides are often children, whose induction into service can include being forced to kill their parents. Somalia, torn apart by contending warlords, has not had a central government since 1991.

Too often the alternative to chaos has been brutal tyranny. Over the course of the 1970s and '80s, the trio of Idi Amin, Milton Obote, and Tito Okello in Uganda murdered more than 800,000 people. From 1972 to 1979, the death toll under President Francisco Marcias Nguema of Equatorial Guinea came to 50,000, or one-seventh of the population.[22] Today, despotism—if less spectacularly bloodthirsty—remains a fixture of African political life. Freedom House's most recent world survey of political rights and civil liberties examined 53 African nations; it rated 21 countries as "not free," and only eight as "free."[23] Arbitrary imprisonment, extrajudicial killing, and confiscation of property are commonplace.

Repression has been accompanied by massive-scale looting. Although other examples can be cited *ad nauseam,* few regimes can match the kleptocratic heights achieved by Mobutu Sese Seko in the country formerly known as Zaire. Mobutu, who ruled from 1965 until 1997, treated the rich natural resources of his country as his own private property. He took personal control of diamond and gold mines, the marketing of cobalt and copper, and the management of Zaire's coffee plantations; some 60 percent of the government's annual revenues were lost or diverted to him and his cronies. He acquired dozens of properties around the world, including orchards and a vineyard in Portugal, a 32-room mansion in Switzerland, and a 16th century castle in Spain. He expanded the airport in his home village of Gbadolite to allow landings by the supersonic Concorde, which he frequently chartered from Air France. His Swiss bank accounts were believed to contain billions of dollars. The country, meanwhile, descended into complete and utter ruin. One chilling statistic tells the broader picture: When it gained its independence in 1960, Zaire's main roads ran 31,000 miles, only 3,700 miles of which were still passable a mere 20 years later.[24]

There is no possibility of economic development under these kinds of conditions. When predators reign, planning ahead is foolhardy; trusting anyone other than the closest intimates is a potentially fatal mistake. Economic horizons are reduced to the shortest of short terms, and entrepreneurial activity (to the extent it exists at all) lurks furtively in the shadows on the smallest of small scales.

Africa fell into the abyss under the spell of collectivism. George Ayittey, a Ghanaian-born intellectual who writes searingly of Africa's tragic post-colonial history, explains the special allure that runaway centralization held for the new African states:

A wave of socialism swept across the continent as almost all the new African leaders succumbed to the contagious ideology. The dalliance and fascination with socialism seemed to have emerged during the struggle for political independence and freedom from colonial rule in the 1950s. Many African nationalists harbored a deep distrust and distaste for capitalism, which, with Lenin, they identified as an extension of colonialism and imperialism. Consequently, they interpreted freedom from colonial rule as freedom from capitalism as well.[25]

The result was economic, institutional, and political catastrophe. Natural-resource industries were nationalized, and agriculture was ensnared in a mad tangle of price controls and confiscatory marketing boards. Economic centralization not only stifled the discovery process of competitive markets; it also precipitated an orgy of corruption. Once national wealth was under government control, the temptation to exert that control for private enrichment proved irresistible. Meanwhile, the logic of central planning proved a handy excuse for centralization of political power, as fledgling parliamentary democracies were quickly dispatched by a rogue's gallery of military dictators and Presidents-for-life. Political violence then escalated to sickening levels: If power meant fantastic riches, how could any other outcome be possible? And all the while, as chaos and savagery consumed the continent, the sweet perfume of socialist ideology helped to mask the stench of putrefaction.

It is the intimate connection between Africa's disastrous lack of government on the one hand and its woeful excess of statist tyranny on the other that Thomas Friedman completely fails to grasp. African governments do too little today in large part because in the past they presumed to do too much. Instead of undertaking the vital but unglamorous responsibility of building market-friendly institutions, they actively wrecked those markets that existed in pursuit of grandiose schemes of centralized control. In many cases, they destroyed in the process their societies' capacity for generating new markets—and thus for overcoming the mistakes of the past. Africa's plight is therefore not, as Friedman imagines, a rebuke to excessive enthusiasm for free markets. On the contrary, Africa today reveals the dead hand of collectivism at its most oppressive.

* * *

The security of property and contract rights cannot be safeguarded in a vacuum. Ultimately, the quality of market institutions is inseparable from the structure of political institutions. What the rules are depends crucially on who gets to make them and how.

A country's legal framework functions to the extent that its political system succeeds in meeting two different and conflicting challenges. First, it must produce a government strong enough to enforce rules and uphold their integrity against powerful private groups that seek to hold themselves above the law. At the same time, the political system must constrain government officials from placing themselves above the law. James Madison summed up the problem over two centuries ago in the *Federalist Papers*. "In framing a government which is to be administered by men over men," he wrote, "the great difficulty lies in this: you must first enable the government to control the governed; and in the next place oblige it to control itself."[26]

There is no magic formula for meeting these challenges. Autocratic governments with blood on their hands have sometimes succeeded, while democratic governments have sometimes failed miserably. On balance, though, both theory and history point to a link between accountability to the broad public and a functional rule of law.

The most obvious threat to legal order posed by dictatorship is the absence of any institutional constraints on power. Human nature being what it is, that absence is all too often a recipe for disaster. The dolorous political history of the 20th century is packed with confirmations of Lord Acton's dictum: autocratic regimes, accountable to no one, that have preyed on their own people like wolves among sheep. Nothing is more destructive to legal order than a rogue government bent on plunder. No property is safe, no agreements can be relied upon, and, consequently, no complex division of labor is possible. Economic life remains stunted and impoverished, confined to small-scale, short-term activities that lie low and hide from the rapacious gaze of predatory government.

Even if an autocratic government is more or less able to control itself, its control over those it governs is often deceptively fragile. Dictatorships are chronically unstable because they lack any institutional mechanism for transferring power. And since the stakes of gaining or losing power are so high, transitions are frequently bloody. They can also be highly disruptive: Groups that flourished under the favor of the old regime are suddenly targeted for persecution under the new. Political instability thus translates into legal instability, which once again undermines the kind of large-scale, long-term investments upon which prosperity in a modern industrial society depends.

Finally, just because a government wields unrestricted power doesn't mean that it is firmly in the saddle. Indeed, a regime's resort to repressive measures is often an indication of how tenuous its grasp on power really is. To maintain power without broad public support, many autocratic governments find it necessary to use special subsidies and privileges to buy the allegiance of other power centers within society. The auctioning off of state favors can end up badly compromising the regime's own autonomy—thus the spectacle of a seemingly all-powerful government that, in fact, is the pawn of powerful private interests. The weak but despotic government is incapable of upholding secure and stable property rights, which now are vulnerable to the depredations of multiple predators.

Nevertheless, history does provide examples of so-called "benevolent dictatorships": regimes that, although they suppress political dissent (and sometimes brutally), exhibit decent restraint when it comes to plundering the property of their citizens, and maintain security and stability long enough to promote sustained economic growth. Indeed, many of the fastest-growing economies of recent times—Chile, Korea, Taiwan, Hong Kong, Singapore, Indonesia, Malaysia, Thailand, and China—began their ascent (and in the cases of China, Malaysia, and Singapore, continue it) by combining a lack of political rights with tolerable security for property rights.[27] Those recent success stories, concentrated as they are along the Pacific Rim, gave rise to notions of an "Asian model" of politics as well as economics—a model that supposedly demonstrated that development proceeds best without too much democracy.

Special circumstances allowed those high-performing economies to escape the usual sad destiny of autocracies. A combination of external and internal factors oriented their leaders toward promoting long-term growth instead of maximizing short-term plunder, and at the same time shielded political life from takeover by economically destructive narrow interests. For many of those economies, the threat of communism was enormously important in shaping the incentives of political leaders. In Korea and Taiwan, Southeast Asia and Chile, leaders were acutely aware of their vulnerability in the face of the communist challenge, and were therefore determined to repel that challenge with broad-based economic growth. In Taiwan and China, leaders were further chastened by past failures: Chiang Kai-Shek knew that endemic corruption had contributed to his downfall on the mainland, while Deng Xiaoping was resolved to turn China away from the mayhem of the Cultural Revolution.

At the same time that leaders in those economies were unusually disposed toward controlling themselves, many were also unusually well positioned to exert control over those they governed. Specifically, they were relatively immune from pressure and manipulation by privilege-seeking private interests. The Hong Kong colonial government, controlled from distant Great Britain, did not have to answer (at least directly) to its subjects. The Nationalist government in Taiwan was also a kind of foreign occupying power: Mandarin-speaking refugees from the mainland who dominated the Taiwanese-speaking natives. Accordingly, narrow interests in Taiwan had little access to state-granted favors. In Korea, General Park Chung-Hee launched his country's amazing economic rise by initiating a ruthless crackdown on business elites in 1962. Like countless plundering autocrats, he jailed most major business leaders and expropriated their holdings; but then, contrary to type, he agreed to release them and their property in exchange for support for a new export-led growth strategy. The power of vested interests attached to the old import-substitution policy had been shattered.

Despite their successes, the growth-friendly autocracies of recent times have had a pronounced tendency to outgrow themselves. The progress of wealth creation breeds new power centers within society, which over time grow increasingly restive about their exclusion from political decision-making. Governing cliques find themselves under mounting pressure to share power—hence the gradual process of democratization seen in Chile, Korea, Taiwan, and Thailand. Under these conditions, autocratic rule is especially vulnerable in the event of a sharp economic downturn. These regimes stake their claim to legitimacy on economic performance; when performance nosedives, that claim begins to dissolve. The 1997-98 financial crisis was thus a debacle for the Asian model of politics as well as of economics: In Indonesia, the seemingly all-powerful Suharto regime toppled in a matter of months; in Korea, the election of Kim Dae-Jung as president marked the first-ever victory by an opposition candidate; and in Thailand, a new, more democratic constitution won parliamentary approval. On the other hand, the Malaysian *reformasi* movement proved abortive, and the current regimes in Singapore and China still look secure. But now it seems that Asia's pro-growth autocrats are clinging to the past rather than defining the future.

The present era of globalization has rejoined the causes of economic liberalism and democracy under a single banner. In Latin America and, to a lesser extent, Africa and East Asia, dictatorships—

benevolent and otherwise—have given way to popular rule, just as statist controls around the world have given way to markets. The association of economic and political freedom is by no means novel: In the 19th century, liberal reformers sought both to extend the franchise and remove obstacles to market competition. It was only the advent of the Industrial Counterrevolution that put the two causes at odds. Economic liberals grew suspicious of popular sovereignty in response to the rise of mass collectivist movements; at the same time, collectivists campaigned for "economic democracy" as the complement to political freedom or—more radically—as the only real democracy.

But though it appropriated the rhetoric of democracy, the Industrial Counterrevolution proved highly congenial to monstrous tyranny, as the enslavement of millions living in so-called "democratic republics" so grimly demonstrated. The belief in centralization was all too easy to carry over from economics into politics. Rationality meant top-down control, and for those who pursued this logic to its limits, it followed that both the chaos of the marketplace and the chaos of "bourgeois" democracy were equally useless anachronisms. Meanwhile, those collectivists who retained their allegiance to political freedom were often hard pressed to condemn even the most hideous crimes committed in the name of their ideology. They excused the "excesses" of "democrats in a hurry"; the centralizing tyrants mocked their naïve apologists as "useful idiots."

The combination of despotism and collectivism throughout the old Communist bloc and the Third World set the stage for the present-day reunion of political and economic liberalism. Revolutionary governments used the promise of accelerated development (and, of course, terror) to substitute for the lack of a popular mandate; moreover, belief in that promise emboldened political leaders to use terror when necessary. Consequently, as disillusionment with economic centralization spread around the world, the justification for autocratic rule began to erode. At the same time that momentum for market-based liberalization was building, popular resistance to repression hardened while despots were losing the will to spill more blood. And thus the overlapping and mutually reinforcing waves that have swept the planet over the past couple of decades: political and economic reform, democracy and free markets.

The recurring historical connections between democracy and free markets are not accidental: There is a deep affinity between the two ideals. Both systems are animated by the fundamental liberal value of autonomy: The market order upholds individual autonomy against top-down control, while democracy upholds collective autonomy against any narrow ruling class. In other words, the genius of both systems is to rely on decentralized decision-making. The market holds producers accountable to consumers, while democracy requires politicians to seek the consent of voters. The market is always open to new investments and new ideas; likewise, democracy allows new political movements to spring spontaneously from any quarter of society.

Because of its decentralization of power, democracy offers the surest foundation for protecting the legal order within which market competition unfolds. Popular government offers clear advantages over autocratic rule with respect to both controlling the governed and controlling itself. Laws blessed with the mandate of popular consent are much less subject to challenge and defiance; furthermore, the peaceful transfer of power ensures that legal protections are shielded from internal convulsions. Democracy thus fortifies the legal framework with legitimacy and stability. At the same time, by holding rulers accountable to the broad public and maintaining open avenues for outsiders to challenge incumbents, popular government guards against abusive ruling cliques that would place themselves above the law. It is no coincidence that the world's most advanced market economies are also stable democracies.

But the process of democratization is strewn with pitfalls. For just as market competition needs an infrastructure of legal institutions in order to function properly, so too does democracy require proper political institutions to fulfill its promise. Democracy is more than just free elections and majority rule, just as free markets are more than the absence of government controls. When democracy is not ensconced in an appropriately supportive political culture, its forms may be present but its substance will be sorely lacking.

Democracy is supposed to mean more than broadly inclusive procedures. It is also supposed to produce broadly inclusive results. The policies of a popular government should reflect public opinion, not the back-room maneuverings of scheming cliques; they should serve the general welfare, not the grasping of narrow interests. The true democracy is government of the people, by the people, and for the people. But that ideal cannot be attained—indeed, not even a recognizable approximation of that ideal can be attained—without a long and tortuous process of political development.

Countries just beginning the transition to democracy often lack even rudimentary institutions for holding selfish interests in check. In such countries, the substitution of competitive elections for autocratic rule can prove, at least initially, a hollow victory. A fundamental problem remains: As before, state power is still treated as the private possession of the rulers. Only now, power is not seized by armed might; instead it is bought and sold. In this degraded and corrupted form, democracy is a kind of commercial enterprise: Politicians invest in power by purchasing votes and doling out favors, and then reap the rewards in graft and lucrative privileges. As a result, the market order—and the great public good of growth and opportunity it provides—is doubly embattled. It is distorted and deformed from above by a tangle of special-interest quotas, licenses, subsidies, and controls, and is simultaneously undermined from below by a legal system that too frequently sides with the highest bidder.

Immature democracies are especially prone to this kind of dysfunction because of a basic rule of political organization. As the economist Mancur Olson made clear in his groundbreaking work on the subject, different types of groups in society have different capacities for organizing and asserting their interests in the political arena. Because of the "free-rider" problems associated with collective action, it is much easier to organize small groups with narrow, focused interests than large groups with broad, diffuse interests. Consequently, in countries without longstanding traditions of popular participation in political life, narrow interests that seek their own selfish gain at the expense of the general welfare have a natural head start in jockeying for power.

Nonetheless, there is hope—over time. If basic democratic rights can be maintained, the organization of interests will continue, and the laggards—the broader, more diffuse interests—will begin to catch up. Meanwhile, as economic growth proceeds, the variety of narrow interests will proliferate. As a result, the task of raiding the public trust for private gain becomes much harder. It is now necessary to overcome resistance from a growing number of conflicting narrow interests as well as the opposition of increasingly vigorous organizations that claim to speak for the public good. Moreover, public attitudes change with economic development. As more and more people move from the villages to the cities and integrate their lives into the national, and world, economy, the general interest in a growing, thriving economy becomes increasingly relevant to them. They begin to expect more from politicians than an envelope full of cash on election day; they begin to expect, and demand, good policies.[28]

Thailand's political history over the past generation provides a case in point. Until the 1970s, it was a volatile, if relatively benign, autocracy dominated by the military and royal bureaucracy. Political life was confined to members of a small ruling class; while often enlivened by coups and failed plots, it did not involve or engage the great body of a mostly rural society. The 1970s, though, saw democratic activism and the rise of political parties that represented the interests of newly powerful elements of Thai society—namely, the Bangkok business elite (mostly ethnic Chinese) and the so-called *chao po* or provincial bosses.

The *chao po* had gotten rich in resource-based industries, government contracting, and a host of illicit enterprises—jewelry smuggling, gun running, the drug trade, and prostitution. At home, they translated their wealth into influence through patronage and liberal distribution of cash. And in Bangkok, they converted their ability to deliver votes into political power—which they, in turn, used to get even richer.

As the military's political strength gradually declined, the provincial bosses became the dominant force in Thai politics. With a winning populist style, they pursued a single, simple goal—maximizing wealth and advantages for themselves and their friends. Their chief rivals were the business interests and growing middle classes of Bangkok, who tended to favor cleaner government and more professional economic management. The balance of power between the provinces and the capital turned, though, on this fundamental fact: The Bangkok metropolitan area accounts for about half of Thailand's total economic output but only about 10 percent of its population. Thus, although the urban middle classes wielded considerable influence, the provincial bosses controlled the votes.

The mismatch between metropolitan wealth and provincial power, amidst the backdrop of fading but occasionally reassertive authoritarianism, put Thai politics in a turbulent cycle of corruption, crackdown, democratic agitation, and reform. The 1988 election of a civilian government was the major breakthrough that brought the *chao po* to national power. The government of Prime Minister Chatichai Choonhavan was called the "buffet cabinet" because the ministers took an "all you can eat" approach to enjoying the perquisites of office. By 1991 Bangkok and the military had had enough; a bloodless coup ousted Chatichai and installed a caretaker government of well-respected technocrats to clean up the mess.

The generals then tried to reclaim power for themselves, but Bangkok was outraged. In May 1992 thousands camped out in the streets to protest the drift toward authoritarianism. A ruthless attempt to disperse the protesters killed hundreds, until the king—intensely revered but usually nonpolitical—called for the bloodshed to stop. In September 1992 a new election pitted the pro-democracy "angels" against the pro-military "devils"; the angels, led by Chuan Leekpai, carried the day. But by 1995 the voting power of the provinces could no longer be denied, and new elections brought a government led by Banharn Silpa-archa—known as the "walking ATM" for his shameless embrace of money politics—and a motley cast of cronies. Endless scandals caused the Banharn government to fall in 1996, but the new government led by General Chavalit Yongchaiyudh was little better.[29]

The financial meltdown of 1997 gave new impetus to political reform. Rule by the provinces was discredited by its complicity in the economic disaster, and Chuan Leekpai and his Democratic party returned to power. More important, a new reformist constitution was able to win passage in Parliament. Among other important structural changes, the constitution calls for the creation of various independent watchdog bodies—an Election Commission, a Human Rights Commission, a Counter-Corruption Commission, and a Constitutional Court—whose purpose is to increase transparency and restrain the corrupting influence of money politics.

So far the new constitution has had mixed results. In the first direct election of Senators in March 2000 (formerly the Senate was an appointed body and stuffed with hacks), the Election Commission tossed out the results in 78 of the 200 races because of vote-buying, and then ordered multiple rounds of polling before all the results were pronounced clean—an impressive flexing of reformist muscle. On the other hand, the Human Rights Commission was effectively neutered when it was placed under executive branch control and staffed with yes-men. And in January 2001, telecom tycoon Thaksin Shinawatra led his new Thai Rak Thai ("Thais Love Thais") party to an overwhelming victory in parliamentary elections on a populist platform—despite the fact that Thaksin was under indictment from the Counter-Corruption Commission for failure to meet financial disclosure requirements. Thaksin was later cleared of the charges against him in an intensely controversial court decision.

Anand Panyarachun, a highly respected former prime minister and principal architect of the new constitution, is philosophical about Thailand's messy political evolution. "We have been progressing well over the past nine years," he told me in January 2000. "We have now had several successions of power in a constitutional context"—that is, without a coup. Looking ahead, he is optimistic that the new constitution will succeed in cleaning up Thai politics, "but we'll need two more general election cycles, perhaps another seven or eight years," before the effects are really visible. "Sometimes, when you're flushing a toilet," he said with a laugh, "you need to do it two or three times."[30]

It must be understood, though, that merely getting rid of the most vulgar forms of political corruption does not dispense with the threat that narrow interests pose to democratic governance—and to the liberal market order. That threat—what James Madison in the *Federalist Papers* called the problem of "faction"—is ineradicable; at best it can be contained. "The friend of popular governments," Madison wrote, "never finds himself so much alarmed for their character and fate as when he contemplates their propensity to this dangerous vice."[31] What was true over two centuries ago remains true today. Although democratic government aspires to policies that reflect a broad public interest, it is always highly vulnerable to the usurpations of narrow groups—what Madison called "factions," and we call "special interests"—whose superior organizational ability allows them to bend public power to their own private ends.

In today's developed democracies we see that vulnerability exploited to the nth degree. The mad proliferation of organized lobbies, their dominance of a now incomprehensibly arcane policymaking process, and the resulting alienation of ordinary citizens from what transpires supposedly in their name—all of these dreary commonplaces of contemporary political life are too familiar to require elaboration here. Their combined effect is to rob democracy of its highest promise, and degrade the public good of market competition with a thousand encrustations, great and small, of narrow-interest privilege.[32]

If this malady is ever to be remedied, the lost wisdom of James Madison and his fellow framers of the U.S. Constitution must first be recovered. Over two centuries ago they saw clearly what today is all but forgotten: The best hope for containing the problem of faction lies in constitutional limits on government power. With their elaborate system of checks and balances, the restriction of government powers to those specifically enumerated, and reservation of rights to the people on which no government can intrude, they sought to craft a constitution that would act as a series of institutional filters—through which would pass the rambunctious, faction-ridden rough-and-tumble of political activity and from which would emerge only those policies that bear a plausible relation to some broadly shared and relatively stable public good.

In the United States, much of the framers' constitutional vision was swept aside during the 1930s to clear the way for the lunge toward centralization. Meanwhile, none of the other industrialized democracies ever did more than dabble with constitutional limits on government power. In recent decades, the pioneering work of Nobel Prize-winning economist James Buchanan has reawakened academic interest in constitutional design.[33] But the project of liberal political reform—of bringing popular government within the discipline of constitutional limits—remains in its infancy. For many years to come, therefore, the market order's political foundation will always be shaky at best.

Notes

1.   Hughes, *American Genesis*, 269-71.
2.   World Bank, *India: Policies to Reduce Poverty and Accelerate Sustainable Development* (Washington, D.C.: World Bank, 2000), 76-77.
3.   World Bank, *Adverting the Old Age Crisis: Policies to Protect the Old* and *Promote Growth* (New York: Oxford University Press, 1994), 123.

4. Friedrich Schneider and Dominik H. Enste, "Shadow Economies: Size, Causes, and Consequences," *Journal of Economic Literature* XXXVIII (March 2000): 77-114, 100-01.

5. Hernando do Soto, *The Mystery of Capital: Why Capitalism Triumphs in the West and Fails Everywhere Else* (New York: Basic Books, 2000), 32-33.

6. Ibid., 34-35.

7. There are sizable shadow economies even in the developed world. In Denmark and Germany, for instance, over 20 percent of working-age adults are believed to engage in significant unreported economic activity. In Italy, the figure may be as high as 48 percent. Examining 20 developed countries, Schneider and Enste found an average ratio of informal output to official GDP of 15.1 percent. Schneider and Enste, "Shadow Economies," 102, 105-06.

8. Friedman, *The Lexus and the Olive Tree,* 350.

9. Paulo Mauro, "Corruption and Growth," *Quarterly Journal of Economics* 110 (August 1995): 681-712.

10. Gwartney and Lawson, *Economic Freedom of the World: 2000 Annual Report,* 10, 86.

11. Transparency International, "New Index highlights worldwide corruption crisis," June 27, 2001.

12. World Economic Forum, *Global Competitiveness Report 2000* (New York: Oxford University Press, 2000), 94, 247-252.

13. Pablo T. Spiller and Mariano Tommasi, "The Institutional Foundations of Argentina's Development," preliminary draft, August 27, 1999.

14. Interview with staff of Fundacion del Tucumán, June 6, 2001: interview with Ignacio Colombres Garmendia, June 6, 2001.

15. Pamela Druckerman, "Argentina, Land of Fiscal Loose Cannons," *Wall Street Journal,* March 2, 2001.

16. Ana I. Eiras and Brett D. Schaefer, "Argentina's Economic Crisis: An 'Absence of Capitalism,'" Heritage Foundation Backgrounder no. 1432, April 19, 2001, 3.

17. Joshua Goodman, "Argentina's Provincial Profligates," *Business Week,* January 29, 2001 (International edition).

18. Interview with author, June 6, 2001.

19. Adrián C. Guissarri, "Costos de la Justicia y Efficiencia en la Asignacion de Recursos" ("Costs of Justice and Efficiency in the Allocation of Resources") Proyecto Justicia y Desarrollo Economico (Project on Justice and Economic Development), Buenos Aires, June 1998.

20. This point is central to Douglass North's analysis of economic history. See North, *Structure and Change in Economic History,* especially pp. 33-44; see also Douglass C. North, "Institutions, Ideology, and Economic Performance," in *The Revolution in Development Economies,* 95-107.

21. Mancur Olson, *Power and Prosperity: Outgrowing Communist and Capitalist Dictatorships* (New York: Basic Books, 2000), 173.

22. See George B. N. Ayittey, *Africa Betrayed* (New York: St. Martin's Press, 1992), 120-21.

23. Freedom House, 1999-2000 Freedom in the World survey, Available at www.freedomhouse.org.

24. See Ayittey, *Africa Betrayed,* 253-62.

25. Ibid., 103.

26. James Madison, "Federalist No. 51," in Alexander Hamilton, James Madison, and John Jay, *The Federalist Papers* (New York: New American Library, 1961 [1787-88]), 322.

27. Indeed, in Chile's case, the government pursued a program of explicitly liberal economic reform.

28. My point here is that the proliferation of organized interests provoked by economic development helps to promote mature and stable democracies. Olson made a similar point in his last and posthumously published book. Olson, *Power and Prosperity,* 30-34. In an earlier work, however, he attempted a very different argument—namely, that the unchecked growth of organized interests in stable democracies tends, over time, to undermine economic development. Mancur Olson, *The Rise and Decline of Nations* (New Haven, Conn.: Yale University Press, 1982). Writing in the early 1980s, Olson contrasted the lower economic growth of Great Britain and the United States with the more dynamic performance of Japan and West Germany, and ascribed the difference to the fact that economically harmful narrow interests had been wiped out in the latter two countries by their defeat in World War II. In the former pair of countries, on the other hand, narrow interests had continued to accumulate like so many barnacles, gradually and progressively hindering wealth creation with steady build-up of special-interest privileges. History has not been kind to Olson's thesis. The United States and Great Britain have staged dramatic restructurings over the past 20 years, while Germany and especially Japan have stumbled off the high-growth path. Although it is true that the interests of narrow groups often conflict with the general

interest in market competition, the long-term effect of the steady growth of such groups is ambiguous. As discussed in the text, an increase in the number of groups that are jostling for privileges can make it harder for any one group to succeed; also democratic stability breeds organized groups with steadily broader interests, which then act as a check on narrow-group lobbying. Furthermore, and perhaps most important, it seems that narrow groups can eventually overreach: Public frustration with poor economic performance can discredit the self-serving claims of narrow interests and allow public-spirited market reforms to carry the day. That is what happened in Great Britain and the United States; in Japan and Germany, on the other hand, the public's patience with declining economic prospects has not yet been exhausted.

29. This account of recent Thai political history up to the Asian crisis relies heavily on Pasuk Phongpaichit and Chris Baker, *Thailand's Boom and Bust* (Chiang Mai, Thailand: Silkworm Books, 1998), 216-43.

30. Interview with author, January 28, 2000.

31. James Madison, "Federalist No. 10," in Hamilton, Madison, and Jay, *The Federalist Papers,* 77.

32. For an interesting commentary on the hypertrophy of organized lobbies, see Jonathan Rauch, *Government's End: Why Washington Stopped Working* (New York: Public Affairs, 1999). Rauch relies heavily on Mancur Olson's work for the theoretical framework of his own reporting and analysis.

33. The literature of "public choice" constitutional economics spawned by Buchanan's work is vast and growing, but a good introduction is James Buchanan, *The Limits of Liberty: Between Anarchy and Leviathan* (Chicago: University of Chicago Press, 1977).

THE PERILS OF REGULATION: A MARKET-PROCESS APPROACH

Israel M. Kirzner

Introduction

Economists have for at least two centuries debated the merits of government regulation of the market economy. In recent decades, however, this debate appeared to die down, and for a number of years it seemed that economists, with very few exceptions, subscribed to (and indeed helped propagate) a strongly approving view of extensive government intervention in the marketplace. Only recently has the pendulum of professional opinion begun to swing away from a definitely interventionist position, permitting a renewal of the classic debate about government regulation of the economy.

The position in favor of extensive government regulation of the market, of course, must be sharply distinguished from the views of radical critics of capitalism. The interventionist position, unlike that of radical critics, in general thoroughly appreciates the role of the market system in the efficient allocation of resources. The interventionist position fully accepts the central theorem of welfare economics concerning the Pareto optimality achieved, on appropriate assumptions, by the competitive market in general equilibrium. Intervention, however, is said to be required by the real-world impossibility of fulfilling the assumptions needed to hold for a perfectly competitive equilibrium to prevail. Because of chronic "market failure" attributable to the violation of these assumptions, the interventionist position deems it essential that government actively modify the operation of the free market by extensive, even massive, doses of intervention and regulation. The interventionist position holds that the market economy, suitably modified by a judicious combination of government controls on prices, quality of outputs, and the organization of industry, can achieve reasonably satisfactory results. This position came to be so entrenched in professional opinion that, supported (as it always has been) by the layman's intuition, interventionism became a virtually unchallenged orthodoxy.

Only recently has this orthodoxy begun to crumble. Both the layman and the economist have come to suspect that government interventions, especially those limiting competition and controlling prices, are consistently responsible for undesirable consequences. Confidence in the ability of government officials to construct a useful program of controls that would correct "market failure" without generating new problems attributable to government action itself has been rather thoroughly shaken. For many members of the public, and even for many economists, the crumbling of orthodoxy has come as a sharp surprise, if not a jarring shock. Economists now must rethink the theory of the market. They have begun to see that the assumption that the market can approximate a competitive equilibrium is more robust than hitherto believed. They have argued that government regulation produces its own undesirable distortions in market outcomes. Finally, economists have begun to understand that the political economy of regulation tends to ensure that market interventions are far more likely to be undertaken to further the well-being of special interests (not excepting those of the regulators themselves) than of the public at large.

This essay, too, draws attention to problems that appear to be the inescapable results of government regulation of the market. However, the approach taken here differs substantially from those just mentioned in that it does not postulate instantaneous or even rapid achievement of a general equilibrium in the free market; nor does it emphasize the undesirable distortions in equilibrium conditions introduced by government regulation. And to simplify matters, the discussion will relate to controls assumed to be deliberately introduced and enforced by legislators and officials intent on nothing but the welfare of the consuming public. The position developed here argues that intervention tends to interfere harmfully in the *entrepreneurial process* upon which the most basic of the market's virtues (conceded in principle by its interventionist critics) must surely depend.

To avoid misunderstanding, it should be emphasized that I do not wish to minimize the impact of those implications of regulation upon which my own argument does not rest. There can be little doubt that much regulation has been inspired, consciously or not, by considerations other than the goal of contributing to the public weal.[1] And the propensity of government interventions to generate tendencies toward suboptimal equilibrium configurations has certainly been amply demonstrated by economists from Bastiat to Friedman.[2] I merely contend that, valid though these approaches to a critique of interventionism undoubtedly are, they do not exhaust the phenomena to be explained. To sharpen the presentation of the approach taken here, regulations are assumed to be introduced and enforced with only the public welfare in mind. Many of regulation's undesirable consequences undoubtedly can be attributed to the tendency for regulation to serve the interests of regulators. I maintain that, quite apart from such difficulties, regulation generates economic confusion and inefficiency. This confusion and inefficiency are perceived more clearly by assuming, for the sake of argument, that those *other* difficulties (arising out of the regulators' self-interest) are absent.

Interventionism and Socialism: A Parallel

The surprise and dismay experienced today by so many economists and others at the manifest failure of well-meaning interventionist measures to create anything but inefficiencies of their very own is reminiscent in many ways of the surprise and disquiet experienced some sixty years ago when Mises first demonstrated on theoretical grounds, the inability of a socialized economy to perform the economic calculation needed for social efficiency. It is instructive to pursue this parallel further, for properly understood, Mises's theoretical argument regarding the socialist (that is, nonmarket) economy suggests useful insights into the problems of the hampered (that is, regulated) market economy. It was the earlier failure (by Mises's readers) to understand the operation and function of the market economy that led them to assume uncritically that a socialist society, in principle, need encounter no difficulty in the attainment of social efficiency. The realization that this assumption was far from obviously justified occasioned the surprise and disquiet following Mises's famous article. The now crumbling orthodoxy upon which the interventionist approach until very recently has rested reflects misunderstandings concerning the operation and function of markets. And those misunderstandings bear a remarkable likeness to those pointed out by Mises, and later by Hayek. These deep-rooted misunderstandings, in turn, appear responsible for the surprise and dismay occasioned by the realization that government regulation may itself be the problem rather than the solution it had so obviously seemed to be.

The hampered, regulated market, of course, is not at all the same thing as the fully socialized economy which Mises and Hayek studied. In the socialized economy there is no market at all, free or otherwise, for the services of material factors. In the socialized economy, therefore, there can be no market prices for such factor services. This absence of market prices is crucial to the Mises-Hayek critique of socialism. The regulated market economy, on the other hand, no matter how hampered it may be, *is* unquestionably a market economy, in which prices emerge through the interplay of profit-seeking market transactions. The Mises-Hayek critique of socialism, therefore, is certainly not applicable, as it stands, to the regulated market.

A brief review of the Mises-Hayek critique of socialism nonetheless proves helpful for a critical appraisal of regulation. For the Mises-Hayek discussion offers an appreciation for the operation of the market process by revealing the enormous difficulties confronting socialist planners trying to emulate the market economy's achievements without a market. This discussion also reveals the hazards besetting the path of regulators seeking to improve on the market's performance. Just as the attempt to seek social efficiency through central planning rather than through the spontaneous market process, in the Mises-Hayek view, must necessarily fail, so too, for essentially similar reasons, must attempts to control the outcomes of the spontaneous market by deliberate, extra market, regulatory action necessarily tend to generate unexpected and wholly undesired consequences.

I turn, therefore, to a brief review of the debate on socialist economic calculation, drawing particular attention to a widespread failure to appreciate fully certain important elements in the Mises-Hayek critique. It is these important elements, indeed, that will be found to be the basis for this essay's critical analysis of government regulation of the market economy. These elements underlie our perception of the parallel between a critique of the regulated market on the one hand and of socialism, without any market at all, on the other.

Mises and Hayek on Socialism

Mises's demonstration of the economic calculation problem facing the socialist planning authorities was first presented in 1920.[3] The demonstration was subsequently repeated in more or less similar terms (with critical attention paid to the attempts of socialist writers to respond to his challenge) in several of Mises's later works.[4] Hayek first addressed the problem in two essays, which respectively introduced and summed up the debate concerning socialist calculation (in the volume of essays on the subject that he edited in 1935).[5] An important third essay, published in 1940, contains Hayek's most complete appraisal of the issues.[6] Many writers on the Continent, in England, and in the United States attempted to meet Mises's arguments, the best known socialist contribution being that of Oskar Lange.[7] A thorough survey of the state of literature at the onset of World War II, provided by a Norwegian economist, was made available in English in 1949.[8]

For Mises, the defining element in socialism lies in its collective ownership of the means of production, in particular land and capital. It follows, therefore, that under socialism there exists no market for these factors of production or for their services; without private ownership, there can be no market exchanges between individual owners; and without market exchanges, of course, there can be no ratios of exchange—that is, there can be no market prices. Mises finds in the absence of factor prices the essence of the difficulty. Without prices, socialist decision makers (the central planners and their subordinates, the managers of socialized enterprises) do not have available relevant indicators (prices) of the relative economic importance of the various factor services in their various alternative uses. Socialist planners cannot know whether the allocation of a unit of a particular resource to a specific line of production is more or less desirable than its replacement by some quantity of another resource which is technologically capable of substituting for the first. Planners cannot know in advance where efficiency is likely to be attained, nor do they have any way of assessing ex post whether or to what extent such efficiency may have been achieved.

Professor Armentano illustrates Mises's point by imagining a socialist director choosing between the construction of a power plant that uses fossil fuel and one that uses nuclear fuel. Since the state owns all of the resources, no objective money prices exist for any of the alternative projects' required resources. The socialist planner has no way of knowing which project is cheaper, which promises the greater return on investment, which, in sum, offers the most efficient way to produce electricity. "If and when the power plant is built at a particular point with particular resources, it will represent an 'arbitrary' and not an economic decision."[9]

Hayek's most complete discussion of the problem of socialist calculation appeared in 1940 as a review article analyzing particularly the contributions of two socialist economists, Oskar Lange and H. D. Dickinson.[10] Both Lange and Dickinson conceded that economic calculation is unthinkable without factor prices.[11] They pointed out, however, that a price need not mean merely an exchange ratio established in a market; the notion of price, they maintained, can be understood more broadly as "the terms on which alternatives are offered." Using price in this broader sense, they argued, there is every possibility for setting up a socialist economy in which "prices" are announced by the planning authorities and are used as guides in the decisions of socialist managers (who are instructed to obey specified rules in which these "prices" appear). These writers believed the authorities could handle the adjustment of prices on the basis of trial and error, with the relation between perceived supply and demand indicating to the authorities where adjustments should be made. In this fashion, the socialist writers held, a socialist economy could achieve an efficient allocation of resources without markets in the material factors of production, and without profit-maximizing entrepreneurial decisions.

Hayek's critique of the Lange-Dickinson proposals was long and detailed. He considered their approach to be a vast improvement as compared with the earlier socialist reactions to Mises, in which the nature of the problem was hardly perceived at all. Yet he continued to find the Lange-Dickinson proposals seriously deficient both in their perception of the problem to be solved and of the practical difficulties confronting the suggested solution. The difference, Hayek wrote, between the "system of regimented prices" proposed by the socialist economists "and a system of prices determined by the market seems to be about the same as that between an attacking army in which every unit and every man could move only by special command and by the exact distance ordered by headquarters and an army in which every unit and every man can take advantage of every opportunity offered to them."[12]

Some Thoughts on the Socialist Calculation Literature

Despite Hayek's powerful critique of the Lange-Dickinson proposals, the postwar textbook literature, curiously, came to present the results of the interwar debate as if Mises's original claim (to have demonstrated the impossibility of economic calculation under socialism) had been decisively refuted by Lange, Dickinson, and Lerner.[13] Several writers have noted that this view conveyed by the literature is seriously mistaken.[14] A careful review of the debate surely reveals that the Lange-Dickinson Lerner solution hardly comes to grips with the difficulties that Mises and Hayek explained. The textbook literature did not so much ignore the arguments of Mises and Hayek *as it failed to understand the view of the market process, which underlies their critique of socialist calculation.* Indeed, the authors of the socialist proposals themselves offered their solution from a perspective on the nature and function of the market economy that differed sharply from the "Austrian" perspective shared by Mises and Hayek. My purpose in drawing attention to this defective view of the market reflected in the Lange-Dickinson literature is not merely to throw light on the socialist calculation debate (an issue only tangentially relevant to our own theme of efficiency in the regulated market economy); for the insights into the market process expressed in the Mises-Hayek view and overlooked in the Lange-Dickinson proposal become crucial to a critique of the economics of regulation.

Lange's response to Mises placed much emphasis on the *"parametric function of prices,* i.e., on the fact that. . . each individual separately regards the actual market prices as given data to which he has to adjust himself."[15] For Lange, each person in the market treats prices as if they were equilibrium prices to which he must adjust himself passively. If the market prices happen *not* to be equilibrium prices, then these market prices must somehow change "by a series of successive trials"—prices rising where demand exceeds supply, and so on.[16] Lange does not address the question of *how* market prices actually change if each person at all times considers prices as given data to which he must silently adjust himself.

For Lange, indeed, the function that prices play in the efficiency of markets is simply the function that the equilibrium set of prices would fill. Prices, that is, provide the parameters to guide market participants in engaging in the set of activities that are consistent with equilibrium conditions. Lange understandably held that this function of prices could be simulated in a socialist economy.

Socialist managers can be given lists of "prices" to which they can react according to well-defined rules (analogous to, but of course not identical with, the "rule" that capitalist decision makers are assumed to follow: that is, to maximize profits), Lange believed the task of ensuring that the lists of "prices" would be those required to ensure overall efficiency in the socialist economy could be fulfilled by again simulating (what he thought to be) the market trial and error procedure.

But here lies Lange's cardinal misunderstanding: he assumed that there exists in the market a procedure (involving "a series of successive trials") whereby prices are somehow adjusted toward equilibrium *without essentially altering the "parametric" character and function of prices* (that is, without departing from the supposition that each person separately regards market prices as given data, which he is unable to change). The market process through which prices are adjusted toward equilibrium, however, is a process in which prices are *not* treated as given parameters but are themselves hammered out in the course of vigorous and rivalrous bidding.

In emphasizing exclusively the "parametric" function of market prices. Lange misunderstood the central role of the market. The primary function of the market is *not* to offer an arena within which market participants can have their decentralized decisions smoothly coordinated through attention to the appropriate list of given prices. The market's essential function, rather, is to offer an arena in which market participants, by entrepreneurial exploitation of the profit opportunities offered by disequilibrium prices, can nudge prices in the direction of equilibrium. In this entrepreneurial process prices are *not* treated as parameters. Nor, in this process, are prices changed impersonally in response to excess demand or supply. It is one thing for Lange to assume that socialist managers can be motivated to follow rules with respect to centrally promulgated given "prices" (in the way capitalist decision makers can be imagined to treat given equilibrium market prices).[17] It is quite another to assume that the *non*-parametric function of price in the market system, the function dependent on entrepreneurial alertness to opportunities for pure profit, can be simulated in a system from which the entrepreneurial function has been wholly excised.

That Lange did not understand this nonparametric function of prices must certainly be attributed to a perception of the market system's operation primarily in terms of perfectly competitive equilibrium. (Indeed, it is this textbook approach to price theory that Lange explicitly presents as his model for socialist pricing.[18]) Within this paradigm, as is now well recognized, the role of the entrepreneurial quest for pure profit, as the key element in bringing about price adjustment, is completely ignored. It is not difficult to see how Lange could conclude that such a (nonentrepreneurial) system might be simulated under socialism.

Mises and Hayek, by contrast, saw the price system under capitalism from a totally different—an Austrian— perspective. For these writers, the essence of the market process lies not in the "parametric" function of price, and not in the perfectly competitive state of equilibrium, but in the rivalrous activity of entrepreneurs taking advantage of disequilibrium conditions. The debate between Lange-Dickinson on the one hand and Mises-Hayek on the other can best be understood as a clash between two conflicting views of the price system. Mises's views on the market as a process have been expounded extensively in a number of his works.[19] The idea of the market as a *dynamic process* is at the very heart of his system. Hayek's perception of the price system was articulated (during the same period in which his critical essays on socialist calculation were written) in a remarkable series of papers on the role of knowledge and discovery in market processes.[20]

That the postwar textbooks incorrectly presented the debate on socialist calculation as having been decisively won by Lange must be attributed not to ideological bias (although this may not have been entirely absent) but to an utter failure to understand the flaws in Lange's discussion (flaws that Hayek indeed had identified). Not recognizing the Austrian background of Hayek's critique, Anglo-American economists saw in Lange a cogent application of standard price theory; Hayek's critique simply was not understood.

The Market Process: An Austrian View[21]

Before returning to the theme of efficiency in the regulated economy, it is useful to review some Austrian lessons to be drawn from the socialist calculation debate. The Austrian understanding of the market as a dynamic process of discovery generated by the entrepreneurial-competitive scramble for pure profit may be spelled out in terms of a brief discussion of several key concepts. A sensitive appreciation of these ideas will alert us to problems raised by government regulation of the market that might otherwise easily be overlooked. It is partly because the terms convenient for the exposition of these concepts also are used in non-Austrian contexts, with rather different meanings, that the ideas developed here are so often misunderstood and therefore require brief elaboration.

Competition. What keeps the market process in motion is competition—*not* competition in the sense of "perfect competition," in which perfect knowledge is combined with very large numbers of buyers and sellers to generate a state of perennial equilibrium—but competition as the rivalrous activities of market participants trying to win profits by offering the market better opportunities than are currently available. The existence of rivalrous competition requires *not* large numbers of buyers and sellers but simply *freedom of entry.* Competition places pressure on market participants to discover where and how better opportunities, as yet unnoticed, *might* be offered to the market. The competitive market process occurs because equilibrium has not yet been attained. This process is thwarted whenever nonmarket barriers are imposed blocking entry to potential competitors.

Knowledge and Discovery. As Hayek has emphasized, the competitive market process is a discovery procedure.[22] If all that needed to be known were already known, then the market would already have attained full equilibrium, the state in which all decisions correctly anticipate all other decisions being made within the market. An institutional device for social organization that mobilizes existing knowledge and brings it to bear upon decision makers is necessary because realistically people never do have command even over all the information that is already known somewhere.[23] Market equilibrium is thinkable only if we can presuppose the full mobilization of existing knowledge; so also centralized economic control would be thinkable (whether by Lange-Dickinson—Lerner proposals or other devices) if we could assume existing knowledge already to be fully mobilized. It is just because, without a market, such prior mobilization is so difficult to assume that a market is seen to be a prerequisite for economic calculation.

The competitive market process is needed not only to mobilize existing knowledge, but also to generate awareness of opportunities whose very existence until now has been known to no one at all.[24] The entrepreneurial process, moreover, disseminates existing information through the market. The process itself is a continual one of the discovery of opportunities. The discoverer of these opportunities himself, at least, has had no inkling whatever of their very existence. The market, in other words, is not merely a process of search for information of the need for which men had previously been aware; it is a discovery procedure that tends to correct ignorance where the discoverers themselves were totally unaware that they indeed were ignorant. A realization that the market yields knowledge—the sort of knowledge that people do not at present even know they need—should engender among would-be social engineers who seek to replace or to modify the results of the free market a very definite sense of humility. To announce that one can improve on the performance of the market, one must also claim know in advance what the market will reveal. This knowledge is clearly impossible in all circumstances. Indeed, where the market process has been thwarted, in general it will not be possible to point with certainty to what *might* have been discovered that has now been lost.

Profit and Incentives. In standard treatments of price theory, decision makers are assumed to maximize utility or "profit." The profit for which entrepreneurs are so eager (and which for Austrians drives the market process) is not that "profit" maximized by the firm in the standard theory of the firm. The standard theory assumes that the firm confronts definitely known and given cost and revenue possibilities. For the theory of the firm, therefore, to maximize profits does not mean to *discover* an opportunity for pure gain; it means merely to perform the mathematical calculations required to exhaust the *already fully perceived* opportunity for gain that the given revenue and cost curves might present. The urge of would-be entrepreneurs to grasp profit, by contrast, is the force which *itself reveals* the existence of gaps between costs and revenues. This distinction is of considerable importance.

It is elementary to the theory of the market that the market performs its functions by virtue of the *incentives* it offers to those who make "correct" decisions. For example, the incentive of the higher wages offered by industries in which the marginal productivity of labor is greatest attracts labor to more important uses. Such incentives tend to ensure that once a superior use for a given factor (or group of factors) is discovered, it becomes worthwhile for factor owners to forgo alternative ways of putting their factors to work. This is well understood. What is not always understood is that the market also offers incentives for the *discovery* of new opportunities (for the most useful employment of factors), that is, for the exploitation of opportunities that until now have remained unexploited. These opportunities have remained unexploited *not* because of high costs, and not even because of the high cost of searching for them. They have remained unexploited simply because of sheer oversight, possibly including oversight of the opportunity to find them through deliberate search. Pure entrepreneurial profit is the market form in which *this* kind of incentive presents itself. The availability of pure entrepreneurial profit has the function not of outweighing the costs associated with withdrawing inputs from alternative uses, but of alerting decision makers to the present error of committing factors to uses less valuable to the markets than others waiting and able to be served.

Market Prices. Market prices in the Austrian view are not primarily approximations to the set of equilibrium prices. Instead, they are (disequilibrium) exchange ratios worked out between entrepreneurial market participants. On the one hand, these exchange ratios with all their imperfections reflect the discoveries made up until this moment by profit-seeking entrepreneurs. On the other hand, these ratios express entrepreneurial errors currently being made. Market prices, therefore, offer opportunities for pure profit. And we can rely on these opportunities to create a tendency for market prices to be changed through the rivalrous bidding of alert entrepreneurs. The course of market prices, in other words, is closely bound up, in *two* distinct ways, with the incentive system of pure entrepreneurial profit. First, the configuration of market prices at any given moment must be attributed to the pure profit incentives that have until now determined bids and offers. Second, this present configuration of market prices, together with existing and future conditions of supply and demand, is responsible for the opportunities for pure profit. The discovery and exploitation of these opportunities will constitute the course of the market process in the immediate future. From this perspective on market prices it is not difficult to perceive how small must be the resemblance to them of any centrally promulgated set of socialist "prices." The entrepreneurial drive for pure profit plays no role at all in the determination of socialist "prices."

Regulated Market Economy

I shall assume, as noted at the outset of this essay, that government regulation of the market economy is generated by dissatisfaction with market outcomes. Legislators or other government officials (perhaps in response to public outcry, or in anticipation thereof) are disturbed either by the high price that certain would-be purchasers are asked to pay in the market or by the low price (for example, farm prices or the wages of labor) received by certain sellers in the market; or they are disturbed by the quality of goods or services being offered for sale (for example, because of the absence of safety devices) or by the unavailability in the market of goods or services that they believe to be important. They are disturbed by the conditions under which workers are expected to work, or they are disturbed by the pattern of income distribution generated by the market, by unemployment, or by "profiteering," or by the side effects (such as environmental pollution, or spread of disease, or exposure of the young to pornography) generated by uncontrolled market activity.

Hoping to correct what are perceived to be unsatisfactory conditions, the government intervenes in the market. It seeks to replace the outcomes expected to result from unchecked market transactions by a preferred configuration of prices and outputs, to be achieved not, as under socialism, by replacing the market by central ownership of factors, but by imposing appropriate regulations and controls. The laissez-faire market is replaced by the regulated market. Price ceilings and price and wage floors, transfers of incomes, imposed safety standards, child labor laws, zoning laws, prohibited industrial integration, tariff protection, prohibited competition, imposed health warnings, compulsory old age pensions, and prohibited drugs are all examples of the countless controls that well-meaning public officials impose.

In the face of these controls, regulations, and interventions there remains, nonetheless, a genuine market both for factor services and for consumer products. Government controls constrain and constrict; they rearrange and repattern the structure of incentives; they redistribute incomes and wealth and sharply modify both the processes of production and the composition of consumption. Yet within the limits that such controls impose, buying and selling continue, and the constant effort to capture pure entrepreneurial gain keeps the market in perpetual motion. Government regulations drastically alter and disturb opportunities for entrepreneurial gain, but they do not eliminate them. These controls thoroughly influence the prices that emerge from the interplay of entrepreneurial competition. But unless directly mandated prices are involved, exchange ratios still reflect the outcome to date of the entrepreneurial process.

Traditionally, criticism of government intervention involves one of more of several general lines of argument.[25] First, critics may argue that the admitted failure of market outcomes to meet successfully the aspirations of regulators is a result not of market failure to achieve peak efficiency, but of inescapable scarcity. If costs are fully taken into account, efforts to improve outcomes must be found to be doomed to failure or to lead to even less preferable outcomes. Second, critics may agree that from the viewpoint of the value system adopted by the would-be regulators market outcomes might be improved upon. But, these critics maintain that the market faithfully reflects consumers' values. Regulation in such circumstances therefore must violate consumer sovereignty, if not consumer freedom.

Third, critics may argue that the unwished-for market outcomes are to be attributed not to the free market, but to earlier government interventions in the market which have hindered the corrective forces of the market from doing their work. Additional regulation, it is then pointed out, either may be unnecessary (since the earlier interventions can simply be eliminated) or may compound the problems. Fourth, critics may argue that whether or not the undesirable outcomes of the market are (in the sense appropriate to economic science and not necessarily from the viewpoint of the regulators' values) to be regretted, government regulation is simply incapable of achieving improvement. The technology of regulation is such that its full costs outweigh by far any benefits that may be achieved.

The Austrian lessons drawn from the preceding survey of the debate about socialist economic calculation suggest that another set of considerations, until now not sufficiently emphasized in the literature, deserve to be included in the list of causes to which one might attribute the failures of regulation. These considerations constitute a separate line of criticism of government intervention, to be added to the other lines of criticism (where one or more of these may be relevant).[26]

Government Regulation and the Market Discovery Process

The perils associated with government regulation of the economy addressed here arise out of the *impact that regulation can be expected to have on the discovery process, which the unregulated market tends to generate.* Even if current market outcomes in some sense are judged unsatisfactory, intervention, and even intervention that can successfully achieve its immediate objectives, cannot be considered the obviously correct solution. After all, the very problems apparent in the market might generate processes of discovery and correction superior to those undertaken deliberately by government regulation; deliberate intervention by the state not only might serve as an imperfect substitute for the spontaneous market process of discovery; but also might impede desirable processes of discovery the need for which has *not* been perceived by the government. Again, government regulation itself may generate new (unintended and undesired), processes of market adjustments that produce a final outcome even less preferred than what might have emerged in the free market.

Here I discuss critically the impact of government regulation on the discovery process of the unregulated market at four distinct levels. First, I consider the likelihood that would-be regulators may not correctly assess the course the market might itself take in the absence of regulation. Second, I consider the likelihood that, because of the presumed absence of entrepreneurial incentives operating on government decision makers, government regulatory decisions will fail to exploit opportunities for social betterment waiting to be discovered. Third, I consider the likelihood that government regulation may stifle or inhibit desirable discovery processes which the market might have generated. Finally, I consider the likelihood that government regulation may influence the market by creating opportunities for new, and not necessarily desirable, market discovery processes which would not be relevant in an unregulated market.

The Undiscovered Discovery Process

We assumed earlier that regulation is demanded because of undesirable conditions that emerge in the market in the absence of regulation. But the urge to regulate, to control, to alter these outcomes must presume not only that these undesirable conditions are attributable to the absence of regulation, but also that the speedy removal of such conditions cannot be expected from the future course of unregulated market events. To attribute undesirable conditions to absence of regulation, moreover, also may require the denial of the proposition that were a better state of affairs indeed feasible, the market probably would have already discovered how to achieve it.

More specifically, many demands for government intervention into the market rest on one or both of two possible misunderstandings concerning the market discovery process. Demand for government intervention, on the one hand, might grow out of a failure to realize that the market already may have discovered virtually everything worth discovering (so that what appears to be obvious inefficiency might be able to be explained altogether satisfactorily if government officials had all the information the market has long since discovered and taken advantage of). Demand for regulation, on the other hand, may stem from the belief that unsatisfactory conditions will never be corrected unless by deliberate intervention. Such demands for regulation might be muted, that is, were it understood that genuine inefficiencies can be relied upon in the *future* to generate market processes for their own correction. (This second misunderstanding itself may rest on either of two bases. First, the tendency of markets to discover and eliminate inefficiency simply is not recognized. Second, by contrast, it is assumed, far too sanguinely, that market processes are *so* rapid that our awareness of an unmistakably unsatisfactory condition proves that some kind of market "failure" has occurred and that one cannot rely on future corrective processes.)

These misunderstandings, so often the foundation for demands for intervention, surely derive from an unawareness of several basic principles of the theory of market process. These principles show that, first, were knowledge perfect, it would be inconceivable that unexploited opportunities could yet remain for rearranging the pattern of input utilization or output consumption in such a way as to improve the well-being of all market participants; second, the existence of such unexploited opportunities, reflecting imperfect knowledge throughout the market, expresses itself in the unregulated market in the form of opportunities for pure entrepreneurial profit; and third, the tendency for such pure profit opportunities to be discovered and exploited tends more or less rapidly to eliminate unexploited opportunities for improving the allocation of resources.[27] These principles of the theory of market process suggest that if genuine inefficiency exists, then (perhaps because of a recent sudden change in conditions of resource supply, of technology, or of consumer tastes) the market has not yet discovered *all that it will surely soon tend to discover*.

These principles may be denied either by expressing a lack of confidence in the systematic tendency for imperfect knowledge to be spontaneously improved or by attributing to the market the ability to attain equilibrium instantaneously (that is, by assuming that ignorance is not merely a disequilibrium phenomenon, but that ignorance disappears the very instant it emerges). Both denials may lead to demands for government intervention. The denial based on a lack of confidence about improving knowledge leads to the belief that current inefficiencies will not tend to be corrected spontaneously (and also to the propensity to see inefficiency where the market *already* has made necessary corrections). The denial based on the belief in instantaneous correction of disequilibrium conditions leads to the view that existing inefficiencies somehow are consistent with market equilibrium and that therefore extramarket steps are called for to achieve correction.

The Unsimulated Discovery Process

Government regulation takes the general form of imposed price ceilings and floors, of mandated quality specifications, and of other restraints or requirements imposed in interpersonal market transactions. The hope surrounding such government impositions, I continue to assume, is that they will constrain market activities to desired channels and at desired levels. But what is the likelihood that government officials, with the best of intentions, will *know* what imposed prices, say, might evoke the "correct," desired actions by market participants? This question parallels that raised by Mises and Hayek with respect to "market" socialism.[28] Government officials in the regulated economy do enjoy the advantage (*not* shared by socialist planning officials) of making their decisions within the framework of genuine market prices. But the question remains: How do government officials know what prices to set (or qualities to require, and so forth)? Or to press the point further:

How will government officials know if their earlier decisions were in error and in what direction to make corrections? In other words, how will government officials *discover* those opportunities for improving the allocation of resources, which one cannot assume to be automatically known to them at the outset of a regulatory endeavor?

The compelling insight underlying these questions rests heavily on the circumstance that officials institutionally are precluded from capturing *pecuniary* profits in the market, in the course of their activities (even though they are as eager as anyone else for entrepreneurial "profit" in the broadest sense of the term). The regulators' estimates of the prices consumers are prepared to pay, or of the prices resource owners are prepared to accept, for example, *are not profit-motivated estimates*. The estimates are not profit motivated at the time of an initial government regulatory action, and they are not profit motivated at each subsequent date when modification of a regulation might be considered. But estimates of market demand conditions or market supply conditions that are not profit motivated cannot reflect the powerful, discovery-inspiring incentives of the entrepreneurial quest for profit.

Nothing in the course of the regulatory process suggests a tendency for as yet unperceived opportunities of resource allocation improvement to be discovered. Nothing ensures that government officials who might perceive market conditions more accurately than others will tend systematically to replace less competent regulators. There is no entrepreneurial process at work, and there is no proxy for entrepreneurial profit or loss that easily might indicate where errors have been made and how they should be corrected. What regulators know (or believe they know) at a given moment presumably remains only partly correct. No systematic process seems at work through which regulators might come to discover what they have not known, *especially since they have not known that they enjoy less than complete awareness of a particular situation.*

The problem raised here is not quite the same as the one identified in other literature critical of government intervention. It is often noted, for example, that government officials are not motivated to minimize costs, since they will not personally benefit from the resulting economies.[29] The problem raised here differs importantly from such questions of incentives for adopting known efficiencies. For even if one could imagine an official so dedicated to the citizenry that he would ensure the adoption of all known possible measures for cutting costs, one cannot yet imagine him somehow divining *as yet undiscovered* techniques for cutting costs. What the official knows, he knows, and what he knows that he does *not* know, one may imagine him diligently undertaking to find out, through appropriate cost-benefit-calculated search. But one can hardly imagine him discovering, except by the sheerest accident, those opportunities for increasing efficiency of which he is completely unaware. The official is not subject to the entrepreneurial profit incentive, which somehow appears continually and successfully to inspire discovery of hitherto undreamed of possibilities for eliminating unnecessary expenditures. Nothing within the regulatory process seems able to simulate even remotely well the discovery process that is so integral to the unregulated market.

The Stifled Discovery Process

The most serious effect of government regulation on the market discovery process well might be the likelihood that regulation, in a variety of ways, may discourage, hamper, and even completely stifle the discovery process of the unregulated market. Indeed, that much regulation is introduced as a result of unawareness of the market's discovery process already has been noted.

Government regulation plainly might bar exploitation of opportunities for pure entrepreneurial profit. A price ceiling, a price floor, an impeded merger, or an imposed safety requirement might block possibly profitable entrepreneurial actions. Such restraints and requirements may be designed to block *particular* activities. If so, the likelihood is that since the possibility of such activities is so clearly seen and feared, the blocked activity may provide standard rates of return, but *not* particularly profitable ones in the entrepreneurial sense. Regulated restraints and requirements, though, are also likely to block activities that have *not* yet been foreseen by anyone, including the regulatory authorities. Regulatory constraints, that is, are likely *to bar the discovery* of pure profit opportunities.

That government regulation diminishes competition is common knowledge. Tariffs, licensing requirements, labor legislation, airline regulation, and bank regulation reduce the number of potential participants in particular markets. Government regulation, therefore, is responsible for imposing monopoly like inefficiencies ("deadweight" welfare losses) upon the economy. But such losses by no means constitute the full impact of the countercompetitive measures often embodied in regulatory constraints.

The beneficent aspect of competition in the sense of a rivalrous process, as noted earlier, arises out of *freedom of entry*. What government regulations so often erect are *regulatory barriers to entry*. Freedom of "entry," for the Austrian approach, refers to the freedom of potential competitors to discover and to move to exploit existing opportunities for pure profit. If entry is blocked, such opportunities simply may never be discovered, either by existing firms in the industry, or by regulatory authorities, or for that matter by outside entrepreneurs who *might* have discovered such opportunities were they allowed to be exploited when found.

From *this* perspective on regulation's anticompetitive impact, it follows that much regulation introduced explicitly to *create* or *maintain* competition is no less hazardous to the competitive—entrepreneurial process than are other forms of regulation that restrict competition. Entry of competitors, in the dynamic sense, need not mean entry of firms of about equal size. For example, entry might imply the *replacement*, by merger or other means, of a number of relatively high-cost producers by a *single* low-cost producer. Antitrust activity designed ostensibly to protect competition might *block* this kind of entry. Such regulatory activity thus blocks the capture of pure profit, obtainable in this case by the discovery and implementation of the possibility of lowering the price to consumers by taking advantage of hitherto unexploited, and perhaps unsuspected, economies of scale.

The literature critical of government regulation often draws attention to the undesirable effects of imposed prices. A price ceiling for a particular product or service (rent control, for example) tends to generate artificial shortages (of housing). A price floor for a particular product or service, (minimum wages, for example) tends to generate an artificial surplus (teenage unemployment!. These important, well-recognized consequences of imposed prices flow from the efforts of the regulators to legislate prices at other than equilibrium levels.

Quite apart from the discoordination generated by such imposed prices in the markets for *existing* goods and services, price (and also quality) restraints also may well inhibit the discovery of wholly new opportunities. A price ceiling does not merely block the upper reaches of a given supply curve. Such a ceiling also may inhibit the discovery of as yet unsuspected sources of supply (which in the absence of the ceiling would have tended to shift the entire supply curve to the right) or of as yet wholly unknown new products (tending to create supply curves for wholly new graphs).[30] The lure of pure profit tends to uncover such as yet unknown opportunities.

Price and quality restraints and requirements and restrictions on organizational forms operate (in a generally understood but not precisely predictable way) to inhibit entrepreneurial discovery. Price ceilings, for example, not only restrict supply from known sources of natural gas (or from known prospects for search), but also inhibit the discovery of wholly unknown sources. Drug testing regulations, as another example, not only reduce the flow of new pharmaceutical drugs where successful research might have been more or less predictable, but also discourage the entrepreneurial discovery of wholly unknown research procedures. Against whatever benefits might be derived from government regulation and intervention, one is forced to weigh, as one of regulation's intrinsically immeasurable costs, the stifling of the market discovery process.

The Wholly Superfluous Discovery Process

There is yet one more aspect of government regulation's complex impact on the discovery process. Whether intended by the regulatory authorities or not and whether suspected by them or not, the imposition of regulatory restraints and requirements tends to create entirely new, and not necessarily desirable opportunities for entrepreneurial discovery.

That such opportunities may be created follows from the extreme unlikelihood that government-imposed price, quality, or quantity constraints introduce anything approaching an equilibrium configuration. These constraints, on the contrary, introduce pure profit opportunities that would otherwise have been absent, as they simultaneously reduce or possibly eliminate other opportunities for pure profit that might otherwise have existed. This rearrangement of opportunities for pure profits, of course, is unlikely to be the explicit aim of regulation; nor even, indeed, is such rearrangement ever likely to be fully *known* to the authorities. Market ignorance is a fact of economic life. It follows that the replacement of one set of (unregulated) prices by another set of (partly regulated) prices, simply means that regulation has generated a possibly major alteration in the pattern of the discovery process. The now regulated market will tend to pursue the altered discovery process.

This regulation-induced alteration in the pattern of market discovery is closely related to the often noticed circumstance that regulation may result in a different set of equilibrium market consequences. Such consequences, moreover, may not have been correctly foretold by the authorities and, indeed, may be wholly undesired by them. Regulation often imposes costs not immediately recognized.[31] Unless, quite fantastically, the regulatory authorities (somehow all acting in completely coordinated fashion) are perfectly informed on all relevant data about the market, they will not generally be able to perceive what new profit opportunities they create by their own regulatory actions. Inevitably, therefore, the imposition of a set of regulatory constraints on a market must set in motion a series of entrepreneurial actions that have not been anticipated and, therefore, that may well lead to wholly unexpected and even undesired final outcomes.[32]

The one kind of new "profit" opportunity created by regulation that is by now well anticipated, though hardly desired of course, involves bribery and corruption of the regulators. There is widespread understanding of the unwholesome channels into which the entrepreneurial quest for pure profit inevitably tends to be attracted if arbitrary restraints on otherwise profitable activities are imposed.[33]

The basic insight underlying these conclusions, in sum, is a simple one. The competitive entrepreneurial process, being a process of discovery of the as yet unknown, can hardly be predicted in any but the broadest terms. The imposition of regulatory constraints necessarily results, therefore, in a pattern of consequences different from and, most plausibly, distinctly less desirable than what would have occurred in the unregulated market. One might therefore refer to this unplanned, undesired pattern of consequences of regulation as the wholly superfluous discovery process.

Discovery, Evidence, and Illustration

The preceding discussion is theoretical and general, providing no hints of possible verification of its conclusions. While this discussion relies on highly plausible insights into the character of human action, a reader may believe himself justified in demanding evidence that might support the discussion's rather strong conclusions. Yet such evidence can hardly be furnished, and it may be instructive to spell out the reasons.

Evidence About Discovery

Econometricians have endeavored to measure the consequences of particular economic policies. Much of their ingenuity and sophistication has been called forth to grapple with the formidable problem of describing *what might have occurred* in the absence of particular policies. The problem of describing concretely what might have happened but did not, it should be noted, exists even in situations in which all the alternatives before relevant decision makers are clearly defined, so that one at least knows the list of options from among which choices would have been forthcoming. The problem derives from the circumstance that it is not possible, without more or less sophisticated conjecture, to be confident as to which of an array of options a particular decision maker *might* have selected in hypothetical circumstances.

This problem becomes infinitely more formidable if one wishes to describe, in specified hypothetical circumstances, *what might have been spontaneously discovered.* Here the problem is not merely that a particular decision maker's preferences are unknown. The problem is that one cannot imagine what specific, now unknown opportunities might have been discovered in the relevant hypothetical circumstances.

One should not be surprised, therefore, that the losses from the regulatory stifling of market discovery processes are difficult to single out. Indeed, one should not be surprised that analysis, too, has tended to overlook such losses. Therefore one can only hope to draw brief attention to studies that perhaps can provide some illustrative flavor of the kinds of losses attributable to regulatory constraints, to which I have sought to direct attention. For purposes of such illustration, I draw on work focusing on the discovery process initiated by the lure of entrepreneurial profit in technological innovation and in corporate entrepreneurial endeavor.

Discoverers: Innovators

Much recent work by economists is devoted to gaining insight into the process of technological innovation. A small part of that work has considered the impact of government regulation on innovative activity at the technological frontiers. Although the authors of these studies are not primarily concerned with the impact of regulation upon entrepreneurial incentives, it is difficult to read their work without noticing its direct relevance to this essay's concerns.

A 1971 Brookings Institution volume, for example, was devoted to a symposium examining technological change in regulated industries (in particular electric power, telecommunications, and air and surface transportation).[34] In the analytical framework within which this examination was conducted, brief attention is paid to the thesis (attributed, perhaps too hastily, to Schumpeter) that it is "the incentive to earn very large profits" which "spurs entrepreneurs to introduce new techniques," so that the limits on possible profits imposed by regulatory commissions may inhibit such innovation.[35]

A similar possible link between regulatory constraints and the possible slowing down of the processes of technological discovery is noted particularly in the context of drug research in the pharmaceutical industry. The classic paper by Professor Peltzman, examining the impact of the 1962 drug amendments upon drug research, together with the work of others, has led to widespread discussion of the possibility that drug research in the United States lags seriously behind that of other countries.[36] Peltzman's results do not prove that regulation inhibits entrepreneurial discovery, which means the discovery of hitherto unknown opportunities, unknown even in the sense that it had not been known that they were there to be discovered. That is, Peltzman's findings would fit in equally well with a theory of search based on the assumption of awareness of discoverable opportunities waiting to be researched if the cost were not too high. Nonetheless, once attention is focused on entrepreneurial discovery, it is difficult to avoid linking Peltzman's results with the postulation of an entrepreneurial discovery process hampered by regulatory constraints.

Discoverers: Insiders

Another important area in which the role of entrepreneurial discovery has been explicitly explored is that of decision making by corporate managers. In his definitive study of the issue, Henry Manne discusses the impact upon the exercise of entrepreneurship in the corporate firm of regulatory restrictions on insider trading.[37] Manne's study thoroughly examines the entrepreneurial role and its expression in a world of corporations. The study identifies the incentives of entrepreneurial profit needed to evoke the entrepreneurial role and the part that insider trading, in the absence of regulatory prohibition, might play to provide profit opportunities to reward entrepreneurial success. Restrictions on insider trading, Manne shows, no matter how plausible the motives underlying the regulatory restrictions may appear, tend to inhibit the exercise of entrepreneurship in corporate firms.[38]

Conclusion

This essay draws attention to some less obvious drawbacks of government regulation of the market. These drawbacks are rooted in the way regulatory restrictions, restraints, and controls interfere with the spontaneous discovery process that the unregulated market tends to generate. These drawbacks are also to be clearly distinguished from other disadvantages that flow from government intervention.

The peculiar character of the perils of regulation identified here closely parallels certain economic problems associated with the operation of the socialist economy. The review of the Mises-Hayek criticisms of the possibility of economic calculation under socialism provides a classic source for an Austrian perspective on the market process, and simultaneously the review provides important lessons for an understanding of the dangers inherent in regulation.

Recognition of these dangers can be most helpful in explaining the inefficiencies and the stagnation that appear so consistently to beset modern interventionist economies. It is in the nature of the subject, however, that the recognition of these perils does not lead easily to the provision of clear-cut examples of such regulatory damage. Nonetheless, in a modest way it is possible to illustrate these perils from contemporary discussions of palpable problems.

An emphasis on the perils of regulation that arises out of concern for the market process does not, in and of itself, justify the absolute condemnation of government regulation of the market process. Such condemnation would require full consideration, in addition, not only of other perils than those discussed here, but also of the hoped-for benefits sought through regulation of the market. Ultimately, public policy must depend on the value judgments of the policymakers or of those they wish to serve. But, no policy decisions with respect to government regulation can be properly arrived at without a full understanding of all the dangers inherent in such regulation. And such a full understanding arises particularly out of studying the market process of entrepreneurial discovery.

Notes

1. For the literature on private incentives for public regulation, see George J. Stigler, "The Theory of Economic Regulation," *Bell Journal of Economics and Management Science* 2 (Spring 1971): 321; reprinted in Stigler, *The Citizen and the State* (Chicago: University of Chicago Press, 1975); Richard A. Posner, "Theories of Economic Regulation," *Bell Journal of Economics and Management Science* 5 (Autumn 1974): 335-58; Sam Peltzman, "Toward a More General Theory of Regulation," *Journal of Law and Economics* 19 (August 1976): 211-40.

2. The most trenchant recent criticisms of government regulation from this perspective include Ludwig von Mises, *Human Action* (New Haven: Yale University Press, 1949), part 6; Milton Friedman, *Capitalism and Freedom* (Chicago: University of Chicago Press, 1962); Friedman, *An Economist's Protest* (Glen Ridge, N.J.: Thomas Horton and Daughters, 1972).

3. Ludwig von Mises, "Die Wirtschaftsrechnung im sozialistischen Gemeinwesen," *Archiv für Sozialwissenschaften und Sozialpolitik* 47 (April 1920): 86-121; reprinted in *Collectivist Economic Planning*, trans. and ed. Friedrich A. Hayek (London: Routledge and Kegan Paul, 1935).

4. Ludwig von Mises, *Socialism: An Economic and Sociological Analysis*, trans. J. Kahane (New Haven: Yale University Press, 1951) part 2, sect. 1; this edition is translated from the second German edition (published 1932) of Mises's *Die Gemeinwirtschaft* (originally published in 1922); see also Mises, *Human Action*, part 5.

5. Hayek, *Collectivist Economic Planning*.

6. Friedrich A. Hayek, "Socialist Calculation: The Competitive 'Solution,' " *Economica* 7 (May 1940): 125-49; reprinted as "Socialist Calculation III: The Competitive 'Solution,' " in Hayek, *Individualism and Economic Order* (London: Routledge and Kegan Paul, 1949).

7. Oskar Lange, "On the Economic Theory of Socialism," in Oskar Lange and Fred M. Taylor, *On the Economic Theory of Socialism*, ed. Benjamin E. Lippincot (New York: McGraw-Hill, 1964).

8. Trygve J. B. Hoff, *Economic Calculation in the Socialist Society*, trans. M. A. Michael (London and Edinburgh: Hodge, 1949).

9. Dominic T. Armentano, "Resource Allocation Problems under Socialism," in *Theory of Economic Systems: Capitalism, Socialism, Corporatism*, ed. William P. Snavely (Columbus, Ohio: Merrill, 1969), pp. 133-34.

10. Hayek, "Socialist Calculation III." Reviewed particularly were Lange, "On the Economic Theory of Socialism," and Henry D. Dickinson, *Economics of Socialism* (London: Oxford University Press, 1939).

11. Thus they agreed with Mises and Hayek that efficiency is impossible without indicators of value and that any hope of solving the problem by direct mathematical methods (for example, by solving the Walrasian equation system) is illusory.

12. Hayek, *Individualism and Economic Order*, p. 187.

13. Abba P. Lerner, *The Economics of Control* (New York: Macmillan, 1944).

14. See most recently Murray N. Rothbard, "Ludwig von Mises and Economic Calculation under Socialism," in *Economics of Ludwig von Mises*, ed. Laurence S. Moss (Kansas City: Sheed and Ward, 1976).

15. Lange, "On the Economic Theory of Socialism," p. 70.

16. Ibid., pp. 70-71.

17. This assumption, of course, is vulnerable to serious question. See James M. Buchanan, *Cost and Choice* (Chicago: Markham, 1969), chap. 6; G. Warren Nutter, "Markets without Property: A Grand Illusion," in *Money, the Market, and the State: Essays in Honor of James Muir Waller*, ed. Nicholas A. Beadles and L. Aubrey Drewry, Jr. (Athens: University of Georgia Press, 1968). It is important to note that the argument stated in the text does *not* depend on any doubt concerning managers' ability and motivation to obey rules. Were socialist managers to be given price lists, then we may assume for the purposes of the present discussion that they *could* make decisions *as if* they were intent on maximizing "profits." (Of course, the profits maximized in equilibrium contexts are not pure entrepreneurial profits. This distinction is discussed later in this essay.)

18. Lange, "On the Economic Theory of Socialism," p. 65-72.

19. Particularly in Mises, *Human Action*, chap. 15.

20. Hayek, "Economics and Knowledge," "The Use of Knowledge in Society," and "The Meaning of Competition," all reprinted in *Individualism and Economic Order*. In this respect the work of Austrian-born Joseph A. Schumpeter is of considerable relevance for the Austrian view of the market; see particularly Schumpeter, *The Theory of Economic Development*, trans. Redvers Opie (New York: Oxford University Press, 1961); this work first appeared in German in 1912 and was first translated by Opie in 1934. See also Schumpeter, *Capitalism, Socialism and Democracy* (New York: Harper and Row, 1950), chap. 7.

21. This section draws freely from my *Competition and Entrepreneurship* (Chicago: University of Chicago Press, 1973), and *Perception, Opportunity, and Profit* (Chicago: University of Chicago Press, 1979).

22. Friedrich A. Hayek, ea., "Competition as a Discovery Procedure," in *New Studies in Philosophy, Politics, Economics and the History of Ideas* (Chicago: University of Chicago Press, 1978).

23. See Hayek, "Economics and Knowledge," "The Use of Knowledge in Society," and "The Meaning of Competition."

24. See Kirzner, *Perception, Opportunity, and Profit*, chaps. 2, 8, 9.

25. Once again, we assume away criticisms based on the view that regulation may be motivated not by the wish to benefit consumers, but by the wish to benefit the regulators and those they regulate.

26. While these considerations support a stance critical of regulation, in and of themselves they do not necessarily declare regulation to be wrong, or even inefficient. Given sufficiently strong value judgments on the part of would be regulators—whether in favor of environmental purity, of an egalitarian distribution of wealth, of freedom from pornography or disease, of national prestige, of the enrichment of the arts, or of whatever—criticism of intervention, from the perspective of these value judgments, may (properly) carry little weight. The economist's task, however, is to spell out as fully as possible the consequences of alternative policies, so that policy decisions at least will not be taken on the basis of erroneous assessments of their likely consequences. The discussion in the following pages does not offer an airtight case against intervention but draws attention to possibly grave perils of intervention, perils that seem to have been taken fully and explicitly into account neither by the literature critical of interventionist policies nor, a fortiori, by the uncritical proponents and supporters of government regulation.

27. Here an improvement in the allocation of resources (given the initial pattern of resource distribution) is defined as a change in the pattern of input utilization and/or input consumption that improves the well-being of each member of the economy. Although this definition is close to the norm of Paretian welfare economics, it does *not* invoke the notion of aggregate welfare.

28. "The Austrian finds no detailed explanation in welfare economics of how government is supposed to obtain the information necessary to carry out its assigned tasks. The knowledge required . . . is not to be found collected in one place, but rather dispersed throughout the many members of the economy." Stephen C. Littlechild, *The Fallacy of the Mixed Economy: An "Austrian" Critique of Economic Thinking and Policy* (London: Institute of Economic Affairs, 1978), p. 40. See also Gordon Tullock, *The Politics of Bureaucracy* (Washington, D.C.: Public Affairs Press 1965), p. 124: "Administrative problems . . . could . . . be of such complexity that the centralization of information necessary to make decisions effectively in a bureaucracy might not be possible."

29. It is even most cogently pointed out that the very notion of cost, seen from the perspective of the regulator, is unlikely to coincide with any notion of cost that one might wish to consider relevant to the quest for efficiency. See Buchanan, *Cost and Choice*, chaps. 5 and 6.

30. Professor Machlup valuably refers to the "fertility of freedom" in generating discovery of new possibilities. Fritz Machlup, "Liberalism and the Choice of Freedoms," in *Roads to Freedom: Essays in Honour of Friedrich A. von Hayek*, ed. Erich Streissler (London: Routledge and Kegan Paul, 1969), p. 130.

31. Murray L. Weidenbaum, "The Impact of Government Regulation" (study prepared for the Joint Economic Committee, Subcommittee on Economic Growth and Stabilization, United States Congress, July 1978). See also Ernest C. Pasour, "Hide and Seek: Hidden Costs of Government Regulation," *World Research INK* 2 (December 1978): 5.

32. "There is ample evidence that imagination and innovation are not stilled by restrictive legislation—only diverted to figuring out ways around it." Freidman, *Economist's Protest*, p. 149.

33. See, for example, Nicholas Sanchez and Alan R. Waters, "Controlling Corruption in Africa and Latin America," in *The Economics of Property Rights,* ed. Eirik Furubotn and Svetozar Pejovich (Cambridge, Mass.: Ballinger, 1974); Edward C. Banfield, "Corruption as a Feature of Governmental Organization," *Journal of Law and Economics* 18 (December 1975): 587-605; and Simon Rottenberg, "Comment," *Journal of Law and Economics* 18 (December 1975): 611-15.

34. William M. Capron et al., eds., *Technological Change in Regulated Industries* (Washington,D.C.: Brookings Institution, 1971).

35. Ibid., p. 8. See also chap. 2.

36. Sam Peltzman, "An Evaluation of Consumer Protection Legislation: The 1962 Drug Amendments," *Journal of Political Economy* 81 (September-October 1973): 1049-91. See also David Schwartzman, *Innovation in the Pharmaceutical Industry* (Baltimore: Johns Hopkins Press, 1976).

37. Henry G. Manne, *Insider Trading and the Stock Market* (New York: Free Press, 1966).

38. Although there are many other studies illustrating the hidden distortions generated by regulation, I do not cite them here, since they do not obviously call our attention to the market discovery process and its modification as a result of the regulatory constraints.

BUREAUCRACY VERSUS ENVIRONMENT—THE BEAT GOES ON

Terry Anderson and Donald Leal

Although efforts to reserve millions of acres in the political domain were under way during the late nineteenth century, Mr. and Mrs. W.W. Beck were doing their part to preserve one little corner of the world on the outskirts of Seattle, Washington. In 1887, they bought several parcels of land with giant fir trees reaching 400 feet in height and 20 feet in diameter. The Becks built a pavilion for concerts and nature lectures and added paths, benches, and totem poles. Ravenna Park soon became immensely popular. Visitors paid 25 cents a day or $5 a year ($3.60 and $72, respectively, in 1999 dollars) to enter the park. Even with the fees, 8,000 to 10,000 people visited the park on a busy day.[1]

As the Seattle population grew and conservationist sentiment developed, residents began to lobby for acquiring more public parklands, including Ravenna Park. In 1911, the city bought Ravenna from the Becks for $135,663 following condemnation proceedings. Shortly after the city's acquisition, according to newspaper accounts, the giant firs began disappearing. The Seattle Federation of Women's Clubs confronted Park Superintendent J.W. Thompson with reports of tree cutting. He acknowledged that the large "Roosevelt Tree" had been cut down because it had posed a "threat to public safety." It had been cut into cordwood and sold, Thompson conceded, but only to facilitate its removal and to defray costs. The federation asked a University of Washington forestry professor to investigate. When the women brought the professor's finding that a number of trees had been cut to the attention of the park board, the board expressed regret and promised that the cutting would stop. By 1925, however, all the giant fir trees in Ravenna had disappeared.[2]

Some people still blame the destruction of the trees on a 1925 windstorm; others blame it on automobiles and chimney smoke. But it was the bureaucracy that destroyed what the Becks had saved. Park employees took advantage of their access to the park and cut down trees to sell firewood. Park Department records charge Superintendent Thompson with abuse of public funds, equipment, and personnel, plus the unauthorized sale of public property. Even if he and his subordinates were not direct culprits, they had allowed the cutting to go on.

The Ravenna Park debacle occurred at a time when leaders of the early conservation movement were touting public ownership as the only way to conserve America's natural resources. In their view, the greed of private owners was an insurmountable obstacle to conservation. Yet, in the case of Ravenna Park, private owners protected natural treasures, while public agents destroyed them. Even an outcry from public watchdogs could not prevent the eventual destruction of the giant fir trees.

Could similar controversies and results occur with political resources today? Unfortunately, the answer is yes, and on a much larger scale than the incident at Ravenna Park.

Timber Beasts versus Tree Huggers

The U.S. Forest Service, with an annual budget approaching $3 billion and over 38,000 full-time employees, is the largest natural resource agency in the federal government. It oversees more than 191 million acres of national forests and is required by law to manage its lands for multiple uses, which include timber production, livestock grazing, mineral and energy production, fish and wildlife habitat, wilderness protection, and public recreation. While the agency does collect revenue from the sale of timber, grazing allotments, minerals, oil and gas, and certain recreational activities such as camping, it is not required to generate a profit. In fact, most of the revenues it collects go to the U.S. Treasury, and expenditures by the agency are appropriated by Congress. Not surprisingly, the agency regularly runs huge deficits. Over the 1994-1996 period, for example, the Forest Service spent an average of $3 billion per year, while receiving $914 million in revenue from the timber, recreation, grazing, minerals, and other uses.[3] Recreation incurred the largest average annual loss of $355 million, followed by timber with a loss of $290 million, and grazing with a loss of $66 million.[4]

Though recreation generates the largest deficit, timber production remains the most controversial activity on national forests. Over the past three decades, environmentalists have argued that the Forest Service overemphasizes this activity at the expense of environmental amenities. Moreover, they contend that because timber production loses millions of dollars each year, it should be eliminated. Timber interests counter that the agency gives wilderness values too much attention and that the Forest Service loses money selling timber because the agency has been inundated with costly regulations and administrative red tape that have driven up program costs.

The fact that the Forest Service loses millions selling timber indicates that something is drastically wrong with the program. (The same can be said for the other programs that lose money, such as recreation.) But it is insufficient to conclude that the program should be eliminated. The appropriate fiscal question is: Does the program have the potential to make money for the taxpayer?

Consider national forests in Montana, where federal timber sale programs frequently lose money. Comparisons with state-run forests in Montana indicate that selling timber from national forests in the state does not have to be a money-losing proposition.[5] Montana state and national forestlands are often adjacent to one another, and surveys by silviculturists have shown that these lands have essentially the same timber-growing potential. Yet Montana's state-owned forests netted more than $13 million selling timber over a five-year period (1988-1992). Over the same period, the ten national forests in the state lost nearly $42 million selling timber! Data on state timber operations in Washington, Oregon, and Idaho show that Montana is not unique.[6]

These dramatic differences do not originate on the revenue side of the equation, but are due to differences in management costs. Not only are state and national forests located in the same land base, both are multiple-use forests. And state foresters must carry out the same duties as Forest Service personnel, including overseeing road building and reforestation and conducting environmental analyses. Yet state foresters operate at much lower costs than the Forest Service—and not only because they are paid less. The Forest Service uses over twice the number of personnel as do state foresters in preparing and administering timber sales for a given volume of timber harvested. State forests also have much lower road building costs because they build relatively inexpensive roads that last only as long as the logging proceeds, in contrast to the national forest's permanent road system. Hence, the state's roads average about $5,000 per mile in construction costs, while the Forest Service spends at least $50,000 per mile.[7]

What explains the fiscal difference between state and national forest timber operations? In a word, incentives. By law, state foresters must maximize returns from their lands for public schools. Their jobs are on the line if they do not do so. Forest Service personnel have no such requirement. If they lose money selling timber, taxpayers make up the losses. In other words, Forest Service personnel have little incentive to control costs or maximize the net value of the timber they sell.

Further indication that the Forest Service operates under perverse economic incentives comes from a recent review of timber harvests and agency spending. From 1991 to 1996, timber harvests, still the dominant source of revenue, fell from an annual average of over 8 billion board feet to less than 4 billion board feet.[8] Yet, Forest Service annual spending changed very little over this period, hovering around $3 billion per year. More puzzling is the fact that while timber production declined 69 percent from 1981-84 to 1994-96, the share of the Forest Service budget devoted to timber actually increased 10 percent. Meanwhile, the proportion of spending devoted to recreation increased only 3 percent, while recreational use on national forests increased over 50 percent. Recently, the fastest growing segment of the Forest Service budget was general administration, increasing from 19 percent of total expenditures in 1992 to 32 percent in 1996.[9]

Perhaps the pain of the Forest Service's poor economic performance would be reduced if national forests were in a state of ecological health, but perverse economic incentives also lead to perverse ecological incentives. An environmental audit, ordered by the Montana state legislature and conducted by professionals (including environmental-group representatives) reviewed forest practices in Montana in 1992 to ascertain how well foresters protected watershed from the impacts of logging. The audit found that the state ranked higher than the Forest Service.[10] Similarly, an inquiry by the General Accounting Office into U.S. Forest and Bureau of Land Management planning for the period from February 1988 to August 1990 found that the two federal land agencies were not meeting objectives for sustaining wildlife populations.[11] The inquiry found that only one-third of the 51 wildlife plans containing 1,130 wildlife-related actions had been completed.

Equally disturbing is the increasing risk of catastrophic fires occurring on many national forests. Decades of fire suppression has led to a huge buildup of fuel from understory growth and changed the species composition of many national forests. According to U.S. Forest Service fire expert Steve Arno, once-open ponderosa pine forests in the Intermountain West have given way to densely growing stands of Douglas fir because, unlike ponderosa pine, fir is shade tolerant and is able to grow in the thick forest understory that now characterizes many national forests in the region.[12] These stands of fir are also very susceptible to insect infestation. The result is a huge buildup of diseased and dying trees, adding further to the fuel load.

And the fire condition in the Intermountain region is only the tip of the iceberg. Forest Service chief Michael Dombeck recently testified before Congress that nearly 40 million acres, or 21 percent of all national forestlands, are classified as at high risk of catastrophic fire.[13] With the recent steep decline in timber harvests in the 1990s, the risk of fire on national forests can only increase.

The fiscal and environmental problems that plague our national forests are the results of institutions, not people. To expect forest managers to set aside self-interest and objectively weigh the benefits and costs of multiple-use management is to ignore the information and the incentives that confront them. Forest managers are not supposed to manage the national forests to maximize returns, but they can and do manage in ways that maximize budgets at the expense of taxpayers without ensuring environmental quality. Bureaucrats in general have a propensity to expand their staff and budgets because such expansion provides higher salaries, more prestige, and more power. In the case of the Forest Service, timber revenues are generated when trees are harvested, with a percentage of the receipts retained by the bureaucracy. In addition, timber harvests mean a larger road-building staff and more budget for timber management. With little revenue generated from recreational or environmental amenities and less staff required to manage wilderness, these values have received less attention than traditional commodities.

Organized wilderness advocates, however, are increasing pressure for making larger expenditures on recreational and environmental amenities and devoting more land to these uses. Even if the pendulum swings in this direction, controversies will not disappear. With the costs diffused among all taxpayers and with benefits concentrated, environmentalists consider no price to be too great for saving wilderness. For example, when a group of environmentalists and local landowners discovered that a timber company was planning to cut tress from four sections (2,560 acres) in the Greater Yellowstone area, they asked Congress to buy the property for $800 per acre, an amount the landowner was eager to accept, since timberlands in the area are worth only approximately $500 per acre. Such pressures will only increase Forest Service deficits and fuel a backlash from commodity interests whose jobs depend on the forests. The bureaucratic process does little to encourage either fiscal or environmental responsibility.

Park Upkeep in Peril

Fiscal and environmental controversies surround the National Park Service as well. The mission of the Park Service is "to promote and regulate the use of the . . . national parks . . . which purpose is to conserve the scenery and the natural and historic objects and the wild life therein and to provide for the enjoyment of the same in such manner and by such means as will leave them unimpaired for the enjoyment of future generations."[14] But national treasures such as Yellowstone National Park are far from "unimpaired for the enjoyment of future generations." Sewage treatment systems in the park are so old that they cannot handle the wastes generated during peak visitation periods.[15] Recent monitoring reveals that treated wastewater is contaminating waters that feed Old Faithful as well as popular trout streams, such as Iron Springs Creek. At times raw sewage is actually dumped into meadows as an alternative to dumping it directly into streams and lakes. The park's road system is also crumbling. In August 1998, a part of Grand Loop Road, a popular road in Yellowstone that provides opportunities to view wildlife such as grizzly bears, had to be closed because it posed a hazard to vehicles and threatened passenger safety.[16] The road, which was last resurfaced in 1942, is presently inundated with potholes. Though the Park Service spent some funds in 1998 from higher entrance fees to patch and fill the potholes, these repairs failed to last through the summer.

In his book, *The National Parks Compromised*, former director of the National Park Service James Ridenour recognized the impact of "park barrel politics" on the nation's treasures. He states that "the government has just not taken care of these beautiful treasures" and goes on to describe a visit to Sequoia National Park when he was director. "I noticed water running down the pavement and upon closer look, I noticed toilet paper. The old sewer system was overloaded and the pipes were clogged up. I couldn't believe it—here we were trying to set the environmental standard for the nation and we were in blatant violation of the standards ourselves."[17] Writing in *National Geographic*, John G. Mitchell said, ". . . parks were created 'for the enjoyment of future generations.' For many, that 78-year-old promise is eroding."[18]

The Park Service wants more money from Congress for park upkeep, but reports reveal that the Park Service may not be wisely spending the funds it has. For example, the agency spent $330,000 in 1997 building an outhouse complete with two composting toilets and state-of-the-art foundation to withstand earthquakes in a remote area of the Delaware Water Gap National Recreation Area in Pennsylvania.[19] The cost seems exorbitant, given the fact that there is no running water and the facility has to be shut down during winter because the two composting toilets will not work in freezing temperatures. The agency is also building two other, more expensive outhouses in Glacier National Park.[20] Designed by six architects and engineers employed by the Park Service, the multimillion-dollar structures will serve only a few thousand of the two million people who visit Glacier each year. Typical of government projects, this project is loaded with high overhead. By the end of 1997, the project incurred $860,000 for the cost of "design and construction supervision teams" in regional offices in Denver.

Not all of the blame can be laid at the doorstep of the Park Service because politicians with high seniority direct money toward pet projects instead of needed park infrastructure at Yellowstone. One high-ranking Pennsylvania lawmaker garnered $8.3 million in land acquisition and construction money for the Delaware Water Gap National Recreation Area in his district. The park, site of the infamous outhouse, received more money for new buildings and trails than Yellowstone, Grand Teton, and Glacier combined. Recently retired Park Service director Roger Kennedy said more money is spent on "congressionally identified" projects than on agency-recommended projects.[21] Crown jewels such as Yellowstone, however, often lose in the battle for congressional pork because congressional delegations from low population states have less clout than their high population counterparts. Journalist Frank Greve notes, "The Old Faithful area . . . suffers from a leaky, overwhelmed World War II-era sewage treatment plant" because with two low-seniority Wyoming delegation lawmakers, Yellowstone's construction problems are not high priority on Capitol Hill.[22]

An impaired Yellowstone National Park stems from the fact that about 90 percent of the Park Service budget comes from taxes by way of congressional appropriations. Under this financing approach, politicians who hold the purse strings are able to direct major park spending. This means they have the power and the incentive to create pork barrel projects. By directing the agency to carry out expensive, unnecessary park initiatives in their own districts, politicians are able to promote local economic development and more jobs. But they also drain funds from the more mundane but necessary maintenance activities at parks such as Yellowstone. A park such as Yellowstone may eventually garner enough attention from Congress through a disgruntled public, but in the meantime natural resources are threatened. Moreover, when money is appropriated, there is an incentive to spend it on high visibility projects instead of behind-the-scenes projects that actually save the environment. Park Service officials would rather attend ribbon-cutting ceremonies at new visitor centers and campgrounds than at sewage treatment plants.

The Water Pork Barrel

Problems in our national forests and parks are more than matched by the havoc wreaked by mammoth federal dam projects in the western United States. The era of construction is all but over, but these projects continue to exact a heavy toll on the environment. One of the most egregious examples involves the forced closing of California's Kesterson Wildlife Refuge, an important stopover for millions of waterfowl. The culprit was an usually high level of selenium, a naturally-occurring chemical, that is benign at low levels but lethal at high levels. Biologists found that as a result of the selenium poisoning, wild duck eggs often did not hatch, and when they did, grotesque deformities were common. The source of the selenium-laced water that found its way to Kesterson was California's Central Valley Project, an irrigation project that provides subsidized water to farmers in the San Joaquin Valley. Further investigation has revealed that the selenium contamination extends to thousands of evaporation ponds in California's Central Valley and to the rivers that flow into San Francisco.[23]

Another example, one that has taken on tragic proportions, is the precipitous decline in wild salmon stocks in the Pacific Northwest, which salmon supporters contend is due to federal dam projects. As if often the case with these projects, the governmental planning process did not take into account the impact of dams on wild salmon. Initially there were not even fish ladders to allow adult salmon migrating upstream a passage around the massive concrete barriers, so that three dams in the Columbia Basin completely blocked fish passage to historical spawning grounds of some four million salmon and steelhead.[24] And now we understand that even if the fish can get upstream, the smolt have trouble finding their way back to the ocean without assistance from a stream current.

The loss of wild salmon runs on Idaho's Snake River, a major tributary of the Columbia, shows just how bad the situation is. Salmon were the main source of food for the Shoshone-Bannock and Nez Perce Indians for centuries before white settlement in Idaho. Furthermore, until the 1960s, when dam construction began along the Snake River, "Snake and Clearwater rivers supported a thriving salmon fishery."[25] Since 1962, Snake River chinook, sockeye, and coho have all shown drastic declines and are listed under the Endangered Species Act (ESA). Thus, if these salmon go extinct, "the fishing communities and Indian tribes along the Snake River basin will have lost a valuable resource, regardless of whether salmon remain throughout the Columbia basin."[26]

From the Kesterson Wildlife Refuge to the Snake River, water problems are the by-product of the federal government's water pork barrel. For 80 years, the Bureau of Reclamation (BuRec), the agency responsible for making the "desert bloom like a rose," and the Army Corps of Engineers have spent tens of billions of taxpayers' dollars to bring subsidized water to farmers, public utilities, and selected industries. Through interest-free loans and extended repayment schedules, these beneficiaries pay only a fraction of the cost of storing and delivering water. Irrigators whose runoff ends up in Kesterson, for example, pay less than 10 percent of the cost to store and deliver the water.[27] BuRec's efforts have resulted in engineering marvels such as Glen Canyon Dam and Hoover Dam, but the water that continues to flow so cheaply to the few at the expense borne mostly by taxpayers has created environmental problems of tragic proportions.

Again the fiscal and environmental problems inherent in federal water projects are not the fault of bad managers. They result from an institutional framework that does not discipline federal managers to be either fiscally or environmentally responsible. Moreover, the system builds an iron triangle among politicians, water users, and bureaucracies that is difficult to dismantle. If the discipline of free market environmentalism were at work, massive, subsidized water projects would not be built, higher water prices would encourage efficiency, and polluters would be liable for the damage they produce.

Behind Canada's Cod Curtain

Political pressures and bureaucracies being what they are, public resource managers simply do not have the incentives to make decisions that lead to sustainable resource use. Nowhere is this more apparent than in the collapse of Atlantic Canada's groundfish fisheries. For centuries, a rich groundfish fishery dominated by cod, haddock, and other groundfish sustained Canada's east coast. Cod landings alone fluctuated around 500,000 metric tons during the fist half of the twentieth century. In the 1960s, landings increased dramatically, thanks to foreign fishing and to an increase in the fishing capacity of Canada's domestic fleet.

Over the next two decades, the Canadian federal government continued to expand the domestic fleet, promoting what it called an "expansionist development philosophy" centered on creating jobs.[28] The government set catch limits above sustainable levels for groundfish stocks in order to satisfy the "economic needs of fishing communities."[29] It encouraged entry into the fishery by providing construction and insurance subsidies, tax breaks, and loan guarantees to fishers, boat owners, and processors. Finally, it maintained a labor force well in excess of what could be sustained in the long run by providing overly generous unemployment insurance benefits relative to fisher incomes. Thus, in 1990, unemployment insurance benefits for self-employed fishers in Atlantic Canada were on average $6,600 per year, while income from fishing was only $8,100.[30]

Scientists were predicting dire consequences for Atlantic Canada's groundfish stocks if those policies continued, but the government paid little heed. A 1982 government task force "suggested that the economic viability of the industry, maximization of employment subject to income constraint, and Canadian harvesting and processing should be priorities."[31] By the beginning of the 1990s, the scientists' predictions had come true. Groundfish stocks had collapsed to numbers never seen before. Spawner biomass of the northern cod stock had gone from a high of 1.6 million tons in 1962 to just 22,000 tons in 1992.[32] The story was repeated on a lesser scale for hake, halibut, redfish, haddock, plaice, and flounder. Forced to respond to the collapse in fish stocks, the government declared a moratorium on fishing for cod and many other groundfish. All told, some 500,000 tons less fish were being caught in the 1990s than in the previous decade. Needless to say, the fishing industry has been devastated, with thousands of workers being thrown out of work. Meanwhile, the government has done little to respond to the basic problem of too many fishers chasing too few fish. As a Price Waterhouse study noted, "Although the income-support programs have been effective at providing emergency income support, they have failed to reduce significantly the number of fishers in the industry."[33]

The collapse of Atlantic Canada groundfish stocks serves to illustrate three problems of politically controlled resources:

1. Politicians tend to choose actions with short-run payoffs. In this case, expanding employment in the fishery served to garner votes for the next election, even though such actions proved to be ecologically, economically, and socially disastrous in the long run.

2. Politics can and does override sound science. An internal government document critical of management of the fishery charged that scientific information was "gruesomely mangled and corrupted to meet political ends."[34] The document went on to accuse fishery managers of "scientific" deception, misinformation, and obfuscation."[35]

3. Politicians and governmental decision makers are not held personally accountable for their decisions. Since the 1992 moratorium on fishing, 40,000 fishers and processors have been thrown out of work, but no one in government has been fired, demoted, or even reprimanded.

The World Bank

Established in 1944 at an international monetary conference in Bretton Woods, New Hampshire, the World Bank's mission is to make loans to poor countries for economic development.[36] As of 1997, the bank and its affiliates had over 10,000 employees and $183 billion in loans outstanding.[37] The bank is actually owned by 180 national governments, also referred to as the bank's shareholders. A subset of these shareholders, industrialized countries such as the United States, provide the capital for the bank to lend to poor countries for large-scale development projects such as irrigation, reclamation, and infrastructure, and for broad economic programs such as agricultural resettlement. As noted in various World Bank documents, the bank selects projects that either cannot attract sufficient private capital or that "the private sector alone has found unworthy of investment."[38] Moreover, when one World Bank affiliate, the International Bank for Reconstruction and Development, makes loans at just below commercial rates, another, the International Development Association, makes heavily subsidized loans with funds from triennial grants from industrialized countries. These are long-term loans (35 to 40 years) at no interest and with only a 0.75 percent annual service charge. The World Bank is able to operate in this manner because its loan capital comes from taxes imposed by industrialized countries on their citizens. This also means that there is very little connection between the ability of the bank to obtain funds for future lending and the economic performance of its loan portfolio.

Evidence in recent years indicates that a growing number of the World Bank's projects are in financial trouble. A 1992 report prepared by a high-ranking World Bank official found over one-third of the World Bank's $140 billion in projects to be failing and that deterioration of the bank's loan portfolio was "steady and pervasive."[39] Among the official's noted observations were the bank's "systematic and growing bias towards excessively optimistic rate of return expectations at appraisal" and an "approval culture" in which "staff perceive appraisals as marketing devices for securing loan approval."[40] "Appraisal," the official observed, was equivalent to "advocacy."[41] The official also found widespread noncompliance with the World Bank's loan conditions. Between 1967 and 1989, for example, borrowers had complied with only 25 percent of the financial covenants for the bank's water supply projects.

A number of World Bank development projects have not only been poor economic performers, but also have been catalysts for environmental destruction and social chaos. One of the more notorious examples is the Northwest Region Development Program, known in Brazil as Polonoroeste. Between 1981 and 1983, the World Bank lent a little over $443 million for the paving of Brazilian national highway 364, a 1,500-kilometer stretch of road that connects "Brazil's populous south-central region with the rain forest wilderness in the northwest"; for the building of "feeder and access roads at the frontier end of the highway"; and for 39 rural settlement centers to attract settlers.[42] The intent was to support settlers in raising tree crops such as cocoa and coffee for export. Once the program was under way, however, the Brazilian colonization agency, INCRA, became overwhelmed by the influx of tens of thousands of settlers. Settlers were unable to obtain land titles, agricultural services, and credit. To survive, settlers were forced to burn once-pristine rain forest and plant beans, rice, and maize for food. Crop failure after a year or two on the poor, exposed soils forced many of the colonists to move back to the populated south-central region. Meanwhile, the program increased the rate of forest destruction in a region the size of Oregon from 1.7 percent in 1978 to 16.1 percent in 1991.[43] In addition, settlers and the indigenous population were ravaged by disease. More than 250,000 people were infected with malaria.[44] Some Indian tribes experienced epidemics of measles and influenza, with infant mortality rates reaching 50 percent.[45] Murders, including the highly publicized assassination of Chico Mendez in late 1988, death threats, and assaults were other by-products of the program, as land conflicts among rubber tappers, Indian tribes, cattle ranchers, and settlers were played out.[46]

Brazil was not the only place where a World Bank project wreaked havoc on the environment and caused social unrest. From 1976 to 1986, the World Bank lent about $500 million for another massive resettlement program known as Indonesia Transmigration. The goal was to resettle millions of poor people from the heavily populated inner islands of Indonesia to the sparsely populated outer islands and to provide support for the settlers in the growing of cacao, coffee, and palm oil for export. The outer islands contained 10 percent of the world's remaining tropical rain forest and were inhabited mainly by indigenous tribes. In total, this World Bank program is credited with "the 'official' resettlement of 2.3 million people, and for catalyzing the resettlement of at least 2 million more 'spontaneous' migrants."[47] Like Brazil's Polonoroeste, promised support for settlers failed to materialize, and many settlers were forced into subsistence agriculture that later proved fruitless due to the poor soil conditions for a few years following forest clearing. In wetland and swamp areas, up to 50 percent of the setters were forced to abandon their sites.[48] Meanwhile, the program led to widespread destruction of rain forest. According to World Bank documents, between 15,000 and 20,000 square kilometers out of a total area of 40,000 to 50,000 square kilometers of rain forest had been cleared as a result of World Bank sponsorship of Transmigration.[49] Equally dismal was its social record. In 1986, the World Bank's own review of the program indicated that 50 percent of the families on program resettlement sites were living below the poverty level, estimated at the time at $540 per year. Ironically, if given the amount the World Bank paid to install a family at a resettlement site, $7,000, a household could have lived above the poverty level for at least 13 years.[50]

As these two examples demonstrate, economic development is not merely a matter of alleviating capital shortages with government funds; institutions matter. A growing economy going hand-in-hand with environmental quality requires free markets and a strong system of property rights. Countries where property rights are weakly enforced, where the rule of law cannot be counted on, and where government agencies have little accountability tend to have stagnant economies and very little environmental protection.

Conclusion

Why do the U.S. Forest Service, the National Park Service, and the Bureau of Reclamation carry out policies that fall far short of environmental protection and fiscal accountability? Why did the Canadian government destroy the cod fishery, and why does the World Bank subsidize destruction of the developing world's environment? Environmentalists who recognize the problem of subsidized destruction of the environment often answer that the cause is people and therefore call for changes in administration. But such an approach overlooks the fact that environmental travesties go beyond people and party lines. Logging may have declined temporarily in the 1990s, but the bulk of spending on U.S. national forests remains with timber production. Yellowstone National Park is found wanting of modern sewage treatment, but Congress ignores the problem, choosing to spend lavishly on elaborate outhouses or on adding parks of questionable national park status. The building of large-scale federal water projects may have slowed in the 1990s, but the environmental travesties are still being felt in terms of lost salmon runs in the Pacific Northwest, and there is little to suggest that the government will fix the problem in the near future. Ignoring the advice of scientists to reduce the number of fishers, the Canadian government subsidized the expansion and eventual collapse of the Atlantic cod fishery. World Bank loans that led to the destruction of tropical rain forests that began in the 1970s and continued through the 1980s demonstrate that public funding is not the solution to economic growth or environmental protection.

The perverse results described in this chapter occur because of institutional failure. In government agencies, bureaucrats have incentives to provide constituents with the products and services they want at little or no cost to them. Entrepreneurs in this area are rewarded with larger staffs, more authority, and larger budgets, but they do not face the reality check of profitability. Moreover, to the extent that they have a single constituency, such as irrigators vis-à-vis the Bureau of Reclamation, there is little incentive for the bureaucracy to consider other values. Increasing the farmers' incomes with cheap water becomes the primary goal, even if there are perverse environmental consequences. Where there are multiple constituencies, such as those confronting the Forest Service, the political arena becomes a battleground where the developmental interests are pitted against environmental interests in a zero-sum game. Unfortunately, the process is costly to the groups themselves, to the taxpayer, to the economy, and often to the environment. The path to harmonizing economic growth with environmental integrity must include clearly defined property rights and a strong rule of law protecting those rights.

Notes

1.   Terry L. Anderson and Jane Shaw, "Grass Isn't Always Greener in a Public Park," *Wall Street Journal*, May 28, 1985, 30.

2.   Ibid.

3.   All dollar figures are in 1996 dollars.

4.   Holly Lippke Fretwell, *Public Lands: The Price We Pay*, Public Lands Report No. 1 (Bozeman, MT: Political Economy Research Center, August 1998), 1, 12.

5.   Donald R. Leal, "Turning a Profit on Public Forests," *PERC Policy Series* No. PS-4, (Bozeman, MT: Political Economy Research Center, September 1995), 4–5.

6.   Fretwell, *Public Lands*, 6.

7. Ibid., 8–9.

8. Ibid., 16–17.

9. Robert F. Smith, chairman, *Statement*, Hearing to Review the Forest Service Timber Sale Program. Committee on Agriculture, U.S. House of Representatives. Photocopy, June 11, 1998.

10. Bill Schultz, *Forestry Best Management Practices Implementation Monitoring* (Missoula, MT: Montana Department of State Lands, 1992).

11. U.S. General Accounting Office (GAO), *Forest Service Decision-Making: A Framework for Improving Performance*, GAO/RECD-97-71 (Washington, DC, 1997), 32.

12. Steve Arno, "The Concept: Restoring Ecological Structure and Process in Ponderosa Pine Forests," in *The Use of Fire in Forest Restoration*, USFS Intermountain Research Station INT-6TR-341, June 1996, 37.

13. Michael Dombeck, Forest Service chief, congressional testimony, March 18, 1997.

14. National Park Service Organic Act, 16 U.S.C.1.

15. Michael Milstein, "Park Water Risky," *Billings* [Montana] *Gazette*, July 5, 1998.

16. "Yellowstone Closes Part of the Grand Loop Road," *Island Park News*, August 14, 1998.

17. James M. Ridenour, *The National Parks Compromised: Pork Barrel Politics and America's Treasures* (Merrillville, IN: ICS Books, 1994), 108.

18. John G. Mitchell, "Our National Parks: Legacy at Risk," *National Geographic* 186 (October 1994): 54.

19. "U.S. Park Service Spends $333,000 on Outhouse," *ENN Daily News*, October 8, 1997.

20. Edward T. Pound, "Costly Outhouses Monuments to Red Tape," *USA Today*, December 15, 1997.

21. Frank Greve, "Senior Legislators Claim Funds for Pet Projects," *Washington Post*, December 1, 1997.

22. Ibid.

23. Richard W. Wahl, *Markets for Federal Water: Subsidies, Property Rights, and the Bureau of Reclamation* (Washington, DC: Resources for the Future, 1989), 197-219; Kathleen Rude, "Ponded Poisons," *Ducks Unlimited* 54 (January-February 1990): 14-18.

24. Northwest Power Planning Council (NPPC), *Columbia River Basin Fish and Wildlife Program* (typescript copy), Portland, Oregon (February 1994): 2-13.

25. Idaho Department of Fish and Game (IDFG), "Can We Bring Back Salmon Fishing?" in *Saving Idaho's Salmon*. Pamphlet issued by IDFG, Boise, Idaho.

26.   Andrew Herr, "Saving the Snake River Salmon: Are We Solving the Right Problem?" *PERC Working Paper* No. 94-15. Bozeman, MT: Political Economy Research Center, August 26, 1994.

27.   Richard W. Wahl, "Cleaning up Kesterson," *Resources* 83 (spring 1986): 12.

28.   Elizabeth Brubaker, "Property Rights: Creating Incentives and Tools for Sustainable Fisheries Management," in *Fraser Forum* (BC, Canada: The Fraser Institute, April 1998): 10.

29.   Ibid.

30.   R. Quentin Grafton, "Performance of and Prospects for Rights-Based Fisheries Management in Atlantic Canada," in *Taking Ownership: Property Rights and Fishery Management on the Atlantic Coast*, ed. Brian Lee Crowley (Halifax, Nova Scotia, Canada: Atlantic Institute for Market Studies, 1996), 145.

31.   Task Force on Atlantic Fisheries [Canada], *Navigating Troubled Waters for the Atlantic Fisheries*, report (Ottawa, Canada: Ministry of Supply and Services, 1982), 60.

32.   C.A. Bishop, E.F. Murphy, M.B. Davis, J.W. Baird, and G.A. Rose, *An Assessment of the Cod Stock in NAFO Divisions 2j + 3k*, NAFO Scientific Council Research Document 93/86, serial number N2771, 1993.

33.   Price Waterhouse, *Human Resources Development Canada: Operational Review of the Atlantic Groundfish Strategy* (Ottaw, Canada: Price Waterhouse, 1995).

34.   Brubaker, "Property Rights," 10.

35.   Ibid.

36.   Bruce Rich, *Mortgaging the Earth: The World Bank, Environmental Impoverishment, and the Crisis of Development* (Boston: Beacon Press, 1994), 7-8.

37.   "Once It's Here . . .," *The Economist*, March 1, 1997, 19-20.

38.   Rich, *Mortgaging the Earth*, 77.

39.   World Bank, Portfolio Management Task Force, *Effective Implementation: Key to Development Impact*, report (Washington, DC: World Bank, October 2, 1992), 4.

40.   Ibid., iii, 4, 12.

41.   Ibid.

42.   Rich, *Mortgaging the Earth*, 27.

43.   Ibid., 28.

44.   Ibid.

45.   Ibid.

46.   Ibid., 28-29.

47.   Ibid., 36.

48.   Ibid.

49.   Ibid.

50.   Ibid., 36-37.

HOMESTEADING THE OCEANS

Terry L. Anderson and Donald R. Leal

A s one of the world's largest commons, oceans provide a challenge for free market environmental solutions. Outside the territorial limits of sovereign countries, only weak treaties limit the use of ocean resources for fishing, mineral or energy development, shipping, and garbage disposal. With few restrictions on entry, a tragedy of the commons can occur, resulting in such problems as pollution and severely depleted fish stocks.[1] The Food and Agriculture Organization of the United Nations reports that 25 percent of the commercial fish stocks in the world are overfished and another 44 percent are fully exploited.[2] Moreover, pressure on the commons is increasing, as new technologies raise returns to exploiting ocean resources. For example, new drilling techniques make deep-water oil exploration and production feasible; shipping technologies are increasing the size of oil tankers and the potential for oil spills; and far-ranging vessels equipped with sonar, onboard processing, efficient harvesting devices, and refrigeration allow fishing fleets to deplete ocean fisheries.

Ocean fisheries are also being exploited by recreational fishing. In 1996, 9.4 million anglers spent 103 million days catching cod, flounder, bluefish, salmon, striped bass, mackerel, and other popular game fish in U.S. marine waters. In fact, the catch of some species by saltwater angling enthusiasts has had a greater impact on population size than the activities of commercial fishers. Sport anglers, for example, are allocated 68 percent of the total allowable catch in the king mackerel Gulf of Mexico fishery. The growing influence of saltwater sport-fishing, coupled with commercial harvesting, has intensified pressure on ocean fish stocks.[3]

These rising demands and new technologies are creating pressures to change the rules governing access to ocean resources. Historically, access to resources beyond narrow territorial waters (typically 3 to 12 nautical miles from shore) was open to anyone for the taking. Gradually, however, coastal nations have begun to exert greater control over resources lying farther off their shores. The move to fence ocean resources began in 1945, when President Harry Truman claimed that the United States had exclusive rights to mineral and hydrocarbon resources lying on or under its continental shelf. What followed was a steady procession of declarations by coastal nations to extend claims to resources lying within 200 miles off their shores. These claims have converted coastal waters from a regime of largely open access and high-seas freedom to one with significant national controls over resource uses.[4]

Like the evolution of property rights to land and water on the American frontier, extending territorial limits is not the final solution to the problem of open access to ocean resources. As economist Ross Eckert points out, the conversion of open access to limited access "does not guarantee the improved allocation of ocean resources" but is "only a first step for removing the inefficiencies that result from communal rights."[5] Over 20 years have elapsed since the United States extended its territorial limits to 200 miles from shore, but a significant number of fish stocks are still being overfished. In a 1998 report to Congress on the status of U.S. fisheries, the National Marine Fisheries Service (NMFS) categorized 90 stocks as being overfished and 10 stocks as approaching an overfished condition.[6] Table 1 lists some of these species.

In contrast to an earlier period, today's problem with overfishing cannot be blamed on foreign fishing. The foreign vessels that depleted fisheries in waters off the United States during the 1960s and 1970s have been mostly removed in an effort to encourage the development of the domestic fishing industry. Notably, domestic fishing effort did rise substantially during the 1980s and early 1990s, putting pressure once again on the reproductive capacity of fisheries in U.S. waters. After two decades of regulation imposed on our own fishers, the striking result has been the continued decline of key fish populations. As with reforms in land resource policy, the key to effective fishery policy lies in a property rights approach.[7]

The Ocean Commons

Ocean fisheries provide the classic case of the tragedy of the commons,[8] because many species of fish are mobile and access is difficult to monitor. Therefore, the rule of capture often dominates; any fish left by one fisher is available to another. Rather than leaving fish to grow and reproduce, the incentive is to harvest the stock before others do. With each fisher facing this

TABLE 1: Sample of U.S. Fish Stocks Being Overfished, September 1998

New England	Mid-Atlantic	South Atlantic
Atlantic sea scallop	scup	king mackerel (Gulf group)
American lobster	summer flounder	
Atlantic cod, Gulf of Maine	black sea bass	Gulf of Mexico
American plaice	bluefish (except Gulf of	red snapper
witch flounder	Mexico)	Nassau grouper
winter flounder, Gulf of Maine		jewfish
winter flounder, southern	Main Hawaiian Islands	red drum
New England	pelagic armorhead	
	squirrel fish snapper	South Atlantic
North Atlantic	longtail snapper	red drum
swordfish		jewfish
blue marlin		Nassau grouper
white marlin		vermillion snapper
sailfish		red porgy
		black sea bass

Source: National Marine Fisheries Service (NMFS), *Report to Congress: Status of Fisheries of the United States*, September 1998, website: http://www.nmfs.gov/sfa/98stat.pdf.

incentive, the end result is for the fish stock to be overexploited. Whether the population of fish ends up becoming extinct ultimately depends on the cost of capturing the last fish in the stock. Because these costs tend to rise exponentially, declining fisheries have historically reached commercial extinction before biological extinction; that is, the additional cost of capturing the few remaining fish exceed the returns, so that it has become unprofitable to continue fishing.[9]

Nonetheless, open access to the resource frequently results in a lower than optimal (if not total depletion of) stock and in overinvestment in fishing effort. As long as the cost of taking an additional fish is less than the value of the fish, a profit can be earned. But with open access, not all costs will be taken into account. Another fish taken from the stock can reduce the reproductive capacity of the fishery and raise search and capture costs for other fishers. Because these added costs are external to an individual fisher who considers only his costs and benefits, over time there will be too many fishers in the fishery. In addition, open access encourages a rate of exploitation that will be too rapid. Being the first to exploit the fishery allows the highest returns, because the costs of finding and catching fish will be lowest. This race to the best fishing ground is often manifest in the form of overcapitalization in radar, sonar, faster boats, and larger nets. The result is lower profits for the too many fishers investing in too much capital to catch too few fish.

Economist Frederick Bell provided one of the first empirical verifications of overexploitation of an open-access fishery. In his examination of New England's northern lobster fishery in 1966, he found that an efficient output of lobster would have occurred at 17.2 million pounds. To attain this output, the efficient number of lobster traps would have been 433,000. However, during 1966, Bell found that fishers employed too much capital—891, 000 traps—to harvest too many lobsters—25 million pounds.[10]

For many of the world's ocean fisheries, government control has replaced no control. Today's tragedy is that government control has not prevented overexploitation in fisheries, but has greatly increased costs.

Regulating the Ocean Fishery

Instead of relying on a property rights solution, government regulation has been the traditional mechanism for controlling overexploitation of the ocean commons. Unfortunately, there are inherent problems with regulation because the regulators do not own the resources and do not face economic incentives to manage it efficiently. For the fishery, most regulatory schemes have focused on sustaining the maximum yield, that is, in allowing the largest quantity of fish that can be caught year after year without depleting the stock. Economists argue that this yield is usually not the yield that maximizes profits, however, because it ignores economic variables such as discounted returns of future catches and the costs of present and future extraction.[11]

On the whole, regulatory schemes focusing on maximum sustainable yield and ignoring economic factors have led to lower profits and economic wastes in United States fisheries. Regulatory policies in the United States before 1976, for example, attempted to reduce catch and maximize sustainable yield by raising the cost of fishing. In the Pacific salmon fishery early in the twentieth century, regulators prohibited the use of traps first perfected by the Indians, who caught the salmon when the fish returned to spawn. With the elimination of traps, fishers chased the salmon in the open oceans. The substitute for traps became very expensive, with sophisticated equipment that still allowed fishers to overexploit the resource. When the number of fishers and the length of the season were restricted, entrepreneurs bought bigger boats, sonar, and more efficient nets. To plug these holes in the dike, regulators then established other layers of regulations controlling seasonal limits. The salmon catch was ultimately curtailed, but the approach generated economic inefficiency, as more labor and capital were applied to catch fewer fish. As fishers were forced to fish longer in less productive areas with more expensive equipment, economic waste reduced the net value of the fishery. In 1976, Francis T. Christy, Jr., estimated that the overcapitalization and overuse of labor in American fisheries cost $300 million per year, or at a 6 percent interest rate, $5 billion in perpetuity.[12]

In addition to the overcapitalization, the regulatory process sometimes spurred absurd restrictions. For example, Maryland oystermen at one time could use dredges but had to tow them behind sailboats on all but two days of the week, when motorized boats were allowed. And in some Alaskan fisheries, fishing boats were limited to 50 feet in length.[13]

Such restrictions often favored one user group over another. After examining data on regulation policies during the 1960s and 1970s, economist James Crutchfield concluded that the regulatory process had "generated an ever-increasing mass of restrictive legislation, most of it clothed in the shining garments of conservation, but bearing the clear marks of pressure politics." The overwhelming majority of these restrictions, Crutchfield decided, reflect "power plays by one ethnic group of fishermen against another, by owners of one gear against another, or by fishermen of one state against another state."[14] The combined costs of regulations led Robert Higgs to conclude:

> The social resource waste has therefore grown steadily larger over time. Today, from a comprehensive point of view, the Washington salmon fishery almost certainly makes a negative contribution to net national product. The opportunity costs of the *socially unnecessary* resources employed there, plus the *socially unnecessary* costs of government research, management and regulation, are greater than the *total value added* by all the labor and capital employed in the fishery.[15]

Meanwhile, despite these costs, many fisheries in U.S. coastal waters during the early 1970s were either in trouble or on the verge of it.[16]

The Magnuson Fishery Conservation and Management Act of 1976 tried to remove some of these regulatory inefficiencies by setting a new direction for fishery policy. It extended the nation's marine management jurisdiction from 12 to 200 miles offshore and encouraged the development of domestic fisheries. Eight regional councils were established with the authority to manage fisheries under their jurisdiction. Notably, the act does not mandate the standard of maximum sustainable yield, but rather stipulates that fishery management plans may "establish a system for limiting access to the fishery in order to achieve optimum yield."[17] Optimum yield in this case must take into account economic variables, such as interest rates, fish values, and the cost of alternative technologies.

While the Magnuson legislation was a step in the right direction, significant problems remain for regulators. The legislation encourages licensing entrants as a way of limiting the number of fishers or vessels in a fishery, but limiting entrants "cannot prevent crowding, congestion, strategic fishery behavior, racism and capital stuffing."[18] Controlling the intensity of effort remains a thorny problem, because fishers are substituting fewer larger boats for more smaller boats. The result is that "rising fish prices constrained by a limited number of vessels, and unconstrained by any sort of territorial limit, has led to vastly increased individual fishing capacity."[19] Even with licensing, regulators find that a few powerful fishing vessels, can do in a few minutes what used to take days. The bottom line is that the Magnuson Act has not rebuilt many declining fisheries in U.S. waters. According to a 1999 status report on U.S. marine resources by the National Marine Fisheries Service, 34 percent of the fish stocks of known status are overutilized—i.e., fished with excessive fishing effort—and many of these remain significantly below their historic levels and continue to be overfished (see Table 2).

Complicating the regulation of commercial fishing is recreational, or sport, fishing. With the impact of recreational fishing in U.S. coastal waters, several fish stocks have come under pressure, forcing regulators in some instances to take drastic action. For example, in 1987 the National Marine Fisheries Service banned commercial fishing of king mackerel after recreational fishers from Texas through southeastern Florida exceeded a 740,000-pound catch limit. Meanwhile, tension has grown between recreational and commercial fishing interests. Commercial fishers fear that recreational fishers under the guise of conservation have become highly influential in setting

TABLE 2: Representative List of Stocks, 1999

Geographic Area	Overfished	Overcapitalized
New England	Atlantic cod, silver hake, red hake, winter flounder, summer flounder, witch flounder, American plaice, goosefish, sea scallops, American lobster	Atlantic cod, silver hake, red hake, summer flounder, winter flounder, witch flounder, American plaice, goosefish, sea scallops, American lobster
Atlantic	black sea bass, scup, tilefish, wolffish	black sea bass, scup, tilefish, wolffish
Gulf of Mexico	red snapper, Nassau grouper, shallow groupers	red snapper, Nassau grouper, shallow groupers
South Atlantic	vermillion snapper, red snapper	vermillion snapper, red snapper
Caribbean	Nassau grouper	Nassau grouper

Source: National Marine Fisheries Service (NMFS), *Our Living Oceans: Report on the Status of U.S. Living Marine Resources*, 1999, U.S. Department of Commerce, NOAA Technical Memorandum NMFS-F/SOP-41, website: http://spo.nwr.noaa.gov/olo99.htm.

policy at both the state and federal levels. Recreational fishers complain that fisheries must not be managed solely for commercial interests and that they have as much right to the resource as commercial interests do. The management districts for both the South Atlantic and Gulf Coast fisheries have experienced intense pressures from these two groups.[20]

The conflicts between commercial and sport interests have led to concerted efforts by both groups to gain stronger footholds in regional fisheries management councils. Historically, the regional councils of the National Marine Fisheries Service were dominated by representatives from commercial fishing interests. This dominance may be changing, as recreational interests have managed to gain more political influence. Meanwhile, the turf battles have left questions concerning the regional councils' effectiveness in managing fish stocks:

> As the battle between user groups has intensified, many observers have questioned whether NMFS and the councils, in their desire to satisfy every demand for a piece of the resource pie, have lost sight of their fundamental responsibility to protect the health of fish stocks.[21]

Individual Transferable Quotas

A relatively recent innovation in fishery management that is an improvement over a strictly regulatory approach is a system of individual transferable quotas, or ITQs. An individual quota entitles the holder to catch a specific percentage of the total allowable catch, generally specified by a government agency. This system is attractive for several reasons. First, each quota holder faces greater certainty that his share of the total allowable catch will not be taken by someone else. Under the current system, an individual's share of the total allowable catch is determined by who is best at capturing the fugitive resources. With ITQs, holders do not compete for the shares, so there is less incentive to race other fishers. Second, transferability allows quotas to end up in the hands of the most efficient fishers—that is, those with the lowest costs and who can pay the highest price for the ITQs. Less efficient producers and inputs move to other industries. As a corollary, ITQs encourage progress in reducing the cost of catching fish and enhancing the quality of the fish delivered to markets. Fishers who adopt new cost-reducing or quality-enhancing methods make more money with their quotas and are in a better position to purchase quotas from those who are less efficient. This is in marked contrast to regulations, which encourage overinvestment in the race for fugitive resources.

New Zealand and Iceland employ ITQs as a major component of their fisheries management system, and both have experienced considerable success in reducing the race to catch fish. The deplorable state of many of New Zealand's inshore fisheries and a government favorable to market solutions led to the introduction of ITQs in 1986 into 29 commercial fisheries. Today, fish stocks are generally healthy, and the value of fisheries is represented by quota value has grown to nearly $1.4 billion.[22] ITQs are also encouraging cooperation among fishers in enhancing fish stocks. For example, overfishing before the introduction of ITQs decimated the paua (abalone) fishery. With ITQs, quota holders in the Chatham Islands stopped competing with one another and instead agreed to limit their catch and invest in research, forming the Chatham Islands' Shellfish Reseeding Association to enhance the production of paua.[23] Similarly, quota holders in the orange roughy, scallop, rock lobster, and snapper fisheries are investing in various research efforts to enhance fish stocks.[24]

Like New Zealand, Iceland has enjoyed success with ITQs as its main approach to managing fisheries. For example, the herring fishery was suffering from too many vessels and too few fish prior to ITQs. With introduction of ITQs, the fishery has improved markedly. Stock biomass is greater than at any time since the 1950s, and economic performance is vastly improved. In 1980, the first full year of ITQs, over 200 vessels took part in the fishery. Fifteen years later, in 1995, there were less than 30 vessels in the fishery. Yet the fewer vessels were harvesting twice as much herring as the 200 had in 1980. Productivity, as measured by catch per unit effort, has increased by a factor of five. There is also strong evidence of higher efficiencies in the capelin (a smelt-like fish) fishery. Since introduction of ITQs, total tonnage of the fleet has been reduced by 25 percent and fishing effort has contracted, with total days at sea reduced by 25 percent.[25]

A number of other countries are using various forms of ITQs in selected fisheries with success. For example, individual vessel quotas[26] in the British Columbia halibut fishery have helped spread out landings over a nine-month period, compared with a mere six days prior to their introduction. As a result, fishers supply the market with fresh halibut for a much longer period during the year, and their catch commands a much higher price. Further, the number of active vessels has decreased, reducing fleet crew payments and fixed costs.[27]

Australia's national government is using the ITQ system for the southern bluefin tuna fishery. Prior to ITQs, severe cutbacks in the total allowable catch and fleet capacity were required to sustain the fishery. After only six months under ITQs, the fleet capacity in the fishery had been reduced by 60 percent, as those who intended to stay in the fishery bought quotas from those who could earn more by leaving. As an indication of increased value of the fishery, ITQs began selling for just under $1,000 per ton on October 1, 1984; they sold for $2,000 per ton five and a half months later.[28]

Prior to ITQs, Greenland's offshore fishery in shrimp was largely open access. As a result, the fishing fleet expanded exponentially and individual catches and profitability became progressively smaller. Following introduction of ITQs, fleet size contracted and individual catches and profitability rose.[29]

To date, ITQs have been adopted in four federally managed fisheries in the United States.[30] The longest-running one is the Atlantic surf clam fishery. Prior to ITQs, the fishery had been suffering from overcapacity and long periods of downtime for crew and equipment. Allowable fishing time had to be steadily shortened due to increases in harvesting power. By the end of the 1980s, a surf clam vessel was allowed to fish only six hours every other week during the season. Under ITQs, the number of active vessels went from 128 in 1990 to 50 in 1997, thereby reducing excess capacity in the fishery. Those in the fishery were making better use of their resources. Fishing hours per surf clam vessel, for example, went from 404 in 1988 to 1,400 in 1994. In addition, ITQs improved vessel productivity to record levels. After two years under ITQs, catch per vessel almost doubled to 47,656 bushels.[31]

The Alaskan halibut fishery is a more recent example of ITQs in the United States. High fish mortality from abandoned gear, declining product quality, and hazardous fishing are some of the reasons ITQs were implemented in 1995. Following the introduction of ITQs, the length of the fishing season went from an average of 2-3 days per year between 1980 and 1994 to an average of 245 days per year under the ITQs. The longer season has meant that fresh fish is supplied to fish markets for a longer period during the year, thus product quality is improved. The longer season also allows fishers to fish during periods of good weather, thereby reducing hazardous fishing. The annual number of search and rescue missions for halibut fishers reported by the U.S. Coast Guard decreased significantly following introduction of ITQs. In addition, ITQs are helping conserve the resource. Managers report that unwanted fish mortality due to lost or abandoned gear went from 554.7 metric tons in 1994 to 125.9 metric tons in 1995, the first year of ITQs.[32]

Despite their growing acceptance, ITQs are not without criticism. Parzival Copes argues that ITQs can experience problems in bycatch fisheries.[33] These are fisheries in which the harvest of one species results in the harvest of another species. In New Zealand, ITQs are used in multispecies fisheries, and lessons learned indicate that this form of management can work if sufficient flexibility exists for balancing catches after the fact by acquiring additional quota holdings for bycaught species. Still, matching the mix of quota held to catches is problematic, and excessive bycatch has occurred in certain New Zealand fisheries. However, fishers appear to be making adjustments in their operations recently so that fewer overruns are occurring.[34] In addition, Copes argues that ITQs will not solve "high-grading," the tendency of fishers to discard smaller fish in hopes of catching larger, more valuable ones. High-grading appears to be a problem in some ITQ fisheries, but there is theoretical evidence that its occurrence depends on the conditions of each fishery.[35] Also, in certain fisheries, such as a lobster fishery where mortality from fish discarding is low, high-grading can be beneficial to the long-term health of the fishery.

There are two other potential problems with implementing ITQs that can negate their benefits. First, given that ITQs are generally set by a bureaucratic regime, there is the question of what incentive or ability bureaucratic managers have to establish the efficient level of harvest. The standard is to approximate the maximum sustainable yield. As discussed previously, this is usually not the yield that maximizes profits. To the extent that fishers can carry quota over into the next season or catch more in the current season by borrowing against future quota, they may adjust toward the economic optimum, but these options may not be available because of restrictions on quota transfers. In addition, even when sufficient scientific information on the condition of the stock is available to set a maximum sustainable harvest, political pressures can cause managers to ignore such information and instead allow unsustainable harvests. If the total catch is set too high, an ITQ fishery will suffer stock depletion.[36]

The second potential problem with ITQs stems from the time and money that would-be quota holders are willing to invest in order to secure claims to valuable quota rights. In other words, the race to catch fish will be replaced by a race for the quota.[37] If the quotas are allocated at random, by auction, or on the basis of historical catch prior to anticipation of ITQs, such investment will be minimized. However, if quotas are allocated on the basis of historical catch that anticipates the allocation, fishers will overfish in an effort to increase their share of the quota. Alternatively, if bureaucratic discretion determines the allocation, fishers will invest in influencing the decision. In either case, at least some of the potential profits from the ITQ fishery will be dissipated through the race for the property rights.[38]

Full Property Rights

Where feasible, a superior approach to either regulation or a politically managed ITQ system is to allow the establishment of full property rights. Exclusive rights to fishing areas are certainly not new. Robert Higgs found that Indians along the Columbia River had well-established rights to salmon fishing sites long before whites came to the area. "In some cases, these rights resided in the tribe as a whole; in other cases, in families or individuals."[39] The Indians developed effective technologies for catching the salmon and avoided overexploitation by allowing sufficient upstream migration for spawning purposes. Their "conscious regulation of the fishery played an important role in maintaining its yield over time."[40] Unfortunately, "legally induced technical regress" resulted from Washington State allowing interception of salmon at sea by whites and legislation that outlawed traps and effectively eliminated Indian fishing rights. This legislation ran counter to British common law, which had a place for private rights to coastal fisheries:

> . . . when we consider that there were already, in 1200 AD, in tidal waters, territorial fishing rights in England and a form of territorial salmon rights throughout the world in the 19th century, the legislative process can only be said to have reduced the characteristics of individual fishing right.[41]

For fish that are not mobile over wide ranges, property rights can be defined by specifying ownership of ocean surface area or of ocean floor, so-called territorial use rights in fisheries (TURFs).[42] Oyster fisheries along the U.S. coasts offer a useful contrast of how property rights can improve resource allocation. Using data from oyster fisheries in Maryland, Virginia, Louisiana, and Mississippi from 1945 to 1970, economists Agnello and Donnelley tested the hypotheses that private ownership of oyster beds would generate more conservation and higher returns for fishers than open-access beds.[43] Under open access, we would expect fishers to take as many oysters as early as possible, with the result being diminishing returns later in the season. Agnello and Donnelley found that the ratio of harvest during the earlier part of the season to that of the later part was 1.35 for open-access oyster beds and 1.01 for private beds. After controlling for other variables, they also found that fishers in the private leasing state of Louisiana earned $3,207 per year, while their counterparts in the open-access state of Mississippi earned $807 per year. These findings support the expectation that private property rights solve the open-access problem.

The same property rights solution has been applied to other local fisheries. Some parts of Maine's lobster fishery continue to offer an example of private, community control of access. Anthropologist James Acheson describes the 100-year-old territorial system as a system "under community control" and at the same time "owned by the State." In order to harvest lobsters in a particular territory, fishers must be members of a "harbor gang." Nonmembers attempting to harvest lobsters are usually sanctioned by these extralegal harbor gangs. Though the system is not officially recognized by the state of Maine, it is recognized by Maine lobster fishers and has a significantly positive impact on productivity.[44]

Like parts of Maine's lobster fishery, a number of fishing communities around the world have avoided overexploiting fish stocks for decades by limiting entry and managing the use of coastal fishing grounds.[45] A large network of Fishing Cooperative Associations (FCAs) governing much of Japan's nearshore fisheries provides and example of a government-sanctioned community system. By law, FCAs own the fishing rights to specific territories extending as far as five and a half miles seaward.[46] The community approach, however, is not costless to maintain, and those that are not recognized by governments can easily succumb to governmental interference. For example, after decades during which local fishers successfully managed a coastal fishery in Valensa, Brazil, the Brazilian government decided to modernize fishing equipment by making nylon nets available to anyone who qualified for a bank loan arranged by the government. The local fishers who had been managing the fishery did not qualify for the loan and did not have enough capital to purchase the nets on their own. Unfortunately, they were displaced by a few outsiders hired to fish the Valensa fishing grounds with the nylon nets. The local management system crumbled as old and new fishers fought over fishing spots, and eventually the fishery was overharvested and, ultimately, abandoned commercially.[47]

Economists Johnson and Libecap observed that even though private territorial rights in the Gulf Coast shrimp fishery were not formally recognized by federal and state governments, fishers historically resorted to informal contracting and the use of unions and trade associations to mitigate open-access conditions.[48] Fishing unions were particularly active from the 1930s through the 1950s, implementing policies along the Gulf Coast to limit entry, conserve shrimp stocks, and increase members' incomes. Such efforts by unions and fishing associations eventually met their demise in the courts, which refused to exempt the collective action of associations and unions from antitrust prosecution:

> A cooperative association of boat owners is not freed from the restrictive provisions of the Sherman Antitrust act . . . because it professes, in the interest of the conservation of important food fish, to regulate the price and the manner of taking fish unauthorized by legislation and uncontrolled by proper authority.[49]

Although scarcity and competition limit the effectiveness of unions and associations, those organizations can provide an alternative for limiting entry and negotiating price agreements with wholesalers and canneries.[50] For a short time, they succeeded in internalizing the cost of regulations and conserving shrimp stocks. But as this situation revealed, any agreement establishing property rights to resources is difficult to maintain if the government declares it illegal.

The tradition of property rights is gaining popularity with the dramatic growth of aquaculture. From 1984 to 1995, world aquaculture grew from 6.5 million metric tons to 21 million metric tons.[51] With aquaculture, there is potential for increasing fish production while reducing pressure on wild stocks, though, as discussed below, there may be problems from pollution and escapement. Because investment in aquaculture requires secure property rights and because property rights are more likely to evolve where the costs of establishing rights are lower, sessile species, such as oysters, have the most promise. As noted earlier, private rights to oyster beds in some states have led to greater productivity.

The emergence of salmon ranching indicates that a solution based on property rights can also be applied to anadromous species that return to their original spawning ground. But before salmon ranching can realize its full potential, property rights problems have to be worked out. For example, a ranch operator has control over his stock only while the salmon are in captivity—before they are released and after they return for spawning. Otherwise, the salmon reside in the open sea beyond the rancher's control. Under conditions of the open range, the rancher may lose a substantial portion of his investment to natural mortality and commercial and sport fishers. Some of these problems can be overcome if there is better coordination between ranchers and commercial fishers. For example, because "restrictive ocean fishing season, depleted stocks of other species and low public smolt release levels raise the profitability from private aquaculture," economists Anderson and Wilen conclude that salmon ranchers would be willing to pay for a reduced season length and for reduced public smolt releases in return for receiving compensation from those who catch ranch fish in the ocean.[52]

This problem is similar to the one faced by British salmon sportfishers. In many cases, the fishers own fishing rights on the streams, but they are disturbed by the alarmingly depleted salmon stocks that return to spawn. The reductions are the result of increased commercial harvests, especially by fishers who have netting rights at the mouths of rivers.[53] To combat the problem, the Atlantic Salmon Conservation Trust of Scotland, a nonprofit group, has purchased 280 netting rights at a cost of $2.1 million and expects to reduce the netting catch of salmon by 25 percent.[54] Most have been purchased from private owners, but some have even come from the Crown. The idea of this buyout program began in Canada, where the federal government bought and retired commercial netting rights in New Brunswick, Nova Scotia, and Quebec.

Wild Atlantic salmon recovery was given another boost with temporary purchases of ocean salmon netting rights in Greenland and Faeroese fisheries. In 1989, Icelander Orri Vigfússon developed a proposal to buy commercial salmon netting rights held by fishers in Greenland and the Faeroe Islands. The Atlantic Salmon Federation fully supported Vigfússon's proposal and began raising funds immediately. In 1991, Faeroe Islands fishers agreed not to exercise their netting rights in 1991, 1992, and 1993. In return, they received $685,500 not to fish for salmon. As a result, in 1993, nearly twice as many salmon returned to their native rivers in Iceland and Europe.[55] In the same year, Vigfússon temporarily bought out netting rights of fishers in Greenland for 1993 and 1994. The buyout paid fishers $400,000 each year and reduced salmon netting off Greenland from 213 metric tons to 12 metric tons.[56] Such arrangements, which Vigfússon and the federation hope to make permanent through a comprehensive financing and job training program, are possible because the legal environment has established a system of transferable netting rights over which Vigfússon and fishers can contract.

Another approach that eliminates interactions between fish ranchers and fishers is based on raising salmon in pens. When the salmon reside in pens their entire lives, there are no losses due to commercial and sportfishing in the open ocean. This method has proven highly successful for the Norwegians, who are the leading international producers of Atlantic salmon. Salmon farmers and ranchers in the United States still face political opposition from commercial fishers, who have sought government protection of their markets, and from environmentalists, who fear that salmon farming will lead to more pollution of bays and inland waters. In 1987, commercial fishers in the Pacific Northwest convinced Alaskan state authorities to impose a one-year moratorium on net-pen salmon farms, and protests from local environmentalists in Washington have led the state to impose stringent guidelines in siting salmon farms.[57] More recently, pen-reared Atlantic salmon operations in Maine have encountered opposition from seaside residents who do not want salmon farms spoiling their viewsheds and from regulators who perceive domestically raised salmon as a threat to wild salmon stocks.[58] In response, aquaculture interests cite scientific evidence that shows that salmon farming meets state water quality standards and poses little threat to wild salmon stocks.[59] In addition, they contend that the science used in salmon farming could be used to encourage survivability of strains of wild salmon.[60]

Institutional roadblocks also stand in the way of other private operations. In Maryland, out of some 9,000 acres of privately leased oyster grounds, only 1,000 are in production; 280,000 acres remain public. Privatizing Maryland's Chesapeake Bay oyster fishery faces the problem of weak enforcement of private leases. "It's hard to find an oyster ground that hasn't been poached upon," complained a planter on the Tred Avon River. "It's the main reason why so many people are reluctant to take their ground and invest their money in it."[61] Obviously, to realize the full potential of aquaculture in the United States, institutional barriers must be removed and the defense of private property rights must be strengthened.

Japan has led the way in establishing private property rights to fisheries. The Japanese took bold steps to allow the privatization of the commons because access to foreign fishing grounds was being more and more restricted by legislation like the Magnuson Act. The Japanese government now initiates the property rights process by designating areas that are eligible for aquaculture. The Fishing Cooperative Associations are then given the responsibility of partitioning these areas and assigning them to individual fishers for their exclusive use.

An exclusive right to harvest resources from a marine area allows an entrepreneur to invest in improvements and to capture the benefits of his or her investment. Consider the story of Ocean Farming, Inc., a company in the business of fertilizing the seas to enhance growth of phytoplankton, which in turn nourishes fish production. Based on actual experiments, company president Michael Markels estimates that with continuous fertilization, about one thousand tons of catchable fish per square mile can be produced each year. Recently, Ocean Farming entered into a contract with the Republic of the Marshall Islands giving the company an option for exclusive fishing rights on up to 800,000 square miles of deep ocean. Once harvesting starts, Ocean Farming will pay RMI $3.75 per square mile of ocean optioned or 7 percent of the value of the catch, whichever is more. Ocean Farming can charge other companies to fish the waters, and the firm has agreed to allow previous small-scale fishing to continue.[62]

This same approach could be used for may other fisheries that lend themselves to satisfactory control of resources within a given area. For example, suppose the National Marine Fisheries Service allowed people to "homestead" sections of the ocean within the 200-mile limit and harvest bottom fish from their homestead. One company, Artificial Reefs, Inc., recently completed a multifaceted artificial reef structure off the waters of northwestern Florida to enhance recreational fishing and provide an area for skin diving. The project was financed with grants, but it could have easily been financed by a potential owner of the area where the reef was deployed.[63] Experiments with sinking oil drilling platforms have demonstrated the success of this approach in improving fish stocks, so it is but a small step to encourage such investments through property rights. Owners of such homesteaded areas could catch the fish themselves, lease out fishing rights, or even lease recreational fishing rights.

There is sufficient evidence that the costs of defining and enforcing property rights for nonmigratory fish are low enough that we should lower the institutional barriers to such homesteading. In the Gulf waters off Alabama and Florida, even a very limited sense of ownership has spawned private provision of artificial reefs. These two states allow private entities to create reefs out of certain permanent structures in parts of their territorial waters. The reefs are considered public property as soon as they hit the water, but the sense of ownership that comes from knowing the exact location of a reef has been enough to encourage private initiative.[64] Unfortunately, the tenuous nature of reef ownership limits the potential for more privately created reefs.

For highly migratory fish, one property-rights solution is to establish the ITQ as a private property right—not a privilege revocable by the government—and allow the transition of managing the fishery from the government to the quota holders themselves. Like shareholding in a public company, "[h]olding an ITQ will allow large numbers of fishers . . . to come together and cooperate" in regulating fishing and coordinating their fishing with other uses.[65] The costs of obtaining stock information, making management decisions, and monitoring and enforcing decisions "need not be higher—and can be much lower—than when these services are performed in a uniform way by a government agency." If there are some fisheries where costs are higher, then, as is done in New Zealand, fishers can literally hire the government agency to perform the services.

The New Zealand ITQ management system appears to be moving ever closer to a real system of privately owned fisheries. For example, Challenger Scallop Enhancement Company, Ltd., whose shareholders are the owners of scallop ITQs, manage the fishery through contracts that allow the company to collect money for research and monitoring and enforcement of daily catch limits. They have even contracted with fishers in other fleets to reduce adverse environmental impacts from other fisheries on the scallop fishery.[66]

Conclusion

While they are by no means the final solution, current ITQ systems are a positive step toward addressing the tragedy of the commons in ocean fisheries. Their immediate benefit cannot be denied from the standpoint of ending the race to catch fish. Furthermore, the more secure they are as property rights, the more compelling it is for fishers to take a longer view of the resource. As is the case in New Zealand, ITQs have stimulated cooperation among fishers in enhancing fish stocks. It appears they make it "easier and cheaper" for fishers holding quotas "to act collectively" in managing the size of their catch.[67]

Unfortunately, the success of ITQs and collective action by fishing associations or communities stimulate political action by special interest groups that want a share of the growing pie. In countries where ITQs have become prevalent, some argue that the income generated by ITQs is a windfall to quota holders and belongs to the government.[68] Unfortunately, these conflicts focus only on how to carve up the pie, not how to make it even larger.

In addition, while ITQs offer considerable advantages, determining the size of the total catch remains a governmental function. Fishery regulators determine total catch based on biological sustainability and economic factors. Unfortunately, regulators are susceptible to political pressures from the special interest groups they regulate, who then become important bureaucratic constituents in the budgetary process. The incentive for pleasing such groups by maintaining an inefficient industry size can be strong enough to overshadow the objectives of efficient production and sustainable future catches.

A superior solution for species with limited range is to establish private property rights to their territories. Aquaculture in coastal areas is one example. There is also evidence that if the barriers to property rights to areas farther seaward are removed, entrepreneurs will invest in homesteading the oceans. In addition, we tend to overlook the extent to which communities hold de facto property rights to coastal fisheries around the world. While many are at risk from government interference, occasionally some arrangements are afforded legal recognition.

Establishing property rights will not be easy for highly migratory species, but, as in the frontier West, we can expect increasing efforts at definition and enforcement. Notably, technologies already exist that can facilitate defining and enforcing property rights in ocean fisheries. For example, transmitters on manatees use satellite telemetry to provide exact location, individual identity, water temperature, and the direction the individual is headed. "Devices can also be placed on board a fishing vessel to constantly relay its exact location via satellite, to identify whether it belongs in a certain area. . . . Heat-sensitive satellites cannot only monitor a ship's location, but can also use its heat profile to tell if it is towing nets or not."[69] In addition, a team of scientists in Kailua, Hawaii, have developed a same-day DNA field test to monitor whale stocks in the wild, and Norway is developing a DNA register on minke whale stocks.[70] For tracking individual whales, most promising are various tags that can be attached to a whale by firing a tag-carrying dart into its blubber. Each tag is actually a data-collecting and broadcasting unit capable of transmitting radio or sound waves.[71]

In the meantime, there are a number of steps that can be taken immediately to improve ocean fisheries. They include: implementing ITQ systems as property rights, removing legal roadblocks to managing fisheries collectively, providing legal recognition of territorial fishing rights, and refraining from further governmental redistribution of fishing rights. If carried out, such steps will move us a long way toward a free market environmental solution to the ocean commons problem.

Notes

1. For an example of pollution at sea, see Ronald Mitchell, "International Oil Pollution of the Oceans," in *Institutions for the Earth: Sources of Effective International Protection,* ed. Peter M. Haas et al. (Cambridge, MA: MIT Press, 1993), 183-247. For two examples of stock depletion close to home, see Michael De Alessi, "Fishing for Solutions: The State of the World's Fisheries," in *Earth Report 2000: Revisiting the True State of the Planet,* ed. Ronald Bailey (New York: McGraw-Hill, 2000), 87-89.

2. Food and Agriculture Organization of the United Nations (FAO), *The State of World Fisheries and Aquaculture 1998,* on-line version, website: http://www.fao.org/docrep/w9900e/ w9900e.00.htm.

3. U.S. Department of the Interior, Fish and Wildlife Service, and U.S. Department of Commerce, Bureau of the Census, *1996 National Survey of Fishing, Hunting, and Wildlife-Associated Recreation* (Washington, DC: U.S. Department of Interior, November 1997); Nelson Bryant, "Fishing Licenses Are At Issue," *New York Times,* February 5, 1989; Gina Maranto, "Caught in

Conflict," *Sea Frontiers* 35 (May-June 1988): 144-151; National Marine Fisheries Service (NMFS), *Our Living Oceans: Report on the Status of U.S. Living Marine Resources,* 1999, U.S. Department of Commerce, NOAA Technical Memorandum NMFS-F/SPO-41, on-line version, website: http://spo.nwr.noaa.gov/fa3.pdf.

4.   Ross Eckert, *The Enclosure of Ocean Resources* (Stanford, CA: Hoover Institution Press, 1979), 4.

5.   Ibid., 16.

6.   National Marine Fisheries Service (NMFS), *Report to Congress: Status of Fisheries of the United States,* September 1998, on-line version, website: http://www.nmfs.gov/sfa/98stat.pdf.

7.   National Marine Fisheries Services, *Our Living Oceans,* website: http://spo.nwr.noaa.gov/national.pdf; National Marine Fisheries Service (NMFS), *The Economic Status of U.S. Fisheries, 1996,* U.S. Department of Commerce, National Oceanic and Atmospheric Administration, National Marine Fisheries Service, December 1996, on-line version, website: http://www.st.nmfs.gov/econ/oleo/oleo/html.

8.   The term "tragedy of the commons" was taken from Garrett Hardin, "The Tragedy of the Commons," *Science* 162 (December 1968): 1243-48.

9.   For a classic article on the commons problem, see H. Scott Gordon, "The Economic Theory of a Common Property Resource: The Fishery," *Journal of Political Economy* 62 (April 1954): 124-42. See also Colin W. Clark, "Profit Maximization and the Extinction of Animal Species," *Journal of Political Economy* 81 (August 1981): 950-60.

10.   Frederick W. Bell, "Technological Externalities and Common-Property Resources: An Empirical Study of the U.S. Northern Lobster Fishery," *Journal of Political Economy* 80 (January-February 1972): 156.

11.   See Tom Tietenberg, *Environmental and Natural Resource Economics*, 2d ed. (Glenview, IL: Scott, Foresman and Company, 1988), 258-64.

12.   J.A. Crutchfield and G. Pontecorvo, *The Pacific Salmon Fisheries: A Study of Irrational Conservation* (Baltimore: Johns Hopkins University Press, for Resources for the Future, 1969); "The Flaw in the Fisheries Bill," *Washington Post*, April 13, 1976.

13.   Francis T. Christy, Jr., and Anthony Scott, *The Common Wealth in Ocean Fisheries* (Baltimore: Johns Hopkins University Press, for Resources for the Future, 1965), 15-16; Crutchfield and Pontecorvo, *The Pacific Salmon Fisheries*, 46.

14.   James A. Crutchfield, "Resources from the Sea," in *Ocean Resources and Public Policy,* ed. T.S. English (Seattle: University of Washington Press, 1973), 115.

15.   Robert Higgs, "Legally Induced Technical Regress in the Washington Salmon Fishery," *Research in Economic History* 7 (1982): 82.

16. Clarence G. Pautzke and Chris W. Oliver, *Development of Individual Fishing Quota Program for Sablefish and Halibut Longline Fisheries off Alaska* (Anchorage: North Pacific Fishery Management Council, 1977), 2.

17. Pub. L. No. 94-265, sec. 303(b)(6), 94th Congress, H.R. 200, April 13, 1976.

18. Anthony Scott, "Market Solutions to Open-Access, Commercial Fisheries Problems," paper presented at Association for Public Policy Analysis and Management 10th Annual Research Conference, Seattle, October 27-29, 1988, 7-8.

19. Ibid.

20. Maranto, "Caught in Conflict," 145.

21. William J. Chandler, ed., *Audubon Wildlife Report, 1988/1989* (San Diego: Academic Press, 1988), 48.

22. Based on an exchange rate of US$0.69 for every NZ$1.00. See Tom McClurg, "Bureaucratic Management versus Private Property: ITQs in New Zealand after Ten Years," in *Fish or Cut Bait*, ed. Laura Jones and Michael Walker (Vancouver, BC: The Fraser Institute, 1997), 103.

23. Rodney P. Hide and Peter Ackroyd, "Depoliticising Fisheries Management: Chatham Islands' Paua (Abalone) as a Case Study," unpublished report for R.D. Beattie Ltd. Centre for Resource Management, Lincoln University, Christchurch, New Zealand, March 1990, 42, 44.

24. Michael De Alessi, *Fishing for Solutions* (London, England: The Institute of Economic Affairs, 1998), 43; Peter Hartley, *Conservation Strategies for New Zealand* (Wellington, New Zealand: New Zealand Business Roundtable, 1997), 97.

25. Ragnar Arnason, "Property Rights as an Organizational Framework in Fisheries: The Cases of Six Fishing Nations," in *Taking Ownership: Property Rights and Fishery Management on the Atlantic Coast*, ed. Brian Lee Crowley (Halifax, Nova Scotia: Atlantic Institute for Market Studies, 1996), 120-21.

26. As the phrase implies, individual vessel quota allocate percentage shares of the total allowable catch to individual vessels. Like ITQs, these shares are transferable.

27. Christopher Sporer, "An Intelligent Tale of Fish Management," *Fraser Forum*, December 1998, 12-13.

28. William L. Robinson, "Individual Transferable Quotas in the Australian Southern Bluefin Tuna Fishery," in *Fishery Access Control Programs Worldwide: Proceedings of the Workshop on Management Options for the North Pacific Longline Fishers*, Alaska Sea Grant Report no. 86-4 (Orca Island, WA: University of Alaska, 1986), 189-205.

29. Arnason, "Property Rights as an Organizational Framework in Fisheries," 113.

30. ITQs are innovative yet controversial for the feared effects on communities and special interests that have invested in the status quo of strictly regulated fisheries. As of this writing, a moratorium on adopting ITQs in other federal fisheries has been imposed by Congress since 1996.

31. National Research Council, *Sharing the Fish: Toward a National Policy on Individual Fishing Quotas* (Washington, DC: National Academy Press, 1999), 293; National Marine Fisheries Service (NMFS), *Economic Status of U.S. Fisheries, 1996.*

32. National Research Council, *Sharing the Fish*, 312.

33. Parzival Copes, "A Critical Review of the Individual Quota as a Device in Fisheries Management," *Land Economics* 62 (August 1986): 278-91.

34. National Research Council, *Sharing the Fish*, 108.

35. Ibid., 108-110.

36. This occurred in the initial stages of Iceland's ITQ fisheries, but was later rectified. See National Research Council, *Sharing the Fish*, 329.

37. For complete discussions, see Terry L. Anderson and P.J. Hill, "Privatizing the Commons: An Improvement?" *Southern Economic Journal* 50 (1983): 438-50, and Terry L. Anderson and P.J. Hill, "The Race for Property Rights," *Journal of Law and Economics* 33 (April 1990): 177-97.

38. Hide and Ackroyd describe this problem in the context of New Zealand's efforts to establish ITQs. See Hide and Ackroyd, "Depoliticising Fisheries Management."

39. Higgs, "Legally Induced Technical Regress," 59.

40. Ibid.

41. Scott, "Market Solutions," 19.

42. Francis T. Christy, "Paradigm Lost: The Death Rattle of Open Access and the Advent of Property Rights to Regimes in Fisheries," paper prepared for the 8th Biennial Conference of the Institute of Fisheries Economics and Trade, Marrakesh, Morocco, July 1-4, 1996, 14.

43. Richard J. Agnello and Lawrence P. Donnelley, "Prices and Property Rights in the Fisheries," *Southern Economic Journal* 42 (October 1979): 253-62.

44. James J. Acheson, "Capturing the Commons: Legal and Illegal Strategies," in *The Political Economy of Customs and Culture: Informal Solutions to the Commons Problems*, ed. Terry L. Anderson and Randy T. Simmons (Lanham, MD: Rowman and Littlefield Publishers, 1993), 69-83.

45. Donald R. Leal, "Community-Run Fisheries: Avoiding the Tragedy of the Commons," *PERC Policy Series* No. PS-7 (Bozeman, MT: Political Economy Research Center, September 1996).

46. Ibid., 13.

47. Ibid., 6-7.

48. Ronald N. Johnson and Gary D. Libecap, "Contracting Problems and Regulation: The Case of the Fishery," *American Economic Review* 12 (December 1982): 1007.

49. 15 U.S.C.A., sec. 522.

50. Johnson and Libecap, "Contracting Problems and Regulations," 1008.

51. De Alessi, "Fishing for Solutions," 109.

52. James L. Anderson and James E. Wilen, "Implications of Private Salmon Aquaculture on Prices, Production, and Management of Salmon Resources," *American Journal of Agricultural Economics* 68 (November 1986): 877.

53. Nelson Bryant, "A Scottish Group Protects Salmon," *New York Times*, January 8, 1990, S-13.

54. Terry L. Anderson and Donald R. Leal, *Enviro-Capitalists: Doing Good While Doing Well* (Lanham, MD: Rowman and Littlefield Publishers, 1997), 103.

55. Ibid., 135.

56. Sue Scott, "Greenland Salmon Fishery Ends," *News Release Communiqué*, Atlantic Salmon Federation, St. Andrews, New Brunswick, Canada, August 1, 1993.

57. Edwin S. Iversen and Jane Z. Iversen, "Salmon-farming Success in Norway," *Sea Frontiers* (November-October 1987): 355-61; Cheryl Sullivan, "Salmon Feedlots in Northwest," *Christian Science Monitor,* July 23, 1987. See also Robert R. Sticker, "Commercial Fishing and Net-pen Salmon Aquaculture: Turning Conceptual Antagonism Toward a Common Purpose," *Fisheries* 13 (July-August 1988): 9-13.

58. Carey Goldberg, "Fish Farms Breed Fight Over Way of Life," *New York Times*, website: http://www.nytimes.com, August 28, 1999; Margot Higgins, "Atlantic Salmon Protection Expected," *Environmental News Network,* October 15, 1999, website: http://www.enn.com/enn-news-archive/1999/10/101599/asalmon_6485.asp.

59. Letter and fact sheets on salmon breeding and habitat impact from Melissa Field, Schiedermayer & Associates, n.d.

60. Ibid.

61. Merrill Leffler, "Killing Maryland's Oysters," *Washington Post*, March 29, 1987.

62. Bruce Yandle, "The Commons: Tragedy or Triumph?" *The Freeman*, April 1999, 32.

63. "Artificial Reef 'Neptune' Complex Deployed," *Environment News Service*, May 26, 1999, on-line version, website: http://ens.lycos.com/e%2Dwire/may99/may269901.html.

64.   De Alessi, *Fishing for Solutions*, 61.

65.   Anthony D. Scott, "The ITQ as a Property Right: Where it Came From, How It Works, and Where It Is Going," in *Taking Ownership*, 97.

66.   De Alessi, "Fishing for Solutions," 99.

67.   Scott, "Market Solutions," 23.

68.   Ronald N. Johnson, "Implications of Taxing Quota Value in an Individual Transferable Quota Fishery," *Marine Resource Economics* 10 (1995): 327-40.

69.   De Alessi, "Fishing for Solutions," 108.

70.   Gregory B. Christainsen and Brian C. Gothberg, "The Potential of High Technology for Establishing Tradeable Rights to Whales," paper presented at "The Technology of Property Rights," 1999 PERC Political Economy Forum, Bozeman, Montana, December 2-5, 1999.

71.   Ibid.

THE MEDICAL MONOPOLY

PROTECTING CONSUMERS OR LIMITING COMPETITION?

Sue A. Blevins

Executive Summary

Nonphysician providers of medical care are in high demand in the United States. But licensure laws and federal regulations limit their scope of practice and restrict access to their services. The result has almost inevitably been less choice and higher prices for consumers.

Safety and consumer protection issues are often cited as reasons for restricting nonphysician services. But the restrictions appear not to be based on empirical findings. Studies have repeatedly shown that qualified nonphysician providers—such as midwives, nurses, and chiropractors—can perform many health and medical services traditionally performed by physicians—with comparable health outcomes, lower costs, and high patient satisfaction.

Licensure laws appear to be designed to limit the supply of health care providers and restrict competition to physicians from nonphysician practitioners. The primary result is an increase in physician fees and income that drives up health care costs.

At a time government is trying to cut health spending and improve access to health care, it is imperative to examine critically the extent to which government policies are responsible for rising health costs and the unavailability of health services. Eliminating the roadblocks to competition among health care providers could improve access to health services, lower health costs, and reduce government spending.

Introduction

> I am myself persuaded that licensure has reduced both the quantity and quality of medical practice. . . . It has forced the public to pay more for less satisfactory medical service.
> —*Milton Friedman*

Although broad-based health care reform has temporarily moved to the back of the public agenda, there remain serious problems of cost and access in the American health care system. The underlying reason for those problems is the lack of a functioning free market in health care in this country. There is privately owned health care, but there is not a living, vibrant free marketplace in health care like there is in other products and services.

Healthy markets have certain common characteristics. On the supply side, there is a choice of providers, in competition with one another, trying to gain customers on the basis of price and quality. And on the demand side, there are consumers seeking the best deal for their dollar. In today's health care system, neither of those conditions obtains.

During the 1994 health care reform debate, much attention was given to the demand side of the market.[1] That attention led to the development of ideas such as medical savings accounts to make health care consumers more cost conscious.[2]

However, true reform requires that the supply side of the health care market be addressed as well. Currently, a wide variety of licensing laws and other regulatory restrictions limits the scope of practice of nonphysician professionals and restricts access to their services. Moreover, at the same time that it is restricting the practices of nontraditional health care professionals, government is providing subsidies for the education and training of physicians who fit the medical orthodoxy. The result has been the creation of a de facto medical monopoly, leading to less choice and higher prices for consumers.

Therefore, true health care reform must involve ending the government-imposed medical monopoly and providing consumers with a full array of health care choices.

The Demand for Alternative Therapies

Every year millions of Americans seek providers who offer health care therapies that are neither widely taught in medical schools nor generally available in U.S. hospitals. Researchers from Harvard Medical School studied the health care practices of U.S. adults and estimated that 22 million Americans sought providers of unconventional care in 1990. The study, reported in the *New England Journal of Medicine*, estimates that in 1990 Americans made more visits to providers who offered unconventional therapies than to all primary care physicians—425 million compared to 388 million visits.[3]

Researchers estimate that 34 percent of Americans used at least 1 of 16 unconventional therapies, such as chiropractic, herbal, and megavitamin therapies, in 1990.[4] Back problems were the most commonly reported "bothersome or serious" health problem for which consumers sought nontraditional services.[5]

There is a great willingness to pay out-of-pocket for providers who offer unconventional health services. The Harvard researchers found that total projected expenditures on providers of unconventional care amounted to $11.7 billion in 1990. Nearly 70 percent—$8.2 billion—of that amount was paid by the consumer, rather than insurers or government. By contrast, only 17 percent of the bill for total physician services was paid out-of-pocket in 1990 .[6]

According to U.S Census data, receipts for nonphysician providers[7] grew by 83 percent— from $10.3 billion to $18.9 billion—between 1987 and 1992,[8] while physician receipts increased by 56 percent, from $90 billion to $141 billion. Census data show that employment by nonphysician establishments grew by 50 percent, while jobs in hospitals and physician offices increased less than 20 percent between 1987 and 1992.

Medical schools are responding to the consumer demand for unconventional health services. To date, 34 out of the 126 medical schools nationwide have started or are developing courses that focus on "alternative medical practices."[9]

It should be noted, however, that medical schools rely heavily on federal subsidies, while training for nonphysician providers is predominantly funded with private money. For example, all of the 17 chiropractic schools in the United States are privately funded; none are state owned.[10] By contrast, 76 of the 126 medical schools are state owned.[11]

At a time when government is looking for ways to reduce health spending, it should examine closely the supply side of health care reform. Some experts have raised concerns about an oversupply of highly trained specialists who rely heavily on government funding for training, while at the same time licensure laws and federal reimbursement regulations restrict nonphysician providers from entering the health care marketplace. An overview of the current supply of selected health care providers is presented in Table 1.

TABLE 1: Supply of Selected Health Care Providers, United States

Type of Provider	Number
Acupuncturists (nonphysician)	6,500
Chiropractors	45,000
Doctors of osteopathy	32,000
Homeopathists[a]	3,000
Massage therapists	9,000
Midwives	
Certified nurse	4,000
Lay	6,000
Total	10,000
Medical doctors	
Primary care	195,300
Nonprimary care	391,700
Total	587,000
Naturopathic doctors	1,000
Nurse practitioners	21,000

Source: Data on acupuncturists, homeopathy, N.D.s (1992), chiropractors, D.O.s (1993) and massage therapists (1994) from Office of Alternative Medicine, NIH, *Alternative Medicine: Expanding Medical Horizons*, NIH publication no. 94-066 (Washington: Government Printing Office, December 1994); data for M.D.s (1992) from Martin Gonzalez, *Socioeconomic Characteristics of Medical Practice 1994* (Chicago: AMA, 1994); data for midwives (1995) from Diana Korte, "Midwives on Trial," *Mothering*, (Fall 1995); and data for N.P.s (1991) from Mullan et al., p. 145.

[a]The estimated 3,000 health care practitioners who are licensed to use homeopathy include acupuncturists, chiropractors, dentists, naturopaths, nurse practitioners, osteopaths, physicians, physician assistants, and veterinarians. Office of Alternative Medicine, National Institute of Health, p. 82.

Any serious reform of the U.S. health care system must address the medical monopoly. Barriers to entry into the health care marketplace are partially responsible for high health costs and lack of access to primary and preventive health care.

Individual Choice and Freedom to Contract

Professional licensure laws and other regulatory restrictions impose significant barriers to Americans' freedom of choice in health care. Clark Havighurst, the William Neal Reynolds Professor of Law at Duke University, has pointed out, "Professional licensure laws have long made the provision of most personal health services the exclusive province of physicians. Obviously, such regulation limits consumers' options by forcing them to use highly trained, expensive personnel when other types might serve quite well."[12]

Yet the freedom to contract—the right of individuals to decide with whom and for what services they will dispose of their earning—is one of the fundamental rights of man. As Chief Justice John Marshall said in *Ogden v. Saunders*, "Individuals do not derive from government their right to contract, but bring that right with them into society . . . [e]very man retains [the right] to . . . dispose of [his] property according to his own judgment." Indeed, legal philosophers and ethicists, such as Roger Pilon, Richard Epstein, and Stephen Mecado, convincingly argue that the rights of property and contract are fundamental rights upon which all others are based.[13]

Accordingly, individuals should have the legal right to decide with whom they will contract for the provision and coordination of their health care services: doctors, midwives, nurse practitioners, chiropractors, spiritual healers, or other health care providers. Any restriction denies Americans the right to make decisions about their own bodies.

The Rise of Medical Licensure

Although protection of the public is often cited as the reason for medical licensing and limiting access to unconventional therapies, history indicates that professional interest was more of an overriding concern in the early enactment of those laws. The latter theory reflects economist Paul Feldstein's perspective that health associations act like firms: they try to maximize the interests of their existing membership.[14]

Medical licensure was first introduced in England in 1442 when London barbers were granted charters to perform certain procedures. The charters authorized "barbers" to treat wounds, let blood, and draw teeth.[15]

In the United States, the earliest health professional licensure law was enacted by Virginia in 1639. That law dealt with the collection of physician fees, vaccination, the quarantine of certain diseases, and the construction and management of isolation hospitals. Other early colonial acts denied nonphysician practitioners any standing in civil courts to collect fees. In 1760 New York City became the first American jurisdiction to prohibit practice by unlicensed physicians. Subsequently, many other cities and states introduced licensing requirements.[16]

During the early part of the 19th century, the United States experienced an era known as "free trade in medicine." A historical vignette in the *Journal of the American Medical Association* explains that during the mid-1800s, botanics and homeopathy were in great demand.[17] Those alternative health practices were a powerful counterforce to regular medicine. Most state licensure laws that granted special privileges to physicians were repealed because of the widespread consumer demand for botanicals. During the period, the United States was one of the healthiest nations, with the world's lowest infant mortality rate.[18]

However, the self-interest of physicians soon began to assert itself. The repeal of licensure laws "triggered a movement that led directly to the formation of the American Medical Association."[19] The AMA was determined to protect physicians from competition by nonphysician health care providers. Consequently, licensure laws arose again, beginning about 1870. By 1895 nearly every state had created some type of administrative board to examine and license physicians.[20]

Another study of the early development of medical licensing laws in the United States reports that the goals of the AMA in supporting licensing appear to have been to (1) restrict entry into the profession and thereby secure a more stable financial climate for physicians, (2) destroy for-profit medical schools and replace them with nonprofit institutions, and (3) eliminate other medical sects such as homeopaths and chiropractors.[21]

History reveals that the AMA was influential in linking physician licensure with strict educational standards that (1) restricted entry into the health care marketplace and (2) increased the cost of medical education.[22]

Paul Starr, in his Pulitzer prize-winning *The Social Transformation of American Medicine,* examined the consolidation of medical authority between 1850 and 1930. Starr notes that before 1870, requirements for physician training were minimal and that many medical schools were for-profit.[23]

Medical education began to be reformed around the late 19th century. Starr describes the competitive climate of the period: "Despite the new licensing laws, the ports of entry into medicine were still wide open, and the unwelcome passed through in great numbers. . . . From the viewpoint of established physicians, the commercial schools were undesirable on at least two counts: for the added competition they were creating and for the low image of the physician that their graduates fostered. Medicine would never be a respected profession—so its most vocal spokesman declared until it sloughed off its coarse and common elements."[24]

In 1904 the AMA established a Council on Medical Education with a mandate to elevate the standards of medical education. Two years later the council inspected the 160 medical schools throughout the United States and approved of only 82 schools: 46 were found imperfect, and 32 were declared "beyond salvage." But organized medicine's professional code of ethics "forbade physicians from taking up cudgels against each other in public," and the report was never published.[25]

Instead, the AMA commissioned an outside consultant to investigate and report on the status of medical education in the United States. Abraham Flexner of the Carnegie Foundation for the Advancement of Teaching was commissioned to do a study of medical education. Flexner, an educator with a bachelor's degree from Johns Hopkins, visited each of the 160 U.S. medical schools and released his recommendations in 1910.

Flexner decided that the great majority of medical schools should be closed and the remainder should be modeled after Johns Hopkins.[26] The AMA used the Flexner report in its campaign to abolish medical schools outside its control. With physician licensure already in place, it was relatively easy for the AMA-dominated state examination boards to consider only graduates of medical schools approved by the AMA or the Association of American Colleges, whose lists were identical. In many states the requirement was statutory.[27]

One result was a significant decline in the number of proprietary schools, which had been very prominent until the early 1900s. Although the number of medical colleges had decreased from 160 to 131 between 1900 and 1910, the release of the Flexner report facilitated the closure of an additional 46 medical schools between 1910 and 1920.[28]

By 1930 only 76 medical schools remained in the United States. In 1932 the chairman of the Commission on Medical Education—Harvard University president A. Lawrence Lowell—reported that "the definition of standards and the efforts of leaders in the medical profession were very influential in eliminating the proprietary and commercial medical schools."[29] Lowell also concluded in the 1932 report on medical education that "the budgets of many schools have increased from 200 to 1,000 percent during the last 15 years."[30]

Women and African-Americans were disproportionately affected by Flexner's recommendations. In 1905 and 1910 women medical students numbered 1,073 and 907, respectively. Five years after the Flexner report was released, the number of women medical students had been cut nearly in half from 907 to 592.[31] Starr notes, "As places in medical school became more scarce, schools that previously had liberal policies toward women increasingly excluded them."[32]

There were seven predominantly black medical schools in existence before the Flexner report, but only two remained after its release.[33] As a result, the number of doctors serving African-American communities declined. For example, blacks in Mississippi had 1 doctor for every 14,634 persons[34] compared to 1 doctor for every 2,563 persons nationwide in 1930.[35]

Many small towns and rural communities were affected by the new educational standards and associated licensure laws. AMA president William Pusey concluded that "as you increase the cost of the license to practice medicine you increase the price at which medical service must be sold and you correspondingly decrease the number of people who can afford to buy this medical service."[36]

The Flexner report also had a significant impact on nonphysician health care providers. Within 10 years after the Flexner report, approximately 130 laws were passed regulating at least 14 health-related occupations.[37] Some nontraditional specialties were virtually wiped out. Take homeopathy, for example. By the end of the 19th century, an estimated 15 percent of physicians practiced homeopathy, the use of natural remedies to stimulate the body's natural healing responses. There were 22 homeopathic medical schools and over 100 homeopathic hospitals in the United States.[38] Early supporters of homeopathy included Thomas Edison, John D. Rockefeller, and Mark Twain.[39] Four years after the Flexner report, the President of the Institute of Homeopathy, Dr. DeWitt Wilcox, shared his perception of organized medicine:

TABLE 2: Graduates of Selected Medical Schools and Nationwide Total Examined by State Boards in 1931

Medical School	Number Examined	Percentage of Failures
Albany Medical College	8	14.3
Boston University School of Medicine	55	10.9
Cornell University Medical College	59	6.8
Georgetown University School of Medicine	139	17.3
Hahnemann Medical College and Hospital of Philadelphia	89	3.4
Howard University College of Medicine	63	11.1
New York Homeopathic Medical College & Flower Hospital	88	11.4
Syracuse University College of Medicine	46	8.7
Total examined nationwide and percentage of failures	5,576	6.3

Source: A. Lawrence Lowell et al., *Final Report of the Commission on Medical Education* (New York: Association of American Medical Colleges, 1932), appendix, Table 87.

The American Medical Association is fast degenerating into a political machine bent on throttling everything which stands in its way for obtaining medical supremacy. It has made an unholy alliance with the Army and Navy Medical Departments, and together they propose to own and control every medical college in this country, all the State, municipal and university hospitals, and get within their grasp all the examining and licensing boards in the United States.[40]

By the late 1930s the practice of homeopathy had largely disappeared from the United States. The new rating system for medical schools was influential in eliminating homeopathic colleges nationwide.[41]

It is commonly thought that homeopathy disappeared because of its poor quality of education. But history shows that physicians graduating from two of the last homeopathic colleges—Hahnemann Medical College and New York Homeopathic College—passed examinations at a rate comparable to physicians from schools that were maintained (see Table 2).

Medical Licensing Today

Today states use three mechanisms for regulating health professionals: (1) licensure, the most restrictive form of regulation, makes it illegal to practice a profession without meeting state-imposed standards; (2) certification, granting title protection to persons meeting predetermined standards (those without the title may perform services, but may not use the title); and (3) registration, the least restrictive form of regulation, requiring individuals to file their names, addresses, and qualifications with a government agency before practicing.[42]

Professional health care associations have been influential in setting the standards for licensure laws in the United States. Feldstein has identified ways in which health care associations limit competition: the first approach, Feldstein notes, is simply to have substitute providers declared illegal.[43] If substitute providers are prohibited, or if they are severely limited in the tasks they are legally permitted to perform, then there will be a shift in demand away from their services. That approach has been used with lay midwives. In addition, states impose professional "scope-of-practice" regulations that prevent nurse practitioners from functioning independently as primary care providers.[44]

Another approach to limiting health care competition—used when licensure and scope-of-practice restrictions fail—is to restrict or limit substitute providers' services from payment by government health programs. That approach has been used by organized medicine, for example, to limit access to chiropractic treatment. Medicare regulations prohibit reimbursement to chiropractors for services they are licensed to perform in all 50 states. The federal reimbursement regulations appear not to be based on empirical evidence: the federal government's Agency for Health Care Policy and Research recently released national guidelines that recommend spinal manipulation as a safe and cost-effective treatment for acute back problems.[45]

The following examples show how the medical monopoly has used the power of government to restrict the practice of a variety of nonphysician health care providers.

Midwifery

At least 36 states restrict or outright prohibit the practice of lay midwifery.[46] Consequently, only 5 percent of all births are attended by midwives in this country,[47] compared with 75 percent of all births in European countries.[48] Americans' low usage of midwifery does not correlate with high-quality birth outcomes: the United States has the second highest caesarean rate in the world[49] and the fifth highest infant mortality rate among Western industrialized nations.[50]

There are an estimated 10,000 midwives in this country who fall into two categories: the certified nurse-midwife and the lay midwife (or "direct-entry" midwife). Certified nurse-midwives are registered nurses with two years of advanced training who most often work under the supervision of a physician and practice in clinic or hospital settings. Certified nurse-midwives represent approximately 4,000 of the 10,000 midwives nationwide.

By contrast, lay midwives enter the profession directly from independent midwifery schools or through apprenticeship. They are trained to meet individual state requirements for licensure, registration, or certification. But unlike certified nurse midwives, most lay midwives practice independently in consultation with physicians, not under direct physician supervision. About half the 6,000 lay midwives are associated with religious groups,[51] and a majority of home births in the United States are attended by lay midwives.[52]

Safety is most commonly cited as the reason for prohibiting or restricting lay midwifery in 36 states. Those licensure laws and regulatory restrictions, however, do not appear to be based on empirical findings of childbirth outcomes.[53] For example, the National Birth Center study on nearly 12,000 nonhospital births found a neonatal mortality rate for midwife-assisted births comparable to that of hospital births.[54] Another study examined 1,700 home births attended by lay midwives in rural Tennessee. Researchers found at-home midwife-assisted births to be as safe as physician-attended hospital deliveries.[55]

Many people attribute midwives' record of success to the fact that they do not assist with high-risk deliveries. To address that issue, researchers excluded physicians' high-risk cases from their study of lay midwives in rural Tennessee. The *American Journal of Public Health* reports that even with comparable low-risk deliveries, lay midwife-assisted home births were as safe as physician-assisted hospital births. Moreover, physician-attended hospitals births were 10 times more likely to require intervention (forceps, vacuum extractor, or caesarean section) than midwife-assisted home births.[56]

Those findings are supported by international studies. In the Netherlands—where more than 32 percent of births are attended by lay midwives at home-research shows that the perinatal mortality rate was lowest in cities that had the highest proportion of home births.[57] A study on Dutch births by the British journal *Midwifery* concluded that perinatal mortality was "much lower under the noninterventionist care of midwives than under the interventionist management of obstetricians."[58]

Midwives are considerably less expensive than traditional obstetric care providers. According-ing to the Health Insurance Association of America, the average physician-attended birth costs $4,200; Midwives Alliance of North America reports that the average cost of a midwife-assisted birth is $1,200.[59] Americans could save $2.4 billion annually if only 20 percent of American women increased their access to midwives.[60]

Most important, though, is that women report significant personal and psychological benefits from midwife-assisted births. Since the early 1970s, a home birth renaissance has been sparked by feminist politics, the women's health and holistic health movements, back-to-nature ideology, and health consumerism.[61] A study of the home birth movement in the United States concludes, "Members have chosen their alternative form of care not through faulty understanding of medical principles and practices, but as a result of active and reasoned disagreement with them. The home birth movement is one of a number of lay health belief systems currently flourishing among middle class populations."[62]

As a result of midwives' success, a wide range of health organizations, including the American Public Health Association, National Commission to Prevent Infant Mortality, and World Health Organization, advocates the expanded use of midwives. The strongest advocacy has come from the women's health movement with support from the Boston Women's Health Book Collective, National Black Women's Health Project, National Women's Health Network, and Women's Institute for Childbearing Policy. The benefits of a low-intervention approach to childbirth are also supported by the General Accounting Office and the Office of Technology Assessment.[63]

Despite midwives' record of safety and mothers' reports of psychological and personal benefits, the medical community continues to enforce licensure laws that restrict women's birthing options.[64] A past president of the American College of Obstetrics and Gynecology (ACOG) denounced home birth as a form of "maternal trauma" and "child abuse" during the late 1970s.[65] A decade later, ACOG released statements that "discouraged the use of birth centers until better data were available."[66]

Midwives are continually placed under considerable legal and biomedical scrutiny. An award-winning women's health writer, Diana Korte, recently examined the number of midwives on trial across the country. According to Korte, at least 145 midwives in 36 states have had legal altercations with the medical authorities. One case involved the arrest of a rural Missouri midwife.

> At 2:00 a.m. on a January morning in 1991, seven law enforcement officers in bulletproof vests ransacked the birth center of a rural Missouri midwife, removed all of her computer disks, and destroyed files and other materials. Although the Missouri Nursing Board had previously authorized the birth center, the county prosecutor charged the midwife with eight felonies and several misdemeanors for practicing medicine without a license.[67]

Parents rarely make complaints about midwives: most legal altercations stem from the medical community.[68] Archie Brodsky, a senior research associate at the Harvard Medical School's Program in Psychiatry and the Law, noted that 71 percent of obstetrician-gynecologists had been named in one or more liability claims as of 1987. By comparison, only 10 percent of midwives had experienced legal claims at that time; lay midwives are even more rarely sued.[69]

The medical community often refuses to provide backup support to women who choose to deliver at home, despite midwives' record of safety and low malpractice claims. A recent pilot study of childbirth choices found that 20 percent of mothers delivering in the hospital setting would have preferred a nonhospital delivery, but no medical backup support was readily available.[70] Another study at the Medical College of Pennsylvania found that women met forceful resistance from physicians when they disclosed their plans for home delivery. Accordingly, the study notes,

> A number of women found it ironic, and even unconscionable, that physicians who criticized home birth as unsafe also refused to provide the prenatal care which all would agree would increase the safety of pregnancy and birth under any circumstances. Some concluded on these grounds that these physicians' motivation must have more to do with self-interest (in terms of power, authority, and money) than with interest in the health and safety of their patients and their babies.[71]

It should be noted, however, that fear of malpractice may have played a large part in the physicians' decisions to refuse backup support. Further, as Figure 1 illustrates, medical attitudes about midwifery and home births vary greatly among physicians and geographical areas. States that grant legal status to lay midwives in the form of licensure, certification, or registration include Alaska, Arkansas, Arizona, Colorado, Florida, Louisiana, New Hampshire, New Mexico, Montana, Oregon, South Carolina, Texas, Washington, and Wyoming.[72]

Nurse Practitioners

Particularly in underserved areas and long-term care facilities, registered nurses with advanced training—nurse practitioners—are able to provide most basic health services provided by physicians, and at lower costs. The American Nurses Association estimates that of the 2.1 million registered nurses nationwide, approximately 400,000 deliver primary care.[73] Many of them are practicing in managed-care organizations under the supervision of physicians. Some 21,000 nurses have received advanced training at graduate schools of nursing and are licensed nurse practitioners.

FIGURE 1: Legal Status of Direct-Entry Midwifery in the United States, April 1995

Prohibited through statutory restriction or judicial interpretation; or unless licensed before a certain date

Legal by statute, but licensure unavailable

Not legally defined but not prohibited

Legal through judicial interpretation or statutory inference

Legal by licensure, certification, or registration

Research shows that between 75 and 80 percent of adult primary care, and up to 90 percent of pediatric primary care, services could be safely provided by nurse practitioners.[74] A study by the Office of Technology Assessment found that the outcomes of nurse practitioner care were equivalent to those of services provided by physicians, and that nurse practitioners were actually more adept in communication and preventive care. The Office of Technology Assessment study also indicates that increasing access to nurse practitioner services could be especially advantageous for the home-bound elderly.[75]

Another study examined the outcomes of a nurse-managed clinic that was opened to provide primary care services to more than 2,000 low-income children and their families in an underserved Texas community. Research shows that after the clinic was opened in 1991, emergency room visits by pediatric Medicaid recipients decreased by 27 percent at the largest emergency room in the county. In addition, the pregnancy-induced hypertension rate was reduced from 7 to 3.3 percent over a three-year period, preventing costly hospitalizations.[76]

The economic loss from inefficient use of primary care nurse practitioners is estimated to be between $6.4 billion and $8.75 billion.[77] A meta-analysis conducted by the American Nurses Association in 1993 showed that nurse practitioner care resulted in fewer hospitalizations, higher scores on patient satisfaction, and lower cost per visit—$12.36 compared to $20.11 for physicians.[78] In addition to projected savings on direct health services, the taxpayer burden for training nurse practitioners is approximately one-fifth the cost of training physicians.[79]

Despite empirical evidence that nurse practitioners can safely provide primary care, many states impose scope-of-practice regulations that prevent nurses from practicing independently as primary care providers. Nurse practitioners derive their authority from various state nurse practice acts.[80] However, some states give their medical boards regulatory control over boards of nursing. That gives one profession full veto power over the rules and regulations of its competitors.

Moreover, scope-of-practice regulations often dictate that nurses must work in coordination with physicians. For example, 48 states grant nurse practitioners prescriptive authority but mandate that nurses must have a written practice agreement or work in collaboration with a physician.

As of January 1995, only 10 states granted nurse practitioners the legal right to prescribe drugs independent of a physician.[81] Moreover, even some of those states limited the independent nurse practitioner's prescription authority by law to 72 hours.[82] What that means for competition is that consumers—for example, elderly Medicare recipients who live in rural areas—would have to visit independent nurse practitioners every three days to renew prescriptions. Barbara Safriet, associate dean of Yale Law School, argues,

Medical practice acts remain overly broad and indeterminate, with concomitant and unnecessary restrictions in the licensure and practice acts of nonphysician providers. If we are to achieve our goal of offering high-quality care, at an affordable cost, to everyone who needs it, we must ensure that all health care providers are able to practice within the full scope of their professional competencies.[83]

States' scope-of-practice regulations shield the full market demand for nurse practitioner services because nurses are not legally free to compete in the health care market. A 1993 Gallup poll found that 86 percent of consumers would be willing to use nurse practitioners for basic health care services. Only 12 percent stated that they would be unwilling to see a nurse practitioner.[84]

This analysis does not in any manner call for increased government regulations that would force Medicaid or Medicare recipients to substitute nurse practitioner care for physician services. Instead, it argues that Americans should not be restricted from choosing low-cost alternative practitioners and forced to subsidize an oversupply of highly specialized physicians. Let nurse practitioners legally compete in the health care market and allow consumers to choose among qualified health providers on the basis of quality and cost.

Chiropractic

The chiropractic profession has faced significant challenges by organized medicine for over 100 years. For example, between 1963 and 1974 the AMA operated a Committee on Quackery with an intent to "expose the charlatanism of chiropractic." The AMA urged members to lend "their full support to the continuing vigorous attack on medical quackery and to the education program on the cult of chiropractic."[85]

Although the AMA certainly had every right to criticize medical practices with which it disagreed, the organization soon resorted to lobbying the government for restrictions on chiropractic practice. Today, chiropractors are subject to numerous restrictions on their scope of practice.[86]

In addition, the AMA recommended that Congress exclude payment for chiropractic services from federally supported health programs.[87] As a result, Medicare recipients are restricted from using the full range of chiropractic services. Medicare policy limits patient access to chiropractors this way: Medicare reimburses chiropractors for performing "spinal manipulation" but requires that a diagnostic spinal xray be taken before chiropractic treatment. The catch is that Medicare does not reimburse chiropractors for performing x-rays, even though they have the training and are licensed to perform x-rays in all 50 states.[88] That policy gives the medical profession control over managing back problems among elderly Americans.

Ironically, the federal government's Agency for Health Care Policy and Research (AHCPR) recently released national pain guidelines that recommend spinal manipulation for the common complaint of acute low back pain.[89] It is estimated that 80 percent of all adults suffer from back pain at some time in their lives,[90] and an estimated 91 percent of older adults (ages 65 to 74) report back problems.[91] The AHCPR estimates that Americans could save over $1 billion annually by using noninterventionist approaches for managing back pain, even if only 20 percent of practitioners followed the agency's recommendations.[92]

International research supports the U.S. findings that chiropractic is a safe and cost-effective method for managing back pain. A study published by the *British Medical Journal* reports that chiropractic treatment was more effective than outpatient hospital management of low back pain. British researchers estimate that if the 72,000 patients who show no contraindications to manipulation but are referred to hospitals for back care each year were instead referred to chiropractors, the British health system could reduce days of sickness absence by 290,000 and could save 2.9 million pounds in social security payments over a two-year period.[93]

Consumers are quite satisfied with chiropractic treatment. The *Western Journal of Medicine* reports that patients of chiropractors were three times more likely than patients of family physicians to report that they were very satisfied with their treatment for low back pain—by a score of 66 to 22 percent.[94] A 1991 Gallup poll found that 90 percent of patients regard their chiropractic care as effective and that approximately 80 percent consider the treatment costs reasonable.[95]

In 1976 four chiropractors filed an antitrust lawsuit against the AMA, 5 of its officers, and 10 other medical organizations including the American Hospital Association, charging them with criminal conspiracy to destroy chiropractic. Plaintiffs alleged a conspiracy that included (1) preventing medical doctors and doctors of osteopathy from associating professionally with chiropractors, (2) defining it as unethical for MDs to accept referrals from chiropractors, and (3) prohibiting chiropractors from using hospital diagnostic laboratory and radiological facilities, among other things.

In 1987 the AMA was found guilty of illegal conspiracy: the AMA's anti-quackery activity was in violation of U.S. antitrust laws,[96] yet restrictions on chiropractic scope of practice and reimbursement remain in place.

Vitamins and Herbs

For years mainstream medicine has suggested that individuals who use unconventional therapies—such as vitamin therapies and herbal products—are not acting according to scientific rationale and therefore need to be protected by the government.[97] The president of the National Council Against Health Fraud (NCAHF), William Jarvis, has suggested that regulators are failing to protect the public against quackery. Jarvis explains that "the real issues in the war against quackery are the principles, including scientific rationale, encoded into consumer protection laws, primarily by the U.S. Food, Drug, and Cosmetic Act. More such laws are badly needed."[98]

Jarvis suggests that promoters of a free-enterprise society are paving the way for organized quackery. He notes that "in recent years, a free-market ideology, advanced by Friedman in his book *Free to Choose*, has gained an influential following" and that "the only way to enjoy both the benefits of a free-enterprise health marketplace and avoid the abuses of quackery is to balance the situation with sound consumer protection laws, enforcement, and education."[99] More recently, a member of NCAHF and president of the Consumer Health Information Research Institute has received a special citation from the FDA for combating health fraud.[100]

One way the FDA combats health fraud is to pull herbal products from the shelf if manufacturers make specific health claims about their usefulness without first obtaining FDA approval. Some providers have even been subject to criminal prosecution. But getting herbal remedies through the drug approval process is unrealistic. Botanicals are not patentable (although they can be patented for use); and the cost of their approval as drugs would be difficult to recover. The total cost of taking a new drug to the market in the United States is close to $400 million, and it takes nearly 15 years to complete the procedure.[101]

Meanwhile, Americans are expressing an increased interest in nutritional and herbal therapies. And according to the World Health Organization, about 4 billion people—80 percent of the world population—use herbal remedies for some aspect of their health care. Yet in the United States the FDA often considers herbal remedies to be worthless or potentially dangerous.[102]

Health care regulators defend their position as necessary to protect consumers. But contrary to conventional expectation, users of unconventional therapies are well educated and have higher-than-average incomes.[103] Even in countries with socialized health systems that provide access to conventional medical care for all citizens, users of unconventional therapies and practitioners are usually from higher social classes.[104] A study of complementary medicine in the United Kingdom suggests that patients from higher social classes presumably have the opportunity to research and explore the possibilities of complementary medicine and to pay for it.[105]

Protecting Consumers or Limiting Competition?

There is little actual evidence that medical licensing improves quality or protects the public.[106] Medical economist Gary Gaumer, reviewing all the available literature on medical licensing, concluded,

> Research evidence does not inspire confidence that wide-ranging systems for regulating health professionals have served the public interest. Though researchers have not been able to observe the consequences of a totally unregulated environment, observation of incremental variations in regulatory practice generally supports the view that tighter controls do not lead to improvements in the quality of service.[107]

Even the Federal Trade Commission has concluded that "occupational licensing frequently increases prices and imposes substantial costs on consumers. At the same time, many occupational licensing restrictions do not appear to realize the goal of increasing the quality of professionals' services."[108]

Licensing laws may actually put the public more at risk by lulling consumers into a false sense of security. Terree Wasley points out in *What Has Government Done to Our Health Care?* that most state licensing laws permit all licensed physicians to perform all types of medical services, even those for which they are not specifically trained.[109] For example, in Massachusetts physicians are licensed to perform acupuncture even though they may not have received special training.[110] That situation disturbs nonphysician acupuncturists who receive more hours of acupuncture training than do most licensed physicians.[111]

Feldstein points out that licensure laws focus at the point of entry into the medical profession, not on continuous monitoring. Once medical professionals are licensed, there are no requirements for proving that they are fully trained to perform the most up-to-date procedures.[112] Some states do not require continuing education, so there is no guarantee that a physician is current with the most recent techniques and information.[113] Feldstein points out that

> state licensing boards are responsible for monitoring physicians' behavior and for penalizing physicians whose performance is inadequate or whose conduct is unethical. Unfortunately, this approach for assuring physician quality and competence is completely inadequate. . . . Monitoring the care provided by physicians through the use of claims and medical records data would more directly determine the quality and competence of a physician.[114]

In his 1987 Cato Institute book, *The Rule of Experts: Occupational Licensing in America,* S. David Young, a professor of accounting and finance at Tulane University, reviewed the literature on a wide variety of occupational licensing restrictions, including medical licensing, and found that "licensing has, at best, a neutral effect on quality and may even cause harm to consumers."[115]

While the public safety benefits of medical licensure are clearly questionable, nearly all economists recognize that professional licensure laws act as a barrier to entry that decreases competition and increases price. As Victor Fuchs wrote in 1974, "Most economists believe that part [of physician's high incomes] represents a monopoly return to physicians from restrictions on entry to the profession and other barriers to competition."[116]

One of the earliest studies of the impact of licensure on physician income was done in 1945 by Nobel Prize-winning economist Milton Friedman and Simon Kuznets. Friedman and Kuznets found that the difference in income between professional and nonprofessional health care workers was larger than could be explained by the extra skill and training of the professionals. A large portion of the variation, they concluded, was due to licensing restrictions. In addition, they concluded that the difference in mean income of physicians and dentists was caused by greater difficulty of entry into medicine than into dentistry.[117]

Friedman and Kuznets's conclusions have been confirmed by numerous other studies. For example, William White examined the effect of licensure on the income of clinical laboratory personnel and found that in cities with stringent licensing restrictions income was 16 percent higher than in cities with less stringent restrictions, with no variation in the quality of testing.[118]

Lawrence Shepard examined the fees of dentists in states that recognized out-of-state licenses and those that did not. He found that in states that did not recognize out-of-state licenses, dental fees were 12 to 15 percent higher.[119] A study of Canadian health care indicated that occupational licensing, combined with mobility restrictions and advertising restrictions, increased health care costs by as much as 27 percent.[120] Gaumer found that both fees and provider incomes were higher in states with more restrictive licensure requirements.[121]

Interesting confirmation that physician licensure is related more to a desire to increase physician incomes than to concern over public health and safety can be found in a 1984 study by medical economist Chris Paul, who found that the year that a state enacted physician licensing was related to the number of AMA members in the state.[122] Paul concluded that decisions by states to require licensing of physicians were more likely a result of special interests than of the public interest.

As the Friedmans note, "The *justification* [for licensure] is always the same: to protect the consumer. However, the *reason* is demonstrated by observing who lobbies at the state legislatures for imposition or strengthening of licensure. The lobbyists are invariably representatives of the occupation in question rather than its customers."[123]

Subsidies and the Medical Monopoly

In addition to using government to restrict competition, the medical monopoly also turns to government for subsidies. For example, most physician training is subsidized by the federal government.

In 1927 student fees accounted for 34 percent of medical school revenues.[124] Today less than 5 percent of medical school revenues comes from tuition and fees. Instead, medical schools rely heavily on federal and state support.[125] In 1992 total medical school revenues amounted to $23 billion.[126] State and local governments provided $2.7 billion.[127] The federal government paid at least $10.3 billion to medical schools and hospitals for medical education and training (Table 3). Additional revenues were obtained from charges for services, endowments, and private grants.

Medicare payments to hospitals represent the largest source of federal funding for medical education and training.[128] Medicare pays for physician education and training in two ways: First, hospitals receive direct payments from Medicare based on the number of full-time-equivalent residents employed at each hospital. Second, Medicare increases a hospital's diagnostic-related group payments according to an "indirect" medical education factor, based on the ratio of residents to hospital beds.[129]

The average Medicare payment to hospitals was more than $70,000 per resident for both direct and indirect education subsidies in 1992. An estimated 69,900 full-time-equivalent interns, residents, and fellows were eligible for Medicare reimbursement in 1991.[130]

TABLE 3: Taxpayer Support for Physician Education and Training, 1991-92

Source	Billions of Dollars
Medicare	5.2
Federal research, training, and teaching	5.1
State and local governments	2.7
Total	13.0

Sources: Fitzhugh Mullan et al., "Doctors, Dollars, and Determination: Making Physician Work-Force Policy," *Health Affairs* Supplement (1993), p. 142; and Janice Ganem et al., "Review of U.S. Medical School Finances 1992-93," *Journal of the American Medical Association* 274 (1995): 724.

Medicare paid hospitals $1.6 billion for direct medical education expenses and dispensed $3.6 billion for indirect medical education adjustments in 1992.[131] Of the total $5.2 billion that Medicare paid to hospitals for training, approximately $0.3 billion was appropriated for training nurses and allied health professionals.[132]

Medical schools and teaching hospitals receive additional federal funding from the National Institutes of Health, the Department of Veterans Affairs, the Department of Defense, and the Health Resources and Services Administration (Title VII) program. Federal funding for research, training, and teaching amounted to at least $5.1 billion in 1992.[133] That money was awarded to medical schools and affiliated hospitals in the form of grants and contracts. Supporting biomedical research in medical schools is one way the federal government supports medical education without appearing to do so directly.[134]

As Feldstein has pointed out, "There is no reason why medical students should be subsidized to a greater extent than students in other graduate or professional schools."[135] That point has also been suggested by Uwe Reinhardt, a professor of political economy at Princeton University, who recently noted,

> In the context of academic medicine, this inquiry should begin with the question of why the education of physicians is now so heavily supported with public funds, when similar support has never been extended to other important professions, for example, students in law schools or graduate programs in business. . . . In truth, the case for the traditional heavy public subsidies to medical education and training has simply been taken for granted . . . it never has been adequately justified.[136]

A less direct form of subsidy is the ability of the health care establishment to direct government payments from the Medicare and Medicaid programs to "approved" providers and hospitals. As already discussed, chiropractors and other nontraditional providers have generally been excluded from Medicare reimbursement. Furthermore, in order to be eligible to participate in Medicare, a hospital must be accredited by the Joint Commission on Accreditation of Health Care Organizations (or the American Osteopathic Association in the case of osteopathic hospitals). The JCAHO, which the *Wall Street Journal* describes as "one of the most powerful and secretive groups in all of health care,"[137] is a private organization with a board dominated by members representing the AMA and the American Hospital Association.

As several medical economists studying the issue have warned, in as much as Medicare is a major source of hospital revenues, "the influence of the JCAHO can be used to limit hospital competition and to protect physicians [against competition] from other groups of providers by denying them access to hospitals or influence within hospitals."[138] Thus the medical monopoly is able to use federal funds to reward its members and restrain its competitors.

Conclusion

What should government do if it is serious about cutting health spending and improving access to affordable health care? The first step should be to eliminate the anti-competitive barriers that restrict access to low-cost providers, namely licensure laws and federal reimbursement regulations. Americans should not be forced to substitute providers against their will; rather, they should be free to choose among all types of health care providers.

Instead of imposing strict licensure laws that focus on entry into the market but do not guarantee quality control, states should hold professionals equally accountable for the quality of their outcomes. That will reduce the need for strict licensure laws and other regulations that are purported to protect the public at large.

The time is right for eliminating barriers to nonphysician health care providers. Many Americans are seeking low-cost nontraditional providers and even choose to pay out-of-pocket for their services. Breaking the anti-competitive barriers of licensure laws and federal reimbursement regulations will provide meaningful health reform, increase consumer choice, and reduce health care costs.

Notes

This study was supported, in part, by the Institute for Humane Studies, George Mason University.

1.   For a detailed discussion of the demand side of health care reform, see Stan Liebowitz, "Why Health Care Costs Too Much," *Cato Institute Policy Analysis* no. 211, June 23, 1994.

2.   For a complete discussion of medical savings accounts, see John C. Goodman and Gerald L. Musgrave, *Patient Power: Solving America's Health Care Crisis* (Washington: Cato Institute 1992).

3.   David Eisenberg et al., "Unconventional Medicine in the United States: Prevalence, Costs, and Patterns of Use," *New England Journal of Medicine* 328, no. 4 (1993): 246-52.

4.   Eisenberg et al. examined therapies not widely taught in U.S. medical schools nor generally available in U.S. hospitals. Therapies included acupuncture, biofeedback, chiropractic, commercial weight-loss programs, energy healing, exercise, folk remedies, homeopathy, hypnosis, imagery, lifestyle diets

(e.g., macrobiotics), massage, megavitamin therapy, prayer, relaxation techniques, self-help groups, and spiritual healing.

5. Daniel Q. Haney, "Study Finds Adults Pay $14 Billion Annually on Offbeat Medicine," *Philadelphia Inquirer*, January 28, 1993, p. A6.

6. Estimate based on amount spent out-of-pocket for all physicians' services in 1990 = $23.5 billion, cited by Eisenberg et al., p. 251; and total amount (out-of-pocket, private insurance, and government) for all physicians' services in 1990 = $140.5 billion, cited by Katharine R. Levitt et al., "National Health Spending Trends, 1960-1993," *Health Affairs* (Winter 1994): 15.

7. Office of Management and Budget, *Standard Industrial Classification Manual* (Washington: National Technical Information Center, 1987). Nonphysician providers include acupuncturists, audiologists, chiropractors, Christian Science practitioners, dental hygienists, dieticians, hypnotists, inhalation therapists, midwives, naturopaths, nurses (not practicing in hospitals, clinics, or offices of medical doctors, nursing homes, HMOs, or home health care), nutritionists, occupational therapists, optometrists, paramedics, physical therapists, physicians' assistants, podiatrists, psychiatric social workers, psychologists, psychotherapists, speech clinicians, and speech pathologists.

8. U.S. Department of Commerce, Economics and Statistics Administration, Bureau of the Census, *1992 Census of Service Industries: Geographic Area Services, United States,* publication no SC92-A-52.

9. Joseph Jacobs, "Building Bridges between Two Worlds: The NIH's Office of Alternative Medicine," *Academic Medicine* 70 (January 1995): 41.

10. Paul Brown, "Chiropractic: A Medical Perspective," *Minnesota Medicine* 77 (1994): 21; National Center for Health Statistics, *Health, United States,* 1992, p. 149.

11. Fitzhugh Mullan et al., "Doctors, Dollars, and Determination: Making Physician Work-Force Policy," *Health Affairs*, Supplement 1993, pp. 138-51.

12. Clark Havighurst, "The Changing Locus of Decision Making in the Health Care Sector," *Journal of Health Politics, Policy and Law* 11 (1986): 700.

13. See, for example, James Dorn and Henry Manne, eds., *Economic Liberties and the Judiciary* (Fairfax, Va.: George Mason University Press, 1987).

14. Paul J. Feldstein, *Health Associations and the Demand for Legislation* (Cambridge, Mass.: Ballinger, 1977), p. 15.

15. A. Lawrence Lowell et al., *Final Report of the Commission on Medical Education* (New York: Association of American Medical Colleges, 1932), pp. 151-53.

16. Ibid.

17. Lester S. King, "Medical Sects and Their Influence," *Journal of the American Medical Association* 248 (1982).

18. Lawrence Wilson, "The Case against Medical Licensing," in *The Dangers of Socialized Medicine*, ed. Jacob Hornberger and Richard Ebeling (Fairfax, Va.: Future of Freedom Foundation, 1994), p. 59.

19. King, p. 1222.

20. Lowell, p. 156.

21. Ronald Hamowy, "The Early Development of Medical Licensing Laws in the United States, 1875-1900," *Journal of Libertarian Studies* (1979).

22. Reuben Kessel, "Price Discrimination in Medicine," *Journal of Law and Economics* 1 (1958): 20-53.

23. Paul Starr, *The Social Transformation of American Medicine* (New York: HarperCollins, 1982), pp. 79-144.

24. Ibid., pp. 116-17.

25. Ibid., p. 118.

26. Flexner called for the adoption of five principles that reflect the model of education developed at Johns Hopkins University School of Medicine in 1893. Those include (1) a minimum of two years of undergraduate college; (2) a four-year curriculum, with two years in the basic medical sciences followed by two years of supervised clinical work in both inpatient and outpatient hospital services; (3) regular laboratory teaching exercises; (4) a high level of quality instruction be maintained through the use of full-time faculty; and (5) that medical schools be university based. Anthony R. Kovner, *Health Care Delivery in the United States* (New York: Springer, 1990), p. 73.

27. A. R. Pruit, "The Medical Marketplace," in *Politicized Medicine* (Irvington-on-Hudson, N.Y.: Foundation for Economic Education, 1993), pp. 23-33; Milton Friedman and Rose Friedman, *Free to Choose* (New York: Harcourt, Brace, Jovanovich, 1979).

28. Lowell, appendix, Table 104.

29. Ibid., p. 11.

30. Ibid., p. 283.

31. Ibid., appendix, Table 116.

32. Starr, p. 124.

33. Ibid.

34. Ibid.

35. Estimate of 1 doctor per 2,563 persons nationwide based on U.S. Census data, total U.S. population = 122,775,046 in 1930; and the total number of physicians in 1932 = 47,914. Lowell, appendix, Tables 62, 63.

36. Starr, p. 126.

37. Charles Baron, "Licensure of Health Care Professionals: The Consumer's Case for Abolition," *American Journal of Law and Medicine* 9 (Fall 1983): 388.

38. Office of Alternative Medicine, NIH, *Alternative Medicine: Expanding Medical Horizons*, NIH publication no. 940-66 (Washington: Government Printing Office, December 1994), p. 82.

39. Burton Goldberg, *Alternative Medicine: The Definitive Guide* (Puyallup, Wash.: Future Medicine, 1993), p. 277.

40. Editorial, "Medical Organizations in Annual Session: The AMA Meeting," *Journal of American Osteopathic Association* 13 (1914): 650.

41. Goldberg, p. 277.

42. Pamela L. Brinegar and Kara L. Schmitt, "State Occupational and Professional Licensure," in *The Book of States* (Lexington, Ky.: Council of State Governments, 1992), p. 567.

43. Paul J. Feldstein, *The Politics of Health Legislation: An Economic Perspective* (Ann Arbor: Health Administration Press, 1988), p. 81.

44. Colleen Kochman, "Nurse Managed Clinics: Improving Access to Health Care for Children," *Invitation to Change: Better Government Competition Winners, 1993* (Boston: Pioneer Institute for Public Policy Research, 1993), pp. 3-22.

45. Mark L. Schoene, "Federal Acute Back Pain Guideline Recommends Medication, Spinal Manipulation, and Exercise: Most Patients Can Safely Defer Specialized Diagnostic Testing," *Back Letter* 10 (January 1995): 1.

46. Diana Korte, "Midwives on Trial," *Mothering* (Fall 1995): 52-59.

47. Stephanie J. Ventura et al., "Advance Report of Final Natality Statistics, 1992," *Monthly Vital Statistics Report: Final Data from the Centers for Disease Control and Prevention—National Center for Health Statistics* 43 (October 1994): 17-18.

48. Chris Hafner-Eaton and Laurie Pearce, "Birth Choices, the Law, and Medicine: Balancing Individual Freedoms and Protection of the Public's Health," *Journal of Health Politics, Policy and Law* 19 (Winter 1994): 815.

49. Francis Notzon et al., "International Differences in the Use of Obstetric Interventions, *Journal of the American Medical Association* 263 (1990): 3287.

50. George Schieber et al., "Health System Performance in OECD Countries, 1980-1992," *Health Affairs* (Fall 1994): 102-8.

51. Korte, p. 57.

52. Ventura, p. 71.

53. Hafner-Eaton, pp. 817-19.

54. Judith Rooks et al., "Outcomes of Care in Birth Centers: The National Birth Center Study," *New England Journal of Medicine* 321 (1989): 1804.

55. A. Mark Durand, "The Safety of Home Birth: The Farm Study," *American Journal of Public Health* 82 (March 1992): 450-53.

56. Ibid.

57. Hafner-Eaton, p. 818.

58. Archie Brodsky, "Home Delivery," *Reason*, March 1992, pp. 28-31.

59. Hafner-Eaton, p. 831.

60. Estimate based on 20 percent of 4,065,000 births in 1992 and savings of $3,000 from midwife-assisted services. Ventura et al.

61. Bonnie B. O'Connor, "The Home Birth Movement in the United States," *Journal of Medicine and Philosophy* 18 (1993): 150-51.

62. Ibid., pp. 152, 171.

63. Brodsky, p. 33.

64. P. A. Stephenson and M. G. Wagner, "Reproductive Rights and the Medical Care System: A Plea for Rational Health Policy," *Journal of Public Health Policy* (Summer 1993): 174-82.

65. O'Connor, p. 167.

66. Rooks, p. 1804.

67. Korte, pp. 54-55.

68. Ibid., p. 55.

69. Brodsky, p. 32.

70. Hafner-Eaton, p. 814.

71. O'Connor, p. 170.

72. Korte, p. 57.

73. Steve Sternberg, "Introducing—Dr. Nurse," *Atlanta Journal/Atlantic Constitution*, August 15, 1993.

74. Kochman, p. 8.

75. Office of Technology Assessment, *Nurse Practitioners, Physician Assistants, and Certified Nurse-Midwives*, Health Technology Case Study 37, OTA-HCS-37 (Washington: U.S. Government Printing Office, December 1986), pp. 5-10.

76. Kochman, p. 11; P. Capan et al., "Nurse-Managed Clinics Provide Access and Improved Health Care," *Nurse Practitioner* 18 (1993): 53-55.

77. Len M. Nichols, "Estimating Costs of Underusing Advanced Practice Nurses," *Nursing Economics* 10 (September-October 1994): 350.

78. Kochman, p. 9.

79. Barbara Safriet, "Health Care Dollars and Regulatory Sense: The Role of Advanced Practice Nursing," *Yale Journal on Regulation* 9 (1992): 437.

80. J. W. Gilliam II, "A Contemporary Analysis of Medicolegal Concerns for Physician Assistants and Nurse Practitioners," *Legal Medicine* (1994): 133-80.

81. Jurisdictions that grant nurse practitioners prescriptive authority independent of physicians include Alaska, Arizona, Iowa, Montana, New Mexico, Oregon, Vermont, Wisconsin, Wyoming, and the District of Columbia. Linda J. Pearson, "Annual Update of How Each State Stands on Legislative Issues Affecting Advanced Nursing Practice," *Nurse Practitioner* 20 (1995): 16.

82. Linda Minich, American Nurses Association, Washington, Personal communication, September 1995.

83. Barbara Safriet, "Impediments to Progress in Health Care Workforce Policy: License and Practice Laws," *Inquiry* 31 (1994): 310-17.

84. Candice Owley, "Broadside against Nurses," *Washington Post*, December 27, 1993.

85. American Medical Association, *Digest of Official Actions: 1959-1968* (Chicago: AMA, 1971), pp. 334-36; "Quackery Persists," editorial, *Journal of the American Medical Association* 221 (1972): 914.

86. "Chiropractic Scope of Practice," American Chiropractic Association, Washington, March 1993.

87. American Medical Association, *Digest of Official Actions: 1969-1978* (Chicago: American Medical Association, 1980), p. 248.

88. American Chiropractic Association, Arlington, Va., Personal communication, September 1995.

89. Schoene, p. 1.

90. Daniel Cherkin et al., "Patient Evaluations of Low Back Pain Care from Family Physicians and Chiropractors," *Western Journal of Medicine* 150 (1989): 351.

91. Robin A. Cohen et al., "Trends in the Health of Older Americans: United States, 1994," *Vital and Health Statistics from the Centers for Disease Control and Prevention/National Center for Health Statistics*, series 3, no. 30 (April 1995): 79.

92. Richard A. Knox, "Agency on Medical Cost-Effectiveness Fighting for Life," *Boston Globe*, July 23, 1995, p. 16.

93. T. W. Meade et al., "Low Back Pain of Mechanical Origin: Randomized Comparison of Chiropractic and Hospital Patient Treatment," *British Medical Journal* 300 (1990): 1435.

94. Cherkin, p. 351.

95. Richard Leviton, "Hands on the Back May Be the Best Treatment, Says U.S. Government Study," *Alternative Medicine Digest* 1 (1995): 33.

96. Brown, pp. 2125; Editor, ACA Journal of Chiropractic, *American Medical Association Issues Revised Ethics Opinion on Chiropractic as Litigation on Antitrust Suit Is Concluded* (Arlington, Va.: American Chiropractic Association, 1992).

97. See, for example, Julian B. Roebuck and Bruce Hunter, "The Awareness of Health-Care Quackery as Deviant Behavior," *Journal of Health and Social Behavior* 13 (1972): 166; James H. Young, "The Persistence of Medical Quackery in America," *American Scientist* 60 (1972): 324; Lois D. McBean et al., "Food Faddism: A Challenge to Nutritionists and Dietitians," *American Journal of Clinical Nutrition* 27 (1974): 1071-78; Faith T. Fitzgerald, "Science and Scam: Alternative Thought Patterns in Alternative Health Care," *New England Journal of Medicine* 309 (1983): 1066; Marc Galanter, "Cults and Zealous Self-Help Movements: A Psychiatric Perspective," *American Journal of Psychiatry* 147 (1990): 54351; Andrew A. Skolnick, "FDA Petitioned to 'Stop Homeopathy Scam,' " *Journal of the American Medical Association* 272 (1994): 1154-56; Thomas L. Delbanco, "Bitter Herbs: Mainstream, Magic, and Menace," *Annals of Internal Medicine* 121 (1994): 803-4.

98. William T. Jarvis, "Quackery: A National Scandal," *Clinical Chemistry* 38 (1992): 1574-86.

99. Ibid., p. 1575.

100. Tim Beardsley, "Fads and Feds: Holistic Therapy Collides with Reductionist Science," *Scientific American* (September 1993): 39-44.

101. Thomas M. Lenard et al., *Interim Report: The Future of Medical Innovation* (Washington: Progress and Freedom Foundation, 1995), p. 7.

102. Office of Alternative Medicine, pp. 183-206.

103. K. Danner Clouser and David Hufford, "Nonorthodox Healing Systems and Their Knowledge Claims," *Journal of Medicine and Philosophy* 18 (1993): 102; David J. Hufford, "Epistemologies in Religious Healing," *Journal of Medicine and Philosophy* 18 (1993): 175-94.

104. Stephen Fulder and Robin Munro, "Complementary Medicine in the United Kingdom: Patients, Practitioners, and Consultations," *Lancet* (1985): 542; Mathilde Boissett and Mary-Ann Fitzcharles, "Alternative Medicine Use by Rheumatology Patients in a Universal Health Care Setting," *Journal of Rheumatology* 21 (1994): 148.

105. Fulder and Munro, p. 542.

106. See, for example, Sidney Carroll and Robert Gaston, "Occupational Licensing and the Quality of Service: An Overview," *Law and Human Behavior*, September 1983.

107. Gary Gaumer, "Regulating Health Professionals: A Review of Empirical Literature," *Milbank Memorial Fund Quarterly* (1984).

108. Carolyn Cox and Susan Foster, "The Costs and Benefits of Occupational Regulation," Federal Trade Commission, October 1990.

109. Terree Wasley, *What Has Government Done to Our Health Care?* (Washington: Cato Institute, 1992).

110. The Commonwealth of Massachusetts's Acupuncture Statute (M.G.L. c, 112 ss. 148-62) states that "nothing contained herein shall prevent licensed physicians from practicing acupuncture."

111. Judy Foreman, "Acupuncture: An Ancient Medicine Is Making Its Point," *Boston Globe*, May 22, 1995, p. 25. Foreman reports that the national organization for physician-acupuncturists (American Academy of Medical Acupuncture) requires 200 hours of acupuncture training for membership. The national organization for nonphysician-acupuncturists (National Commission for the Certification of Acupuncturists) requires more than 1,000 hours of acupuncture training before candidates take the exam for national certification.

112. Paul J. Feldstein, *Health Policy Issues: An Economic Perspective on Health Reform* (Ann Arbor: Health Administration Press, 1994), p. 189.

113. Wasley, p. 42.

114. Feldstein, *Health Policy Issues,* pp. 189-90.

115. S. David Young, *The Rule of Experts: Occupational Licensing in America* (Washington: Cato Institute, 1987), p. 53.

116. Victor Fuchs, *Who Shall Live?* (New York: Basic Books, 1974), p. 20.

117. Milton Friedman and Simon Kuznets, *Income from Independent Professional Practice* (New York: National Bureau of Economic Research, 1945).

118. William White, "The Impact of Occupational Licensure on Clinical Laboratory Personnel," *Journal of Human Resources* (Winter 1978).

119. Lawrence Shepard, "Licensing Restrictions and the Cost of Dental Care," *Journal of Law and Economics* (April 1978).

120. Timothy Muzondo and Pazderka Bohumir, "Occupational Licensing and Professional Incomes in Canada," *Canadian Journal of Economics* (November 1990).

121. Gaumer, p. 397.

122. Chris Paul, "Physician Licensure and the Quality of Medical Care," *Atlantic Economic Journal* 12 (1984): 18-30.

123. Friedman and Friedman, p. 240. Emphasis in original.

124. Medical school revenues totaled $11,983,863 in 1932. Sources of income were as follows: student fees, $4,057,304; endowment income, $2,784,527; state and city, $2,574,973; and other, $2,567,059. Lowell et al., Table 104 and p. 283.

125. Uwe Reinhardt, "Planning the Nation's Health Workforce: Let the Market In," *Inquiry* 31 (Fall 1994): 250-63; Janice L. Ganem et al., "Review of US Medical School Finances, 1993-1994," *Journal of the American Medical Association* 274 (September 6, 1995): 724, Table 1.

126. Janice L. Ganem et al., "Review of U.S. Medical School Finances," *Journal of the American Medical Association* 274 (1995): 723-30.

127. Mullan et al., p. 142.

128. Congressional Budget Office, *Medicare and Graduate Medical Education* (Washington: Government Printing Office, 1995), p. 10.

129. Ibid.

130. Mullan et al., p. 143.

131. Ibid.

132. Ibid., pp. 142-43.

133. Ganem, p. 724, Table 1.

134. Kovner, p. 73.

135. Feldstein, *Health Policy Issues*, p. 189.

136. Reinhardt, pp. 253-54.

137. "Prized by Hospitals, Accreditation Hides Perils Patients Face," *Wall Street Journal,* October 12, 1988.

138. Sherman Follard, Allen Goodman, and Miran Stano, *The Economics of Health and Health Care* (New York, Macmillan, 1993), p. 583.